The Fijian wooden figurine (*matakau*) on the cover of this book is held in the National Museum of Victoria in Melbourne, item 2530, 62.2 cm in height, with feet in the form of dowels as if to be held erect. One arm is missing. Exact significance to Fijians is not well understood and might vary with the locality. *Matakau* were iconic, considered a spirit but not necessarily worshipped or prayed to. This *matakau* is somewhat similar to the famously named *Bui ni Nakauvadra*.

Fijian-English Dictionary

with notes on
Fijian culture and natural history

Ronald Gatty

Copyright © Ronald Gatty 2009
G.P.O. Box 120
Suva, Fiji

USP Library Cataloguing-in-Publication Data

Gatty, Ronald
Fijian–English Dictionary : with notes on Fijian culture and natural history
Ronald Gatty. – Suva, Fiji : R. Gatty, 2009.

340 p. : ill. ; 25 cm.

ISBN 978-982-98047-1-6

1. Fijian language—Dictionaries—English 2. Fijians—Social life and customs
3. Natural history—Fiji I. Title.

PL6235.4.G27 2009   499.5321

CONTENTS

Foreword by Ratu Kamisese Mara — 1
A First Few Words — 2
Preface — 2
Brief Notes on the Language — 4
Abbreviations and Notes — 6
Acknowledgements — 7
A — 9
B — 10
C — 37
D — 55
E — 82
F — 83
G — 84
I — 92
J — 94
K — 95
L — 131
M — 149
N — 178
O — 184
P — 188
Q — 192
R — 201
S — 213
T — 243
U — 281
V — 287
W — 315
Y — 323
Fiji Traditional Calendar — 334

FOREWORD
by Ratu Sir Kamisese Mara

Fiji is at the same time a new nation and also one rich in cultural heritage and tradition. While adapting to progress, to economic development, to taking our place as a nation in the modern world, Fijians are mindful that we are a Pacific Island people, people with a proud tradition with customs, language and a way of life that gives us our own identity and stability of social structure, ways of living together and sharing in social responsibilities. We do well to respect our own heritage, culture and customs that are so well reflected in the language of our people.

It is to this purpose that Professor Gatty writes, for an appreciation of our language in the context of traditional culture, yet showing the adaptability of the language to what is modern in Fiji. English-speaking people may thus learn much of value in understanding and appreciating the bases of our thought, our social life, our ways of farming and fishing, our arts, crafts, songs and ceremonies, and our ways of talking and thinking about what is new or modern.

Fijians too, especially those who live in towns remote from their home villages, may learn and appreciate aspects of their own culture and language that their parents knew better before them. Also they may improve their English which is a second language to most of us, though it is now the official language of our country. Certainly it is necessary in most responsible positions of employment.

Ronald Gatty is well qualified to write on this subject. He spent some of his early years in these islands and villages working as a fisherman and diver. Ronald left us as a young man to study in the U.S., later becoming a professor. He has returned to us often, exploring further in Fijian traditional culture and taking a strong interest in Fiji as a developing nation. I am sure his books will be useful to our own Fijian people, to other citizens and residents of Fiji and also to the many visitors who come to Fiji each year.

K. K. T. Mara

A FIRST FEW WORDS

This book is written both for Fijians, and for foreigners. So many Fijian youngsters speak a jargon that could hardly be understood by earlier generations of Fijians. And being raised and living in towns, our youngsters know little of the older customs, and little of their heritage of animal and plant life that is briefly described in this book. Their English too, is often limited at best, as a second language, with a rudimentary vocabulary – though English is necessary for employment and advancement in the modern world. This book should help them.

Similarly, few foreigners understand much of Fijian language, though they live here for years and some settle permanently. Virtually all Fijians have a working knowledge of English so knowledge of the Fijian language is not absolutely necessary. But there is no easy way for foreigners to relate to Fijians more completely without understanding local language. The *Alliance française* offers courses to the general public that along with this book should help with a closer understanding. Both University of Fiji and University of the South Pacific offer accredited courses. But the Fijian heritage involves more that just words of the language. It includes the natural environment and native custom, ethnology and social psychology.

Tourists and visitors are often impressed with the apparent open friendliness with which they are greeted. If visitors stay long enough they will come to learn that relationships are not nearly so simple and open. The ways of the Fijian, the social context, the thinking and feeling can be vastly more complex than they ever dreamed – but that at first is not revealed. People think they understand when they understand nothing. This book is a first, very small step trying to demystify the enigma that is the Fijian. It is only a beginning on a journey of understanding that is never-ending.

The Nature Garden (and Spice Garden) at Wainadoi, near Suva, show off many of the trees, bushes, fruits, vegetables, medicinal plants, dye plants, and scented flowers that have been important to Fijians (and spices to the Indians). Both for overseas visitors and locals, especially schoolchildren, there are demonstrations of how these traditional plants have been used and much of the lore that has been lost.

A tour of the forest canopy can take visitors around tree-tops of the jungle where they experience the view and the sight and sound of birds. Colourful parrots are always an attraction. You call and sometimes they will answer. In wonderment, you view the dancing streams and thick, dense jungle down below. This has been my home for thirty years, following the early and formative years of youth in these islands.

The Nature Garden and Spice Garden at Wainadoi have been featured on television in Australia, New Zealand and Canada with demonstrations of how to use the plant materials. This is an effort to preserve and promote what has been useful in Fijian culture. People from other lands can learn something from Fijians. And young Fijians might come to appreciate more of their own heritage and with this dictionary, learn a little English at the same time.

PREFACE

This is a handbook for practical understanding of Fijian language, as commonly understood speech one might hear around Suva. Words from Fiji's regional languages or dialects are listed only if they have become part of the common vocabulary that many Fijians understand. Included also are notes on natural history and brief explanations of Fijian customs and culture where they may be important.

The only other readily available dictionary has been Capell's with many obsolete entries and a lack of modern words and idioms. This dictionary tries to present the language as it is now. Capell's so-called *A New Fijian Dictionary* was first published almost seventy years ago, compiled mostly from missionaries' notes of much earlier generations. Revisions of 1957 and 1968 added or corrected scientific names for plants, fishes and birds without much change in any of the rest. That is archaic! So a new dictionary is needed.

Fijian language is particularly rich in emotion, feelings, the physical senses, social and family relations, and the context of village life and subsistence farming. It is strained and much less useful in coping with the multitude of foreign contexts, employment, urban living, technology, and novel artefacts that pervade modern life almost everywhere. Anglicisms and borrowed words, so-called "loan words", dominate in many situations that begin to sound artificial. To turn on a light or turn it off, you *on-taka* or *off-taka* instead of *Me waqa* or *Me boko*.

As spoken around towns the new Fiji-speak has often hurt my ears. Just as well, perhaps, that deafness with age has faded my hearing almost completely. Fijian begins to sound like English in translation with many English words pronounced in a Fijian style. The context of life is very different from ancient times. The old life-style and old languages barely survive anywhere but in remote villages. Already 100 years ago Basil Thompson wrote a book entitled *The Fijians: A Study in The Decay of Custom*. And the language and culture have changed a very great deal more since that time.

This dictionary has many gaps, omissions and no doubt a number of errors. There was no methodical checking for completeness. Words and expressions were gathered and noted them down as a quiet pastime of evening hours. I have been a scavenger of words and languages. I was raised partly in Fiji, with my family owning Katafaga Island and a home in Suva. Fijian studies then became an idle and casual pursuit in my adult life as a scientist and professor, and later years, as a horticulturist with a tropical garden and a small collection of horses in Fiji. My formal training in language has only been French, German and Latin. (My wife of fifty seven years has been a classical philologist, steeped in Greek, Latin and medieval languages from the Sorbonne, and Cornell University.) I had been admitted directly to the Graduate Programme at Cornell University without the benefit of undergraduate training. This set an academic record that has since been matched by several other students during the passing years.

My interest in language has been a sideline to a deep interest in cultural anthropology and social psychology. Language is an approach to understanding a culture. For a doctorate at Cornell University, I minored in Anthropology with the distinguished scholar A. Holmberg and tried to help Charles Hockett, professional linguist who at the time was struggling with his interest in Fijian language. For me Fijian was a language learned during youth without any formal instruction.

Fijian conversation is very sensitive as to who is talking to whom. Relationships of regions, tribes, clans, extended families and nuclear families are all relevant but usually invisible to outsiders. There are privileges, courtesies and taboos that depend on those relationships. Some people may not speak with certain others, brothers and sisters for example or in some cases, children and a parent. Virtually everyone is related to everyone in some way that determines the conditions of mutual speech. Formal Fijian speech has an overload of verbiage with protocol and politesse. It may border on a mannered preciosity that can be quite boring.

Still today, though, Fijian patterns of thinking and feeling are very different from anything foreigners might expect. Fijian culture and social interconnections are difficult if not impossible for an outsider to penetrate. Fijian openness is never as open as it would seem. Questioning a Fijian on any sensitive issue is rather like peeling an onion. Layers are removed but nothing much is revealed at the inside.

Fijians usually pretend their thoughts and feelings are congruent with those of a stranger or a foreigner. They avoid disclosing potential discord of their different motivation, different social aims, very different manners and private behaviour. And some can be masters at hiding their self-interest. The Fijian smile presents a disarming front. The smile serves to charm, disarm, and put the visitor at ease. Sometimes it is a mask for dissimulation and manipulation. More often perhaps, it may be genuine, especially in the case of children.

A Fijian individual living in a traditional Fijian context exists within a social system that is much more structured than a European usually experiences. Within Fiji, the system leaves little room for an individual to act independently of the group. At the same time, for the individual, that system can be helpful and supportive emotionally. Emphasis is on human relationships, extended family, and clan, and to a lesser extent, the tribe and territory, and quite importantly, their church with their own Fijian versions of Christianity. But these social involvements and commitments can be preoccupations that limit an individual's development as an individual and dissipate the personal resources. Social demands can exact enormous amounts of time, effort, energy, even money, food and other consumables.

Commoners have been restrained by their elders and by their chiefs who with very few exceptions, have little education, and all too often, are marked by self-interest. Young people are discouraged from expressing opinions or openly asserting themselves as individuals. Still now, Fijians hardly dare "talk up" directly. Many men, especially, have been very considerably repressed. From early childhood all Fijians are taught severely not to ask questions and not to speak their minds. It is understandable that Fijians might become secretive about their own feelings and thoughts. They have had so little personal privacy.

It is not easy to understand Fijians and the common fallacy of foreigners is to think they do. Perhaps this modest dictionary will help with a little understanding of the language and some of its cultural context. That would be a beginning.

BRIEF NOTES ON THE LANGUAGE

I have wanted to write this book as a dictionary with very little grammar, syntax or other formal aspects of language that might be boring to read. Al Schutz's *The Fijian Language* covers those aspects only, exhaustively and exhaustingly in something like a thousand pages. (Univ. of Hawaii, 1985.)

Originally Fijian had no written language and spelling has varied considerably since writing was introduced. There have been differences as to how words or letters should be combined or separated – such as *e daidai* or *edaidai* (meaning "today"). The word for "the knife" has been seen as *nai sele* or *na i sele* or *na isele*. That little letter "*i*" transforms the root-word of the verb *sele* into a noun. On 11 March, 2008, the Fiji Cabinet has determined that all should follow a newly imposed Government system, and I try to oblige, reluctantly. Along with imposing a few other rules, they insist we attach that little "i" to the noun. Thus *na isele* is "correct" by Cabinet decision.

Government officials are trying to enforce rules of spelling that differ from common practice. Teachers, most of all, resist the change. I believe writers of dictionaries should follow what people do, as the people write and like to read, rather than trying to dictate a scheme for "proper" spelling. George Bernard Shaw tried to rationalise English spelling with absolutely no success.

Fijians' compound words are made up from simple words but it has not always been clear if they are to be written joined together as one word or to be separated by a space. To make things easier for the novice, I have sometimes placed spaces between the little component words, or in a few cases I have used a hyphen to separate them. It will be easier for foreigners to follow the meaningful parts. But in fact, Fijians virtually never use a hyphen, and most often run words together when they write. Some Fijians may find my hyphens annoying, and my spacing of words to be awkward. My apologies for that.

A problem arises with the alphabetic arrangement. Readers may have to search about to find the word they want. I tend to put compound words close to the root-word that is their base, rather then in strict alphabetical order.

Glottal stops may replace "t" or "k" in some areas but locals are not much bothered by this. In Fiji we are accustomed to the fact the the "v" of mainland Fiji is likely to be replaced in Lau by an "f", and a "b" replaced by a "p" and a "t" replaced by a "j", these changes being an influence of Tonga. In the western part of Viti Levu, the "d" might be replaced by a "t". We take that in our stride because in Fijian language, unlike English, it is the vowels mainly that give meaning to a word, not the consonants.

Some teachers of Fijian language have thought it useful to invent Fijian words for the vocabulary of formal grammar. *Abaca* (pronounced "Ambatha") refers to the ABCs, the alphabet. A sentence is referred to as a *yatuvosa*; a letter of the alphabet is *matanivola,* a capital letter is a *matanivola levu,* while a lower case is *matanivola lailai.* A full stop (a "period" in USA) is *digo*, a comma *koma*, a colon *koloni*, a question mark a *cegu taro,* and *ikovu* a bracket. A noun is a *nauni*, a *kilanauni* an adjective, a root-form or verb is *vu*, but a *vuwale* the intransitive form of a verb, and *dewa* indicates the transitive form of a verb. A prefix is *ikuri liu.* An acute accent as *itoqa cabe* and a grave accent might be *itoqa siro.* Et cetera will appear as *kei na so tale.* A number of these words are known to very few Fijians and it would seem to me much simpler just to use the English expressions without creating new Fijian words for them.

Fijian language as spoken today is a modern Anglicised Fijian, because the context of Fijian life today corresponds closely to the European context of schools, and sports, and jobs and urban life in a money economy. That is remote from village life that was more the context of my youth. So many youngsters today are *susu madrai,* literally raised on European bread in the urban context, and know little of village culture or their own heritage. Many have never visited the village of their father and a fair percentage have never been "written down" as belonging to a certain tribe, clan, and village. A relationship to the parental village is often no longer relevant. It can even be an unwanted burden. Mixed marriages, with Europeans, Indians, Chinese and Polynesians lend to this trend, and there has been an enormous amount of inter-breeding over the last couple of centuries. That may well bode well for future of Fiji society to give stability with more homogeneity. But what evolves as Fiian language become a polyglot mixture of ancient Austronesian, Proto-Central Pacific language of the Fiji, Samoa, Tonga complex, indigenous Melanesian, with later Polynesian, and European overlay and a few Hindi words thrown in. The loan words from English are so many and so obvious that I omit most of them from this dictionary. I try to retain the original or ancient root-words, many that go back to Proto-Polynesian sources. In a few cases I show the Tongan or Samoan cognates. It is the earlier, indigenous cultures that interest me, far more than the modern aspects.

Verb-forms

Verbs are not conjugated in Fijian. For verb-forms, a word is shown in this dictionary in its basic form, and then the suffix or suffixes attached that make it transitive. For instance, the word *sele, seleva* is listed. That is *sele* for the root verb-form meaning "cut", made transitive as *seleva* for "cut it" (some say *seleta*. There are lots of local variations in the languages of Fiji.) Another listed verb is *moku, mokuta*; this is the basic verb *moku* "hit" with its added suffix to become *mokuta* "hit something or someone" or "hit it", as a transitive form of the verb. A suffix may also include an implied preposition, meaning "for" or "with", for example. *Cicivaka na isele* means to run with the knife. *Ciciva* means to run for the knife.

The suffix *–raka* or *–laka* make a verb more forceful. Repeated syllables also may emphasise the effect of a verb. And a verb may serve equally as a noun or adjective.

Common prefixes are *vaka*, creating an adverb, or *vei* or *veivaka* or *dau* that precede a verb-form. These are not all listed but when they do appear, they are normally found next to the root word they modify. Listing them all separately would burden the volume with too many pages of fairly obvious material.

Noun-forms

There are no different genders for nouns and no different plural forms for all but a very few adjectives. The only general plural is one that implies a set or group, formed by placing *vei* before the noun. Thus *kau* plant, *veikau* forest. *loga ni dalo* taro planting-bed, *veiloga ni dalo* taro garden as a set of *dalo* planting-beds.

Some nouns have a suffix that indicates a possessive pronoun. For clarity here (but not in everyday writing) I separate the suffix with a dash. *Liga-na* means "its/his/her hand". My hand would be *ligaqu*, your hand *ligamu*, etc. I leave the details for grammarians to explain.

Adjectives normally follow the noun. Thus *na koli* the dog, *na koli loaloa* the black dog. And there are just a very few adjectives that differ in the plural. *lalai* small, is the singular, and *lalai* is the plural. *levu* is big, with *lelevu* as a plural. *balavu* is long or tall, with *babalavu* the plural, *leka* is small in the singular, *leleka* small in the plural, applied to more than one thing.

Pronouns

Pronouns are perhaps the most unusual aspect of Fijian for the foreigner. The words for "you", "we", or "they" vary as to how many people are involved. And the "we" also varies as to whether the people being spoken to are included or excluded. Readers may learn the details elsewhere.

Possessive pronouns may differ slightly if they refer to foods, or to beverages. Fijians distinguish carefully between being the "owner" of food (or beverage), and being the one who will consume it. *Na noqu kakana* is food that belongs to me. *Na kequ kakana* is food that is mine to eat myself. *Na noqu ti* is tea that belongs to me but *na mequ ti* is tea that is mine for me to drink. And curiously, Fijians reckon that they "drink" melon and some other fruits, ice cream, and medicinal pills.

Stress and accents

Stress is almost always on the second-to-last syllable of a word. A very few important exceptions may be indicated in this dictionary by underlining the stressed vowel. Some language teachers use what is called a macron, a line over the vowel, but neither mark is ever used in ordinary writing or printing of Fijian.

C*a*waki is a sea-urchin, for which the first syllable is stressed in pronounciation, not the second to last, which is customary. Underlining in this book may also indicate the prolonging of a vowel when that affects the meaning. *Dredre* refers to smiling or laughter. *Dredre* refers to a difficulty. Such underlining is done here only as a very occasional aid to pronounciation and meaning. It is not usually done here for long vowels unless it is thought absolutely necessary. In fact, Fijian is often spoken so fast that there is hardly any audible difference. Also, words are run together, as in French, and often in English, unlike the clipping distinction of each word, as can be the case in German speech or even Latin, as I have heard it spoken by present-day classicists when they are talking to each other in a university atmosphere.

The structure of a Fijian sentence is quite unlike English structure. An English sentence normally runs from subject to verb to object, as in "The man wrote the book". A Fijian might put that as "wrote the book the man". And Fijian most commonly uses the root-form, the basic, stative or passive form of the verb, rather than the transitive, active form. But this book avoids the topic of syntax.

Fijian is also less direct, more wordy and periphrastic, using allusions rather than bluntness and simple clarity. Preciosity and politeness are fundamental as they are in Japanese, especially in formal situations. Traditionally one never mentions a person's name and rarely mentions the name of a place. These facts were communicated in a roundabout way, or implied in a context. These things are changing, of course, as Fijian drop some of the old prohibitions and their syntax begins to mimic the European way of saying things.

Omitted to save space are a vast number of English words that are pronounced and spelled in Fijian fashion but can be readily understood and need not be included. For examply, I include *basa* for bazaar only because the English equivalent may not be obvious. Archaic words are included only if they have continuing significant relevance in understanding Fijian culture and history.

ABBREVIATIONS AND NOTES

Some words may be shown as Archaic, Anglicism (a English notion expressed in Fijian), Slang, Insults, Vulgar. And a few abbreviations are used:

n. noun-form. **v.** verb-form. **abbrev.** abbreviation. **adj.** adjective. **adv.** adverb., **lit.,** literally. **Eng.** direct copy of an English word. Some words may serve as nouns, adjectives, verbs or adverbs with little or no change. But the structure and grammar of Fijian is not directly applicable or comparable to European languages.

Words from various regions, or parts of those regions, are occasionally shown in paretheses. They include Lau, Rewa, Colo East, LomaiViti, West(ern Viti Levu), Cakau(drove), Vanua Levu, Nadro(ga), Navosa, Ba, Ra, Kadavu, or words from a few other places or languages: Polyn(esia), Samoa, Tonga, Hindi. There are significant variations in Fijian language(s) and dialects. Many Tongan or Samoan words are close cognates of their Fijian equivalent and a few of these words are listed. The contact with Central Polynesia has been close certainly as early as 1000. For an extended period, the same language was shared in eastern and northern Fiji, and what later became Samoa and Tonga. One might refer to that as Proto-Central Pacific and some of that ancient etymology is persists in present-day Fijan language. The Proto-Polynesian Lapita people were in Fiji some three thousand years ago though most moved on to the east. The influence of Proto-Polynesians and then Polynesians on Fijian culture has been profound. Much of what is thought of today as Fijian culture has its origin in Tonga, especially from the last 750 years with active inter-communications. Samoa but also Rotuma and Futuna have also had effect.

ACKNOWLEDGEMENTS

The notion of writing this book came about from conversations with my friend the late Semesa Sikivou, former Minister for Education, Fiji's first Representative to the United Nations and earlier, Headmaster at Queen Victoria School. At his own insistence, he spent many Saturday mornings reviewing my writing with a critical eye. I began this particular book only at his urging. Also Ratu Kamisese Mara took a personal interest and read many sections of my early work with encouraging comments. He was kind enough to write a foreword for this book several years before his untimely death. He had been a close family friend and my personal friend for many years, and freely shared knowledge, as did Semesa Sikivou.

Similar encouragement came from the late Solo (Solomone) T. Bulicokocoko who has been a leading light in curriculum development, to teach Fijian language and culture to Fijian students. We spent many days together, comparing notes as he himself wrote source material on legends, culture and language, much of it still used in schoolrooms of Fiji.

For plant names it has been a great help to have had the advice and writings of my dear friends, now deceased, B.E.V. Parham, his son John Parham, and A. C. Smith; also for trees, the German Forestry Project. For birds and terrestrial creatures the writings of Paddy Ryan, Fergus Clunie and Dick Watling have been bountiful sources. Both Watling and botanist Hal Moore have given me an appreciation for the palms. (I had been a field assistant to Dr. Moore on his botanical collecting expeditions in Central America in the early 1950s.) And Fiji's Fisheries Department has provided scientific names of some aquatic creatures. In anthropology and archeology, I was greatly stimulated by conversations more than half a century ago with the late Ed Gifford. And the late Aubrey Parke has been a soul-mate in the search for knowledge of early Fiji. We both saw that much of what Fijians think to be Fijian tradition and culture has evolved since the influx of Tongans and Tongan culture (such as the notion of paramount chiefs and the hierarchal ceremony of kava drinking).

For a few words from the various different regional languages, aside from my own very limited knowledge, use has been made of articles by the late Bruce Biggs, Andrew Pawley, and by P. Geraghty. In quite a number of cases I have referred to Capell's dictionary to check what he has listed. I do not dwell on his errors.

Very helpfully, George Hazelman has carefully read through this dictionary, raising a number of questions, and discussing the usage of many words and correcting some of my errors. Fijian might be considered his native language, along with English. Without his help I might never have completed this work as I edge past my eightieth year. Memory fades and deafness takes a toll almost completely.

For finally putting the book together, Detlef Blumel is a professional who has no peer, and has kindly given much of his time including the design of the book cover. George Bennett was kind enough to draw the charcoal sketch of the author. Ms Sagale Buadromo, Director of the Fiji Museum, has graciously permitted the use of a photograph of the Fijian idol (matakau) on the front cover. Dom Sansom has given some good advice on printing and Rod Ewens' knowledge of handicrafts was a big help. I am very grateful to these people who have helped bring this book to completion.

I am very grateful also, in a final editing, to have had the help of Mr. Joe Hewson, who was Senior Education Officer (Secondary) of Fiji's Education Department. He had the patience to read through the manuscript and offer comments and his personal encouragement. His involvement, however, was personal, and does not imply official sponsorship by the Department of Education. Also, the late Tevita Nawadra was quite supportive. He had the opportunity to study the manuscript and commented at some length, taking precious time in the last year of his life. Nawadra was strongly opposed to rules imposed by the Institute of Fijian Language and Culture with the support of Cabinet, but he made no public issue on the matter. Privately, Nawadra expressed regret that I was accommodating in complying with the rules set up by the Institute. And I note in the vernacular newspaper *Nai Lalakai* that Nawadra and other Fijian writers have ignored the imposed system of spelling.

In early years, Semesa Sikivou went through my writings as a benevolent despot and sternly added many words. He taught me a great deal, as indeed he had taught a few generations of Fijian students. But that was many decades ago.

After basic completion of this manuscript there was published a new dictionary *Na iVolavosa Vakaviti* in 2007, almost 1000 pages, sponsored by the Department of Fijian Language, written over some 30 years by many dozens of civil servants and a few consultants. It is an overwhelming, compendious work of many years and many native Fijian teachers. They were writing in Fijian to Fijians. With my own translations to English, I have adopted many of their useful entries that had been omitted from my earlier manuscript. My book, written by me alone, is much more limited, containing far fewer of the "loan words" that they list very extensively, and fewer regional or local words that are unknown to most Fijians.

My own volume dwells much more on aspects of the culture and natural history and is of course a Fijian to English dictionary. So the two dictionaries serve different purposes. Again, I have tried to restrict the scope to common knowledge which is really only my own quite limited knowledge. Only the errors are mine. I merely arranged the material in a format intended to be useful.

My interest now turns to a series of volumes that I have been writing for more than half a century of idle evening hours. The *Tribes of Fiji* is an effort to outline the history of the tribes and clans of Fijians in several volumes, much of that already completed. One might think of these books as social archeology, for Fiji has little to show in physical archeology. The first volume concerns Naitasiri Province with focus on the *KaiColo* highlanders, the "real Fijians", as they themselves say: *Keitou na kaiViti dina*. Tailevu Province will follow, and then the others. Villages are listed, with tribes and clans, often with comments as to their origin, their chiefly titles and traditions or specialties, and relationships with other Fijian people and places.

As with this Dictionary, I began writing the series of volumes *Tribes of Fiji* a great number of years ago, only as a set of notes for my own understanding. Perhaps these notes may interest others, though there are a very great many gaps and certainly some errors. No one person can take account of so much detail. The hope is that some readers might correct my work and add to the research in years to come. This could help support a feeling of identity for Fijians in these times of fast-moving change.

A

A is usually pronounced as in "far", and more rarely as in "cat". In Lau, the letter **y** may be pronounced in front of **a** at the beginning of a word or a person's name that begins with an **a**. For example, the title Adi may be heard as Yadi. The word for tuna fish may be heard as **atu** or **yatu**.

a "a" or "the", an indefinite or definite article, not referring to any one specific person or thing but to a generality. *a lawa* law, or the law (as a general concept). *na lawa* the (specific) law. *A vosa taumada* foreword (to a book).

Adi Lady, as a form of address, usually followed by a first name. Adi is sometimes sounded as Yadi under influence of Lau. When followed by a name, Adi may be heard abbreviated informally as Di, as in Di Lala for Adi Lalabalavu, and this short version is not disrespectful. Like the man's chiefly title Ratu, this form of address was limited to the eastern coast of Viti Levu but has become commonly adopted by chiefly women throughout Fiji. The origin may come from the Ra word *yadi* (also used in parts of Tailevu), meaning to take, as a chief takes up a woman when he takes her as a wife. But that is idle speculation.

Adi Senitoa n. Hibiscus Festival usually held annually in August in Suva with parade and floats. A "Queen", Adi Senitoa, is selected. A great deal of rain usually falls during this week, giving the local expression "Hibiscus weather". *senitoa* Hibiscus rosasinensis, Malvaceae, the introduced, ornamental hibiscus flower.

agelo (or) **yagelo** (Eng., Rom. Cath.) n. angel.

agelosi (or) **agilosi** (Eng., Prot.) n. angel.
Idiom: *agilosi* flattering reference to a beautifully natured girl.

Ailadi (Eng.) Ireland.

aisi (Eng.) n. ice. *aisi boloko* ice block.

aisikirimu (or) **aisikirimi** (Eng.) n. ice cream, that Fijians usually spell as one word.

Ajibisovi (Eng. Angl. Church) n. Archbishop. Syn.(Rom. Cath.) *aravikavo, arekavikavo*.

akaude (Eng.) n. account (bank).

ala, alaca (Cakau) v. to remove wood from fire, to reduce or extinguish the flame; usually one hears *alaca na buka* or *me ala na buka*. (*buka* firewood). The word may be written, less often heard, as *yala, yalaca*. Abbrev. of *tala, talaca*.

aliva 1. n. millipede; three harmless types, one small and brown, one small and black, one large and black, which leaves a yellow stain when its belly is touched, the yellow fluid irritating to human skin.

aliva 2. (Bible) alpha, used in the expression *aliva kei na omeka* from beginning to the end, lit., from alpha and omega, first and last letters of the Greek alphabet.

ALTA (Eng. acronym) n. Agricultural Landowners and Tenants Act, which has governed the leasing of native land.

"alto" (or) **alato** (Eng.) alto singing voice. Syn. (Lau) *kanokano*.

"ambar" (Hindi) n. white-fleshed turmeric, used fresh for pickles, especially by Gujerati Indians, or raw in salads as a refreshing ingredient. Introduced plant. Some is grown commercially by Tailevu Fijians and exported by Gujerati. The plant is shorter and flatter than yellow turmeric, and is somewhat more susceptible to root-rot fungal disease.

aniciuramu (Eng.) n. anthurium, a genus of plants of South American origin. These attractive durable flowers, usually bright red, are grown commercially by some Fijian women who sell to hotels. Very few local people know that this plant is quite toxic.

"apei" (Rotuma) n. very fine white mat woven by Rotumans from pandanus leaf, a principal item used in ceremonial exchange. Leaves from this variety of pandanus, called "sa'aga", are brought to mainland Fiji from Rotuma.

apolo (Eng.) n. apple (imported from Australia, New Zealand).

apositolo (Bible) apostle.

Araneke! (Interjection) Cheat! (usually at card games). Syn. *Ereneke!*

asa (Bible) n. ass (the animal). None in Fiji.

asipirini (Eng.) n. aspirin. Due to successful marketing, aspirin these days is largely displaced by the omnipresent, more expensive Panadol, much used by urban Fijians.

au I (or) me. Pronoun, 1st person singular. As the subject of the sentence it can become *Oi au* or *O yau*. Preceded by a vowel it may become *yau*: *Raica e dua vei keirau, o Seru se o yau*. See one of us (two, exc. the one being talked to), either Seru or me. Following the particles *me* or *ni* it becomes abbreviated as *meu* and *niu*, sometimes seen as *me'u* and *ni'u*. Syn. (Tonga) *au*. (Colo East, Namosi) *'u*.

aua (Eng.) n. hour. Also spelled *auwa*. *ena veiaua kece* at all hours. *ena veimama na aua* in half an hour.

avisaki (Eng) n. haversack.

avorosa (Slang) n. lazy person who shirks work. This is a man's name but how it has come to take on a lazy implication is an elusive story.

B

B is always pronounced **mb**, as in "number". Lauans sometimes substitute a **p** for the mainland Fijian **b**. This letter **b** does not exist in the local language of Drekeniwai, near Nasavusavu, Vanua Levu Island.

ba 1. n. edible stalk of taro, considered a delicacy, steamed with the skin removed. Lemon and chili pepper are sometimes added as a modern touch, not traditional. It is also a special ceremonial gift-food for mothers of newly born babies. *cola ba* (of a man) to bring taro, with stalks attached, to a new mother. *dreke ba* (of a woman) to bring taro stalks to a new mother. Syn. *baba*.

ba 2. (Rewa) n. taro, Colocasia esculentum, an edible root-crop, staple food. Syn. *dalo*.
Idiom: *Ba Rewa!* "Hi beautiful!" (or) "Hi handsome!" Young Fijians are much given to jocular greetings amongst their own people or related people. And most everybody is related in one way or another. This expression rather dated.

ba 3. n. as in *ba-ni-ika*, fish fence, usually made of reeds. Fish are caught by the movement of the tide or coastal currents.

iba 1. n. game, contention, riddle. *veiba* quarrel, dispute.

iba 2. n. guess, bet, belief. *Noqu iba o Seru.* My bet is on Seru.

iba 3. n. (Archaic) trolling lure, often made of shell, as a Samoan and later, Tongan artefact. Binding was done with inner bark of *roga* (Pipturus argentus). Trolling was unknown to Fijians who fished almost exclusively within the lagoon.

ba, bataka v. to deny, argue.

veiba, veibataka v. to argue, to argue about (something). *veibataki* disputed.

baba 1. n. slope, hill. *veibaba* hilly slopes. See *Baba Siga*.

baba 2. n. ceremonial food taken to a new mother and baby, usually the skinned stems of taro, as a vegetable delicacy. See *ba*.

baba-na n. cheek (of the face), side, as of the body.

vakababa v., n. to block (as a fallen tree might block a road), to impede, hold back, prevent. Also, to move sideways.

babakau n. wall of wooden house, also a fried pastry turnover eaten at breakfast.

babale n. dolphin, a mammal. This word is not commonly known. Dolphins are not referred to in any of the well known myths or legends.

babani (West) n. species of freshwater eel, Gymnothorax sp. Syn. *dadarikai*.

Baba Siga n. popular nickname for Macuata Province where, as the name implies, there are sunny slopes.

baca n. worm, bait, as in fishing, or by extension, an enticement that has duplicitous intention. As a verb, *baca, bacana* to put our bait, as on a hook. *baca ni qele* earthworm.
Idiom: *baca kuita* a special enticement, very likely to succeed, a "hooker" that will win over the person being enticed. (*kuita* octopus). *O iko baca cava?* What bait (enticement) are you using? *Na baca kuita*. Something special, that will succeed.

baca (Kadavu, Lau) sick, illness, injury. Syn. *tauvimate*.

baci 1. a rather formal word, difficult to translate; it approximates "thus", or "then" or "again", implying a repetition. The word may be used to indicate a result or consequence of something that is stated earlier. *E rawa meu baci cakava tale.* I could or would do it again. *Au baci raica tale mada.* I wish I could see it again. *Sa baci voleka tale tiko na gauna ni balolo.* Once again the time of *balolo* is close by. *Sega ni dede, sa baci lesu mai.* Before long, he/she will return.

baci 2. (Vanua Levu) penis, male sexual organs. Syn. *boci* (uncircumcised). See *qala-na, uti-na*.

badamu n. a common swamp eel in fresh or brackish water. It is reddish brown in colour with a yellowish belly. Slow-moving, it is often caught by hand. The presence of algae called *de ni duna* ("eel excrement") indicate its presence, and one can see the air holes in the mud. Relative to other eels they are slow-moving. The flesh is a little brownish and slightly oily when cooked, usually grilled with the skin on, after gutting, or cooked in a leaf-wrapped package in the earth-oven.

bagi after all, therefore, thus, then (in the preceding senses), as a matter of course, as an affirmation. This is a rather formal word used by the older generation.

bagi (Lau, Kadavu) n. tooth. Syn. *bati*.

bagitaka (Eng.) v. to hit, "bang", smash it/him (marbles as a game), a word said by some children but not in general usage.

bai n. fence, stockade. *vakabai* fenced. *viribai-taka* to fence, set up fences. *Viribai* can refer to stockades, ancient war defenses, and is often used figuratively to mean prepare for imminent war or, these days, any serious conflict. *baitaka na iteitei*. to fence in the garden. *bai ni ika* fish fence. *baivatu* stone enclosure, stone wall. *bainivuaka* pig-pen, pig stye. Syn. *ba ni ika, bavatu,* etc.

baigani (Hindi) n. eggplant, an introduced food in areas of Indian influence.

Idiom: *E sega ni dua na nomu baigani.* It is none of your business.

"bainj" (Hindi "sister") n. form of address speaking to a mature Indian woman.

"baiya" (Hindi "brother") n. form of address to an Indian man.

baka n. very large native tree, Ficus obliqua, with drooping branches and hanging roots. Growth can start as an epiphyte, and smother the mother tree. Believed formerly to be associated with spirits. They are conspicuous by the Queens Road near Navua. Inner bark formerly used for cloth when *masi* not available. White latex has been used to entrap birds. Fruits are a fig, maturing to yellow orange, then red, throughout the year. Often confused with F. prolix, an introduced, similar, sacred tree of India, which has fruits that turn black while F. obliqua fruits turn yellow, orange and red, and F. obliqua fruits all year round. There is confusion as to which species is referred to by the Fijian names *baka ni Viti* and *baka ni valagi*. Confused also is F. tinctoria. Syn. (West) *yayawa*.

Idiom: *Vunibaka ga sa tevoro.* Beware the power of a big man; he may appear magnificent but he can be dangerous, literally, The *baka* tree (banyan tree) has its own devil.

Idiom: *Sa kamusu na baka.* a great chief has died.

baka n. a type of branched coral.

bakava adj., n. crazy, silly person. Reference is to St. Giles Hospital, a mental hospital in Suva, suggesting the metal fencing (which in fact does not enclose the place).

bakewa n. remora, pilot fish that attaches itself to sharks. Edible but not tasty, Echeneis naucrates.

baku 1. adj. bitter, astringent in taste, such as the taste of immature bananas.

baku 2. n. foreskin of a penis, excised in ceremony of circumcision. By extension *baku* may refer to the penis of people who are not circumcised.

Idiom: *Baku!* insult, usually joking, of someone who is thought ineffectual. Syn. sometimes used for Indo-Fijians *Kulina*, literally "skin".

bakui n. Hydra, according to Neyret, one of the Cnidarians (jellyfish, sea anenomes, polyps, and including hydra), tiny, with tiny tentacles. Gov't dictionary has this listed as Ophiolepsis superba.

bala n. male sea turtle (green turtle), Chelonia mydas.

bala! interjection, implying surprise or disappointment.

bala, balata v. push into water (person, anchor, other things), or shove into some place, put into (prison): *Me bala na ikelekele!* Drop the anchor! *bala ki na vale ni veivesu* put into prison. The word implied shoving, pushing. There is a New Year's Eve custom of heaving people into the water.

balabala n. tree fern, Cyathea lunulata and other species. Splinters from tree ferns cause dangerous and lingering pain and are a common injury in the bush, especially to bare feet. Tree fern wood is useful as a means of keeping fire a long time; it burns very slowly. The firm spongy pith in the stem of mature tree ferns is cut into round shape for children to use as a ball. Soft scales at the apex of the trunk serve to stuff cushions. Syn. *loulou* (source of the place-name Naduruloulou. a Government agricultural station.)

Idiom: *mate vakabalabala* to die childless, like a tree fern. The tree fern has no suckers or seeds and Fijians did not know it breeds by spores.

Idiom: *vula i se na balabala* lit. month when the *balabala* flowers, i.e., never, since the tree fern has spores, not flowers or seeds.

Idiom: "blondie", a word sometimes used by prisoners for the soft upper part of a tree fern after it has been cut off. It is very fair colour, and is slimy. With round hole cut in it, it has been used as a vagina for sexual relief.

balabala sa n. tree fern, Cyathea affinis, tall and very thin but solid, very hard trunk, and thus much more durable wood. It is distinguished by a lighter leaf-stem colour, finer leaflets and less branching of the leaves.

balagi n. edible Surgeon fish around the reef, Acanthurus sp.

balaka n. a palm useful for its very thin, straight and hard stem, formerly used for spears, Balaka species.

balala v. to stick through (spear, nail, knife) without gripping.

balavu adj., n. long, tall. (Fijians use the same word for both concepts.) length, height. *na kena balavu* its height (or length). *babalavu* plural, one of the very few adjectives that takes a plural form. See *cere, cecere,* height applied to high places, hills, mountains. See also *dede,* for length of time.
Idiom: *vuaka balavu* lit. "long pig" or "tall pig", meaning a human body intended for eating.

balawa n. Pandanus fruit, and by extension, the introduced pineapple due to similarity in appearance of the fruit. In the Viti Levu highlands, *balawa* usually refers to an edible bush pineapple with very small fruits, now growing wild. (Cultivated pineapple is re-planted every two years with suckers because the fruits become much smaller after the first two years.) Pineapples originated in central America. Well established commercial variety is the Ripley Queen, small, very thorny, very juicy and sweet. The Serene (Sydney) varieties are types of Smooth Cayenne, much larger and with only small thorns at the tips of leaves. *vatu ni balawa* whale-tooth (*tabua*) formerly placed in a grave; certain coastal Fijians (not highlanders) believed that a dead man's spirit would throw the *tabua* at a certain Pandanus palm to gain entry to the afterworld.

balawa viriki (Archaic) After the mid-1700s, when whale-teeth were introduced to Fiji and became symbolic, a legendary custom developed: the notion that after dying, a man's spirit would pass Udu Point (*Mua-i-udu*) where there was supposed to be a pandanus tree and he should throw a whale tooth at it. If successful, he could pass on to the other world. *viriki* thrown at.

bale v. to die (of a person) polite, honorific term, especially for chiefs. *bale drokadroka* v. to die young

bale adj. noble, honorific term used only in the combination *na Turaga bale* the noble chief, *na Marama bale* the noble lady.

bale, baleta v., adj. to be the cause of, often meaning to be at fault, to blame. *Sa bale vei koya.* He/she is to blame. He/she was responsible. *Sa baleti iko.* It is because of you.

bale, baleca v. to fall from upright position (onto), usually of something tall, a person or a tree.

baleca adj., adv. disrespectful (words, behaviour). *Ke tau baleca na noqu vosa, meu vosoti.* If my words are disrespectful, please be patient with me. inappropriate in behaviour. *baleca na nomu ivukivuki.* Your behaviour is inappropriate. Syn. *sakasaka.*

vakabalea v. to topple, to set down.

bale (Nait.) v. to go. *E bale ivei o koya?* Where is he/she going? *taubale* to walk.

bale, bale-taka v. to go on, pass by, cross over, usually on foot. *taubale* to walk, go on foot. *bale dodo* to follow the "stretch" (path, road, river, but perhaps especially, the continuing ridge of a hill).

balebale (Lau) n., v. cooperative work, various households doing a task together. Syn. *solesolevaki.* The concept is that many hands make light work. Working alone is slow and arduous. This is a very important, useful custom in Fijian villages.

ibalebale n. meaning. *A cava na kena ibalebale?* What does it mean? *ibalebale-rua* double meaning (this is a modern Anglicism). *balebale-rua* to have a double meaning, homonym.

vakaibalebale adj. meaningful, has meaning.

balei (Colo East, Namosi) n. snake. This is a totem of tribe Naleya at village Nasava, Noemalu District, Naitasiri. A closely related word, *Baleni,* refers to a ten-headed snake godess around village Vunikodi, Macuata Province, and there is there a clan called Baleni. The title Rokobaleni exists among Waimaro Fijians, tribe Navakavu, villages Muaivuso and Togalevu, at the coast of Rewa Province. The implication is that of a snake, though present-day locals are unaware of that connection. A distinctive fern that grows around tree trunks is known as Snake Nest in Cakaudrove (*sova ni gata*) and on the Waidina River of Colo East (*sova ni balei*). Sold as a large household ornamental, this plant is often known among Europeans as Antler Horns or Staghorn, names not listed in my botanical references. Syn. *gata.*

veibaleyaki adj. indeterminate, ambiguous, going this way and that way. *Sa veibaleyaki tiko na uluna.* His/her head is nodding this way and that way.

balekana n. var. of breadfruit with small, long fruit that has smooth skin. It matures early and may be eaten when it falls, which is implied in the name.

baleravu n. fire-torch of bamboo or other improvised bush material used still today to light one's way at night around the village. The word implies the damage done if the torch falls. Traditional housing is very combustible and houses usually built close together. For such torches highlanders used bamboo while coastal Fijians normally used dried coconut spathes (flower shoots) called *bawara.*

balesi broken off but still hanging (as with a tree-branch).

baleta 1. because (or, in a question) because of what, why. *Baleta na cava?* (or) *Baleta?* Why? (Because of what?).

baleta 2. concerning, as in *na veika baleti au.* the things concerning me (about me).

baleta 3. guilty, at fault, to be the one concerned. *Sa baleti koya*. It is his/her fault. *Sa baleti au*. I am to be blamed, am guilty. responsible, at fault. *Sa baleti iko ga*. It is just because of you (You brought it on yourself.) Syn. *Sa bale vei koya*. He/she is at fault. *Sa bale vei au*. I am at fault.

bali, balia v. to knead, as of Fijian *vakalolo* pudding, or modernly, dough for baking. (Fijians anciently had no knowledge of yeast or leavened bread.)

balia (Vanua Levu) n. mad, insane, mentally unstable, of a person.

balibali or **balikali** adj. clumsy, of a person.

baloa black, or blackish, usually of skin colour. Fijians can be colour-conscious and will sometimes remark on how dark or light a person's skin is. Traditionally, many of the blacker, "true" Fijians of the highlands have felt disadvantaged. They have in several places accepted as chiefs immigrant Tongans, who have fair skins, as for the Noemalu, and at the Nadroga coast. On a few occasions, Fijians have accepted Europeans as incoming chiefs (Clan Naulucavu, for example, at Nakoroṣule, and also the *kaiNadakua* in Sawakasa, Tailevu). Fijian mothers are often proud to have a light-skinned child. Skin bleaches (whiteners) are advertised in the Fijian language newspapers, as are hair-straighteners. This topic is a sensitive one, and a complicated one. Black warriors of the Fiji highlands have had a great reputation as mercenaries in Tonga and also in the Tui Kaba conquest of Lakeba Island accomplished by the "Black Regiment", literally "Black Pigs" *Vuaka loa*, famous for their courage and fighting skills. They were proud of being black.

balobi sulu n. bolt of cloth, *lobi, lobia* to fold. *e va na balobi sulu* four bolts of cloth. Bolts of cotton cloth are important gift items at some modern Fijian ceremonies. (In coastal areas, barkcloth has been used, especially in areas of Polynesian influence.) The long stretch of cloth is strung out on display, brought forward by a procession of women, showing it off. Highlanders never had the mulberry barkcloth, and never had such grand ceremonial displays.

balolo n. an edible sea-worm, the annelid Eunice viridis (formerly Palolo viridis), found only in certain places, but not at Viti Levu. *Balolo* appears once or twice a year at only about 100 coastal locations in Fiji but at any one place it may not recur annually, or may occur only once (as at Lakeba). Elsewhere, outside of the usual places, Fijians may never have seen it or tasted it, but they have all heard of it. Early in the morning the annelids rise in a spiral from coral sand, brown male sperm sacs and green female egg sacs in the form of worms that intertwine and fertilise, squirming to the surface. By the time the sun becomes strong, around eight o'clock, they will disappear. The transparent eggs become invisible and the thin coloured skins seem to evaporate to nothing. The *balolo* also exists in Samoa, Tonga, and the islands off Japan. *qoliva na balolo* fish for the *balolo*. *tagava na balolo* net the *balolo*. Collection may involve many village people. When quantities are great, much will be given away. It is contrary to custom that *balolo* be sold, but Lautoka market now does have some, cooked, for sale.

On Vanua Levu it occurs only on the northeastern coast from Saqani to Udu, and on the southeastern coast from around Nasavusavu to village Dakuniba. Geraghty also names some islands around Vanualevu:- Kia, Cikobia, Naqelelevu, Rabe, Yanuca, Taveuni (at Vuna and Lavena), Qamea, and Laucala.

Other locations are in LomaiViti (Tokou, Ovalau, Wakaya), Yasawa (Mamanuca, Waya), Lau (Lakeba, Naidi, Susui, Avea, Udu at Kabara, Vanuavatu, Vatoa), around the south coast of Kadavu (village Muani and according to Geraghty, from Nabukelevu to Galoa, and Soso to Vacalea), and off the south coast of Vatulele Island.

At Lakeba Island, various of the villages have a different seafood that they call their *balolo*, which appears in abundance only once a year. Village Tubou has the true *balolo*. Nukunuku has the fish *nuqa*. Waciwaci has the red land crab *lairo* in late November to December, and the *salala* fish in April. Vakano has the unicorn fish *ta*, and a type of bill fish *saku*. Saqalau has the shark *qio damu*. Drano has the fish *tugadra*, similar to the *salala*, and also the fish *kalawa*. Waitabu has the land crab *lairo* and the small black reef eel *boila*. Elsewhere in Fiji, village Namara in Tailevu has the fish *nuqa* that is their *balolo*. *vula i balolo lailai* October-early November, when the *balolo* has its minor season. *vula i balolo levu* November-early December, when the major season may occur, according to the phase of the moon and the weather, and other factors unknown.

Rising of *balolo* usually occurs 7 to 9 days after the full moon, from midnight to 4 am, on the falling tide, lasting into the early daylight hours. The rising is often preceded a day or two by the appearance of scum on the surface of the sea. At this time, in many places, Fijians are fearful of "red tide" that causes the flesh of certain reef fish to become poisonous to humans.

At western areas of Fiji, *balolo* occurs usually earlier than in eastern areas. In Samoa, however, it is a couple of weeks earlier.

In the early morning, until about 8 am, the annelids are sieved up in tins, fine-mesh nets, and cloth, as they spiral in thick streams to the surface from the sandy bottom. (I have observed them and swum amongst them as a diver.) Males are brownish and the females are green but otherwise they look similar. When exposed to the sun, they appear to dissolve, leaving only a few drops of water which then evaporate. The segment of the animal that rises is composed almost entirely of tiny transparent eggs or sperm covered by an extremely thin, fragile coloured skin that itself becomes virtually invisible when burst open.

Balolo are eaten raw, living and writhing, or cooked in the earth oven, all with some joyous ceremony. They can be frozen, and they can be fried. There is a tradition of first presentation (*isevu*) to the chief, then a wide distribution to relatives and friends. Rain often falls after the *balolo* have risen. *Sa cabe cake mai na balolo.* The *balolo* are rising. *taga-va na balolo* net the *balolo*. *na te ni balolo* the sea scum remnant of the *balolo*. Syn. (Kadavu) *baya*.

Idiom: *E kua gona ni balolo, me na kua sara.* "Now or never", If this opportunity is not grasped, the chance will be lost. Lit. if you do not take the *balolo* now you won't have any -- the occasion passes quickly.

Idiom: *Balolo sara.* It won't happen quickly (it takes a long time for the *balolo* to re-appear).

Idiom: *balolo ni vakananu* sorry, you have missed out on that.

balu-na n. cheek (part of the face).

Idiom: *balu bilo* the vulgar trick of some men, say, who try to force a mouthful of *yaqona* beverage into the mouth of a young woman, as might be done if their peoples are *tauvu dredre*, kin-groups, closely related in a very hard joking relationship with the people playing tricks on one another. The Waimaro people of Matuku Island in Lau are related this way with Waimaro people of the eastern highlands of Viti Levu. When the two peoples meet, great liberties are taken that can be humiliating and very frightening to youngsters. Real injury is never done.

balubalu adj. chubby-faced.

bameni (Eng.) n. bar-man (who serves drinks).

bameti (Eng.) n. barmaid (who serves drinks).

"banana-face" (Youthful Slang) adj. "freckle-face", a taunt directed against white kids or part-Fijians.

bani 1. (Eng.) n. bun (as from a bakery). Modernly, a Fijian breakfast is a fried or boiled *bani* for which there are many local names. In urban areas on Good Friday a primitive Fiji version of hot cross buns is imperative, and replaces virtually all other breads. These are very simple, virtually tasteless buns, sold by the dozen, each one marked crudely with a red cross painted on with food-dye. It is a necessary ritual, not at all a gastronomic occasion, rather like the concept of a birthday cake, which modern urban Fijians also insist on. The cross must be red colour.

bani 2. (Eng.) n. band (musical). *Au sa laki sara bani.* I am going to watch a band play. More fully the term is *matabani* band.

ba ni ika n. fish fence to catch fish, usually made of upright reeds fastened together with strips of *walai* vine. Some are erected seasonally to catch seasonal runs of fish such as the *ki*. *ba kele* permanent fish fence, usually made of stones. Depth is usually four to six feet at high tide and virtually empty or very shallow at low tide. An inner collection area is known as the *malevu* and there may be as many as three of these. A stone fish fence is known as *moka*.

banuve n. caterpillar, general term. Banuve has been a name of a Vunivalu chief on Bau Island. Syn. (Lau) *nuve*.

baosi (or) **bausi** n. (Slang, Eng. "purse") **1.** purse. **2.** a small gift, or action, usually to attract the affections of someone of opposite sex. In mild, good-humoured reproach, one might say *Kua ni bausi!* Don't try try flattery!

baovi, baovi-taka v. to cook a food (usually fish) wrapped in leaves, grilled on hot coals of the fire. Syn. *tavusala, tavusalutaka*.

ibaovi n. any leaves used to wrap a cooked food.

baqe (Eng.) n. bank.

bara (Eng., Slang) wheelbarrow(s), much used at Suva Public Market with boys offering for a fee to carry shoppers' produce to the buses and taxis.

baraca (Eng.) n. brother, used as a form of address, and title in some of the Christian sects. Male members of the American denomination Assemblies of God may be referred to as Brother. Some teachers at Roman Catholic schools are referred to as Brother. Outside the various denominations, in ordinary life, "brother" may be vulgarly abbreviated as *"Bro"* in the style of lower class American speech.

barasi (Eng.) brush. *barasi ni bati* toothbrush.

baravi n. sea-coast.

bareki (Eng.) n. barracks (military).

Ba-rewa! (Slang) adj. pretty, handsome, often called out as affectionate greeting amongst young urban people of opposite sex. A somewhat dated expression. Syn. *Uro!* (lit. fat, as opposed to lean meat. The crisp fat of pork is considered a delicacy.) Antonym: *Balekade!* (lit. "Fallen fruit!", a coconut or other fruit, fallen from the tree before it is ripe), exclamation of rejection, usually in response to *Ba Rewa!* implying that the other is a loose woman.

bari, baria v. to gnaw, nibble at something hard, done by rats and bats as well as people. Idiom: *bari sui* n., adj. of a person, lazy, dependent on others, begging, demanding. Lit. gnawing at bones.

bari-ni-savu n. edge of a waterfall. Syn. *batinisavu*.

bari-ni-vatu n. cliff.

basa, basa v. to level, fit together, correspond with as to position. *Au a basa na basi.* I arrived at the same time the bus arrived. *Na kau me rau veibasai.* Place the two pieces of wood in position together. *basa* (Lau especially) to be just in time for something or someone.

basa (Eng.) n. bazaar, a common Fijian way of raising money for community purposes (church, school), a custom learned from Europeans. Usually it involves the sale of cakes, coconut oil, mats, and more recently, barbecue lamb chops and fried sausages. It is a social occasion.

basaga 1. adj. branched, divided. Syn. *besaga* (or) *basoga*.

basaga 2. n. starfish, generic term.

veibasai opposite. *veibasai kei na i kelikeli ni basi.* opposite the bus-stop.

ba seisei n. taro leaf-stems (*baba*) stripped of skin, for food, a delicacy of Fiji, best steamed lightly, often served in coconut cream. Symbolic gift, uncooked, brought by relatives to mothers of newborn babies. (*sei* split). Syn. *baba, dolodolo*.

basi (Eng.) n. bus. *waraka na basi.* wait for the bus. *vodo e na basi.* get on the bus. *calata na basi.* miss the bus. *na ikelekele ni basi* the bus-stop. *basiteni* n. bus stand, often referring to a central bus stand in town.

Idiom: "Tailevu no *leqa*, no *basi*, paidar". This is a proud exclamation, vaunting the qualities of Tailevu. A curious tri-lingual saying (English, Fijian, Hindi), lit. There's no problem in Tailevu. If there is no bus we can walk. The notion is that Tailevu is a relatively flat province. If there is no bus one can walk almost anywhere.

Idiom: *Qarauna o na sega ni "vodoka na basi ni Lokia!* An apocryphal, legendary rumour has it that Ro Lala exclaimed this to her husband Ratu Kamisese Mara, lit. "Be careful or you won't climb on the Lokia bus!" Implication is that he should be more considerate of her or he would not succeed in mounting her in sexual union. Village Lokia is a junction point where, after crossing the Rewa River, Rewa people can take a bus to Suva, and Ro Lala of course, was a lady of Rewa.

basi, basia v. to spread open with fingers, e.g. of coconut-shell partly opened but not completely separated. Idiom: *vakabasibasi* to sit or lie down suggestively exposing one's private parts (with or without underwear).

basika 1. v. to put through, as thread through a needle.

basika 2. v. to make known. *Me basika vei iratou na itukutuku.* Let them know the message. (Suddenness is implied.)

basika 3. v. to appear, emerge, come into view. *babasika* more emphatic or abrupt an action, to burst into view. Virtual syn. is *lasika*, though that is usually less sudden, more gentle or slow.

basikeli (Eng.) n. bicycle. Little used by Fijians.

basiteti (Vulgar, Eng.) n. bastard, said as an insult.

basoga branched, having branches, divided. *na babasogasoga* the multiple branching. *na basogo ni gaunisala* the branch in the road (where it divides). *na veibasoga ni kawa* n. the division of kinship lineage. Syn. *basaga*.

basoritaka v. to close (basket, sack, door) with little sticks threaded together.

basovi n. sp. beautiful and magnificent giant fern with huge bulbous base and virtually no trunk, fronds spreading out 18 feet, Angiopteris erecta, Marattiaceae. One of the possible hosts to the *dalo* beetle.

basu, basuka v. to break open, break down (house, crate), spread open (mouth, basket). *basuraka*, more forceful. *basu lawa* law-breaker, lawbreaking. *basuka na vale* break down the house. *basuvale* break-in (of a house).

bata (Eng. "butter") butter. May refer to margarine.

batabata n., adj. cold, chilly, usually of weather. *vakabatabata-taka na kakana* cool the food. See *liliwa* (which can apply to a person, water, the wind or an object). Syn. (Colo East) *kudukudua* cold. By ext., *batabata* may mean cold in a figurative sense, concerning a person's behaviour, or the failure of a meeting, or a game that has not been carried off well and has been a failure. *batabata* may also modernly (as an Anglicism) refer to a cold as an infectious malady, runny nose, coughing, sneezing.

bateri or **batiri** (Eng.) n. battery (electrical). Syn. *beteri*.

bati n. warrior caste, usually referring to a traditionally specialised clan serving a chief. These days the functions are only ceremonial, for example at funerals or installation of chiefs. *veibatiki* serving as warriors to another group of people, one tribe or village in a traditional relationship to another. *bati balavu* warriors who are a first line of defence, fighting away from the chief's home. *bati leka* warriors who are a last line of defense for the chief, household warriors, and may have the duty of handling a dead chief's body. Two tribes that are *veibatiki* have food prohibitions in each other's presence. Warriors may not eat pork or sometimes, plantain; the others may not eat seafood or coconut products. Historically, such warriors were not always loyal; they could trade their favours with different chiefs.

bati- as a prefix, indicating a taste preference supposedly common to a certain region of Fiji, said mockingly, as a joke or competitive jibe by people of another region. These jibes formerly came mainly from a people who are related, especially as *tauvu,* but these days it all becomes much more general. *bati via* refers jokingly to Rewans, who are supposed to eat a lot of *via,* the giant corm Cyrtosperma chamissonis that thrives in swampy Rewa. (In fact the original relationship was only between Noco in Rewa, and Nayau in Lau Province. Other such expressions are:

bati balei said of the kaiNakelo, by the people of Tokatoka, implying they eat a lot of *balei*. *balei* is a regional word for snake, mostly heard in Naitasiri and Namosi.

bati busa people of Natokalau, Ovalau Island, implying they eat a lot of the fish *busa,* a garfish (Hemiramphus far).

bati dairo people of Moturiki Island, especially by people of sub-Territory Naqaliduna who are under the Roko Tui Kala centred at village Taviya, Ovalau Island. *dairo* is a sandfish that may be eaten raw.

bati dalo, people of Bua Province.

bati daroro people of Navatusila in the western highlands.

bati dogo people of Bureta by Lovoni people on Ovalau Island.

bati drokai people of Dravuwalu, Kadavu Island.

bati ivi people of Beqa Island for eating Polynesian chestnut *ivi*.

bati kaikoso people of Verata for eating that shellfish.

bati kalavo people of Tokatoka, by Nakelo people, who claim their neighbours eat rats *kalavo*.

bati kawai people of Macuata. *kawai* type of cultivated yam.

bati kulu people of Vuda, Sabeto, or Vatukarasa (Nadroga). *kulu* breadfruit.

bati lumi people of Gau Island. *lumi* an edible seaweed.

bati maoli Lauan people for their eating (cooked) papaya *maoli*.

bati me people of Kadavu Island, who supposedly eat goats *me*.

bati niu Korocau people by their *tauvu* of Kocoma. *niu* coconut.

bati paileve Laucala people, by their *tauvu* of Vuna, Taveuni Island. *paileve* is form of Fijian *madrai,* a fermented starch-food commonly known as *bila*.

bati pata people of Buca, Cikobia, Naqelelevu, Udu or Yacata Island. *pata* is a type of plantain.

kai pota Vuna people, by those of Laucala. *pota* is taro leaf, steamed or cooked in earth oven, supposedly a local specialty food.

bati qari people of Namara, Tailevu Province, related to sea crabs *qari*.

bati qina people of Vuma, usually by the people of Tokou, Ovalau Island. *qina* is a small type of sea urchin.

bati sara people of sub-Territory Naqaliduna, Ovalau Island, especially by those of Moturiki Island and Natokalau. *sara* is a tiny, edible, silver, sardine-like fish of the coast.

bati sore Lovoni people, by those of Bureta, referring to seeds of *dawa* fruit.

bati soro Namata people, by people of Namara. *soro* Fiddler crab, Uca sp.

bati vala Volivoli villagers, Nadroga Province. *vala* nuts of Barringtonia sp., more usually referred to as *vutu kana*.

bati vea people of Nairai Island. *vea* over-ripe breadfruit. Properly this applies only to tribe Qalilevu of village Vutuna, and specifically only clan Bete, but modernly, this has been generalised to all of Nairai Island. (The name Vutuna derives from Futuna Island of nearby French Polynesia; these are the only people on Nairai Island who do not relate to Bau Island.)

bati- as a prefix, indicating some characteristic of the person. (*bati* tooth).

bati digidigi choosy eater (*digi-taka* choose).

baticalucalu gobbles food fast, usually said of children but may apply to gluttony of an adult.

bati vou person who prefers immature fruit to mature fruit. Often said jokingly of an older man who has an eye for young girls (*vou* new). Syn. *bati ka vou*.
bati kamica sweet-toothed, liking sweet foods or snacks.
bati dredre giggly person. *dredre* laugh.

bati-na 1. n. edge, of some object. *bati ni teveli* edge of the table. *bati-ni-wai* water's edge, riverside, seaside. *bati ni savu* edge of a waterfall. *bati ni lovo* edge of the earth-oven, and by extension, in Lau, the extended family, who can share the same food resources. *bati ni cakau* edge of the reef. The edge of a garden, or hem of a cloth is *bele-na*.
Idiom: *ena bati ni tanoa* lit., around the (edge of a) *yaqona* bowl. Gossip and yarning are both implied.

bati-na 2. n. tooth. *cavuta na bati* pull out the tooth. *daunibati, daubati* (or) *daucavubati*, the older term. dentist. Syn. (Lau, Kadavu) *bagi*.
bati sila tusk, canine tooth.
bati-ni-sucu n. milk teeth, first set of teeth of a baby.
bati lutu toothless person or person with few teeth (*lutu* to fall).
bati qoru gap-toothed.
bati qesa person has rotten teeth (*qesa* charred black).
bati kopa having brown-stained teeth (*kopa* copper).
bati votu or *bati vusi* buck-toothed, over-bite.
bati lasu (or) *bati sui* false teeth. *lasu* false, *sui* bone.
bati cavu false tooth or denture that may be removed. *cavu* v. to pull out.
Idiom: *Vosa mada o iko, e rovu e liu na batimu.* You go ahead and talk first, because you are my elder (your teeth sprouted first). Usually said humorously when two people begin talking at once.
Idiom: *bula i bati-na* lives only to eat, gluttonous.

batibalavu 1. n. migrant shore bird, Bat-tailed Godwit, Limosa lapponica, visits Fiji October through March, spending the northern summer in Alaska or Siberia. Syn. (Lau) *bajikaciwa*.

bati balavu 2. (Archaic) n. of a clan or tribe, frontier warriors as a first line of defence for a chief and his domain. See *bati leka*.

batibasaga n. scorpion, lit. "split toothed".

batikaciwa (Lau) n. Bar-tailed Godwit, large migrant bird, wader with upturned bill, often seen on mudflats. Syn. *batibalavu*.

batikadi n. bandit, guerilla fighter, formerly used for wild man, "bogey man" of the bush, living alone, an imagined threat to straying people (or children who may be naughty, and so cautioned by their mother) In fact such wild men existed, social deviants, psychologically disturbed people, outcasts who did not fit into very rigidly controlled village society. I discovered such a young man hiding in the jungles of Namosi in the 1990s. I fed him and kept him and he followed me around like a pet. He was mentally deficient, and escaped from his own family who treated him like a slave and beat him. The Police required me to return him to his family who ultimately beat him excessively, and he died. He had never hurt anyone and never tried to defend himself.

bati leka (Archaic) n. of a clan or tribe, traditional household warriors and guards for a chief and his village. Contrast with *bati balavu* frontier warriors at a first line of defence.

bati loa n. species of swimming crab that has black claws (*batiloa*)

bati madramadra n. medicinal herb, Bidens pilosa, Compositae, common weed, macerated in coconut oil and applied externally in massage for painful muscles, bruises.

bati ni kete-na n. stomach just below rib cage on each side of person's body.

bati ni lovo (Lau) n. extended family, intimately related, lit. "edge of the earth-oven", implying the sharing of food. Syn. *tokatoka*.

bati-ni-siwa n. fish-hook, formerly made of wood or shell. *wa ni siwa* fishing line. Line fishing was not customary in most parts of Fiji. Tongans and Samoans introduced the concept.

bati ni toro n. razor blade. *toro, toroya* to shave. *itoro* razor. Fijians formerly used a piece of glass and before that, the sharp edge of a chipped shell. When razor blades became common, they were sharpened by rubbing against the inside of a cup.

batiri n. mangrove (*tiri*) swamp at edge of sea or river. A recurring place-name. Very useful breeding ground for fish and other marine life.

Batiri n., adj. valencia-type oranges grown at Batiri, Macuata. This has been a failed plantation programme sponsored by the Fiji Government. Mis-management continued for years.

bativou (Idiom) adj., n. person who prefers green fruit rather than fruit that is fully mature. This is fairly common in Fiji. By extension, a person who is attracted to younger people of the opposite sex, usually said of men who are attracted to younger women. *vou* new.

bau 1. a word that can have several meanings: just (or) indeed. A modifier that adds decisiveness or affirmation in a very polite form by softening a statement or request. *Au sa bau lako.* I'll just go; *e dua bau* just one. *Sa bau vakacava na teitei?* Just how is the garden? *A cava sa bau tukuna na boso?* Just what did the boss say? *O bau wili kina o iko.* You are definitely included. There can an implication of once or ever, or in the negative, not once, never. *O sa bau cakava?* Have you ever done it? *Au a sega ni bau rogoca na yacana.* I have never heard his/her name. *Au a sega sara ni bau moce ena bogi koya.* I did not sleep at all that night.

bau, bauta 2. v. to accompany, supportively, to do something, go somewhere together.

vakabau v. supported, approved.

vakabauta v. to believe in a supportive sense.

bau 3. (Colo East) v. to go. *Au sa bau* I'm going. *veibauyaki* go here and there. Syn. (Bau) *lako*.

bau 4. n. sp. of tree, Pittosporum brackenridgei, useful timber, fruit eaten as a snack.

bau 5. n. small riverine fish, Ophieleotris aporos, Eleotridae, a significant food in the Viti Levu highlands. Syn. *ika bau, kaqa, sika.* (Waidina) *tauci*.

baubau n. a Fijian sickness, believed caused by spirits or witchcraft; generally failing health, weakness, confused thoughts. Baubau happens to be a name associated with the mother of Cakobau, the name of her house-site on Bau Island. It is also an old place-name in the Tailevu mainland. See *drimi*.

baunova (or) **baudova** (Eng.) v. bound over by court, with conditional suspended sentence for minor offenses.

bausa (Eng.) n. bowser. petrol station, gas station (U.S.A).

bausi (Eng.) n. purse, wallet.

bauta v. to recognise, realise, acknowledge some quality or characteristic.

bau vudi n. tree, Palaqium spp. and Burckella sp., Sapotaceae, timber often used to make punts.

bavelo n. simple dug-out canoe, made from one log with no outrigger, still occasionally used in the highland rivers, as well as coastal areas, and smaller islands.

ba via n. an old traditional variety of taro, much favoured still, with yellowish coloured flesh, excellent taste and pleasantly chewy texture *wadrega vinaka*.

bavulu n., adj. (Eng. "bloody fool") dopey, *bavulu levu* really dopey. Bauan *doce*. This expression is by now perhaps somewhat archaic.and also a rather low-class expression.

bawara n. spathe (unopened flower shoot) of coconut palm, also the dried calyx, the outer sheath of the spathe, used as torch in walking outdoors at night. (Viti Levu highlanders, having no coconuts, more normally used bamboo for torches at night.) Gilbertese but not Fijians have known the art of making alcohol, a type of arrack, from unopened spathes. It is shaved thinly at the tip each day and the juice drips into a small container. A plant rich in tannin may be used to arrest fermentation. A "wine" can be produced, or a strong alcohol.

Idiom: *basu bawara* of a person, to break free, break out from constraints such as discipline at home, village, or military. A spathe bursts open as it dries and matures, and reveals its flowers.

be adj., n. stubborn self-will and judgmental nature. *dau be* stubbornly negative.

bebe ni gusu-na n. lips (of the mouth). Syn. *tebe ni gusu*.

bebe n. moth, butterfly (pronounced with both vowels prolonged).

bebe n. vagina. Syn. *maga-na*. Words not normally pronounced but *maga!* may be heard in swearing, expressing sudden disappointment, as with the French exclamation "merde!". Syn. (Vanua Levu) *ele*. See *manene*.

beca (or) **beci** adj., v. to disrespect, look down on something or someone. *kakua ni dau veibeci* don't look down on people. *na nona vosa beca baleti au.* his disdainful words about me.

becerui apparently agreeable but in fact uncooperative.

becuru n. eyebrow. Syn. *vacu-na*.

beitaka v. to accuse, blame. *viribeibei* blames others.

veibeitaki n. accusation.

dauveibeitaki n. prosecutor (court).

Beika n. surname of Thomas Baker, Methodist missionary killed in interior Viti Levu 1867. He is referred to as *Misi Beika*. A main hall is named Baker Hall,
Beika Olo at the Methodist School, Davuilevu. *Misi Peka* may be a preferred spelling.

beka perhaps, maybe. *vakabeka-taka* v. to doubt (something).

beka 1. n. may refer to small insect-eating bats but more usually to the large, very visible Flying Fox, three species, mainly the Polynesian Flying Fox. It is eaten especially by hill tribes, caught by prickly vine nets, or by stoning, or by shaking a tree where one hangs. When the tree is shaken, the bat falls to the ground, temporarily disoriented. Fijians have usually boiled the bat whole, and then easily pluck off the fur. They eat the guts after squeezing out the gut, which is not considered dirty. In the highlands the bat was usually grilled (*tavu*) over a fire.

Fruit bats can become very friendly pets, and can be stroked on the neck and on the nose. They may be let to fly free and the males especially, will return to a person who has fed them. They eat fruit of bananas, papaya, the *sa* tree, *kavika* tree, and flower shoots of the *yaqoyaqona*. They have excellent vision, and sense of smell but cannot echo-locate, as the smaller, insectiverous bats do, who live around caves. They scout around dusk, flying alone, in pairs, and sometimes in a pair of couples. In certain locations at certain times they may appear as a great cloud of thousands; this is thought to be a sign of impending bad weather with the bats looking for food in advance. Settling into a tree at night, bats may fill the tree. Against a torchlight their eyes may gleam like a thousand little lights, a fascinating sight. The *beka dina* sleeps more in daytime. The *beka lulu* is active in daytime, and has much lighter colour fur. Syn. (Tonga) *peka*. (West) *bekwa*. (Kadavu) *doli*.

Idiom: *beka ni bogi* (Slang) person who is active only at night.

Idiom: *lako vakabeka* to take one's own food when going somewhere, find one's own food, not depending on others. Syn. *vuka vakabeka*.

Idiom: *samusamu beka* to stand around doing nothing (usually when others are working).

Idiom: *tuvani vaka bati ni beka* very neatly arranged (like the teeth of a bat).

beka 2. n. By ext., a boil in the armpit, very painful, causing a person to hold up the arm, like a bat-wing. This is fairly common among Fijians. Syn. *kirikiribeka*.

vakabekabei v., n. pet, pamper (person, animal).

bekabeka ni mata-na n. eyelash(es). *dakudaku ni mata-na* eyelids.

belavu n. fenced area containing dairy cattle.

bele 1. n. edible leafy vegetable shrub, Abelmoschus manihot, Malvaceae, often grown at edge of garden, as implied by the name. (The name also means "to sprout", of young leaves for the edible parts picked and these do sprout easily.) See *bele-na*. The edible leaves are mucilaginous and bitter but cooking water is often consumed, neither bitter nor slimy if it is not stirred too much. Medicinal use of leaves, heated over a fire and then placed on boils. Also juice extracted to ease menstruation or childbirth. The plant is propagated by cuttings. Syn. (Namosi, Colo East, Rewa) *vauvau (ni Viti)*. (West) *waci, sasau*. (Kadavu) *momoke*. The variety of names might suggest that this green was introduced separately from various parts of eastern Melanesia. It was indigenous to Southeast Asia, still widely cultivated in Malesia. Available all year but mainly December, January. *Bele damudamu* is hardier, more durable, less susceptible to rot, smaller somewhat tougher leaves; *bele vulavula* and regular green *bele* are two other cultivars. *Bele sukau* (or) *sukau* refers to the edible young leaves of the small tree Gnetum gnemon, Gnetaceae. *sani, sanita* pluck, harvest, leaves such as *bele*. *na sani bele* the harvesting of *bele* leaves.

Idiom *gunu wai ni bele* to be humiliated, reprimanded, lit. to drink the (inferred, distasteful) water from cooking *bele*-leaf.

bele 2. v. to sprout (of tree-leaf shoots). *Sa bele mai na vu-ni-kau* The soft leaf-shoots of the tree are sprouting (implying impending fruiting), esp. of forest trees and fruit-trees. *belebele* v. implies a multiplicity of sprouting.

bele-na 1. n. edge, hem (garden, cloth, etc.). **2.** crest of a wave, *bele-ni-ua*. **3.** cock's comb.

beleti 1. (Eng.) n. belt.

beleti 2. (Eng.) "belt", Ribbon fish, Trichiurus haumela, silver colour, edible. Syn. *tovisi, tovici*.

beli n. freshwater fish, gobi, 3 inches, edible though head is discarded. As a kind of "whitebait" (a N.Z. term), *beli* are born in the sea, move up to freshwater, where they are known variously as *cigani* or *cinani* or, around Navua, Namosi Province, *ta-nene*. Syn. *siri-beli*. *beli* are strictly seasonal.

belo n. Reef Heron, Egretta sacra, mottled, grey or white colour. Often seen around rivers. May nest fairly far inland. Syn. (Suva) *sako*.

Idiom: *domo ni belo* person who has only tea for lunch or dinner.

Idiom: *Sa suru na belo.* Work is done for the day; the job is finished. Lit. the heron has sneezed. (Time to go home.)

belu, beluka v. to bend, of something strong but soft, such as tin. See *lobi, lobia* for bending or folding soft flat things such as mats, cloth.

bena, bena v. to treat hair with dye (usually black, sometimes orange), lime, or ashes. *ibena* n. hair dye. Fijians women usually like to have lustrous black hair and must dye it to have that colour. Formerly the men dyed their hair and some still do. Leaves of the tree *manawi* were often used. Viti Levu highlanders used the nuts of *makita* tree to treat their hair. A common, inexpensive commercial dye is Bigen, most commonly used these days, purchased at Chinese shops.

bena v. to overuse something, to use excessively. *bena na yaqona* to overuse *yaqona*.

benisini (Eng.) n. "benzine", the local English for petrol, gasoline. The somewhat different white benzine for Coleman lamps is referred to as *benisini vulavula*.

benu n. garbage. *biuta na benu* throw out the rubbish, garbage. *na wai benuci* the polluted water.

ibenubenu n. place for throwing garbage. *kava ni benu* garbage tin.

benu-ca v. to discard rubbish indiscriminately.

benu vakaca v. n. to litter. This is a modernism, of course. Virtually everything a Fijian used was organic plant material that decomposed naturally.

beqaravu (Eng.) n., adj. bankruptcy, bankrupt.

bera 1. not yet. *sa bera* not yet. *sa bera ni lako* not yet gone.

bera 2. late. *Keitou sa bera mai.* We (several) are late in coming. *Keitou sa bera sara.* We are too late. *Bera! Bera!* You are late! (school, job). *cakacaka bera* (Ang.) v. to work late. *vakabera* v. to delay, to cause to be late (person, work).

bera 3. before, in *ni bera ni* . . . : *Ni bera ni o lako* Before you go. *Ni bera ni'u lako* . . Before I go . . . Or *ni bera na* as in: *ni bera na nona siga ni sucu* before his birthday.
Idioms *bera na liva* quick as lightning. *Beranaliva* The Phantom (comic book character).

berabera slow (vehicle, boat, horse, person). *Keitou sa berabera.* We (several) are slow. *vakaberabera* to slow it down.

berata v. to miss, to be late for. *berata na basi* miss the bus.

bese, besetaka v. to refuse (it). *au sa bese ni cakava* I refuse to do it. *Bese!* No! I/we refuse what your are asking. (Only youngsters would talk so bluntly, among themselves.)

vakabesebese v. to strike (of workers).

beseni (Eng.) n. basin.

beta in full bloom (of a plant).

beta (Nait.) n. an ornamental plant Coleus sp., red or yellow, variegated, often grown next to houses. In Bauan, *lata*. Fijian women drink an infusion of the leaves of the red variety believing it will prompt menstruation because of the red colour.

bete 1. n. priest, traditional Fijian, or Roman Catholic or Anglican. In eastern Fiji the *bete* were in many places associated with a specific local clan (*mataqali*). Among people speaking western dialects there was usually no special clan of priests. Priests were consulted mainly prior to war, though chiefs were not always convinced of the authenticity of their powers. Priests also functioned in many cases in handling the body of a dead chief.

bete 2. v. to snap off (branchlet).

bete-na n. usefulness, purpose. *E sega na betena.* It is of no use.

beteri (Eng.) n. battery. Syn. *bateri*.

beti, betia v. to pluck (fruit, flower), usually with a twisting motion. *betibeti* (or) *betia vakalevu* pick many (applies to small fruit).

beto (Colo West) n. lit. mens' house, but referring to the basic kin-group of Colo West where the now standardised types of units called *yavusa* and *mataqali* were unknown. Among highlanders, adult men lived in such a men's house, one for each extended family. Wives and children lived separately. Syn. (West) *bito*. (Colo East) *bure*.

bevu, bevuya v. to thatch (old-style Fijian house). *ibevui* n. thatch. Leaves of the swamp plant *misimisi* are probably the most durable thatch. This word might not be known by Fijians living in towns.

bewa n. ceiling beam of house.

bi 1. (Archaic) n. fence at the shore to enclose live captured sea turtles. The same word applies to a collection of ten turtles to be presented at some very important traditional ceremony.

bi 2. adv., adj. heavily, heavy (only for special uses). *sa tau bi na uca* it is raining heavily. This is a root-word used to express heaviness or importance. (See the following words and expressions.) *ena domo bi* in a deep voice. *ucu bi* stuffed nose.

vakabi v. to place weight on, move the centre of gravity to another place by shifting the weight, as in a sailing boat, to shift the weight to one side or another to stay on a more even keel.

ivakabi 1. n. paperweight, or any object used to weigh down and hold something in place.

ivakabi 2. n. stress or emphasis on a syllable (a modern term). Usually in Fijian pronounciation stress is on the second-to-last syllable of a word.

bia (Eng.) n. beer.

biau (Polyn.) n. wave(s). *ena dela ni biau* on top of the wave. *wasawasa vakabiau* very rough sea.

bibi adj., n. heavy, weighty, serious or important (problems, talk), severe (as in *Sa rui bibi na itotogi* the penalty is too severe), weight (as in *E vica na kena bibi?* How much does it weigh?); *loloma bibi* much love (a common way of ending informal letters), or written more fully *loloma bibi tu yani*. *tiko bibi* of a woman, pregnant, lit. heavy (with child). *na nona tiko bibi* her pregnancy. *e na yalo bibivoro* in greatest sorrow.

vakabibi especially, most importantly (in enumerating thoughts). *gadreva vakabibi* especially desire, seriously desire. *Vakabibi vei ira* especially for (to, or among) them.

bibivoro adj. overcome with sorrow.

bici n. a bird, Banded Rail, Gallirallus philippensis, now extinct on the main islands, due to the introduced mongoose and also feral cats but common on small islands where those animals are absent. Often walks or scampers rather than flying. Can become charmingly cheeky and rather unafraid when accustomed to people. Syn. (Nadro.) *kuma*. (Kadavu, Lau) *bisi*.

Idiom: *Keteketekete ni bici na lomalagi* fair clear sky with light strips of cloud, like the breast of the *bici*.

Idiom: *E lauta na bici na kena ikolo*. He/she gets what is deserved (usually a just punishment). The punishment fits the crime.

bika, bika 1. v. to press down.

bika, bika 2. v. to refuse a favour that is asked in a presentation ceremony (usually a gift of whale-tooth) by a return-gift of a similarly valuable thing (another whale-tooth). See *dirika*.

bikabika v., n. a funeral ceremony where women sit on pile of mats on which coffin will be placed. They keep vigil, attend to the coffin and grieve for the dead. This is a traditional function of certain women only but modernly, others may also attend.

bikena v. (Rare) achieve by careful planning, manipulation.

bikini 1. (Eng.) beacon, as for sailors.

bikini 2. (Eng.) bikini bathing suit of women. (*pikini* n. diaper for baby.)

bila n. a form of Fijian "bread" *madrai ni Viti*, dense and chewy, made of fermented but unleavened starchy root-crop, usually cassava these days but formerly, traditionally, from *ivi*, Polynesian chestnut. Grated coconut and sugar is sometimes used in the preparation. Wrapping is with leaves, usually of *masawe* (= *vasili*= *qau*), Cordylene terminalis. Village Naila, Tailevu, has a reputation for making famously good *bila*. It is sold in the Suva market as a snack food.

sikivoro is a somewhat similar food. Idiom: *na kena bila* refers to one's specialty, a special skill or talent that a person has.

bila v. to crack something using a stone. *na bila niu* the cracking open of coconuts with a stone.

bili, bilia v. to set out (*wasea*) portions of food (*ibilibili*) to be shared formally at a *magiti* feast, usually at the end of the ceremonies. Extremely sensitive important task of the *tuirara* who may have the advice of others. Recipients attending the ceremony will feel offended if they are not alloted a fair share, and they are watching closely. Idiom: *ibilibili o tuirara* Excessively large share selfishly kept by the *tuirara* for himself. The person dividing up goods to be shared may be accused of favouring himself.

bili, biliga v. to push. *tamata biligi* n. outcast. *veibili* push each other *veibilibili* accuse each other.

Idiom: *bili ni mua* idiom, lit. "shoving off" (of boat, departing), by extension, ceremonial giving and drinking of *yaqona* to a person departing.

ibili ni koro n. outskirts of village.

bilibili 1. n. raft, usually of bamboo, made in Colo East, Wainibuka, and Namosi to descend the river system to the coast. The Wainimala and Wainibuka Rivers, and then the Waidina River all flow into the Wailevu River (Rewa River), that leads south to the Suva area. Propulsion is by the current, and by poling and pushing, as implied by the word. Fijians may live on the raft for three days or more. Platform was advisable for bananas, not to get soaked, but not necessary for taro which withstands the wetness well. Bananas were grown in the highlands, but also taro and *yaqona*, and then transported down to the coast, to sell around Suva or Nausori. The rafts never make the return journey and thus may be referred to as "HMS no come back". In some cases they have been sold cheaply for use in building in the lowlands, where bamboo is more scarce. *bilibili* are still reasonably common, because it is expensive to rent punts with outboard motors, or trucks for the roads that now penetrate the highlands of Viti Levu.

ibilibili 2. n. portion of feast food shared out. It is placed out, often pushed there (as implied by the word), in a heap. The quantity and quality are noted very carefully by recipients who are sensitive to any slight.

bilo n. cup. *bilo iloilo* glass (for drinking). *bilo kava* tin cup, *bilo yaqona* cup of *yaqona*, *bilo ni yaqona* cup for *yaqona*, a smoothed half-shell of a mature coconut. Cups did not exist in any form in olden times. Water and even *yaqona* was normally lapped up. Sometimes a temporary cup was improvised by folding a leaf but that was used only for carrying a little water a short distance. It was then lapped up or poured into someone's mouth.

Idiom: *bilo cicila* undependable, cannot be relied on (person), lit. like a leaky cup.

Idiom: *bilo vata* words that might be said in humour, suggestively, by a man to a woman, as in *Daru sa bilo vata, kedaru.* We, we two share the same cup, have much in common, and should have an intimate relationship.

vakabilo has a cup, is supplied with a cup. As an idiom, a person can be said to be *vakabilo*, meaning bewitched, having magical powers derived from pouring a cup of *yaqona* to an evil spirit. Once a Fijian relates to a "devil" (*tevoro*) in this way to carry out his (usually evil) wishes, he must regularly continue to pour cups of *yaqona* to his devil, or great misfortune will befall him. In effect, in Faustian fashion, he has made a pact from the devil and cannot withdraw from it. In a very different context, *vakabilo* may refer to someone of chiefly rank, as if they have been installed by having been given the official cup to drink, i.e. they have been *vagunuvi*.

bini (or) **pini** (Eng.) n. peas, cooked, dried and salted, sold in the street as a snack. The same word may apply to green beans, mostly the very long beans grown by Indians, eaten as a vegetable. *pini* may also refer to clothes-pins, or paper-clips used in an office.

bilobilo n. kneecap.

bini, binia v. to pile up.

ibinibini n. pile, heap.

vakabira v. to attach (as brooch to a dress, etc), stick up (as with thumbtack, something on the wall, etc.), put up (poster on the wall). *vakabira na sitaba e na mata ni waqa ni ivola.* Stick a postage stamp on the front of the envelope.

biri adj. bulging, of body veins, muscles, usually from exertion.

biri, biria, birika v. to set, prop up, of a snare to catch birds, pigs; set open, of umbrella, mosquito net. *birika* implies more force. *Birika na nomu taunamu.* Open up your mosquito net.

bisa, bisa 1. v. to complete something difficult.

bisa, bisa 2. v. to fall suddenly, to pour down, of rain usually but could apply to mud in a landslide, or anything that flows. *bisa* to rain on something.

bisa, bisa 3. v. to arrive, come or occur suddenly (not a common expression). *au bisa ga yani na nona lako tiko.* I just arrived as he was going.

bisikete (Eng.) n. biscuit, usually referring to the local breakfast biscuits, such as Lee's brand or Punja brand. Fijians often dunk *tonia* biscuits in tea and slurp them, especially those with poor teeth. *bolomo* refers to a thorough soaking or dunking.

Idiom: *tei bisikete.* refers to planting biscuits, a joking, but unkind remark made about Rotumans, as if they were incompetent gardeners. Expression comes from a supposedly true event. A man of a specific Rotuman family, a man of feeble mind, got the notion of planting biscuits.

bisinisi (Eng.) n. business. *na dau (ni) bisinisi* the businessman. *caka bisinisi* to "do" business (a modern Anglicism). *cicivaka na bisinisi* to run the business. Also an Anglicism.

bisopi (or) **bisovi** n. bishop (R. Catholic or Anglican).

bitalaka v. to throw forcefully. *bitalaki* thrown forcefully, as a man from a motorcycle, or a boat in a storm, thrown ashore.

bite n. dew. Syn. *tegu*.

biti! (Eng.) Bitch! in vulgar insults among women, sometimes called out in friendly, jocular manner to a woman who is too elaborately dressed, or putting on airs. Not as vulgar as it would sound in English.

bito (West) n. clan, or extended family. Syn. for extended family: *tokatoka* in central and parts of eastern Fiji. (Lau) *batinilovo*. In the west, the earlier immigrants (before arrival of the Nakauvadra people) had no concept of tribe

yavusa.. The western *bito* or *beto* corresponds to the highlanders' *bure*, essentially a clan or large extended family, the key kinship unit. In the highlands these adult men all lived together in their *bure*. There could be several *bure* in a village. Wives and children lived separately from the men in houses *vale*.

bitu n. bamboo. *bitu ni wai* n. bamboo container formerly used for water in formal mixing of *yaqona* beverage, still occasionally used at formal ceremonies. Three main species: *bitu kau* the indigenous Schizostachyum glaucifolium, large and woody, not at all flexible, used for cooking in highlands, for carrying and storing water, and for rafts (*bilibili*), as well as for wall posts set vertically or horizontally. Much more common is the introduced *bitu dina*, "true bamboo", Bambusa vulgaris, a flexible bamboo, thinner, not as strong, the flattened stem often interwoven in sections to form house-walls, which is not an indigenous technique. *bitu sici* Bambusa multiplex, a very thin-stemmed introduced var. of bamboo; children make a whistle *sici* from this species and it is occasionally used as an ornamental shrub, or to create a fence

Green, immature bamboo is not a wood that endures unless treated chemically. The "fur" at the growing tip can cause irritation if it touches one's skin. Some Fijians are aware that bamboo shoots are edible but they have been eaten only very rarely.

The only knife known to highlanders was improvised from split bamboo, which is extremely sharp but dulls easily. Sharpness was restored by pulling away some with the teeth. In the highlands, where the earth-oven was unknown and there were no clay pots, cooking was done in sections of bamboo, held over the fire, and turned, so it would not burn. This was referred to as *vuki*, from *vuki, vukica*, meaning to turn over. Syn. (Kadavu) *duvu*. (Polyn.) *kofe* and cognates *'ofe, ohe. ko'e*.

Idiom: *Vaka la e boko na buka bitu.* ended suddenly, as a fire of bamboo goes out suddenly, leaving no coals.

Idiom: *Vaqara bitu* said of or by women, to go look for a man for sexual and romantic purpose. The rationale behind this is probably the similarity in shape of the young bamboo sprouts to an erect penis. One comparable expression for men is "to capture red-feathered parrots" *tobo kula*, when they are on the look-out to find a woman to have sex. To have these expressions with sexual implications does not necessarily mean that many Fijians did these things but that they have talked about it.

bitu ceguvi (or) **bitu ucu** n. (Archaic) nose flute musical instrument formerly used by men or women, blown through one nostril. Virtually no one has the skills today and we have practically no knowledge of the type of music. The instrument was uncommon and quite unknown in the Viti Levu highlands.

biu, biuta 1. v. to put, to place. *biuta ena kovate* put it in the cupboard. Syn. (Colo East) *bite, biute*.

biu, biuta 2. v. to depart, to leave. *biuti Suva* leave Suva. *biuta na vanua* leave the country. *na biu vanua* the emigration, departure for overseas, the emigrants. (*curu vanua* immigrate).

biu, biuta 3. v. to discard, cast (anchor). *biu-iyaragi* to disarm, disarmament. *biuta laivi* v. to throw it out, throw it away. Syn. (Rewa) *kavotaka* v. to throw it out.

biubiu v. to leave, depart. *Sa biubiu ena noa* He/she/they departed yesterday.

biubiu n. people departing, those people who are leaving or the departure itself.

veibiu v., n. to leave each other, and by ext., to divorce, divorced. *veisere* separated (of a couple). *Rau sa veibiu kei na watina.* He/she divorced his/her spouse. *Daru sa veibiu eke.* Let us leave each other here.

biu cakacaka v., n. to go on strike, the strike, work stoppage, strikers.

biukila (Eng.) n. bugle, trumpet, also the Trumpeter brand of cane-knife, preferred by many Fijians, who refer to it with their version of the brand name.

biuvuli n., v. school-leaver(s), to quit school.

bo root-word used in many combinations, meaning squeeze. *veibobo* massage.

bo 1. n. boil (Med.). This is a common complaint, probably due to crowded living and sleeping conditions in many Fijian dwellings. Infection can occur through mutual touch, through any slight abrasion of the skin, a fact unknown to most Fijians. *Sa vakamatana na bo.* The boil has come to a head.

bo 2. n. species of edible fish along the shore and at reefs, Lutjanua gibbus, reddish body with black tail and dorsal fin, the back somewhat swollen. Syn. *kakedamu*, (Lau) *boa*.

ibo 1. n. traditional hibiscus-fibre (*vau*) as for straining *yaqona* at ceremonies but may be made from other fibres, or even a cloth. It is squeezed to release the liquid. Same concept for squeezing medicinal plant extracts, more usually then referred to as *ivulo*, often made from coconut fibre cloth.

ibo 2. n. traditional medicinal oil for massaging, of several sorts, usually coconut oil or *dilo* oil, both used only by coastal Fijians.

ibo 3. n. edible annelid, soapstone seaworm, up to ten inches in length and a quarter of an inch in width. Chewy, whitish brown flesh eaten raw, often after marinating in lemon juice. Also used as bait. It burrows into limestone at the shore in holes that are clearly visible. Siphonosoma australe. Other species may be known as *vetuna*.

bobo eyes closed. *bobo mata dua* one eye closed. *vakabobo* type of mat with no wool edging.
bo, boka v. to squeeze, press.
veibo n., v. wrestle, wrestling (as a sport), more traditionally Polynesian than Melanesian. *veibo liga* arm-wrestling; tradionally, Fijians did arm-wrestling lying down.
bobo, boboka v. to clench (the fist), close (the eyes), squeeze (fruit, trigger of gun), massage (the body), *vakabobo, vakaboboka* v. to feel by pressing (in checking on something such as maturity of fruit). *boboka na matamu* close your eyes (usually covered with the hand, as in children's games of hide and seek). *boboka na ivaka-sa-ribariba* squeeze the trigger.
veibobo n., v. body-massage, a highly evolved skill in Fiji. This is considered by eastern highlanders to be an introduced coastal concept. Highlanders never developed any body oil-lotions.
boboraka v. to squeeze rapidly and forcefully many times, as in squeezing orange juice, or in softening a mango for eating. (Fijians make an opening in the mango skin with their teeth, then suck out the flesh, if the fruit is ripe.)
bobota 1. adj. pleasantly plump and soft (human body, fruit) with an implication of rosiness and ripeness of the flesh, or approaching full ripeness.
bobota 2. adj. of the body, covered with blisters, pimples.
bobula n. slave. *bobula-taka* v. to enslave. Slavery was very common among coastal Fijians (areas of Polynesian influence). Slaves were not usually bought or sold but were sometimes given to political allies (Cakobau gave some Lovoni slaves to the Tui Cakau but he sold many of them to white planters). Usually they were war captives. Commoners were sometimes virtual slaves to the chieftains, but often happy enough, accustomed to that servitude. In some places still today, dependant relatives may be treated as virtual slaves within a family. The Tui Cakau has in a previous generation used prisoners as slave labour on his farmland.
boci adj., n. uncircumcised, for a male adult a despised characteristic, implying he never became a man. A person known to be uncircumcised is the butt of jokes and derision. Circumcision is an important ceremony for all Fijian boys growing up. By contrast, most Fiji Indians are not circumcised.
bodaka n. blister, callus, hardened skin on hand or foot, from abrasion or work, typically on the hand from use of cane knife, or foot from ill-fitting shoe.
bo-dra n. ulcer. *bodra ni davuibuco* stomach ulcer.
bogi n. night. *Sa bogi mai.* Night is falling. *Sa bogi mai na vanua.* Night is coming over the land i.e., night is falling. *ena bogi* last night. *Bogi!* a courtesy called out at night when passing an occupied house, or intending to enter it. (This is a *tama,* traditional greeting at the entrance of a house; inside, the host will give a traditional response.) The passing of a number of days is spoken of as the number of nights that have passed. Feasts mark certain numbers of days that have passed after a birth or a death: *bogi va* four nights, a ceremony 4 days after a death, birth, or circumcision, *bogi tini* "ten nights" ceremony 10 days after a birth, especially of chiefs. *bogi drau* 100 nights (after death, when formal mourning period ceases). *bogi walu* eight nights, is a certain type of seasonal storm that lasts a week to ten days of ugly blustery, cold, wet weather. Syn. (Colo East) *bo*.
Idiom: *droka na bogi.* stay up all night.
vakabogibogi v. to do something until nightfall. *Au a mai vakabogibogi toka e bati ni wai.* Until nightfall I stayed by the water's edge.
bogicaka (or) **bogivaka** v. to do something, usually work, right into the night, usually gardening or fishing. *laki siwa bogivaka* go fishing till nightfall.
bogilevu tutu n. the dead of night, midnight. *bogilevu* in the middle of the night.
bogi-rua n. refers to day before yesterday or the day after tomorrow. *Au a yaco ena bogirua.* I arrived the day before yesterday. *Au na lako ena bogirua.* I will leave the day after tomorrow. *rua* two. *bogi* night(s). Fijians count in nights, not days.
iboi n. smell. *na kena iboi* its smell (pleasant or unpleasant).
boi, boica 1. v. of a person, to smell (a thing). **2.** of something, to have a smell. *sa boi vinaka (ca).* it smells good (bad). *boilevu* smells very bad. *boi kamakama* has a burnt smell. *boi bunobuno* smells of sweat. *boi kuvukuvu* smells of smoke. *boi mimi* smells of urine. *boi-sa-reguregu* smells delicious (of food). *boi sisiva* has a fishy smell. *vakaboiboi* v. to put on perfume,
Idiom: (Ra) *boi-tilitili.* bad smell. (somewhat vulgar).
Idiom: *E na boi ga mai na da.* A misdeed will always be found out. Lit. The smell of excrement will always become apparent.
boia n. a plant, tall, 20 feet, wild species of ginger family, Alpinia boia, leaves used to wrap food for cooking in earth oven. Also known as *boboia* or *vava, boe, boeboe*. Wild pigs favour the stalks as food, pigeons and parrots eat the small fruit.

boiboi da n. medium size tree, offensive-smelling, small white flowers that become black, remaining on the tree, long sharp leaves, Geniostoma vitiense, Loganiaceae. Good firewood when dry. Lit. the name means smelling like excrement. Bark used medicinally for urinary problems.

boi-da smells of excrement, as of clothes or a baby' diapers.

boila n. a small rather inoffensive but pesky moray eel common at some reefs, not usually eaten. It can bite people but very rarely does.
   Idiom: *E sega na ika, ka laukana kina na boila.* When there is no fish we can always eat *boila* eels, i.e., we can always "make do" with what is at hand.

boi mimi smells of urine (mat, mattress, blanket), usually from a child. Syn. *boiriri*.

boiri v., adj. dizzy, feel faint.

vakaBoitaci n. v., (Vanua Balavu, Lau) to snack on traditional starch-food (*kakana dina*) while drinking tea, but only after a meal, a curious local custom of village Boitaci, sometimes adopted by other villagers of Vanua Balavu Island.

boivutuka v., adj. to smell musty, as of clothes, mats that need to be sunned out.

boka v. to see. Syn. *rai-ca*. A saying from Lau, widely used in Fiji, is the idiom *Sagasaga ya, e boka ya.* Yes, go ahead and try it and you will see (the consequences).

boka n. (Colo East, Namosi, Waidina) *dalo*, taro, a staple starch-food that grows only as a cultivated plant, the main cultivated starch-food in the eastern highlands. Much of their starch-food was wild yams.

boka n. gifts brought to a village after a long absence, to compensate for one's not having been present for funerals of people who died during that absence. This can be a heavy expense. The necessity of bringing such gifts might delay the return of villagers now living elsewhere.

bokasi n. var. of breadfruit *uto* that gives its name to the Wainibokasi River not far from Suva. Small tree, small fruit with a smooth skin. The leaves have rough gritty surface.

boko, bokoca v. to extinguish (fire, a people, a Christian sin), turn off (an electric light or appliance). *mataboko* blind. *kawa boko* extinct (animal species, Fijian kin-group). *na bokoci* the extinction. *iboko* eraser (at school or office). *boko-buka* fire-fighting.

bokoi 1. n. a kind of soft Fijian pudding or mash, made with coconut cream and sugar. The main starch-food ingredient is often a pink-fleshed plantain, and these days, grated cassava, a special food of Wainikeli. Syn. or similar *lote*. (Lau) *sepo*.

bokoi 2. n. a sort of wild Malay Apple, small tree, Syzygium richii, around the coast, edible fruit somewhat like the *kavika*. Flowers white petals with yellow stamens, often used for personal decoration and pleasant scent. Syn. (Rewa) *oqori*.

bokola n. human body for cannibal use, living or dead, now a common serious insult.

bola 1. n. matting or temporary wall thatching made of split coconut leaf-fronds, sometimes used for food presentations. See *bola, bola.*

bola 2. (Slang) n. Said in English, "nice *bola*" upon seeing a pretty girl, a remark attributed to Prince Charles during a visit to Fiji. (Pondering the etymological basis for this is probably fruitless). The expression is somewhat dated and trite.

bola 3. n. type of round basket of coconut leaves, often used for food at feast presentations *magiti*.

bola, bola v. to split with axe or heavy knife.

bolarua v. to split in two with a heavy blow. *e rua* two.

bolabola n. temporary shelter or shed made of coconut fronds, usually split down the middle of the stem, the two sides interwoven. Often made for occasions when many people will assemble. See *vakatunuloa* temporary shed, these days often using sheets of corrugated iron, usually borrowed or rented.

Bolatagane (Tongan *Bolotane*) n., adj. Britain, British, a term of respect not much used these days. The word has been adopted as a native title in Macuata.

bole, bolea v. to challenge. *na bolebole ni 1990s* the challenge of the 1990s (as seen in a newspaper *Nai Lalakai*; that replicated word appears more often as a verb.) Physical challenge is an important concept to Fijians. *Erau a veibolebolei me rau veivacu.* They (two) challenged each other to a boxing match.

ibole 1. n. challenge. In Fiji, various regions have a challenging cry, heard today usually at football matches. From Ra Province, for example, one might hear *Ma'e na ma'e!* Fight to the death!

ibole 2. n. slogan of identity, as for example *manu dui tagi*, "birds of a different feather", for Kadavu people.

boli n. dimple, as a natural depression on the cheek.

bolo n. a small dark-coloured snake, Fiji Burrowing Snake, Ogmodon vitianus, reportedly blind and certainly timid, but deadly poisonous, more so than a cobra (fortunately absent in Fiji). Juveniles sport a white chevron on the top of their head. Extremely few Fijians have ever seen one and most do not know of its existence. One never hears of anyone being bitten by the snake and it normally scurries off and disappears very quickly. Paddy Ryan suggests it is probably nocturnal. Living in the rain forest and jungle for decades, I have encountered it only once. They are perhaps best known in Namosi Province and Colo East, where they have been eaten. They live in dead, rotting vegetation. Highlanders catch them with a forked stick. Some believe they render it harmless by rubbing the snake's mouth and teeth with the cut stem of *via milamila*, Alocasia indica, Araceae, which has a very irritating sap. Curiously, this is spoken of as "sawing" (*varo, varota*) the teeth. It would seem to be a dangerous treatment.

bologa, bololaka v. to heave, throw heavily, an object, a kick or a punch. To smash into pieces.

bolomo v., n. to steep or dunk a starch food e.g., chunks of breadfruit most commonly but also taro, in coconut cream (*lolo*), or a biscuit in tea, a favoured and acceptable way of eating. Steeping tends to soften starch foods which is helpful to older people whose teeth are weak. *toni, tonia* to dip or dunk.

bona v., n. adj. stink. putrid. Occasionally used pejoratively to a person; also, in children's game of tag *veibona*, the word is exclaimed to mean "you are 'it'!" Syn. (Kadavu) *busi*.

Boni Vilive n. Burns Philp, major department store, Australian origin now under the name of Courts. Often written as one word. Now mainly known for its clock tower in central Suva.

bono, bonota (or) **bonata** v. to stuff, to block, to plug up or dam (hole, stream of water). *ibono* dam, plug. *bonata na vanua galala* close off the open spaces.

bonu n. swamp eel or mud eel sp., very thin body up to a meter long but hardly more than an inch in thickness, pointed nose, lives beside creeks, in drains, thriving in mud. It never lives right in the creeks but only alongside. A good food, to be caught with care by hand but it bites when grabbed. One can reach into the slender mud holes but the *bonu* can move as easily in reverse as it can forward. Brown on the back, white underneath. One type is the *bonu loa*, which is short and has more distinctive beak-like head. The other, longer type is the "true" *bonu dina*. Fijians do not consider *bonu* as a type of eel (*duna*), possibly because it does not live in creeks or rivers. There is a river named Wai-ni-sulu-bonu, a tributary into the Wainadoi, near the coast of Namosi.

bora, borota, boralaka v. to bawl out, reprimand.

bore, borea v. to wash, usually of utensils or food. *bore vakawai* to rinse without washing completely. See *dere*.

borete n. shrubby fern, Acrostichum aureum, Pteridaceae (or Adiantaceae), that has edible young leaves, a delicious vegetable, normally lightly cooked, like *ota*, and can be eaten raw. Sometimes used as medicine. It grows by the mangrove shore or in brackish, boggy areas, and is unknown at sandy shores and in the highlands. It is never cultivated. Syn. *boresi, babasiga, caca,* (Lau,, Cakau) *vativati*.

boro 1. (Lau) n. virtually any green vegetable.

boro 2. n. certain edible shrubs and small plants, virtually all of genus Solanum, family Solanaceae, formerly important in the diet, now mostly neglected, replaced by *bele* and *tubua*, and to some extent by European vegetables (English cabbage) or oriental greens (Chinese cabbage, mustard greens). Cooking is by boiling, formerly by steaming. Only rarely sold in the market.

- *boro dina* Solanum uporo, formerly S. anthropophagorum, smooth leaves, small tomato-like fruit yellow or red. Seeman considered the plant a digestive that was eaten in association with human bodies in cannibal times. Eastern Polynesians have used the red fruit in floral necklaces.

- *boro sou, sou,* (or) *sousou* S. repandum, shrub with edible leaves when well cooked in boiling water. Seeman mentions this was eaten with yams, or cooked in soups. *sou* suggests something that occurs early. S. Savage mentions the edible fruits shaped like very small papaya with a pleasant aromatic smell, as used by maoris of eastern Polynesia.

- *boro gaga* (or) *rokete* is introduced, hot chilli pepper, Capsicum frutescens, (so-called because of similarity to some species of Solanum genus in their form of plant and shape of leaves). Quite a few Fijians now use chilli, in curry, in

  tomato sauce, in a Tongan coconut-cream sauce called *miti* for seafood, and on a salad-seaweed *nama*. Idiom: *boro gaga* reference to sarcastic, hurtful speech.

- *boro wa* (or) *tokoi* edible leaves of woody liana or shrub with long hanging branches, wild or semi-cultivated at low altitude from Malesia eastward to the Marianas and Fiji, Deeringia amaranthoides, Amaranthaceae.

- *boro ni yaloka ni gata* S. nigrum. Black nightshade.

boro, boroya v. to paint, apply (ointment etc.). *boro pouta* v. to apply talcum powder to the head, usually of a dancer, as a compliment *fakawela*, a Lauan custom, now adopted elsewhere. Formerly Fijians painted with colour their faces, as with war-paint, and in coastal areas and small islands, to colour their bark-cloth. (Viti Levu highlanders painted nothing but their faces.) The word now applies to painting of any objects.

boroboro v. to wallow, as a pig does, smearing itself in mud, to cool itself, since it cannot perspire.

iboro n. paint, ointment. Anciently, Fijians used face-paint mostly in time of war. One of its functions was to help conceal the identity of the warrior. *qele boro damudamu* "red-lined" native land of extinct clans which has reverted to the Government, with some later re-allocated to native clans. *iboro ni vava* n. shoe polish. Some young men make a living in Suva shining shoes. *iboro ni gusu* lipstick. *iboro ni liga* fingernail polish.

dau boroboro n. painter, sign-painter, graphic artist.

vaka-boro-vulavula-taka (Ang.) v. literally, to "whitewash", cover up some ulterior purpose of improper behaviour.

bosa n. tree-fern stump appearing at ends of a house roof-ridge.

bose n. meeting for the purposes of discussion, conference, council, council meeting. *bose vakoro* village conference. *Bose Levu Vakayabaki* Annual General Meeting A.G.M. of company, association, or social club. *Bose ni Tikina* District Council. *Bose Yaco* n. Cabinet (of government). *Boselawa* Parliament (lower house composed of elected members of Parliament). *Bose Levu Vakaturaga* Great Council of Chiefs founded by the British in the 1870s as the Council of Chiefs; its own members later added the adjective Great. In 2007 a set of office buildings for the Council was planned to cost F$30 million as an exercise in grandiosity. *bose-kacivi* n. formal meeting called for special occasion. *bose-kara* n. meeting planned but then deferred.

bose, bosea v. to confer, discuss in conference.

bosebose v., n. to chat, chatter, yarn, talk idly, yatter.

boso n. boss, often used as an informal form of address to one's employer, a term often used ingatiatingly when a person wants something.

boso, bosoka, bosoraka v. to squish or squeeze together and soak, knead lightly, as pounded *yaqona* in water, or ingredients in cake-mix, or mixing grated coconut before squeezing out (Syn. *lobaka*) the coconut cream (*lolo*), or swishing around edible seaweed (*lumi*) in water to clean it. This may not include the forceful kneading of bread, or the hard squishing of clothes when being washed by hand. It is a lighter motion. *lumi boso* n. type of edible seaweed, cooked, water discarded, squished, chopped, served often with *miti* sauce.

bosucu n. snail, slug. *wa bosucu* very common introduced weed, Mikania micrantha, Compositae, a creeping vine that smothers gardens, "Mile-a-minute". Snails are damaging particularly to vanilla plants. They may be impeded by copper wires, copper sulphate, or by caffeine, even from coffee grounds. Modern treatment is with pellets of iron phosphate, not dangerous to dogs, cats.

bota adj. ripe, of fruit (implying a change of colour), seeds, and boils (Med.); yellowed or red and mature, of deciduous leaves; reddish colour of the sky.

Idiom: *Sa bota ira na vanua* the sky is red, in the evening forecasting good weather or in the morning predicting bad weather, as in *Sa botaicake na vanua*. Uncertain as to whether this is an indigenous notion or was adopted from Europeans "Red sky at night, shepherd's delight".

bota n. blister (Medical).

botana v. to paste. *ibotani* patch or thing intended to adhere.

bote, botea v. to break, burst out or in, fish from a net, burglar into a house, to undo, break down, break apart. *kacabote* explode. *kaca* split.

botebotekoro n. goatweed, very common herb with soft leaves introduced from central America, Ageratum (two species), Compositae. The name implies that it bursts into villages. After ground is cleared this weed does grow up very quickly. It is easily pulled out. Almost every Fijian knows that it is useful in stopping bleeding of small cuts and has curative healing properties when applied externally on wounds. It is also taken as an internal medicine for gastritis or other stomach pains but especially diarrhoea. The name *botebotekoro* applies also to an herb, Synedrella sp.) Syn. *suguvanua*. (West) *usuusu-vanua*.

boti uncommon root-word, implying something that happens suddenly, or unexpectedly, bursting forth, without any prior action of a person. *E boti mai na co ca.* Weeds just grow up.

botiki (Colo East) n. a var. of edible wild yam; root grows vertically often six feet deep, stem angular in cross-section. By contrast, the more common wild yam *tivoli* root grows horizontally to the soil surface with a stem round in cross-section. Both have thorny stems.

boto 1. n. ground frog, Platymantis vitianus (not P. vitiensis, which is the tree frog *ula*). About four inches long, twice the length of the tree frog. Inhabits rain forest but in some cases, the shore, such as at Viwa, according to Paddy Ryan. The colour is consistently dull brown/grey, while the tree frog may take on highly varied coloration. Like the tree frog, it has no tadpole phase of growth, differing in this from the introduced toad, or many frogs in other lands. Tiny young frogs emerge directly from the large eggs. Neither frog is equipped to live in the water, and the skin membranes between the toes are minimal. Unlike the tree frog, the ground frog has no adhesive sucker pads on its feet. Both types of frog were significant items in the diet of Viti Levu highlanders. Syn. *dreli.*

boto 2. n. toad, Bufo marinus, native to South America, introduced from Hawaii in 1936 with the misguided notion it would control insect pests in the canefields. In fact, it has become a dreadful nuisance. Poison glands at the side of the neck repel potential enemies. They exude a while fluid that can seriously irritate human skin. They are ground feeders, very probably competing with the Fiji ground frog.

boto 3. n. (Eng.) punt, a European-style boat, often flat-bottomed, usually 16-18 feet in length, often made of the timbers *bauvudi, mavota* or *dakua,* propelled by poling or by outboard engine. Now often made commercially of fibreglass with more rounded bottom. This has been a common form of local transport on major rivers and at seaside. At sea, it has replaced the sailing cutters of earlier years, having the advantage of an engine. In deeper river areas the *boto* has replaced some of the bamboo rafts *bilibili.*

boto-na n. bottom (not of a person's backside), underside. *na boto ni yava-na* the bottom of his/her foot/feet. *ena boto ni tuvatuva* at the bottom of the class (classification, arrangement), *boto ni kato* bottom of the *kato* box/basket, *boto ni sauloa* bottom of the sea, *boto ni ituitui* end of the string (of something, such as small fish). *boto ni drau ni pepa* bottom of the page.

botoboto pure. *kai Idia botoboto* pure Indian person (not mixed breed).

botoilevu abrupt, abruptly; rapid, unpleasant or unfortunate termination. *Sa tini botoilevu.* It ended abruptly. *curu botoilevu* v. to enter (or depart) brashly, without proper protocol (as many Tongans were thought to have done in early years.) Syn. *curu botolaki.*

botolaka v. to heave out or down.

botolaki adv. roughly, crudely, without showing proper respect, as in *curu botolaki* to enter/exit without proper courtesy. Syn. *botoilevu.*

botonikete-na n. lower abdomen.

bou (Polyn. pou) n. central house-post; appears in some place names *Nabouwalu* eight house-posts, *Naboutini* ten house-posts. Such words are used for place-names, indicating what was originally a Tongan settlement.

boulu (Eng.) n. bowl.

bouta (Archaic) n. a function of certain clans only in certain parts of Fiji, special service for the chief, usually the duty to bury him when dead. Clans often have a traditional function, such as fishermen (*gonedau*), spokesman for the chief (*matanivanua*), warrior (*bati*), priest (*bete*), empowering the chief (*na sau*), and *bouta,* occasionally spelled *bauta.* The functions are maintained usually with appropriate ceremony. The divisions are more elaborate in coastal areas of Polynesian influence and less elaborate among tribes in the interior of Viti Levu.

bovu n. a well known common shrub or small tree, much used as a general digestive medicine for babies, and to help control overheating of a baby; Mussaenda raiateensis, formerly M. frondosa. Tiny yellow flowers subtended by very large sepals that look like huge white petals. One uses the inner bark of stem or branch and the leaves. Syn. *vobo.* (West, Bua, Macuata) *bobo.*

bovoro v. to crush open, crack (as of a nut).

bowai (Archaic) n. type of pole-shaped fighting club.

bowiri dizzy, faint standing up. *wiri* suggests spinning.

bu 1. n. coconut at the drinking stage, with a very small amount of gelatinous flesh. *bu sosou bu* with little or no flesh to eat. *kabata na bu* climb up for the *bu. la'i kaba bu mai.* go climbing to fetch down *bu. vakavidika na bu.* tap, snap the fingers against the *bu* to test it. *sau, sauca na bu* to cut or pierce the *bu* for drinking. *diri, dirika na bu* crack the top off the *bu. vida, vidạ na bu* split, cleave open the *bu.* See *drokai* for coconut with gelatinous flesh but also drinkable liquid.
Idiom: *bu ni Bau* a poor substitute (because Bau has so very few coconuts that one could never obtain a fine drinking-nut at the right stage of maturity).

bu 2. n. form of address for grandmother (father's mother). Syn. *bubu.* (Lau) *pu, pupu. bu levu* great grandmother. *bu-na* n. grandmother.

bua 1. n. Tahiti gardenia, Gardenia taitensis, Rubiaceae, indigenous in Vanuatu, Fiji, Tonga, probably Samoa, aboriginal introduction to Hawaii. The name is *tiare* from French Polynesia where it is the national flower of Tahiti. Flower usually white, propellor-shaped, delightful scent. *pua* is an ancient Polynesian name meaning "flower", and sometimes refers to certain specific flowers in the various

Polynesian languages. *bua* is a Fijian version of Polynesian *pua*. **2.** Gardenia augusta, larger flower, now very common, introduced by Europeans, native to Japan, China, now pantropic.

bua (ni vavalagi) n. frangipani, introduced, native to central America, cultivated pan-tropical, deciduous, Plumeria rubra, with fragrant pink or red flowers, leaves dull grey with acute tips, some vars. white with yellow throat, Apocynaceae. P. obtusa fls are white, lves shiny, evergreen, with obtuse tips, perfume more discreet or delicate, origin West Indies. Planting by cuttings. Seeds rarely viable.

bua (ni Viti) n. indigenous woody plant of the bush, with fragrant white flowers becoming yellow to orange at maturity, through the year but evident October through March especially, with notably long corolla tube, Fagraea berteroana, Loganiaceae. Fruits are orange to red. Since ancient times, flowers have been favoured for floral garlands worn around the neck. Though the tree may reach 20 meters, it is often seen as quite a small tree growing on the side of other trees as an epiphyte. The wood is fine-grained and twisted, but good for carving. Bua Province in Fiji owes its name to this flower, and the name of prominent early settler from Verata, named Buatavatava. The plant has mystical but undefined significance in Fiji but among East Polynesian maoris, the plant, known as *pua*, has been sacred, the branches symbolic of the path that spirits take after the death of a person. Syn. *buadromo*.
Idiom: *Dui seva ga na bua ka a tea.* Everyone gets what he deserves from his own actions, lit. everyone gets the flower (*bua*) he/she has planted.

buabua 1. n. large tree of coastal areas, Guettarda speciosa, Rubiaceae, durable timber. Dark-coloured bark. Cream white flowers and fruits. Flowers scented, used in garlands and for scenting coconut oil, small green fruits. Syn. *buatoka, buabua-ni-sawana*.

buabua 2. large forest tree, Fragraea gracilipes, Loganaceae, flowers white or pale yellow, scented. small round white fruits, extremely durable timber that can withstand salt water, for building wharf posts. Due to valuable timber, many have been removed from the forest. A river is named Wainibuabua at Wainadoi, Namosi Province. Same genus as *bua ni Viti*. Syn. (Kadavu) *botu*.

buawa adj. unclear to the vision, as if misty or fogged over. By extension, unclear or vague of notions or understanding.

bubului-taka (Anglicism) v. to promise, swear on oath. *bubului vua na Kalou* swear to God. *Rau a vosa bubuluitaki e rua na turaganilewa vua na Peresitedi.*
Two magistrates were sworn in by the President. *Bubului sara ga!* I swear it's true! (informal exclamation). *na vosa bubului* the swearing in.

bubu adj. water-logged, soggy, as of some cooked starch foods, or of soil and the ground after heavy rain.

bubu, bubuca v. to "drink" a soft ripe fruit such as a mango, by biting a hole and then sucking out the flesh. On does not "eat" a soft fruit (melon, plum, ripe mango, and even ice cream or medicinal pills), one "drinks" them.

ibuburau (Archaic) n. indigenously Fijian wooden plate from which *yaqona* was sucked up and drunk, the drinker (usually a priest) kneeling or lying down. In the highlands especially, improvised *ibuburau* are still made in the bush, usually at garden locations by men working there. Leaves of *dalo* or *via* or plantain serve as waterproof lining to a shallow pit dug in the ground. Fern leaves (*vuti*) serve as a strainer. The custom of drinking *yaqona* this way, sucking it up, is called *burau*, formerly customary in the highlands. These days, out in the bush, men might more often use a cup improvised from a folded leaf. The concept of a regular serving bowl such as the clay *dari*, or wooden *tanoa* bowl (from Tonga), is much more recent. The word *tanoa* is Samoan.

bu-na n. grandmother. *na veibuni* the grandmother and grandchild(ren). *bubu* or *bu* grandma.

buca n. flatland, plain. *bucabuca* flat. *buca ni ivalu* battlefield.

buca adj. dirty and still, of water, as in *wai buca*.

bucekovu adj. refers to children with very distended stomachs. Could apply to pot-bellied adult.

bucina 1. v. set out to sprout (seeds, cuttings planted) *Sa bucini.* It is set out for sprouting.

bucina 2. v. to conceive (of an idea, plan of action). *bucini e loma* conceived privately or secretly. This is an ext. of the basic meaning, to sprout.

buco n. var. of breadfruit, large long fruit with rough skin and no seeds.

bue v. to boil actively (water or other liquid such as tea). *na buebue ni wai katakata* the boiling of hot water. *bue* does not refer to the food or anything else that is being boiled (such as pandanus leaf for weaving.) Syn. *buebue* which can also refer to anger boiling over.

bui n. grandmother, respectful form of address for a woman who has reached upper middle age, or is elderly. It may also be a nickname for a child who is named after the older woman. Similarly, a small boy may be referred to as *Tukai*, Grandpa, if a grandfather is his namesake.
Idiom: *na nomu bui* your wife (said to a man of mature age).

bui-na n. tail (physical). *bui ni gata* snake's tail, *bui ni ose* horse's tail. *bui ni ika* fish tail.
Idiom: *loki buina* Lit. tail between the legs (as a dog), for being afraid, running away or quitting in fear.

bui ni ga n. type of haircut this supposedly resembles the backside of a duck. This has been fashionable. A somewhat shortened version has been known as *bui ni soqe* "pigeon's tail".

bui ni gone n. respectful term for elderly woman who is or could be a grandmother, sometimes used for fertility godess of locality which may be represented by a
carved wooden figurine. As a form of address, one may say, for example, Bui-Sireli for the grandmother of Sireli.

bujia (Eng.) n. butcher. Fijians are just trying to use the English word. Syn. *butia*.

buka 1. n. firewood, fire. *ta buka* to cut firewood. *ca buka* to gather firewood.
Idiom: *Maca na wai ka boko na buka.* The cupboard is bare, or no more kava, tobacco, food. Lit. No more water and the fire has gone out.
Idiom: *kuvu na buka me laurai* you won't be caught (seen), go ahead and do it, suggesting to someone to do something illicit.

buka 2. n. children's game with two teams. Single goal post is at each end of a field. One child calls "*Buka*" and runs for the opponents' post. The other team will try to touch him.

buka, bukana v. to add wood to a fire, build up an on-going fire.

bukana v. to instigate, as in stirring up trouble. *daubukana* n. instigator.

bukana v. to tempt. *Mo kua ni bukani au.* Don't tempt me. See *baca*.

buke (or) **bukebuke** n. mound, as for planting yams etc. *Nabukebuke* n. super-tribe that predominates in all of Namosi Province. Idiom: *dravusani ga na buke e cere.* the important person (such as a chief) is to be favoured.

bukete adj., n. pregnant. *bukete vatu* false pregnancy. By ext., *bukete* may refer to fruit of *duruka* becoming plump, mature. Syn. *Sa tawa na matana*.
Idiom: *bubului vaka bukete* to make false promises.

vakabukete-taka v. to impregnate, make (a woman) pregnant.

buki, bukia v. to fasten, to tie (a knot). *bukia na vere* conspire to trick. *ibukibuki* knot, bond. *Keirau bukia tu* we (2 exc.) have planned ahead, are committed. *ulu buki* hair tied in a knot or "bun" behind the head (usually of a woman with soft hair).

buki ni liku (Archaic) n. former custom of fastening a traditional skirt (*liku*) on a young woman at the time of marriage.

buki vere n., v. conspiracy, conspiring, to plan an attack, which will often be by conspiracy and treachery.

ibukibuki n. knot, or bond formed deliberately.

buku, bukuya v. to tie (as of a knot).

ibuku n. knot (as tied in a rope).

veibuku v. to agree (as in setting an appointment), to plan something together. *veibuku* n. appointment, agreement for something scheduled.

buku, bukuta v. to plan, arrange to do something together. *bukuti* adj. planned, agreed upon, as a verb, persuade to go along with. *A bukuti au ko Seru me keirau laki vakasasa.* Seru persuaded me to accompany him going pig-hunting. *E tiko na noqu veibuku.* I have an appointment.

buku v. bulge out, as in *Sa buku mai na sucuna*, usually referring to a girl maturing, Her breasts are bulging.

buku-na n. heel, as in *buku ni madrai* heel of the breadloaf. In some dialects, *kubu-na*. *kubu ni ivava* heel of the shoe. *buku ni dakai* n. stock or butt of a gun. Idiom: *Buku levu!* (Vulgar) Big ass! big bum.

bukubuku ni yava-na n. heel of the foot.

bukuta v. to invite or persuade someone to accompany another person or join in some activity, a trip, a social occasion, or task to be done.

bula v., n., adj. to live, life, live; by ext. hello. *mate bula* knocked unconscious, medically in a coma (or) worthless, of a person. *ilavo bula* cash money. "*yau bula*" money. *bula vakawati* n. married life. *tamata bula* n. adult (no longer a youth or girl), able to perform fully adult functions in the community. *bula i yavei* (or) *bula yavoki* v., n. drifter, vagabond, lone person who lives by what he can pick up here and there, thus not a full participant in society. *ika bula* live fish (but may refer to a turtle). *bula vinaka* to be well, healthy. *veika bula* n. living organism(s), including all plants, animals, microorganisms. *bula* adj. erect, of a penis. Syn. *droi*. (The opposite is *mate*.) By ext., an

Anglicism, *bula* may mean "to save", as in *E rawa in bula e $3.9m.* It is possible to save $3.9m (by reducing the size of the civil service).

bula 2. n. crown of thorns, Acanthaster planci, a camouflaged starfish with as many as 20 short "arms" with poisonous, needle-like spikes. Waders should be careful where they tread! *Bula* feed at night on coral polyps, leaving behind the white skeleton of dead coral, devastating huge areas of reef. Its main known predator is the triton shellfish, Charonia tritonis, all too often collected for sale to tourists, and thus now rare. This may explain explosive growth of *bula* populations in certain areas. Divers are paid to gather *bula* (carefully!), removing them from the reefs. Alternatively, some divers spike formalin into them to kill them.

vakabula 1. v. say "hello" *Bula!* often to be replied to by *Bula vinaka!* Syn: (Cakau) *Bula vina'a!* (Nasavusavu, Wailevu and Bua) *Bula re!* (Macuata) *Bula sia!* (Lau) *Sa malo!* (West) *Cola vina!* Such regional expressions can be deliberate, revealing where a person comes from.

vakabula 2. v. to save, to revive. *vakabula* save his/her/their life. *na iVakabula* the Saviour. *na ivakabula* the saving(s), as in retail sales "specials", the reduction from regular price. *na ivakabula ilavo* the saving(s) of money. *E sega tale ni vakabulai rawa.* It is still not possible to revive it/him/her.
Idiom: *vakabula ika levu* the big one got away, you missed your big chance lit. the big fish was saved (by escaping). .

bulabula 1. adj. healthy. *Bulabula vinaka tiko?* How are you? (In good health?) It is customary to respond with *Vakalailai*, implying that you are doing fine, in good health. In Fiji *bulabula vinaka* usually means a person is plump, a Fijian sign of good health. *ika bulabula* fresh fish.

bulabula 2. adj. fertile, productive, as of land. *qele bulabula* fertile land. *ibulabula ni qele* chemical fertilizer.

bulagi adj. stale, of food, and thus not always to be eaten. *Mai, kana bulagi!* Come, eat some leftovers with us! (That may be said from modesty that the prospective host has only simple food available.)
Idiom: *bulagi katakata* "hot" news, very latest news.

bulago n. food kept for journey, picnic. Syn. *ivaqa*. May refer to food previously cooked. Idiom: *bulago mai na koro* news from the village, rural news, usually of passing interest.

bulago, bulagoca v. to give food to someone, but by extension, to convey important information or gossip. Also to entertain, usually with entertaining news, interesting story.

bula tawamudu n. small plant of the coast, especially stony areas, often grown beside houses, Kalachoe pinnata, Crassulaceae. Curious feature of fat, waxy leaves that can live a very long time without water. A leaf is often put inside a book where it will stay viable, eventually sprouting new roots from the edge of the leaf giving the impression it can live forever (*bula* to live, *tawamudu* forever). Warmed over a fire, the leaf is sometimes applied to a boil with the notion that will help the healing process. Syn. (West, Macuata) *cakamana*.

bulebulewa adj. slippery, slimy, mucus, (eel, some fish, live coral, inner bark of hibiscus).

bulewa 1. n. a slippery, granular but soft coloured coral, Alcyonaceae. By ext. *dela-bulewa* refers to groupers, species of fish that lives around such coral.

bulewa 2. n. conjunctivitis, certain type of eye infection, usually of children.

buli n. cowry shell. Large white cowry shells have chiefly significance. Two large white ones, *buli vula* (Ovula ovum) are often fastened at the head of a *yaqona* bowl (*tanoa*), with another white cowry at the end of the sinnet cord *watabu*, leading in the direction of the chief or honoured guest. This fairly obviously represents the male genitals. No one should walk between the *watabu* and the chieftain or guests to whom it is pointing. At informal session, one may have to pass in front of the *tanoa* but should bend down and touch the *tanoa* respectfully, in passing. The *bulivula* is sometimes mounted on the inside walls of a chief's house, as a mark of chiefly status.

bulibuli n. landmark used by surveyors, putting a pile of rocks over a landmark peg.

bulikula n. Golden Cowry, Cypraea aurantium, prized by Europeans, once thought to be very scarce and valuable. Formerly, a chief or priest might wear one as a pendant, hight on the throat. These shellfish are most often found off the Nadroga coast.

bulileka n. cowry shell, Ovula costellata, small and white, often worn around the neck of women performing a traditional exhibition dance *meke*. Properly, in earlier times, only a chiefly woman would wear this ornament.

buliloa n. common cowry shell, Cypraea tigris.

Buli n. traditional title of certain chiefs (followed by a place-name), Macuata, Bua Provinces, a title borrowed by Colonial administration for the government Fijian official administering each Old District

(*Tikina makawa*), discontinued for a time after 1948, replaced by District Commissioners of United Provinces. Later the smaller Old Districts were re-instated, and the United Districts discontinued.

buli, bulia v. to form, shape, create, manufacture. *buli vacu* v. to form a fist, clench the fist (as for punching). *talanoa buli* fictional story. *ibuli madrai* loaf of bread. *ibuli kasivi* glob of spit. *ibuli koula* ingot of gold. Syn. for *ibuli* is *ibulu*. *E bulitaki levulevu*. He/she is heavily built (fat). *ibulibuli* n. shape, form.

Dauveibuli n. Creator, usually referring to a Christian concept of God.

ibulibuli n. shape, form, figure or build (person).

bulibuli koya self-promoting, conceited, full of oneself.

buli-na (Colo and Tailevu) n. buttocks, bum (U.K), ass (U.S.), properly *mu-na*.

buliloma adj. self-willed.

bulikia n. (Archaic) type of warclub made of a tree root.

Bulou n. title of chiefly lady as a form of address just before the name, especially in Kadavu. This is equivalent to the title Ratu, modernly used for chiefly men, though formerly (and properly) restricted to Verata.

bulou n. edible wild yam, Dioscorea pentaphylla, similar to *kaile*.

bulu, buluga v. to clench, squeeze, and release in the hand, as in preparing grated cassava for puddings, or as a child might make globs of mud to throw.

bulu, buluta v. to bury. Also to fill, as of tooth cavities. *buluta na qara ni bati-na*. May also imply the hiding of money, saving it out of sight of others.

Idiom: *bulu we ni yava* lit. "bury footsteps", informal ceremony drinking *yaqona* by a host and his group, to discuss visitors who have departed. The visitors need not be discussed further after this event. In a sense, their departing footsteps are buried. Also referred to as *e dua ni tanoa ni bulu yava*.

veibulu n. funeral, burial. *na veibulu vei Seru* funeral for Seru.

Bulu (Archaic) n. underworld, legendary place where people lived after death. It is said to be located just west of Naicobocobo, Bua, where spirits departed by jumping off at a certain location. *Ratu mai Bulu* a former god of Tailevu especially.

bulu-taka v. to pile up earth (at a planting-mound, as for yams, taro, *yaqona*, ginger)

bulubulu 1. n. small shark believed to be blind, sometimes eaten when better seafood is not available. Seen seasonally common around the shore, especially very early in the year. This may be the young of a sand shark that lies half buried in the sand, and can be dangerous to people.

bulubulu 2 v., n. to hide or conceal something, particularly when a person is thought to be acting meanly, unsharing of what they have (money, for example) that other people want: *e dua na ka na bulubulu toka vei iko* your concealment (of money, etc.) is really something. *Kakua ni bulubulu* Don't conceal what you have that might be shared out.

ibulubulu 3. n. burial place, grave. The use of graves is now adopted by highlanders. Formerly in the highlands a burial place was concealed or a corpse was buried under the house, where it would be less exposed to potential witchcraft. In some places caves were used for corpses. The idea of elaborate graves comes from Tonga. In Fiji, the concept of cemetaries was introduced and required by colonial authorities. *vatu ni ibulubulu* gravestone.

Idiom: *bulubulu boro vulavula* to cover-up by external appearances only, as whitewash on a grave merely covers up a rotted corpse within.

bulubulu 4. n. ceremony of forgiveness, "burying" resentments. Commonly this ceremony is be performed after a man elopes with a girl. This is a type of informal marriage in Fiji. The man will later go to the girl's family and present a whale tooth. v. *bulubulu-taka*. *E dodonu me bulubulutaki Mere*. A whale tooth should be presented to Mere's parents for her being taken away. (They cannot very well refuse.) *ibulubulu* usually a whaletooth given as a request for forgiveness.

bulukau n. button. *bulukau taba* n. push-button. *bulukau coba* shirt-button(s) at neckline. *qara ni bulukau* button-hole. The notion of buttons was of course introduced by Europeans.

bulukau-taka v. to button up.

bulumakau n. cattle, beef. *bulumakau yadru* mature bull. *bulumakau sele* steer, castrated bull. The word derives from Tonga.

bulusiti (Eng.) bullshit, nonsense.

bulutoka (Archaic) n. wooden, so-called "cannibal fork" used by chiefs and priests; each fork was normally given a name, often obscene. Now to be seen only in a museum. Copies are made for the tourist trade. Fijians with certain functions were not to touch food so they were fed by others, or used such forks.

buluwai n. timber tree, Garcinia pseudoguttiferae, Clusiaceae (Guttiferae), same genus as the introduced mangosteen. Fls and frts are used to scent oil. Totemic plant in Ra Province, villages Nayavuira, Nasau, Namarai, Dama. Name refers to concealing (*bulu*) the private parts of a woman (*wai*), possibly due to shape of the leaf and also the yellow sap. Bark is dark brown to black. Branches straight, horizontal. Prop roots at base of trunk. Fls throughout the year, white to yellowish, pink to red at later stage. Fruits red at maturity. Syn. *buliwai*, (Vanua Levu) *bulumaga* which has clear sexual indications (*maga* vagina). (Vuda, Ba) *sueri*.

bune (or) **buneko 1**. n. (Viti Levu and LomaiViti) Golden Dove (more accurately, Lemon Dove), Ptilinopus luteovirens, male bright yellow, female deep green. The call is unique and distinctive, somewhat like the bark of a dog. The general word for dove is *ruve* (Polynesian *lupe*).

bune (or) **buneko 2**. (Vanua Levu and Taveuni) Orange dove, Ptilinopus victor, male bright orange, female deep green. The call is unique and distinctive, like the tick or tock of a loud clock.

buno n. sweat, perspiration; *buno ca.* sweat from fear. *buno sivia* considerable or excessive sweating.

bunoca v. to try very hard, lit. to "sweat" over something.

bunobunoa adj. sweaty. *Au sa bunobunoa ena levu ni noqu cakacaka.* I am sweaty from the amount of my work.

bunokata n. prickly heat, heat rash.

bunotaka v. to sweat, sweat for it (as a worker sweats for his pay), sweat over it (some work). In saying the word a Fijian will sometimes pass a hand over the brow. Idiom: *Bunotaka!* Lit. "You sweat for it", a sharp refusal in response to an unreasonable request for something to be given free. This is usually said in good humour.

bura (West) bad.

bura, buraca v. to ooze, ooze onto, as of water, mud, or blood from a wound, or pus from a sore, ejaculate from sexual climax. *laburabura* n. pimple(s).

bura, buraka 1. v. to stick (it) with hand-held spear through mud or sand, as in spearing eels, or finding turtle eggs in the sand. *na bubura duna* the poking into the mud to locate eels.

bura, buraka 2. v. to spit out quickly, as of bad food or bad water.

buracimi n. (Medical) yellow jaundice.

buradela n. very top of the (human) head.

buraka v. to spit out from the mouth solid material (fibre, fruit seeds, food that is too hot).

burau n., v. drinking of *yaqona* by sucking it up from a flat dish (formerly, by priests) or from a leaf-lined pit in the ground (by highlanders). The technique of using a wooden serving-bowl (*tanoa*) or clay bowl (*dave ni yaqona*), and coconut drinking cups was introduced from Tonga in the early 1800s. *ibuburau(-ni-bete)* flattish wooden dish used by priests for sucking up *yaqona*, now seen only in museums.

bure 1. n. house serving a special function, as for visitors, or (in olden times) a men's house for a clan in some parts of Fiji. Tourist resorts now refer to cabins as *bure* but this is a modernism. (*icili* would be more "correct" in older Fijian.) *bure ni sa* large community house, or men's house for meeting and sleeping (an old Melanesian custom no longer current in Fiji, never known in Nadroga and some other places). Wives and children lived separately from men in pre-Christian times. In the highlands of Viti Levu the *bure* was the basic social unit, equivalent to clan (*mataqali*) of the some lowlands. As a men's house, that *bure* bore the name of the clan. *bure ni kadi* nest of the black biting ant. *bure ni pi* hornet nest. *bure ni oni* beehive. *bure kalou* (Archaic) traditional temple, lit. "spirit house".
Idiom: *tiko e bure* to get circumcised with ritual stay at home for 4 days for healing, for boys, formerly in a separate house, isolated from women. The same term is used for girls staying home at her first menstruation. One also hears *tu i bure*.

bure (Anglicism) n. "House" at a boarding school where each child as assigned to a dormitory with membership in one "house". Such "houses" may compete in various sports within the school.

bure adj. muddy, of water; *burebure* very muddy, of water.

bureburei n. (Colo East) muddy floodwater. *Taukei ni Wai Bureburei*, chiefly Waimaro title of Colo East, based at the highland village Nairukuruku, Naitasiri Province. This chiefly lineage actually came from Ra and is thus not itself of highland origin. Most Fijians know of the title by its Bauan translation: *Taukei ni Waluvu*. (*waluvu* n. flood). Supposedly, this chief controls the rain and floodwaters that greatly affect the Rewa delta. This is even talked of today, some Fijians taking it seriously. A couple of village elders insist that they do add the final letter "i" to this word.

Burebasaga n. honourific name for the traditional, extended territory of Rewa, lit. "Divided House", originating from Verata. Since around 1820 the leading chief is the Roko Tui Dreketi, having overthrown the former chiefly Vunivalu lineage, a branch of the people in Namosi Province. Included in the extended territory (*matanitu*) is Beqa, Kadavu, Vatulele, and west through Nadroga. (Orginally that included only coastal Nadroga and part of Kadavu. Northern Nadroga still does not feel a part of this territory.)

buredela-na n. very top of the head at its highest point. *kesu-na* is the crown of the head, the depression at the back of the head.

bureitaka v. to be reluctant to give, to refuse something wanted by someone else.

buroburogo or **buruburogo** adj. stingy, mean, ungiving, selfish, keeps things to oneself instead of sharing (and thus the behaviour "stinks").

burogo n. stink-bug. When disturbed it gives off a strong odour that can cling to a person.

buroro v. to sprout up abundantly, of seeds, plants, weeds. Also refers to breaking out of many pimples, usually on children. May even apply to occurence of many troublesome flies in a house.

Burotu n. after-life paradise, floating island of Central Proto-Polynesian mythology that sometimes recedes beneath the sea, inhabited by beautiful women and things that have a reddish tone, including coconuts. The myth is especially associated with the Waimaro people on Matuku Island and it is said to be located near that island. Reference is sometimes made to Burotu-kula, associating the colour red *kula* with Burotu. Stories tell of men who visited Burotu and returned. It seems that Matuku Island was in most extremely early times settled and greatly disputed by Proto-Polynesians. Part of their interest was almost certainly the collection of the red feathers of the Fijian parrots *kula*. Syn. *Pulotu* in Lau.

Idiom: *Eda sa mai tarai Burotu sara.* We (many) are on top of the world, enjoying the best of everything, in Paradise.

buru, buruka v. to squeeze and crush with the fingers, or pinch, as with chilli pepper for use as a condiment, or with a cigarette butt to extinguish it. Applies also to a private signal pressing and moving the fingers; it may be between the sexes as an expression of interest, or may be just a private signal man-to-man, or woman-to-woman, to direct attention secretly to someone else of interest.

burua-sika v. to splatter, spurt out, as juice from mushy fruit, watery stool of diarrhea.

buruburogo adj. stingy, unsharing.

burugone v. to attempt abortion by physical means. Syn. *vakalutu na gone*, implying abortion by any means.

buru-lago adj. lazy, doing nothing, wasting time, as if just swatting flies.

busa 1. n. an edible Garfish, half-beak, that skims as it swims, Hemiramphus far. Three black spots on each of the two silver sides. Syn. *buse*. Iconic fish of Yaqeta Island where it is eaten.

busa 2. n. an area of thick underbrush, low forest.

busi (Slang) n., adj. stink.

buta 1. v. cook, cooked, of food. *vakabutari* cooked. This is a general word. *saqa, saqa* v. refers to cooking in a pot, traditionally referring to steaming, though modernly referring also to boiling. *ura buta* n. type of prawn that is red naturally (as though it were cooked), at Vatulele, Naweni, and VanuaVatu, Parhyppolyte uveae, not eaten.

Idiom: *itukutuku buta katataka* "hot" news.

Idiom: *kana buta* lit., eat food that is cooked and ready, refering to a person who might help with work at the later stages but expects to be fed or rewarded as if he had helped substantially.

Idiom: *buta droka* trying something at which one is inexperienced, lacking full knowledge, not yet competent, new on the job, a greenhorn. The usual meaning of *buta droka,* mentioned above, refers to food half-cooked, not completely cooked, usually from an earth oven opened prematurely. (It is not always easy to judge the right timing.) Syn. *butu-kara.*

buta 2. burned, scorched, of person or part of their body, blisters may be implied, caused by strong sun, heat or friction. Despite dark skins some Fijians may be burned by the sun, and may be afflicted with sun cancer. *bubuta* having many blisters. *buta* may refer to a boil ready to burst.

buta-na n. (Vulgar) bum, rump, buttocks of person or animal. Sometimes used as insult, which may be joking, showing a consciousness of racial colour: *Buta vula!* White ass! or *Buta loaloa!* Black ass! A general insult would be *Buta karokaro!* Pimply ass! In Suva, men may call out "Nice *buta!*" to a girl they admire. And they may hear as a fast answer "Cost *tabua!* " ("It would cost you a whale-tooth!") which implies "You would have to marry me." It is all said in good fun, if a little vulgar. *buta dauloloma* n. easy girl, an easy "lay". Syn. *mu-na,* the proper word.

vakabutara v. to cook. *vakabutari* cooked.

butara v. to remove food from pot or oven and put it on plates.

butako, butakoca v. to steal. *dau butako* thief. *butabutako* thieving. Finding and taking things for one's own use or one's own family has been a major source of sustenance in Fiji. This is not necessarily to be thought of as stealing if the things taken are not being used immediately by the "owner" or if the "owner" has an abundance. Gathering from the bush or nearby vicinity has always been a major part of subsistence life. Taking from one's widespread set of relatives without asking is considered quite normal. The notion of personal possession was not sacrosanct. This was a consumer society of goods that were almost all disposable and very few things could be kept personally or permanently by an individual. Taking something would not be thought of a stealing if it would not greatly inconvenience the "owner". On the other hand, Fijians can be angry if someone takes coconuts or fruit from a tree they consider theirs. Looting of salvaged goods, as from a fire, flood, or shipwreck, would be considered quite customary. Syn. (Lau, Kadavu) *driva, drivata*.

veibutakoci n. adultery, from *butako* to steal.

buto n. dark, darkness. *mata buto* fainted. *buto leka* short night of summer (or can refer to an eclipse). *butobuto* very dark. *yalo butobuto*. adj. unenlightened, ignorant, selfish. *buto ni vanua* inland, middle of the land or island. (This is the origin of the name of inhabitants of flatlands of what later came to be called Bau Island, the *Butoni(vanua)* people, replaced by tribe Mataisau and super-tribe Kubuna.)

butobuto n. adj. darkness, very dark, ignorant (referring to pre-Christian times) *ena gauna butobuto . . .* in pagan times . . .

buto adj. dark, of colours. *damudamu buto* dark red (deep purple).

buto-na n. navel, belly-button. Syn. (Tonga) *pito*. (Vanua Levu) *vicocico*.

Butoni n. a turtle-fishing people of Polynesian type, formerly residing at Ulunivuaka (on Bau Island), now residing mostly in LomaiViti. The name is short for *Buto-ni-vanua*, meaning the middle of the land. These people were expelled from Bau and settled in central and eastern Fiji.

butu, butuka v. to tread on, trample on. This word may also apply to treading very lightly on a friend's foot as a secret signal to notice something going on that should not be spoken about. *butu qele* walk the land, looking over the property. *vakabutuka na noqu qele* walk around my land. *butu vatu* firewalking. *butu-voroka* v. to step on and crush.

Idiom: *buturaka* to beat up (someone).

Idiom: *butu kai* to dance, usually the Fijian *taralala*. See *taralala*.

Idiom: *Au butuka tu*. I am standing (on) my ground, a defiant response to someone from another place who is acting with presumption. This might be said by a Viti Levu highlander, an original indigenous Fijian, to a Fijian from the smaller islands, a *kai-yanuyanu*.

Idiom: *butu cala* "to put one's foot in it", i.e., to make a gaffe of impropriety in traditional custom, such as speaking out of turn in a formal situation.

Idiom: *vakabubutu* to desire and try for something novel. *Au sa vakabubutu tiko e dua na ka vou*. This can almost imply a notion of keeping up with the Jones.

ibutubutu (Archaic) n. woven mats to stand on during Christian ceremonies, weddings, or baptism. Mats are given to the minister after the ceremony.

butubula, butubula-taka v. of a wife, to return to her paternal clan, separating from her deceased husband's clan, after his death. This is done by formal ceremony, usually with the presentation of a whale tooth *tabua*, referred to as the *ibutubula*. Traditionally, theoretically, a woman moved to her new husband's village when she married. For practical reasons, this is not often the case in these modern times. But in formal terms, a woman "belongs" to the husband's village even if she does not actually live there.

butubutu n. doormat, carpet. Refers mostly to mats *ibe* woven of pandanus leaves.

ibutubutu 1. n. mat where man and wife stand for marriage ceremony; these will afterwards be given to the officiating minister. Also a long series of mats on which high chief walks, entering a village. These notions are all modern. **2.** doormat of a modern dwelling. This may be simply a sack. It is customary for shoes to be removed before entering a house.

butudravu n. first occurence of menses in a girl. A girl stays home (*tiko e vale*) for four nights during which relatives and friends bring gifts (clothes, barkcloth, pandanus mats), followed by a feast *bogi va*. She will now stay close to her mother and sever close relations with her former friends who are still children. Traditionally, she must also avoid boys and men. These customs are fading in urban areas.

butukilikili (Colo East) adj. very beautiful, of a young woman.

butu-muri v. to follow in one's footsteps, sometimes of many people following one. The word may be used literally or figuratively. *Mo butumuri au de o qai lutu*. Follow in my footsteps lest you fall.

buturaka v. to beat up (person). This may occur when men feel they or their families have been slighted. *buturaki koya* to beat him/her up.
buturara n. floor (house or any building), deck of a ship, area for walking around.
butusiri, butusirita v. to trip over something, in treading.

C

The letter **c** is pronounced as a soft **th**, as in *this*, not hard as in *thanks*. In a few places the **c** may be pronounced as an **s**, as an ancient local form in Nalea and Nasava in the upper Wainimala territory of Viti Levu Island, at Wainimakutu at the headwaters of the Wainikoroiluva River, and Tavea Island in Bua Province. These local variations cause no difficulty in our common understanding.

ca n. the letter "c". *ca levu* capital "C". *ca lailai* lower-case "c".

ca adj., n. bad, evil. See *vakacaca*.

ca v. to gather, as in *ca buka, cava buka* to gather firewood. See *canu, canuma*.

ca, cata v. to dislike, have no liking for, to hate. *catacata ni mate* (Lau) hate to die.

cabacaba adj. unkempt, disheveled, ill-behaved.

caba, cabana v. to join (of people). *cabana na kalavo* join the club. *cabana na laga sere* to join in the singing, joining the singer who leads off. *laga, lagata na sere* to lead off the song.

icaba n. colleague(s), chum(s), campanion(s), gang, group of people with a common interest or of the same age.

cabacaba n. a flat type of edible crayfish, slipper crayfish, Paribacus sp. Syn. *vavaba*. Idiom (Lau): *cabacaba* n. person who sticks his nose into other people's affairs.

cabe, cabeta, cabe-taka 1. v. to go up, climb up (slope but not steps, ladder or tree). *cabeta na baba* climb up the hill. *cabetaka na isele* go up with the knife. *Sa cabe na balolo mai Sese.* The *balolo* (edible sea annelid) rose at (the village of) Sese. **2.** v. to emerge from the water, after swimming or collecting shellfish. **3.** v. to land or come ashore from a boat.

icabecabe n. ascent, steep path, rising (of the sun, for example), landing (ashore, usually).

vakacabecabe adj. step-relative, as in *na tinaqu vakacabecabe* my stepmother. *na tamamu vakacabecabe* your stepfather.

cabo, cabora (or) **vakacabo, vakacabora** v. to offer formally, as in presenting *yaqona* at ceremonies such as *isevusevu* (greeting), *soro* (surrender), or *bulubulu* (asking forgiveness). The same word is used for presenting a whale-tooth. Also *vakacabora na masu* offer the prayer.

cabola adj. broken or cracked open, as of dropped egg, husked coconut, green jak-fruit, ripe melon, unripe pineapple, or of husked coconut cracked from overheating, exposure to sun. Syn. (Vanua Levu) *(k)abola*.

cabolo v. to make a sudden loud noise. *Sa cabolo na kaila.* The shouting burst forth. *Sa cabolo na dakai.* The rifle-shot rang out. *Sa cabolo na katuba.* The door slammed shut. *na caca-bolobolo ni gasau ni dakai.* the crackling of gunfire. *na cacabolobolo ni dakai ni vanua* the continued roaring of artillery. *cabolo ni saga* (Vulgar idiom) to fart loudly. *saga* thigh.

cabota v. to break or burst, of string, rope, or sail of sailboat.

cabura v. covered with discharge, as of a sore. See *bura*.

vakacaca, vakacacana 1. v. to damage (it), to harm. *vakacacani* destroyed, severely damaged. Idiom: *vakacacana na gone yalewa* to take the girl's virginity. *vakacacana* v. to spread damaging rumours.

vakacaca 2. n. damage. *Rabailevu na vakacaca ni cagilaba.* Damage from the hurricane is widespread.

caca, cacavaka v. to exaggerate, overuse superlatives, exclamations.

icaca (ni kuro) n. potsherd, broken pieces of pottery. *icaca ni veleti* broken pieces of plate. Potsherds are the main archeological artefacts found in Fiji from the immigrant Lapita people as early as 3,000 years ago. These were Proto-Polynesians who were sea-going sailors. Most moved off to the east.for reasons unknown.

vakacaca "and then some", plus a few, as in the expression *e tini vakacaca* ten and then some, a little more than ten.

vakacacalevu n. great destruction (war, hurricane), holocaust.

dauvakacaca n. vandal, hoodlum, terrorist.

caca v. to catch fire and then spread quickly, of fire, but also by extension, rumours or news. Idiom: *Rogo i Viwa, qai caca vakabuka.* Heard at Viwa, then the story will be spread like wildfire. (Viwa was thought to be a centre of gossip.)

cacali v. to talk about, or sing about, to comment about. As a noun, may modernly refer to "literature" in academic curricula. In either old or modern usage this is a word not commonly known.

vakacacali n., v. things to be talked about, to keep in mind, worth knowing and remembering. As a modernism, Fiji's Education Department now uses the word *cacali* for "literature" in the academic curriculum. It is based on the notion of selecting out things, as one picks out the lice from a child's head. See *vakacakulei*.

cacavukavuka adj. intermittent, as in *ena domo cacavukavuka* in a broken voice (halting, hesitating, not smoothly flowing).

cacawale adj. impermanent, perishable, something that will not last. Syn. *caca rawarawa*.

cadra v. to rise, of sun, moon or star, just appearing, to appear or happen suddenly, a plant sprouting, peace in a time of war. *na icadracadra ni siga* dawn, sunrise.

cadri v. to fly up or out (paper in the wind, chip of wood), hit hard, sent flying (person).

cadruti v. to speed, rush, dash. *Sa dua na ka na nona cadruti yani.* That's really something, how fast he takes off.

caga (Archaic) n. a unit of measure: span of hand from tip of thumb to tip of little finger, with fingers stretched out. One speaks of *caga dua, caga rua*, one span, two spans, according to the length thus measured. Usually used for barkcloth *masi* or for woven mats. *Cagawalu* is the name of an important god of Moturiki, and then also of super-tribe VusaRatu on Bau Island, then ultimately elsewhere.

caga (Ba) n. part of body all around the hips, sometimes used pejoratively: *caga levu!* big ass! In Nadroga *caga* may refer to a woman's private parts.

cagau n. internode (of plant stem, as in bamboo), a space between two or more objects (such as the nodes of a plant-stem). See *tagau, togo-na*.

vakacagau going along smoothly, to be underway (as of work, a meeting, sailing of boat). *Sa vakacagau tiko na tei yaqona.* The planting of *yaqona* is going along nicely.

cagi n. wind, breeze. *cagi mudre* light wind, breeze. *cagi bula* fresh, pleasant, lively breeze. *cagi tataba* gusts of wind. *cagicagi* breezy, well ventilated, aired. *tabu cagi* kerosene lamp (hurricane lamp). *sala ni cagi* windpipe (human, animal). *Sa rui cagicagi.* It is very windy (speaking of the weather). *cagi laba* n. hurricane. *Sa liwa mai na cagi.* The wind is picking up. *liwa, liwava* to blow (of the wind), to blow on.

Idiom: *kana cagi* nothing to eat.

Idiom: *me ikacikaci ni cagi.* to die far away from home (overseas).

Idiom: *sa cagi na vuna.* All is in order, the work is proceeding correctly, people in control know what they are doing.

Idiom: *cagi ni doi* n. blustery wind that blows during the lunar month when the shrub *doi* (Alphitonia spp.) blossoms (small, white), around the month of May.

Idiom: *cegu cagi bula* or *loma cagi bula* to have had nothing to eat.

vakacagicagi v., n. to relax, take a break, intermission, rest-period.

ivakacagicagi n. intermission (as in a programme of entertainment), rest period, tea-break.

cagilaba n. hurricane, defined as a wind of 64 knots (72-82 mph) or more. Hurricane season is approx. Nov through April. *laba* murder.

cagina 1. v. to ventilate, to air out by letting the air in.

cagina 2. v. to be whisked away, disappear quickly, things, people, food.

cagi ni Vugalei (or) **cagivugalei** n. disease of the skin sometimes said to involve prickly heat. Capell 2nd ed. has it listed as Herpes zoster. Syn. (Lau) *lewavoki* with blisters around the hips, and when fully circled, the person is thought to die. This is sometimes considered a "Fijian disease" not readily explained by modern medicine.

cago n. turmeric, Cucurma longa, Zingiberaceae, aboriginal introduction, semi-cultivated and now grown as a commercial root crop (especially at Namara and Waibau, Tailevu, and at Wainadoi, Namosi), formerly for medicinal protection, painted on mother and new-born baby. The plant in fact does have antiseptic value, and is used for this purpose in India and other parts of Southeast Asia. It has become naturalised and does not require re-planting, as commercial ginger does. Fijians also use *cago* to colour barkcloth yellow. Fijians never used it for food or edible spice until they learned to buy curry powder, which is about 25% turmeric powder. Turmeric is commonly called *rerega* or *rereqwa* in the western part of Viti Levu. Fresh it is used by Gujerati in making pickles. There is also a white type of turmeric, used mainly by the Gujerati. The word *cago* is modernly also applied to commercial ginger, more properly *cago ni vavalagi*. Syn. (Kadavu) *qumu*.

Idiom: *cagocago* the colour of turmeric.

cagolaya n. a semi-cultivated ginger, Zingiber zerumbet, the root still used often by Fijians in a concoction to ease symptoms of a cold. These days also used for asthma, diabetes, and thrush with undetermined effectiveness. (Fijians learned of diabetes from Europeans.) Syn. *layalaya*, (Lau) *cagola*. (Colo East) *danidani*. (West) *dalasika*. (Kadavu) *sago*. See *drove*.

cai, caita v. to fornicate, a word one can pronounce only in very limited context, but a word one can virtually never write. It occurs almost only in extremely vulgar swearing, such as *Veicai!* That is the

reciprocal form of the verb. *veicaiyaki* (Vulgar) f—k around, here and there. *Veidauci* n. fornication (polite word). Cf. *veiyacovi* sexual intercourse, the formal, correct term. *yaga-siri* a vulgar term.
Idiom: *caivosa* glib-tongue; smart and all too quick to give defensive answers to any embarrassing question asked, "back-talk", especially from children to adults. Americans might say "smart-ass", not to be said in polite society.

caka, cakava v. to make, to do. *Me caka mada.* Please do it. *cakava oqo* do this. *caka nomu ga* "do your own thing". *caka-cala* (Church) v. to sin. See *kitaka* to do, a more rarely used word. Syn. (Kadavu) *jila.* (Lau) *vala, valata.*

cakacaka n. work. *tamata cakacaka* worker. *iliuliu ni cakacaka* foreman, work-supervisor. *vakacakacakataka* v. to employ (person, people). *cakacaka-taka* v. to work for it. *na kena cakacakataki* the way it works, how to work it.

cakacaka ni liga n. handicraft(s). This is, of course, a modern expression.

cakacaka-mate n. life-sentence in prison.

vaka-cakacaka v. to reveal, demonstrate, as of a special skill or power. *Sa vakacakacakai koya dina na qaqa qo.* He really showed his special power for this victory.

vaka-cakacaka-taka v. to put (someone or something) to work, give work to a person.

caka-i-ba n. magic done by sleight of hand for spectators, an introduced idea.

cakamana n. magic by supernatural or special powers; miracle (a concept introduced by Christian missionaries).

cakau n. reef. Syn. (Tonga) *hakau.*

vakacakau v. as in *laki vakacakau* go out to the reef at low tide to gather whatever food one finds, small fish, crabs, crayfish, octopus, shellfish.

cake 1. up, upwind and by implication, an easterly direction. *tu cake* to stand up. *lako e cake* to go up. *na Tu i cake* honorific name of Lau, the windward archipelago (*yatu,* here abbrev. as Tu). Idiom: *mai cake* up in the highlands. Only context can indicate whether the Fijian is talking of a higher place or a windward place. Syn. (Colo East) *colo,* that gives rise to the word *kaiColo* highlander (of Viti Levu). (Tonga) *hake.*

cake 2. more (in certain contexts), especially used to create comparatives, as does the English suffix "-er": taller, longer, blacker. *Sa vinaka cake na draki* the weather is better. *balavu cake* longer, taller. *dredre cake* harder (*dredre* hard). But note: *e dua tale* one more. *eso tale* some more.

caki, cakitaka v. to deny (an allegation), dispute (an assertion), take to task. *A sega ni cakitaka o Seru.* Seru did not deny it.

cakule, cakulea v. to search for lice in the hair, poking around with the fingers. Parents might do this with children. They usually bite the louse to crack it, and then they swallow it. *me vakacakulei na gone* have the child de-loused. Syn. *vakacecele.*

vacakura v. to walk fast, showing off, having exhibitionist manners.

cala, calata v. to be wrong, make a mistake, miss a target, to miss a bus, fail to hear the news, etc.). *cala* n. error, mistake. *Na nona itukutuku e veicalati vakalevu.* His/her report is quite erroneous.

vakacala v. to declare as false, to disagree, to consider it wrong.

vakacalacala v. to distort, falsify, mislead, deliberately miss the target.

cali n. (Archaic) war club that is shaped as a blade.

calidi v. to detonate, flash with a sharp noise (gun), click (closing a lock), flashing punch (boxing), popping of fat in a fire, small firecracker. This does not refer to an explosion. By ext., *Calidi!* can be an exclamation indicating that something is extreme: Fantastic!

caliva v., adj., n. to gleam, gleaming, shiny, reflective, polished (mirror, glossy paint, bald pate, face or body with sweat or oil, water reflecting the sun, shoes). *Sa caliva vinaka na nomu vava.* Your shoes are polished nicely.

calo, calova v. to hollow out, as in carving a wooden drum (*lali*), or dugout canoe (*bavelo*).

calove, calovetaka v. to place leaves around food being cooked, to protect it.

calucalu (or) **vakacalucalu** v. to gobble food down fast, as a child might do.

cama n. outrigger. In Lau, by ext., a close chum or inseparable aide. *camakau* outrigger canoe.
Idiom: *vodo i cama.* to be completely dependent on others, lit. to ride on the outrigger of the canoe.

camakau n. single-hulled sailing boat with outrigger. The forward-sloping, horned masthead supports the sail. Some 140 such boats were in operation in Lau in the 20th century, though the length was 7 to 9 meters, in contrast to the 30-meter length reported by Wilkes in 1845. These older, longer boats required a crew of 40 men. An equiv. Tongan craft was the *hamatafua.*

camana v. to follow the lead singer, or leading instrumentalist, as back-up and as chorus. *icamani* (Catholic) response of the congregation, in recitation.

cameme adj., v. talkative, non-stop talker, facile speaker, to babble, quick to gain fluency in local speech (of child or newcomer). May be said to someone in a jocular way,

canu, canuma v. to gather (firewood, shellfish, edible seaweed). *na canu buka* the gathering of firewood. *Me tou laki canu kai.* Let's go gathering mussels. May apply to certain fruits. See *ca buka*.

caqe, caqeta v. kick (forward direction of foot) as a football. *mataveicaqe* n. football (rugby) team *caqelaka* v. to kick very forcefully. *veicaqe* to play football. *taceqe* to stumble, stub the toe, to trip (on something).
Idiom: *tamata vakaicaqe* influential person (today often implying rich and thus powerful).
Idiom: *caqe veva* lit. kick paper around, meaning to fool around doing nothing.

icaqe n. spur, as of a rooster, or a warclub.

caqou v., n. thumping sound, when something solid is struck.

caqu v. to walk hurriedly.

caquru v. to crackle, crunch, as a fresh biscuit being eaten. See *quru, quruta*.

cara, cara, carata, caramaka v. to clean off, sweep off (a place), such as a path, or a place for earth-oven, usually outdoors. Can include gathering up as of rubbish. *were cara* clean off all vegetation down to the bare ground. *cara bulubulu* to clean off weeds, grass from cemetery or gravesites, a regular community task.
Idiom: *cara sala* lit. clear off the path, but referring to efforts to renew earlier relationships between villages, or between individuals and their villages. By contrast it is said that the path to the village (or between the villages) is overgrown -- sa *tubua na sala ki na koro* -- when the relationship has been neglected, or set aside deliberately. Sometimes obligations are thought to be onerous, or relationships have soured.
Idiom: *cara kuvu* v. to run at full speed, lit. stirring up the dust.

caracara 1. adj. strong, willing, fast, effective, of a person cleaning up some mess.

caracara 2. v. to wipe up, clean off, as of the bottom after relieving one's bowels, or making a mess.

carawai v. to clean oneself off with water after relieving oneself.

cara, carata 1. v. to confiscate.

cara, carata 2. v. to finish something (food, money) quickly and have no more.

cara, carata 3. v. (Lau) to run away fast to escape.

caraqa refers to a bald spot or place where the head hair is cut away. There are many synonyms.

carawa bobota adj ripe, of fruit, as indicated by bright colour.

cariba v. to spring up, spring back, of branchlet, usually, or chip of wood when chopped, bounce (of a ball). *na vakacaribariba* the spring-trap. *Sa cariba na bai.* The trap is sprung. See *riba* and *ribariba*. *cariba* may refer to a person being quick.

caroba v. to flap, like the wings of a chicken, the sail on a sailboat. To fall in fainting, or losing one's footing. To break, of a tree branch.

carubi v. to be in full swing, hyped up at this time. *Sa carubi sara tu ga na lutu sobu ni vakalala sitoa* the store sale is in full swing. May refer to the bursting out of song.

cau, cautaka v. to make a formal contribution, usually an expected one, presented at some traditional occasion. *Mo dou mai cau.* Come (you several) and give.

cau 1. n. formal contribution to a *soli* usually of money, or presentation-goods (mats, bolts of cloth, kerosene etc.) at ceremonial occasions. Such contributions play a major rôle in the life of a Fijian. *Nomudou cau e $200.* Your (several) contribution is to be $200. A person's worth is to some extent reckoned on the visibility of giving, which may prompt a Fijian to borrow what may be difficult to repay. A Fijian will be shamed for giving little, especially if he is known to have the resources. Anonymous giving would be rare for a Fijian. Because of this system, it is difficult for a Fijian to accumulate personal capital. Even if he does accumulate possessions or some capital, he might as a consequence be looked down upon as greedy, selfish, ungiving. Syn. *soli*.

cau 2. n. (Vanua Levu, Lau, Rewa, Kadavu) Ironwood tree, Casuarina sp., Bauan *nokonoko*. In earlier times thought to be an abode of spirits. Unless it is sharp, an axe bounces off this tree. Often used for making clubs that were thrown.

cau 3. (Vanua Levu) not. *Au na cau lako.* I won't go.

cau-na n. leftover food. There are prohibitions about eating the leftover food of a high chieftain, or of certain others. *vakacau* v. to eat leftovers.

cauraka v. to speak out, make a statement about (something).

caucau 1. n. wind that blows from mountains to the sea, late at night through very early morning. On the larger islands, it can be a very cold wind, in the low 50s° F. Idiom: *kana caucau* walk around idly outdoors at night/early morning. *Ia, evei ga o kana caucau tu mai kina o iko?* Well, just where are you running around at night? *va-kana-caucau-taka* walk around idly at night with someone (usually a baby); in Colo East this is considered unhealthy for the baby during the late night, but a healthy thing to do once the very early dawn begins to break.

caucau 2. n. well known ornamental shrub, Cestrum nocturnum, Solanaceae, flowers on a shrub can be either purple or white. The white flowers especially are highly scented in the evening. Syn. (Vanua Levu) *senibogi*.

vakacaucau ni ravu n. distinctive, traditional war cry of a tribe. In many cases, these are still remembered. Many were recorded by the Native Lands Commission.

vakacaucautaka v. to congratulate, applaud, express admiration or appreciation.

vakacau-oca v. to grumble with fatigue, to say one is "fed up"; burdensome. *oca* tired. *Sa rui vakacauoca na levu ni soli ni lotu.* The amount of contributions exacted for the church is very burdensome.

caudre adj. lit up, aflame, alight, burning with flame. *waqa* refers to burning or being alight (as of a lamp) but not necessarily with flame.

caudre, caudreva v. to light (a flame, a light or lamp). *caka me caudre na buka* make the fire flame up. *caudre na matana* his/her eyes lit up. *Sa caudre na livaliva mai Rewa.* Electricity now lights up Rewa. Syn. *vakawaqa, vakawaqara* (that does not imply a live flame).

vakacaudreva (or) **vakacaudre-taka** v. to fan a fire alight.

cauravou n. young unmarried man, considered a youth. Such a man is not expected to be responsible for making independent decisions. This stage of life extends much later in life among Fijians than among Europeans. A man is not usually considered responsible until he is married. Formerly, men usually remained unmarried till age at least 28, often to around 34. Modernly, marriage is occuring much younger for men.

cauve, cauvena v. to carry, over the shoulder basket (*ketekete* or *isu*), or something crooked over the shoulder or arm, such as bunch of bananas (with curved stem over shoulder), or a lame person who needs help walking. (= *caube, caubena*). Not common.

cava 1. why (in a question) *baleta na cava?* why? (because of what?)

cava 2. what, which (in a question). *Na cava oqo?* What's this? *Cava o cakava?* (or) *O cakava na cava?* What are you doing? *A cava o kaya tiko?* What are you saying. *na lori cava?* which truck? *Na cava?* What? (asking a person what they want, or to repeat what they said -- this is a modernism, rather brusque and familiar; it is much more polite to say *O?*) *A cava na betana?* What is the purpose? *Me i cavai na ka oqo?* What is this thing for? *A cava o lakova?* What are you going for?

cava 3. in the expression *cava ga*: whatever. *ena veivanua cava ga* in whatever places.

vakacava how. *vakacava?* How are things? What's up? *Vakacava o koya?* How is he/she doing? *Me caka vakacava?* How to do it?

cava, cavaraka v. to reach a place or time when something has been completed, end of voyage, end of story or letter. *Sa cava mada eke na noqu talanoa.* My story ends here. *nomu cavacava* where you end up. *cavaraka* to make a full disclosure, to disclose it fully.

vakacava, vakacavara v. to complete, to finish (a task).

vakacavacava n. tax, a new concept. Formerly this word referred to tribute exacted by a dominant tribe. Prior to the dominance of Bau, Verata had a very extensive system of tribute that extended far into Vanua Levu. See *qali*.

vei-cava-takini refers to how people are related.

cava n. sp. of cone shell, Conus marmoreus, that can sting painfully, even dangerously, formerly used in coastal parts of Fiji for presentations, just as a whale-tooth would be used today. There are no good, early written accounts of the usage of this shell as a revered presentation item and none used as such have been preserved in museums.

cava n. hurricane, heavy gale. This is an older, traditional central Polynesian word. The more recent and now commonly used word for hurricane is *cagilaba*, lit. "murderous wind".

cavea, cavena v. to hang up, usually clothes to dry, sometimes fishing nets. *na caveni isulu* the hanging up of clothes.

cavi (Archaic) n. penis, cock, circumcised as required by custom, an old word not commonly heard. *boci* refers to the uncircumcised penis, and may imply an Indian male, since many Indians are not customarily circumcised and virtually all Fijians are. *cavi-i-tamamu* ("Your father's penis") is a somewhat archaic insult. *Roko Cavi* (Sir Penis"), also called *Mai Nasoni* is an ancestral spirit at Naweni, in Cakaudrove Province.

cavilaka v. to defame, speak badly of someone.

cavu, cavuta 1. v. to pull up or up and out with a little effort, as in harvesting taro or ginger, pulling a cork, unplugging bath-tub, pulling up an anchor *na cavu cago* the harvest(ing) of ginger. *na gauna ni cavucavu* the time of harvest. *ulucavu* n. wig. *cavulaka* v. to uproot indiscriminately. *veicavuyaki* to tack (sailing canoe, sailboat), from the ancient notion of having to pull up the mast at each tack.
Idiom: *cavu* to elope.
Idiom: *cavu ikelelele* departure of boat, ship, pulling up anchor (or by extension, leaving a mooring, departing the harbour).
cavu, cavuta 2. v. to beat, as in beating a record, or setting a record *cavu isausau*.
cavu, cavuta 3. v. to pronounce, enunciate (word, sentence, speech), to cite. *cavu-qaqa-taka* to recite (such as verses of a *serekali*). *cavuyaca, cavuyacataka* to tell a person's name, usually of informants to the police or courts, or to elders of the village. *cavu-qaqa-taka* v. to recite, as of a poem or *serekali*.
cavu 4. v. to arrive or appear on the field, formally as a group, dancers for an exhibition dance, or women making a formal presentation of bales of cloth or other goods to the person(s) of honour at a welcoming ceremony.
cavuikalawa n. progress, forward step, literally or figuratively. *na imatai ni cavuikalawa* the first step of progress.
icavuti 1. n. title, name by which a person or group is identified, the (usually honorific) name by which a kin-group is known or, less commonly, their plant, fish, or other animal.
icavuti 2. totem of clan (*mataqali*) or tribe (*yavusa*) may be indicated by this word but properly, there is no unique word for totem in Fijian languages. Only a few kin-groups are known by the name of their totem and among the more Melanesian Viti Levu Fijians of highland origin it is usually forbidden to pronounce the name of the totem. For this reason *icavuti* is not an appropriate translation for the word "totem". Mostly among Viti Levu highlanders and former highlanders, true totems exist as secret symbols of the people's fertility and reproductive capability and thus, in a sense, their ability to survive. Mere mention of the name of a sacred totem could formerly have drastic consequences, including sexual abuse, stripping and dousing. (These days one might be splashed with water and/or required to drink an enormous volume of *yaqona* as punishment.) Many if not most of Fiji's kin-groups have no sacred totems. They do not exist in Lau, Burebesaga (Rewa, Beqa, Kadavu), most of LomaiViti beyond Ovalau, and with perhaps rare exceptions, do not exist in Vanua Levu, Taveuni or Bau. They are conspicuouly absent in areas of Polynesian influence. What Fijians may call their plant, their fish or their bird is often a local distinction or feature for which they are known, or for which they have a high regard, or some thing associated with their ancestral spirit that can be a shark, a dog, or a stone, some sand, or a piece of water. In one case, it is a type of driftwood in the river. In some cases there are true totems with reproductive and fertility significance, and in other case merely iconic features of importance in local custom and tradition and sometimes, their tribal spirit, *kalou*, such as a dog. Unknowingly, in its investigations, the Native Lands Commission, persisted in demanding to know the local totems in every area and was given many fanciful answers that were entered into official records. Similarly, Fiji's Education Department gathered totemic information published in 1984, and much of this is fanciful.
icavucavuti (ni vosa) n. pronounciation, enunciation. Syn. *itautau ni vosa*.
icavu 1. n. a particular pleasure one takes in something. Not a common word. It may be a grand-child, a boat, etc. *ukucavu* adj. all decked out, dressed up grandly (person).
icavu 2. perfect match for a person, piece of clothing, necktie, hat, haircut, lipstick colour, costume jewelry, any added feature that makes the person more attractive.
cavu isausau v., n. refers to the setting of a new record, as in sports achievements. The term originates from the custom of pulling up (*cavu*) the marker (*isausau*) of the past record throw of the obsolete traditional sports javelin (*itiqa*).
cavuivuvu-taka v. pulled up, out of the ground, with the roots.
cavuka 1. v. to snap, snap off, of cord, rope.
cavuka 2. n., v. (Slang) to go into a mental fit, have a nervous breakdown, go crazy, lose one's mind, be out of touch with reality. *E tauvi koya na cavuka.* He/she has had a mental fit. *E cavuka tiko o koya.* He/she is having a fit. The word may be used light-heartedy or humorously. *O cavuka tiko?* You going crazy? (asked rhetorically). The notion is that some connection to the mind is disconnected suddenly, has snapped.
cavu mai v. to come from (person and their place of origin). *E cavu maivei ko koya?* Where does he/she come from?
cavutu 1. n. place that one comes from.

cavutu 2. v. to set off on a trip, voyage.
veicavuyaki v. to flap about as of a boat's sail, with a change of wind, or of the boat's direction).
cavuru v. to lose the hair on one's head. *E cavuru tiko na uluqu.* I am losing the hair on my head (becoming bald). *cacavuruvuru* lose absolutely all the hair on one's head.
cawa n. steam, water-vapor, visible breath.
cawa v. to steam. *cawa sese* to steam away forcefully, excessively, usually of a cooking pot.
cawadru v. to snap off (as a rope might snap). *wadru* or *wadruca* suggests stretching. or stripping, as in stripping off leaves from the edible terrestrial fern *ota*.
cawaki n. sea urchin eaten raw, sometimes cooked very lightly. It can be rather liquid. The delicate taste is a contrast to its murky appearance. To render the spines harmless, one can dip the sea urchin in hot water. This was a favourite food of Ratu Kamisese Mara. Tripneustes gratilla. Syn. *deru, gasagasau,* (Macuata) *gaca*.
cawi v. to fly off or out suddenly in the air, as with a wood-chip from chopping, a stone or spear that is thrown with sudden vigour.
cawiri v. to be spinning, as an electric fan or as with a person's head feeling like it is spinning, dizzy, perhaps from exposure to the sun, as a soldier on parade. By ext., may also mean to dash off, to rush somewhere. *Tou cowiri tale!* Let's have another dance! Syn. *cowiri, co-iri*.
ce root-word, used alone or attached in other words, implying spread out, extended, scattered. *daliga ce* protruding ears that stick out (like Prince Charles of the U.K.)
ceacea (Rare) adj. pale. Syn. *vulaci*, the more common word, often used for the facial complexion.
ceba 1. cross-eyed. Syn. *mataceba*.
ceba 2. v. to flutter, flutter down, as of leaf, feather, sheet of paper; falling, stagger about (drunken person), dart here and there (small fish, birds), move about unsteadily, to swerve. *ivolacebaceba* pamphlet. *taceba* to stagger (drunk person, wounded animal), veer about on the road (vehicle). *mata ceba* looks one way with head directed another way, squint to the side, cross-eyed. *vakaceba* v. to glance to one side (eyes only). *cici vakacebaceba* run zig-zag, darting here and there (such as the evasive action of a rugby player with the ball) *veicebayaki ena gaunisala* swerve or veer this way and that way on the road (as a drunken driver might do). *mata veicebayaki* with eyes glancing back and forth from one side to the other.
cebe, cebeta v. to cut (circumcision), slice (bread, sandwich meat), to skin (animal), to nick (as with pen-knife), slash lightly, superficially, cutting where there is little resistance. Syn. *tava, tava*.
cebo n. arse. *Mata vakacebo!* Vulgar exclamation that a person's face looks like an arse.
cebu, ceburaka v. to shake out, flap, as of mat to air it, shake off the dust, to wave, as a person might do, a flag in the wind.
cece v. to skitter, as a spear might do hitting the ground, or a thrown stone, on the ground or on the water. Could apply to a small boat speeding on the water.
cecebuya v. to cause to flutter, fly (of flag, laundry on line), to wave a flag backwards and forwards.
cecekala v. to wake with a start, wake up abruptly. *Era yadra cecekala ena mataka ni Tusiti.* They (many) woke up suddenly on Tuesday morning.
cecekia adj. huge, enormous, of a man, an event. *gu cecekia* enormously energetic.
cece, cecega v. to pull out, pull up, lift up something thin, light, such as a mat, blanket, band-aid, bark-cloth; to slice, remove skin. *ucu cega* pug-nosed, turned up nose, usually of a person. See *cega,*
cecere adj. very high (mountain, tree, person), exalted, lofty (ideals). *itutu cecere* exalted position. See *cere*. Syn. *cecelevu*, usually of a mountain.
cecevula adj. pale. Syn. *vulaci, ceacea*.
cedru, cedruma v. to slurp in sipping, as Fijians have done normally drinking soup, tea; suck (smoking pipe). Syn. *ceru, ceruma,* more common usage. *macedru* hiccups. Idiom: *cerumi au, au na cerumi iko.* to have too much of a good thing. Have too much of something and it will make you sick, implying to be like a child who consumes too much sugar cane (*dovu*).
cega, cega v. to lift up by one side, as of mat, page of a book, opening up leaves of a leaf-parcel (usually of food, *ikovu, isala*). *me cega na ivola ena taba tini* open the book at page ten. *bati cega* buck-teeth. *ucu cega* snub-nose, pug-nose. See *cece, cecega*.
Idiom: *gusu cega* person who cannot keep a secret.
cegacega (or) *cega* n. type of small giant clam *vasua*, Tridacna sqamosa.
cegu, ceguva v. to breathe, breathe in, take a rest, relax, be relieved. *cegu cake!* breath in! *cegu sobu!* breathe out! *ceguva* breathe it in (as of oxygen, in hospital). *cegu leka* asthma, breathing difficulty, *me cegu mada* take a break. *cegu levu* breathe heavily. *wacegucegu* pant, puff, out of breath. *Sa cegu na yalo-na.* His/her mind is relieved.

cegu, vakaceguya v. to rest, take a rest, relieve, terminate (employee).

icegu n. breath, as expelled. *vakatabuicegu* v. hold the breath. *Sa leka na noqu icegu.* I am out of breath. *cegu oca* out of breath (from exertion).

cegulado v. to splutter, choke when a beverage goes down the wrong way, impeding proper breathing.

ceguleka asthma, an indigenous, fairly common affliction. May refer to other difficulty of breathing. Syn. (Lau) *ceno*.

cegu levu v. to gasp in fear, surprise, emotion, or fatigue,

icegu levu n. full stop (at end of a sentence). (U.S.A.) period. This Fijian word is the invention of schoolteachers, as are all words of grammar.

cegu oca 1. n., adj. out of breath (from exertion).

cegu oca 2. n. asthma. Syn. (Lau) *ceguji*.

icegu kurau n. exclamation mark. A word invented by schoolteachers.

icegu taro n. question mark: ? A word invented by schoolteachers.

ceguvaka v. to breathe on (something).

vakacegu, vakaceguya v. to retire (as with age), resign (from employment). *ovisa vakacegu* retired policeman. *ivola ni vakacegu* letter of resignation. *siga ni vakacecegu* sabbath, Christian day of rest. *vakaceguya* put it/him/her to sleep (as of animals)..
  Idiom: *vakacegu vakadua* "passed away", dead (polite form).

ivakavakacegu n. place to rest up (as on a voyage).

cei who, whose, whom, what is the name? pronoun used in questions, and always preceded by a particle at the beginning of the question, as: *O cei ?* Who? *O cei oqori?* Who is there? *O cei li?* Who could that be? *nei cei* whose? *vei cei?* to whom? *O cei na nomu koro?* What is the name of your village?

ceka, cekata, cekeraka v. to open up, usually a parcel, often of leaves enclosing cooked food from an earth-oven.

cekalu v. to whistle, as a passing bullet, to whir like propeller blades. *kalu* to whistle.

ceke n. enlarged testicles, from elephantiasis. A legendary Waimaro characteristic that for them implied great power. See *tatuku*.
  Idiom: *ceke dada* (vulgar slang) coward, impotent, ineffectual.

ceki, cekitaka v. to deny.

cele, celeka v. open up, usually of last stage of opening up an earth-oven, separating the leaves that cover the food.

cele, celea v. probing physically hair on the head to detect and catch lice, usually on children. see *vakacecela*.

vakacecela, vakacecela (na uluna) v. to separate the hair (of the head *ulu-na*) and pick out the lice, often done for children. Lice are usually then eaten. They are first cracked between the teeth to kill them. Syn. *cele, celea.* c

celua n. having soft, distinctive long hair, as with person, dog, or cat.

cemuri, cemuria v. to chase, force to go, send person(s) away, or simply run after to catch a person or animal.

ceno n., adj. coughing spasm, wheezing breath, bronchial infection, asthma, asthmatic. Syn. *cegu oca*.

cere n. traditional competition as part of formal welcoming ceremonies, such as at a wedding reception. It involves a running race by male visitors chasing local young women who bear prizes of traditional goods (whale-tooth, barkcoth). At Sawani the ceremony was performed to welcome the return of their own chief after an overseas visit. Formerly, *cere* referred to the prizes themselves rather than to the ceremony. By extension, the term *cere* might apply to mats or other gifts brought to a person who has acquired a new boat, or a new car, as a matter of wonderment and admiration, gifts to be placed on the new acquisition. Perhaps implicity, the donors might expect to benefit from the acquisition.

cere, cereva v. to perform the *cere* ceremony of welcome for people, or for a new boat or vehicle, mostly in Lau I seem to remember. *Sa cerevi na waqavuka vou* the new aeroplane's arrival has been made official with ceremony. May celebrate a variety of occasions, welcoming and congratulating. Syn. (Lau) *rova, rovata*.

cere, cereka v. to lift away partly (mat, carpet, box), or open up, raise slightly, tip up on its side (box, suitcase); *cereka na ligamu* open up your hand.

vakacerea v. to raise up.

vakacerecerea v. to elevate, to hold up supportively, usually with praise for some person(s), or occasion or act, raising in esteem.

cere adj., n. high, height (outdoors, of natural objects such as mountain). *na cere ni ulunivanua* the height of the mountain. To describe people as being tall, or time as being long, the word *balavu* is used. *E 200 fute na kena cere.* Its height is 200 feet. *Raba* is width, *raraba* is wide though they may be synonyms. See *cecere*.

cerebu v. to scatter, fly off in all directions, as children scampering off and away, or birds taking off in all directions, scattering. Idiom: *cerebu* (Slang) n. *kati*, a means of collecting money for some good cause, people paying to "buy" certain playing cards, and someone winning a modest prize (sugar, flour, a vase) if one of their cards is selected out from a shuffled pack of cards.

ceru, ceruma v. to slurp, sip. Slurping soup or tea is proper and normal manners in the Fijian village. Syn. *cedru*.

cerudi v. to blow the nose. Fijians have traditionally done this by holding one nostril with a finger and blowing away. Residue is often wiped away with the shirt or tee-shirt. Formerly the back of the hand was used. See *wadruca*.

ceu, ceuta 1. v. to poke (as a finger in eye), flick (out of hole), prick and pull out (as flesh from univalve shellfish), prick and open (a boil on the body). *vakaceuta mai na vosa* bring out the words (that have been repressed or suppressed). *iceuceu* children's game, flicking bits of wood out of holes in the ground.
Idiom: *ceu ibe* pick at a mat one is sitting on, a very common nervous gesture with the fingers, when one is being reprimanded. One sits as far away as possible, facing away if possible, but certainly diverting the eyes away from the accuser. The head is bowed low.

ceu, ceuta 2. v. to carve (wood usually) but also to engrave, incise or scratch on any surface some writing, diagram or drawing,

ceuceu n. the action of carving (usually of wood). Fijians themselves did virtually no decorative wood-carving except on war-clubs and in making spears, and wooden bowls, or neck-rests. Some of the best carving in Fiji was done by Maori natives, early Tongans, and Polynesian Fijians of Fulaga. *dau ceuceu* wood-carver, sculptor. These days various objects are carved as souvenirs for tourists. Some are good replicas of Fulaga carving but most are fakes that never existed as Fijian artefacts.

ceva n. south. *ena ceva kei Suva* to the south of Suva. *na tokalau cevaceva* the southeast tradewind (*tokalau* = northeast). *Bulou ni Ceva* lit. Lady of Kadavu, name of a Kadavu ship. Fijans had no compass and did not define directions as NSEW. Their directions were named from directions of the wind but have been adapted to match the European compass directions. *Naceva* is a place-name in Kadavu. *na Ceva ni Pasifika* the South Pacific. *vualiku* north, northerly wind.
Idiom: *Naceva* polite ref. to Kadavu island (because it is to the south of Viti Levu). This is sometimes said in Fijianised English *Na Sauca* (The South). Or Kadavu is referred to as little New Zealand because it lies to the south.

ceva ira southwest. *ceva* south, *ra* west. *vua-i-ra* northwest.

cevaceva n. seasonally cool wind from the south around the month of March (*vula-i-magomago* or *vula-i-vila*) when cultivated yams are being harvested. This can be a time of fairly dry, ruffled weather during the latter half of the hurricane season (roughly November through April). The wind is thought to be related to some dry skin conditions, and a chapping of the lips.

vakacevaceva (or) **vale vakacevaceva** n. open-sided shelter improvised of layers of branches, leaves.

veicevacevai adj. arranged in layers, stacked, stratified.

ceva (or) **diligo** n. abalone.

cevaruru v. whirr, buzz, whiz, whistle (insects, blowing wind, missile such as an arrow or bullet).

cevata congealed (blood, sap, coconut oil), frozen, as in *wai cevata* ice. *lumi cevata* a type of edible seaweed that is cooked and then congeals as it becomes cool, and may be kept in a refrigerator.

cevu v. to make a sharp plosive sound, to burst out (as in song, setting the tone), blurt out, puff out (as in pronouncing a "*p*" or a "*b*"), to make the sound of small explosion (bamboo cannon, rifle shot), sharp twang or zing (bow releasing an arrow). *vaka-cevu-ya* v. to set the tone or mood, as of a conversation, or a meeting, *vakacevuya na veivosaki*. It is an assertive act.

cevua n. false sandalwood, small timber tree with large white scented flowers, spherical, juicy, purplish brown fruit, and having very fragrant, hard white wood similar to *yaro*. Vavaea megaphylla, Meliaceae, wood used by Indians for incense.

cevuga n. red or white flowered ornamental ginger plant, Amomun cevuga or Geanthus cevuga, with flowers used in garlands or to scent coconut oil. The name also applies to Alpinia purpurata. By comparison, bush sandalwood (*yasiyasi*) resembles true sandalwood only in the type and shape of leaf; it has not special scent and the timber is brown, subject to cracking.

cewa, cewava v. sit up on (box, chair, log).

ci, cita v. to fart, to fart deliberately (at something or someone), indicating gross disrespect. *icici* n. rectum. Syn. *sivi, sivita*.

veidauci v. to have sexual intercourse. See *cai, caita* (more vulgar) v. to fornicate, *vei-yacovi* (a formal, polite form) n. sexual intercourse.

ciba v. to faint, be knocked out (boxing), to die (polite term). *Sa cibati koya*. He/she fainted, collapsed. This may be the matter of heat, dehydration, as for soldiers on parade ground.

ciba (Slang) as in *Sa ciba!* That settles it! That is decided! Syn. *Set!*

icibaciba n. legendary place where a dead person departs for the next world. There are about three of these located around Fiji. They are usually in a direction from which their original migration came. There is one on the coast of Bua Province, at Naicobocobo, one at Udu Point, Macuata, and one at Naiqoro at the east end of Kadavu Island. At the very tip of Udu there was indeed a pandanus palm standing in 2003, though thought not to be the original *balawa,* at which a dead person's spirit should throw a *tabua,* to gain entry to the nether world.

cibi, cibina v. to coil up (rope, pandanus leaves for making mats, snake). *cibini* coiled up. This coiling is with less tension, less pulling action than the verb *vivi, viviga* that would apply to a bandage, or the rolling of a hand-made cigarette.

icibicibi (or) **icibini** n. coil, as in *icibini voivoi* coil of *voivoi* leaves (for weaving mats).

cibi, cibitaka v. to rejoice (over something), celebrate (victory), formerly to dance joyously to celebrate victory, now usually after sports, previously after battle. *cibitaka na qaqa* celebrate the victory.

Idiom: *vakacibicibi* v. egotistical, to be proud of one's own accomplishments. *sa dau vakacibicibi koya ko Seru*. Seru is so proud of himself. Syn. *dokadokai koya*.

cibi n. Formerly this was a dance of triumph after combat. Since 1939 it has come to mean a brief dance of combative challenge performed by Fiji's national rugby team before a major match. In brief, the words of challenge are : *"Tei vovo! Tei vovo! Ia Ia Ia! Rai tu mai! Rai tu mai! Oi au na viriviria na kemu bai!"* Ratu Bola of the Vusaradave, Bau Island, composed the football challenge at the request of Ratu George Cakobau. (Originally, the initial words have been heard as *Tei voavoa* rather than *Tei vovo*.)

icibi n. seed of woody *walai* vine Entada phaseoloides, formerly used as a rattle attached to ankles of celebrant dancers. It is also now used decoratively in various tourist souvenirs.

Also called *ilavo*, or *ilafo* (from the Polynesian name) the seeds were formerly used in a game (*veilavo*), as counters to be flicked on a woven mat, knocking away another seed. The huge coin-shape of the seeds gave rise to the Fijian word for money *ilavo*.

For snack-food called *revereve* in Colo East, the kernel is grilled, sliced thinly and added to wild poisonous yam *kaile mila* (*koile gaga* in Colo speech) that has been cooked (these days boiled), then grated into a basin through which fresh water flows. The washing and the addition of *icibi* offsets the irritating ("itchy" *mila*) qualities of the yam. The resultant mush is hung in a cloth to drain, and then eaten. But first fruits must be formally presented to the chief at Nadakuni, for example. The Waimaro people say the mash tastes like ice cream. It has the texture of mashed potatoes with a little taste added by the slices of *icibi* seeds.

Highlanders of Viti Levu made no oil for the body but they formerly chewed *icibi* and rubbed that on the skin for the oil content.

Children have used *icibi* for the detachable head of sporting javelins used in their playful version of the competitive game *veitiqa*, now obsolete.

cibura v. to fart and defecate at the same time.

cici, ciciva, cicivaka v. to run, run after, run to (someone, something). *cicivaka* to run with (taking something). *ciciva na polo* to run for the ball. *ciciva yani na vale* run toward the house. *cicivaka na cina* v. to run with the lamp. *cicivaka na polo* v. to run with the ball (as in rugby). Syn. (Colo East) *dosi, dosive*.

icici n. anus (Vulgar: arse hole). Syn. *mata ni da, ivoco*. *ci, civa* (or) *cita* v. to fart, to fart at (someone)

cici levu! vulgar insult: Big asshole!

cici, ciciga (or) **cicia** (*na niu*) v. to cut (as of copra). *na cici niu* the copra-cutting. Also applied to extracting the nut-flesh of *vutu kana* (to be eaten), Barrigtonia sp. The motion is that of incision, then scooping out, as in removing coconut meat from within the coconut shell with two or three cuts, then applied leverage with the knife. There is considerable skill involved to do this fast. *Cicia* may be the origin of the name of Cicia Island or it may be from an ancient word for the Trochus shell, now known as *sici*.

cicila adj. having unwanted holes, of clothes, pots, roof; leaky.

Idiom: *bilo cicila* unreliable, not to be depended upon (of person), lit. leaky cup.

cidre adj. on the verge of death, or close to death (person, animal) as indicated by physical signs, belly-up (of fish). Syn. *civedre*.

cidroi adj. undisciplined (child or youth). *gone cidroi* undisciplined child who acts on his own without helping out at home, prodigal son (Biblical). See *droi*.

cigani n. tiny. freshwater river fish, Sicydiaphiinae, sub-family of Gobies, a Fiji version of "whitebait" migrating upriver when they are tiny, netted in large numbers during October, November, around Navua, for example. Adults spawn in freshwater, the young developing in the sea. Syn. *tanene*.

cigi, cigita (or) **cigiva, cigilaka** v. to caulk (boat), close or fill in a chink, or small gap. Of people, to push their way into or through a crowd of people.

cigogo v. to squint (of a person), failing, fading light (lamp, candle). Syn. *sigogo*.

cika n. infection of eye, conjunctivitis.
Idiom: *Sulukui na vudi, e dua e cika?* You are trying to hide something from me, as if I could not see clearly? Literally, Ripening stalks of plantain are cut and covered with leaves on the ground but they do not deceive the birds. This proverb is credited to the *kikau* bird (Ra Kikau). *cika* is conjunctivitis, here suggesting blindness.

cike, cikeva v. to implore, ask persistently. *vakadre cike* persistently failing to comply with requests, never listens. *O sa dau cikeva na ka.* You always persist for what you want.

cikecike adj. demanding, exacting, "difficult", "pushy". *cikecike matua* very demanding, persistent in a constructive way. *cikecike ca* excessively demanding, in a destructive way.

cikinovu n. centipede, up to 18 cm in length, nocturnal, consuming insects, the front two legs modified as poisonous pincers with dangerous sting. They appear seasonally, often around houses or entering houses. *Cikinovu* was one of the names of Cakobau.
Idiom: *malumalumu vakacikinovu* looks harmless but is dangerous like a centipede, usually said of a man.

cila, cilava v, to shine, of sun, moon, stars, to shine on (something). *sa cila na siga* the sun is shining. *E sega ni cilava na nona vakasama.* His/her thoughts are not brilliant. *E a cilava vinaka na yaqona na siga nikua.* The yaqona was shined on nicely by the sun today (to dry it after harvesting and washing). *na cilavi-siga* the sunshine, the shining of the sun. *vakacilavi siga* to sunbathe.

cili, ciliva 1. v. to cut open, pierce open, slice lightly with a surface cut. *ciliva na ika* clean the fish (cut out guts). *ciliva na bo* lance the boil. *Me cilivi na gone tagane.* The young boy(s) should be circumcised.

cili, ciliva 2. v. to stitch up, repair holes (as of fishnet).

icili n. lodging, house for visitors to the village, well constructed shelter for a temporary stay. *vakaicili ena otela* to stay in the hotel. Modernly, hoteliers refer to tourist cottages as *bure*. More traditionally they would be called *icili* for temporary accommodations. In villages, a sleeping area might be provided in a large *bure ni sa* (non-existent in Nadroga and some other places), intended for visitors or for meetings.

vakaicili v. to stay temporarily at a house or shelter, take a room (hotel) or lodging. *vakaicili-taka* to provide accommodations, as for visitors.

cilo n. (Medical) blood in the faeces.

cilu, ciluma 1. v. to pick at, remove one or a few things from inside a pile of them, "fish around" for something selectively. Syn. (Slang., Eng.) *samarini*.

cilu, ciluma 2. v. of birds, bats, to peck at, maturing fruit for example.

cina, cinava v. to illuminate, cast light on, usually by lamplight or torch. *cina* lamp, torch. *cina livaliva* electric light or torch. *cina tabucagi* kerosene lamp. *cina benisini* Coleman lamp using white spirits (and now also, the petrol or "super" used as car fuel). *mata ni cina* n. light bulb.

ciokarasi (Eng.) n. theocracy. Some Fijian Christians have wished to make Fiji a church-controlled state, especially after the first military coup in 1987. Their views have not been widely accepted by others.

ciqi, ciqira v. to stick pointed object into something, close or fill in a chink or small gap *ciqimaka* is more forceful. *ciqira na peni ena ulumu* stick the pen into your hair (frequently done in bushy hair of Fijians). *ciqira na sote* tuck in the shirt. *ciqira na isulu* tuck in, do up the *sulu*. *sa rui ciqi* it is tucked in too tight. *ciqira na mata-iloilo* put on the spectacles. *ciqira na sau ni daliga* put on the ear-rings.

ciqo, ciqoma 1. v. to catch, receive (ball, other object) in the hands.

ciqo, ciqoma 2. v. ceremonially to accept a gift ritually presented (whale tooth, or *yaqona*). *Au ciqoma ena yalo marau* I joyously accept it. By extension, this can suggest acceptance and agreement to a request that is being made. An offered whaletooth is usually an integral part of any serious request. Even without the whaletooth (or other offering), *ciqoma* can mean to aquiesce, agree to a request, or accept. *ciqoma na lewa ni bose* to receive and accept the decision of the council. By ext., may imply social acceptance, as in *sega ni ciqomi raraba* not widely accepted (in social terms).

ciqo baca v. of fish, to nibble the bait (*baca*) without being caught by the fishhook. Also said of a person whose words or activities are disruptive of a conversation.

ciri, cirima v. to drift (of an object), set it adrift. *vakaciri salusalu* ceremonial feast, after learning a new exhibition dance (*meke*), symbolic of throwing floral necklaces into river or sea. *vakaciriciri* drift down the river (of people, usually on rafts, deliberately). *Sa ciri yawa na noqu vakasama.* My thoughts are drifting far away. Idiom: *sa ciri ko Beqa.* usually said of a child, about to cry, with the face distorted. Lit. Beqa Island is drifting away.

Ciri (Name) na Ciri, who in English are referred to as the Ciri Twins, Nacirikaumoli and Nakausabaria, who killed the pet fowl Turukawa of Degei at Conua, Nakauvadra. They were expelled and departed with Rokola, master carpenter at village Narauyabe, and founder of the *Mataisau* (or) *Matasau* people who then dispersed down the Wainibuka River, reaching Rewa, with one branch settling on Bau Island, the others scattered. The Twins disappeared but have been claimed to reappear, or be about to reappear at various occasions. The notion of a return persists still today. It has sometimes been thought they will bring great riches in cargo cult fashion.

vakaciri loloma touching, deeply affecting the emotions with pity or sympathy. *yaloyalo vakaciriloma* touching movie.

ciri mai v., n. (Viti Levu) insulting term for offshore islanders (from Kadavu, Lau, Vanua Levu, LomaiViti, all areas of Tongan influence), who have recently come to Viti Levu and are often thought to behave presumptuously. Implication is that they just drifted to Viti Levu and do not belong there; they are not "real Fijians" (*kaiViti dina*), though in fact a great number of them had originally emigrated from Viti Levu. Syn. *qalo mai*.

ciu, ciuva v. to stream out, as steam from a kettle, air from a punctured tyre.

veiciu (Archaic) v., n. string-figures to form cat's cradles in a whole variety of forms, using both hands, an old game for children, especially girls and young women.

civa n. breastbone.

civa n. pearl oyster, Pinctada margaritifera (Meleagrina margeretifera), edible. *mata ni civa* n. pearl. Fijians traditionally did not gather or treasure pearls or any other gems, though white cowry shells were used to symbolize power and chiefly authority. Pearlshell came to be used in breastplates (see *civavonovono*, below), made by Tongans to be worn by Fijian chiefs. There is no gold-lipped pearl in Fiji and pearls are rare in natural black-lipped pearl. All are cultured pearls. In the 1970s a Japanese established a small cultured pearl enterprise on the coast of Ra. Another one has been more recently established in Nasavusavu Bay, Vanua Levu, by Justin Hunter, and another has been planted at Malake Island. Seeded pearls take some three years to mature and can live for ten to twelve years. Harvest is usually in March and August. Very large, delicious rock oysters from Sydney were introduced to Mago Island long ago. Fiji also has a small mangrove oyster, or rock oyster *dio*, Ostrea sp., not now usually eaten. (They are small and hard to open.)

civaciva n. species of small pearl oyster, Pinctada martensi, often eaten. Near a Vanua Balavu village one may see piles of discarded shells.

civa vonovono n. (Archaic) round breast-plate of black-lip pearlshell, often with some strips or pieces of whaletooth, made by Tongans. In Tonga there had been the notion that a breast-plate might impede the arrows of Fijians. (Tongans themselves traditionally used bows and arrows only for chiefly sport, not in war.) Bau gave some of these breast-plates to Viti Levu chiefs who co-operated in accepting Christianity and Bauan leadership. Syn. *bulutoko* also referring to breast-plates.

civedre v. to roll or turn up the eyeballs, showing fatigue, unconsiousness, or impending death, or just as a gesture of boredom, or exasperation. Syn. *civele*.

civi, civia or **civita** v. to peel, pare, or chip off the skin (raw yams, taro, cassava; fruit such as *wi*). *civicivi* peelings. Chipping or carving more deeply into the substance would be *ceuta*. See also *sivi, sivita* for a chipping action that would give shape, as to a club or spear, or even a pencil being sharpened.

civicivi (ni yaqona) n. peelings and chipped pieces of sun-dried kava rhizome (*lewena*). The skin is removed only in areas of Tongan influence (Lau, Cakaudrove, Kadavu) to make a whiter beverage that is less bitter, which is then preferred by Polynesians. The peelings are used to adulterate powdered kava sold in the market. They add a bitterness and unpleasant taste. This skin was used by European manufacturers of neutraceutical kava as a source of kavalactones and that may explain to toxicity that resulted in a ban on those pills.

vakacivo v. to express a wish after spitting out a light spray of the dregs from a cup of *yaqona*. Usually the individual's wish is for fair weather, good crops, good health. These days, spitting is less common than previously, but it is still polite form to express a wish. Modernly one may make a motion of spitting without actually doing it, before expressing the wish.

civocivo n. gust(s) of wind. *cagi vakacivocivo* gusty wind.

ciwa n. nine. *tini ka ciwa* 19, *ciwasagavulu* 19, *ciwa na drau* 900.

co, comaka v. to stick it into or through, leaving it there, of spear in the body, of a cutting (cassava, hibiscus) to be planted in the soil.

ico̱ n. Black-naped Tern, or Crested Tern named for the habit of swooping. Syn. *dre̱*. Another tern in Fiji is the Sooty Tern.

co̱ n. grass, small plant, herbaceous plant (not woody). *co ca* n. weed. *covuata* n. cereal grain such as wheat, rice, corn (maize), jacob's tears. (*covuata* would be rare usage, as by a technician in the Agric. Dept.) *veico̱* n. grassland. *cocona* (Lau) overgrown, as of a garden.

co̱, cova v. of a hawk, tern, frigate bird, to swoop down and carry off its prey.

co̱ boi n. lemon grass, Cymbopogon citratus, Fijians sometimes use this herb as a substitute for tea. Syn. *bucago, bucavu*. (West) *irabo*.

co drogadroga n. introduced weed, low-lying, tiny leaves that close up when touched. Prickly nettles, with tiny, round pink flowers. Often found around paths and dirt roads. Mimosa pudica. Syn. *co gadrogadro*.

Na iCobocobo n. jumping-off place after death, to move to the next world, a location on the coast of Bua Province. There are a few different jumping-off places in Fiji, one of Kadavu Island, for example.

co, cova v. to swoop down, plunging, of a predatious bird, to catch its food at the ground (rat, chicken, lizard) or water (small fish), or pounce as a cat might do in catching a mouse. *Cocova!* Go for it!

Coba! exclamation when a target is hit.

coba, cobara, cobaraka v. to stick a sharp object into something, where it will stay, nail in wood, a stake or fence-post in the ground, do up buttons on shirt. *vakacobara na ivako* to nail, hit the nail. *Ni viri e dua na toro, e na cobacoba wavoki na kau.* When a pig-stye is set up, sticks will be stuck in the ground all around. Syn. *tekiteki-vaka*.

cobo, cobota v., n. to perform a ritually respectful or politely appreciative gesture, clapping one's hands across each other (not parallel), to make a deep, resounding noise. *cobota na vulagi dokai* clap resoundingly for the honoured visitor. *vakacobocobo* ritual performance of such clapping. *cobo bitu* in dance music, using a section of bamboo (*bitu*), to hit the ground rhythmically with the open end to maintain a resounding beat. (In many parts of Fiji this was in early times the only musical instrument.) *derua* is an alternate word for bamboo used in this way, though more exactly *derua* refers to the round and smooth surface of the internal closure at the internode of bamboo. (Thus the term *derua* is also used mockingly for a man's bald pate, when no hair grows on his head.) *A ivakacobocobo* n. ritual clapping of thanks, as traditionally done by hosts at the end of an *isevusevu* ceremony, receiving a presentation of *yaqona*. The *cobo* these days is most often heard after a person has consumed a bowl of kava, clapped three times, or in Kadavu, that can be five times. Older Fijians may still *cobo* to show appreciation for some act or gift, instead of saying words of thanks, such as *vinaka*, which is modern custom. In rural areas, people may *cobo* for a chief who has finished eating a meal. Formerly, they might *cobo* "after a chief had spoken, after he had belched (*nderekonataka*) or broken wind (*thi*) . . . before someone spoke to him and after speaking to him." (Roth, *Fijian Way of Life*, p. 95.)

cobo (Colo) n. ass-hole (vulgar). It is because of this local meaning that people of Colo highlands use *'obo* for the Bauan *cobo*, to indicate the ritual of appreciative clapping of the cupped hands. (The clapping of the hands held parallel and flat is quite different, done to indicate applause, a custom adopted from Europeans.)

cobo, cobora 1. v. to cover, usually a plate or bowl of food, using another plate, or to cover something being dried in the sun (*yaqona* or pandanus leaf), placing a sheet of tin on top to protect from the rain.

cobo, cobora 2. v. turn upside-down, plate, cup, saucepan, pot, box.

coci n. hare-lip, as in *gusu coci* cleft palate.

coco v. to fall down forwards. Syn. *colovu*.

ico̱co̱ n. coarsely woven floor-mat made of pandanus.

cocoko adj. compactly woven, of pandanus mats, leaving no gaps.

codo, vakacodo (or) **codoya** or **codoka** v. to insert, put one thing inside another thing. *codoka na livaliva* plug it in (electric appliance). *sinucodo* chain (of inter-connected links). *codoya na peni ena kena isogo* insert the pen into its cap.

codro adj. rough, hard to control (of a person, or hair on a person's head). *e na gauna codrocodroa eda sa lakova tiko.* In the troubled times we (many) are going through.

codro v. to intrude into a conversation or the affairs of others, to intercede, pushing oneself forward inappropriately.

coga n. barb (as in a barbed hook). *moto vakacoga* n. barbed spear. *talanoa vakacoga* story with a barbed intention. *cogacoga* many-pronged, as of a fishing spear or set of fish-hooks.

coge, cogeva v. to be angry about nothing. *Kua ni cogeva na ka e sega ni yaga.* Don't get angry about unnecessary things.

icoi v. at a meal, the garnish (meat, fish, for example) eaten along with root-crop (taro, yam, cassava) or other starch food (bread, biscuits, rice); at a tea, the garnish might be biscuits or cake that supplements the tea beverage. The basic item of any meal is the starch food, traditionally the Fijian root-crops, the "true food" *kakana dina* as distinct from the garnish *na kena icoi.*

coka n. diarrhoea. These days diarrhoea is often effectively treated by the chewing leaves of guava, an introduced tree. It is an effective herbal remedy. *Au coka.* I have diarrhoea. *oso na kete-na* v. to have constipation.

coka, coka v. to spear (something), to pierce. *coka na ika* v. to spear the fish. *gusu coka* n. sores around the side of the mouth. *coka na uto* an obsolete game, spearing breadfruit (*uto*). *cokadra* n. dysentery. (*dra* blood).

Idiom: *cokacoka na vula.* too ambitious, striving for the impossible, lit. trying to strike the moon (*vula*) with a spear. By ext. this may refer to a person desiring a certain romantic match that is utterly impossible.

Idiom: *cokaidrauna* all dressed up, with great attention to personal appearance.

icoka n. beam(s) as used in house-building.

cocoka v., n. spear-fishing (underwater or above water). *O laki cocoka?* You are going spear-fishing? See *coka, coka*. See also *sua, suaka*.

cokataka v. to throw a spear. *cokataka na moto* v. to throw the spear.

vakacoka v. to spear, stab, poke repeatedly with a long, sharp object..

cokacoka v. to poke repeatedly (as in nervous gesture, say of child, poking or tapping his school-desk with a pen).

cokacoka-taka v. to throw many spears, or throw long objects (bamboo, poles) from one place to another.

coka i drauna v. Idiom: beautiful to see, fitful,, and perfect; to be all dressed up in finery. Can apply to a room, a building, a boat as well as a person.

coke n. shoots, sprouts, young new branches growing from an older plant: also sharp side-branches of shrubs and trees that can be hurtful, like thorned citrus branches.

coki, cokia v. to fold up or roll up and take in, usually into house, things left outdoors, clothes drying on a line, mats being aired, Pandanus leaves being dried, usually because of impending rain or nightfall. *cokia na taunamu* to open up the mosquito net. *na coki isulu* the bringing in of the drying clothes. Can refer to rolling up sleeves.

coko 1. n. yaws, frambesia, ulcers on the body, formerly a common disease in the South Pacific, now virtually eliminated, caused by a spirochete, Treponema pertenue. Infection occured mostly with children ages 5 to 12 and boys more than girls. Infection caused by body contact through a cut or scratch. Infection provides immunity to re-infection of yaws, and also to a closely related sub-species, syphilis. Ulcerous yaws around the rectum or in the mouth are referred to as *medre*. Formerly a severe indigenous problem, yaws have been successfully controlled by anti-biotics, tablets or injection thanks to an American doctor funded by the Rockefeller Foundation in the 1950s. Only older Fijians might know this word and problem. Syn. (Lau) *tona*.

coko 2. n. syphilis, a most extremely serious sexually transmitted disease (STD), very closely related to yaws caused by a sub-species of the same spirochete. *tona* n. gonorrhoea. There is no clear distinction in the minds of many younger Fijians.

coko, cokota 1. v. to catch (fish on line, in net, in trap, animal in trap or by spearing, person by some trick). In the highlands spears were used for pig-hunting but not for fishing. *Sa coko kina o koya.* He/She is implicated, caught up in that.

coko, cokota 2. v. to wrap up and tie a parcel, usually food or firewood, with leaves (such as *via, vuti, balabala*). *cokota na idrekedreke* to wrap and tie the parcel (to be carried on the back of the person or horse). *Me coko na laca.* Furl the sail (of a boat).

cokoi, cokoya v. to tie up, as in closing certain types of basket such as the *idrekedreke*, that is borne on the back.

cokocoko 1. n. shells strung as a necklace, such as very small cowry shells. The shells are pierced and joined together by a cord (now often a nylon cord). Traditionally piercing is done by knocking the shells with a rock.

cokocoko 2. n. fishing-net weights made from heavy shells pierced with a hole.

Cokonaki n. (Lau, Tongan Tokonaki) Saturday, implying the collecting of food before the Sunday Sabbath, a custom imposed by Methodist missionaries.

cokonaki n. vegetables to be cooked and eaten with meat or fish.

cokovaki adj. of the land, leasehold under old tradition, common in Rewa, where the Waivau, Vanualevu, and Vuci people, for example, held land as tenants, providing food and goods in return for usage rights to the land.

cokovata-taka 1. v. to unite, join together. *Eratou sa cokovata ena nodratou vakasama.* They are united in their thoughts. *Matanitu Cokovata kei Vuravura* United Nations Organisation.

cokovata-taka 2. v. to tie together (ropes, prisoners).

cokovata-taka 3. v. to add together, put together *cokovatataka na lima kei na ono* add together five and six. Syn. *soqoni rau na lima kei na ono. soqoni vata.*

Cola! (Nadroga) Hello! Syn. *Bula!* (Nadroga) *Muju cola vina! Bula vinaka!*

cola, colata v. to carry on the shoulder (man), carry in mouth (dog). *icolacola* burden carried this way. *cola isau* back-up, enforce chiefly authority. *Keitou colacola oqo?* We are going to carry all this (on our shoulders)?

Idiom: *E dua ga na siga ni cola qele* Let's try hard and finish up this work, we can finish it today, lit. it is only one day of carrying soil.

Idiom: *cola vatu* traditional obligation, bringing many gifts to the village after a long absence. Because of this heavy expense, some villagers living away may have to delay their return to their home village.

icolacola 1. n. burden (to be carried on the shoulder).

icolacola 2. n. fleshy part of the upper shoulder that bears the weight of a shouldered burden.

cola rara v. of a visiting team, to defeat the home team on its own ground (*rara*).

cola vanua v., n. to carry out traditional responsibilities to the clan, the chief and the Territory, also in modern times, to the nation. Bear the burden of representing the nation (as soldiers or as national athletes competing overseas). This is an important concept to traditional Fijians. Syn. *cola sau.*

cole, coleva n., v. call for help, cry out for mercy. *colecole* call repeatedly for help. Syn. *ole, oleva.*

colo (Interior Viti Levu) up (as opposed to down), by extension, the interior highlands of Viti Levu. *KaiColo* Highlander. *Colo i Suva, Colo i Nadroga, Colo i Ba* place-names, highland territories upland of place named. Early highland provinces were Colo East, Colo West and Colo North, later, in 1945, all merged into other provinces to suppress highland separatism and independence.

Slang: *kaicolotaka* transitive verb, implying that a person is naïve, or dumb, or unfamiliar with what is understood or taken for granted by better informed people. To be amazed, seeing something for the first time.

colovu v. to somersault, go head over heels, fall forward when running. By ext., may refer to falling upside down, and imply capsizing, as of a boat. Syn. *comatai.*

comolaka v. to shove or manhandle a person by shoving, pushing, or to shove or toss things in a careless manner.

conaka v. to spread out and cover (floor, table, inside a basket) with some covering such as grass, leaves and/or mats, or table cloth. The intention here is usually to soften a hard, bare surface. See *coni, conia.*

coni, conia v. to cover the earth-floor of house with dried grass (*co*), and also then to cover that with woven floormat (*na icoco*).

iconi (Nait.) n. floor mat.

coqa, coqa and **coqaraka** v. to bump hard, crash. *au coqa na tamata* I bumped the person hard (as in rugby). *Au a coqaraka na tamata.* I bumped the person hard, deliberately. *Sa coqa na motoka.* The car is crashed.

veicoqacoqa v., n. to oppose, to conflict with. *Me kua ni veicoqacoqa na gagadre ni iTaukei.* The wishes of indigenous should not come into conflict.

coqa-dro, coqadro-taka (Modernism) v. to hit and run, as with an automobile.

coqa v. (Slang) as an improvised meal, to eat tinned fish (usually a cheap "salmon-style" mackerel) inserted into a whole loaf of bread that is cut lengthwise. Bread helps alleviate the oiliness of the cheap and salty tinned fish.

coqe v., n. to hop on one leg at a time, to skip.

cori, coria v. to thread a needle (for sewing or thatching), to patch up (usually a damaged or worn mat or net). *icori ni taga* n. coarse "needle", usually improvised, to sew up a sack (*taga*). *corivaka* v. to close up as of a sack or basket with coarse threading.

cori, corita 1. v. to pierce (as a cow's or pig's nose to fit a ring). 2. to capture or retain an animal or person, usually using a rope, tether. 3. to string (necklace) by piercing the shells, to string flowers in a garland (*cori salusalu*). *na coricori ni salusalu* the threading of garlands. 4. to scratch the flesh deeply (barbed wire).

veicori adj. prickly, thorny, spikey (barbed wire, some thorny plants). *Na wa vuka e dau veicori.* The vine *wa vuka* is thorny. See *gadrogadro*.

coricori adj. itchy (clothes), rough, raspy (beard of man, also some vines with small thorns that can be painful).

coro, coroga v. to sting with a burning sensation, as with some prickly plants or from touching a hot object, as from the stove. *veicorogi* stinging, as of prickly plants such as the hairy leaves of the tree *salato,* or some jellyfish.

coro, coroga (or) **coroya** v. to singe off hair from pig before butchering or cooking; by extension (Slang) to gossip damagingly about an old love. *Kua ni dau coro.* Don't keep telling bad tales about a lost romance. Also may mean to "back-bite", tell vengeful, damaging stories. May imply wishful romantic thinking, especially of youngsters.

coroga n. type of coral formerly used to grate food. Live, it may cause a stinging sensation to a person's touch. Fungiidae sp. In the highlands a type of rock called *sule* is used for grating.

coroalidi v. to splutter, crackle as of burning firewood, oil from a frying pan.

corocoro n. a small reef fish, to 7 inches, red and silver; before the fish can be eaten, scales are best removed by grilling the fish in fire. Spines can prick painfully.

corocoro adj. rough (coral, pitted limestone). *surisuria* adj. of stone, to have a somewhat rough surface, but not jagged or cutting.

corovudi v. Idiom: usually of youngsters, to yarn, gossip, laugh and dream about their their desires, goals, fantasies, youths about girls and visa versa. One may discern this group behaviour at a distance. Syn: *tavu vudi*.

cou adj., n. bald (person). *ulu cou* has a bald patch. *ulu tasi* bald with a shaved head. Syn. *drisi, derua, drika*.

covi, covia, coviraka v. to pick, usually leaves, either for medicine or for culinary use such as covering pots or earth oven. May also apply to *bele,* the leaf vegetable. *na covicovi* the picking (as of such leaves).

icovi n. award, prize (in competition, lottery). Old word, previously applied to awards for battle performance, *icovi ni dra,* for killing. Syn. *icocovi*. *Tomika na nomu icocovi.* Pick up your prizes.

icovi koroi ni ivalu n. military medal. This is a modernism of course, though *koroi* was a title given at a certain stage of warrior success.

covu n. place of refuge for octopus in or among rocks or reef. Syn. (Vanua Levu) *sovu*.

covu, covuta v. to bite off, peck at, rip off, break off, as with a piece of food with the teeth.

covu-laca n. waterspout, whirlwind. These are extremely dangerous, destroying a boat, killing the sailors. It is rather more specific and limited in area than a tornado on land. *laca* n. sail.

cowiri v. to spin as of a propeller, the head, to feel faint, or dizzy under the sun with the head spinning. *cocowiriwiri* more forceful or continuous whirling. Syn. *cawiri, coiri.* May be used figuratively, to spin off, run off, dash off.

cu (or) **cucu** v. to bend over and turn one's buttocks to someone, usually in disrespect or in teasing disrespect. *cu!* a vulgar cry of contempt. *vakacucu* to show contempt by stooping, bending over (*cuva*) and showing one's bottom to someone. This is most often done in jest to mock people related as *tauvu,* having an historical traditional relationship that permits this. This action is not always contemptuous or humorous; in some cases the word *vakacucu* or *vacucu* may apply to bending over, to do something at ground level. Syn. *solimu, solimu-na*.

cua n. sticks on both sides of hand-net, for holding it, as when catching prawns, or small fish. *lawa vakacua* hand-net with such handles.

cudru, cudruva, -vaka (-taka) v. to be angry. *cudruva* angry at (someone). *cudruvaka* angry about (something). *Kakua ni dau cudrucudru.* Don't always be angry.

vakacudru, vakacudruya v. to cause to be angry (person, animal, god). *Au sa vakacudruya na turaga.* I have made the chief angry.

cui n. clitoris, a word not usually spoken. Syn. *toi, toitoi*.

cuki, cukita, cukiraka v. to dig up (garden), turn the soil. *cuki vovo* make a garden-plot by digging up the cleared land (*ivovo* garden plot) *cukita na buke* dig up the garden planting-mound(s). *sa dau cukiraka na iteitei na vuaka* the pigs always root up the garden.

cula, cula v. to pierce (with needle), sew (clothes, sailcloth), give injection (hypodermic). *na culacula* the sewing. *misini ni culacula* sewing machine. *culacula vata* stitching together. *icula* n. needle, table fork. *icula liga* n. sewing-needle for hand-stitching. In early times needles were used only for sewing sails of pandanus leaf; some were made of human bone.

veicula (Modernism) v., n. to give an injection or vaccination, as at a medical clinic. *icula-ni-veicula* hypodermic needle for medical injections.

icula ni bokola (Archaic) so-called "cannibal fork" sometimes used by chiefs and priests and, as with war-clubs, were often given a personal name, some of them quite vulgar. They were carved of wood, usually with four prongs. On view at Fiji Museum and modern copies are sold as tourist souvenirs.

culaliga, culaligataka v. to sew by hand (not sewing machine). *culailiga* hand-made. *liga* hand. Formerly, there was no stitching done except coarsely for sails of pandanus leaf or for thatching of houses.

cule n., adj. as in *vatu cule*, limestone, limestone rock, common around Suva, common on some small islands like Katafaga, in northern Lau Province. *Sule* is a related highland word for a different, jagged type of stone.

cumu 1. n. rectum. Syn. *icici*. The anus is *sona*.

cumu 2. n. Trigger fish, Balistes sp., edible, common at the reef of a lagoon.

cumu, cumuta v. to butt with the head (by person, goat, bull, pig), to root (pig) Idiom: *sere ni cumu* informal group-singing by men seated cross-legged, facing each other with head down in a closed circle (*sigi-drigi* is a related term).

cuqa n. a common illness of babies, small children, over-heating of the body. It can be dangerous and even fatal. Various herbal remedies are used for this and may or may not be effective; at least they make the mother feel better. Syn. (Lau) *reu*.

cuqe adj. restless, of a person, animal.

cuqena v. to prop up, prop open (some container). May be used figuratively, to be supportive to a person, or for a cause. *icuqeni* (*ni katuba*) n. door-stop. *cuqena na kumuni ilavo* be supportive of the collection of money. A window-prop (common in older wooden houses) may be called *idumu*.

cuqe, cuqeta v. to knock (someone) with the elbow as if to prompt them.

cuqu, cuqtita, cuquraka v. to butt with the snout (pig), usually knocking down plants in quest for food, or to root in the ground. *cuquraka* to do so forcefully.

cuqu, cuquma v. to grab roughly and hold close (person).

cuquru v. to crackle, as of a hard biscuit being crunched. Syn. *caquru*.

curu, curuma v. pass through a doorway, an entrance or exit (house, cave, forest, village, a piece of land). *curuma* v. may refer to officially opening some new edifice or event. *curutaka* to bring something in. *Curu mai!* Come in! (when speaker is already inside). *Curu yani!* Go inside! (speaker outside). *curu ki loma* go right inside. *curu ki tuba* go outside. *curu-qara* return to its hole, as of crab, fish, moray eel. There is a special meaning of *curu, curuma*, referring to a devil *tevoro* "entering" a person and possessing that person, taking control of the person. See second idiom, below. Syn. (Rewa) *ruku, rukuta*.

Idiom: *curu vakaiToga* leave or enter a house, room, in an unmannerly way, as early Tongans were thoughts to do, without excusing oneself. Many early Tongan Christians are said to have behaved abominably in Fiji with little respect for Fijian custom. For many of them, Christianity was a facade they used in dominating Fijians.

Idiom: *curumi tevoro* "possessed" by a spirit, common occurrence, body thrashing about, shouting, out of control, not conscious of one's words or actions. The *tevoro* has "entered" the person and may speak through the person, using that body as a vehicle (*waqawaqa*), as a presence. In handling such cases, one tries to control the victim's movements and shout at him/her literally to eat the spirit (*Kania!*). This whole event may be a form of psychological release in a traditionally highly controlled society. A person may not be held responsible for what is said or done while possessed by a devil. People in attendance may throw food, such as pieces of taro, at the victim, or spit on them to help exorcise the devil. Syn. (Rewa) *ruku, rukuta* to enter a person (of a devil).

Idiom: *curu vale* v. to abscond with someone else's spouse, usually said of a man taking another man's wife or simply taking in a mistress.

Idiom: *tamata curu-suka* repeating offender who is repeatedly in and out of prison, but may refer to someone who repeatedly goes in and out of some place such as a medical clinic or hospital.

Idiom: *curu uciwai* of old traditional custom, to be watered down, replaced by modern custom, just as river water is altered by tidal seawater at the river mouth.

curu botea v. to barge in (or out), to enter or leave abruptly.

curuma v. to open officially some new building or enterprise (new church, school, provincial building etc.) with ceremony. *na kena curumi* its official opening.

curumaka v. to insert, as in threading a needle, for example. Might refer to something analagous.

vei-curu-maki intermittent, inter-twined. *E veicurumaki siga kei na uca* It is raining while the sun is shining. *E veicurumaki na lewe ke na uro.* The flesh (of the meat) in marbled with streaks of fat.

curumivale v. of a woman usually, to move in to live with a man who is not her husband.

icurucuru n. fee for admittance, as for a theatre, dance, sport stadium. Also school fees. *icurucuru ni gone* customary bringing of whaletooth when eldest child of family visits the home of close relative, for which there will be a reciprocal gift of equivalent value. *ivodovodo* fare charged, as in a bus.

vakacuru 1. "possessed" by a spirit, usually when it is a deliberate or voluntary and welcome condition. This word is used for shamans, soothsayers, and formerly, Fijian traditional priests *bete*. 2. v., n. deposit, payment. *lai vakacuru-ilavo ena baqe* make a deposit in the bank.

dau vakacuru n. witchdoctor. A devil enters the person, and in some cases "owns" the person, rather a Faustian notion, very real to Fijians. People who are believed to be involved in witchcraft may be attacked violently.

curumaka v. to push or poke something into another thing, as one does in thatching a house.

veicurumaki adj. intermittent, unscheduled, inserted out of the usual, regular order, new, introduced; may refer to official meetings or elections. *na bula veicurumaki* the introduced, modern life (as contrasted to the older, more traditional Fijian way of life).

curumi possessed, as by a devil. The person becomes merely a vehicle for the devil. Any words or actions are those of the devil. This is a common occurrence among Fijians. This notion provides a forgivable rationale for temporary unacceptable behaviour, nervous breakdown or mental illness. The condition may last for part of a day, or for a prolonged period of time. Recovery to normal condition is often quite complete as if nothing had ever happened. *dau veicurumi* of a person, often possessed by a devil.

curumi-wai v., adj. soggy, of breadfruit or root-crop such as taro, when improperly cooked.

curu oso 1. of the mind, crowded and thus at least temporarily confused by many different feelings or thoughts. Too many things on one's mind.

curu oso 2. packed full of people, as of a bus, dance floor, theatre, town on busy shopping day.

curu oso 3. to fill as of a space, an environment, to pack in but usually only in certain contexts, as of a fragrant scent, any smell, or the wind that may blow through a room.

curusuka, curusuka-taka v. to return repeatedly to some place, a clinic, hospital, even a prison as a repeat offender.

curutaka v. to bring in.

curuvale Idiom: n., adj., v. gossip that causes trouble, usually said of a woman.

curu vanua (Ang.) v., n. to migrate. *Eratou a curu vanua mai ki Viti.* They (several) immigrated here into Fiji. *Eratou a curu vanua yani ki Ositerelia.* They (several) emigrated to Australia. *Tabana ni curuvanua* Immigration Department.

vakacuru, vakacuruma or **curumaka** v. to put inside, insert. *vakacuruma na kateni ena rumu* put the carton in the room. *curumaka ena nomu taga* slip it in your pocket. *laki vakacuru ivola* go post some mail (sometimes slang for going to the toilet). *vale ni vakacuruivola* post office.

vakacuru-ilavo (Anglicism) v. to invest, deposit money (as in bank account). *na dau ni vakacuruilavo* the investor, depositor. *na vakacurumi ni ilavo* the investment.

vakacuru vosa Idiom: gossips, person always saying bad things about people.

cuva, cuvata or **cuvara** v. to bow the head; to have the face down (people, pots, dishes, box) *sa cuvata na ibe na yalewa ena talitali* the woman bows her head over the mat, weaving.

cuvacuva face down, stooped posture. *dabe cuvacuva* to sit with head bowed down (usually in respect, shame, sorrow). *moce cuvacuva* to sleep, lying face-down, head in the crooked arms. *Au kilai koya ena nona icuvacuva.* I recognize him by his stooping posture. As a place-name *Cuvacuva* refers to a location on the border of Tailevu and Ra where super-tribe Nasautoka suffered defeat, presumably surrendering to Christianity. They were bowed down in defeat but were not slaughtered which suggests this happened during Christian times.

vakacuva, vakacuvara v. to turn upside down, turn over and down. *Mo savata na kuro qai vakacuva* (or) *vakacuvara.* Wash the pot then set it upside-down. *Sa vakacuvari na kuro?* Is the pot turned over?

D

The letter **d** is pronounced as **nd**. The combination **dr** is pronounced with the **r** trilled, as the **r** is always trilled quite strongly.

da (or) **eda** we, us (many, inclusive of person spoken to), pronoun. As the subject of a sentence *da* is sometimes preceded by the letter e written as a separate word: *e da*. Used as a syllable in other pronouns, *da* indicates "we" in various contexts: *edaru* we two. *edatou* we three (or we few). *eda* we (many). *Me da cakava* Let us (many) do it.

da n. human excrement but sometimes of animals. Syn. (Kadavu) *meso*. *boi da* small tree spp., Geniostom, Longaniaceae, greenish white flowers with a foetid smell, around March. See *veka*.
Idiom: *korokoro da* pile of rubbish (often figuratively, sometimes literally), pile of excrement.

daba adj. seasonally plump, of mud lobster and rock lobster crabs, usually around April. This is the time of egg-bearing and considerablel meat.
Idiom: *Sa daba o iko!* You're really something, you're great!
Idiom: *Sa daba!* That's swell, great!

idaba n. packet, coil (as of Fiji tobacco, that is sold retail as a length of twisted coil, unrolled from a ball).

daba, dabara (or) **dabana** v. to tie up a bundle, usually of homogeneous things, stacked together.

dabe 1. adj. too soft, overly mature, of breadfruit.

dabe 2. n. seat (in parliament); sitting (parliament).

dabe, dabeca v. to sit, sit upon (chair etc), sit for (exam). *dabe vakadodonu* sit up straight. *Dabe e cake!* Sit up! (on chair), said to respected Fijian visitor who is seated on floor. *dabeca na ibe* sit on the mat. *dabe vakayalewa* sit with both legs together, at one side, as women sit. *dabe vakatagane* (or) *dabe vakaToga* to sit cross-legged. as men sit. Syn. (Rewa) *drata, dratava*.

dabe, dabera, dabelaka v. to set something down, parcel on the floor, pot on the stove. *dabelaka* may refer to sexual position, woman seated on top of the man in intercourse.

vakadabera 1. v. to seat someone, have them sit down.

vakadabera 2. v. of a future house, to decide on a location.

vakadabera 3. v. to take one's bride to her new home.

idabedabe n. chair, place to sit, seat (incl. seat in legislature); *idabedabe laca* canvas deck-chair. *idabedabe lobi* folding chair. *idabedabe ni ose* saddle. *idabedabe ni vale ni vo.* toilet seat.

dabea n. moray, conger eel, Gymnothorax undutus or Lycodontis javanicus in *Ika ni Waitui*, as published by the Institute of Fijian Language and Culture. Can be large, up to an unusual three meters long, with no scales and no fins. In Rewa sometimes referred to jokingly as "saltwater pork" *vuaka ni waitui,* because Rewa has so few wild pigs. The *dabea* flesh is eaten but not prized. Sacs of poison at the neck must be removed. There are some reefs, as at Mago Island, that are virtually infested with this eel. Very dangerous if attacked or feels threatened. It does not go out of its way to attack people but will attack very swiftly if imposed upon in its territory. Of camouflaged colour, and often keeping still, it may not be observed by the diver. Strangely, this predator has two sets of jaws, one set in front that grasps its victim, then a second set, the pharyngeal jaws that advance to force it back into the throat, to the esophagus. Unlike most fish predators, the moray does not use suction to consume its prey. (Details published by Drs. Mehta and Wainwright in *Nature,* 2007). Its flexible, multiple jaws allow it to consume large fish. It holds its grip, not having to bite twice. More dangerous than the moray bite is the very deadly poisonous nature of moray flesh due to "red tide" ar certain places and certain times, more deadly than any fish.

dabi n. puzzlenut tree, Xylocarpus granatum, Meliaceae, 30 to 60 feet, growing around mangrove. Big round fruit is poisonous. Bark is brown, smooth, and almost shiny white in places, used for red dye. An infusion of the bark is drunk as a remedy for thrush *macake,* a fungus infecting the tongue and mouth. Rind of the nut makes black dye. As the name implies, the nut separates into segments that seem impossible to assemble back together. Syn. (Lau) *leqi*. (West) *leqileqi*. (Nadro.) *lokoloko*.

dabibi n. heavy wet mud in mangrove swamps, riverside or on flats where washed down by rain, or flood. It can later become fine-grained alluvial loam when dry, not clumpy like clay soil. It is also the soft mushy mud often dug out from drains. Lit. "heavy excrement".

dabo (Med.) n. wen. *dabo wai* cyst, blister. *Sa vakadabo na dakuqu.* My back is blistered.

dabo (or) **daboa** adj. feels soft, nicely ripe (of fruit), usually tested by squeezing. May also refer to a matured boil, ready to burst. See. *dreu* ripe. *dada* too soft, ripe.

dabui, dabuya v., adj. to deceive or trick, tricky, deceptive, usually used in word combinations: *veidabui* deceptive (person), *veidabui-taka* to trick (a person).

dabuiloa adj. bruised, of people or fruit.

dada adj. too soft, overly ripe (fruit, taro, breadfruit, fish), soft, swampy (land), weak (human body). *yago dada* soft, weak of body (human). *dada weruweru* of food, soft, soggy from over-cooking.
  Idiom: *liga dada* "butterfingers".
  Idiom: *dadayalewa* have a "soft spot" for women, fond of women.
  Idiom: *yava dada* (or) *saga dada* having weak legs, usually from age, or infirmity; *yava-na* leg, *saga-na* thigh.
  Idiom: *vosota noqu dada* pardon my thoughtless or hurtful words.

vakadada v. to mash it up (taro, potatoes, pumpkin), make it very soft.

dadada adj. weak, of a person.

dadaga weak, exhausted, worn out, usually from exertion, of the body. Syn. *wawale*.

dadaka (or) **dakadaka** adj. slack, of a tether, rope or binding that needs tightening. *vaka-dadaka-taka* v. to slack off (rope, binding).

dadakulaci n. a harmless coastal sea snake, the banded sea krait, striped vertically yellow and black, often seen sunning itself ashore on rocks where it will mate and lay eggs, ten to twenty at a time, Laticauda colubrina and L. laticaudata. The venom is poisonous but the snake never bites people. Children sometimes play with them. They are not to be confused with the true sea snake, which often swims around flotsam and never comes ashore. The true sea snake is similar in appearance but extremely dangerous. There are two species of true sea snakes: Hydrophis melanocephalus, with a black head as indicated by its Latin name, that never comes on land. It lays its live young in the sea. More common is the yellow-bellied sea snake Pelamis platurus. Pelamis is often found around flotsam.
  Idiom *drua dadakulaci* boy and girl twins. (The snake has starkly coloured alternating yellow and black vertical stripes.)

dadamuria "copy-cat", one who imitates others. *muria* to follow it.

dadarivia adj. slippery.

dadarikai n. sp. of freshwater river eel. It is dark-coloured with white or yellowish spots, dorsal fin yellowish, Gymnothorax sp., Muraenidae. Not usually eaten. Of a feisty, vicious nature and will bite the hand that tries to catch it. Same family as the dangerous saltwater moray eel (*dabea*). Syn. (West) *babani*. (Vanua Levu) *verici*.

daga n. source of water, spring, well. See *vure*.

daga, daga (or) **dagava** v. to raise up, tilt up, of face, head. This is how water was drunk from a cup or pot in earlier times, by tilting the face up and pouring water into the mouth. The mouth itself never touched a drinking vessel.
  Idiom: *dau daga* idle, just gazing into space, inattentive to one's surroundings. *Sa rui levu na nomu dau daga!* You just stay around doing nothing and thinking nothing!

daga adj. slack, lost its resilience, of an elastic band or rubber band (*wa drega*). *Sa daga tu na wa drega oqo.* This elastic is slack.

dagadaga adj. tired.

dago-na n. trunk, main part of body where it is largest or heaviest (tree, person, boat, clay pot), usually when positioned horizontally. *dadago* "bone-tired". See also *tolo-na*.

dagole v. to droop, as of a person's head, lolling with sleep, or a limb, hanging slack.

dai n. animal or fish trap, by extension, can apply to persons. *Au na cakava e dua na kena dai.* I will lay a trap for him. *viria e dua na dai* to set a snare or trap. *daira* n. deathly dangerous trap for wild pigs (and formerly for humans) being a deep hole in the ground, often with sharp bamboo pointing upwards to spike the pig as it falls. This type of trap is located on a known pig-path and is concealed with leaves. Some still exist for pigs, and can be dangerous for people.

dai v. (Lau, Cakau.) to lie, tell falsehoods. *daidai* liar.

daidai 1. n. today, sometimes seen as *e daidai* but more properly as *edaidai*. Also meaning:- in these times, at the present time, these days.

daidai 2. adj. false

daiga n. indigenous wild plant that emits putrid odour when flowering, Amorphophallus campanulatus, Araceae, found from India throughout the Pacific to the Marquesas. Reasonably well known around the coast. Edible part is the round corm (6" wide by 3" to 4" high, weighing about 9 lb) with a depression on top from which the flowering shoot grows compactly. The mother plant dies back as the sprout emerges beside it. *Daigai* is harvested after the leaf has died back and the plant is dormant. The corm is poisonous when raw. Grated and cooked, it is believed to aid fermentation of a Fijian storage-food called *madrai*. Indians eat it as a starchy vegetable they call "suran". In the market *daiga* is sometimes called "Indian yam" though it is not a yam. The name *daiga* applies in Samoa as well as Fiji.

daimani (Eng.) n. diamond. Under Christian influence, Fijians now use wedding rings that may may include diamonds.

dainimati (Eng.) n. dynamite. Stolen dynamite is sometimes used by illegal fishermen. Source of dynamite has been the gold mines.

dairekita (Eng.) director (usually company director).

daiosisi (Catholic, Anglican) diocese.

dairo n. sandfish, bêche-de-mer *dri*, Metriatyla scabra (or Holothuria scabra), eaten by coastal Fijians raw or cooked (boiled for a few hours), also exported for the Chinese market. Found in muddy sand, seagrass beds and reef flats, .5 to 3 meters depth. Harvesting is often done toward evening at high tide. From over-harvesting, stocks have become severely depleted. Efforts are underway to breed sandfish to be restored in the wild. Raw, it may be marinated in lemon juice or eaten plain, along with its orange-yellow gut, after cleaning. Only the internal white lining is discarded. Fijians clean the skin off by scraping against rocks. Europeans usually find it tough and tasteless. The skin is of pale, sandy colour, brownish cream or brownish grey colour, sometimes brownish green, with black spots, creases horizontal to body. *Bati dairo* refers to people of Moturiki, a jocular insult, indicating that they like to eat *dairo*. Syn. (West) *tero, sero*. (Macuata) *taro*. (Nadro.) *jero* (or) *sero*. (Kadavu) *valiki*.

dakai n. gun, formerly a bow (for shooting arrows), which is now called *dakai titi*, implying it was made of mangrove aerial roots (*titi*); this was the case only on the coast where the mangrove grows; in the highlands, *yasiyasi* branches were often used to make bows. Bows were used in fighting only by Melanesian Fijian men and women, never by the Tongan Polynesians. Guns are very carefully regulated in Fiji. *dakai lekaleka* hand-gun. *dakai wai* water-pistol. *dakai bitu* bamboo play-cannon to explode kerosene at festive occasions, especially New Year. *dakai ni vanua* artillery cannon. *vaka-dakai* armed with gun(s). *dakai ni vakatatalo* toy gun.

da-kanakana adj. gluttonous.

dakoba 1. heavily padded, fully filled out, soft, comfortable (Fijian padded house-floor, a chair, sofa, bed, pillow).

dakoba 2. pleasantly plump (person). *balu dakoba* chubby cheeked. *yalewa dakoba vinaka* plump, nicely filled out woman. In seeking a wife, Fijians generally prefer that to a slender woman. Syn. *dabosa.*

dakudaku ni mata n. eyelid(s). *yaloka ni mata-na* eyeball(s). *bekabeka ni mata-na* eyelash(es).

daku-na 1. n. back (person, thing, place). *Daku* or *Dakui* common place names, referring to location at back of an island, the lee side, protected from the S.E. direction of the tradewind. *ena taudaku ni koro* at the outskirts of the village. *veinadakui* back-to-back. *Nomu taudaku ga rau qai yaco mai.* You had just left (turned your back) when they both arrived. *daku rodu* n. hunchback, or *daku vusi* n. hunchback, literally like a cat with an arched back.

daku 2. n. an in-law of opposite sex, formerly considered to be a likely marriage partner, if the spouse dies. If an elder brother is married and dies prematurely, his younger brother may be expected to marry the widow, as her back-up, so to speak. Two such people may call each other as "Daku", as a form of address. The custom persists in some places.

daku 3. before, especially in the following expressions that are idiomatic: *ena daku ni kuila* before Cession 1874. (*kuila* flag) and *ena daku ni lotu* before Christian times.

vaka-na-daku, vakanadakuya v. to turn one's back to (person, thing or place), to leave behind, and by extension, to turn one's back on, as a form of rejection.

vanadaku departure, leaving, as in *Na nomu vanadaku ga rau qai yaco mai*. They (two) arrived just after you left.

dakua n. large forest tree with useful very white timber, Fiji kauri, Agathis macrophylla (= A. vitiensis), Araucariaceae, a gymnosperm, often used to make punts. The circumference can be up to six meters, though logging has removed most of the very large ones. Syn. *dakua makadre*, so named for the exuded resin (*makadre*), used for glazing of clay pots near the coast, and in the highlands, formerly, to be ignited as a type of very smoky candlelight. Winged seeds are in the conspicuous female pine-cone (8x10 cm), while on separate trees the male cones are barely 5 cm long. Pollination by wind. The leaves are waxy, the young ones are four inches in length, twice as long as the mature leaves, exuding white latex when cut.

dakua salusalu n. large forest timber tree, brown wood, superior to *dakua* for building and furniture, Retrophyllum vitiensis (= Decussocarpus vitiense), Podocarpaceae (or) Taxaceae, from New Guinea to

Fiji. Bark smooth, dark brown to near black. Lvs opposite in pairs, each leaf with prominent midrib. The cones are very small, with male and female on separate trees. Resin inflammable.

daku ni kuila before Cession (1874). *kuila* flag.

daku ni tuba n. outside the reef, in the open sea. *e tuba* outside.

Dakuwaqa n. a major Fijian god in the form of a huge shark, associated with Cakaudrove, especially Benau people who came from Tonga via Beqa island. He can change his form, even appear like a human, but is not malicious. Libations are still sometimes poured to him, especially to protect divers, and he is still a significant force in Fijian beliefs. A shark representing Dakuwaqa is sometimes seen near the shore when the Tui Cakau is being installed. Some Fiji Indians believe that Dakuwaqa has taken the earthly manifestation of Sai Satya Baba (1926-), the magician guru avatar.

dala, dalaga v. to open wide the mouth (human, animal), as in gaping, yawning, or gasping in astonishment, or responding to a dentist's request. The word applies as Fijians used to drink water by throwing the head back, pouring water in the mouth with their lips far from the water-container. In early times Fijians never drank with the lips touching any cup, bottle or jug. That was changed with enamel mugs and cups, proper teacups and the *bilo* for drinking kava, an introduction from Tonga. None of these were used in ancient Fiji.

dalagataka v. inadvertently say too much, to "run off at the mouth". *Kua ni dalagataka na ka o sega ni kila.* Don't talk about things you know nothing about.

dalama adj. gluttonous. Syn. *dakanakana*.

dalasai 1. v. to fall backwards, facing up (humans, animals). This might happen when slipping, walking on muddy ground.

dalasai 2. n. a flying insect, about 1 cm, that lands on its back; turning right side up, it takes to the air again.

dale (or) **daledale** adj. or n. daffy, dumb in a harmless funny way, gremlin-like in manners, behaviour, said especially of the Serea people (Waimaro highlands) but extending throughout Waimaro areas of Wainimala and Waidina Rivers on Viti Levu Island. Village Serea, at the base of Wainimala River is closely associated with the gremlins (*iveli*) of the forest. Syn. *sauvou*.

dali 1. n. rope, string.
Idiom: *silima na gau ni dali* interrupt, break into a conversation.

dali 2. n. to speak a certain dialect or language. *O dali vakacava tiko?* What dialect are you speaking?

dalice n. deciduous coastal tree now more commonly known at *tavola*, conspicuously horizontal branches, edible nuts. Terminalia catappa, Polynesian chestnut. Dalice is an ancient name. River in Tailevu is named Waidalice. It provided a river passageway to the Wailevu (Rewa River), leading ultimately to the Colo East highlands from the eastern coast of Viti Levu.

daliga-na (Proto-Polynesian) n. ear. *vakadaliga* to listen carefully, often by cocking the head in direction of the speaker. *Me vakarorogo na daligamu.* Listen very attentively, don't miss a thing. *dre daliga* pull the ear (a painful school punishment, also a harmless and painless children's game.) *Vosa lo e qara ni daligana.* Speak very quietly into his/her ear. *daliga ce* protruding ears, ears that stick out from the head (like Prince Charles of the U.K.) *daliga kabi* ears close to the head. *lobe ni daliga* (or) *bele ni daliga* ear-lobe(s). *sau ni daliga* ear-plug or ear-ring. *sau-ciqi* is a more modern term. It was anciently imperative to have an ear-plug. *sau-lili* pendant ear-ring. *sau-kabi* ear-ring that is set on the ear by a screw or clamp. *daliga rogorogo* very keen hearing. *dalidaliga, dalidaligana* v. to listen closely, attentively. *vakatudaliga* to pay attention. Syn. (Tonga) *telinga*. Close cognates of this word appear throughout the Pacific, even among aborigines of Taiwan
Idiom: *tara na daliga-na* of children, to dare to fight by touching or pulling the opponent's ear. A sharp, painful pull on the ear is a common punishment for a naughty child.

daliga tuli (Lau) adj. deaf (*tuli* or *dule* ear-wax).

daliga vara adj. deaf. Syn. *didivara*, *didi*.

daliga n. a kind of edible "mushroom" (fungus), ear-shaped, growing on dead trees, known as Jew's Ear in English. Fijians soak them overnight, steam them (these days maybe boil them), and would normally serve them with coconut cream sauce (*lolo*). Related types of fungi are commercial food products in China, usually sold dried.

dalo n. taro, Colocasia esculentum, Araceae, an aboriginally introduced root crop. Baked, it can be kept a long time, useful in early long voyages. *Dalo* and cultivated yams are the most prestigious root-crops for feasts and presentations. The young leaves are cooked and eaten as a green vegetable called *rourou*. The leaf-stems, called *baba*, are skinned and eaten also, as a fine vegetable and as a food for new mothers and babies. *Dalo* is planted with the crown from the top, or from suckers that grow alongside the mother plant. Fijians do not normally plant in rows. Using a digging stick (*doko*), they make a hole for the sucker or the top. Varieties of taro include: *mumu* (yellow-coloured flesh), *vavai, samoa, tausala ni Samoa* (often exported; the Samoan word *tausala* means "lady"), Samoa hybrid (black stem), *toakula* (pink stem), *dalo ni Toga, ba-via* (superb tasting, small taro). *dalo yaca* taro grated for making pudding. *dalo vavi* taro roasted in earth-oven. See *dalo ni tana*, a quite different species. Syn. (Naitasiri) *sulo*. (Colo East) *boka*. (Rewa) *ba*. (Tonga) *talo*.

Idiom: *drau ni dalo* "cry-baby", based on the fact that *dalo* leaves can be torn very easily.

Idiom: *suasua vadrau ni dalo* water off a duck's back, lit. wet like a *dalo* leaf (that in fact, is impervious to water).

Idiom: *vaka e cavu na dalo matua*. done easily and quickly, just as mature *dalo* can be pulled out of the ground so easily.

Idiom: *Na dalo e tei ka vakasulina*. Lit. Taro is planted and has suckers, meaning that a woman has responsible, caring parents who must be approached to have the woman in marriage. She is not just an individual.

dalo ni tana n. cultivated starch food, perrenial, Xanthosoma sagittifolium, Araceae. From a large "mother" corm, may smaller corms grow and are harvested a few at a time. Leaves are edible when cooked, as are many *dalo* leaves.

dalobi 1. n. large roll or bolt of cloth as in tailor shop, also seen at Fijian ceremonies as presentation gift when it is unrolled, spread out in a long train of cloth carried by a chain of women who display it as they approach the distinguished visitor(s). **2.** n. stack, usually of folded cloth or clothing items.

dalo yaca n. Fijian type of pudding of grated taro (*dalo yaca*), packaged in leaves, roasted with caramelised coconut cream (*lolo buta*) added.

dama-na (Colo) n. paternal grandmother.

damanu n. very well known and useful endemic timber tree with pink timber and yellow-brown bark, Calophyllum vitiense, Clusiaceae. Fragrant fls 2 cm diam. in clusters in the axils of lvs, 4 white petals and 4 sepals, stamens with conspicuous white anthers. Fruits all year round, similar to the related *dilo* nut, 3-4 cm diam and turning purple or black at full maturity. Secondary species with the same Fijian name is C. leptocladum, red-brown bark tinged yellow with white blotches; no petals, 4 sepals with conspicuous white anthers; tiny white fruit 1.5 cm diam. There are two other, minor species of this genus. In parts of Polynesia, *tamanu* may refer to that related, important coastal species of the *dilo* nut, Calophyllum inophyllum, which contains a useful oil for massage. Syn. *dilodilo*.

damele adj., n. inept, ineffectual, awkward, clumsy, droopy, thought to be characteristic of some people. Sometimes used jokingly *Damele!* "Butterfingers!" when someone has done something clumsy.

damola n. kiln drier (for copra, cocoa usually). Syn. *domola*.

damole n. sp. of shrub. Syn. *tamole* or *tomole*, Limnophila rugosa, but the name also applies to the herb basil (Hindi tulsi), Ocimum basilicum, quite widespread but hardly used by Fijians who used virtually no herbs or spices.

damu 1. brown, dull red, auburn colour, russet.

Idiom: *ulu damu* person with hair that is not the usual dusky black, but tinged with orange, auburn, or even fair tints. These genetic characteristics may change as one grows up. Sometimes the orange or reddish tints are achieved with lime or dye.

damu 2. n. edible fish, mangrove jack, red snapper, Lutjanus argentimaculatus or L. bohar, coastal and riverine, large scales, these days caught on a fishing line. Similar to the *kake*. The reef variety can be poisonous due to "red tide", and is best avoided, especially October-November, at the time of *balolo*, but the poison may persist as late as March. Syn. *bati, batidamu*.

damudamu 1. red. *qele damudamu* red soil, acidic latersol. *mata damudamu* red-eyed (of fatigue). *qele boro damudamu* land red-lined, from extinct clans, now classified as state land, or in some cases, reallocated to clans that have little land.

damudamu 2. fair-skinned, usually referring to Fijians with some Tongan ancestry, as in Lau, Cakaudrove, Kadavu. This is an old word, now rather dated.

damudamu 3. as in *kai Idia damudamu* ("Red Indian"), from cowboy films, a term sometimes used in slang for the people of NaWi village, Buca Bay, Vanua Levu. These people often cross over to Taveuni for shopping, and have a reputation of causing trouble like a bunch of wild Indians. To a less extent, people of Tunuloa have a similar reputation.

damule v. to be dozing off, sinking into sleep. Syn. *sosovu*.

damusa adj., n. skin colour pink or reddish, healthy, shiny, sometimes from sunburn. *balu damusa* rosy-cheeked. *sa damusa na yagona ena katakata ni siga.* his/her skin is sun-burned.

dani n. fairly common whitish discoloration, pale blotches on a person's skin caused by a fungus, Tinia versicolor. Most often treated medically with salicylic acid. Selenium sulfide (often found in anti-dandruff shampoos) is also useful in modern treatment.

dania (Hindi dhaniya) n. coriander, Coriandrum sativum, herbal spice used by Indians for the bitter-tasting fresh leaves, and also, quite separately, for the bland dried seeds that makes up as much as 25% of curry powder. Urban Fijians often eat curry and buy prepared curry powder. Only rarely would some Fijians use coriander directly.

danidani n. plant, Polyscias spp., Aralaceae, commonly grown near houses, small yellow leaf, leaves sometimes used as tea. *danidani ni Solomoni,* P. scutellaria, probably very early intro. from Solomons and/or Vanuatu, with large round green leaf, used as medicinal herb, edible though not often eaten. P. cumingiana is modern introduced ornamental, "yellow prince", becoming bright yellow in the sun, common hedge plant with fern-like leaf, sometimes used in floral necklaces (*salusalu*). Syn. (West) *dalidali,* (Tonga) *tanitani,* (Samoa) *tagitagi.* Caution: *danidani* may also refer to *cagolaya,* the medicinal Zingiber zerumbet in Suva, Naitasiri, Waidina, Wainimala, Wainibuka, Nadrau, used mostly as a cough medicine.

danisi (Eng.) v., n. dance (modern, non-traditional). *na idadanisi* the style of dancing. *vale ni danisi* night club.

daniva n. common small, year-round salt-water food fish, Goldspot Herring, Heklotsichthys quadrimaculatus or Sardinella filiense. Travels in schools, caught by netting near the shore. The size is that of a large sardine. Best cooked over an open fire. Delicious flavour. Some Fijians in the West have developed the skill of putting the whole cooked fish in their mouths, removing the bones by tongue and mouth movement, and spitting out the bones intact. Around Nasavusavu, this fish (and the smaller sardine-type fish called *sara*) are rather used as bait. Schools may be fished with double hooks without bait, snaring the fish by chance.When *daniva* are chased by larger predators, they fling themselves out of the water, often landing on the beach. Clupeioid poisoning, particularly from the viscera, may kill on consumption, especially October through February. Also, deadly poisonous *daniva* may result from explosions, as of dynamite blasting around a reef or from hurricane damage of a reef.

danoto adj. soft, spongy, as of a cake or a pillow, but springing back when pressed as plastic foam would do. Also applies to a person's flesh, contrasting it, say, to a hard, muscular body. Not in common usage.

danuya v. to weight down something so as not to budge, such as a stone on a mat outdoors, not to be blown by the wind. Syn. *tabika.*

da-qaqi constipation. A word not widely known. *da* excrement.

dara, darama, daramaka 1. v. of something, to move or be moved or inserted into or through a confined space. A fish into a coral hole, a snake into vegetation, a fieldmouse into the grass, ball rolling under some heavy object, a stout person through a narrow passageway.

dara, darama 2. v. Unless some other object is stated or implied, *dara* refers to a man trying to force a woman, or at least make forced sexual approaches (touching the breasts, private parts): *lai dara ena bogi* go take a woman by force at night. *darama na yalewa* rape the woman. *dau dara* obsessed with sex, usually of a man. See *kucu, kucuva* to rape.

dara, daramaka 3. v. to put on, slip into and wear (some object worn on the body, inc. seat belt of a car). *daramaka* can apply to rings, clothing, shoes, hat, pair of glasses, condom. *Na cava e dara tiko o koya?* What is he/she wearing? *daramaka na mama* slip on the ring. *daramaka yani na nomu ivava.* put on your shoes.

Idiom: *dara kulikuli* v. to put on some clothing though the person is not properly bathed.

dara yame (Anglicism) v. to stick out the tongue. *yame* tongue.

darai n. type of Fijian pudding, starch food (taro, cassava, perhaps breadfruit) cooked, mashed, with addition of coconut cream *lolo droka.*

darama adj. clear, cleaned, of vegetation on land to be planted, or path, or compound; bald or close, clean shaven or a human head; clear, of *yaqona* beverage that has had the fibre strained out. *Darama saka na yaqona vakaturaga.* "The *yaqona* is strained clean, Sir", traditional words pronounced when *yaqona* has been formally prepared, and ready to be served.

darava (Nait., Lom., Verata) n. doorway, entrance. Swinging doors never existed in ancient Fiji. Entrances were closed, especially at night, by some covering such as matting or a plaque of interwoven palm leaves. A house has two doorways, one at the bottom end where cooking was done and less important people could enter, *na darava i sue,* and a more formal entrance at the side where important people would enter, *na darava levu.* In fact, this was a development in Colonial times. Originally there was usually only one doorway. Syn. *katuba.* (Vanua Levu) *takari.*

dari n. simple bowl made of clay or wood, formerly used for serving food or *yaqona*, also perhaps for liquid hair-dye. In some areas, such as Rewa, where there is little timber, clay bowls are still used for serving *yaqona*. The Samoan concept of a wooden serving bowl (*tanoa*) for kava was introduced from Tonga in the early 1800s. Pottery was made in only a few coastal places in Fiji, virtually all by women of Tongan origin. Syn. *sedre*. See *takona*.

daridari-via slippery to walk on.

daro, vakadaroya 1. v. to defer, delay, postpone, cancel. *Sa daro na qito.* The game is postponed, cancelled. *lai daroya na ilakolako ni tou na sega ni lako* go defer the trip because we (several) won't be going. *vakadaroya na qito* to defer the game (to another day). *Me daro na qito.* The game should be deferred. *na daro* n. the delay, deferment, postponement

daroi, daroya 2. v. to smooth out, often of muscles in gentle massage, but also of removing creases from clothes or mats.

daru or **edaru** we, us (two, inclusive of person spoken to). *Daru lako!* Let's go! (the two of us).

daseni (Eng.) n. dozen. Rather creatively, some highland vendors in the Suva market will explain when questioned, that a dozen now means ten instead of the twelve you thought it did.

dasila, dasilataka v. to crush, smash (of something soft, fruit stepped on, a sandwich that has been sat on, a person run over by car). *butu-dasila-taka* to crush by treading on (something). *dasila* badly injured, of a person. *dada silasila* badly crushed. See *siki, sikita*.

datou we, us (three, or a few more, inclusive of person spoken to), often abbreviated to *tou*. *Tou lako!* Let's go! (we three or more).

datuvu n., adj. ineffectual, given up trying with a lack of consistent and persistent will to accomplish anything, or to finish a task. Lit. to pound and crush excrement (*da*), formerly claimed to be the afterlife punishment of ineffectual warriors. *dau dadatuvu rawarawa ke sa oca.* gives up easily when tired.

Idiom: *Au sa datuvu sara ga vei kemudou.* I really give up on you people (several). You are hopeless.

dau 1. root-word, either standing alone or often used as a prefix that modifies verbs and nouns, implying frequency, customary behaviour, competence. When it is a prefix, the whole word may be found in this dictionary under the word that is adjoined to it. *daubutako* thief. *daunivosa* spokesman (in a modern sense). *daunifika* auditor. *dau sasaga* one who keeps trying. *gonedau* professional fisherman (formerly a function of certain kin-groups). *dau veivacu* boxer. *dau bisinisi* businessman. *dau bokobuka* fireman. *daulotu* church-goer. *dau-kaulotu* missionary (often referring to Fijian preachers in western Melanesia). *dau yalewa* girl-chaser. *dau tagane* man-chaser. *dau dara* sex-driven. *daunivucu* composer of group dances (movement, music and words). *dau rairai* seer, said to be a teller of the future or the truth, prophetic visionary. *dau va-tevoro* practitioner of black magic, *dau va-gunu* herbalist and medium who may do evil or counteract evil. *daugunu* heavy drinker. *daukosa* heavy drinker of kava. *dau taurilavo* n. cashier (as at a shop). *Dau raici koya, au cudru.* Whenever I see him/her, I get angry.

dau 2. n. expert, appearing in the expression *na kena dau* the expert.

Daucina n. a spirit-god that pursues women to take his pleasure. He may assume the form of a familiar man, even a husband, and seduce a woman. At night he may be seen walking with a lamp (*cina*), as implied in his name. To avoid him, women may eat their meals at a toilet or out-house. He is known by various names in different regions, Kanakana-da, and Saroni (Cakaudrove). There is an active belief in the existence of Daucina.

dau kata v., adj. given to biting (dogs, sharks, snakes).

dau vakata vuaka n. pig-hunter who uses dogs and knife (not a gun). Pig-hunter with spear is a *dau vakasasa*. Considerable skill and experience are needed for this. It can be dangerous.

dauca v. to fornicate, to have sexual intercourse outside of marriage.

vei-dauci n. adultery, committing of adultery.

Daulevu n. title of chief of tribe Mataisau, people of Tongan origin, traditional carpenters, boatbuilders settled on Bau Island.

daumaka adj. pleasant, delightful, nice (of thing, or an occurence, or characteristic, but not of a person as such). *Sa daumaka na draki.* It is pleasant weather. *Sa daumaka na nona igu.* His/her enthusiasm is delightful. *Daumaka!* Lovely! Perfect! Great! *Na masima e vaka-daumaka-taka na ikanakana ni kakana.* Salt makes the taste of food delightful.

daunibati (or) **vuniwai-ni-bati** (Anglicism) n. dentist. In earlier years the terms was more commonly *dauveicavubati* toothpuller.

Daunifika Levu n. Public Auditor.

dau vakamolimoli adj. soft-hearted, of person. See *moli*.

daurairai (or) **daurai** n. person who foresees, foretells the future, or reveals facts of the past while in a trance. After a Christian prayer (these days) and a bowl of kava with some ceremony, the sage reveals the needed information. Syn, *dau- kilakila*.

dau-rai-vuli n. school inspector.

dausiga n. famine from drought.

dausoko n. sailor. *soko* to sail.

dau-va-curu n. traditional medium who can be possessed by spirits, often to do evil to others. The spirit enters (*curu*) the person possessed.

dauvagunu n. traditional medium who mixes and pours *yaqona* to the spirits (*tevoro*), requesting favours, even including a person's death, or counter-acting such witchcraft.

dauvana n. shooter, marksman, formerly an archer before guns were introduced. Also a diver who fishes with a spear or spear-gun. *vana* to shoot.

dauvavana n. hunter (with gun). This was a name given to a brother of the Tui Cakau who shot the invading Tongan, Wainiqolo, at Wairiki in 1862 when Ma'afu forces invaded Taveuni.

dauve-na 1. n. sister-in-law of a woman, a mutual relationship, a woman related to another woman, her husband's sister, or that sister as related to her brother's wife. *Dauve* is also a form of address mutually used by such women. 2. mutual relationship of daughters whose parents are brother and sister. The woman-to-woman relationship is referred to as *veidauveni*. In Colo East the closest equivalent term is *raiva-na*.

Dauveibuli n. Creator (the Christian concept).

dauveiqia n. tattooer. In early Fiji, only women were tattooed, around the lips, groin and upper thighs. This made them more eligible for marriage.

dauveivakaisini n. person who often deceives, or is secretly vindictive. *kaisi* common lout, social scum, low-class people.

dauveivaka-laboci n. person who tricks people. *lobo* to be stuck, *lobolobo* swamp.

dauvere n. tempter. *dauvere-taka* to tempt by tricking.

Daunivere n. Satan. *vere* deceitful trick.

dava n. a noxious weed, Koster's Curse, Clidemia hirta, Melastomataceae, introduced. The leaves may be crushed and used as soap, raising a lather. The crushed leaves are also placed on cuts to stop bleeding and aid healing. The small purple berries are delicious. The fruit has been noted in April but may extend to other months.

dave 1. v. to flow (liquids, usually river, tide or blood). *Sa dave na dra.* the blood has started to flow. *na dave* the flow. *vakadavea* v, to cause to flow, as in making a drain to let water flow. Nadave is a place-name in Tailevu Province.
Idiom: *vakadave-dra* make war, lit. make blood flow.

dave 2. (Archaic) platter for chiefs, priests. One carved of *vesi* is illustrated in the book *Yalo i Viti* by Fergus Clunie.

daveta n. reef passage for boats. Formerly could mean any kind of passage, even on land.

Daveta Levu n. legendary place near Bau where Bauans resided after death. Bauan ancestors live there doing the same daily things as living Bauans do. It is said to have been located near a reef. The main entrance to Suva harbour is also referred to as Daveta Levu. Daveta Levu is also the name of a tribe in Tailevu.

davila smooth.

davilai n. flounder, two species of flat fish, Pleuronectiformes sp., and Bothus sp., which is quite a bit larger.

davo, davora (or) **davoca** v. to lie down, lie on. *Sa davo koto.* It is lying there. *davoca na ibe* lie down on the mat. *vakadavora na gone lailai ena idavodavo* lay the child down on the bed.

idavodavo n. bed, regular place to lie down, sleeping mat. *idavodavo* may also describe mats prepared by a husband's relatives for a newborn baby. Syn. *imocemoce*, (West) *idaradara*.

vakadavora v. to lay (something) down, knock down (as in boxing), cause to lie down. *vakadavori na paipo* lay down the pipes.

davui n. trumpet shell, Charonia tritonis, Ranellidae. The familiar name Triton is the name of a son of Poseidon, legendary god of the sea. Fijians use it as a trumpet, these days mostly rural fishermen who announce their return with fish to sell. It is also blown ceremonially at the funeral ceremonies for high chiefs, mostly blown from the side. The triton shellfish helps control crown-of-thorns which destroy live coral reefs. Unfortunately, tritons are over-harvested, for sale to tourists. Their populations are in danger. In western Fiji, a different but similar shell was used, the Bursa, blown from the end. The verb *uvu* is used for the blowing of the trumpet-shell.

davuibuco n. stomach.

davuke n. pit in the ground, dug for fermenting and storing a Fijian starch food called *madrai*. This has been Fijians' principal means of storing food (aside from yam storage houses and sun-drying of fish). Starch-food mashed and so stored may be breadfruit, taro, *kawai*, arrowroot, Polynesian chestnut, plantain, sweet potato, cassava. Fruits used may be those of Malay Apple (*kavika*), or even the mangrove (especially on Fulaga island, and at Bureta on Ovalau). The pit is usually lined and covered with plantain leaves and weighted down with stones. Syn. (Lau) *lua*.

davuki (or) **davuke** n. hole or pit in the ground that has been dug out, as for burial grave or for harvesting large wild yams. *dau kele davuki* gravedigger (a job done in Suva by prisoners).

dawa n. semi-cultivated indigenous fruit with sweet translucent and delicious flesh (rather like a lychee) around a large seed, Pommetia pinnata, Sapindaceae. The seed was formerly eaten as a famine food, after soaking for several days, and cooking. *Dawa sere* is a var. with pink skin while *dawa moli* has green skin. *Samuta na dawa* to harvest *dawa* fruit by striking the branches, beating them to loosen and release the fruit which appears March through May. There has been a belief that double fruits may be offered to a woman to improve her chances of having babies. Syn. (Tonga, West, Kadavu) *tawa*. Idiom: *kena na isamu ni dawa* he/she suffered from someone else's actions.

dawa, dawaca (or) **dawaka** v. to cross over (river, creek, road). *e dua na dadawa* a crossing (place to cross) but not usually a bridge, can be a ladder or steps up to a house. The verb applies in tree-climbing, to branches that allow one to cross to the next tree. *sa dawa na mate* the sickness is transmitted, infectious. *vakadawa* to transmit. *vakadawa na itukutuku* transmit the message. *vakadawa-i-lago* stay in the doorway, inadvertently blocking it (bad manners). See *dewa*.

dawai n. unmarried adult, widow, widower. There is often pressure on an unmarried person to find a marriage partner. In early times a man often stayed single till the age of 35 years.

de 1. lest (something will happen). *Au sa lako i vale, deu qai tauvimate* I'll go home lest I get sick. *Qarauna, de dua na kemu dogo!* Watch out, or you might get struck with a stick! *Totolo mai, de ko qai bera!* Hurry up or you will be late! *De da mani guilecava* Lest we forget.

de 2. perhaps, probably, maybe. *De sa lako ko koya.* He/she may have gone, must have gone, has probably gone.

de 3. would, might, as in *Au nanuma ga de o ni via raici koya.* I think you would like to see him/her.

de dua perhaps, maybe, there might be. *De dua na nomu ilavo levu.* You might get a lot of money. *De dua beka.* Perhaps.

de ... me (or) **mo** Idiom: It would be ... if .... *De vinaka me cakava.* It would be good if it were done. *De daumaka mo cakava.* It would be great if you would do it.

de-na n. excrement (usually animal). *de ni oni* honey (*oni* bee). *Demu sara!* vulgar insulting expletive. *de ni toa* chicken manure. *de ni duna* certain algae that grow in swampy places, indicating the probable presence of swamp eels *badamu*. See *da*.

dede 1. for a long time, take a long time. *Sa rui dede o iko.* You take so long. *Sa dede na noqu tiko eke* I have been here a long time. *Sa dede daru qai sota.* It has been a long time since we met. *O na dede mai?* You are going to be late in coming? *A cava o vakadedetaka mai?* What delayed you in coming? *Kakua ni dau vakadede.* Don't always take so long (be so late). *dede vakalailai* after a while.

dede 2. n. duration, span or extent of time. *na dede ni qito.* the duration of the game. *na kena dede* the (its) duration.

dedena n. crusty or damp yellow discharge from the eyes, sometimes from excessive fatigue, sleep, an indication of exhaustion and/or ill health. Syn. *denadena* as in *mata denadena*, having eyes with these characteristics.

vakadege (or) **vakadigi** v. to poke out the tongue at someone. *Jone vakadegei Mere tiko* Jone is sticking out his tongue at Mere. *Na veidege sa dua na itovo ca.* Sticking out one's tongue at a person is bad manners.

Degei n. founding ancestral spirit-god, immigrant to Fiji, who assumes the form of a giant snake living in the Nakauvadra mountains of Ra Province. He is harmless and usually rather indifferent to human affairs. Sometimes mentioned as being a younger brother of Lutunasobasoba, who led a fairly recent immigration hardly more than a few hundred years ago. There is sometime reference to Degei I and a later Degei II. The name derives from the snake flicking out its tongue. Legends tell of his pet fowl Turukawa being killed by the Ciri Twins at a place called Conua at the Nakauvadra Range, which brought on the Nakauvadra wars as a result of Degei's anger. The Twins were exiled, and were swept away along the Wainibuka River, downstream in a flood from their refuge at village Narauyabe, village of Degei's Tongan canoe-builder Rokola who was protecting them. That village had been successfully attacked by Vueti, from Verata, a champion for Degei. Vueti late became the first Roko Tui Bau, and founder of super-tribe Vusaratu of Kubuna Territory. Thunder has been attributed to Degei moving about in his Nakauvadra cave. Offerings were left at that cave.

degelaka v. to slam (something) down.

deguvacu v. to raise, to waggle eyebrows, but usually only once, as a subtle but very clear indication of assent, agreement. A Fijian does not feel it necessary to give a verbal response, which is sometimes frustrating to foreigners who want explicit verbal commitment. Raising the chin is also a clear indication of agreement. *vacu* eyebrow. Syn. *dolevacu*.

degi n. soot. Sometimes used for blackening, as for barkcloth by women or the face by men and has been used for tattoos.
Idiom: *samu degi*. to be doing nothing of any importance, as in cleaning out soot from the fireplace, a criticism for choosing an easy job.

dei firm, fixed in place. *Sa dei tu na duru.* The post is fixed in place. *tu dei* permanent(ly). *Sa cakacaka tu dei mai kea.* He/she is working there steadily (permanently). *cakava me tudei* make it permanent. *O iko sa sega ni rawa ni tu dei.* You cannot be steady. *Sa dei tiko na veivosaki.* The discussion is settled (completed). *Me da toka dei toka* Let us (many) stay steady in our purpose, our work. (That second *toka* is redundant but may sometimes be said.)

ivakadei n. deposit, as in lay-by for purchase of retail goods.

deidei n. sp. of edible land crab, dark in colour with white-tipped claws.

deivaki firmly. *Au vakabauta deivaki.* I firmly believe it.

vakadeitaka v. to ascertain, confirm, affirm, ensure, make sure, establish (facts), steady up. *Vakadeitaka na siga tou na sota kina.* Confirm the date when we will meet. *ivakadei ni vale* frame of the house. *ivakadei ni sausaumi.* deposit in payment.

deke 1. n. river fish like a large *vo loa*, edible, to 15 inches, very few bones. There are several species of fish named with *deke* as a prefix.

deke ulu 2 v. to stand on one's head, or fall head-first, or dive into the water head-first Syn. (Vanua Levu) *doko ulu*. Idiom: *dokodoko ulu* to be wasted from excessive drinking.

deki (Eng.) n. video deck.

dela-na top. *ena dela ni vanua* on the hilltop. *ena dela ni teveli* on top of the table. *na delana* n. hilltop. *Dela-da*. alternative name of the licentious spirit-god Daucina, lit. "On Top of the Excrement".

delabulewa n. large edible fish, grouper, Epinephelus spp., that may be poisonous with ciguatera, especially October-November during *balolo* season.

deladela n. mons veneris, female private parts.

delakautaka v. to knock on the head, kill with a club, a word fallen into disuse.

delamaca stranded high and dry (*maca*), out of water.

delana n. hilltop. *na veidelana* the hills. Delana can be a person's second name.

delanimati n. section of reef exposed at low tide. *mati* tide.

dela ni yavu n. home (a very formal, honorific expression).

delavuvu n. roof, ceiling.

dele (Archaic) n. joyous, erotically vulgar dance of women, welcoming returning successful warriors with corpses for cannibal food. Syn. *wate*.

dele, deleva v. to make a formal request for community help in a substantial task such as house-building, clearing of new land. *idele* is the quid pro quo to show appreciation for the help.

vakademena v. to pet (child, dog).

demokarosi (Eng.) n. democracy, a word that might not be understood in the same way by all Fijians. Western-style democracy goes sharply against the grain of Fijian chiefly system. It is hardly compatible with the concept of paramount chiefs introduced from Tonga and consolidated by the British hierarchal system of indirect rule. Spelling may vary.

de ni ose n. literally "horse excrement", small shrub, Sida acuta, rhombifolia, used, twigs used as toothbrush, branches as a broom at Korolevu, Navosa. This replaces the *sasa* broom of coconut mid-ribs, used in coastal areas where coconut palms thrive. (In Colo East, small branches of *makita* are used as a broom.)

de ni ruve (or) **de ni soqe** n. plant used in Rewa as soft underlayer for mats in old-style Fijian houses, and also for thatching roofs, Typha domingensis.

de ni varo n. sawdust. *varo* to saw.

deqi (or) **deqe** (Eng.) n. dengue fever, seven-day fever, breakbone fever. Mosquito vector for the virus Aedes aegyptae, eggs deposited in wet containers, ditches, live for several weeks, hatching when water level rises. Female must feed on blood before it lays about 100 eggs three days later, once every 4-7 days. Larvae become adult in 10-14 days. Females feed in early morning or evening and only the female transmits the disease; one bite is sufficient. The closely related Ross River fever, introduced from Australia, is often more serious.

dere, derea and **vakaderea** v. to clean off, wash, of a person, referring to their private parts. Formerly, or perhaps in certain regions, the word has been applied to more general washing. See *dere neke*, below.

deredere v. (Lau) to wash one's private parts.

derekona v. to belch, burp. This word seems little used today. Custom has been for a guest to belch at a dinner, showing appreciation for the food. The host might also belch. No apology necessary. Syn. *qeremavu, dorokana*.

dereneke n. spawning of land crab (*lairo*), October through December, when they march to the sea to discharge their eggs. A delicacy is the orange coloured attachment holding the eggs. The eggs themselves are not eaten. The crab wash off (*dere*) the eggs to disseminate them. Male land crabs have a brown attachment that is eaten with the seafood seasoning called *miti*. *Dereneke* usually occurs after the full moon, following the rise of the *balolo* (edible annelid, sea worm), Oct.-Nov.

derogo v. to clear the throat with mouth closed. (*terema* is with mouth open).

derua n. The indigenous Fijian musical instrument used to accompany ceremonial dances (*meke*). It is a section of bamboo a couple of feet long, open at the bottom end, to be struck vertically on the ground setting a beat to the music. The top node is white and bare, like a bald pate, and is thus used as impolite slang for a bald person. The *derua* and the nose-flute were two indigenous Fijian musical instruments and the nose-flute was rare, used only by a few Polynesians. Even more rare was the Fijian equivalent of the Jew's harp, made of bamboo.

dete n. small of the back and lumbar area of the body.

deu lest I, sometimes seen as *de'u*.

vakadeuca v. to transmit, pass along, a disease, a thought, a command, an object. Syn. *vakadewa-taka*.

devo n. soapstone, limestone, which may have a thin layer of soil on top. This is common in the area of Suva city. Fijians dug caves into the limestone.

dewa, dewaca v. to spread out, transfer (usually words, written or spoken, or sickness). *Sa dewa vakatotolo na vosa.* The word spreads fast. *Sa dewa ga.* It is only hearsay. **vakadewataka** translate (language), transfer or pass on (something). *dau vakadewa vosa* translator, interpreter. *na idewadewa* the funnel, strainer (as for tea). See *dawa*.

vakadewa n. translation, v. to translate.

dewa n. (Anglicism) A newly invented word for a suffix attached to the root-form of a verb (*vu*). For example, with the root-word for "hit or strike, club or kill" *moku*, one may attach a suffix to create the transitive form, as in *moku-ta* to hit it/him/her. Such innovative words are thought useful by some language teachers.

dewa, dewava v. to catch, spread, as of a disease. **matedewa** n. infectious disease. *na dewa ni mate* the spread of the sickness. *na veidewavi* the transmitting (as of disease), the infecting.

di root-word. empty, silent (house, container), out (tide). *Sa di na mati.* The tide completely out. *mati didi* very low tide. *di caracara na mati* very low tide. *Sa lala didi na vale.* The house is completely empty. **didi** (or) **didivara** deaf.

vakadi rorogo silent (house, forest, people individually or in a group). *Me vakadi rorogo mada.* May we have silence, please. May imply to listen in silence, or imply that silence is golden. Fijians are not usually expected to respond when listening; deadpan expressions may give foreigners the impression Fijians are not listening or do not care. This is only sometimes the case.

dia (Eng.) deer, now also often a term of affection, dear. Deer were introduced to Wakaya Island but nowhere else in Fiji. The Fiji Army was asked to cull their numbers very severely. As in New Zealand, they damage natural vegetation.

dia, diaka v. to throw knife (handle first). *diaka na vunikau* to throw a knife at the tree. **veidia** children's game, throwing knives into ground. Anciently, hard reed-stems were used before knives were introduced.

dia-na n. handle (knife, axe, shovel, spear, umbrella). **vakadiataka** affix a handle to it.

dibi-na n. from hip to upper thigh of body. *sui ni dibi-na* hip bone. **saga-na** n. thigh. Idiom: *lali dibi* show appreciation by clapping a hand resoundingly on thigh.

didi, didivaka v. to grumble, complain. *O koya didivaka na kena.* He/she complains about his/her food. *dau didi* person never satisfied. *Kakua ni dau didi.* Don't always complain. *Na cava o didivaka?* Why are you grumbling?

didivara deaf. Also *didi*.

vakadidike n., v. to inspect closely, now used for the English word "research". *vakadidike vakaiwiliwili* (Anglicism) n. quantitative research study.

dige v. to make faces (like a child), to tease. *Kua ni vakadigei koya.* Do not make faces at him/her.

digi, digia and **digitaka** v. to choose, select, vote, elect. *idigidigi* n. choice. *bati-digidigi* n. choosy eater *dauveidigitaki* n. selector, as for rugby and other team sports to choose members of the team.

veidigidigi n. election. *na iwasewase ni veidigidigi* the electoral constituency.

digo 1. n. mole (on body), and perhaps by extension, birthmark or distinctive freckles.

digo 2. n. cricket (insect).

digo 3. n. full stop, period (U.S.A.), a word devised by school-teachers in teaching grammar. Syn. (Eng. "full stop") *vulusitovu*

digo, digova v. to inspect, examine carefully and ponder. Admiration may be implied in some cases. *dau didigo* observant. *didigo* v. to continue examining carefully. See *dikeva*.

Dike (Eng.) man's name, Dick.

dike n. central branch of a bunch of coconuts.
Idiom: *Tara na dike ni niu qai kevu.* lit. touch the coconuts but then come right down, as if a person climbed a coconut palm for the nuts but quit the effort after reaching close to the goal, but not accomplishing what he set out to do.

dike, dikeva v. to look into, inspect, examine carefully (as in medical check-up). *Dau vei-va-didike* Inspector (police). *yaco e valenibula me ratou laki dikevi.* get to hospital for their (few) check-ups.

dikevi vakavuniwai n. medical examination, check-up.

dikedike n. a type of firefly.

dilikatoa n. a type of terrestial glow-worm.

diligo n. abalone. Syn. *ceva*.

dilio n. a migratory coastal bird, Pacific Golden Plover, visits Fiji September through April, having flown south from Siberia and Alaska. Seen on coastal grasslands or inland along rivers. Syn. *doli, dolidoli.*
Idiom: *kunekune vayaloka ni dilio.* impossible to find, just as it is impossible to find the eggs of the *dilio* bird which in fact does not lay eggs in Fiji.

dilo n. seaside tree, Calophyllum inophyllum, Clusiaceae. Timber used for ribs of a punt, or a boat keel, and also for making wooden drums (*lali*), furniture and utilitarian wooden items.. Oil of the nut is used for massage; a little is exported. Known as *tamanu* in some Polynesian island groups (and *damanu* is the Fijian name for a closely related species). Flowers and fruits all year but nuts abundant maturing in April. Inner bark has white latex. The bark itself is thick and very strong. White petals and sepals are four, with very conspicuous globe of yellow anthers. The seed is bitter, inedible but can supply oil for massage. Lvs oblong, stiff, dark green with yellow central vein and margins. Children were formerly punished by whipping with branches of the *dilo* tree.
Idiom: *vakuli-ni-dilo* very strong (of a man), implying not easily hurt, having a tough skin.
Idiom: *waiwai dilo* to sweet-talk someone to get what is wanted, smooth talk, as if applying the oil.

vakadiloya v. to criticise. *dau vakadiloi* person who criticises a great deal. The implication is of being whipped with a branch of the *dilo* tree.

veivakadiloi n. criticism.

dina 1. adj. true, real. n. truth. *dina, dinata* v. to tell the truth, to believe it, accept as true.

dina 2. although, as in expressions such as: *Dina ni sa rawa, e sega ni cakava.* Although it was possible, he/she did not do it. *Dina ni sa levu na vale, sa lailai ga na lewe ni matavuvale.* Although there are many houses, the family households are small.

vakadinadina-i-koya adj. haughty, self-contained, failing to recognize and inter-relate with others, deceiving oneself. Syn. *vakadinadina.*

ivakadinadina n. witness, testimony, evidence, proof. Fijian language makes no clear distinction between evidence and proof. *na soli vakadinadina* the giving of testimony. *Vakadinadina i Jiova* Jehovah Witnesses, an American Christian denomination now established in Fiji.

vakadinadina-taka v. to verify, certify, confirm.

vakadinata v. to agree with (something), accept as true, to comply.

dinamati (Eng., dynamite, Slang) n. gorgeous, usually of a woman but may apply to a man.

dinau n. loan, debt. *dinautaka* v. to borrow money (or) take goods on credit, a modern concept to Fijians that they do not always adapt to easily. Traditionally *dinau* referred to obligations incurred that require reciprocal action. Loans in a European sense did not exist. Traditionally, reciprocity might be accomplished by various favoured actions at a different time, to different members of the family or social group. It was best not be seen as a direct person-to-person return favour, which might be thought vulgar. *na ilavo dinautaki* the borrowed money.

dio n. Rock oyster, small, edible but not often eaten, usually found around mangroves. Hard to open. Dendostrea sp. Idiom: *rabe dio* just a follower, who accompanies people doing a job.

diqiri (Eng.) degree, as in navigation, geometry. The letter **q** here is often pronounced as a **k**.

diri, diria (or) **dirika** v. to crack open (coconut, egg, bamboo), to clink forcibly. *veidiri-ulu* bang two children's heads together (as punishment).
Idiom: *dirika na tabua* ceremonial giving of whaletooth in response to one presented, signaling a refusal (usually of wedding proposal). See *dirika* below.

diria n. a species of river eel, usually in clear water (not muddy), fresh or brackish. It is tawny coloured with a white to yellowish belly. The flesh is white and not at all oily; it may be boiled, or grilled with the skin on.

diridamu n. Abrus precatorius, seaside vine with small and beautiful, brilliantly black and red seeds, extremely poisonous (cyanide), formerly used for necklaces, now forbidden by law because people might unknowingly chew on the seeds. Syn. *leredamu*.

dirika v. to present a whaletooth, declining a request that came with a whaletooth, as a request for a certain wife in marriage, or request to have a widow remain at her husband's village after his death. (Custom is for a widow to return to her original village.) The teeth should be of equivalent value.

diro n. brackish water in ponds, often used by people on the smaller islands for bathing, washing clothes.

dirovu n. swampy mangrove area at the shore, usually near river-mouth, where small fish and crabs are abundant. Syn. *veitiri*. *tara dirovu* go fishing, crabbing by hand or small nets at such a place.

diva v. to long for, desire (person, home, a certain food) with nostalgia often implied. *Au diva meu lako.* I wish I could go. *Au diva na noqu daulomani* I long for my beloved. *Au diva na veigauna sa oti* I miss the old times. *na veigauna divi* the times remembered. *e dua na gauna divi* a time to be remembered, an unforgettable time. *Au diva lo voli me . . .* I secretly dream that . . . *na kena idivi* n. that which is desired, dreamed of.
Idiom: *Wai ni diva, sega ni kabita* tears of futile desire.

doa n. heartwood of a tree. In the eastern highlands, *doa* is favoured for making fire by rubbing two pieces of wood, a hard piece against a soft wood base. *doa* can also refer to driftwood that floats downriver. Curiously, it is the plant totem of one highland tribe at village Tavia and the name is never to be mentioned there. This is an example of a rarity, a totem that is not a living thing.

dobui n., v. adj. river flood, fast-running river current, to surge powerfuly, gush, of a current or burst of water. *Sa dobui yani na uciwai.* The river (or stream) gushed away. Syn. *tacoka*.

doce adj. outspoken in unhibited manner, overly candid, lacking respectful behaviour, mostly from being naïve, awkward, immature, daffy, having an unguarded nature. *Sa doce tu na nona ivakarau.* His/her behaviour is lacking in proper manners.

dodo, dodoka v. to extend, stretch out (arm, legs), lie down in extended position (person), lay out (as of *voivoi* leaves on the ground, to be cured in the sun) *vakadodo* stretch (oneself), as on waking up. *Lai vakadodo ekeya.* Go stretch out (and rest) over there. *dodoyava* v. to extend the legs. *vakadodoka* straighten it out. Used figuratively sometimes, as in *E sega ni tadodo rawa vakavinaka e dua na soqo vakaViti ke sega ni tekivutaki vakavanua.* A Fijian meeting cannot proceed well if not begun by proper Fijian custom with ritual.

dodo liga v., n. to extend a (helping) hand, reach out and help. *liga* hand.

ivakadodo-rairai (Anglicism) n. telescope, binoculars. *vakadodorairaitaka* look at it through the telescope.

vakadodo-sasa to be lying about with feet extended, as with several people sleeping on the floor (very common in Fiji), or dead soldiers lying about on a battlefield.

dodo-lua to feel nauseous, as if to vomit. *lua* to vomit.

dodomo v., n. to be deeply in love, with strong physical desire. n. passionate feeling of love and desire. *dodomo lo* v., n. secret love, undisclosed.
Idiom: *Na nomu dodomo sa vaka e dua na tiaina dreu.* Your love won't last (it is like a ripe banana).
Idiom: *dodomo mate wale.* futile love that has no hope.

dodonu 1. straight. *Sa dodonu na gaunisala.* The road is straight. *tu vakadodonu* stand up straight.

dodonu 2. correct, right. *Sa dodonu na nomu itovo.* Your behaviour is correct. *Sa dodonu ki na matanitu me cakava.* It is right for the government to do it. *vakadodonutaka na nodra pepa na gonevuli* correct the students' papers. See *donu*. Syn. (Tonga) *totonu*.

dodonu 3. (Anglicism) n., right(s), as in human rights, one's rights under the law, women's rights. This is modern usage, of course, much used in recent times.

dogadoga adj. dopey, awkward, clumsy thus sometimes inadvertantly disrespectful.

dogai weakness and sickness of body and confused mind that in Fijian belief inflicts a younger man who has sexual intercourse with an older woman.

dogo n. black mangrove, sturdy tree, Bruguiera gymnorrhiza, growing in firm mud, usually a little more inland than the red mangrove (*tiri*) which is distinguished by its having drooping aerial roots. *Dogo* becomes a more substantial tree and has "knee roots" (pneumatophores) for air that grow up out of the ground. It has small black oval fruit and white flowers (to 3 cm), with calyx of eight lobes. The fruit and the soaked, cooked germinating seeds of B. gymnorrhiza are edible. The wood is used for firewood. The bark is very high in tannin and was formerly used as a preservative for wood and for fishing nets which were soaked in an infusion of the bark. The bark provides a brown stain used for colouring barkcloth. *veidogo* n. mangrove swamp. Syn. (Lau) *dogokana*. (Nadro, Ba) *lailai*. (Serua) *tiri*. (Kadavu) *togo*. See *tiri, tiriwai*.

doi n. a small forest tree though rarely the trunk may be 75 cm in circumference, Alphitonia zizyphoides and A. frangulnoides, Rhamnaceae, often growing near a river limited to 300 m. altitude. Syn. (Lau) *selavo*. From a distance it is recognized by its small, fine leaves. Flowering of white blooms is around April to May, taken as a sign that cultivated yams are mature. *vula i doi* a traditional lunar month, around April-May, when weather is thought to be unsettled, wet in Viti Levu. Whitish bark, smelling of sandalwood when cut. Young lvs and twigs covered in brown hair. Wainadoi ("Doi River") is a river and a freehold rural settlement and plantation area, 22 km west of Suva, by the Queens Road. It is now known for spices grown there and a Nature Garden, visited by tourists and school children. There is a village on Ono-i-Lau Island that bears the name Doi.

doina v. to attach by a string, usually crabs such as *lairo*. *e dua na idoini lairo* a string of *lairo* crabs. A set of crabs are usually sold on such strings.

doka n. horizontal top ridge, usually of house. *doka ni ucu-na* ridge of the nose.

doka v. to respect, honour. Fiji motto: *Rerevaka na Kalou ka doka na Tui*. Fear God and respect the King. *Sa ka dokai na nomu itovo*. Your behaviour is honourable. *Au dokai iko*. I respect you. *vulagi dokai* guest of honour, honoured guest.

dokadoka adj. overtly disrespectful (usually showing off), conceited, proud in a bad sense. (*vaka*)*dokadokai koya* egotistical, egocentric, proud of oneself.

dokana n. ridge, as of a range of hills or mountain. See *tokaitua*.

doketa (Eng.) n. doctor. Syn. *vuniwai*.

dokete (Eng.) n. docket (as for a sale), invoice, document.

doko 1. n. sharp, hard digging stick for planting taro, yams, still widely used. The pole is sometimes discarded after a single use. *doko ni niu* sharp stick (or metal bar) for husking coconuts.

doko 2. (West) n. taro. Syn. *dalo*.

doko 3. number of mulberry bushes cut for production of bark cloth (*masi*), ten or one hundred.

doko ni vudi n. a delicious edible fish, feisty to catch on a line, long-nosed emperor, sea bream (according to Rob Wright), or grey snapper, Lethrinella mineatus (or perhaps L. xanthocheila), similar to a *sabutu*, upper parts faded yellow, striped blue/green mouth, often found around reef entrances, but some times at some places dangerous to eat because of ciguatera (red tide) poisons in the food-chain. The curious name possibly derives from the shape as seen by early Fijians (and rather implied by the Fijian name) rather like an improvised support for a fruit-heavy plantain "tree", pointed at one end and deeply forked at the other. (P. Geraghty suggested this derivation.) Syn. *kacika*.

doko ulu v. to dive head-first (as into water) or simply head for some other place.

dokodoko ulu (Slang) very drunk, wasted from excessive drinking.

dola (Eng.) n. dollar.

dola, dolava v. open, open it; today, the word can apply to almost anything but not usually the mouth. *Dolava vei au!* Open up for me! *dolava na kava* to open the tin (can of food). *dalaga* to open the mouth.

dole premature(ly). *biu vuli dole* quit school prematurely (too young). *sucu dole* born prematurely. *mate dole* died prematurely.

dole, dolea v. to respond, or reciprocate, with words or an act (saying, giving, permitting something), usually in a ceremonial context. *dolea na vosa* respond to the speech, summarizing it, often with appreciation. *idolei* n. the act of responding. *na idole* n. the response itself, the actual repayment or reciprocal gift. *veidolei* repayment (as a concept). In most places of Fiji, for example (but not at Udu), it is customary for hosts to reciprocate the *isevusevu* of *yaqona* presented by visitors introducing themselves and their purpose. Reciprocity has been an essential aspect of Fijian culture. In some cases it can be a return favour for what has been obtained by *kerekere* requests. Traditionally, but perhaps less so today, *kerekere* has been part of a continuing, reciprocal social relationship. (Modernly especially, the custom may become exploitive among relatives.) *Na veika kece e dau kerei vei koya ka a mai dolei tale.* Everything asked of him has been reciprocated in some way. The reciprocity is often subtle, not directly an obvious repayment. Too direct a repayment might be considered inappropriate and even vulgar. Properly a mutual bond is affirmed in any exchange. It is a continuing process that reinforces the relationship.

dole n. (West) crevally (= trevally). Syn. *saqa*. *dole* may refer to a very young crevally.

dolele v. to reach out.

doli 1. (Eng) dolly, doll as a girl's toy. May sometimes be applied to a woman who is made up carefully or elaborately. Also, an abbrev. of the name Dolores.

doli 2. or **dolidoli** n. bird, Wandering Tatler, Heteroscelus incanus, very common migratory shore wader, breeding in North America, though some stay in Fiji round the year. Sometimes flies far inland on Viti Levu. Known throughout Polynesia. Distinct white stripe from above the eye to bill and a dark stripe below that.

dolo, dolova, dolovaka v. to wriggle or crawl, writhing on the stomach (baby unable to walk, snake writhing on the ground, soldier crawling forward cautiously on the ground, in combat). *gone dolodolo* n. baby at the stage of crawling about on its tummy. *dolovaka* v. to crawl bearing something, as a soldier might crawl carrying his rifle.

dolo, doloka v. to snap off, usually of fruit from a plant (corn, sugar-cane, cauliflower, pineapple, *duruka*), or snap in two (corn, sugar-cane). *dolodolo na painapiu* picking the pineapples. See *kidoloka* v. to snap off more forcefully.

dolo ni cakau n. section of reef exposed at low tide. See *delanimati*.

dolou n, dried, broken-off branches of breadfruit used as a first firewood in setting a fire. They burn fast but do not last long and do not form coals that linger. Useless as timber. Idiom: *buka dolou* fast work on some project but yielding only a quick solution that will not have an enduring effect.

domi, domica v. to sip, suck (child the breast, man the pipe), drink through a straw.

domidomi v., adj. suckling, as in *gone domidomi*, a suckling baby. May apply to child sucking the thumb or other object.

domo-na 1. n. neck. *ilobi ni domo* neck-wrinkles. *Sa domo-dali ko koya* He/She hanged himself/herself. (That form of suicide never existed in ancient times.) *Au sa domodali sara ga.* I am all choked up (worries, emotion). This is a modernism.

domo-na 2. n. voice. *na domodra na taba gone* the voice of the children. *vosa e na domo-i-levu.* say out loud. *domo-i-levu* adj. loud. *domolailai* speak in a soft voice, not very audible, weak voice. *vosa e na domo mamasu* speak in a pleading voice. *domo drogadroga* hoarse voice. *domobi* (or) *domo bibi* deep voice, bass voice. *domo vadugu* deep, resonant voice. Idiom: *katoa na domo.* lot of words but little action.

domobula-taka v. n., adj. to be terrified; terror; -*taka* terrified by (something).

vakadomobula adj., adv. horrifying, frightening.

domodali v. n. to hang oneself. The hanging of a person. Strangling with a cord was traditional in Fiji, but not hanging. Most unusually, Cakobau treacherously imposed the hanging penalty on his close relative Ratu Mara Kapaiwai in 1859, who had rebelled against Cakobau in the Rewa-Bau wars of the mid-1850s. Kapaiwai had been deliberately misinformed as to his safety in returning to Bau. Memory of Cakobau's deceit lingers on.

domodomo-qa adj. courageous, unafraid to speak out.

domodua (Anglicism) v., n. solo (as in singing). *domorua* duet.

domona n., v. to desire, lust for, love (physical desire). *na dodomo* the desire, lust, love. *Au domoni iko.* I want you, desire you. By ext., *domona* can refer to a very strong desire or passionate desire to do something or have something specific. Can be a physical object. Idiom: *Veidomoni e sega ni kena wai.* There is no cure for love.

domoqa n., adj. person who cannot listen or do as asked.

domorua (Anglicism) n. duet, literally two voices.

donu correct, straight, exact. *Sa donu oqori* That is correct. *Donu!* Correct! Okay! *e loma donu* exactly in the middle. *lima donu na kaloko* exactly five o'clock. *tu donu* straight ahead. *vuki donu* behaves correctly, obedient, of a child. See *dodonu*.

donuya, donumaka v. to match (in many different senses), be level with, coincide in time or place, to meet up with, to correspond to, to be allowed or approved. *Sa donuya na basi o koya.* He/she got on the bus on time. *E donuya yani o koya na coqa oya.* He/she was there at the time of that crash. *veidonui* to be opposite each other, correspond to each other, parallel. *me rau veitaudonui na teveli* match up the two tables (fit them together). *E navuci me veitaudonui na tayabe ena kena rogoci na kisi.* It was planned that the march coincide with the hearing of the court-case. *veidonui* coincide, as in *na vula-i-sevu, via veidonui kei na Feperueri* the (lunar month) *vulaisevu* coincides approximately with the month of February. *dabe donui Iliesa* to sit facing Iliesa. Syn. *donumaka.*

va-donui koya proud of oneself, conceited.

ivaka-donu-mata n. approval of a request of a bride for marriage. Opposite is *iduguci,* the whaletooth given to the family of prospective groom, politely declining the request.

vakadonuya v. to approve. *Keu vakadonuya.* If I approve of it.

veivakadonui n. approval. Modernly, one can say *solia na veivakadonui* to give the approval (translated quite literally from the English.)

donu n. an edible fish, coral trout, rock cod, salmon cod, Seranus maculates. Also Plectropomus leopardus (salmon cod, reddish colour) or P. laevis (mottled colour) and Cephalopholis argus.

dora v. to burst open, open out (flower bud, leaves of sensitive plant.)

doroka v. pull back the foreskin of the uncircumcised penis (*boci*).

dorokona v. to belch, burp. Syn. *derekona, qeremavu.*

dosa v., n., adj. stiff, unbending, rigid, inflexible, usually applied to the body or, part of the body, leg, arm, as from paralysis or an accident, or rigor mortis in death. As a verb *dosa* refers to limp walking with rigid leg(s), as a partial cripple, person using a crutch having a leg in a plaster cast. It could apply to a clown walking on stilts. Syn. *wadokau* stiff, a word sometimes applied to frozen things such as food.

dosi n. (Insult) derogatory term for an Indian, or a person thought to act like an Indian, or who favours what is thought to be an Indian viewpoint.

dou you (three or a few) as the subject of the sentence. *Mo dou* . . . You (few) should . . . *Dou bula!* Good day! Hello! (to several people together).

doudou n., adj. courage; brash, and brave (if successful), foolhardy (if not successful). *E a cakava vakadoudou o Seru.* Seru did it bravely, without fear.

Idiom: *Na doudou na ka ni mate,* Courage is the way to get killed,
na datuvu na ka ni veiwali. while cowardice is a matter for joking.

douvaka v. to be brash (toward someone or about something. *Sa douvaka na vosa vei iko o Seru.* Seru is not afraid to talk to you.

dovi, dovia and **dovilaka** v. to break off food in the hand using thumb and fingers. In the village, Fijians may still normally eat with the hands.

idovidovi (ni kakana) n. thumb. Pieces of food are normally broken off with the thumb and fingers.

dovisere (Archaic) n. a measure of length, approx. three feet, from middle of the chest to end of outstretched arm, approx. half of a fathom. See *katu*.

dovu n. sugar cane. *dovu kama* brown sugar. *qaqi ni dovu* sugar mill. *sitima ni dovu* sugar-cane train. *gunu dovu* chew and suck sugar cane (it is considered a beverage). Indigenous sugar canes were known in Fiji and probably aboriginally introduced, used for thatch but not generally used for making sugar. As a snack the commercial varieties of the cane are chewed for the sweetness, especially by young people who have strong teeth.

dra v., n. blood, sap (of plant). *dra tabu* first-born child. *E dra tiko na ucuna* His/her nose is bleeding. *dravaka* blood-red. *coka dra* have blood in the faeces. *dra vata* related (of people). *dra mate* black bruise. *dradra* bloody, too rare (of cooked meat). *buta dra* of meat, cooked rare. *E maca nomu dra.* You have anaemia. *dra balavu* continued bleeding.

-dra as a suffix to certain nouns, meaning that it is integral to them (many people). *yava-dra* their legs. *tama-dra* their fathers. Such hyphens are never written in Fijian. This suffix serves as a possessive pronoun.

dradrakita adj. sticky, viscous, as mud can be, or Fijian pudding *vakalolo,* or a cake-mix before cooking. By ext., progress of discussion at a meeting might appear to drag, or move slowly, ponderously. This can be virtually synonymous with *drakidrakita* See below.

dradraluka adj. tasteless (food, lacking salt), distasteful (of manners and behaviour, and of a person). *Sa dradraluka na tamata dau kerekere.* People who always ask for things are abhorrent.

dradranu adj. tasteless, lacking good flavour. Often this would imply a lack of salt. *tuituina* salted appropriately. (*kamikamica* suggests tastefulness and not just sweetness). Syn. *dranu.* (Colo East) *daladalau.*

draiva (Eng.) n. driver. *draiva ni taxi.* taxi-driver.

draiva-taka (Eng.) v. to drive (a vehicle).

draka-na (Macuata) n. lips. (Lau) mouth.

Idiom: *Draka ni kemu!* taunt, refers to one's mouth as if the person had lips like an asshole.

drakai (Lau) tired. (Bau) *oca. Sa vakadrakai au.* It wore me out, made me tired.

draki n. weather. *dau ni draki* (Anglicism) n. meteorologist.

drakidrakita adj. stiff or sticky to mix (pudding ingredients), gluey of texture, thick (of mud), difficult, slow and tedious (of a meeting). *Sa drakidrakita na bula.* Life is difficult. *Sa drakidrakita na gaunisala.* The road is difficult. *e dua na gauna drakidrakita* a troubled time. See *dregadregata*.

drakulu adj. chafed, of body or body parts, by abrasion, scraping (as from a fall), scratching, or burn.

drakusi v., adj. to be scratched (as by cat, thorns).

drala n. spp. tree, Vitex trifolia and/or Erythrina variegata, more commonly the latter. (Seemann cites only Erythrina sp.) The native, wild *drala* has trifoliate triangular leaves, thorny branches, spreading crown, altitude under 400 m, growing to 15 m. The commonly planted, introduced ornamental var. has green leaves with pronounced yellow streaks and the branches have no thorns. *Drala* flowers red, inflorescence to 45 cm., in July, August and September, attracting the *kula*, Collared Lory. That flowering is a traditional signal to plant yams. Used as living fence and for nitrogen-fixing characteristic.

dralawa n. vine with edible beans, Canavalia maritima, Papilionaceae. Flowers pink to mauve, long pods with large brown seeds. Syn. *drautolu*.

drali, dralia v. to daub and "work in" with the hands. *dralia na ulumu ena lase* daub you hair with lime (typically, implied mixture of lime, conditioning from *makita* nuts, and red mud), ashes on occasion, or modernly, a hair colorant or conditioner. For hair conditioner or relaxant, this may imply an excessive application.

draloa n. or adj. bruise, bruised.

drama (Eng.) n. theatrical play, in Fiji mostly children's re-enactment of biblical stories done in a childish but funny way, often accompanied with much laughter. *dau-ni-drama* (Ang.) actor, actress.

drami, dramica v. to lick. *gone dramidrami* baby at toothless stage. *drami-liga* taste with the finger (jam, cake-icing). *drami, dramica* may apply to oral sex on a woman.

Idiom: *drami toka* I'll believe it when I see it happen, wait and see (sarcastic, when another makes assurances), sometimes accompanied by a gesture, like a cat licking the back of its paw.

Idiom: *drami yame* to tell tall stories, to tell fibs, lit. lick the lips.

Idiom: *E drami nona vale lailai.* He/she has a "runny stomach" (usually said of a child). Implied is mucous fluid.

Idiom: *dramica na vusi* lit. the cat licked it up, meaning some food is so relished that it disappeared quickly, or something has been stolen secretly.

dramu (Eng.) n. drum, either for band music, or as a container, eg., 20 or 200 liters.

dramukai (Archaic) n. legendary and mysterious creature of the bush around Waimaro country along the Waidina River and west into Namosi Province, associated with the legendary Little People (*na Leka*) and the gremlins (*na veli*) who play a significant role in the culture of super-tribe Waimaro of the eastern Viti Levu highlands. To some of the highlanders *kaiColo*, the *veli* are a part of current life and are occasionally encountered. (Some of their visits have been reported at Wainadoi, Namosi, in the 1980s and 1990s.)

drano n. lake.

dranu adj. fresh (of water) as in *wai dranu* fresh water (not saltwater). *dradranu* tasteless. Syn. for fresh water *wai droka*.

dranu (or) **dranudranu** (or) **dradranu** (or) **dradraluka** adj. tasteless, lacking salt.

vakadranu v. to rinse in fresh water (usually after having been soaked in saltwater), in washing cloths, pots, people bathing. Syn. *dranu, dranuma*.

dranuma v. to test by tasting a touch to see if a food lacks salt or is appropriately salted.

dranu, dranuma v. to use a plant or part of a plant or an herbal concoction to avert evil magic or spirits (*tevoro*); it may be drunk or mixed with oil to be anointed, or it may be burned for the smoke to exorcise bad spirits. Also to plant a shrub or small tree, such as the *vasa* (Cerbera manghas, Apocynaceae), or the *qai damu* (Cordyline terminalis), which are set out around the garden to ward off evil spirits or even theft. This is still done today though the effect is now less sure. *idranumi* n. the plant material used to fend off evil spirits or theft. (Theft of crops becomes a serious problem in many areas.)

drasa adj. dirty brown, or reddish brown colour, as a characteristic of being soiled (usually cloth), or rusted (iron), or oxidised (freshly cut fruit). A child may have soiled its underwear, or clothes soiled by slipping in the mud. May even apply to a food such as banana or apple that turns brown after being cut and exposed to the air.

drasa (or) **drasadrasa** having sore eyes, reddish and feeling granular. Can be from conjunctivitis, exposure to smoke of a fire, dust of a dirt road, or simply fatigue.

dra-tabu n. eldest child. Syn. *ulumatua*.

-dratou suffix to certain nouns, as a possessive pronoun, meaning that it is an integral part for several people. *luvedratou* their children (of several parents). *kedratou* their food (of several people).

drau 1. hundred. *e dua na drau* one hundred. *drau vakadrau* hundreds of hundreds. *budrau* var. of coconut with many very small nuts.

drau or **o drau 2.** you (two), as the subject of a sentence. *Drau moce!* Good-bye, you two!

-drau 3. as a suffix to certain nouns, possessive pronoun meaning that the thing belongs to two people. *na luvedrau* their child(ren), of two parents.

drau 4. n. thatch for roof or wall of house. Properly, at least in the highlands, this is usually leaves of *duruka*. Nadrau is well known village in the Viti Levu highlands.

drau-na n. leaf. *drau ni veva* sheet or page of paper. *drau ni balabala* fern-tree leaf. *na drau ni ulumu* your hair (on head). *na drauniulu* the hair (of the head). Soft body hair is *vuti-na*.
Idiom: *coka i drauna*. all dressed up in finery.

draudrau adj. leafy, as in *kakana draudrau* green (leaf) vegetables.

draudrau (ni masi) n. patterned design, usually traditional and regionally characteristic, used to fill in white spaces of barkcloth. Traditionally this was often stenciled through a plantain leaf, now more commonly used X-ray film obtained from health clinics. *draudrau ni Moce* local *masi*-design used at Moce island. See *kupeti*.

draunikau n. witchcraft, black magic. *vakadraunikau* or *vakadraudrau* practise witchcraft. Witchcraft is believed to be very much alive. Sickness and death are often attributed to witchcraft when they may in fact be due to other causes.

drauniveva n. page of paper.

drautolu (or) **dralawa** n. littoral vine with edible beans, white flowers all year, Canavalia sp., Papilionaceae.

drava 1. catch nothing fishing or diving. *Sa drava na siwa.* The line-fishing yielded nothing. This word is not pronounced till after the event, to avoid bad luck. *vanua drava* poor, unproductive land. May also apply to a reef where little seafood is to be found.

drava 2. won't listen or obey (requests or persuasion yield nothing), usually said of a child.

drava, dravata v. adj. persistently to beg or demand (something).

dravia adj. smooth, hairless, shaved clean (person, animal), slippery.

dravidravia adj. very slippery (path), shiny (leaves, body), sleek.

dravo n. (Verata, Wainibuka, Rakiraki) reed, Miscanthus floridulus, Poaceae. Syn. *gasau,* (Nadro) *hina*. Useful for walls, arrow shafts, fish fence, supports for growing yams. Name of a village in Bau District.

dravoci adj., v. skinned (fish, cattle), de-barked (tree), is peeling (of person's skin). *Sa dravoci tu na kulina ena kati ni siga;* His/her skin is peeling from sunburn.

dravu n. ashes. *dravusa* wood-ashes. *dravu-i-siga* drought. *vanua dravu-i-siga* desert. *matadravu* fireplace for cooking, formerly in a lower corner of the house. *sa dravukasi na yagomu* your skin is very dry. By extension, *dravu* has come to mean the colour grey. Idiom: *veiqe dravu* to fight amongst themselves.

dravubuto adj. dark grey colour.

dravuloa adj. grey colour, usually of hair. See *sikoa*.

dravudravua adj. poor (people, land). *vakadravudravua-taka* v. to impoverish.

Dravudravua n. *Lotu Dravudravua*, Church of the Poor, properly the Spiritual Congregation of the Poor, an indigenous Christian sect founded 1954 by Sakaia Loanaceva of village Mua, Batiki Island, led (1993) by its President, Sitiveni Gusuivalu who lived at village Tacirua, near Suva and claimed a membership of 2000. Members often dress distinctively, the men in white gowns and the women in a white dress with a red *sulu* showing below the dress. There are 36 male preachers but leadership has been totally autocratic, including choice of the script of teaching. Meetings are held in private homes. There are no church buildings. There are no prohibitions of food or drink and no tithing. Although women have no formal role, one is not supposed to criticize the behaviour of one's spouse. Reliance is on individual conscience. This is essentially a breakaway group from the authoritarian discipline and monetary contributions exacted by Fiji's Wesley (Methodist) Church which has not always been accountable for its funds But then neither has the Church of the Poor. A breakaway branch is said to allow certain sexual permissiveness and sexual obligations. Main settlement is at Naboro. Leader died November, 2006, replaced by a man called Peter who lives with his wife Josie at that settlement.

dravusa n. ashes, burnt wood-coals. See *dravu*.

dravusa kulukulu Idiom: certainly not possible. The reference is to "cool ashes". *Kulukulu* is the base of a hearth that is permanently embedded with ash residue. This idiom can be used by itself as an interjection, or used in a sentence. *sa bau dravusa kulukulu au qai cakava* I most certainly will not do it. *E dravusa kulukulu na vosa* Without there being anything at all said . ..

dravuisiga adj. as in *vanua dravuisiga* scorched earth, desert, impoverished land.

dravukasi adj., n. dirty grey. Syn. *dravusa, dravuseka*.

dravutu n. physical symptoms of a woman's pre-menstual syndrome.

dre, dreta, drelaka v. to pull. *vakadreta* to urge, convince. *vosa ni vakadre*. words of persuasion, advice. *vakadretaka vei iratou* persuade them (of it). *dretaka mai na velovelo* haul in the rowboat. *dretaka na wa bosucu* pull off the creeper (Mile-a-minute, fast-growing weed that covers farm crops). *vakadretaka na dali* tighten the rope. *veidre* tug-of-war, as a sport or game, formerly using a *walai* vine as a rope. *mata dre* chinky-eyed (Oriental), in Fijian this is familiar but not insulting. By extension, *dre, dreta* may mean to insist, to press one's opinion, to persuade.
Idiom: *Sa dre tiko na mataqu.* I'm still not quite awake yet (partial closure of the eyes).
Idiom: *Sa dre ko Malolo.* The sun is setting. (Malolo Islands are in the west of Fiji, off the coast of Nadi). May imply that something is coming to an end. May alternatively imply the wasting of time, doing nothing. Syn. *moku siga*.

drecala v., adj. of a person, contrary, difficult, stubborn, uncooperative, to go one's own way, contrary to the will of others.

vakadrecike adj., n. listless, lacking motivation, stubborn, disobedient.

dredre 1. difficult, also firm(ly) as in *tabu dredre* strictly forbidden. *vakadredre-taka* make it difficult. *dredreta sara vakalevu ko ira na lewe ni koro* make it very difficult for the villagers. *Eso na ka e vakadredretaki* some things are restricted. (Though spelling is the same as the word for "laughter", this *dredre* is pronounced with drawn-out, prolonged vowels as indicated here by the underlining.)

dredre 2. close, intimate, fast (friends), precious. *itokani dredre* intimate friend. *tauvu dredre* bound in a close *tauvu* relationship (which permits privelages and intimacies). *iyau dredre* precious goods. *na veidredreti* the mutual affection.

dredre, dredrevaka v., n. to laugh. *dredre kaikaila* to shout with laughter. *dredre kubukubu* to smile broadly, chuckle, laugh to oneself. *E kacabote noqu dredre.* I exploded with laughter. *mata dredre* has a smiling face. *bati dredre* fond of laughter. *dredrevaka* to laugh at. *vaka-tubu-dredre* to make people laugh. *na veidredrevaki* the laughter. Syn. (West) *mali*. Idiom: (Lau) *dredre ni sima*. giggle to cover shame, embarrassment.

drega n. gum (trad. the latex of tree) used to glue things, or for children to chew, glue. Chewing gums include breadfruit, jak fruit, *sorua, bulilewa* (or *bulimagailewa*). *wa drega* rubber band (office, school), or elastic band (as on underpants). *cegu drega (ni vava)* v. sniff glue, usually of the type shoemakers use, sometimes done by school-age children, as a dangerous drug.

drega, dregata v. to glue it or them. *dregata ena lalaga* glue it to the wall.

dregadregata sticky, gummy (usually implying clay in soil). *na qele dregadregata* the sticky soil. On the main islands there is a great deal of volcanic latersols of stickly red clay under a thin organic layer of good soil. *Sa dregadregata na yagoqu* my body has become sticky (perspiration, etc.).

dreke n. large cavity (diverse applications). *dreke ni wai* n. mouth of the river. *dreke ni waqa* n. hold of the ship, where the cargo is loaded. *dreke bi* overloaded, very heavily loaded, usually of a boat.

dreke, dreketa v. to carry on the back (of person or animal). *Sa dreke bi na ose.* The horse is carrying a heavy pack. *idrekedreke* burden carried on the back (food, firewood, soldier's knapsack, Pandanus leaves for weaving). *dreketi* carried on the back, a term used as a place-name in Rewa and Macuata. This is usually a woman's way of carrying heavy things.

drekea adj. low or virtually empty, of water in a pool, or the tide, a cooking pot or tea-pot.

drekedreke-vuata n. firefly.

dreke-ni-wai n. canal, creek. *na drekeniwai ni Nubukalou* Nubukalou Creek (in Suva). Drekeniwai has been a village of native Bauans (*kaiBau*), near village Nayavu by the Wainibuka River, and also at District Navatu, Cakaudrove. See *uciwai* river, stream.

Drekula (Eng.) Dracula, a fiction familiar to many Fijians.

drelaka v. to yank hard, to pull forcefully. See *dre, dreta*.

dreli 1. adj. (Lau) blunt (knife, axe, spear). Syn. *mucu*.

dreli 2. n. frog, usually referring to the Fiji Ground Frog, Platymantis vitianus, though the name and the two endemic species of frog are unknown to most present-day Fijians. (The other endemic frog is the much smaller Tree frog *ula*, Platymantis vitiensis that has adhesive pads on the feet.) Located on Viti Levu, Vanua Levu, Taveuni, Koro, Gau, Kadavu and Viwa. The colour varies with the environment.

The female is up to 10 cm is length, while the male is usually only three-quarters the size of the female. Eggs laid, some 40 at time usually in rotted wood during February and March, requiring four or five months to hatch. The *dreli* can swim, and can jump as far as a meter. The ground frog has been become rare on the larger islands due to the ravages of the mongoose, and feral cats. All such animals have been common foods for the highlanders *kaiColo*. The frog is not to be confused with the introduced and very common toad (*boto*) which has become a nuisance in the wet zone. Syn. *boto (ni Viti)*.

dresu, dresuka, dresulaka v. to tear (paper, cloth, sail of a sailboat). *kadresu* torn. *dresulaka* v. to tear forcefully.

vei-dresu-qa-ni-bulu v., n. noisy heated argument (here likened to the tearing of a coconut husk), fierce contest of matched opponents (boxing, rugby).

dreta n. clay suitable for pottery, mud suitable treatment of human hair;

vakadreta v. to stress (the importance of something).

vakadreti-taka (Eng. bandage)v. to bandage. *ivadreti* n. bandage. sSyn. *vadreti-taka*.

dreu 1. adj. ripe, ready for eating (usually fruit, including breadfruit). *vakadreutaka* to ripen fruit (leaving it in sun, or enclosing in bags). *veidreu* children's game of touch and chase, often played in the water. *boi dreudreu* smells ripe. Fijian do not necessarily prefer very ripe fruit, and will often reject it if there is any bruise or any insect damage.

dreu 2. (Nait.) n. banana. Naitasiri was a major producer of bananas for export as organised by the British. After Independence this export industry died due to failure of responsible marketing with quality control.

Dreu! familiar, informal and friendly form of address between people of Nadroga and Cakaudrove, often used between men and women, with a smile. Macuata people use the more full expression *Draka dreu!* meaning Sweet lips!

dreve adj. futile, ineffectual, ineffective, unsuccessful (person, plan of action, remedy, medicine). Something that does not work. Applied to a person, *dreve* suggests someone who cannot do anything right. *Sa dreve na sasaga* The effort is futile, ineffective.

drevula n. edible starkly white shellfish, small, round, Polinices albumen. Syn. (West) *tidre*.

drevula kata (Medical) a patchy, whitish discoloration of skin.

dri 1. n. sea cucumber, bêche-de-mer, of genera Holothuria, Bohadschia, Actinopyga or Thelanota spp. Most Fijians themselves eat only the sandfish *dairo*, usually raw. This species and other types they sell to Chinese traders for export. Named other species include: *sucuwalu* (H. fuscogilva, dark brown or creamy white, sometimes with blotches, all covered with sand, with eight nipple-type nodules), greenfish (*lokoloko ni qio*), *loaloa* (H. whitmaei), *dri loa, dri damu* (reddish brown), *tarase* (brown, Actinopyga mauritana), *dri loli* (A. miliaris), *sucu drau* (Prickly Redfish, Thelenota ananas, with papillae prickles all over its body) and *dri vula* (Bohadschia sp.). Noting that tiny fish come out from the *dri vula*, some Fijians believe that this sea cucumber is giving birth to *ika sa* which later becomes a fairly big fish that they catch and eat. Some say the *dri vula* is mother to the moray-like eel called *tunatuna*. *Dri vula* is whitish, similar to *dairo* but much bigger, and has pronounced teats. *wai ni dri* soup made from slitting the black *dri* and removing the sticky white or pink strands from the inside, which are then washed and cooked in fresh water for half an hour. (Red or bright orange sticky strands are not to be used.) Natewa people have traditionally prepared black *dri* for the Tui Wailevu, The *loaloa* is gutted, cleaned, cut into pieces and wrapped in plantain leaves. That is left to rot for four nights. It stinks awfully but it is boiled and then eaten by the Tui with great relish. *sili dri* to gather *dri,* to dive to collect *dri*. Syn. (Nadro.) *ki*.

Idiom: *volitaki dri* n. (Slang) prostitute, *volitaka dri* v. to go around as a prostitute. Implication is from the notion that a woman's private parts may be symbolized by a sea cucumber. Literally the reference is to sell (*volitaka*) sea cucumber.

Idiom: *volitaki kai koso* same meaning as above, implying a resemblance of the *kai koso* shellfish (Arca sp.) with a woman's private parts.

Significant trade in bêche-de-mer had begun by 1830, boomed in the 1840s but was finished around 1850. European ships sold in Manila for the market in China and the ships returned home with silk, tea and sugar. A minor trade continues today on a modest scale, individual Fijians diving and selling to Chinese merchants who export it.

dri 2. v. to bounce off, rebound (ball, wood chip), ricochet.

Idiom: *sa dri yani* "over to you people", said by a person who finishes telling a story. Someone should respond and take over with another yarn, or a response.

Dri 3. n. Waimaro highlanders of Colo East on Viti Levu Island, known earlier as fierce black warriors, *Dri loa,* black like some *dri* (sea cucumber, see above) and extremely agile to dart here and there in fighting, as implied in the rebounding suggested by the verb *dri* (see above). *dri* thus has double meaning.

dridri adj. plump, fully filled out, as a woman's breasts, or the body of a baby or young person. This is thought to be a positive feature.

drigi, drigita v. to bump into (people, animals). *drigita yani* push one's way into the crowd. *veidrigiti* too crowded in. *veidrigidrigi* so crowded, people bumping into one another (as of people on dance floor). *osodrigi* crowded with people moving about.

drika 1. adj. bald. *ulu drika* bald-headed (no hair at all). Syn. *cou*.

drika 2. (Rewa, Colo East) n. or adj. cold (of person feeling it). *Sa vakadrikai au na cagi.* The wind has given me a chill, has chilled me.

drili adj. smooth, sleek, usually of the skin.

driloa adj. very black, almost a shiny black (of person), like a black (*loa*) sea cucumber (*dri*). Fijians are quite conscious of skin-colour differences among people and often comment on it. Fair-skinned youngsters are often favoured. Dark-skinned indigenous Fijians often originally accepted light-skinned Polynesian (and sometimes Europeans) as their chieftains and ancestral spirits. However, *Dri loa* has been a proud reference to Viti Levu highlanders of super-tribe Waimaro, feared warriors, dark-skinned of Melanesian origin. Proudly, they consider themselves the "real Fijians", *kai Viti dina*.

dri loli n. bêche-de-mer species, Actinopyga miliaris, of commerical value. Dark brown, lighter below, long thin papillae, average 20 cm, depths 1-10 meters, found at reefs, sandy lagoons. Round, cylindrical body, ball-shaped when disturbed.

drimi n. a certain itchy, fungal affliction of the skin with pimples or blisters, sometimes said to be ringworm. Fijians have believed *drimi* can come from the wind, from the spirits themselves, or from witchcraft, in which case it can be fatal. *E dua e cakava tiko na kemu drimi.* Someone is causing your *drimi* illness. Natively, virtually all illness was thought to be caused by someone casting a spell and that notion persists still today. Fijians often believe that European medicine is ineffectual against *drimi* and a few other "Fijian sicknesses" (*tauvimate vakaViti*) such as *raberabe*, and *sau*. Some of the problems might be psychogenic. Syn. *drimu*. See *baubau*.

dri qala n. a small bird, Scarlet Robin, Petroica multicolor, on Fiji's four largest islands, a red-breasted robin. Also found in Savai'i and Upolu in Samoa. Males especially have a starkly red breast with dark head.

drisi 1. adj. bald. See *cou, ulu drika*.

drisi 2. adj. as in *mata drisi*, having haggard features or complexion, often with bloodshot eyes. This is thought to be from poor life-style, such as excessive drinking, staying up late at night.

drisi 3. n., v. to whistle sharply, as if to attract attention, like the call of the *kula*, the collared lory, Phygis solitarius. In various parts of Fiji the *kula* bird is referred to as the *drisi* (or) *drusi*. Formerly it was valued for the red feathers, especially by Tongans who collected it in Fiji, especially for trading to Samoa. Tongans engaged many Fijians in this effort.

driti, dritia 1. v. to cut off (cloth from a roll of cloth), tear off (leaves of a plant, usually for food or medicine). *e dua na isulu driti* a length of cloth.

driti 2. n. an edible leafy vegetable, Amaranthus sp,, named from the action of tearing off the leaves. Amaranthus spp. also go by the names of *tubua* and *moca*. Aboriginal intro. Sold at markets.

driu adj. wide-eyed, as in *mata driu*. Can be natural or by emotion. *E driu na matana niu vakaraitaka vua.* He/she was wide-eyed when I showed it to him/her.

driva, drivata (Lau) v. to steal. *dau drivadriva* habitual crook.

drivi n. a small black edible, salt-water mussel Modiola lithophaga.

dro v. to run away, flee. *dro vakayawa* run far away. *dro vata kei au* run away with me. *dro mai vei au* run to me (words of a popular song). *dro vua* run to him.
  Idiom: *dro bula* get out alive, survive.
  Idiom: *O sa dro tiko ena loma ni yaloka.* You can't get away (just running around in circles), lit. run away inside an egg.

idrodro (Bible) n. refuge for an escaping person, hiding place, referring to the *Koro ni Drodro* of the Old Testament, cities of refuge for Israelites.

drodro, drodrova v. to flow, to flow to or over, usually a river, ditch, canal, sweat, some heavy leakage. *drodro yauyau* flow plentifully.

drodrolagi n. rainbow. *lagi* sky.
  Idiom: *vakasiri drodrolagi* very fast, lit. as a rainbow might jump. *E vakasiri drodrolagi mai na waqavuka.* The aeroplane is coming in fast.

dro (na lewe ni yago-na) v. to have a muscle cramp.

vakadrodro, vakadrodroya v. to cause to flow, usually water or electricity, as in putting in a water conduit, or an electric line.

drodrolu n. deep soft mud. Syn. *lolobo*. See *soso*.

drovaka v. to escape, run away from (person, thing, a fight). *drovaki koya* run away from him. *Sa dro vakai koya*. He ran away by himself.

drotaka v. to escape, run away with (person, thing). *E rau sa veidrotaki* They (2) ran away together, eloped. Syn. *veicavu*. Traditionally, most marriages were arranged. Lovers by choice have usually had to elope, arranging afterwards for "forgiveness" (*bulubulu*) by bringing gifts (whale-teeth, mats) to the woman's family.

idrodrodro n. current, flow (of liquid), wake of a boat or ship.

drodro, drodroga v. to flow with the current (of person or thing).

drodro, drodrova v. to flow (of liquid), against or toward.

droga (or) **drogadroga** adj. hoarse (of voice). Some stories relate that this word gives rise to the name of Nadroga Province but the place-name existed earlier, inland.

droga-oso n. (Medical) congested lungs, "flu", influenza.

drogadroga-wale n. third finger, ring finger of the human hand. Fijians reckon this as the fourth finger *na ikava ni qaqaloniligana*. Syn. *idaradara ni mama*. *mama* n. ring.

droi v. to rise, erect, of penis. Syn. *drui, bula* (in this context).

droini (Eng.) n. drawing (picture). Fijians anciently developed none of the graphic arts except the use of stencils for designs on barkcloth, and men painting their faces in stark colours, preparatory to war. Now there are some gifted graphic artists. *idrodroini* n. graphic arts.

droini, droini-taka (Eng.) v. to draw (picture). *dau droini* n. artist (pictorial).

droka 1. raw, not cooked (any food). *butadroka* undercooked (of any food) and by extension, inexperienced of a person.
Idiom: *droka i wai* usually of children, reluctant to get into the water and bathe.
Idiom: *Adi droka na bogi* young women who are active in the night.

droka 2. fresh, as in *wai droka* fresh water.

drokadroka adj., n. green (colour), usually of vegetation but can be fish, (but not water or the sea), green (uncured) of firewood, timber. Modern tendency is to use this word for anything green as perceived by Europeans, if it were an abstract colour defined as part of the colour sprectrum. Fijians had not developed the notion of abstract colours as such. Their names of colours were always associated with specific objects.
Idiom: *mata drokadroka* fresh, gleaming face, youthful face, baby-face.

drokai n., adj. almost mature, of coconut, with flesh fully formed but not hard, usually with green-skin husk or very light tan. Skin inside the shell is light tan, not yet darkened. It is a good stage if one is eating the meat as an improvised meal. The water is still drinkable, not so laxative as water of the completely mature coconut. *Drokai* may also mean mature but not yet soft-ripe, of a fruit like guava (introduced). Syn. *kade*.

droka-i-wai adj. usually said of a child who has not bathed frequently or properly.

droku 1. v. to join in the singing as a back-up to the lead singer, as with a chorus. See *camana*.

dro(k)u 2. (Vanua Levu) sated, had enough to eat. Syn. *mamau*.

drolo adj. very muddy, especially of watery mud. Syn. *drodrolu, soso*; words based on *lobo* refer to very sticky mud. The word *Drola* was used for the name of a coastal bay of Nacula Island in the far west of Fiji, and it implies murky water, there caused by brown algae. Here a branch of super-tribe Vusaratu settled and call their chief the Tui Drola and Drola became the name of their tribe. Closely related is the word and notion of a snake god named Tui Drolo, of the Colo East highlands of super-tribe Waimaro. He is the ancestral spirit (*kalou vu*) of clan Nakorovatu, tribe Waimaro, who have resided at villages Nakorosule and Nakida. Fact is quite probably that this snake is the eel known as *dadarikai*, that inhabits such sloshy mud. Highlanders using the title Tui indicates an earlier close contact with Verata and Tongan influence. Tongans did use Viti Levu highlanders as mercenary warriors, slaves, and collectors of red *kula* feathers for trade to Samoa. There is a village Vaimaro (= Waimaro) in Vava'u, Tonga.

drolo, droloka v. to "work", massage heavily, muscles that are cramped. See *dro*.

drolua adj. lacking any body hair (*vuti-na*).

dromela adj. **1.** soggy, water-soaked of overcooked root crops.

dromela adj. **2.** out of tune, of a singing voice.

dromodromo yellow. Also refers to the disease yellow jaundice or yellow of an egg. May be synonymous with *dromodromoa*.

dromodromoa adj. yellow, or lightly orange-yellow as in dried turmeric (*cago ni viti*) or the dried mace (= aril, in botanical terms) of nutmeg.

dromu, dromuca v. to sink below in water. *vakadromuca* to push it under water. *sa dromu na mata-ni-siga* the sun has set. *ena vula sa dromu* during last month, some time last month. Idiom: *Sa dromu na nona matanisiga* He/she is getting old. lit. his/her sun is setting.

Idiom: *Dromu na vula, dromu vata kei na kena kalokalo.* lit. The moon sets and its star sets with it, meaning the death of one person can quickly bring on the death of a spouse, close relative or associate.

idromudromu (ni siga) n. sunset, setting of the sun.

dromucaka, dromutaka v. to submerge (something) in a liquid, usually water.

dromu-na n. bottom end of the yam, a soft part that is eaten rather than being used as planting material. *kobe-na*, the middle part of the yam is eaten or, for the outside that has skin, may be planted. That is the *vaci*, the parts of the *kobe-na*, that are to be planted. The head of the yam is *na ulu-na* which is planted.

drose n. edible white or colourless jellyfish, the "Upside-down Jellyfish", that must be cooked in hot water to be eaten. This sting in made innocuous by hot water. This is a special food for the chiefs of Verata. (Blue jellyfish is to be avoided). *Drose* is also a common food of hawkbill turtles. *canu drose* gather jellyfish. Cassiopea spp. Syn. (Kadavu) *drodro*, (Lau) *yalove*.

droso hoarse (of voice). Syn. *droga*.

drotini n. pennant, ensign, flag. *na drotini ni Peritania* the British ensign. Syn. *kuila* flag, now usually referring to a national flag.

drove 1. "a variety of seaweed, Ulva sp., Ulvaceae, giving its name to the Province of Cakaudrove", according to Capell. It is more likely that the Cakaudrove name derives from a native species of the ginger family.

drove 2. (Cakau. & Nadro.) n. a native ginger, Zingiber sp. In different parts of Fiji, different species of ginger bear this name. One of the main species bearing this name is Geanthus cevuga, a tall ginger with fragrant large white flowers used in garlands and to scent coconut oil, a species also called *cevuga* though that name also may refer to Alpinia purpurata.

drove 3. n. a type of edible sea-hare.

drovili adj. good looking. *drovidrovili* very good looking, of a person.

drua 1. n. double, twins. *drua-i-valu* (or, in Cakaudrove) *drua vesi* male twins. *drua tabua* female twins. *drua dadakulaci* boy and girl twins. *drua-i-tolu* triplets. *Rau drua o Seru kei Opeti*. Seru and Opeti are twins.

drua 2. v. large type of double-hulled ship built in southern Lau during the 1800s. The invention was Samoan, the carving mostly Tongan, and the timber Fijian *vesi*, much of it from Kabara or Fulaga. The last one was the *Ratu Finau, Tui Nayau*, built at Fulaga in 1913-14. The *Rusa i Vanua* was built at Fulanga Island and sailed to Lakeba Island, 118 feet in length, with a deck 50 x 20 feet, six feet from keel to deck. The *Ra Marama* was built at Somosomo, given to Cakobau who gave it to King of Tonga, made three trips to Tonga, returned to Cakobau, was 102 feet long by 18 feet wide with mast to 68 feet. Crew of 140 men. After Cakobau died, it was returned to Taveuni and left to rot. Very few *drua* existed after 1875 when British administration became well established.

drua 3. duplication or replication of a syllable (*tago*) in the formation of a word, such as *ruarua* meaning "both" from the word *rua* "two". School-teachers invented this term to help describe Fijian grammar while avoiding the use of English words. *drua-balavu* (or) *druadina* refers to replications that have two syllables (*tagoirua*), as in *ilakolako*, or three syllables (*tagoitolu*) as in *qiqiqi*. If only a single syllable is repeated, as in *rorogo*, the replication is known as a short one: *drualeka*.

drudru, drudruga v. to slit and remove outer skin with inner bark of shrub, such as mulberry, in production of bark-cloth (*masi*), wild hibiscus (*vau*) for fibre, cinnamon bark for quills, and skin of cassava, preparatory to cooking. Also to remove bark from plants like *qatima*, Urena lobata, to obtain cordage. *drudru na kulina me wa.* remove the skin to make cordage. Also may refer to skinning of animals.

drudru adj. dull-witted, of a person.

drudrula adj. tasteless, off-flavour, of water that is stale, brackish, not clean and fresh, or of the juice of some fruits such as melon, mango, pineapple when they are off-flavour.

druga n. windpipe of throat, bronchial tube(s).

drugudrugu(a) ad. smelly (person, place, thing).

drugu, druguta v. to add bass voice(s), chorus, to the singing lead. *na idrugu* the chorus. *druguta!* join in! (the chorus). *laga sere* to lead off a song.

druka 1. to fail, lose (game, fight). *vakadruka* to defeat. *vakadrukai* defeated.

druka 2. by extension, idiomatically, to be amazed, astonished, dumbfounded. *vakadrukai e na kena levu* astonished at the amount of it. *Au sa druka ena nomu yaloqaqa.* I am astonished by your bravery. *veivakadrukai* amazing.

druma adj. stupid, awkward, inept.

drusi harsh loud whistle to catch someone's attention.

druti, drutia, drutilaka v. pull off leaves of grass, trees, as for making Fiji medicines, or pulling out weeds by hand. May also apply to a rope snapping from a forceful pull. Often used of children or two women fighting, pulling the hair aggressively.
  Idiom: *drutia* v. to dash off to escape suddenly.

druti (Nait.) v. to nip, pull our grass or weeds, and may extend to cleaning lawn around house or cleaning a garden.

drutidruti v. weeding, pulling of weeds by hand, *drutilaka* if done forcefully.

dua 1. one (as a cardinal number). *e dua, rua, tolu* one, two, three. *e dua na drau* one hundred. *e dua na tamata* one person (a person, some person). *e dua ga* one only. *duadua* unique, exceptional, special. *duabau* (or) *dua bulu* unique, only one.

dua 2. the indefinite article **a.** *E dua na nomu isele?* Do you have a knife?

dua 3. someone. *Sa lako mai e dua.* Someone came. *Dua mada e taki mai!* Someone pour a drink. *taudua* alone as one person. *yadua* each. *vakayadua* each one (by him/her/itself).
  Idiom: *Dua mai keri!* "Your turn!" (to speak, tell a story, entertain the group). This is said by someone who has just finished telling a yarn.

vakadua *vakadua* ever, once and for all, permanently. *Sa oti vakadua.* It is completely finished. *Sega vakadua!* Never! *sega ... vakadua* never. *vakacegu vakadua* died (polite term). *lako vakadua* gone permanently, forever. *Vosa vakadua* n. Chief Justice.

duabau adj. unique, one of a kind. *na luvedrau duabau* their (2) only child. Syn. *duabulu*.

dua bulu adj. unique, single, only one. *E dua bulu ga.* It is unique. Syn. *duabau*.

duadua adj. unique, exceptional, best.

Dua O! a call to announce one's arrival outside a house, wishing to enter. It should be done from a respectful distance. The response is *O i Dua!* for the visitor to enter. Several people inside may add to the welcome, crying out *Dua O!* Such calls are referred to as *tama*, which can be a verb or a noun. The exact words vary from region to region. The tendency today is to drop such niceties except in conservative villages. Some Fijians prefer to approach a house quietly, even secretly, and listen before they make their presence known. In earlier days such behaviour would be punished severely.

duatani adj. strange, different (usually not good), unfamiliar, not the same.

Duatolu Tabu (Roman Catholic) n. Holy Trinity. Syn. *Lewe Tolu Vakalou*.

duavata adj. united. *vakaduavata-taka* v. to unite.

dubi, dubia, dubilaka v. to punch with the fist. *e dua na idubi* n. a punch.

dudu 1. adj. brave in the sense of standing out, willing to express opinions or fight by onself.

dudu 2. adj., n. inflated (balloon, tyre), heaped up, high and full (gravel pile, mountain), swollen, swelled out, protruding (cheeks, stomach, breasts). *gusu dudu* sullen. *sucu dudu* protruding breasts (woman). *dudu i wai* protruding into the water (or sea). *ulu dudu* protruding brow (usually of a person). *na dudu* n. the protuberance.

dudu 3. (Rewa) adj., n. deaf. Elswhere the word is usually *didivara* or *didi*.

vakadudu-i-le adj. difficult (of person), sullen and uncooperative.

dugu n. or v. rumbling sound (sea, pigeon, human's deep voice). *sa dugu mai na domo i Seru ni sa yaco me cauravou* Seru's voice deepened as he became a youth. *vadugu* usually refers to the sound of the sea on the reef.
  Idiom: *dugu ga na saqa lala* lierally, the empty vessel makes a deep resounding sound, an Anglicism adapted from the English idiom, suggesting that the person who has nothing useful to say makes the most noise.

dugua 1. (Archaic) n. Death or severe disability resulting from too close a contact with a chief; magical influence of a chief, an awesome power mentioned by A. C. Reid (*Tovata,* Part 1, p. 20), as the probable source of the name of Tugua Island, in Ha'apai, Tonga, residence of the sacred Tamaha, and part of the estate of Fale Fisi chief, Tu'i Ha'ateiho. Mara Kapaiwai (the early one) visited the Tamaha and revived the connection between Tugua and his native island Moala.

dugua 2. (or) **dugudugua** adj. somewhat soiled or sullied with age and wear, dusty (house, car, object, not usually a person, physically). In describing objects, this is not always negative. *Sa rui dugudugua na nomu vakasama.* You have developed a dirty mind.

duguca v. to make formal request for a woman in marriage. This has usually involved the presentation of a whale tooth with ceremony by the family making the proposal, not the prospective husband himself. *duguca mai na yalewa.* Syn. *vosaki.*

dugu, duguna v. to heap up (clothes, gravel, fruit).

dui particle implying separateness, difference, various, each one, both, individually. *Era dui dro.* They all ran off in different direction. *Dui tamata yadua e kila na nona itavi.* Each person knows what he has to do. *Dui yalona tu na tamata.* People have their own different way of thinking. *Ko Viti e dui tu ga na kena turaga.* Fiji has various chieftains (not only one). *Seru, Opeti, Semesa kei na dui watidratou.* Seru, Opeti, Semesa and their respective wives. *duikaikai* people of various different origins (British, Chinese, Fijian, Indian for example). *duiroka* variously coloured, variegated. *dui yaloyalo* of a different mind, with different feelings, said of people.

Idiom: *dui tu tu* each one located in a separate place.

Idiom: *dui tau tau* of individual things, fallen in several disparate places (fruit from a tree, parts of a car from a crash).

Idiom: *Dui mate ga ena nona ucu ni vatu.* The implication is that each person is ready to die defending his home territory. In fact, practically no Fijian tribe has ever lived for any great length of time in any one place. On the basis of Ratu Sukuna's research, virtually no tribe continued living in the place (*yavutu*) where it was formed. Nonetheless, a close attachment to the land is quickly formed. Here the notion is that when cornered, a Fijian will fight to the death.

duidui adj., n. difference, different, separate. *Duidui mai na ka oqo mai vei na ka oqori.* This thing is different from that thing. *Sa duidui o Seru.* Seru is different from all others. *na kena duidui* the difference

vakaduidui-taka v. to differentiate, discriminate, show prejudice.

vakaduidui-le adj. having independent, different and divisive ways, non-conformist who is indifferent or opposed to the group norms.

duka adj. and n. dirty, dirt. *Sa rui duka na yalomu.* You have a dirty mind. It is an Anglicism to apply this word to the mind. To earlier Fijians, dirt was just physical dirt.

vakadukaduka v. to soil, to dirty.

dukadukali adj. very dirty (but can be cleaned). *Me kakua ni dukadukali nomu ivakarau.* Don't develop bad habits. Syn. *dukaveluvelu.*

duka-veluvelu adj., n. extremely dirty disgustingly dirty.

duki, dukia v. to slap, clap the water making a sound, usually to direct fish into a net or trap.

dula! hush! (affectionate, consoling, for babies, loved ones). After the fact, *dula* implies that the baby has been quieted.

dula, dulaka 1. v. to extend, raise (hand, arm, weapon, tool). *dulaka na ligamu* raise up your hand (arm). It is a modernism to say, in literal translation from English, "raise the hand" *laveta na ligamu.*

dula, dulaka 2. v. to give an order to do something. *Sa dulaka na turaga ni koro na ka me caka.* The village administrator ordered the things to be done.

dulali (Archaic) n. Fijian nose-flute (*bitu vakatagi* or *bitu ceguvi*), now known only in the museum, and in a few coastal areas, unknown in the highlands. Fijians never had any romantic music; that concept is Polynesian. Ramacake was legendary player on Makogai Island whose music attracted the women of Bau. They looked for him in LomaiViti, and he, being very shy, misdirected them to avoid them finding him. He thought himself ugly, possibly due to leprosy.

dule n. ear-wax. *Savata na dule ni daligamu.* Clean out the wax from your ear.

dulu, duluka (Vulgar) v. to fornicate, have sexual intercourse. *veidulu* fornication. Syn., *cai, caita.* See *veiyacovi.*

duludulumata n. (Archaic) ten bundles of *dalo* at a formal presentation ceremony. For such occasions, counting of the goods used this traditional number system, in this case, so many tens of bundles of *dalo*. Some Fijians consider this to amount to be 100 of the taro tubers, assuming ten in each bundle. In fact, it is approximate.

dulumi 1. n. tree-stump.

dulumi 2. adj. bald-headed. A person with a bald shaved head may be referred to as being *tasi dulumi.* Syn. *cou.*

dumu, dumuka v. to open out (umbrella, boat-sail), also, to pick certain fruit by hand or with a long stick to poke tree-fruit (usually poke the fruit-stem) to bring down fruit (breadfruit, mango, *kavika, dawa,* oranges). The implication is of lifting up and then taking down. *me dumu na taunamu* let down the mosquito net (closing it). Also applied to opening the shutter windows, hinged at the top, common of colonial houses but also Fijian houses in modern times. (Traditionally Fijian houses had no windows and also no swinging doors.)

dumudumu-kuro n. edible jellyfish. It is boiled, Netrostoma sp. Syn. *drose*. (Note that *Na iVolavosa VakaViti*, page 148, considers *dumudumu-kuro* distinct from *drose* and, unlike *drose*, not eaten.

duna n. river eel. Three main types are the *diria* (clear-water eel), the *badamu* (mud eel), and the *tautaubale* (rock eel). There is also a moray eel in the rivers, that is not usually eaten, and has a very nasty bite; see *dararikai*, above. *laki ta duna* go catching eels. They are caught by hand, or by hand-net, or light fishing line. Bait used is a shelled shrimp or tiny fish (its natural food), or guts from another eel; worms may be used in daytime. With a line, one patiently lets the eel swallow the bait deeply, then pulls it in easily. The eel is subdued by hitting or cutting its tail, not its head, for the tail is the motive force. In catching by hand, the fingers are inserted into the gills, or directly into the mouth, pushing in hard. To attempt to pull out the finger too soon results in a very painful, injured finger. The eel's teeth are deeply raspy (not like a snake's) and are very effective at removing skin painfully. Eels are edible, but in some areas of the mainland it is an aquatic totem, and is not eaten. Eels breed in the sea, the young transformed into transparent "glass eels" when they encounter fresh water, become darker in colour and, known in English as elvers, they migrate upstream in the rivers, even against forceful currents. (The migration is described by Paddy Ryan, author of *Fiji's Natural Heritage*.) Syn. (West) *tuna*.

durabu adj. disrespectful, a term not much used.

duri 1. v. sit up, straighten up or stand up, make an upward movement. *Duri mada lai kauta mai na ka oya* Get up and bring that thing here. *Duri cake!* Straighten up in a sitting posture, or Stand up! depending on context. *Duri vakadodonu!* Stand up straight! *gone duriduri* baby who has just learned to stand (but not walk).

duri 2. v. to set up, as of a fallen fence post, a flagpole, telephone pole, house-post.

vakaduria v. set it up (bottle fallen over, a club or business that is being established). *vakaduria e dua na bisinisi* (Anglicism) v. to establish a business.

duruduru (ni liga-na) n. elbow. Syn. *duru ni liga*, *ilokiloki ni liga*.

duru-na 1. n. knee (person, animal). *tekiduru* v. to kneel.
Idiom: *ucu mai duru* unbelievable, tall tale (lit. like a nose growing out of the knee).

duru-na 2. n. vertical post (house, telephone pole), keel (boat). Syn. (Polyn.) *bou*. Idiom: *duruvesi* n. key supporter, mainstay (person.) *vesi* is a "noble" wood.

duru 3. prefix or suffix, as in *duruliu* prefix, *durumuri* suffix, words invented by language teachers who try to avoid direct usage of English.

duruka n. delicious vegetable, "Fiji asparagus", Saccharum edule. *duruka vulavula* white *duruka*, grows in damp locations, the unopened flower shoots harvested annually around April. *duruka damudamu* red *duruka*, grows best on somewhat drier ground, and is prone to rot (due to rain penetrating the "husks"), yields twice a year, around March or April and again in November. The fruits of red *duruka* are smaller and in texture are drier than white *duruka*. *Duruka* is perhaps best cooked by grilling over embers, or simmered in coconut cream. Also eaten raw, sliced in salads, by resident Europeans.

dusi, dusimaka v. to point (as with the finger), to indicate, point out.

dusi, dusia v. to indicate, point, to point at. *Dusivaka vei koya na ka me kau mai*. Indicate to him the thing that is to be brought here. *dusia na sala* point the way (the path, or figuratively, the way to do something). Syn. (West, Rewa, Kadavu, Lau) *duci*.

idusidusi n. indicator, indication, instructions, guidelines, suggestions, and by extension, *idusidusi ni turaga* index finger (anciently, only a chief might point with the finger). *ivola dusidusi* n. book or pamphlet of instructions, guidebook, or more simply one may simply say *idusidusi*.

duta v. put together (of two or more things, people, ideas) to be as one. Can be two adjoining pieces of land to be treated as one, tables placed together *vakaduta vata* put them together. *Me rau duta*. Consider them as one. To match up two.

veidutaitaka to compare. *Ni veidutaitaki na isau ni dovu kei na isau ni yaqona . . .* When the price of sugar is compared to the price of *yaqona . . .* *me veidutataki* to match up (two or more things that go together, as sometimes requested in a school exam paper.)

dutua n. wooden "anvil" on which barkcloth is beaten (*samu*) to join the pieces and smooth it out. It is a familiar sound in some outlying coastal villages. *kuveti* n. stencil for applying a pattern design on bark-cloth.

duva (or **tuva**) n., v. plant(s) used to poison fish, the roots pounded and placed in a cloth-like sac, especially Tephrosia sp., Pittosporum spp. and Derris trifoliata, coastal shrub with pale pink flowers, rich in natural pyrethrum. What has been called *duva ni niukini* (New Guinea *duva*), introduced, is D. malaccensis. The poisoned fish are perfectly edible. They float to the surface. Curiously, crustaceans are not affected by the poison. The poison itself is fatal to human if consumed, as evidenced by a case of a suicide. Leaves are also macerated and used to heal wounds, applied externally. *vakaduva na wai* poison the water (with *duva*). By extension, *duva* can refer to black magic: *Kemu duva sa caka tiko.* Black magic is being made against you. Modernly, Fijians may use dangerous agricultural chemicals (often stolen) to poison fish and prawns that they sell by the side of the road.

duva, duvana v. to apply poison deliberately, either to fish (see above) or humans. *duvani* poisoned, of fish or humans. Poison for humans was usually mixed in with *yaqona* to be drunk by the unsuspecting victim. Poisons used included the *duva kalou,* Pittosporum, five species, fish poisons, and in the Naitasiri highlands, *lobau* Brugmansia suevolens, poison for humans, these days more commonly known as *davui* or Angel's trumpet, introduced shrub closely related to Datura, Jimson weed, a known intoxicant. Also *mavu ni Toga,* again a human poison, Antiaris toxicaria, Moraceae, a not very common tree with bright crimson flowers. I have noted it in Tailevu, perhaps an introduction via Tonga. This taxon has provided many of the poisons used for centuries in Southeast Asia. The Fiji variety is somewhat less toxic than some of the Asian ones. In Fiji a poison would only have to disable a person. A club to the head could finish the job.

duvu n. uterus, womb. Syn. *kato ni gone*.

duvu lutu n. Fijian medical problem of women when the womb has seemed to descend. This is adjusted manually by an older woman, and is often done while the patient is seated in water. One uses the verb *sili* for this action, as if bathing. *Sa tarai na nona duvu.* Her uterus has been manipulated.

duvu as used in *vuniduvu,* this refers to a composer of traditional exhibition dances (*meke*). This is a very presitigious position. People formally request the composer to compose a *meke* for them. He composes, trains those people, and then transmits it so that it "belongs" to that group. No other people should perform that *meke* without persmission. The composer is well rewarded. Syn. *daunivucu*.

E

The letter **e** is pronounced just as the **e** in the English words **end** or **bell**.

E 1. particle that may go before a verb beginning a sentence.

e 2. in (or) at (only when the speaker is located at that place). *e Suva* in Suva (speaker in Suva).

e 3. particle in front of some words that indicate location or direction (sometimes it is written as part of the main word): *e loma ni vale* inside the house. *e tuba* outside. *e ra* down, beneath; *e cake* up, upwards; *e daku-na* behind it/him/her. *e mata-na* in front of it/him/her. *ena dela ni teveli* on top of the table. *ena ruku ni teveli* underneath the table. *e ke* here (properly *eke*). *e keri* there (where the listener is, properly *ekeri* or *ikeri*). *e kea* over there (where neither the speaker or listener are located, properly *ekea* or *ekeya*). *e vei?* where? Fiji's official grammarian insists that *e na* should be printed as *ena* though many people do not follow that rule.

e 4. particle that may appear in front of numbers, or quantities: *e tolu* three. *e so* some. *e so tale* some more. *e vica?* how many?

e 5. particle that may appear in front of some words indicating time: *edaidai* today. *vaka-edaidai* current, modern, of these times; *e naica?* when? *ena bogi* at night. *ena gauna ni ivalu* in time of war. *ena noa* yesterday. *ena mataka ni mataka* tomorrow morning. *ena mataka* tomorrow. Again, an official grammarian insists on joining the *e* with the *na*. Actual custom varies greatly.

e 6. particle in front of pronouns especially when the pronoun is the subject of the sentence, or begins the sentence, as in: *e ratou = eratou, e ra = era*. Properly this *e* should be attached, not separated, according to the modern rules imposed by Cabinet decision.

e 7. particle with other meanings, such as concerning, about, for, over, on, with. **7a**. concerning, for. *kudru ena isau ni kakana* angry about the price of food. *yabaki tolu ena butako* three years (prison) for theft. **7b**. on. *rogoca na qito ena walesi* listen to the game on the radio (wireless). **7c**. with. *laki vuli ena veivuke ni sikolasivi*. go to school with the help of a scholarship. Again, Fiji's official grammarian now joins the *e* to the *na*.

ecanolo (Eng.) ethanol, much spoken of as vegetable fuel of the future.

ece 1. (Lau) v. to squat on one's heels.

ece 2. v. to shift without raising (a thing such as a pot on a stove), shift without rising (a person, as when moving closer to a food-mat). A duck is thought to walk in this way: *Sa ece tiko yani na ga*. The duck is waddling away.

ece 3. (Cakau.) v. to sit at rest.

ece 4. (Cakau.) alone. *Oi au ece* (or) *kece*. I alone.

eda we (many). *Eda kila ni da cala*. We (many) know that we are wrong.

edaru we (two people). Also *kedaru*.

edatou we (several), abbrev. *Tou*. Also *kedatou*.

edaidai today Syn. *nikua*.

edita (Eng.) n. editor.

ei (or) **eu** (Interjection) rejection of something clearly unsuitable.

eke (or) **e ke** here, most properly *eke*. *eke ga* right here.

Ekelesia (Roman Catholic) The Roman Catholic Church.

e keri (or) **i keri** there (where you are), most properly *ekeri*.

eketea (Eng.) n. hectare (2.471 acres).

eki adj. disgusting, "yuk", as in *eki na boto mate* the dead toad is "yuk".

ele (Vanua Levu) n. woman's private parts. Syn. *tele*. The word may be used freely in most of Cakaudrove, but not in Bua.

Elei! (Vanua Levu) Interjection of lament, rejection or disgust. *Oilei* is the more common word throughout Fiji.

elevaniti n. (Eng.) elephant. None in Fiji but historically there had been correspondence with U.S. Government as to the possible use of elephants as work animals. Syn. *elefadi*.

eli (Eng.) n. hell.

eli, elica 1. v. to combine two or more food ingredients (in a pot).

eli, elica 2. v. to remove (something). *Elica na buka* Remove some of the burning firewood. Syn, *talaca*.

elikoputa (Eng.) n. helicopter.

Emeni (Eng.) Amen. Syn. *Ameni*.

ena (or) **e na** in, or in the, or during, as in *ena vula sa oti* during last month. *ena rua na siga* in two days. Preferred spelling by official grammarian is *ena* though many educators disagree very strongly.
enanoa tomorrow.
Epereli (or) **Evereli** (Eng.) n. April. The **p** is more common in Lau, Cakaudrove. The **v** is used more often in Tailevu, Naitasiri, Ra.
eqe v. to walk in a lop-sided way, with unequal balance between the two legs. May be due to one or more of several medical causes. One common view is that this is brought on by an irritation of the genitals, sometimes thought to be caused by excessive love-making. *Eqe* may become the butt of unkind jokes.
era they (many) or he/she (of high chief).
era (or) **ira** below, as opposed to *e cake,* above. This applies to relative height but *ira* may refer to the west, downwind of the speaker's location. Similarly *e cake* may refer to an upwind direction or uphill direction.
eratou (or) **e ratou** they (few), properly *eratou.*
esi (Interjection) declining to answer, I am not sure, do not know.
esi (Eng.) ace, as in a deck of cards.
esikote (Eng.) n. escort, usually as a guard for people of great importance. *esikote-taka* to escort, accompany, a dignitary on official mission.
esitimeti (Eng., Methodist) formal estimate of financial needs of a local church for the coming year. Thought and planning is then given as to how these funds can be sourced and what the congregation should be asked to contribute.
eso (or) **e so** some, as in *mai na veivanua e so,* in some countries. Used at the beginning of an expression it is perhaps more customary to separate the spelling, as *e so na tamata* some people.
eteremosio (Eng.) n. extreme unction as last rites for a dying Roman Catholic.
Etikoqe (Eng.) Aide-de-camp, formerly serving the Governor. May be heard as *Tikoqe.*
Eu! interjection of pain, or of rejection, disgust, especially in response to something said, or something offered. As with most expressions, this may be said in jest. One sometimes hears *U!*
evei (or) **e vei** where (as a question).
Evereli (Eng.) n. April. Syn. *Epereli.*
evu v. to grow big, espec. of the body.
evu-evu n. a seaside tree, Hernandia peltata or H. nymphaeifolia, Hernandiaceae, the inner bark often used as an abortifacient. (Scientific tests on rats indicate no such effect - R.G.)

F

There is no letter **f** in mainland Fijian languages. It is the Polynesian equivalent of the Fijian **v** in many words and has been introduced by Tongans on the smaller islands, especially in Lau. Some English or Tongan words with **f** are now sometimes pronounced with that letter. The letter **v** is sometimes used in place of an **f**, except for distinctly Lauan words or for some adaptions of English words.

Faca (Eng.) Father, form of address for Roman Catholic priest.
fafatu (Lau) treat the hair with lime (*lase*) as conditioning.
"faiba" or "fibre" (Eng.) n. fibreglass boat, usually open-topped, operated by an outboard engine. in some places this has replaced the wooden punt and and small cutters used for short trips.
ifaile (or) **ifaele** (Eng.) n. file. *failetaka* v. to file, Fijians' way of sharpening knives. Bush knives (cane knives) are made of soft steel that can be sharpened readily by frequent filing. Knife-filing justifies resting between bouts of hard work cutting weeds, grass.
fainala (Eng.) n. final (in sports), referring to the last championship game. *semi-fainala* semi-finals. Can be used as a verb as well as noun.
faite (Lau) v. to sit cross-legged, as done by men.
faiwa (Lau, from Togan *faiva*) n. expertise, special skill from experience.
faka (Lau) n. spokesman-protocol officer for Lauan chief. The equiv. of *matanivanua* among mainland Fijians. Sometimes pronounced *vaka.*
fakawela (Tonga) n. spontaneous giving of gifts during dances, or functions of two different groups of people, often a man's shirt. May include money slipped into the clothes of dancers, flour sprinkled on their head. Syn. *tibivuru.*
falata or **valata** (Lau) v. to do, to make, Bauan *cakava.*
falawa 1. (Eng.) n. flour. Along with rice and cassava, this is now a main staple starch foods of Fijians, though it is much less nutritious. These introduced starches have been cheaper than traditional root crops and are less perishable. Flour is used for many fried breakfast foods.

falawa 2. (Eng., Lau) a starch food treated as *kakana dina*, "true food", such as taro or yam, cooked in earth oven and eaten at meals with a garnish (*icoi*), or at breakfast with tea. Because of the shortage of home-grown starch-foods in the smaller islands of Lau, store-bought flour is mixed with grated cassava and coconut as a basic food.

fale (Lau) n. house. Traditional Lauan houses follow Tongan style with rounded ends, rather than appearing strictly rectangular. Syn. *vale*. (West) *were, sue*.

"Fale Fisi" (Tonga) n. the clan Ha'a Fale Fisi, of the Tongan royal family, as founded by Tapu'osi, the Tui Lakeba, a Waciwaci chief who married Sinaitakala i Langileka, Tu'i Tonga Fefine, daughter of Tele'a, 29th Tu'i Tonga. The Narewadamu are true *kaiLakeba,* early chiefs of Lakeba, replaced ultimately by the Vuanirewa people of the Tui Nayau who retain a separate but similar affiliation with the Ha'a Fale Fisi. Nayau had been associated with the Moala group, both independent from Lakeba at the time, but Moala leading family was descended from Tui Naosara, son of Kubuavanua who brought back a royal wife from the sacred, royal island of Tungua in Tonga. Tui Naosara settled on Nayau and his two sons were the first Vuanirewa.

famali (Eng., Lau) n. family.
fanala (Eng.) n. funnel.
Faqa! (Interjection) Cheat! (in playing, usually marbles).
Farisi (Bib.) n. Pharisee.
vakafatu (Lau) n. Lauan chiefly serving-bowl especially for kava, the rim inlaid with pearl shell, and having twelve legs instead the the four legs that are more common elsewhere in Fiji. The artefact is Tongan in concept. *Vakafatu* (or) *vakavatu* as an Anglicism, may also refer to a very wealthy person.
fekei (Rotuma) n. traditional sweet pudding with thick coconut cream, sometimes sold in the public market. The starch basis has been mostly taro, sometimes yam. (Yams rarely used in Fijian sweet puddings).
Feperueri (or) **Veverueri** (Eng.) February.
fika 1. (Eng., Lau) adj. to be smart, clever, adept.
  Idiom (Lau): *Meca i a fika ga*, or *Meca qo na fika ga*. Literally, "The thing is to think it through", more figuratively, "(Things will be done) by hook or by crook".
fika 2. (Eng.) v. to calculate.
fika 3. (Eng.) n. arithmetic, figure.
fikataka (Eng.) v. to calculate a total (*isoqoni*) in arithmetic.
fikakere subtraction *na musumusu. 5 musu e rua sa tolu.* Five minus two is three.
fikasoqoni addition *sosoqoni. 5 kei na rua sa vitu.* Five plus two is seven.
fika-vaka-levu-taki multiplication *na vakalevutaki. 5 vakarua sa tini.* Five times two is ten.
fikawase division *na wasewase. 10 wase rua sa lima.* Ten divided by two is five.
"Fire!" (Slang) pron. "faiya!", go ahead! Begin! Let's go!
"fifty cents" (Eng, Slang) a very vulgar taunt, meaning "coward", implying a loose rectum as large as a fifty-cents coin.
filimu (Eng.) n. movie film or photographic film.
fiu 1. (Lau, Tongan "fihu") n. a type of very fine white woven sleeping mat.
fiu 2. (Lau, Tongan "fiu") tired, worn out, done in, fed up. Syn. *oca*.
"fix"-taka v. to arrange, to set up, to iron out (a problem), to fix.
"fix", "fix"-taka v. to try to win over a woman, with a desire to make love, arrange intercourse with or for someone. *Au na qai fixtaka a dua na nomu.* I will get you a partner for making love.
fokisi (Eng.) n. fox, and may refer to someone cunning like a fox. Slang: *yalewa fokisi* prostitute.
foleni (Eng.) v. to assemble in a formal group, "fall in", of soldiers, or children assembled at school.
fomani (Eng.) n. foreman.
fomu 1. (Eng.) n. form (to be filled out). *vakalewena na fomu.* fill out the form.
fomu 2. (Eng.) n. form, as a class of secondary school that in Fiji can extend through Form Seven, in preparation for possible tertiary education.
fue (Tonga) sinnet fly whisk as used by chieftains.
fuloa (Eng.) floor. Syn. *buturara*.

G

The letter G is pronounced as a soft **ng**, as in going, fling. It is not pronounced like the **ng** in anger. In western Viti Levu, **gwa** may replace the **ga**, as in *gwata* for *gata* (snake), or *tagwane* for *tagane* (man) in eastern Fiji.

ga 1. n. duck. *ga ni vatu* Peregrine falcon, rather rare in Fiji. *ga loa* (or) *ga ni Viti* Pacific Black Duck, common wild duck at rivers and coastal shores. Syn. (Lau) *pato*.
Idiom: *sili vaka ga* lit., bathe like a duck, said to a child who takes a quick, superficial bath, not bathing properly.
Idiom: *tamata daku ni ga* person who cannot listen or follow instructions. Words flow off as water from a duck's back, an Anglicism.

ga 2. only, just, a particle used with some words to limit them: *wale ga* only. *wale ga oqo* just now. *o iko ga* only you. *tiko ga* forever, always. in written Fijian this particle is often joined to the word that follows it. The expression *O iko ga!* can have romantic implications.

ga 3. v. mouth open, agape, stare, usually with a blank look. *Ga cake!* open your mouth! (as a dentist might request). *Dalaga!* open your mouth wide (as mother to child, giving medicine). *ga balavu* remain gaping, doing nothing with a blank stare into space. *Kakua ni ga balavu!* Don't gape! don't stare! (to child). *mata gaga* face agape. *ga calucalu* to be at a loose end, idle with nothing much on the mind. *igaga* n. spout, as of teapot.

gacagaca 1. n. guts, intestines. 2. by extension, equipment, spare parts for motors, engines. Syn. *iwawa* intestines.
Idiom: *ivola gacagaca* document, manual.

gade v. to walk at ease, usually for pleasure, take a pleasure trip. *au na gagade tu mai kea.* I will be walking around over there. *vale ni igagade* holiday cottage. *ilakolako vakagade* pleasure trip. *vanua ni igagade ni saravanua* tourist spot. *gade siga tolu* take a three-day trip. Syn. *gadi*. (Colo East) *gadea*.

gadi 1. (Archaic) n. a type of Fijian fighting club.

gadi 2. brother of one's mother or husband of father's sister. See below. Syn. *momo*.

gadigadi 1. n. object of romantic love.

igadigadi 2. n. place to relax and pass the time peacefully.

gadina-na and **gadi** n. a type of family relative, man, mother's brother or the husband of one's father's sister. Bauans use the term *vugo-na*.

gadre, gadreva v. to desire, want, wish for (anything). *Au bau gadreva tu meu lako* I just wish I could go. *na gagadre* the desire.

gadro-na n. palate, extending to the gums. *mate ni gadro* gum disease. *gadro lala* toothless.

gadrogadro adj. prickly, thorny (as of some trees, citrus, sago palm, some liana vines). *wa gadrogadro* a prickly vine, a wild raspberry, Rubus moluccanus. *gadro, gadrota* v. to prickle.

gadrota v. to pierce, as by a needle or thorn. Syn. *qarota*.

gafigafi (Lau) n. finely woven soft cummerbund of pandanus matting made by Tongan procedures, usually intended for formal occasions including church services. It is customary to use worn or somewhat torn matting, to give a sense of humility. This is not worn in the Moala Region (*Yasayasa Moala*), part of Lau Province, and not in some parts of northern Lau Province that are more closely related to Cakaudrove than to the more Tongan culture of Lau.

igaga n. spout, as in small, clay pot for water to be drunk. *ga* refers to mouth agape, since Fijians poured water into the mouth, the pot being held several inches above. Lips never touched the drinking vessel and there were not cups. By ext., *igaga* might modernly apply to the spout on a teapot.

gaga 1. adj. bitter, overly concentrated, distasteful, "hot" (of chili). *Sa rui gaga na kari.* The curry is very "hot". *Sa gaga na wainimate.* The medicine tastes bad.

gaga 2. adj., n. poison, poisonous, toxic, polluted. *vakagaga na wai* to pollute the water. *vakagagai* polluted. *wainimate gaga ni veivaka-mateni-taki* intoxicating drugs (*mateni* intoxicated). *E na rawa ni ko ni gaga kina.* It is possible that you could be poisoned by it. *E rawa ni vagagai ko ira na dau kania.* People who usually eat it could be poisoned.
In ancient times Fijians used at least three species of plant as poisons to be consumed by their enemies. *Duva kalou*, Pittosporum sp., Pittosporaceae, was pounded and mixed in *yaqona* (Capell, p. 64); *lobau*, Brugsmansia suaveolens (formerly Datura candida), also mixed in *yaqona* in Colo East as I have recorded in oral histories; and *mavu ni toga*, Antiaris toxicaria, Moraceae, for which I have insufficient information on how it was used. Antiaris spp. have long been used in Asia as a poison to kill humans. Apparently Fijians did not usually use poison on their arrows or spears. Used as an abortifacient were colourful (bright red and stark black) seeds of *diridamu*, Abrus precatorius, but its deadly cyanide often killed the mother as well as the foetus. Formerly, *diridamu* were used in necklaces, now forbidden due to the dangerous poison. So small and quick-acting, *diridamu* has been used in food for assassinations.

gaga adj. to be sitting idly, not knowing what needs to be done.

gagadre n. wish, desire. *A cava na nomu gagadre?* What is your desire? What would you like?

gagano, gaganotaka v. to desire secretly someone, usually sexually. Somewhat more moderately, *gano, ganova. garo, garova* v. applies to lust for a person, or some thing very greatly desired.

gagano ca n. deep-seated desire (usually sexual, usually futile).

"Gagaj" (Rotuma) n. chief in one of the seven districts of Rotuma. May be used as a title. There is no one dominant chief on the island though one eccentric character has claimed to be "King". The letter "g" is pronounced with a soft "ng", as it is in Fijian.

gagaraka v. to have an excessively strong scent.

gaga-sogo-gusu n. tetanus.

gagata n., adj. very sharp, as of a knife or spear. Syn. *momoto*, as applied to spears, pencils. *gata* sharp (and also, as a noun, for `snake).

gagavo v. desire deeply.

gagoi adj. ineffectual, useless, of a person in any endeavor. A lack of motivation or ability is implied.

gai 1. n. pet pig, or affectionate name for pigs, used to call out to pigs to come and be fed. It has been a Melanesian custom to adopt very young pet pigs, a custom discontinued in Fiji. Formerly, women sometimes nursed them at the breast. Syn. *geti*.

gai 2. (Vanua Levu) v. do not want. *Au gai ni la'o.* I don't want to go.

gai (or) **gaigaiya 3.** n., adj. a colour, light or soft yellowish (can have brownish or dusky tone) usually referring to wilted vegetation or to faded, sullied cloth, not usually to human skin.

galala adj. free, independent, available. *Sa tu vagalala o Seru* Seru is living (and farming) alone, outside of the village and legally free of usual traditional obligations. *na tu-galala nei Viti* the independence of Fiji. *O galala?* Are you available (free)? *Me galala na nomu vakasama.* Free your mind (do not worry). By extension, may indicate that some item of clothing is too large, too slack about the body. *Sa galala tu na nomu tarusese.* Your pants are loose (too big). Colonial authorities established a system whereby a Fijian individual or nuclear family could be released from village and clan responsibilites to be independent (*galala*). Although Ratu Sukuna himself lived independently of any clan or village responsibilities, he discouraged that system for Fijians generally, believing they were not ready for it. The system failed partly because independent Fijians usually lived close to their village, and villagers by custom would not release them from traditional obligations.

vagalala, vagalalataka v. to make free, available, to clear off or out or away. *vagalalataka na teveli* clear off the table. *vagalalataka na vale* clear out the house (make it free, available). *me vagalala na rumu* to vacate the room. *vagalalataki iko mai vei iratou* stay away from them.

gale 1. have one's head tilted to one side and/or supported with a hand, usually indicating lack of interest, attention, relaxed *Sa vagalegale tu ga o Seru* Seru has his head to one side of his shoulder (can be with head in hand).

gale 2. n.,v. to eat, something to eat, idiom from *galegale* jaw. *A cava na ka ni gale?* What is to eat? What are we having for food?

galegale-na n. molar(s), side teeth, side of the jaw.

vagalegale v., adv. to be relaxed, even when doing something. *E a taubale vagalegale sobu mai.* He walked down here relaxedly.

gale, vagaleta 1. v. to need, care about. *Au sega ni galeti iko* I do not need you. *Au sega ni vagaleta na bia* I do not care for beer.

gale, galeta, galeleta 2. v. to care for, desire, to be motivated with interest. *Kevaka e sega ni galeleta na yalomu na cauravou oqori, kakua ni gole vua.* If your heart does not strongly care for that young man, do not go to him. Syn. *galele*.

galili adj. lonely.

ga-litolito adj. of child who is curious, independent, picking up things and leaving them somewhere else; of adult who sees things and picks them up without asking. A loner who is not properly socialised.

galo (Colo) n. night. *Ma lutu mai na galo.* The night is falling. *vakagalo* afternoon. *vakagalo* have dinner.

galu, galuva v., adj. to be silent (of person) speechless, dumb. *Galu!* Shut up! Fijians are taught not to speak in the presence of their elders. *galuva* to be silent in relation to someone or something. See *tiko lo*.

galugalu adj. quiet, silent (person), rarely speaking.

vagagalu adj. silent, as in *Sa dua na bogi vagagalu.* It is a silent night.

galu, galuva, galuvaka v. to be silent, speechless, dumb, to be silent in relation to someone, or some people, *galuva. E galuvi au na ganequ.* My sister may not speak with me (man speaking). *galuvaka* v. to be silent about it, deliberately, to clam up. *vagaluya na gone* to quiet down the child. *Na* *vakagalu ni gusumu!* This will shut you up! *Galu!* Be silent! *Galu na gusumu!* Shut your mouth! *Galu mada!* Quiet down! *vagagalu* to make someone be silent. In the face of direct questions, a Fijian may assume the right to remain silent. (Silence, or non-response may often mean "no" to a request.) See *Tiko lo!*.

vagaluya v. to remain deliberately silent through self-interest, to avoid getting involved or found out, to avoid revealing something. *E so na ka eda dau vakagaluya.* Some things we do not talk about.

veigaluvi n. silence (no people talking). May refer, for example, to the prohibition of speech between father and daughter-in-law. Also, formerly, a brother and sister might not converse.

galui v. do something a second time to do it better. *na kena igalui* the second try, which will complete it. Could apply to burning off garden again, or to an additional ceremony that will satisfy people that it has been done properly.

gane-na n. sibling of the opposite sex, sister (of male), brother (of female). *E rau sa veiganeni.* They (two) are brother and sister. *na gane i Siteri* Esther's brother. This has been a *tabu* relationship, no talking, looking, or any contact, unless the sister is older, acting in motherly role. *na veiganeni* the brother and sister.

ganei n. father's sister, abbrev. from *gane i tamaqu*; now often further abbreviated as *nei*.

ganita v. to be suitable, appropriate, match (of clothes). *Sa veiganiti vinaka na nona vosa.* His/her words were apt, appropriate. *Erau veiganiti na nomu vava kei na nomu vinivo.* Your shoes and your dress match nicely. *E ganiti iko na sote oqori.* That shirt really suits you. *Na ka o ganita!* That's what you deserve! *Na itotogi e veiganiti kei na cala.* The punishment fits the crime. *E sega ni veiganiti me kaburaki ena walesi.* It is not appropriate to broadcast on the radio.

ga ni vatu n. Peregrine falcon. Syn. (Northern Lau) *tuitui*. Black head, breast, flank and thighs striped black on cream. Staple diet is Flying Fox fruit bat, finches, pigeons, some sea birds. Eyrie on cliffs, 3-4 white eggs with brown blotches. Watling says the long pointed wings and long tail are distinctive.

gano, ganova v. to gape or stare with desire, to lust after.

gara, garata v. to snarl wildly, angrily, snort. *ucu gara* makes a wild angry face (or, simply) have large wide nostrils with a flat nose. *Kua ni garata na gone.* Don't snarl at the kid(s). *E garati au mai o koya* He shouted snarlingly at me just now. *Kua ni gara.* don't shout angrily. Syn. *kara*.

garegare v. to like to eat immature fruit, as in pregnancy. Syn. *bati vou*.

garo, garova v. to have a strong desire for (a food or drink), or lust after (a person, sex).

garogaro adj. having rabid desire (a food, drink), or lustful (with sexual desire). See *vorivori*.

gasa v. to want something that will never give satisfaction. *Na ka o gasa!* That's what you yourself wanted! (often said sarcastically).
Idiom: *dau gasa yawa* always wants the inaccessible. Often said of a person who stays away from home, feeling more comfortable elsewhere.

gasagasa adj. tasty, delicious, nicely sweet. *mata gasagasa* cute, sexually attractive (of person). *vagasagasa-taka* v. to make a food or beverage tasty or sweet, as in adding a condiment. *igasagasa* n. sweetener, condiment, such as salt.

gasau n. reed, arrow. *gasau kuro* n. bomb. *gasau nunu* torpedo. *gasau ni dakai* bullet. Various kinds of reeds are *gasau saisai* (= *gasau lailai*) used for multi-pronged fishing spears and formerly for arrows, *gasau dina* used for house-walls, fish-fences. Reeds also served commonly as toilet paper before the innovation of newspapers. (See Roth, *Fijian Way of Life*, p. 40). Flowering of reeds, Miscanthus floridulus, occurs around February-March, signaling a time of flies, and a time of conjunctivitis (*cika*). In western Viti Levu, reeds were commonly used for the walls and roofs of native houses. Syn. (West) *sina*. (Nadro) *hina*.
Idiom: *Daru qai laki sota ki na gasau leka.* We are not likely to meet again, lit. We will meet next at the place where the short reed grows (at Bua, supposedly the jumping-off place to the next world, after death).

gasau-kuro n. bomb. *na vakalutu gasaukuro.* the bombing.

gasau mokimokiti (Archaic) n. cannon balls.

gasi v. (Vanua Levu) to refuse.

gata adj. sharp. *vagata.* to sharpen (knife, axe). *rui gata* very sharp.

gata n. snake, the Pacific Boa, Candoia bibroni, a harmless, nocturnal tree-climber that gives live birth on the ground, a couple of dozen babies at a time, preferably in a damp place. Most of the day is motionless, high in the treetops, so most Fijians have never seen one. (Many Fijians these days live in the cities, towns or suburbs.) The diet is lizards, rats, flying foxes (fruit bats), birds. A common length is one meter but the boa can grow to two meters. Locally, the boa has its colour variations which led people to think there were several species, and the personality can become a quite snappy in some places, Kabara, for example. Males have tiny vestigial claspers or spurs around the cloaca. Formerly, necklaces were sometimes made of the snake's back-bones. Modernly, Fijians might generally refer to all or any snakes as *gata*. In Fiji there are no venomous land snakes that ever bite people. The small, to 15 inch *bolo,* Ogmodon vitiensis, is deadly poisonous but is shy, very rarely seen, and has never been known to bite anyone. The boa was eaten in Taveuni, Ovalau, Namosi, and Kadavu and in the highlands of Viti Levu (Namosi and Colo East) and probably other places. Tavuki people of Taveuni bred snakes for the Tui Cakau to eat. In some places the snake is sacred, and may be a totem. At village Somosomo on Taveuni Island it has had ritual significance. Similarly on Kadavu Island, village Naikorokoro, Sanima District, tribe Suesue, there has been great ritual significance to the snake; they kept a *bai ni gata*, snake pit in a pile of rocks, and practised ceremonies that revitalised the people.

Reverance for the snake brings up a connection between the Vusaratu people of Nacula Island and those Colo East highlanders of tribe Nakorovatu who have revered a snake-god called Tui Drolo where *drolo* refers to murky or muddy water. Nacula's Vusaratu people opted to become Tribe Drola (sic) which again refers to murky waters (from algae) of the bay where they arrived and settled. Nothing more is known of their old relationship. It is well known that the ancestral god Degei takes the form of a snake at the Nakauvadra mountain range in northern Viti Levu. His movements turning over his body in a cave explain any thunder that is heard but he is quite inoffensive, little interested in human affairs, if at all. Degei was the name of a legendary immigrant chief, later deified. Some oral history refers to Degei I and Degei II. Syn. (Colo East, Namosi) *balei*.

gato 1. n. glottal stop that in pronunciation replaces the **t** in parts of Ra and western Vanua Levu, and replaces the **k** in eastern Vanua Levu. *gatotaka na t.* put a glottal stop in place of the letter **t**. *Sa gatotaki na k mai Bua.* The letter **k** is replaced with a glottal stop in Bua. In some Vanua Levu areas both the **t** and the **k** are replaced by glottal stops; this is referred to as *gato rua*, another term newly invented by school teachers.

gato 2. adj. able to speak a local dialect as if from that area.

gato, gatova v. to peer, peek, usually secretly or without disturbing.

gatu (Lau) n. large barkcloth used in presentation ceremonies. There are two kinds, *gatu vakaToga* and *gatu vakaViti*. The Tongan type used freely hand-painted design, mostly with tan colour, and often has writing relevant to the occasion. The Fijian type has more formal geometric design using stencils and often, darker colouring.

gau n. major or principal section or part of something, mid-section, suggesting large size. *gaunisala* roadway, path. *gau ni vosa* main body of a speech. *gau ni kau* chunk of wood. *gau levu* big bodied, stocky (person, animal). Syn. *tolo-na*.

Idiom: *gau kau* beat someone with a stick. In jocular jibing with a person from Gau Island, one hears the term *Gau kau* that calls to mind the supposedly great power of the Gau people. In fact, that power has been more imaginary than real. The expression usually raises a smile.

Idiom: *silima na gau ni dali* to intrude in a conversation, lit. dive for the middle (rather than the end) of a rope fallen in the water.

gau (Onam.) meaow, the cry of a cat.

gauna n. time. *ena gauna vou* in modern times. *ena so na gauna* sometimes. *ena gauna kece ga* at all times. *ena gauna oya* at that time. *ena veigauna eso* sometimes, occasionally. *ena veigauna vakaKaloni* in Colonial times. *e veiveigauna* at various times. *na gauna ni liliwa* (*katakata*) the time of cold (hot) season. *gauna ni vuata* fruit season (tree-fruit: bananas, citrus, etc.) *ena veigauna sa bera mai.* in times to come, in the future. *vagauna* sometimes, occasional, occasionally. *E vagauna ga na kena vua.* The fruit is only seasonal. *vagaunataka na veitau cici* to time the running race. *vakagauna* occasional, occasionally (more commonly *vagauna*.)

Gaunavou n. "New Era", a name adopted by Apolosi R. Nawai (ca. 1877-1946) renegade political dissident, to express the importance of his indigenous movement. He first formed an association called *Soqosoqo ni Gauna Vou*. His commercial enterprise Viti Kabani "Fiji Company" collapsed and he was detained by government authorities at the instance of Ratu Sukuna who had him deported to New Zealand, and then exiled, first to Yacata Island, later to die at Yanuca Island (just off Qamea Island). He had led a flamboyant personal life and had a large following as a sort of indigenous prophet. Some of his conceptual ideas had been good and constructive but his own self-interest, opposition to government, flamboyant life-style and cavalier mis-management led to his own failure. The word *Gaunavou* is still occasionally used by Fijians for some new venture, more mundane than Nawai's vision.

gauniliga-na n. forearm (human).

gaunisala 1. n. road. See *sala* path.

gaunisala 2. n. by ext., means, ways. *Me taurivaki eso na gaunisala me cakava.* Use some means of doing it.
Idiom: *Mo muria na nomu gaunisala.* You are to follow proper protocol, as in the formalities of entering a village, or approaching a chief. Formal communications were supposed to follow traditional paths.

gauniyava-na n. calf (of the human leg).

gavu adj. off-condition, pale, weak, worn out, dirty, of people or materials such as clothes, matting, barkcloth. *gavugavu* cowardly.

gavui adj. useless to others, ineffectual (of a person), uncooperative, listless and lazy, implicitly dirty. In Ra this word can be slang for "naughty". Syn. *gavu-sa.*

gawai adj. mentally vacant, of unfocussed mind, droopy headed, inattentive to present surroundings. May imply sleepy headed.

gede, gedea v. to rock back and forth, to shake, or bob up and down (as in mixing a cocktail). *gedea na gone lailai* rock the baby. *vagedegedea na lori* rock the truck (to move it). *gedea na tavaya ni sucu* shake the milk bottle. *gedea na niu* shake the coconut (to check for presence of internal liquid). *tatagedegede* toss about, as a small boat in rough seas. See *gude, gudea.* Syn. *kurea.*

gedegede rocking about, rumbling (thunder), bobbing up and down (fishing float in the water). See *vude* to bob up and down.

vaka-ta-gedegede-taka v. to classify, set a standard or set an example.

ivaka-ta-gedegede n. class, classification, standard, example (that demonstrates a standard), relative quality. *na ivakatagedegede ni qito.* the standard of playing (sports).

gege v. to open up the ripe *ivi* nut (Polynesian chestnut), or open the *kai* (mussel).

gelegele v. wobble, as something not firmly in place.

vagelegelei adj. proud of bearing.

gera adj., v. lame, to limp. *yava gera* game leg.

vageregere, vageregerea v. to have rhythmic fluctuation, as in the throbbing of a drum (Fijian *lali*). *na vageregerea ni lali.*

gesa v. to crash, usually of something heavy falling.

geti n. pet pig. Syn. *gai.*

gi v., n. buzz, as of mosquitos.

gi, givaka v. to squeak (bat), squeal (pig), yelp (dog, person), buzz (mosquito). *Na cava e givaka na vuaka?* What's the pig squealing about? Children make the sound *gi* in teasing and reproaching each other. It goes with a facial expression and sometimes pinching. In former times, warriors were said to make this sound in attacking.

gilu n. Friendly Ground Dove, Gallicolumba stairii, actually quite timid, brown colour, it "coos" the way a dove should do. By contrast, Peale's Pigeon *soqe,* brownish grey, barks like a dog. Syn. *qila, gila,* Tongan *tu.*

godro v. and n. to grunt, groan, grumble *Sa godro tiko na ketequ.* My stomach is rumbling. Such use of this word might be a Fijian way of expressing hunger. *cegu godrogodro* v. to make a noise when breathing. See *kudru.*

gogo 1. adj. weak from sickness or age, infirm, feeble. *gone gogo* dull child, undeveloped mentally. *Au sa gogo mai niu sa qase.* I have become weak with age. *Sa vakagogotaki au na noqu tauvimate* My illness has weakened me. *Ka kua ni dau gogo nomu itovo.* Don't let your behaviour deteriorate from weakness (lack of resolve).

gogo 2. n. bird species, Black Noddy, Anous tenuirostris, grey colour with white cap, often seen with the very common Brown Booby, Sula leucogaster, *gutulei* or *toro* or *tero,* but is smaller in size. Or may refer to Common Noddy, Anous stolidus, *gogo* or *rosawa* which also has distinctive white cap. Syn. *drelo.*

gole, goleva v. to proceed, turn away or turn toward. *igolegole* n. turn-off, turning off point, turning away (in a new direction). *Lako yani ekea qai gole ki na bati ni wai.* Go over there and then turn off toward the river bank. *Sa goleva vakalevu na yaloqu.* My mind keeps turning back to that. *Qai gole yani vale!* Come over to my house! *Au sa gole mada.* I beg to take my leave.
Idiom: *gole ki (na dua na vanua)* allied with (some more important territory), referring usually to ancient ties between two territories, usually a minor one and a major one. This is an alliance, not a tributary relationship. There was an advantage of mutual protection in this traditional type of relationship.

vagole, vagolea v. to direct (boat, car) toward (some place).

gole, golea v. to push back and forth (tree stump to test if it can be removed, digging stick to plant crops, garden fork in digging planting-mounds, gearshift of car to change gears).

goletaka v. to shake back and forth sharply or forcibly. *goletaka na uluna* shake the head sharply from side to side, as in certain dance motions.

gona thus, therefore, aforementioned, because of that, referring to something previously said or understood.

Idiom: *Koya gona!* That's it! (that's what I've been trying to tell you, that's what I meant).

gone 1. n. child, youngest one (of family); *gone tagane* boy. *gone yalewa* girl. *vagonegonea* childish. *vagone* child-like. *gone yaga* helpful child. *gonevuli* pupil, student (inc. university). *gone biu vuli* school-leaver. *gone tubutubu* adolescent child. *gone dramidrami* baby at nursing stage. *na itabagone* the young generation (children). *gone ni toko* pampered, favoured child.

Idiom: *tamata vagone* person who has a devil (*tevoro*) who is served (as in pouring *yaqona* in tribute) in return for favours that are usually evil. Conceptually, looking after the devil is as looking after a child, requiring attentive care but it is dangerous if duties are neglected. Syn. *vakatevoro*.

Idiom: *Gone Turaga* (or) *Gone Marama* respectful reference to a chief, male *Turaga* or female *Marama*.

gone 2. adj. young. *na itei gone* the young plant(s). *tamata gone* young person. *na itaba gone* the youthful generation. *gone vei au* younger than me. *Oi au gone sara.* I am the youngest.

Gonedau n. traditional type of kin-group serving a paramount chief as fishermen (usually of turtle), or warriors collecting human bodies for chiefly consumption (as in the case of the Lasakau on Bau island). These were sailors of Tongan origin. Their language has some differences from other versions of the Fijian languages.

gonedau n. fisherman.

Gonesau n. chiefly title, centred in Ra province in the area of Nakorotubu. There is confusion and dispute as to the origin and lineage associated with this title. There is no tradition of a formal installation ceremony. Close connection to super-tribe Dewala and the early history of Bau Island. The origin has a very close relationship with Bau. Curiously, this title has no extensive territory and no direct control over any extensive tribe. N. L. C. official report lists the title as Na Sau. (Tribe Dewala itself has become fragmented and dispersed widely.)

gonevou n. first-born baby of a mother. See *ulumatua*.

gonevuli (or) **gone ni vuli** n. school child(ren), young student.

gu n. motivation, physical energy. *Tovolea ena nomu gu taucoko.* Try with all your might. *E malumalumu na nodratou gu.* Their (several) motivation is weak.

igu n. force of effort with powerful motivation. *E kaukauwa na nodratou igu.* Their powerful force is strong. *Nomu igu!* give all your effort! (yelled at athletes). *gudea vakaigu* to shake it vigorously, energetically. *igu matua* diligent, diligence. *Vinaka na igu matua.* Thanks for trying hard.

vagugu, vagugutaka v. to hum, as of a melody, usually when the words have been forgotten.

gu, guta, gutaka, guraka v. to apply effort. *gu vakaukauwa* to try hard. *guta vakaukauwa* to try hard for it. *Guraka!* Really go for it!

Idiom: *lai guguraki* v. go to the toilet (to defecate). This is socially polite usage, more common in the highlands than the Bauan term *veka*. Perhaps the most frequently used polite term is the verb *valelailai*, referring to the physical toilet itself. (No such facility in earlier days. Faeces were concealed to avoid black magic.)

Idiom: *gu vaka tina-ni-gone* to try very hard, like a woman giving birth.

Idiom: *vagugu* v. to rush wildly. *Rau sa vagugu yani me rau yacova rawa made ga na gusu ni qara.* They (two) rushed over to reach the mouth of the cave.

gu ca adj. lacking motivation, energy, lazy. *gu-ca-taka* v. to fail to apply oneself at something. Syn. *gu ce*.

gu calucalu adj., adv. hasty, forceful, slipshod, of a person, or some work or action.

guce, guce-taka v. to fail by lack or motivation or energy, not to be interested or motivated, to give up the effort. *Ira sa guce ena vaqarai iratou.* They (many) failed in the search for them (few).

gude, gudea, guderaka 1. v. to cradle in the arms and gently rock, as with a baby.

gude, gudea 2. v. to shake. *Gudea na vunikau me lutu na vuana* Shake the tree so the fruit will fall. *Gude!* Shake it! supportive cry to dancers (*taralala, tamure* or disco dance, not *meke*). *gudea na* "cocktail" shake the cocktail. Syn. *gede, gedea*.

gudu, guduva 1. v. (Colo East) to pull out, off with the hands. (electric plug, vines off a fruit-tree). Syn. *gutu, gutuva*.

gudu, guduva 2. v. to cut off. *igudu* piece of something that has been cut off. Syn. *gutu, gutuva*.

gugu n. (Archaic) type of sharp-edged, oar-shape warclub, much less wide than the *kinikini*.

guileca, guilecava v. to forget. See *leca*. *guiguileca* adj. forgetful. *na guiguileca* n. the loss of memory. *guiguilecavi dredre* hard-to-forget, unforgettable. Syn. *lecava*. See *liaca*.

gule, gulea v. to press or push back and forth, to test the firmness, as of a tooth possibly loose, of a newly placed house-post in the ground to test its solidarity.

gunu, gunuva v. to drink, drink it. *me gunu di na bilo yaqona* drink dry the cup of *yaqona*. *gunuva maca* drink it dry. *vagunuva na ose* water the horse (give water to drink). *Sa gunu vinaka.* That tastes good (of beverage). Syn. (Kadavu) *somi, somica*.
Idiom: *dau vagunu* person who dispenses herbal medicines.

gunu sevusevu v. to drink water from cupped hands, a relatively modern custom outdoors. More traditionally, Fijians drank directly from streams, putting their face to the water, or from water vessels, by pouring the water into the mouth, with the vessel several inches from the face. Cups as such never existed before the introduction of coconut cups (*bilo*) for drinking kava and no other liquid. Originally, *bilo* referred just to human knee-caps.

veivagunuvi n. installation of a chief (by having him drink the ceremonial cup of kava offered), a custom of most but not all Fijian tribes. For some territories it is said that no installation ceremony is necessary when there is no dispute as to the rightful successor.) Some Christian sects now forbid their members to drink kava. *vagunuvi* installed, of a chief, having drunk the installation cup of *yaqona*.

igunugunu 1. n. flavour, taste of a drink (or melon, orange, ice cream).

igunugunu 2. n. source for drinking water for a village or community.

guru n. colourful Damsel fish of the reef, various species in various colours, but of the same shape, feeding on algae, often fearless of people. Unaffected by poison cells of anemone. With tough prickly scales and tough skin, *guru* is usually grilled on a fire and then skinned. Dorsal spines make the fish hard to handle. This fish has special significance to Waimaro highlanders of Serea and their distant kinfolk who migrated to the shores of southern Viti Levu, centred around village Muaivuso. There it is a totemic fish. In rare usage, *guru* may also refer to a type of large sea turtle, Carreta carreta, Syn. *tuvonu*.

gusu-na 1. n. mouth. *gusuniwai* river-mouth. *gusu coci* harelip, cleft lip. *gusu bona* bad breath, halitosis. *gusu kaukauwa* "big mouth", outspoken, rough mannered. *gusu ca* or *gusugusu ca* back-biter, gossip, uses rough language. *gusugaga* spiteful, hurtful, nasty. *gusu tete* broad-lipped (*tete* lit. spread-out). *gusu kabasu* cannot keep a secret. *gusu macala* clear speaker. *gusu macamaca* voluble, never at a loss for words. *gusu wa* or *gusa tabu wawa* to talk on and on, incessant talker. *gusu ni vosa* spokesman. *gusu-sika* one who cannot keep a secret. *gusu totolo* n. rapid talker, a characteristic of many Fijians, especially in broadcasting; Fijian speech in general is much faster than virtually all Polynesian speech.

gusu-na 2. n.,v. spokesperson, spokesman, with a possessive pronoun suffix; as a verbal form, to speak for (someone, some people), as in *Au gusundratou na gone ni Viti ka keimami tiko mai Niusiladi.* I speak for those (several) of us Fijians who are in New Zealand.

vakagusu adj. verbal or oral (not written).

gusu ni vosa (Anglicism) n. microphone; spokesperson.

gusu rairai ineffectual talk just for the sake of appearances.

gusutaki as in *na wili gusutaki* the reading aloud, reciting, mouthing the words.

gusuwa adj. loquacious with futile talk, babbler.

guta v. refers to a strong feeling of missing someone, or longing to be with someone. *E guta na lomaqu meu raici kemuni.* I long to see you.

guta v. (Vanua Levu) to take it all, using force if necessary, not leaving anything.

gutu, gutuva, gutulaka v. to snap off (twig, string) or pull out and off with the hands (electric plug, vines off a fruit-tree), sever, cut off (rope, cloth from a bolt of cloth), separate off. *gutugutu, gutugutuva* snap off in pieces (string, vine). Syn. *gudu, guduva*. Using an axe or heavy knife on sticks of wood, this word implies chopping across the grain. May be used figuratively as in *tagutuvi mai na nodra vanua dina* of a people, cut off, separated from their own true land. This has been said of Lovoni people, expelled from Ovalau by Cakobau. *ragutu* or *cagutu* snapped off, severed, without that being deliberately done.

gutulei n. seabird, Sula spp., Brown Booby or Masked Booby (never nest in trees) or Red-footed Booby (nests in trees), Sula sp., both very common. Syn. *toro, vava-biau*.

gutuwa v. to run for one's life, to flee. *gutuwa-taka* desperately run off with it.

I

The letter **i** is pronounced rather more like the double **e** in English, as in **queen**, and less usually like the **i** in the word **city**.

Quite a few noun-forms begin with the letter **i** when the noun-form is adapted from a verbal root-form. Thus the word for "the knife" *na isele* is adapted from the verb "to cut" *sele, seleva*. By Cabinet dictum in March 2008, that **i** should be attached as part of the noun-form. Nonetheless, in much common writing in Fiji, the word can often still be seen as *nai sele* or *na isele*. In this dictionary that word would appear alphabetically under the letter **s**, first letter of the root-word *sele*. In ordinary, fast speech, one might not always hear the letter **i** that precedes many nouns.

i 1. of, an abbreviation of *ni* as in: *tama i Seru* father of Seru.

i 2. to (or) to the, an abbrev. of *ki* or *ki na*. *siro sobu ki matasawa* go down to the beachfront.

i 3. alternative, regional pronounciation for the prefix "e" in word combinations helping to indicate direction. *i ra, ira* or *e ra* below (or downwind). *i cake* (or) *e cake* above (or upwind). Those words sometimes used as a suffix to a place-name, as in Nananu-ira Island.

i 4. an attached prefix that indicates a noun adapted from a verbal root-form: *isele* knife (from the verb "cut" *sele*); *idabedabe* seat, chair, saddle (from the verb "to sit" *dabe*). Some Fijians prefer to see that "i" float alone, unattached to the noun.

ia 1. v. to go. *Ia mai!* Come here! *ia i Suva* go to Suva. Syn. *lako*. (Vanua Levu) *la'o*.

ia 2. word that stands alone, indicating a pause, meaning "Well, . . ."

Ia! 3. said rather forcefully, this can be the equivalent of "Hey, you!", catching a person's attention.

ia 4. (or) **ia ka** but, used as a conjunction (*isema*) in a sentence. *Au via lako ia sa sega ni rawa*. I want to go but it is not possible.

ia, iataka 5. v. to take place, occur, to be performed or done. *Sa ia tiko na bose* The meeting is taking place. *iataka na meke* to perform the exhibition-dance.

iauwe! emotional interjection, when a person is surprised, amazed, fatigued, suddenly sorrowful. Syn. *oiauwe*.

ibe n. mat. *ibe ni moce* sleeping mat. *ibe ni kana* mat for serving meals, of cotton cloth or woven pandanus leaves. *ibe vulavula* woven mat with no coloured fringe of wool (*kula*) and no blacking (*somo*) from dyed pandanus leaves. *ibe vakula* mat fringed with colourful wool (formerly red feathers (*kula*). *ibe kilukilu* course-woven floor mat (*kilu* refers to the plain finishing edge with no fringe). *kiluvatu* is a type of mat unique to Udu, Macuata Province, having no fringe but a very strong, straight edge. *ibe vakabati* mat with several layers of wool fringe for covering a bed. *bati ni vasua* mat with large saw-tooth edges. *ibe Papua* decorative mat with intricately interwoven black geometric design, made on Gau Island (and some overseas Melanesian places). *ibe vakavutuvutu* mat with finely sliced pandanus fringe. *ibe kuta* (or) *ibe sasa* mat made from sedge, a specialty of Bua; it is softer but less durable; traces 2000 years old have been found at Sigatoka sand dunes. *ibe ni Tonga* round mat used under dining tables. *tabu kaisi* refers to a very high quality, fine mat made at Ono Island, southern Lau. Most mats are made with leaves of *voivoi*, Pandanus sp., about 40 leaves needed for one sleeping mat, some four feet wide and seven feet long, but as many as 100 may be used. A floor mat is referred to as *icoco*. *ibe ni valagi* rug or carpet. Syn. for mat (West, Vanua Levu) *loga*. (Lau) *yaba*.

ibo n. edible type of worm, often found buried in sand, eaten raw or used as bait, Siphonosoma australe. Syn. *bou*.

idi 1. (Eng.) n. inch. *e lima na idi*. five inches.

idi 2. (Eng.) n. hinge.

Idia n. India, Indian person, people. *kaiIdia* Indian (person), more politely, *turaga ni Idia* or *marama ni Idia* Indian gentleman or Indian lady.

idini (Eng.) n. engine. *idini cavu* outboard motor. Punts with outboard engines have replaced the sailing cutters so common at mid-century. *idini dabe* refers to a boat engine that is installed, not readily removable. *idini ni cina* generator to produce electricity.

idinia (Eng.) n. engineer, mechanic.

Igiladi (Eng.) England. *Bolatagane* is an older term, more honorific. *Peretania* Great Britain.

Ijipita (Eng.) Egypt.

ika (Polyn.) n. fish. *ika vuka* flying fish. *ika bau* sp. of river fish, Eliotris melanosoma or Ophieleotris aporos, Syn. (Kadavu) *vorina*, (West) *miqa*. *ika ni wai droka* fresh water fish. *ika droka* raw fish, but *ikadroka* flagtail, Kuhlia rupestris. *ika ni laca* sailfish, Istiophorus sp., *ika toa* lion fish (see below), *ika vavi* oven-cooked fish. *ika tavu* grilled fish. *ika vakalolo* fish cooked in coconut cream.

tobo, toboka na ika catch the fish. Syn. (eastern Macuata) *koli*. (western Macuata) *qoli*, (Colo East) *ilava*. (Tonga) *ika*.

Idiom: *tobo ika ena vanua mamaca.* lit. catch fish on dry land, i.e., attempt the impossible.

ika bula n. sea turtle, any kind. May also refer to a live fish.

ika loa n. a kind of mullet, Cestraeus sp., a significant source of food from rivers. Viti Levu highlanders caught these in community efforts with large nets, using stone sinkers, and divers to guide the net and drive the fish. These stone sinkers (*vatu-kata-i-lawa*) were the only stone implements ever used by highlanders.

ika ni laca n. sailfish, long-beaked with a huge dorsal fin, the usually migratory Istiophorus sp., rarely if ever caught by early Fijians but now available as people now fish outside the reefs. The flesh is not preferred, partly because of the frequently found holes in the flesh caused by parasitical worms. Normally darkish coloured, sailfish skin sparkles with colour and glistening silver when the fish is excited. They travel in small groups but can come together in large groups, male and female together, to herd small, schooling sardine-like fish into ball shapes, circling them, then individually penetrate that school with thrashing beak to stun the smaller fish, ultimately consuming almost all of them.

ika toa 1. (or) **ikatotoa** (or) **tokalou** lion fish, butterfly fish, Lactoria cornuta, formerly listed as Pterois volitans. Beautiful, floating fins with very long dorsal and pectoral fins equipped with poisonous spines, unfrightened of visitors, confident in its armament.

ika toa 2. Box fish, square in cross-section, very tough body and skin but with a delicious, tender slab of meat on its back that resembles a chicken breast.

ike (or) **iike** n. wooden pounder to beat bark-cloth.

iki a dance motion, to turn sharply the body to face left or right. *ta iki* turned in this way (here the syllable *ta* suggests a cutting motion).

iko you (singular, as object). *vukei iko* help you. *Au na qai solia vei iko.* I will then give it to you. *Ocei? O iko* (or) *Ko iko.* Who? You.

iloilo n. mirror, glass. *mata iloilo* spectacles, glasses. *vaka-rai-ta-iloilo* n. imagination. *vaka-rai-ta-iloilo-taka* v. to imagine it. The only kind of mirror known in Fiji was a reflection in clear pool of water. Such a mirror gives rise to the name of Ratu Sir Joseva Iloilo (he told me) from his mother's use of such a natural mirror on Taveuni.

ilova v. look at, through something transparent (glasses, diving goggles, translucent or reflective like a mirror). By ext. have an x-ray image taken, usually of some part of the human body. See *tirova*. Also see *irova* v. to peep.

inisua, inisuataka (Eng.) v. to insure (in a commercial sense).

io yes. Traditionally, Fijians answered questions with strict logic, as in "Aren't you going to town?" responding with a "Yes", meaning "Yes, I am not going to town." Today usage is confusing. Only conservative village Fijians can be relied upon to retain the correct Fijian logic. Often, instead of giving a verbal answer "yes", Fijians will raise their brow slightly (*deguvacu*), or they may simply raise the chin to indicate agreement. Instead of saying "no" in declining a request, a Fijian may remain silent. In effect, a silent response means "no". It might be considered impolite to say "no". A negative response may be indicated by a slight sideways movement of the head. *vaka-io* v. to say "yes", to approve, to agree. Syn. (Tonga) *'io*.

iqi (Eng.) ink.

ira pronoun: them (many). *o ira kece* all of them. *ira na tamata* the people.

Idiom: *ira vata* they are all the same.

iratou them (few).

iri n. fan. *iri ni buka* fan for fanning fire. *iri livaliva* (or) *iri ni cagi* electric fan. *iri batabata* air conditioner. *iri buli* hand-held traditional fan of woven pandanus leaf, notably from Daku, Tailevu. *iri ni meke* hand-held fans used in exhibition dances *meke*. *Liga i iri* were warriors who carried a large fan in battle confrontations as an indication of fearlessness and display of confidence. (Ligairi has also become a distinguished family name from village Nabalebale, Wailevu, Vanua Levu.)

iri, iriva, irivaka v. *Mo irivi au mada* please fan me. *Me irivi na kakana.* Fan the food (usually to disperse flies). *irivaka na buka* fan the fire. *dau ni iri* trad. person who fans the chief.

iro, irova v. to peer, peep, take a look at (or) *vakairoiro* to keep peering, usually quietly, even secretly. *dau iro* "peeping Tom", Syn. *tokalulu*, (Macuata) *va'alalagi*.

isa! (or) **isalei!** cry of regret, sorrow. Isalei is the name of Fiji's popular song of farewell. That melody and original words were actually Tongan and not at all ancient but has become an icon of Fijian culture with words adapted into a Fijian context.

I'Saka! formal form of address, used at the beginning of a letter, respectfully to draw the attention of the reader. The equiv. of "Dear Sir" or "Dear Madame". May also be used in speech, similarly, respectfully to draw the attention of a listener. *Saka* Sir (or) Madam.

isi (Eng.) n. yeast. Early Fijians had no leavened bakery products and no baking flour.

isi, isia n. tear off, as of twig, flower, piece of bread, newspaper, piece of cloth, to split pandanus leaf for weaving.

Isireli Eng. Israel. This is also used as a man's name *Sireli*.

isiti n., adj. east. *Colo Isiti* Colo East, a former Province in the eastern highlands of Viti Levu Island. There is a very proud tradition to this area and its people.

isou n. very near miss, as with something thrown. Syn. *oisou*.

itini (Archaic, Eng.) agent, commercial agent.

ivi 1. n. Polynesian chestnut, Inocarpus edulis (or) I. fagiferus, Caesalpinaceae. The fruit is a cooked, nutty starch-food eaten in some areas, notably on Beqa Island, and sold at the public markets. Tiny white fragrant flowers, fruits heavily around April, May, June, nuts eaten boiled, grilled, or made into a form of pudding after grating. The heavily buttressed tree grows rapidly in damp areas and can reach giant size. The thin buttresses formerly served as an improvised drum for communicating at a distance. *ivi solo* grated *ivi*. Mainly a coastal tree, widely known, often by similar names, throughout the South Pacific. There are many different varieties. Excellent firewood. Various puddings of *ivi* include *sikovoro, koko, soloi, bila*. Tender leaves are also edible. Syn. (Polyn.) *ifi, ihi, i'i*.
Idiom: *vakaruku ni ivi.* shelter under an *ivi* tree, i.e., having sheltered where the rain leaks through.

ivi 2. n. kidney. *ivi qaqa.* padlock.

J

The letter **j** does not occur in mainland Fijian speech except in adaptions of English words, or in words of the people from Lau and Kadavu where Tongan influence is strong. It often replaces the standard letter **t** as in *ijitoko* for *ititoko*, walking stick. In a person's name such as Jemesa, for James, the intitial **j** may give way to an **s** as in Semesa. The letter **j** appears in some speech of the Navosa highlands that were penetrated by early Tongans; the Tongan *'ikai* for no or not becomes *jikai*.

. . . j a single letter, and thus a sound, appended to any or all Fijian words or names by youngsters affecting to carry on a strange, childish language that they think is cute. It can be difficult to understand their speech. It is even harder to speak it. One might presume this silly fad will pass.

jaba n. (Eng.) "jumper", as in *isulu* and *jaba*, formal cotton dress of Fijian women. The *isulu* extends from waist to ankles. The *jaba* is a sort of bodice on upper body, from the neck down to the thighs, or to the knees, or further down, outside the *sulu*. This form of dress was imposed by missionaries.

jabeni (Eng.) champion, usually in sports.

Jafau n., adj. immigrants from Tonga, specialised boat-builders who settled mostly at Fulaga. They built the famous *drua* named Ratu Finau, its hull (*kata*) 13.5 meters long, 1872-1877.

Jaji as in *Lotu Jaji* (or) *Lotu Tiati* Anglican Church, Church of England. *Jaji* is a Fijian rendition of "George" though there are various spellings of that name. Many Colonial officials were Anglicans and this attracted some upper-class Fijians. Many Solomon Islanders in Fiji are Anglicans. It now remains a minority denomination. The name George became popular after the (self-appointed) George I of Tonga befriended Cakobau around 1855.

jaji, jajitaka (Eng.) v. to charge (battery) or charge some expenditure to an account.

jakete (Eng.) jacket.

Jalesi n. (Lau) Charles. Syn. *Salesi*.

Jamani (Eng.) Germany. *kaiJamani* German person or people.

jameni (Eng.) chairman. Syn. *jiemeni, jemeni*.

Janueri (Eng.) January.

jeke 1. (Eng.) cheque. U.S. check, for transfer of funds.

jeke 2. (Eng.) "Jack" in the royal suite of playing cards. *joka* Joker.

jenereli (Eng.) general (military). *Metia Jenereli* Major General, usually referring to Sitiveni Rabuka who arranged to be given this title after his military coup in 1987.

Jerusalemi (Bible) Jerusalem. Idiom: *Tekivu mai Jerusalemi, . .* Begin at home before worrying about other places. This has been an excuse for nepotism.

Ji (Kadavu) local chiefly title that precedes a place name such as Ji Wailevu.

jia, jiataka (Eng) v. to cheer, to cheer for . . . *jiataka na timi* to cheer for the team.

jiaina n. (Eng. "China") banana, formerly classified as Musa Chinensis. Banana may be distinguished from plantain by its fragile leaf that tears more easily in the wind, and by its more acute form. It is more susceptible to disease than is plantain. Early native immigrants brought several varieties of plantain but no bananas which are much sweeter and do not require cooking. The species has tiny, non-viable seeds. Propagation is only vegetative, by suckers, and movement is only by man. Plant are variable in phenotype, being genetically very motile. Syn. *jaina*. See *tiaina* for more details.

Jiaina (or) **Jaina** China, or Chinese person(s).

jiale (Eng.) Gardenia, "Charley" (= *tiale*), the national flower of Tahiti, Gardenia taitensis, native to Melanesia but aboriginal introduction to Polynesia. A now more common species is G. augusta (formerly G. jasminoides), introduced from the Orient. There are eight other Gardenia species, including G. vitiensis as named by Seemann.

jiemeni (Eng.) chairman. *vukevuke jiemeni* assistant chairman. Syn. *jameni*.

jikai (Western highlands, Navosa, from Tonga) no, not. Syn. *hikai, sega, warai, wara, mino*. (eastern Macuata) *maka*, (western Macuata) *maqa*. These variations are all familiar to most Fijians.

jili (or) **tili** (Tonga) n. hand-net thrown from the shoulder to catch small schooling fish close to shore with the man standing in shallow water. This is Polynesian custom, not Fijian.

jisi (Eng) n. cheese.

Jisu (Bible) Jesus.

ijitoko (Lau) n. walking stick (= *ititoko*), sometimes used to refer to one final bowl of kava, "one for the road", before departure of a guest.

Jiulai (Eng.) July. Syn. *Julai*.

Jiune (Eng.) June. Syn. *June*.

Joka 1. (Eng.) "Joker" in a deck of playing cards.

joka 2. (Eng. joker) person who is showing off, acting important, powerful.

vakajokajoka (Slang) v., adj. to act in a manner of exaggerated self-importance, aggression or power, as in swaggering, "collar up" as is said in Fijian English.

joke (Eng.) n. chalk; also jug. *joke ni wai* water-jug.

jokeliti (Eng.) n. chocolate.

K

Some words may begin with either **k** or **q** such as *kasivi*, *qasivi*, depending on regional dialect. The **k** tends to be used by "true" Fijians of Viti Levu, while the **q** is more common among the island people of Lau, Kadavu or Vanualevu-icake or Vanualevu-ira, where there is a substantial Tongan influence.

For many of the dialects of Cakaudrove and Macuata the **k** is replaced by a glottal stop, as in *la'o* for *lako* (go). But when an introduced foreign word has a **k** sound, the **k** sound is usually retained. In Bua, the **k** is often replaced by an **h**. The fruit (Morinda citrifolia) *kura* becomes *hura*. In parts of Vanua Levu, **k** may be omitted at the beginning of a word. In Fiji as well as many other Pacific languages, it is vowels rather than consonants that serve to anchor the meaning of words.

ka 1. and, a conjunction joining verb-forms. *raica ka rogoca* see it and hear it.

ka 2. that, as in *na ilavo ka sa kumuni* the money that was collected.

ka 3. n. thing. *na ka oqo* this thing; *na ka oya* that thing. *Na Ka Levu* (locally *Na Kwa Levu*) lit. "The Big One" high chief of the coastal region of Nadroga Province. *ena veika kece* in all things. *Minisita ni Veika Vakaitaukei* Minister for Fijian Affairs
Idiom: *Sa dua na ka!* That's really something! (remarkable). *ka lo* secret.
Idiom: *ka ni tagane* or *ka vakatagane* n. male genitals, a polite term.
Idiom: *ka ni yalewa* n. female genitals, a polite term.

ika- 4. prefix to a numeral, indicating "nth" as in a sequence: *na ikatolu* the third. *ikaciwa* the ninth. *kavica* ? raises the question as to which ranking. *kadua* usually means "other" as is *na yasana kadua* the other side. *taura na kadua* take the other one. *na ikarua* the second (after the first), but *karua* refers to a certain family relative of same sex.

ka- 5. prefix of adjective or past participle indicating force, strong action. *kasura* smashed. *kabasu* broken.

Ka! 6. (Slang, affectionate) Hey you! That greeting is sometimes associated with male homosexuals. *Ko Ka* or *Ka oya*. "What's-his-name". *Ka oya* can also mean "That one".

kaba, kabata, kabataka 1. v. climb up. *kabata na vunikau* climb the tree. *kabataka na itukituki* climb up with the hammer. May also refer to climbing a hill.

Idiom: *ivakaba ni sau* dramatic act to assert a demand for rightful title to some authority, such as chiefly position, lit. a means of climbing to power.

Idiom: *kabawaqa* v., n. girls of easy morals who board ships (*waqa*) in harbour, often accepting money for their services. This is a common insult, equiv. of *saqamua* fornicator, prostitute.

Idiom (Vulgar Slang): *kaba* to have sexual intercourse, though for animals this is not a vulgar word. This is the normal way of referring to a male animal mounting a female.

ikabakaba n. ladder, steps, staircase. *ikabakaba ni sere* (or) *ikabakaba sofa* musical scale, staff notation in music.

Idiom: *ikabakaba vou* new habit, new skill, new way of doing things.

kaba, kaba, kabata 2. v. to attack, fight. *kabata na koro* or *kabakoro* v. to attack the village.

kabakoro n. conquest (in war).

kabani 1. (Eng.) n. commercial company, corporation, military company.

kabani 2. (Eng.) n. darling, partner, good friend, companion.

kabasi (Eng.) n. compass. Fijians had no compass and no concept of regularly spaced directions like NESW. Their directions were the directions of the various winds of Fiji. Fijians have adapted readily to the European compass directions *mata ni kabasi*. The term *kabasi* applies also to a compass as used in schoolroom geometry. *noca* north. *sauca* south. *isi* or *isiti* east. *wesi* (or) *wesiti* (or) *ra* west. Previously *ra* meant only downwind, which is in a westerly direction. The common tradewind comes from the southeast in the southern hemisphere and from the northeast in the northern hemisphere of the Pacific ocean, with the doldrums in between. *noca isi* northeast. *noca wesi* northwest. And so on. Fact is, however, Fijian sailors now most often simply use the English word for compass directions without modifying the pronounciation.

kabasu v. to burst, bust (box, door kicked in, clothing from stress, book with broken binding), broken. See *basu, basuka* v. to break.

kabatia n. sea bream, edible reef fish, Thumbprint emperor, Lethrinus harak, resembles the snapper *sabutu*, whitish body, reddish lips, tends to fight the fishing line. The body adopts the camouflage colour of the background adapting to the immediate background in the area nearest the eyes, according to the late Rob Wright.

kabe n. a type of strong string for tying things. A thin string is sliced from the top of the midrib of a coconut-palm leaf. This is often used to sew up a sack after it is filled with copra.

kabe, kabea (Archaic) v. to flourish and threaten with a raised weapon, club or spear.

vakabe-kabea v. of a person or people, speak badly of them, spreading bad stories. *veivakabekabei* n. the action of doing this.

kabelu adj. bent out of shape (corrugated iron, basket). Syn. (Lau) *kapelu*.

kabete adj. chipped (plate, tooth, blade of axe or knife).

kabi, kabita v. to cling onto, adhere onto, to stick. *kabikabi* sticky (can apply to a farmer's soil). *vakabita ena lalaga* stick it to the wall. *na itavuteke sega ni kabi* the non-stick frying pan.

Idiom: *Wai ni diva, sega ni kabita.* Tears of longing for what can never be.

kabi v. to bring alongside, or dock (as of a boat), usually at a wharf.

ikabi n. (Archaic) wooden club formerly used to knock down, burn, and clear away bush before planting crops. Stone axes did not exist in the highlands among the very early indigenous Fijians who immigrated from Vanuatu or the Solomon Islands.

kabibi adj. dented, bent out of shape (car in accident, kitchen pot). May refer to sheets of corrugated iron. See *kabelu*.

kabo, kabota v. to take hold of something hot with the hand(s) protected from the heat by leaves, a cloth, gloves, that protection being called *ikakabo*.

kaboa n. edible saltwater fish, Saluridae sp. catfish. Plotopidae, usually Plotusus arab. Sharp serrated spine in each pectoral fin and in dorsal fin. Young, they stay in schools of a few hundred, often staying burrowed in mud or sand in shallow water, a danger to waders, the pain of a sting lasting several hours.

kabote 1. n. Yellow-breasted Musk Parrot of Viti Levu, Prospeia personata. It cannot be taught to speak very well at all. Flies about in the morning and afternoon. Swooping, jerky flight. Sometimes in pairs. Likes to feed around cassava patches. Often a friendly bird, even loving, especially the female. Syn. *kaka*.

kabote 2. v. to burst. *Sa kabote na vaivo.* The pipe burst. See *bote, botea*.

kabu n. morning mist, fog. *kabukabu* (or) *kabukabua* heavy fog, misty (weather), fogged over, covered with mist (as a mountain might be).

kabu, kabuya, kaburaka v. to scatter (seeds), sprinkle (water).

kabuacara, kabuacarataka v. to put or keep in careless disorder one's personal possessions, tools, equipment, supplies, scattered about.

kabuata limited visibility, usually due to weather conditions and distance. Syn. *kobua* See *buawa*.

kabura v. to seep out, as liquid from a package, as happens sometimes to leaf-parcels of food cooked in an earth-oven. *bura, buraca* to ooze.

kaburaka 1. v. to scatter (as in broadcasting seeds) forcefully.

kaburaka 2. v. to broadcast. *Vale ni Kakaburaki* Broadcasting House.

kabuwacara (or) **kabuacara** v. to spread out at random, scattered here, there and everywhere, spread out, scattered about in careless or sloppy manner (clothes, shoes in a room, tools in a workshop etc.). Syn. *kabuacara*.

kabuya v. to sprinkle, usually something like a powder, or ashes. Ashes may be used in treatment of hair on the head. Powder, either talcum or flour, may be sprinkled over a performing dancer as a mark of encouragement. (Such use of powder is Lauan custom, now done widely in Fiji.)

kaca adj. cracked, split (mirror, stone, skin, leather, wooden or cardboard box). *vakaca* v. to crack it. *kaca na mataka* (Anglicism) break of dawn.

kacabola split open (coconut, breadfruit, bamboo).

kacabote v. to explode, burst, detonate. *vakacabote-taka* v. to explode deliberately. Idiom: *Veitalia na kacabote!* No matter what the consequences! Let's just do it! (a saying attributed to the frog Ra Boto who puffs up his chest in a story for children).

kacabura v. to burst (of a boil, or a fallen fruit). Syn. *kasabura*. See *bura*.

kacau 1. n. small, pelagic, non-migratory bird, quite common, Collared Petrel, or White-Throated Shearwater, Pterodroma leucoptera brevipes. Feeds largely on squid. Grey upperparts, grey breast but white underneath. Syn. (Lau, all petrels) *lafu*. (Kadavu) *lagio*.

kacau 2. n. MacGillivray's Petrel, Pterodroma macgillivrayi. In the South Pacific there are some five species of that genus, some of them quite widespread. But this one is known only at Gau. It was discovered by T. M. Raynor, Medical Officer of the H.M.S. Herald, in October, 1855. He named it for the ship's naturalist. For many decades it was not again sighted. Conservationist Dr. Dick Watling has recently rediscovered the bird, always alone, separate from its mate. The bird is strictly monogamous, and even after the death of the mate, will remain alone for up to five years. The nest is thought to be a burrow but has never been found. Watling and Fiji's National Trust are looking to overseas aid to help learn about the nesting habits, probably with the help of New Zealand's sniffing dogs. All this is thought important in terms of biodiversity. Even the District Council has been persuaded to take an interest.

kacavida v. to crack with sharp sound. Syn. *kavida,* heard as *avida* in major parts of Vanua Levu.

kaci, kaciva v. to call using some form of address (attracting someone's attention), invite (person, animal). But *kaci* may refer to a village headman calling out some announcement in the village.
Idiom: (Vulgar) *O kacivi ga, o sa vude cake*. When alerted, the penis rises to the occasion. Lit. When you are called, you rise to the occasion.

kacibale v. to call out to someone from a distance without concern for disturbance to people in between.

kacika n. large edible fish, Long-nosed Emperor, Lethrinella xanthocheila, reddish belly (as implied in the Latin name), yellowish on upper parts, found around the reefs and feisty to catch on a line. Sometimes, some places, dangerous to eat during *balolo* season due to so-called red-tide poison (cigatuera). Syn. *dokonivudi*.

kacikaci, kacikaciva v. to call out continuously, persistently.

ikacikaci (or) **ikacivi** n. name or title by which a person is addressed, the name they are called when speaking to them, or the name used in referring to them. Traditionally this has almost never been the person's personal name, which was considered impolite. A man whose name is Seru, and who has a son called Manasa may be addressed as Tama i Manasa, and referred to as such. Similarly, formerly, one often referred to a place indirectly by some reference other than its proper name. These words may apply to a group of people, the name by which one refers to them.

ikacikaci ni cagi Idiom: to die far from home, usually overseas, as an example of Fijian indirect manner of speech.

kacimuri, kacimuria v. to call after (someone).

kacivaka v. to announce, to call out publicly, as done by village administrator *turaga ni koro,* in making announcements. *kacivaka yani vei koya* announce it to him, shout it out to him. *kacivaka na vakamau* announce the marriage.

kada, kadava v. (Lau, Vanua Levu) to run, run for it (Bau: *cici, ciciva*). *kada vakina* run with it. *ada, adava* could be heard in Vanua Levu.

kada n. reed or other support for food-crop cultivated vines, yams. *Me vakada na uvi* Put up the yam-vine support.

kade n., adj. medium stage of maturity of coconut when there is flesh and refreshing liquid. Syn. *drokai*.

kadi n. aggressive black biting ant, Odontomachus sp., that nests around rotting vegetation. *kadi vuka* flying ant. *batikadi* formerly, a potentially dangerous lone wild person living in the bush, now guerilla fighter, commando, resistance fighter (World War II), bandit.
Idiom: *vakaseuta na bure ni kadi* lit., scratch into an ant's nest, i.e., inadvertantly stir up trouble.

kadiga adj. old but still edible, of yams, or overly mature sweet potato that may be split.

kadikadi 1. n. River prawn, also found in brackish water, Macrobrachium equideus. The "true prawn" *ura dina* is M. lar, in freshwater, the totem of some tribes. M. rosenbergii is the introduced Malaysian freshwater prawn with no special Fijian name.

kadikadi 2. spying gossip.

kadikadia (Med.) "pins and needles" sensation, prickly feeling.

kadila adj. changed to bright red, of cooked prawns, crab, dyed clothes, a healing wound.

kadiri adj. chipped, cracked, usually of something like crockery. See *dirika*.

kadola forced open (door, box). See *dola* to open.

kadolo broken off with force (branch, banana from stem, pencil broken in two). See *doloka*.

kadrala 1. (Eng.) n. candle.

kadrala 2. (Eng.) n. Roman Candle Tree, Candelabra plant, Cassia alata, a common, introduced garden bush with yellow, candle-like flowers. Juice from the macerated leaves are used medicinally, applied to ringworm.

kadrala 3. (Eng.) n. cassava root when it has the undesirable eating characteristics of a hard, waxy texture and heavy core-fibres that resemble a candle wick.

kadre, kadrę v. to sprout up. Modernly, the word may be used figuratively, as with ideas, thoughts.

kadrę n. vegetative shoot or sprout. *Sa kadre mai na soredra.* Their seeds are sprouting out. *vula i kadrekadre.* sprouting season (yams).

kadresu torn, of something still hanging there. See *dresu, dresuka*.

kadru, kadruva, kadruma, kadruta v. to scratch, usually with the nails, or forcefully, a cat with claws. *-ma, -ta* both imply scratching with force. *wa kadrukadru* barbed wire. *Sa kadruvi au na vusi.* The cat scratched me. *Kadruva na dakuqu.* Scratch my back (to relieve itch). *e dua na ikadru* n. a scratch, or a scraper. See *kaku, kakuva*.

kadrudru n. univalve shellfish, considered a type of *sici*. It thrives in brackish, tidal water. It is prickly, hence the name.

kadua other. *ena yasana kadua.* on the other side.

ikadua first, as the first in some sport, first among things that are counted, as in first century, or reference to a king or queen, as in *Ilisapeci I* Elizabeth I. See *imatai*. See also *isevu* which implies the very first time something has occured. From *ikadua*, there follows *na ikarua*, the second, *na ikatolu*, the third, et cetera.

kai- 1. native, countryman, (familiar term, with place-name added). *kaiViti* Fijian (as a familiar term, not polite in formal conversation). *kaiColo* highland people (of Viti Levu). *kai vata* fellow countryman. *kaivalagi* European. *kaiIdia* Indian. *kai Jiaina* Chinese. *kai Mereke* American. *kaitani* foreigner. *kaiwai* or *kaimua* seaman, sailor. *kai veikau* bush person. *dui kaikai* different kinds of people (usually different races, ethnic groups, or nationalities). *ko ira na dui kaikai* people of different (various) origins. *kaivata* fellow countryman, person of the same territory (sometimes abbrev. as *kai*). *kainoqu* my fellow countryman. *kainona* his countryman.

kai 2. n. score, goal(s) or point(s) in a sport or game. *na kedratou kai* their score. *rawata e dua na kai.* win a point, make a score, goal. *E vica na kai?* What is the score? *E qaqa tiko o Suva ena lima na kai.* Suva is winning by five points.

kai- 3. as a prefix before the name of certain traditional Fijian territories, indicates a member of that particular kin-group, tribe or set of tribes. They are the original people of the territory. Not all Fijians of Rewa are *kaiRewa*. Not all Fijians of Nadi are *kaiNadi*. Even the Tui Nadi is not a *kaiNadi*. On Lakeba Island only the Narewadamu people are *kaiLakeba*.

kai 4 n. bivalve shellfish, mussel, clam, a general term for several genera and species. Commonly sold in Suva is the freshwater mussel from the Wailevu (Rewa River), Batissa violaceae, much of that from around village Kasavu, and some also from Verata territory. *canu kai, canuma na kai* pick up, gather *kai. qe, qeva na kai* dig *kai* out with the hands. *sili kai, silima na kai* to wade (even neck deep) for *kai*. The small bamboo basket used for collection in the Wailevu is referred to as *ikata*; it allows water to flow freely through it but retains the mussels. *butu kai* v. to feel for *kai* with the feet. *gege na kai*

v. to open the *kai*. *vali, valia na kai* v. to separate the *kai* from the shell. *ciciga na lewena* v. to prise out the flesh. *Sa siki na kai.* The *kai* is full and fat, seasonally good. *vadololo* soak in water to remove sand. Syn. (West) *tave*.

Idiom: *butu kai* dance, usually the *taralala*, of European origin in Fiji but now tradition of Fijians. Couple holds each other side by side with movement resembling the shuffling movement of women feeling for mussels with their feet as they tread in the rivers.

kaiColo n. highlander of Viti Levu of Melanesian origin (Vanuatu and Solomon Islands) with a reputation of being proud, feisty, independently minded, with no aristocratic pretentions. Viti Levu has the only original highlanders in Fiji, though some have dispersed to other locations. Quite different, muscular physique and culture compared to lowlanders and Fijians of the smaller islands where there has been an infusion of Polynesian stock. Main centres were the early provinces Colo East, Colo North, Colo West, later incorporated as part of larger provinces, Ba, Ra, Naitasiri, etc., for the central administration to keep control of them. Syn. (Insulting) *siromai*.

kaicolo-taka v. to do something ineptly, to mess it up, to be clumsy about something. This is an impolite reference to highlanders *kaiColo* being simpletons, inexperienced in what is thought to be more evolved ways of coastal Fijian.

kai davatu adj. (Slang) ungiving, stingy, as a clam like a stone (*vatu*) that cannot open.

kaikai n. ponyfish, Laeognathidae nathidae, relatively small edible fish found close to shore. Very often caught these days with small hook and line by urban, spare-time fisherfolk. Syn. *cebe*. In Cicia and Lakeba, according to Geraghty, the Tongan name is used *japajapa*. *kaikai* may refer to more than one species, including Caranx spp.

kaikaia (or) **kaikaiya** adj., n.,v. fatigue, tired from exertion, lifting something excessively heavy.

kai koso n. saltwater surf clam, Ark shell, Andara cornea, the shell ridged and white with serrated edge. Eaten raw or cooked, rich in iron. Sold in the market this is a dangerous food. When stale and rotten it has no bad smell, yet becomes quite poisonous, even causing death. Burglars use it to poison dogs to facilitate breaking and entering. Syn. (Nadro., Macuata) *qeqe*.

kai kuku n. bivalve shellfish, mussel, Mytilidae, generally Modiola tulipa a specialty of the lower Rewa River, supplying the Suva market. The shell is often used to split pandanus leaves preparatory to mat-weaving. Kuku is a place-name, and a name of a people in southeastern Viti Levu Island.

kaila, kailavaka v. to shout out loud, to yell. *Kailavaka yani vei koya.* Call out to him/her. *Kailavaki koya!* Yell at him/her! *kaikaila* v. to shout loudly, as of a crowd. *na ikaikaila* the shouting. *E levu na ikaikaila ena vale ni kuro.* There is a lot of shouting in the kitchen. *Kaila!* is the name of a children's weekly newspaper published by the Fiji Times.

kaile n. high-climbing, semi-cultivated or wild edible yam, Dioscorea pentaphylla, with five leaves, thick round stems very prickly in lowest internodes, twining to the left, counterclockwise. Aboriginal introduction. Three basic varieties, eaten usually when there is a lack of other food, though for eastern highlanders in Viti Levu, this was a staple food. Syn. *bulou, tokatolu*. (Colo East) *koile*.

kaile kubu or **kaile dina** n. "True" (*dina*) *kaile*, the tastiest variety, smooth skin, rather like a potato in texture. Eating quality depends on exact stage of harvest.

kaile mila or **kaile gaga** or **kaile dranu** n. wild, high-climbing aerial yam, D. bulbifera. Only the large hairy underground tuber is eaten, not the more poisonous small round tubers that grow off aerial roots. Stems have a reddish tinge. They twine to the left, counterclockwise (as does true *kaile* but not the cultivated yam *uvi* or the wild yams *tivoli, tikau*). The tuber is bitter and poisonous until cooked thoroughly, grated finely and washed in several changes of running water. This makes a bland starch food with the texture of very soft mashed potato. Fijians may add strips of the boiled seeds *icibi*, from the vine *walai*, Entada phaseoloides, which adds a nutty taste. Some highlanders *kaiColo* of Colo East refer to this as *revereve,* with first fruits *isevu* offered to the chief around April. Traditionally eastern highlanders rarely cultivated yams; their main starch food was cultivated taro or wild yams.

kaile wa n. Tubers of this var. of wild yam have heavy fibres that are spit out after chewing.

kainaka v. (Rewa) to tell.

kainaki v. said, from *kaya* to say. *E kainaki vei iko.* It has (already) been said to you. *E kainaki vakavica vei iko?* How many times has it been said to you? *Sa kainaki . . .* It is said . . . , often beginning a sentence. *E kainaki ni sa yali.* It is said that it is lost.

kai-nako or **kainakoro** n. (Slang) simple village person unfamiliar with town life and the ways of modern urban living. *koro* n. village.

kai-natauni (Slang.) n. town person, unfamiliar with traditional village ways. There is an implication of acting "smart" or "uppity" but lacking proper courtesy and village manners. *tauni* (Eng.) town. Syn. *kai-nasiti. siti* city. Syn. *susu madrai.* lit. raised on (European) bread.

kaininiu n. coconut scraper for making coconut cream. Syn. *kari ni niu*.

kaisi 1. n. low-class commoner, one who is ill-mannered. This is a common and rather serious insult. The syllable *si* here refers to human semen, as if *kaisi* were the result of casual copulation. *itovo vakaisi* extremely vulgar behaviour. *tabu kaisi* n. finely woven mat from Ono-i-Lau, "forbidden to lower-class people". Syn. (Kadavu) *qala*. (Vanua Levu) *aisi*.

kaisi 2. v. torn, split, from *isi, isia* to split, of cloth or wood.

kaivalagi n. white person, "European", as they are called in local English. It would be more polite to say *turaga ni valagi*. By ext., certain playing cards are referred to as *kaivalagi*, those of the royal suite, king (*turaga*), queen (*marama*), jack (*jeke*).

kaivale n. a certain clan or extended family may be traditionally intimate with the chiefly family, virtually part of the chiefly household, but in a subservient capacity. Such a kin-group is referred to as *kaivale*. *vale* house.

kaiwai n, sailor, seaman. *kaimua* crew member of a boat or ship. Idiom: *kana vakaiwai* v. to eat as a sailor does, mostly protein with very little starch-food.

kaka n. a large parrot, from the sound of its squawk. Prospeia spp. The Yellow-Breasted Musk Parrot (mainly on Viti Levu, and does not learn to speak) and Red-Breasted Musk Parrot, widespread on the larger island and can learn to speak. Both can learn to be friendly. Often fly at dawn or dusk, frequently in couples. Call and either bird may answer. They like to feed at cassava patches and on the seeds of *mokosoi* trees. Syn. *koki*. (West) *rove*.

kaka, kakavaka v. to stammer, to stutter.

kakabace n. a small bird, White Rumped Swift, Collocalia spodiopygia. Swoops with jerky flight. Nests in caves, rarely if ever seen to land.

kakaca adj. split, cracked (eggs), smashed into many part (bottles). *Sa kakaca tu na mata ni dau veivacu*. The boxer's face is all cut up. *Sa kakaca tu na yaloka kece*. All the eggs are cracked. Dry earth may be *kakaca*. See *kaca*.

kakadra bloodshot, infected (of eyes), probably conjunctivitis.

kakalawa v. stride with fast long steps. See *kalawa*.

ikakalawa n. short piece of wood across a drain or ditch to step on in crossing. Syn. *ikawakawa* though this may be a much larger crossing.

kakana n. food. Idiom: *kakana dina* "real food", i.e., a traditional prestigious root crop such as taro, yam. Meat, fish, or anything accompanying it would be considered only secondarily, as garnish *icoi*. Starch-food is the main element of a meal. *kakana droka* uncooked food. *kakana buta* cooked food. *kakana draudrau* leafy green vegetables. *vaka ta-kakana* n., v. picnic. See *kana, kania* to eat.

vakakana v. feed itself (people, animals, fish).

kaka-ni-oro n., v. adj. ticklish, bothersome (can't get it off one's mind). *E kakanioro vei au ni kadruvi na yavaqu* My feet are ticklish. *E kakanioro vei au ni ra dau vosavosa na gone*. It is bothersome to me when the children keep chattering. Syn. *sikisikinea*.

kakaraki v. to hock, as in bringing out something stuck in the throat.

kakase n., v. to gossip. This is an often mentioned characteristic.

kaka-seisei split badly in many places (mats, clothes, paper).

kakavaki v. to look forward to something.

kaka-vidavida snapped, chipped (plate, cup) in many places, branch of a tree.

kakavo dry, flaking off, peeling off, of human skin. *Sa kakavo na kulina ena kati ni siga*. His/Her skin is flaking off from sunburn.

kaka-vorovoro broken in many places (glass, the heart). *sa kakavorovoro na utoqu mai loma* my heart is all broken up inside (words of a popular song in Fiji). Such a romantic notion for the heart is an Anglicism. For Fijians, the heart was never a centre of emotion.

kaka-vuruvuru crumbled away in many places (biscuits, cake, bread, bamboo).

kake n. sea perch, Lutjanus russelli, Russell's snapper, the grunt, fish found at reef and mangrove areas, these days caught on fishing lines, which is not traditional with Melanesian Fijians. Polynesians and Micronesians used fishing lines with hooks. This fish has silvery colouring with five or six yellow stripes longitudinally, black spot on either side near the tail. Similar Lutjanus spp. include *damu, bati, tanabe*.

kaki (Eng.) n., adj. khaki.

kako (Eng.) cargo.

kaku, kakuva 1. v. to seize forcefully in the hand(s), to grab a hold of.

kaku, kakuva 2. v. to scratch. Syn. *kadru, kadruva*.

Kakua! Don't! as a forceful expression. Syn. *kua* (though usually less forcefully, depending on the tone or emphasis of speech).

kakula n. Red-breasted Musk Parrot, Prospeia tabuensis, on all larger Fiji islands except Ovalau. Syn. *ka̲ka̲, koki̲, ka kula*. Readily learns to speak. Various sub-species.

kala 1. (Eng.) n. colour. Syn. *roka-na*. Fijians had not developed the concept of abstract colours of a spectrum. Words for colours depended on the objects described. Fijians now tend to follow the European system. *kalavata* refers to clothes of the same colour, as for school uniforms, or a choir or church group that decides to dress in the same colour and type of clothes.

kala 2. v. to lean over, be tilted. *kala yani vua* lean on her/him. *va̲kalakala* leaning slightly. *va̲kalakala-taka* lean it over slightly. *veikalayaki* to sway back and forth. *matanivola kala* italics, lit. "leaning letters", one of those new expressions invented by teachers of language. *Sa kala na siga.* It is afternoon (the sun is leaning low). Caution: in Vanua Levu *kala* may refer to male sexual organs, *qala-na* in standard Fijian.

Idiom: *Sa kala na matanisiga.* He/She is getting old (their sun is setting).

va̲kalakala adj. slanting rather than staying straight up, as of a house, a tree.

kalabuci n. a well known shrub, ornamental and medicinal, usually growing at low altitude, wild or semi-cultivated, Acalypha insulana, Euphorbiaceae, red flowers in a cat-tail, large round leaves. This is a totem at Nalawa in Ra, symbolic of their human genitals; the name of the plant is not to be pronounced in that area. The leaves are an ingredient boiled with Pandanus leaves (after soaking the Pandanus in the mud) to fix the black colour, used along with the leaves of *koka* tree, Bischofia javanica, notably on Gau Island. A red species, A. wilkesiana, *kalabuci damu* is a common ornamental planted by Europeans. Syn. (West) *ruru*.

kalaisiga fern spp. that is open under the hot sun, closes as the sun declines, as implied in the Fijian name.

kalaji (Eng.) n. clutch, as in an automobile.

vakatala-i-siga walk about or work under the hot sun.

kalairoro bowed, as with age or infirmity (people).

kalaroko bowed in posture, from respect.

kalasi (Eng.) class, as in school.

kalasi-taka (Eng.) to classify, to arrange in classes or groups, or by qualities.

kalavo 1. (Eng.) social club, night club.

kalavo 2. rat, mouse. Fijians words did not distinguish clearly between rats and mice, which they considered to be small rats. Mice were inadvertently introduced and are now sometimes called *mausi*. The Polynesian rat (Rattus exulans) was very likely an aboriginal introduction, and rats were caught and eaten in former times, before European sensibilities inhibited the custom. Now the Polynesian rat is restricted mainly to smaller, offshore islands because it cannot compete with two later introductions, the black rat (R. rattus) of the forests, and the Norway rat (R. norvegicus), which usually depends on humans and lives close to them, and close to water, for it is an agile swimmer. Of Asian origin, the Norway rat is also responsible for carrying the flea that is the vector for bubonic plague, which has never been know to occur in Fiji. Surprisingly, there are some fifteen cases a year in the U.S.A.

The black rat has a long tail (longer then the head and body), and is an agile climber of trees, capable of leaping among the tree-tops. The female black rat has ten nipples, while the Polynesian rat has only eight, and the Norway rat has twelve. A short tail distinguishes the Norway rat as it is far shorter than the head and body. The Polynesian rat-tail is about the same length as its head and body. All of the rats have caused serious depradation of birds that nest on the ground, including the aboriginally introduced jungle fowl. (I am indebted to Paddy Ryan for most of these notes.)

kalavo 3. n. (Slang) prostitute.

kalawa, kalawaca v. to step, step over. *kalawaca na ikelikeli* step over the ditch. *E kalawa ga vakavica.* He took just a few steps. Syn. *lakawa*. By ext. *kalawaca* to omit, to skip, or to pass over, improperly but perhaps inadvertantly, some item or some person(s).

ikalawa n. step, as in walking, used sometimes as a crude measure of length.

kalesi broken, hanging down (branch of tree).

Kalevu or **Kwalevu** n. chiefly title at the coast of Nadroga. With some degree of presumption, this title is now considered by the national administration to be paramount in Nadroga Province.

kali n. (Archaic) neck-rest, traditional artefact of carved wood or bamboo, to support the head while sleeping. It also protected a man's coiffure, an important feature of vanity. Now carved and sold only as tourist souvenir. Though no longer used, the neck-rest is comfortable to one accustomed to it. Indigenous Fijians used no soft pillows; that was a European and Tongan innovation.

kali ni qio n. a beautiful, very common bright blue type of starfish, quite useless, "shark's pillow", Linckia laevigata. Syn. *ilokoloko ni qio*.

kali, kalia, kaliraka v. to separate forcefully, to split something, as in the hand. to tear off by hand, as a page from a newspaper. *kaliraka* to grasp away, snatch away, as in *Kaliraka o Nadi na icovi ni rakavi*. Nadi snatched away (from Suva) the rugby prize.

kalikali separated, of a married couple. *Keirau sa veikalikali dede.* We (2) have ben separated a long time.

kali v. to wean (a child or young animal). *ikali ni gone* n. ceremony celebrating weaning of a child, a time also when husband and wife may resume sexual intercourse. This delay of time between births of children is traditional, preceding Christianity.

kali-na n. of banana or plantain, the lower hands on the bunch, thought to be of less good quality and size compared to the upper hands of the fruit. See *veta-i-cake*.

kalia 1. n. edible double-headed parrot fish, greyish light brown in colour, large scales, Bolbometopon muricatus, nibbles at the coral, schools at night.

kalia 2. n (Archaic, Syn. *drua*, now the more common name). A huge obsolete type of sea-going canoe developed mainly by Tongans in Fiji in the last quarter of the 1700s. The ship had great carrying capacity and could beat to windward. It was a major factor in the conquest and trade that brought Tongan influence to dominate and integrate in Fiji. The timber was Fijian *vesi* (Instia bijuga) which was still abundant at Kabara and in parts of Cakaudrove. With its outrigger, the *kalia* hull was partly a proto-Polynesian concept. The bow-shape, mast and sail-plan owe more to Micronesian technique, with stern and bow interchangeable to facilitate tacking. Two famous Samoan builders in Fiji, Lemaki and Leha of Manono Island, are credited with adapting features of the Samoan fishermen's paddling canoe, the *va'a alo*. They added planking, with a simple cutwater bow and an uplifted, tapered stern that were functionally interchangeable when the ship was tacking. Famous *kalia* include the "Draunivia" of Tanoa, 105 feet, built 1820 by Maopo of Kabara. This topic owes much to Fergus Clunie.

kaliko n. (Eng.) calico, but in Fiji, the term covers several sorts of cotton fabric.

ikalima fifth (in sequence). *lima* five. *lima* is a Proto-Polynesian word for "hand".

ka lo n. secret.

kalo (Colo, Nait., Namosi) to bring water (Bauan *taki*). See *talo*.

kalobi dented (car), mis-shapen by being bent, folded over (piping, timber), slumped down (person). See *lobi, lobia, lobika*.

kalokalo n. star. No distinction was made among stars, planets, comets.
  Idiom: *Raica na kalokalo mataidua.* (Anglicism) Knocked silly, knocked out, "seeing stars", severely stunned. *matakalokalo* n. constellation of stars. Only Polynesian navigators had a knowledge of the stars. That knowledge is now mostly forgotten. They were aware that stars maintain a constant declination (celestial latitude) and knew what islands were to be found under which major star's declination. The star Sirius, for example, signals the latitude of Fijian islands.

kaloko (Eng.) clock, o'clock. *E vica na kaloko?* What time is it? *E lima na koloko.* Five o'clock. *Veimama na lima* half past five. *Sa vo tini na miniti me lima.* Ten minutes to five. *kaloko ni liga* wrist-watch. *kaloko ni vakayadra* alarm clock.

kalolo bent or leaning to one side, as a growing plant might be.

kaloni (Eng.) n. cologne, after-shave lotion.

kalou n. spirit, god, many in form and nature, always to be feared. They are everywhere. A Fijian would hardly dare stay alone in the forest at night. Certain places may be especially fearful. Syn. (West) *nitu*.

Kalou n. God, a word adapted by Methodist missionaries for their Christian God and then used also by Roman Catholics and later denominations. Earlier, *kalou* meant "ghost" or "spirit", in some cases tribal gods who might be protective, as in *kalou vu*. These days one tends to refer to spirits as *tevoro*, a word of Tongan origin, meaning devils, a concept that did not previously exist in Fiji. Devils are very real to many Fijians. The ancient Fijian *kalou* might be powerful and sometimes dangerous but they were not perforce evil and they were certainly not satanic.

kalou-ca unfortunate(ly), unlucky.

kalou-gata 1. adj. happy, lucky, blessed. The word seems to refer to the supreme snake-god Degei who is a benign or indifferent creature, certainly not threatening. (*kalou* spirit, *gata* snake.) Modernism: *Mo kalougata tiko!* Be happy! See *Degei*, legendary immigrant chief, later a sacred spirit.

kalou-gata 2. n. good fortune, happiness, blessings.

kalou-ni-wai 1. n. hookworm, or also pinworm that may cause itchiness at the anus when it itches at night. Pinworms emerge at night to lay eggs at the anus. Local people are often accustomed to the pinworm do not feel any irritation. Usual medication is mebendazole pills available in Fiji without prescription.

kalou-ni-wai 2. n. larvae of mosquitos that wriggle about in water. They feed on tiny particles of organic material (such as decaying leaves), moult three times, and then transform to pupae at the fourth moult. Pupae look like black commas. They split and release a fully formed mosquito within three days.

kalou vu n. A spirit-god of some social group (tribe, *yavusa* or clan, *mataqali*), not usually a human ancestral leader (and thus differing from the *vu*, an originating ancestral person, often later considered a spirit, but not worshipped or solicited with offerings at a temple). The *kalou vu* can take the form *waqawaqa* of some animal (often a snake, pig, dog, shark) or reside unseen within some object such as a rock or a war-club. The *kalou vu* was subject of worship and offerings, and was often served by a priest or priestly clan within the tribe and there was often a temple *bure-kalou* for that purpose. There were some 20 temples counted at Bau Island in 1853. The founding ancestral spirit *vu* is is sometimes shared between two peoples who later became divided. They are then said to be related as *vietauvu* to each other. This allows permissive joking and privileges they make take with each other. Similar relations may have resulted from an ancient chiefly marriage between two groups.

kalove bent (as of a nail). *love, loveca* v. to bend.

kalu, kaluva v. to whistle, whistle at. *kalukaluva* (or) *va-kalukaluva* to whistle at (person, people, dog) at a distance. *kaluva na sere* to whistle the song, not custom in old Fiji. Whistling was only used for signaling.

Idiom: *Me sivi na veikau qai kalu.* Don't rejoice till success is certain, don't count your chickens till they hatch, lit. get out of the forest, then feel free to whistle (with a feeling of success).

ikalu n. whistle. Formerly carried by some chiefs in the western highlands of Viti Levu, attached to a cord around the neck. No certainty as to the function of those whistles.

kama, kamaca n., v. to fire, burn, scorch (may refer to sunburn). *wai kama* hot spring, hot acid (sulphuric, hydrochloric). *kama bula* wild fire, hot fire, still burning, spreading. *kama bulabula* burn alive. *kama mate* burned to death. *kama yavu* burned to the ground. *vosa ni vakamakama* inflammatory words, speech. *vakama, vakamaca* v. to set fire, burn it. *vakama tamata* cremate. *E kamaci au na sitovu.* The stove burned me. Idiom: *kama na veigasau* refers to the incredible rapidity with which rumours or surprising news travels about on "coconut wireless".

vaka-maca v. to dry (clothes), usually by hanging. See *mamaca* dry.

kamedre adj. badly tangled (rope, fishing line). *medre* tangled.

kamikamica (or) **kamica** adj. good tasting, sweet, flavourful, nicely salted (food), pleasant (speech, manners, appearance). *wai ni gunu kamica* soft drinks. *vakamikamica-taka* v. to sweeten (something to be consumed), to make it more tasty.

kamunaga n. traditional Fijian riches of ceremonial presentation offerings, especially whale teeth, but including mats and barkcloth. This word is used mostly by people formally accepting such offerings, speaking of them in a complimentary manner.

kamusu cut, broken, rather forcefully. See *musu, musuka* to break off or cut in two.

kana, kania v. to eat, to eat it. *Mai kana!* Come, eat! When eating it is customary, virtually imperative, to invite any visitor or passer-by to share the food. *kakana* n. food. *laukana* usually eaten, eaten, edible. *masu ni kana* grace said before a meal, a strict custom in virtually every Fijian household. *Sa kana vinaka.* It tastes good. *na kanavalavala* n. the part of the human head on each side of the temple, the part that moves when one eats. *vakania na manumanu* v. to feed the animals.

Idiom: *kana bui ni vuaka.* lit., eat pig's tail, refers to a child who cannot sit still, wriggling around like the tail of a pig.

Idiom: *matai via kana vuaka.* lit., carpenter who wants to eat pork, i.e., refers to a person who might pretend to diligence and skills but in fact is only interested in how the work is rewarded.

Idiom: *Sa kua la na kana!* Playful flattering words said before a pretty girl. Implies she is so pretty that it puts you off your food.

Idiom: *kana vosa* to take verbal abuse, get complaints.

Idiom: *kana e loma* eats away inside (disease, hurtful words). *E kana e loma vei au na nomu vosa.* Your words feel hurtful to me.

Idiom: *Kana, kana! Ka o lakova mai.* Lit. "Eat, eat! That's what you came for." Teasing a friend who is passing by during a meal, invited to join in.

kana cagi v. n., an idiom, to eat nothing, as in skipping breakfast or lunch. lit. "eat the wind". Syn. (Slang) *kana "wind"-pai*. *kana wai*, by contrast, refers to a definitive and total loss, as of a team at some sport.

kanace n. blue-spot mullet, seasonal migrants upriver. A secret, sacred totem among a few Colo East kin-groups, as at village Naqara. Valamugil spp. See also *kava*.
  Idiom: *rokoroko vakanace*. lit., show respect like a mullet, i.e., fail to give
  proper respect, just as a mullet skips out of the water to avoid the larger,
  predatory fish.

kanakana (ni bulumakau) n. cow pasture.

ikanakana 1. n. taste, flavour (food or beverage). *Vakacava na kena ikanakana?* What does it taste like?

ikanakana 2. n. piece of land belonging to a clan, used for planting food crops.

ikanakana 3. n. piece of land granted as a food-garden area for someone who is a useful but needful member of the community. The land is not permanently alienated. *e dua na qele me kedra ikanakana* a piece of land to provide for their food.

vaka ikanakana adj. edible, tasty.

kanakana ca v. to eat alone, secretly, very bad manners in Fiji, where one must always offer to share food with other people. Syn. *kana lo*.

kanaki dirty, unkempt, slovenly.

kana kuita v. to beat or flog, give a thrashing. *kanakuita* n. corporal punishment (as formerly, in schools). *kuita* octopus.

kanala (Eng.) n. colonel.

kanalevu 1. glutton(ous), heavy eater.

kanalevu 2. tasteless or tasting "off", lacking a proper taste.

kana lo v., n. to eat by oneself to avoid sharing food, or by extension, to conceal some secret purpose. Not sharing food would be despised behaviour to Fijians.

kanamoce v., adj. **1.** usually after a hard day's work, from fatigue, to eat dinner and go right to sleep without delay.

kanamoce v., adj. **2.** to be lazy, or not having to do any work, just enjoy one's leisure, eat and sleep without taking the trouble of working. This is the most common meaning of the idiom.

kana-sese adj. of pregnant woman, to have crazy, idiosyncratic food desires.

kana-valavala n. lower jaw of the human head, from the notion that it moves *yavala* when a person eats the food. See *galegale*.

kanavata n., v. meal shared with family, friends or colleagues. *vata* together. This is informal, with no traditional ceremony, only the saying of grace before a meal, now customary among Fijians. Sharing of food is very important to Fijians.

kanavoro v. to over-eat, stuff oneself with food to the point of discomfort.

kanawai Idiom: v. to lose badly, usually at some sporting game such as football; lit. to eat water, to get nothing. See *kanacagi*.

vei-kana-yaki v., n. to eat here and there, take food where one can, in different places.

kanedromo n. the bird, Velvet Dove of Kadavu Island, Ptilinopas layardi.

kani n., adj. dry scaly skin, often with blotches, that results from excessive drinking of *yaqona*. *kanikani* refers to serious cases.

veikanikani n. cannibalism.

kani v. afflicted, and seriously weakened. *Sa kani koya na tauna*. He/she is seriously afflicted with elephantiasis. As a prefix, *kani* may refer to specific afflictions, as follows:

kani-rere terrified.

kani-siga sunburn(ed)

kani-tevoro adj., n. of a person, involuntarily possessed by a devil *tevoro*. This is a fairly frequent occurence. The agitated victim is usually held down and attended to, being told to : Eat it! *Kania!*

kani-uca spoiled by the rain.

kanikani ora n., v. to tickle deliberately, tickling, usually the armpits, ribs, soles of the feet.

vakania v. to feed (person, animal). *vakania na koli* to feed the dog.
  Idiom: *vakania na qio* lit. feed the sharks, i.e., to vomit at sea when seasick.

ika ono sixth.

kanu (Archaic) n. decorative pattern markings on pottery. Term used to describe markings on ancient Lapita pottery but also some modern pottery. *na kanukanu* the making of such markings. *kanu, kanuma* v. to make such markings.

kara 1. v. to squawk (parrot), from the sound the parrot makes.

kara 2. v., n. to make obstreperous noise (mainly children). *E tabu eke na kara.* No shouting allowed here.

kara 3. to be thirsty for some beverage (water, *yaqona*, beer). *karamaca* extremely thirsty.
Idiom: *Oi au sa kara.* Make another round of *yaqona*, lit. I am still thirsty.
Idiom: *gunu kara* after drinking kava and wanting to sleep, to realize the need to drink more to enable sleep

kara 4. n., adj. bruise, bruised, of person, fruit.

kara 5. n. ringworm (a common skin fungus of children).

kara 6. adj. not completed, decided upon but not carried out. *bose kara* conference scheduled but deferred. *buta kara* of food, not fully cooked as had been expected.

kara ni ulu n. dandruff.

kara, karaca v. to reprimand, scold. *na karakara* the reprimand.

kara, karavaka (or) **karataka** 1. v. to paddle (boat, canoe). *karataka na waqa i cakau* paddle the boat to the reef. Unlike eastern Polynesians, Fijians apparently had no elaborately decorated oars.

kara, karavaka 2. v. to pole (boat), to pole for something or someone. *ikara* pole for poling a boat.

karadila n. (Eng.) Granadila, mostly referring to the common wild introduced Passifolora foetida, with a small, very hard shell, but the name applies also to the true Granadila, P. quadrangularis, cultivated rarely.

vakarakara adj., used only in an idiom: *rourou* (or) *bele vakarakara* taro leaf (or) *bele* vegetable leaf boiled in water (without any coconut cream) sometimes with salt and onion. (Onion is an introduced, imported food.)

vaka-takarakara-taka v. to make a symbol, sign, action that represents something else. That can be a sign, diagram, picture, enactment or re-enaction, perhaps of a drama, or an historical event.

ivaka-takarakara n. representation, that could include say, a re-enactment of the signing of the Deed of Cession, or a thing, such as an imitation (as a rather modern notion), a sign, symbol, diagram, that represents a thing or an action.

karakara levu v. to talk with unpleasantly loud voice(s), rowdy (as of children) and thus self-assertive and disrespectful.

karakara-visa loud, unpleasant sound grating on the nerves (crackling of radio, children packed in a room, some music bands with electronic amplifiers).

kara-karawa 1. blue (many things, sky, sea, fish). *Sa karakarawa na draki.* It is relatively cloudless day with blue sky. The Fijian colour formerly meant either blue or green, inspired from the colour of some Fiji parrots, which depends on the angle viewed and the light. Modernly, *drokadroka* is used for the abstract colour green, though previously that word would be used mainly for plant material.

karakarawa 2. n. sp. of edible parrot fish blue and green colours, as implied by the name, Chlorurus sordidus, Scarus fasciatus, to 18 cm. Syn. *rawarawa*.

karaki vosa adj. talkative (of person), loquacious, garrulous.

karamaca very thirsty. *maca* dry.

karasi (Eng. "grass") marijuana. *kana karasi* smoke marijuana.

karasini or **karesini** (Eng.) n. kerosene. Also, by extension, a kind of tree that has a wood that catches fire very easily and quickly even when wet. The tree *vesiwai* sometimes goes by this name. That is a very dense wood.

karata v., n. thud, to make a very soft, sudden plosive sound, a far-off gunshot in the distance, a fart, a bag bursting, a coconut falling.

karawa, dark green as of vegetation in the shade. Also the name of a type of shark, possibly Isurus glaucus.

karela (Hindi) Indian vegetable, Momordica charantia, Cucurbitaceae, sold in the public market, naturalised in some places. Syn. *kerala*.

kareti (Eng.) n. carrot, also cart. (Slang) lover.

kari (Eng.) n. curry, turmeric. *tara kari* prepare curry (Fijian adaption of Hindi term "thar kari"). Curry powder normally contains about 25% turmeric powder and at least 25% coriander seed powder. Other ingredients may include cinnamon, clove, chilli powder (not traditionally Indian), and black pepper (the traditional "hot" ingredient).

kari, karia, karitaka v. to grate, scrape with sharp instrument some part of a plant such as coconut flesh, breadfruit; scrape off, for example: midrib of Pandanus leaves for weaving, medicinal bark from tree, outer bark from mulberry stems, for barkcloth., burnt crumbs from toast, mud from a shoe. *karitaka* to scrape forcefully. *ikari* (*ni niu*) coconut-grater.

karia v. to ripen (bananas only, not plantains) by putting salt on the broken-off stems of the hands of bananas and storing in enclosed space (bag, box, hole in ground), where self-generated ethylene gas hastens the process. This is an introduced process.

karikari 1. n. scrapings, such as the skin of *yaqona* branches, either discarded or used as a bitter, cheap adulterant often mixed with the root *waka* or rhizome *lewena* to be used as a beverage. *Karikari ni yaqona* has only one percent kavalactones (the active ingredients of *yaqona*), while the rhizome has 6 to 8 per cent, and the root usually has 9 to ten percent, in some cases up to 15% while 19% has been recorded. Syn. *civicivi* which properly refers to chippings of the skin. Removal of the *yaqona* skin is done by Fijians of Polynesian background, not Melanesians.

karikari 2. n. yard(s) of a sail.

Karipea n., adj. Caribbean, the ocean and chain of islands in the West Indies.

karisi (Eng. "cress") n. watercress, edible leaves, flowers faded pink. Several native species grow naturalised in drains, wet places, but are little used by Fijians. Rorippa nasturtium-aquaticum (or) Ipomea aquatica. A few Fijians cultivate it for sale. Syn. *ota karisi*. (Rewa) *karamua*.

Karisito (Eng.) n. Christ. Syn. (R. Cath.) *Kirisito*.

karobo n., v. dusk, twilight. *Sa karobo mai na vanua* or *Sa lutu mai na karobo*. It is becoming twilight, night is falling. Syn. (Colo East) *galo*. *vagalo* v. to have supper (at dusk, just before nightfall). In the tropics, twilight is quite brief, not prolonged as in temperate climates. Formerly, Fijians normally had their second and last meal of the day before nightfall.

karokaro n., adj. pimples, pimply (person, fruit), scabies. Syn. *karo*. *moli karokaro* lemon, lit. "pimply" citrus.

karoko v. to walk with head down from age, infirmity or respect. Also the name of a village in Cakaudrove.

karona v. to cherish, look after, take care of (child, garden, boat, but usually humans) with emotional involvement. *na veikaroni* love and concern, tender care. *dau karoni* dearly beloved. Cf. *vakamareqeti* treasured, often referring to a treasured possession.

ikarua 1. n. second one in a sequence.

ikarua 2. virtually the same, duplicate, replicate.

karua n. a certain type of family relative: first cousin of same sex if one of the cousins is married (the idea is as a back-up to support the wife if the husband dies). May also apply to two unrelated men who are married to a couple of sisters. Two such related people are said to be *veikaruani*. *Karua* can be used as a form of address, now sometimes used jokingly amongst unrelated people if the potential partner is found to be attractive.

karui adj. worthless, powerless, useless, dirty, ill-behaved (person). *Sa karui na nona itovo* His/her behaviour is unacceptable. Syn. *gavui*.

karuka (Lau) n. small common ground-fern now used in floral decorations. So-called male and female forms viz., *karuka tagane* and *karuka yalewa*, the latter, female form used under house-mats to soften the flooring, Pteridium esculentum. Syn. *koukou, qato*. These names may be used for more than one species. One such is Dicranopteris linearis.

kasa (ni yaqona) n. section of *yaqona* stem with one or two nodes, planted for propagation, or cut and dried as an adulterant to the beverage when it is sold in the form of powder. Virtually all *yaqona* that is sold as powder is adulterated with *kasa* or the rhizome (*lewena*) that has a weaker flavour (lower kavalactone content) than the root (*waka*). That is why Fijians often prefer to buy unpounded kava, and do the pounding themselves.

kasa 1. v. to run aground (of boat), or drift ashore. *vakasa* make a boat go aground. By ext. also, to be admitted to hospital *vakasa e vale ni bula*. And to gather firewood drifting in the water *vakasa buka*.

kasa 2. v. to understand and quickly commit to memory. *loma kasa* quick-learner, intelligent. *vakasa* to make someone understand and remember. *vakasama-taka* ponder, consider, think about it.

ika sa n. partner. *ika sa ni drua* one of a set of twins. Syn. *isa*.

kasabura v. to burst and spurt out (like a boil lanced).

kasaga (or) **manumanu ni cagi** n. Lesser Frigate Bird, Fregata ariel (the much more common species, males with two white patches underneath), or Greater Frigate Bird, F. minor (males all black, female has white throat and breast). Rarely go out to sea more than 75 miles and thus an indicator of nearby land. Cannot land at sea because feathers are not water-repellant and feet not webbed. With long hooked bill it often steals small fish caught by other birds. In breeding season males can display conspicuous red throat-patch. Syn. (Regional) *lasaqa*.

kasala n. a sp. of edible salt-water rock cod, grey background with brown colour markings of a a grouper, to 55 cm. Lodges at holes in the reef. Epinephelus polyphekadion. Same genus as *kavu*. Syn. *se-ni-kawakawa*. (Lau) *kerakera*.

Idiom: *vunau va Ra Kasala* doing the very same thing he/she advises against, thus a hypocrite. *vunau* sermon.

kasalu n. dry twigs, small kindling, usually for lighting fire.

kasa-na n. stem, petiole, pedicule of a plant. Usually applies to fruit or flowers. May apply to other things with a small stalk or handle.

kasami-taka v. to suspect. *Au kasamitaki Seru.* I suspect Seru.

kasari n. dried branched stalk of coconut palm from which the nuts hung, used as a sort of rake or crude broom.

kasa uru v. to fall down amply, as of fruit or coconuts, collapse (tree, house) into a pile. May refer to things in a huge pile.

kase, kaseta v. to slander behind the back, back-bite, gossip about (person). *kaseti au* gossip about me. *kakase* n. gossip.

kasei torn, broken open (clothes). *kasei rua* split in two.

kasere, kakaseresere v. to tear in many places, be torn to bits.

kasese n. scab, as of a cut or wound. Particle(s) of "sleep" in the eye or on the eyelids, or dried spittle, dried mucus on the face. Related to the word *imamaca*.

kasi 1. n. abcess or long-term internal injury as from a fall.

kasi 2. (or) **kasiqarisui** n. a Fijian malady, painful joints, possibly related to arthritis. Somewhat similar in notion is *kasi-qari-lewe*, probably related to rheumatism *sasala*.

kasi 3. n. very fine root-hairs, as of *yaqona*. *wa kasi* sp. of very thin vine.

kasi 4. (Eng.) n. gas. *kasi gaga* poison gas (wartime).

kasi 5. v. to crawl. *kasi lo* crawl secretly. Syn. *qasi*.

kasi 6. n. strip of skin from plantain or banana stem, used as string for binding.

kasi, kasia 1. v. to peel or cut off and away, or fall away (dead leaves, useless stem-skin of banana, pandanus), skin (cassava, fruit). Syn. (Lau) *qasi, qasia*.

kasi, kasia, kasina 2. v. to tie together on a string something such as mud lobsters *mana*, sea crabs *qari* or land crabs *lairo*.

kasikasi n. small hermit crabs sometimes used for bait, Cancer sp.

kasina n. furry sort of "hair" on the ferntree trunk, which indicates maturity and strength of the trunk.

kasiraki attractive, neat, well presented, of a person.

Kasitaba (Eng.) Customs.

kasitati (Eng.) custard.

kasivi n. tiny ant, often appearing in great numbers during rainy weather or even before the rain. Syn. (Lau) *qasivi*.

kasivi, kasivita n. to spit, spit on. It has been custom, falling into disuse, to spit (or simulate spitting) and express one's good wishes (fair weather, good crops) at the drinking of a bowl of *yaqona*, particularly at formal ceremonies. *ikasivi* n. spit. *kakasivi* n. spittoon, usually old tobacco tin or section of bamboo. Syn. (Lau) *kanusi, kanusitaka*.

Idiom: *kasivita na vale* celebrate finishing building of house, usually jovial *yaqona*-drinking, the house-owner as host. The celebration is called *ikasiviti ni vale*. In urban areas the custom has fallen into disuse.

ikaso 1. in the old game of *veitiqa*, the shaft of the javelin to which the head (*ulutoa*) was attached. This was usually made from a reed (*gasau*).

ikaso 2. n. bar that connects a canoe to its outrigger.

ikaso 3. n. child(ren) born out of wedlock, of a chiefly father. *ikaso vesi* when the mother is chiefly, *ikaso dolou* when the mother is a commoner. *vesi* is a strong, durable wood; *dolou* implies that the outrigger can be broken off easily, literally like old dead branch of breadfruit tree that breaks easily.

kasou 1. v. of water, to splash with bubbles, as from a wave or object falling in water, or from boiling.

kasou 2. adj. of a person, to be very drunk. Syn. *mateni*.

kasove adj. swampy, of land.

kasova spilt, from *sova, sova* pour it. *kaka-sovasova* spilt all over the place.

vakasova, vakasova v. to pour water carefully, usually on plants, to water them.

kasura 1. v. to burst open (of a boil, or parcel, bag, basket). *kakasurasura* burst all over the place, such as rice from a bag, many houses in big earthquake

kasura 2. v. to fall apart suddenly, collapse (shed, temporary building)

kasura 3. v. to break-up or disintegrate, of a business, voluntary sports team, political party, club or other group of people.

kata 1. (Eng.) n. cutter (boat), which replaced Fijian canoes. Cutters were much used for Fijian inter-island sailing from the 1920s or earlier, through the 1950s, before the use of outboards engines, motorized boats and scheduled airlines. Fijians are a very motile people and this was an historic era of intrepid sailing. Ports like Levuka and Lautoka were sometimes crowded with cutters. The cutters had no radio or navigational equipment, though some had motors. Only the larger cutters had a compass. Often the boats were overloaded with people and cargo, and hardly ever had life preservers or extra water. Living conditions aboard had no amenities. This word has fallen into disuse since cutters are obsolete. The port of Levuka lost its importance in sea traffic when motorised boats became common. In Macuata and some other parts of Vanua Levu, the word *kata* was also applied to motorised boats, Joe Hewson tells me. Syn. *waqa vakalaca*, the general term for sailboats.

kata 2. (Archaic) n. hull of an outrigger canoe. *cama* n. outrigger.

kata, katia v. to bite (animal, person), sting (insect, a thorny plant), (Lau) itch. *kati mai* have a bite (from fruit, candy etc., inviting someone to share it). *E kati na siwa.* The fish are biting. *ikata* n. bite. *na katakata* the biting (also meaning "the heat". *E sega ni veikati na koli.* The dog does not bite.

vakata v. to hunt with dogs (for pigs, mongoose).

kata-bokoboko adj. indistinct, unclear, blurred, faded (as of an old photo).

katabu v. to refuse by facial gesture, pouting and pretending to spit, as a forceful rejection, as if affronted, a particularly Fijian grimace.

katabulu-taka v. to close both eyes, wink at (person), often in sly, secretive communication.

katadigi-taka v. to cluck the tongue in reproach, regret or surprise. *katadigita* cluck tongue once in strong approval.

katagusu v., n. the equiv. of English "Psst!", sort of hissing or kissing sound made by person, often to attract attention of someone; also the noise of a bat.

kataivanavana adj. of cloth or barkcloth, damaged, worn out, disintegrated, faded and weak from age, humidity, insect damage.

katakata adj. hot (weather, person, thing), hotly spiced (of food, with chilli, an introduced condiment). *yalo katakata* quick tempered. *katakata vinaka* good and hot. *vakatakata-taka* v. to warm it up, heat it up. *Me vakatakata mada na ovani.* Please heat the oven.

Idiom: *itukutuku buta katakata* Idiom: fresh "hot" news, lit. hot from cooking.

Idiom: *katakata vakurokava* become quickly hot then quickly cold (object, person's temperament), like a tin-pot that heats quickly but then cools off quickly. People may begin with great enthusiasm, but may lose interest quickly.

ikatalau n. breakfast food, these days a rather formal word. More modernly, familiarly, one says *gunu ti*, "drink tea", specifically meaning breakfast which may or may not be substantial. Formerly Fijians ate only two meals a day. They often rose at dawn and worked for a few hours before breakfasting. Lunch was never a formal meal. Supper was usually eaten just before nightfall. *katalau, katalautaka* v. to breakfast, to eat for breakfast.

katalautaka v. to have (something consumed) for breakfast. Fijians often eat a piece of cassava, or some flour-based fried food.

katamisi v. to make a sound sucking the teeth, indicating reproach.

kata-remoremo v. to flicker, of a light such as a candle or a failing light.

katariva, katarivata v. to blink or wink deliberately, make a secret signal to someone. Such private signals are common because open talk may be thought to be rude or too revealing.

katasisi v. to signal to someone by making a hissing sound. *katasisitaki au* to signal to me by hissing. In English this might be the equivalent of "Psst!", to attract someone's attention. Syn. *katasiu*.

katasiu v. to make a hissing sound to call someone, or dog. Also said of a kettle hissing, or a steam-pipe, or a cat, snake or mongoose. Syn. *katasomi*.

katasomo n. tinea, athlete's foot or so-called "jock-itch", a fungus, often treated with tolnaftate or other fungicide.

katavatu n. a small Tridacna sp., var. of giant clam that is generally known as *vasua*.

katavida v. to snap (fingers), click (noise of prawns). See *vida*.

katavila (Eng.) n. bulldozer, "Caterpillar".

katavoro v. to bite through and break off with the teeth (sugar cane, nut).

katebe adj. chipped (cup, plate, clay pot).

katela adj. broken, cracked in two (plate, bottle, coconut), separated (land, by flood).

kateni (Eng.) n. carton. *kateni-taka* v. to put things in a carton.
katete v. spread out widely (weed on land, oil spilled on floor, news among people). See *tete*.
kati 1. (Eng. "cut") n., v. card game with the purpose of collecting money for some local cause. At each round, participants "buy" one or more cards at a set price (these days 50¢ up to $1), and win a prize if one of their cards is selected at the cut. Prizes are usually one or more items of food (sugar, rice), or things of practical everyday use (bowl, knives). Cuts are made rapidly so that quite a bit of money can be made, and almost everybody goes home with some prizes. This is a good feeling of social togetherness and *yaqona* is usually served freely by the organiser.
kati 2. (Slang) n. young girl-friend, boy-friend (opposite sex), implying bother and trouble of a self-interested young child; cuteness may be implied.
katikati 1. adj. jealous, spoiled, demanding (child). *kakua ni katikati* don't be a spoiled brat. It seems that some people use this word simply referring to children without implying a demanding or cheeky nature.
katikati 2. v. to sting, as from medication on a cut, scratching or scraping of an arm of leg in falling, prick or scratch of thorns. See *sasa*.
katikati matua (Lau) v. to insist on getting something. Syn. *cikecike*.
kati, katia, katilaka v. to bite (food, prey), sting (insect, irritant such as tiny thorns). *katilaka* v. to bite hard. *katikatilaka* bite very hard repeatedly.
katibi adj. chipped (cup, plate, clay pot). syn. *katebe*.
katiki adj. cracked (tooth, plate); from *tiki, tikica*.
ikatini tenth, tithe (as imposed by certain Christian sects).
kato n. angular-shaped basket, bag, or modernly, a box. *kato kau* wooden trunk (usually for personal belongings). *kato ni lako* travel bag. *kato lili* handbag. *kato ni vosa* n. recorder. (tape or disc). *kato ni iyaya* tool-box. *kato ni vuli* school bag. *kato ni volivoli* shopping bag. *kato ni ki* key-case. *kato ni meli* mail-box. *kato ni ilavo* money-box. *kato* (or) *kisi ni mate* coffin. *kato ni wai* water-container, water canteen (of soldiers) *Kato ni Cakamana* legendary magic basket or box containing precious ancestral objects, lost at sea in a storm in the Yasawas just before one of the later, major migrations arrived at the so-called First Landing near Vuda on the west coast of Viti Levu. *kato ni tu* box or case in which a clan *mataqali* or other kin-group may keep precious records such as lease records, papers from hearings of the Native Lands Commission, lists of registered members, births and deaths, maps of their lands), or precious objects such as historic clubs, axes, breast-plates, or carved images. This is often in a trunk, kept in a private part of the chief's house if it exists at all. Syn. (Rewa) *bola*.
Idiom: *kato ni bula* n. person one depends on.
Idiom: *kato ni dredre* (Slang) lit. "laughing box", person who makes everybody laugh.
katoa 1. adj. abundant, of fish caught. One never uses this word before going fishing. That would be certain to bring bad luck and poor fishing. Idiom: *katoa na domo* lots of words but only talk, no performance.
katoa 2. adj. successful. *lesu katoa mai vanua tani* v. to return successful from overseas.
katokatoni n. recording (usually music), compact disc or tape. *na iyaya ni katokatoni* recording equipment.
Katolika n., adj. Roman Catholic. *na Lotu Katolika* the Catholic church.
ikatolu third.
katona v. to retain, to keep permanently (an object, a thought, a feeling).
katona, katona-taka v. to record (music etc.).
kato ni gone n. uterus, womb. Syn. *duve*.
kato ni mi n. bladder (urinary). *mi* urine.
kato ni vosa n. recorder, as for musical tapes, compact discs.
kato-ni-wai-liliwa n. a rather dated, awkward word for refrigerator or cooler. Modernly on might just hear the word "fridge".
katu, katuma v. to measure in fathoms (approx. 6 feet), with outstretched arms and hands. *vale katu tolu* house three-fathoms in length. *katudrau* ceremonial barkcloth (*masi*), of great length, theoretically of 100 fathoms, for formal presentation. The size of a Fijian house is normally expressed as so many fathoms (*katu*) in length.
Idiom: *vale katu dua* burial grave.
Idiom: *katuwalu* complicated, hard to understand, especially of English or foreign speech.
katukatu v. to run with long steps in the stride. (A *katu* is about 6 feet in length or height.)

katuba n. doorway but modernly that implies a door. Fijian did not have a fixed or hinged door. They used unattached matting or woven leaves as a closure (*isogo*). In the highland a block of wood was sometimes used that was propped up by a stone that covered up half of the doorway. (See Roth, *Fijian Way of Life*, p. 26.) The height of the doorway opening was formerly very low; a visitor could not enter erect. This would delay an attacker. Syn. *darava*. *icurucuru* entrance/exit. Early Fijian houses had only one doorway, usually on the lee side, and no windows. Later Colonial authorities required houses to have at least two doors and three windows.

katuba leka (Anglicism) n. window. Traditional Fijian houses had no windows. *leka* short.

katuba levu n. main doorway of Fijian house where most people enter, at the lower end of the house. Syn. *katuba i sue*.

katuba e loma n. side doorway of Fijian house where privileged people enter. Syn. *katuba i kubu*. This custom developed after the Pax Brittanica.

katuni (Eng.) adj. funny in a ridiculous way, of a person or their behaviour, from the English, as from a "cartoon" character. Syn. *kisitoni, sakisi*.

katuvu v. explode, burst out (laughter, shouting, baloon bursting cannon, bamboo gun, music), punch hard, fight hard, from *tuvu-laka*. In Lau the word is *fufutekateka*.

kau n., adj. plant (small herbaceous plant, shrub, bush, or tree), timber, wood, stick. *vu ni kau* tree. *vale kau* wooden house. A clan's "plant" (*kau* or *kautabu*) is its sacred plant totem, a feature of Melanesian Fijians, especially on Viti Levu. Prohibitions have surrounded such totems and usually, a highland Fijian (*kaiColo*) will not mention the word and cannot discuss the subject when it has fertility and reproductive implications. In some places a certain plant may be iconic, though not a fertility totem. (The Native Lands Commission confuses the two concepts and has erred in believing that all Fijian clans have totems). *kau-vuata* fruit-tree. *kau-salusalu* tree that yield attractive or sweet-smelling flowers or leaves for making garlands, such as *mokosoi*. Syn. (Lau, Kadavu, VanuaLevu) *kacu*.

ikau 1 n. bunch of bananas or plantain. *veta* "hand" of bananas. Syn. (Lau) *ua*.

ikau 2. n. introduction of a book, essay, research report. Syn. *Vakamacala Taumada*.

ikau (ni meke) 3. n. song sung before an exhibition-dance (*meke*) begins.

veikau n. forest, bush. *veikau loa* deep forest, dense forest, remote forest.

kau, kauta v. to take, take away, bring, carry. *kauta mai* bring it here. *kauta yani* take it away (away from the speaker). *Kauta na isele me nomu.* Take the knive as your own (for yourself).

Idiom: *E kauta tu ga na ketena.* He/She comes (to the feast, dinner) bringing only his/her stomach, with no food or gift, just to eat "free".

kauta cake (Anglicism) v. to bring (it) up, as a topic in conversation, an item for an agenda.

kau laivi, kauta laivi v. to reject, to take away.

kau na mata ni gone n. a ceremony of introducing children to their mother's village, bringing substantial gifts (kerosene, mats, bales of cloth). By this, children are formally recognized at the village. (This ceremony is based on the traditional notion that the mother lives away from her own village, having joined her husband's village at marriage; these days that is not so often the case.) Fijian children are not supposed to appear at their mother's village till this ceremony has been performed. After it, they will have the rights and duties of a *vasu*. These days parents often wait to take all their children at the same time, so some of their children may already be in their teens. Commoners now sometimes ignore the custom as being too expensive for them, and formal village relationships not so important.

kaucina (or) **kaunicina** n. tree with edible nut but very hard shell, hard to crack. The nut oil formerly used by small-island people as lamp-oil. (*cina* lamp). Canarium harveyi, Burseraceae, but also two other indigenous species with a small nut, hard to crack, eaten only as an occasional snack. In Vanuatu, and especially parts of the Solomons and Papua-New Guinea there are more cultivars and this nut (larger than the Fijian species) was formerly a major staple food before the introduction of sweet potato and cassava that have displaced it completely. In western Melanesia, the Canarium nut is often know as the galip nut. Colourless sap turns white on exposure. See *yagai*, a Lauan name that derives from a Solomon language. Syn. *kaunigai*, referring possibly to the fact that wild pigs sometimes eat the bark. (*gai* baby pig). The name *kaunicina* may also apply to Haplolobus floribundus; hardened flammage latex formerly used in torches.

kaudamu n. timber tree, Myristica castaneifolia, syn. *maile* in eastern Fiji, closely related to commercial nutmeg, having a very similar fruit but without the taste. Named *kaudamu* for red bark and sap.

kaukauta v. to put on airs, be pretentious, self-promoting, pretending to be on par with higher-class people.,

Idiom: *Kua ni kaukauti iko cake* Don't "put on airs", Don't be pretentious, Don't act "big-time". In speaking English, Fijians might say "Don't put yourself up" or "Don't go around collar-up".

vakau, vakauta v. send off (message, package, person). *Vakau me la'ki lewai mai vanua tani* extradited to be judged overseas. *na ivola sa vakauta mai o Seru* the letter (or book) Seru sent here. *Ke o via vakau ilavo,* . . If you wish to send money, . .

kau baleta v. to intrude by word or action. *kau baleta na tanoa* to walk across in front of *yaqona* bowl *tanoa*, a disrespectful action; at informal grog sessions, when it may be absolutely necessary to walk in front of the *tanoa*, one should bow down and touch the bowl respectufully. *kau baleta na nodatou veivosaki* cut into our (several) conversation.

vakau-caca-taka v. to slander, speak ill of (person).

kaukamea 1. n. (Tongan *ukamea*) iron. *wa kaukamea* steel wire.

kaukamea 2. n. common weed, introduced, Vernonia cinerea, Compositae, leaves crushed and applied to cuts to prevent infection. Syn. *tagi-o-litia*.

kaukaro n. dangerous tree of dense forest, yellow or brown-black sap causing severe itch, blindness, Semecarpus vitiensis, Anacardiaceae. Red inner bark. Lves entire, stiff and leathery, dark green above, grey-green beneath, rounded apex. Frts all year, small to 3 cm, irregularly rounded, ripening orange to purple-black.The dangerous sap solidifies and becomes black on exposure to air. Syn. (Lau, Vanua Levu) *malawaci*.

kaukaua (or) **kaukauwa** adj. strong, tough. Modernly one might hear this word applied to a beverage such as kava, but that is not traditional usage.

va-kaukauwa-taka v. to make it firm, stronger. In spelling, the **w** may be omitted. See *kauwai*.

vakaukaua-i-yago (Anglicism) v., n. body-building.

ikaukau n. goods (mats, sinnet, barkcloth, kava, whaleteeth) brought in formal presentation, exchange, in traditional manner.

kauke n. sp. small land crab, used as bait, not eaten by Fijians. Rotumans eat it raw by sucking on it.

kau kola n. firewood ready to carry, already cut up.

kaulau adj. thorny (of plant).

kauloa n. tree, several different genera, including some of the Ebony family.

kaumoce n. plant(s), Cassia spp., weeds that have leaves folding up at night.

kau ni bati n. jawbone. See *galegale*.

kau ni buka n. wood to be lit by friction in making fire.

kau-ni-kuila n. flagpole.

Kaunisela (Eng.) n. Consul (foreign service). Councilor (as in town council).

kau ni siwa n. (Anglicism) fishing rod. The rather archaic terms *cavo* and *cavocavo* may also apply to fishing with a rod. Fijians never used fishing rods and only very rarely do in modern times.

Kaunitoni n. legendary ship of immigrant Lutunasobasoba and Degei, probably in 1600s, settling at Vuda, then with some of those of this so-called "First Landing", moving on to Nakauvadra. These immigrants arrived long after the much earlier, more Melanesian settlers.

kauta v. to reach, as of a path reaching a village, or the tide reaching to a certain location. This is not common usage. See *kau, kauta*.

kautabu 1. n. sp. prickly plant. Syn. *salato*, Dendrocnide harveyi, tree to 40 feet, leaves and sap causing skin irritation aggravated by water. Planted around ancient Fijian village-fortresses, this would help deter attackers.

kau tabu 2. n. central longitudinal post in house-roof.

kau tabu 3. n. totemic plant associated with a kin-group, clan or tribe, a Melanesian concept of a sacred symbol (*icavuti*) of that kin-group's fertility and reproductive viability. Similarly, the kin-group may have a sacred aquatic totem (*ika tabu*) and/or sacred animal (*manumanu tabu*), that may be a bird or insect. Among some Fijian groups, especially Viti Levu highlanders, it is forbidden to mention names of the local totems. Formerly, drastic consequences could ensue if anyone mentioned the name. That could include sexual assault, stripping of clothes, throwing the culprit in a river. Still today, offenders might be required to drink a huge bowl of *yaqona*, or have a bucket of water thrown over them. Elsewhere, kin-groups or tribes may have iconic plants, plants with which they are closely associated, or are famous for, but are not true totems as secret reproductive and fertility symbols. Beqa, for example is associated with *ivi* Polynesian Chestnut, and Rewa is associated with *via kana,* the root crop, but these are not totems as such.

kauveilatai 1. n. cross, often referring to the Christian cross. *Kauveilatai Damudamu* Red Cross.

kauveilatai 2. n. pile of sticks criss-crossed, usually to keep them dry for fire. This word supplied the origin for the concept of the Christian cross.

kauvaro n. sawn timber. *varo* to saw.

kauvuata n. fruit-tree, or tree that produces edible nuts (*tavola, tarawau* for example) or starch foods (*ivi*, jak-fruit, breadfruit).

kauvula n. a common soft-wood timber tree with compact crown, Endospermum macrophyllum, Euphorbiaceae, endemic on Fiji's larger islands, at altitudes below 900 m. Treated chemically for house-timber and formerly, for wooden boxes. Slightly triangular alternate leaves, spirally arranged. Globose yellow fruit, 8 mm diam, eaten by pigeons. Smooth whitish bark and white timber, as suggested by the name meaning "white timber". Colourless sap. Syn. (Namosi, Colo East) *lekutu*.

kauwai v. adj., to be interested, supportive. *Au sega ni kauwai kina vakalailai.* I am not at all interested in it. I cannot be bothered with it.

kauwaitaka v. to support, believe, care about, be concerned about. *au sega ni kauwaitaka na ka era tukuna* I do not care what they say, don't go along with it. *Kauwaitaka na lotu na levu ni wiliwili ni vakalutu.* The church is concerned about the great number of abortions.

kavika n. fruit of the tree *vunikavika*, semi-cultivated, Malay Apple, Syzygium malaccense, Myrtaceae, under 800 meters, some varieties tasteless, some delicious. (Very similar species, S. jambos and S. samarangense are tasteless.) Exists from Southeast Asia through the Pacific. Fruiting from May to February but mainly around early October, November, December. The flowers are scarlet. Inner bark with salt water and lime yields crimson stain, as does the root. The bark can also yield a yellow dye, according to Gale S. Troxler who studied Fiji bark-cloth. Two main varieties: *kavika damu* or *k. damudamu* (reddish at maturity), and *kavika vulavula* (whitish at maturity).
Syn. (Polyn.) *ka'ika* and cognates. Idiom: *kavika dreu lo* refers to a girl with a beautiful face who as yet does not adorn herself correspondingly with flowers, perfume. Lit., *kavika* fruit ripening secretly.

kava (Cakau.) n. edible fish, though not highly prized, diamond-scale mullet, or square-tail mullet, Liza vaigiensis, yellowish body, yellow tail. Unlike some other mullet (*kanace*), does not migrate upriver. It schools close to shore. Syn. *kanace* (general name for mullet). Waikava is a river on the southern coast of Vanua Levu Island. Waikava was the place of the second Council of Chiefs (actually only a few Roko Tui, salaried heads of provinces with advisory powers only), organised by Governor A. Gordon in 1876. (Only one Roko Tui attended all meetings; others were casual in their attendance.) Later, chiefs decided to call themselves the Great Council of Chiefs though many members were not chiefs. Today the place is a wilderness, with no sign remaining of the historical event. One chiefly family of tribe A i Sokula returned to live there after the Tui Cakau set aside their land on Taveuni to provide for Morris Hedstrom facilities. Syn. (Tonga) *'ava*.

kava 1. (Tonga) n. *yaqona*, the beverage shrub Piper methysticum, familiarly known as grog. Fijians of Polynesian background remove the skin (*civicivi*) from the rhizome (*lewena*) to make a whiter drink that is somewhat less bitter. The root (*waka*) makes a stronger beverage, preferred by many Fijians.

kava 2. (Tongan "kapa") n. sheet metal, corrugated iron, also a can or tin, as of meat or biscuits. *vale kava* n. house made of sheet metal. *kava ni benu* n. rubbish bin.

kava 3. n. tin, can. *kava bulumakau* tinned beef. *kava pamutaki* aerosol can.

kava, kavana v. to roll up (mat, sinnet).

ikava fourth.

kava, kavata (West) v. to comb (the hair). *kavata na ulu-na* comb his/her hair. *ikava* n. comb. These are older words than *seru, seruta*, and *iseru*.

kavera broken, smashed (glass, coconut). Syn. *kavoro*.

kavesi broken off (tree-branch, bunch of fruit like coconuts, citrus, *dawa*).

kaveti n. (Eng.) n. cabbage. *kaveti olo* English cabbage, Brassica oleracea, var. bullata. *kaveti ni Tiaina* Chinese cabbage, several types but perhaps mainly "wong bok", Brassica pekinensis.

kavetani (Eng.) captain.

kavida adj. cracked (coconut, cup, plate, yam), split (wood), sharply divided (people's opinions). Syn. See *vida, vida* to split. See also *kacavida*.

ikavilo n. indigenous temporary drinking cup or vessel improvised from large leaf (plantain, taro). In the interior of Viti Levu there were no cups and certainly no half coconut shells to use as cups. Drinking was normally done by pouring water into the open mouth, or by lapping it up.

Kavitu as in *Lotu Kavitu*, an American Christian sect, Seventh Day Adventists, that retains Saturday as their sabbath, tithes for church contributions, largely vegetarian, follows dietary restrictions of Leviticus, forbids tea, coffee and *yaqona*, tobacco. *vitu* seven.

kavoro broken, cracked, from *voro, voroka*. *ikavokavoro* sherds. *kakavorovoro* smashed completely (bottle, eggs).

Kavu! interjection, usually surprise and disappointment. Syn. *Bala!* (or) *Pala!*

kavu v. to be blown about by wind, as sand (*nuku*) might be, or dust (*kuvu*).

kavukavu adj. dry (skin, as on face, from exposure; throat, as when suffering from a cold).

kavu n. edible fish, a rock cod, grouper, sea bass, jew fish, Promicrops lanceolatus. that can grow large, to 1,000 pounds and a length of 12 feet according to Rob Wright. More commonly, large ones might weigh 400 lbs and extend to seven feet in length. *Kavu* now mainly classified as a couple of species of genus Epinephelus. See *kasala*.

kavuru v., adj., n. to crumble, crunchy, crunched, crumbs, broken into pieces, crushed, from *vuru, vuruka*. By ext., *kavuru* n. butt, stub of a cigarette. *ka ni kavuru* ash-tray. See *kavoro*.
Idiom: *kere kavuru* beg for crumbs, beg for food, but more commonly, to cadge a cigarette.

kawa 1. n. family lineage, progeny (humans, animals, plants). *Na iVola ni Kawa Bula* The Genealogical Records kept of all registered Fijian clans and registered members. *kawayali* (or) *kawa boko* extinct stock (tribe, clan).

kawa 2. n. blood-relative from the father's side of the family. *Bula kawa!* Hello kinsman! (Colo greeting). The equiv. for a relative by the mother would be *Bula vasu!*).

vakawa v., adj. to have children, progeny.

kawa, kawaca v. to walk on (prone tree-trunk, stones) or in (water), in making a crossing, as of mud, swamp, river. *ikawakawa* improvised crossing-place, used as rough bridge. *idewadewa i tai* n. crossing to the other side.

kawa n. fish-trap of wire or wicker with two "pockets" to retain fish.

kawaboko adj. extinct (race, species). *vakawaboko-taka* to exterminate.

kawago n. edible fish, sea bream, upper body yellowish, belly white, Lethrinus nebulosus, caught inside and around the reef. Same genus as *sabutu*.

kawai n. cultivated species of edible yam, Dioscorea esculenta, specialty of certain places with a dry climate, particularly in Tavua, Ra and Macuata. Not as noble a ceremonial food as the regular, more common yam, *uvi*, D. alata, which usually matures later and can grow to a much larger size. Also, by contrast, *kawai* stems twine to the left, counterclockwise, and have alternate (not opposite) leaves. Sometimes referred to as the Chinese yam, or lesser yam. The flesh is drier and whiter than the regular yam, and it is less chewy and perhaps a little sweeter.

vakawai 1. v. to be critical, to criticise. *Au vakawai koya ena nona isulusulu*. I am critical of the way he/she dresses.

vakawai 2. adj. watery, soggy, as a melon might be. Not common usage.

vakawai-taka v. to add water, as to a pot, in cooking.

kawakasa n. bird mainly of the bush, usually heard, not so often seen, near rocks, waterfalls, long tail that droops on landing, Long-Tailed Cuckoo, breeds in New Zealand, arriving in Fiji during April, departing by October, sometimes as late as December.

ikawakawa n. place to cross on foot, usually a foot-bridge improvised (permanently) with a tree-trunk. Fijian villages virtually never had any substantial, safe footbridges no matter how frequently used the crossing. (There have been sigificant exceptions, such as ancient river crossings in Rewa.) *ikawakawa tolo ni niu* n. footbridge of a coconut-palm trunk. Substantial, modern road bridges are referred to as *wavu* ("wharf").

kawakawa n. edible fish, grouper, several species; Cephalopholis spp., Epinephelus spp. Names vary regionally. Bearing this name is the Variegated Grouper that is dangerouly poison.

ikawalu eighth.

ka-wale n. something useless or unimportant, useless thing.

kawa-yali n. extinct stock (tribe, clan). Syn. *kawaboko*. *yali* lost.

kaweki-taka v. to bend (sail).

kaya v. to say, said. Syn. (Rewa) *kanaka*.

kaya with him/her/it. *lako vata kaya* go with him/her/it. *na gone au sa lako kaya ki Lautoka*. the child I went with to Lautoka. Abbrev. of *kei koya*.

ke if. Shortened form of *kevaka*. *Ke au o iko . . .* If I were you . . . . *Ke o lako ki Suva, ke drau sota kei Mere, qai solia vei koya, kevaka e rawa* If you go to Suva and if you meet Mere, give it to her, if possible. When *ke* follows *kevaka* in a sentence, *ke* means "would", i.e. *Kevaka ko a tiko kina, ke o mate*. If you had been there you would be dead.

ke or **eke** here. See *oqo*.

kea or **keya** over there, at that place.

keba (Eng.) n. camp (military, Boy Scouts).

kece all. *kece ga* absolutely all. *ena veika kece* in all things. *na tamata kece* all the people. See *taucoko* whole, all, referring to things rather than people.

keda we (many, incl.). Includes the person spoken to. Our (many) food.
kedaru we (two, incl.). Our (two) food.
kedatou we (several, incl.) Our (several) food.
kedra their (many) food for them to eat themselves. Also their (many) something that is integral to them.
kedratou their (several) food for them to eat themselves. Also their (many) something that is integral to them.
kedrau their (two) food for them to eat themselves. Also their (2) something that is an integral part of each other. *kedrau iyalayala o Ra kei Tailevu* the border between Ra and Tailevu, lit. their border, Ra and Tailevu.
kedru v., n. to snore, to snort. *na ikedrukedru* n. the snoring. This is often caused by a physical or nerve blockage called sleep apnea, a malady that is not recognised by Fijians. It is most common among people who sleep on the back rather than the side.
  Idiom: *kedru toso* v. facetiously refers to someone who shifts about (*toso*) while pretending to be sleeping, moving secretly closer to desired person of opposite sex. Informally, people may sleep fairly close to each other on the comfortable and clean, soft matted floor of a traditional Fijian house.
kei 1. and (or) with. *veitalanoa kei Seru* chat with Seru. *Seru kei au* Seru and I. *kei na so tale* et cetera, and so on. *na nona veimoceri kei na dua na yalewa* his sleeping with a woman. *lako vata kei Seru* to go together with Seru.
kei 2. of (in certain applications, when something is an integral part of another). *na qele kei Viti* the land of Fiji. *na colo kei Ba* the interior highlands of Ba. *Matabose kei Vuravura* United Nations. *na sauka kei Suva* the outskirts of Suva.
kei 3. concerning, on the subject of, about. *na italanoa kei Seru* the story about Seru. *A iTukutuku kei Viti* The History of Fiji. *na irogorogo kei Cakobau* the fame of Cakobau. This implies that something is an integral part of something or someone.
keimami we, us, our (many, excl.). Excludes the person spoken to.
keirau we, us (two, excl.). The person being addressed is excluded from the couple referred to. *Keirau sa veikilai*. We (two, exc.) have met, know each other.
keitou we, us (several, excl.). In speaking to an outsider, a Fijian may refer to himself and his own kin-group as *keitou* we.
ke ka if that is so. *Ke ka, daru lako.* If that is so, let us (2) go.
keke 1. (Medical) n. lumbago, i.e., persistent pain in the lower back.
keke 2. (Eng.) n. cake. Fijians have firmly adopted the custom of baking and eating cakes, even the necessity of birthday cakes in urban areas, especially for children.
kekeli v. to dig in the bush for wild yams such as *tivoli*.
kekeo (Tonga kekeho) n. type of clam shellfish found only at Waqava Island (next to Kabara Island, in Lau), no doubt imported from Tonga. In Fiji, it is a local curiosity.
kele, kelea 1. v. to anchor (boat), stop or park (motor vehicle). *kelea* (the vehicle). *kelea ina wavu* to moor at the wharf. *kele ciri* v. to anchor out, away from jetty or shore. *keleravi, keleravita* v. to anchor (or stop) next to (something, some place).
kele, kelea 2. v. to push down, stick in the ground, usually to set up a fence-post, fish-fence post, sign-post, etc.
ikelekele n. anchor, anchorage (boat), bus-stop, garage, parking place.
keli, kelia v. to dig (a hole, drain). *ikelikeli* ditch, drain. *na kekeli* the digging up of wild yams.
ikeli-musu n. man-made canal. Reference may be to Suez Canal, or more commonly, to the old canal that linked a waterway from Bau to Rewa, joining the Wainibokasi River with the Wainiki River (now the Navuloa River). Without modern tools, making that canal was a remarkable feat. Bau employed the forced labour of Nakelo people, an arduous task without modern shovels or sacks.
ikelo n. bend or turn in a road or river. See *takelo*.
kemesi (Eng.) n. chemist-shop, pharmacy. Syn. *kemisi*.
kemu 1. possessive pronoun: your (one person), food for you to consume. *Oqo na kemu* here is your food. *Oqo na kemu ika* here is your fish (for you to eat).
  Idiom: *Kemu!* (interjection to a person): You deserved that! Serves you right! You had that coming!
kemu 2. possessive pronoun: your (one person) thing or characteristic, as in *na kemu irairai* your (personal) appearance, the way you appear to others. *na kemu italanoa* the story about you, your story. Contrast with *nomu*, "your" that is less personal, less a part of the person.
kemudou you (several), as object of sentence. Possessive "your" and may refer to food to be consumed by you (several). Also used as interjection Oh, you!, in mock reproach.

kemudrau you (two), as object of sentence. May be a very polite form of address to a person.

kemuni you (many), object of sentence. Also used as polite form of address, even to a single person. *na kemuni* your food (many, or very politely, a singular person).

kena 1. its (almost anything). *na kena duidui* its difference.
   Idiom: *Na kena levu* in ending a message, report, or letter: That's all there is to say, to report.

kena 2. his/her/its (food), for that person (or animal) to consume, always as *na kena*.
   Idiom: *vakalevu kena* to restrain oneself, by modesty or shame, not accepting, usually food, when actually one is quite hungry.

kena 3. his/her/its, referring to some integral part of the person or thing. *na kena rewa* its height (tree, building, mountain, never a person). *na kena irairai* his/her/its appearance. *na kena italanoa* the story about him/her/it.

kenavi n. part of woven thing (sinnet, rope, mat) to make it longer.

kenadau n. expert, someone who is adept.

kenagusu n. person adept at speaking.

kenisa (Eng.) n. cancer.

kenivesi (Eng.) n. canvas shoes.

kequ 1. possessive pronoun: my food (to eat), as contrasted to mere possession that would be indicated by the word *noqu*. Also applies to tobacco *na kequ tavako* my tobacco, cigarettes (that I will consume). In humour, a person might address their lover as "*Kequ*". *mequ* my beverage for me to drink (includes fruits such as orange, melon, mango, but also medicinal pills *vuanikau,* and ice cream).

kequ 2. possessive pronoun, first person singular, referring to some essential part of that person. *na kequ irairai* my (personal) appearance. *na kequ italanoa* my personal story (the story about me).

kere, kerea v. to ask for (something), ask of (person). *kere wai* ask for water. *kerea na wai* ask for the water. *kerea vei Pita* ask Pita for it. *kere veivosoti vua* to apologise to him/her, to beg forgiveness (usually in light social matters).
   Idiom: *kere wai* to be seriously needing water.
   Idiom: *mai kere liti-momo-wai* said about a person who comes to ask for one thing, then greedily keeps adding more requests.
   Idiom: *kere cagi* to be "winded", short of breathe from exertion.

ikerei n. gift in a ceremonial presentation, usually a whale tooth, in gratitude for some request granted, often for the use of a piece of land for gardening, the use of fishing grounds, or for the use of a name for a child or a boat. Permission may be required for the use of certain names that "belong" to a family or other kin-group. *ikerei ni yaca* n. gift requesting the use of a personal name, or name for a vehicle (boat, aeroplane) when that name "belongs" to some person or some community.

kerekere 1. please, a word that introduces a request. *kerekere bibi* introducing a serious, earnest request that is extremely difficult for a Fijian to refuse.

kerekere 2. n., v. custom of making demands on relatives, friends, employers, that are difficult or impossible for a Fijian to refuse. Reciprocity occured usually later, perhaps quite indirectly to a close relative, a favour done, some food given, schoolbooks bought, some help with garden labour. It might be considered vulgar to pay back too directly too soon. The system was based on mutual supportiveness that is still quite functional in segments of Fijians society. But the social system has been changing, with some abuses occurring. Nonetheless, a person might be resented if he bluntly declines a request and as a result, Fijians usually have trouble saying "no". It could be thought rude and unkind. Thus it is difficult for a Fijian to accumulate much wealth while living as a Fijian in the Fijian context. Kinship relations are extremely important to the Fijian, not individual advancement, and certainly not individual accumulation of wealth. *kerekere bibi* urgent or pressing request. See *dole, dolea* for the return exchange in response to *kerekere* and for general reciprocity.
   Idiom: *Kerekere, ke sega ni soli, e na qai butakoci* Ask for it; if it is not given, it will be stolen.

kere v. to boil, bubble actively (liquid), purr (cat), wheeze (sleeper, person with cold), reinforced by redup. *kerekere*. *vakerea na wai* to boil the water.
   Idiom: *tabu rogoca na kere ni cakau* said to one who does not listen to instructions or good advice. Lit. does not listen to the sound of the sea against the reef.

ikeri there, in the place where you are (the person being talked to), *kere* preceded by "i" or "e", which may not be heard in certain situations

keria (Eng.) n. carrier, van, truck. This relatively modern, general term has virtually replaced the older term *lori* (Eng.) lorry. The change occured with the popularity of vehicles rented (with driver), to transport goods for Fijians going to and from their villages. Road access to villages has increased greatly in recent years and there is a strong demand for rented "carriers".

kerisimetiki (Eng.) charismatic, referring to the evangelical, demonstative Christian sects that emphasize popular communal singing, speaking in tongues. Assemblies of God is a primary example but there are now several branches of Christian sects that have a so-called charismatic orientation. The origin is from the U.S.A., as are almost all the denominations of recent introduction, following the Methodists and Roman Catholics.

kesa 1. n. a small tree, the long ago introduced Annatto, Bixa orellana, Bixaceae, bark use for dyeing bark-cloth. Seeds supply bright red colorant. In English, sometimes referred to as the lipstick tree.

kesa 2. n. dye as used for decorating barkcloth *masi*, whether or not the colorant is made from this tree or some other plant. Brown is usually made from boiled bark of mangrove tree *dogo*. Black was often formerly made from the candlenut-tree fruit *lauci*. Today on Vatulele, the black is usually made from diesel soot, fixed by mixing it with root-sap of the trees *koka*, or *kaudamu*. *Kesa* may also be a woman's name.

kesa, kesava v. to imprint with *kesa* dye. At Vatulele and at Moce, this is normally done with a stencil (*kupeti* or *kupeji* in Lau), formerly made of plantain leaf, now made of used X-ray film cut with a razor blade. Lauans may use free-form designs in Tongan style. *na kesakesa* the dyeing. *na kesavi ni masi* the dyeing of barkcloth.

kesu-na n. the slight depression at the upper backside of a person's head, crown of the head. *kesu dudu* "pin-headed", i.e., dolichocephalic (person). *kesu sababa* flat-headed at back, i.e. brachycephalic (person). Fiji has both types of skull, indicating various origins. Syn. *buredela-na*.
Idiom: (Anglicism) *mila kesu-na* to be perplexed, not to know what to do or say; lit. to scratch one's head.
Idiom: *solia na kesuna* v. to turn one's back (on someone), showing disrespect.

kete-na 1. n. belly, stomach. *kete levu* big-bellied.
Idiom: *kauta tu ga na ketena* lit. brings only his/her stomach, referring to a person who comes to a feast but brings no food, comes only to eat and makes no contribution.

kete-na 2. n. womb. *bukete* pregnant. *kete gone* (or) *ketekete gone* bears children easily or often (woman). Syn. *kato ni gone, duvu*.

kete-na 3. n. of a woven pandanus mat, the "good", shiny side, in contrast to the back, dull underside.

kete n. (West) n. sub-clan, a type of kinship group, larger than the extended family (*tokatoka*). Some place-names, even in Lau, refer to Kete-icake, Kete-ira, locations of a family group.

ketedromo n. bird, Golden-breasted Whistler, Pachycephala pectoralis, widespread in Fiji and Vava'u, Tonga, especially in mature forest. Many local variations in incidental coloration.

ketedromo n. riverine fish with a yellow belly, Eliotridae.

ketekete n. woven coconut-leaf basket carried on the back by women. Idiom: *lewe ni ketekete* n. land given to a *vasu* by the village. See *vasu*.

keteleka n. type of mullet, smaller and shorter than *kanace*, silver coloured, yellowish tail, travels far upriver.

keu 1. if I, often seen as *ke'u*, an abbrev. of *ke au*. *ke* itself is an abbrev. of *kevaka* if.

keu 2. n. v. to cry, of certain birds (onomatopoeic).

kevaka if. Abbrev. *ke*. If *ke* follows *kevaka* in a sentence, the *ke* indicates the result of the "if". *Kevaka o a tiko kina, ke o mate.* If you had been there, you would be dead.

keve, keveta (Bau) v. to lift and carry in front at chest-height with arms underneath (baby, stack of books). *keve liga* to fold the arms. *ikevekeve* n. what is carried in the arms this way. Syn., more common, *roqo, roqota*.

kevu, kevuta, kevutaka v. to clamber down, climb down (as from tree, roof) or climb down in the direction of. *kevutaka* climb down bringing (something).

keya over there (far away), also seen as *kea* or *e kea*.

ki 1. to, toward (a place). *Kivei* to (specific person, as in addressing a letter).

ki 2. for. *Sa dodonu ki na matanitu me cakava*. It's right for government to do it.

ki 3. (Eng.) n. key. *vakitaka* to lock with a key.

ki 4. n. a small edible fish, surmullet, yellow striped goatfish with a split tail, Upeneus vittatus. Annual appearance in great numbers celebrated at Kaba, Kiuva, Daku and Nasilai at Viti Levu, Nagigi at Vanua Levu, and at Vatoa Island as well as other places. This little fish squeaks when it is touched. Four yellow markings on the side. Village Daku and settlement Kaleli have a tradition of catching *ki* in a fish-fence known as *ba kalou*, elaborately made of vertical reeds bound by a swamp vine *midre*, Stenochloena sp., Blechnaceae. A legend from Vatoa Island tells of this fish and a devil-woman (*Na Viti Lima*, p. 89-95). Syn. (Cakau.) *ose, deu*. (Ba) *kiki*. *voro* (noted in *Na Viti Lima*, p. 93).

ki, kitaka (Eng. "key") v. to set the pitch, usually for a church choir about to sing. *na ki* n. the pitch (musical). See *kitaka* with a different meaning, "to do". *vaki-taka* to lock with a key.

kiakavo (Archaic) n. type of warclub.

kibo v. to retreat into a hole (crab, rat, mongoose). *mata kibo* having the face shrunk back like an owl. See *kino*.

kiboraki koya startled to a state of shock (of person, animal) resulting in sudden concealment, hiding, or crouching.

kida 1. (Eng.) n. abbrev. of kindergarten. Syn. *kidi*.

kida 2. startled, to give a "start" in surprise. *kidakida* easily startled. *kida* is a root-word suggesting something that happens suddenly.

kida 3. v. to break, of dawn. *Sa kida mai na mataka.* Dawn is breaking.

kida-bera v. to realise too late, to have a sudden, belated realisation.

kidacala, kidacala-taka v. to be surprised pleasantly (at something). *E yaco vakakidacala mai na vulagi.* The visitor arrived (pleasantly) unexpectedly. *va-kidacalataki au* surprise me. V*eiva-kidacala* delightfully surprising. Syn. (Rewa) *rika-ca*.

kidava v. a particularly Fijian notion, to have a premonition that turns out correct, often stirred by physical twitching (one's eye, finger, leg) invisible to others.

kida, kidavaka v. to greet or welcome a visitor, introduce a stranger. *na kidavaki* the welcome *na vakakidavaki* the formal greeting, formal introduction, usually with speeches and responses.

kidi, kidia (or) **kidiva** v. to crease (as in folding paper napkins), crimp (cloth), *sorokidikidi* wrinkled (cloth), crinkled (paper), choppy (sea).

kidi 1. (or) **kidikidi** adj. itchy (of body). Syn. *milamila*.

kidi 2 (Eng.) n. kindergarden. Syn. *kida*.

kidolo, kidoloka v. to choke or snap the neck (person, animal), or snap off (flower) forcefully. See *doloka* v. to break off, snap off, as a piece of sugar cane, or a small branch.

kidomoka v. to throttle deliberately (person, animal), to strangle. *kuna* refers to formal, ceremonial strangling, as for widows of a recently deceased chief to accompany him in the next world, and also for the (rare) event of hanging as a punishment, a custom derived from the English. *domo* n. throat.

kidroa, kidroataka v. to be startled, give a "start", be stunned, shocked, as with usually unpleasant surprise.

kidrakidra n. a sucking sound of something removed from a sticky mass, usually used for feet in the mud. Or a startled gasp with unpleasant shock, bad news, sudden fear.

kidroto v. to splash, as of an oar in the water or a stone thrown into the water.

kie (or) **kiekie** (Lau, Kadavu, Macuata) leafy plant cultivated for weaving mats, baskets, Pandanus sp. Syn. *voivoi*.

kikau n. common bird spp. Onomatopoeic name with a very commonly heard call. Wattled Honeyeater. There are two species, a large one and a smaller one. The larger one has a much louder cry and has a larger body. Exists only where there is no concentration of snakes, as noted by P. Geraghty. There are many different synonyms in different localities. Syn. *sovau, visilo*. (West) *kitou*. (Lau) *kaisevau*. (Nadroga) *kikitou*. (VanuaLevu) *kaisau*.

kiki 1. (Kadavu, Lau) n. rattan. Syn. *wa ulo*. This very woody vine can grow many hundreds of yards. It is used in securing house-thatch. Legends tell of it allowing magical transport from Fiji to Tonga.

kiki 2. v. to chirp, as of a small bird.

kikila adj. very timid, extremely shy.

kikilo adj. bumpy (usually of a road), having a lot of "potholes" (*qara ni gaunisala*),

kila adj. wild, shy (of animals).

kila, kila v. to know, recognise. *kilaka* intelligent. *kilaseva* v. to fail to recognise. *Drau sa veikilai tiko?* Do you two know each other? Are you known to each other? Have you met? *E kilai.* It is known.

vakilai recognised, realised. *Vakilai na yaga ni veisusu vinaka.* The value of proper upbringing is recognised.

vakilai yalo-na adj. conscious. *Au a sega ni vakilai yalo-qu.* I was unconscious.

vakata-kila v. to reveal, make known.

ivaka-ta-kilakila n. mark, sign, sign-post, signature, indication, indicator (book-page marker, road-sign, army flag, symptom (medical). *vakatakilakila ni taifote* symptoms of typhoid.

vei-vaka-kilaitaka v. to make the introduction of people, to introduce or present someone.

kilaka adj. intelligent, quick to learn, understand, knowledgeable.

kilakila (or) **va-kilakila** v. to guess. *Kilakilai au* "Guess who I am", a phrase that often begins a childrens' riddle. Similarly one may hear *Kilakila mada* announcing a children's riddle and you are to guess the answer to the riddle.

kilakila adj. secretely sly.

kilaleca, kilalecava, kilalecava-taka v. to mistake one thing or person for another, fail to recognise. Syn. *kilacala, kilacala-taka*.

kila-kasami, kilakasami-taka v. to suspect.

kila-nauni n. adjective, a word invented by schoolteachers.

kilaseva, kilasevataka v. to fail to recognise someone or something, due to passage of time, or changes that have taken place.

kilavaka v. to avoid, mistrust, be shy of.

kilavaki adj. unsociable, uncouth, loner. *vanua kilavaki* wild bushland.

kili, kilica 1. v. to upturn stones, as at the seashore, for shellfish, clear away stones or heavy earth from an oven when effort is required. *vakili vatu* turn up stones. *kilikili* n. small stones tossed onto a Lauan grave, a respectful custom from Tonga.

kili, kilica 2. v. to open an earth-oven (*lovo*) after completion of cooking (*ni sa buta oti*). *cele, celea* v. to clear away leaves or light debris, as in opening up an earth oven. (Also applies to opening up or parting the hair to remove lice.)

kilia (Eng. clear) v. to cast off, as of a boat, departing.

kilikili 1. n. (Lau only) small stones which are dunked in coconut oil and spread on a grave, a ceremony called *vakadranu kilikili* on the occasion of *bogidrau* (one hundred nights after burial).

kilikili 2. adj. befitting, good manners (of behaviour). *sa kilikili vei au meu cakava*. it is fitting for me to do it. *rairai kilikili* suitable, fitting appearance.

kilo a root-word: depression (as in road, pothole, person's face) *kilokilo* having a lot of potholes (road); ravine; *qakilo* valley. *E kilo na baluna* He/she has dimples on the cheeks.

kilu v. to plunge head-first (usually into the river). *Me daru kilu qai lako*. Let us (two) take a dip, then go.

kilu, kiluca v. to make sawtooth edge (mat); *ibe va-kilukilu* mat with sawtooth edge.

Kilivati or **Kilipati** (Eng.) n., adj., v. Gilbert Islands, Gilbertese; by extension, to go diving with a single-pointed spear propelled by stretched rubber. Gilbertese are superb experts at diving for seafood.

kilivatu n. crop, stomach (of birds).

kimomo v. to squint the eyes due to glaring sun.

kina 1. n. jar-shaped fishing trap woven of *wa me* vine.

kina 2. n. piece of weaving material (mat, rope, sinnet) for interweaving to extend the length. *me vakina na magimagi* interleave the sinnet to extend the length.

kina 3. particle. to which, to whom, of which, where. *na vanua sa lako kina*. the place where (to which) he/she went. *na nona itikotiko o koya ko vakau ivola kina*. the address of the person (him/her) to whom you send the letter.

vaka kina similarly, like this, like that.

kini, kinita (or) **vakini, vakinita** v. to pinch between the fingernails as in pulling a splinter, or pinching very hard and painfully, as in punishing a child, or very lightly as in drawing a person's attention in secret signal; to snap off, as in picking *rourou, bele*, or *ota* leaf vegetable; pinch mashed taro to form balls for *vakalolo* pudding. *e dua ni ikini masima* n. a pinch of salt. *kinilaka* v. to pinch (a child) very forcefully, as punishment.

kinikini n. (Archaic) type of wide, thin oar-shaped warclub with relatively sharp edges.

kinivari, kinivarita v. to attract a person's attention secretly by pinching lightly. Syn. *tarakini, tarakinita*, lit. touch by pinching. Such secret signaling is common in Fiji.

kino v. to shrink back, wither, withdraw as into shell, or into hole (marine animal) and thus to disappear; by ext., may apply to a person or animal, making themselves scarce at some impending danger or fear. *mata kino* sunken face, as in illness of a person, or the face of an owl. See *kibo*.

kino, kinoca 1. v. to stifle, withhold a sneeze or cough.

kino, kinoca 2. v.to restrain, to curb, to keep within, defuse (tears, sobbing, anger, feelings of shame or other feelings of emotion, sneeze).

kinoto adj. has a plump, attractive body. *kinokinota* has a very plump and attractive body.

kiobo v., adj. squint, have narrowed eyes, have eyes with megalanthic fold, as do many orientals. Syn. *matadre*.

kiokio n. chicks (many types of young birds), from the sound they make.

kiri, kirica v. to tickle under the armpits.

kirikiti (Eng.) n. cricket (the game), greatly favoured by Polynesians, now being played by more Fijians with coaching and management by Australian aid.

kirikiri-ta v. to tickle the armpits, ribs.

kirikiriwa-na (or) **kirikiri-na** n. armpit(s). *kiriwana* v. to carry under the arm(s). Syn: *kirukiruwa-na*.

kirimi (or) **kirimu** (Eng.) n. cream. *aisikirimi* ice cream.

Kirisimasi (Eng.) Christmas. Also *Siga ni Sucu*. *Kirisimasi-ivi* Christmas eve.

Kirisito (Roman Catholic) Christ. Syn. (Prot.) *Karisito*.

kiro 1. v. to get down (as from a tree or roof).

kiro 2. adj. hollowed out, curved, as dugout canoe; dimple on the human face; or other body depression, as from a wound.

kiro 3. n. a sp. of bird, Black-Faced Shrikebill, only on large islands. May also refer to Polynesian Starling, according to Dr. Watling.

kiru v. to reverberate with rhythmic throbbing sound, or sobbing sound. Could be a child sobbing or a drum perhaps, throbbing; to warble, to whimper repeatedly.

va-kirukiru v. to cry sobbingly.

kisi, kisia v. to shift, move (self or object), usually something heavy, not lifting it high, not moving it far. *kisiraka* to move forcefully. *Kisi mai!* Shift over here! (seated).
Idiom: *kisi kaba* to put oneself up with pretension.
Idiom: *Dabe ena ibe qai kisi ki na tabakau.* to be demoted. After living at a high level, then finding oneself in reduced circumstances.

kisi 1. (Eng.) n. case, box. *kisi kau* crate, wooden box. *kisi ni mate* coffin. See *kateni* cartom.

kisi 2. (Eng.) n. case (court).

kisi, kisiva 3. (Eng.) n., v. to kiss. *kisilaka* to kiss ardently. Fijians never knew any form of kissing, though they did and still do sniff with nose to the face *regu, reguca* as an affectionate greeting or farewell, including the final farewell at a person's death, especially in areas of Polynesian influence. Lip to lip kissing, and respectful kissing of the hand (often done by women) was learned from Europeans. Kissing babies in now common custom as is romantic kissing among the young, though romantic kisses are never done in public. *ikisikisi* n. kissing.

kisi kaba (Anglicism) n., v. (Familiar) pretention, acting pretentiously, lit. to climb on top of a box (case).

kisimausi (Anglicism) "Customs House"

kisitama (Archaic) n. Customs, now more commonely called *kasitaba*.

kisitoni n., adj. ("Keystone" cops of fame in old films) clown, a traditional role, usually mimicking someone known, often in pantomime, spoofing them hilariously, an act that may be done by spontaneously in public by an ordinary person. By extension, a funny person, a person who makes you laugh. For the formal role of a comic who livens up a group-dance (*meke*), the term used is *manumanu ni meke*. He is a funny, very skilled dancer, very adroit, agile, active, spoofing the other dancers to keep them performing at their peak. Syn. *sakisi, katuni*.

kiso v. to hop on one leg. *yava kiso* limp on one leg.

kisokiso 1. hopping, "hop-scotch".

kisokiso 2. n. cramp (of the muscles) or other lameness that causes a person to limp or favour one leg.

kitaka v. to do (something specific). Speaking broken Fijian, some people over-use this word rather than the more appropriate *cakava*. It is somewhat archaic. In modern Fijian of the lower classes *kitaka* can imply sexual intercourse.

kitu 1. n. ball of sinnet (coconut-fibre cord called *magimagi*).

kitu 2. (Lau, Kadavu, Nadro.) n. bird, swamp hen, Porphyrio porphyrio. Syn. *teri*.

kitu 3. n. variety of coconut with very large shell, used as a water container when the shell is green and then dried. Some used for salt water as a condiment to flavour food.

kitu 4. (Archaic) n. pottery jar for water with clay handle, water spout on both sides, no longer used.

kiva (or) **kakiva** v., adj. to act sly, cunning, to act smart for one's age, to be a little too bold, presumptuous, "smart-ass". *mona kiva!* is a form of rebuke, sometimes intended facetiously. *mona* brain.

kivei to (person, as in addressing a letter, customarily written before the name). Also *Ki vei?* Where to?

kivi, kivita 1. v. to turn the head to one side, or to glance to one side with the eyes only; *raikivi* to glance to one side, over the shoulder; *rogo kivi, rogo kivita* cock the head to hear better. *tikivi* at one side, alongside, next to. *E dua na yanuyanu lailai ka koto tikivi Ovalau.* A small island that lies to one side of Ovalau.

kivi, kivita, kivilaka 2. v. to knock someone (usually child) on the head with the knuckles, "dong the head" in Fiji English, a typical Fijian punishment for children, at home and in school. Syn. *qou, qouta*.

Ko indicator of proper name, person or place when used as the subject of a sentence, or when it stands alone. *Ko Viti* Fiji. *Ko Jone* John. The letter "k" is sometimes dropped, as in Polynesian languages.

ko you, singular pronoun, only as the subject of a sentence; *ko iko* used as object. Alternatively one may drop the initial "k": *O* and *o iko*.

koa n. birthmark of dark skin covered with fine hair.

koala (Eng.) n. coal. This is a seldom used word since coal is not used in Fiji. In early days, both Fiji and Samoa were considered potentially useful coaling stations for steamships crossing the Pacific Oceans.

koba, koba v. to punch with the fist, usually with a curved or twisting motion (*vacu, vacuka* might more usually be with straight punch). *ikoba* such a punch.

kobe-na n. bottom end of a yam, always used for eating, rather than as seed-stock for planting. Syn. *dromu-na*.

kobi 1. n. part of the penis removed by circumcision; may refer to a boy who has not yet been circumcised. See *kulina*.

kobi 2. adj. astringent, of taste, as of an unripe banana.

kobi, kobita v. to sting with astringency, can be used figuratively, of a person's speech.

kobiuta (Eng.) computer.

kobo 1. n. sores on the scalp, under the head-hair, usually of children.

kobo 2. v. to knock on the head with the knuckles, either as punishment to a child, or one child to another in hard play or bullying. Syn. *ikivi, ikodi, iqou*, in this sense.

kobua indistinctly visible, of limited visibility, usually due to fog, mist, faded daylight. Syn. *kabuata*.

kobuta 1. adj. misty, foggy.

kobuta 2. n. type of grass.

koca v. to be tired of something, long speeches, dull movie, certain foods. Syn. *oca*.

koco, kocova v. to covet. *kocokoco* greedy, covetous. This is a frequent reproach to children.

koda, koda v. to eat raw (fish, shellfish, seaweed). *kokoda* n. marinated raw seafood with lemon, often also onions, chilli (introduced condiments), a Polynesian concept.

Idiom: *gunu koda* to drink strong alcohol "straight", without diluting in water, fruit juice or soda. .

kodrau v. to scream, squeal, screech (usually of a pig), when fearful, knowing it is about to be killed.

kodro, kodrova v. to bark, at something (of dog). *kodrovaka* v. to bark because of something. *na ikodrododro* the barking.

kodro 1. n. part of a man's hair-do that juts forward in hair-style.

kodro 2. n. a feather stuck up in the hair.

kodro 3. n. a fish, small crevally.

kofe (or) **kofi** (Eng.) n. coffee. Coffee has never been a successful commercial crop in Fiji but overgrown plantations exist, as at Gau island. Fruiting is around May. The ripe fruit is sweet to eat as a snack and even the seeds may be munched, though one spits out the fibre. Until recently, Fijians rarely drank coffee. Tea had been more common due to early British influence. Now there are fashionable coffee shops in the cities, pioneered by John Philp. What is called Fiji coffee is roasted fresh, packed and sold in Fiji after having been grown in Papua New Guinea.

kofesio-taka (Roman Catholic) v. to confess.

kofirimasio (Roman Catholic & Anglican) confirmation.

koge v. to grunt or squeal, as a pig does.

ko i (or) **oi** pronoun particle, *Koi au* I, me. Occasionally this appears (and sounds) as *koi yau*, or *oi yau*.

koi (Lau, Vanua Levu) here.

koila (Archaic) n. flag. Syn. *kuila*.

koile (Colo) n. type of wild or semi-cultivated yam. See *kaile*.

koka n. a useful tree, java cedar, Bischofia javanica, Euphorbiaceae, often used to mark borders because it lives long and endures high winds, heavy durable timber, white with reddish brown heartwood. Clear sap turns red on exposure. Lower altitudes, below 900 m., from China, SE Asia, east to Samoa, Tonga. Trifoliate lves with toothed margins, turning red as they die. Fls small, 2 cm diam., cream to pale green or yellow, edible fleshy frts subglobose, 5 cm diam., maturing to pink to orange-brown. The roots make a yellow dye, bark makes a reddish brown dye which is also used as a medicine. Tongans use the rough bark to colour their bark-cloth. Thought to be introduced by early native settlers. Syn. (Lau) *tea*. (Ba, Vuda, Nadro.) *togotogo*. (Tonga, Samoa, eastern Polyn. *koka*.

koko 1. (Colo) you (Bauan *ko iko*) heard in the highlands of Naitasiri and Namosi.

koko 2. (Eng.) n. cocoa. There are efforts to revive the industry. The problems have been a severely fluctuating world price, black pod disease in rainy areas, and a lack of disciplined care for the trees. There has been a lack of organised, equitable and competent marketing for export.

koko 3. n. Fijian pudding of grated *ivi* fruit (Polynesian chestnut), baked in earth oven. This is a regional food of Rewa, where the tree has been common; it grows in low-lying, wet areas. Also a food specialty of Beqa Island.

koko 4. (Eng.) n. cork usually used as float for fishing line or stopper for a bottle. A piece of coconut husk (*qanibulu*) often serves as a bottle stopper.

koko 5. v. to crow, cackle, croak, of hen, frog, parrot.

kokoraki v. to clear the throat with a kind of cough.

kokoroti (Eng.) n. cockroach.

kokosi (Eng.) n. goose, also now applied to a native bird, Fiji Shrikebill. Geese are rarely kept in Fiji.

kokosi (Lau) to be playful, play a game. *Kakua ni kokosi!* Stop playing!

kokovu v., n. about to burst, of boil, pimple, blister. *kovu* bud.

kola, kola or **kolata** v. to split wood, coconut, dalo with something sharp. *kola rua* split in two. May apply to cutting up of kava, especially the way the basal stem (*lewena*) is chopped up into pieces for drying. *kola musu, kolamusutaka* v. to cut up in pieces.

kolarua, kolaruataka v. to split into two pieces. Similarly, this can be extended to more pieces, as in *kolatolu* three pieces, *kolava* four pieces, etc.

kola (Eng.) n. collar. Idiom: *kola up*, means to go about in a challenging, proud manner, often said of hoodlums, pretentious youths, ready to make trouble.

kolai root word, used as a prefix that implies something close to happening (but usually used as an exaggeration: *kolai mate* see below.

kolai mate Idiom, lit. close to death, or figuratively to be "dying" with desire, as to see someone, or to eat some savoured food. Syn. *kolai ciba*.

koli n. dog. The term does not derive from English "collie". Polynesians raised dogs, fed them a vegetable starch diet, and ate them. Some still eat dogs, as I have recorded from Lakeba, Vanua Balavu, and Gau Island. Killing was by strangulation. But the dog is sacred in quite a number of places, as with the clan Nanuku-ira of the DauLakeba tribe, who have a black dog as their founding spirit. A dog is the iconic animal of a fair number of tribes. Fiji Melanesians have no tradition of keeping dogs for eating but highlanders would eat almost any living thing they could catch and that includes feral dogs and cats, introduced by Europeans. Dogs are often kept to help them in hunting pigs. Fijians have almost never kept dogs (or cats) as close members of the family, as the British do. Caution: in Macuata, *koli* can refer to fish. Feral or domestic dogs in Fiji are sometimes subject to mange caused by the scabies mite, Sarcoptes scabiei, which can be treated with pyrethrin, or its synthetic equivalent, permethrin. Heartworm is also a problem for dogs.

Idiom: *Lesu na koli ki na nona lua.* lit. The dog returns to his vomit. i.e. the criminal returns to his crime.

Idiom: *Sa moce na koli e matadravu.* Lit. the dog sleep in the fireplace (where food is cooked). There is no food at home.

Idiom: *vesu koli* extremely hungry.

Idiom: *koli ni koro* lit. village dog, a person who always stays around in the village.

Koli archaic honorific warrior title, now a common name, sometimes also an abbrev. for Kolinio (Colin).

koliji (Eng.) college.

kolo n. a "Fijian sickness", not readily identified in western medicine, often involving a persistent backache, or for women, a hardness in the abdomen, usually attributed to being chilled by being wet and cold around water, fishing or washing clothes. May involve a headache. Lumbago (*keke*) may be part of the problem.

kolo, kolova, kolotaka v. to hurl (*kolotaka*) a stick or club (*ikolo* the object thrown) with a sweeping, almost horizontal motion, usually now to bring down (*kolova*) fruit from a tree, or to hit a fruit bat with a short stick, for food. Previously certain types of war-club were thrown this way in combat. *kolokolotaka* throw (them) repeatedly, many times. *kolotaka na tauwelu* v. to quit, to throw in the towel, as in boxing, to have had enough and admit defeat, an Anglicism, of course.

ikolo ni matanisiga Idiom: to drink kava in the morning, lit. as if a stick were being thrown at the sun, a waste of time. *ikolo ni bogi* the same, in the evening, night-time.

koloni 1. (Eng.) colony. *ena gauna vakoloni* in colonial times.

koloni 2. (Eng.) colon, as a punctuation mark; a newly invented word.

koma 1. (Eng.) comma, as punctuation in a sentence *(iyatuvosa)*. Again, words invented by school teachers. Syn. *icegu leka*.

koma 2. (Eng.) coma as a medical condition.

koma-lili (Ang.) apostrophe, as a punctuation mark in a sentence. *koma-lili-rua* quotation marks. Words invented by teachers of Fijian language. *lili* to be hanging up, as of clothes on a clothes line.

Komai formal title of a minor chief, followed by place-name, used in Tailevu and Cakaudrove Provinces. Literally, it means "He From . . .". In Cakaudrove, it is pronounced 'Omai.

komada (Eng.) commander.

kome n. part of the cultivated yam that is cut off for cooking and eating. The other part of the mid-section of the yam *(na kobe-na)* is the *vaci*, the outside parts with skin, to be planted. *ta-ulu* n. head of the yam, a piece to be planted. Syn. *dromu-na*.

Komadoa (or) **Komodoa** (Eng.) n. Commodore, as in Commodore Frank Bainimarama.

Komanisi n., adj. Communist. Syn. *Kominisi, Komunisi*.

kominio (Eng.) communion, as a religious sacrament.

Komisana or **Komisina** (Eng.) n. Commissioner. *na Komisana mai na Yasayasa vakaRa* the Commissioner Western (of the government's western division). Reference may be made to *na Talai Veivuke ena Yasayasa vakaRa. Komisina ni Ovisa* Police Commissioner.

komiti (Eng.) n. committee.

kona (Eng.) n. corner.

kona, konataka (Eng.) to corner someone or some animal to capture them, or in the case of people, perhaps just to confront them, as in forceful questioning.

konakona very salty. Syn. *tuituina*.

konetaka, -raka v. shake up, as of a liquid, juice, medicine, cocktail.

Ko ni you (honorific, and only as the subject of the sentence, not the object). Also *O ni*.

konitaraki or **konitareki** (Eng.) n. contract. Usually this refers to a short-term work assignment for Fijians, paid on completion. A great deal of work is done by Fijians this way rather than being paid by the day *(muri siga)*. Syn. *tasi* (Eng. "task")

koniteina (Eng.) n. container (for sea shipment).

Koniveredi (Eng.) n. Conference, a Methodist annual national meeting that is a very major undertaking for the location that hosts the occasion. Many people must be housed and fed. It is considered an honour for the location but it is a very expensive honour.

kopa (Eng.) n. copper. Copper is one of the mineral resources of the Namosi hills that someday may be mined.

kopi, kopitaka (Eng.) v. to copy, to make a copy or copies.

kora v. to make a sound of splattering, as fish jumping, gun firing.

kora n. residual shreds of coconut flesh after expressing the liquid.

kora toni n. condiment of grated coconut fermented in parcels that remain for more than a week in a pile of rocks, steeping in the rise and fall of clean tidal waters at sandy locations. It is a specialty of Lau, sold in the Suva market. Syn. *kota*. May refer to bad smell of genital fluids.

kora v., n. to gargle. By extension, grated coconut condiment that ferments in sandy tidal flats where seawater gargles through it, but also the discarded coconut remains after grating in the making of coconut cream. *kokoraki* gurgling, clearing the throat (of person).

kora (Kadavu) as in *Sa kora*. That's finished, done, complete.

kori (or) **kore** n. a nut-like fruit of a vine *(wa kori)* used for decorative necklaces, Mucuna sp., Fabaceae. Edible nut is an occasional famine food.

koro 1. (Polyn.) n. village; the common meaning of the word suggested a hilltop fortress on a mountain peak in olden days but also included the very compact ring-ditch, moated villages in flatlands such as Rewa. It is only in colonial days that people felt safe to settle in more convenient, lower, exposed places like beaches and riverside locations that they now occupy. (Almost all villages have shifted). *koroturaga* capital city, principal town. *na bula vaka-nakoro* the village life, life in the village. *koro dina* village of one's father, where a Fijian is usually registered as a clan member. *koro-ni-sucu* village where a person was raised (quite often not their *korodina*.) *koro-ni-vasu* village of one's mother, where one is *vasu*, having certain rights, and especially these days, certain responsibilities. *koro-ni-vuli* school. Syn. (Tonga) *kolo*.

Idiom: *were koro* cut the grass and clean up the area around the compound of a house.

koro 2. a root-word, n. or v. pile, heap (stones, coconuts, fruit, yams, bodies). *korokoro* intensive form of the same word. May apply to people being crowded together.

koro 3. (Archaic) one hundred coconuts, a measure used in feast-food presentations.

koro 4. (Tonga "kolo") wicket, in cricket. Syn. *wikiti*. Polynesian influence (Tonga, Samoa) has been significant in cricket. It is a favourite Polynesian sport.

koro galala n. settlement of Fijians on native land, sometimes only one family, separate from the formal village. In principal, village discipline and authority does not effectively extend there.

korokoro da Idiom: lit. pile of excrement, but actually meaning a pile of rubbish, a mess (literally or figuratively), a whole lot of worthless nothing.

koro, korona v. to pile up, to make a pile, usually sand, stones, earth. *ikoro qele* n. pile of earth.

koro makawa n. abandoned village site. In some cases there is sentimental or sacred attachment to the old site, especially if it was the origin-place (*yavu-tu*) where the tribe (*yavusa*) was formed. In many cases, old stone house-sites (*yavu*) remain in place, though in ancient times Fijians moved about a great deal due to perpetual war and internicine conflict, as well as natural disasters or population expansion. Since the Pax Brittanica, Fijian villages have moved to more accessible places, near beaches, streams, roads, schools. Sometimes the old village name is retained for the new location.

koroi n. academic degree, certificate, credential, formerly an honorific name awarded to warriors, now adopted as an ordinary given name.

vakoroi adj. credentialed, i.e., holding a certificate or other credentials.

koro-ni-vasu n. village of one's mother, to which one is *vasu*. A child is normally registered to the father's village. The child should be ceremonially introduced to the mother's village, with goods presented, in a ceremony known as *kau-na-mata-ni-gone*.

korosi (Eng.) n. cross (as a mark made on paper). *toqa ena dua na korosi* to mark with a cross (as on a ballot, a hot-cross bun).

korosi, korositaka (Eng.) v. to cross out, to cross through.

korotini (Eng.) n. quarantine. There are several spellings of this word.

koroturaga 1. n. top of the animal head or human head.
Idiom: *Sa leqa na noma koroturaga.* You are "out of your head", crazy.

koroturaga 2. n. chiefly village or capital (of a nation). *ena koroturaga ko Lodoni* in the capital city of London.

Korovou n. (Slang) reference to Suva City gaol, located at a part of Suva called Korovou. It is named after the Korovou prison, first prison in Fiji, in Navosa, after the "Little War". *Korovou-e-cake* "Above Korovou" refers to St. Giles mental hospital, located above the Suva City Prison.

kosa n. fibrous refuse (to be discarded) from expressed *yaqona*. In fact, less than half of the kavalactone is expressed from the kava fibre when the beverage is prepared. Much of the kavalactone is thus discarded. The word may apply to other fibrous residue after a liquid is expressed.
Idiom: *dau kosa* heavy drinker of *yaqona*.

kosakosa adj. raucous, tumultous noise (amplified music, traffic, children playing, a great number of birds chirping), referring to the noise itself or to whatever is causing the noise. rough, rude, of a person.

Kosipeli n. (Eng.) Gospel.

kosipeli n. (Eng.) small wild plant, Cape Gooseberry, Physalis spp., Solanaceae. Syn. *tukitukiyadre*.

koso root-word, implying a cutting across, truncate.

koso, kosova, kosolaka 1. v. to cut across, person crossing road, river, private land. *kosova na gaunisala* to cross the road. *qalokosova na uciwai* to swim across the river. *na takosova* the cutting across, the crossing over (as in taking a short-cut). *koso dola* to cut open.

koso, kosova, kosolaka 2. v. to cut up something, usually food such as fish, meat into smaller pieces, cut across the grain. *kosolaka* v. chop up. *kosorua* cut into two pieces, *kosotolu* cut into three pieces, etc.

koso 3. abrupt(ly), sudden(ly). *tini koso* to break off, terminate suddenly. *mate koso* to die suddenly. *bogi koso* sudden nightfall (common in the tropics where there is very brief twilight or dusk).

kota n. damp, shredded pieces of *yaqona* root in the serving bowl, not yet fully expressed and strained out as *kosa*, which are the fibres to be discarded. (Actually a very considerable amount of kavalactone remains in the *kosa* and it is wasted but the *kosa* has a bad taste if used to make more beverage.)

kotai n. specialty food, ripe fruit such a mango or *wi* grated, served with shredded coconut and sugar. Syn. *'otai*.

kota-fainala (Eng.) n. quarter-final (rugby).

kote (Eng.) n. coat, woman's blouse. *kote-ni-uca* raincoat.

koti, kotiva, kotilaka v. to cut (hair, grass, paper, cloth). *ikoti* scissors. *veikoti* haircut. *na dauveikoti* the barber. *na kotikoti* the cutting, mowing (lawnmower, bushcutter). *na kena kotivi na raveni* the cutting of the ribbon (Fijians have adopted such European customs of ceremonial openings as for new construction.)

ikoti n. scissors. *vale ni veikoti* hairdresser, barber. *na ikotikoti* the hair-style, the hair-cut. Hair style was formerly a point of vanity for many men; missionaries changed that. *ikoti* originally referred to a sharp piece of shell or shark tooth used to cut shave and cut hair.

ikoti-ni-co n. lawnmower, bush-cutter. *co* grass.

koto n. sea mullet, Mugil cephalus, Mugilidae, identified by a large black spot at base of pectorals. See also *kanace, kava*.

koto, kotora v. to lie, to stay (usual place), be situated (at a place). *kotora* v. to lay down. *va-koto-ra* to lay it down (rather more directly). *koto no* lie there, where it belongs. *Sa koto no.* It's still here (in its regular place). *E kele koto mai Lami na waqa.* The boat lies anchored at Lami. *E koto ki na ceva.* It lies to the south. *E dua na yanuyanu lailai ka koto tikivi Ovalau.* A small island that lies next to Ovalau. *koto-ravita* to lie next to, as a nearby location for something. In Lau, *koto* is syn. with *davo* (to lie down, of a person or animal). In Navosa *koto* means to sit (*dabe* in Bauan). *va-kotokoto-taka na lali* beat the drum at increasing pace for lengthened time (as for school, or a *meke*). *Lawa Virikotori* Act of Parliament.

ikotokoto n. Pandanus mat laid out on the floor of a sleeping area in a house, a place to lie down.

koto lo n. wild yam (*tivoli*) root mature in previous year, still in the ground, useless for eating, but can be cut and replanted. The implication is of something lying (*koto*) hidden (*lo* secretly).

ikou n. Giant Forest Honeyeater, Gymnomyza viridis, resembles the common *kikau* but is much larger. Several regional synonyms.

koukou n. edible terrestrail fern, Pteridium esculentum, often growing in dry, sunny locations, used in floors of traditional Fijian houses underneath the floor-mats (*icoco*) to soften the floor. This made for comfortable sitting compared to modern wooden floors that are hard. Syn. (West) *mata*. (Lau) *karuka*.

kouva v. to call out loudly from far away, to catch someone's attention.

kouvaka v. to call out (to someone), as in the bush, equiv. in purpose to Aust. "coo-eee". It is a sound, not word(s), and traditionally never uses a person's name, though tradition is changing.

koula (Eng.) n. gold. The place-name Vatukoula means Gold Stone, an adopted place-name where the mines are situated on Viti Levu. Metals were all completely unknown to Fijians. By ext., *koula* may refer to gold medal in athletics and also to a gold-coloured package of Benson & Hedges cigarettes. *dau keli koula* gold miner.

kova v. to overlap. *vale va-kovakova* house with tin roofing overlapped.

Kovana (Eng.) n. Governor, as of the Colony in early times. The Governor might set policy, but all government operations were managed by the Colonial Secretary.

kovati or **kovate** (Eng.) n. cupboard. By ext., a glutton.

kove, kovea, koveraka v. to snatch, grab. *na kovekove* grabbing for oneself, selfishness. *tamata kovekove* greedy person.

kove (or) **kofi** (Eng.) n. coffee.

kovesio (Eng.) confession, as in Roman Catholic tradition.

kovu adj. reserved (of land), especially for food gardens. *qele kovu* or *ikovukovu* land set aside and granted for someone's use, a right that may in some cases be inherited, but distinct from ownership. *Mataveivaqaqai ni Qele Kovu* Commission for Special Land Reserves, mostly set aside for use of the specific clans, preventing any lease to outsiders because the land was needed by the locals. Ratu Sukuna proposed this concept to the chiefs in 1936.

kovu, kovuta v. to wrap in bud-shape some food, as with leaves to package *vakalolo* pudding, closed at top. Ten such packages *ikovu vakalolo* would be referred to as one *wai* in the counting system used for grand food presentations. Such bud-shaped packages may also be used for certain foods to be cooked in the earth oven, shrimp, some meats.

kovuta v. to include or enclose.

ikovu 1. n. bud-shaped package, usually of leaf-wrapped food to be cooked in the earth oven.

ikovu 2. (Lau) n. women's dress. Syn. *vinivo*.

ikovu 3. n. parenthesis ( ), a word invented by schoolteachers of Fijian. *ikovurivi* bracket(s) [ ]. *kovuta* v. to include or enclose.

kovula (Eng.) n. corporal.

ikovurivi n. brackets [ ], used in writing a sentence. A neologism invented by schoolteachers.

koya him, her, it. *ko koya* he, she. *Koya!* That's it! *E a cakava vakai koya* He/she did it by himself/herself.
  Idiom: *Koya gona!* That's it, just as I was saying!
koya that one over there, sometimes seen as *ko ya*.
koyakoya v., adj. unchanged, the same as before.
ku 1. v. in some situation of guilt, to be held responsible without complete justification, or to befall with the consequences when not fully justified. Uncommon usage.
ku 2. (Eng. coup) n. military coup. See *vuaviri*.
kua don't. *Kua ni cakava* Don't do it. *Au sa kua ni gunu bia.* I don't drink beer. *Au sa kua mada.* (or) *Sa kua mada.* I'd rather not (politely, I decline). *kua mada* please don't. *Kua sara!* Just don't! *kakua* definitely don't (stronger prohibition).
Kuaranitini (Eng.) n. Quarantine. Various spellings of this word.
kuasi n. forest tree to 15 m., Podocarpus neriifolius, good timber for furniture, fine construction, formerly used for spears, poles, canoes. flowering, fruiting October-November, cherry-like base of fruit, lvs linear-lanceolate, spirally arranged. Male and female cones on separate trees.
kuaya (Eng.) n. choir.
kube, kubeta v. to cling to, to grasp, hang onto, hold tight, haul up, pull in (rope). *kukube* hang on tightly.
kube (or) **kube kau** adj. quite drunk.
kubou n. smoke (from a fire), mist or fog. See *kuvu*.
kubu v. to form buds, beginning to sprout on plant.
kubu v. to flee. *veikubuyaki* to run off in all directions. *Kubu!* Take off! Run! Escape!
kubu, kubuta 1. v. to fill the cheeks out with something (like water, food). sometimes to swill it as in tasting wine or gargling. Modernly, the word can become vulgar, referring to oral sex on a male.
kubu, kubuta 2. v. to remain silent, concealing some thought, feeling, keeping it to oneself.
kubukubu v., n. to gargle, gargling, rinse the mouth, as in morning ablutions. *kubukubuta* to gargle with something, such as a mouthwash, or *cagolaya*, a species of ginger used to ease throat colds. *dredre kubukubu* v. to chuckle, laugh to oneself, laugh quietly.
kubu-na n. butt-end (house gable, rifle, chin, heel of the foot or a shoe), protuberance (flower bud, small promintory of land, pimple or boil on the body). Kubuna is a place-name on the Tailevu coast opposite Bau island. It became the name of a super-tribe, combining tribe Vusaratu and tribe Tui Kaba. Kubuna later became a native state (*matanitu*).
kubuiloqi n. upper, more prestigious, private end of the house where the owner of the house sleeps. Syn. *kubuicake*.
kubu-i-sue lower, less prestigious and less private end of a house where the cooking was done in a corner, in former times. For fire safety, the British required that a kitchen house be built next to the family house which has become the custom. While *sue* can mean "house" in the West, it more commonly refers to the small props, usually three of them, stones or pieces of clay, that held up a Fijian clay pot that always had a rounded bottom. Syn. *kubu-ira*.
kubu lolo n. of a traditonally shaped Fijian house, the rounded ends of gables characteristic of the Polynesian-style houses of Lau Province. The more square ends or gables of Fijian houses are known as being *kubu ravi*.
kucu, kucuva v. to rape, force a woman.
kudru, kudruva (or) **kudruvaka** v. to grumble or groan at (person, situation). Also of a pig, to grunt. *kudruvaka* v. to grumble about something or someone.
kudrukudru-i-Ra Mo Idiom: to be angry or disgruntled about something after the fact, having given no prior indication of dissatisfaction. Fijians may be afraid to speak openly at the time of a decision or agreement. This can result in later back-biting and obstruction to plans, a common complaint.
kudukudua (Colo East, Namosi, Rewa) n., adj. cold. Syn. *batabata*. These words apply to the weather, not to a thing, such as water. *wai liliwa* cold water.
kui n. current (river, sea).
kui, kuitaka v. to flow (current of water), carry or sweep along with the current, as with a piece of driftwood (or the unwary swimmer).
kuila (Tonga) n. flag. Naval flags *drotini* were known to Fijians, mainly in the large coastal states such as Bau. Syn. *koila*. See *tawake* pennant.
  Idiom: *ena daku ni kuila* before Cession (1874)
  Idiom: *na cicivaki kuila 4x100 mita* the relay race (track).

kuita 1. n. octopus, a cephalopod with eight arms, each with two rows of suckers. On males, one arm is modified to implant sperm packets into the female. For feeding, there is a beak and a radula that serves as a file to open crustaceae and shellfish. Movement is by walking or by a type of jet-propelled thrust. Black "ink" helps conceal its exact location and confuse predators. *rubi, rubica na kuita.* beat the octopus (to soften it). The octopus is usually speared, most bountifully beginning around July (Fijian lunar month *vula i cukicuki*), plentiful through August. Larger ones, to five feet in length, are turned inside out to kill them, expertly done by Gilbertese and some Fijians. Such *kuita* can be very dangerous in self-defense. Small octopi, very shy, very sensitive, can be tamed and become quite friendly though always shy and quickly reactive. (I have kept some as pets in a sea garden at Katafaga Island. I love them too much ever to hurt them or eat them.) Octopi are reputed to be very intelligent. They are powerless out of water. Besides eating octopus, Fijians like to use it as a preferred bait on fishing lines. Many Fijians have the curious notion that cats or dogs would lose their coat of hair if they eat octopus. They also believe that to kill a an undesired tree (such as an African Tulip that is hard to eradicate), one has only to plant the beak of an octopus at its base. Syn. (Serua, parts of the West) *sulua* (or) *hulua*.

kuita 2. n. as in *baca kuita* an idiom, meaning a special enticement in human affairs, based on the fact that octopus *kuita* is a preferred, effective bait (*baca*) on a fishing line.

kuita 3. n. octopus, but by extension, a very painful headache, migraine. Syn. *kuitamona, kuitaquruquru*.

kuita 4. n, asterisk, a Fijian word invented by teachers of Fijian language. Syn. *kalokalo*. s

kuita-ni-nubu n. Nautilus pompilius, formerly caught in deep waters outside reefs. Occasionally seen at the surface, the shells sometimes found on beaches.

kuita-nu n. Bigfin Reef Squid, Sepiatenthis lessonicena, calamari, a cephalopod. When small, squid move in schools, sometimes almost immobile, but capable of darting very quickly. Fijians hardly ever caught them which would seem to require specialised nets, fast reaction time, and a lot of luck. Unlike octopi, two of the ten arms are adapted for swimming. They each have four rows of suckers. Squid tend to swim about while octopi tend to clamber about. Large squid exist only in deep water, never encountered by humans. The very large ones are food for the sperm whale which can dive to great depths. Syn. (West) *sulua qalo*.

kuka n. type of small crab, dark coloured with a little red, living among mangroves, often used for bait, best beginning around January. Sesarma spp. Idiom: *Sa ua levu, sa kaba na kuka*. Times are good and we are prospering. Lit. High tide is rising and the *kuka* crabs are coming out.

kuku n. mussel, Modiolus spp., edible. The sharp edge of the shell *kai kuku* used for smoothing and cleaning pandanus leaf preparatory to weaving, and formerly used for cutting small things. Name of a people and village near Suva. Syn. (West) *boro*.

kukuna v. as is *kukuni koya* to hang oneself. In earlier times this was virtually unknown in Fiji. It is much more common among Fiji Indians than among Fijians. See *kuna*.

kukuva v. to grasp, usually another person's hand or some support such as a rope or the branch of a tree, to prevent a fall, or to prevent slipping into deep water, or a drowning.

kukuvu adj. worm-eaten, as of fruit.

kukuwalu n. cultivated plant introduced by Tongans and particularly associated with Bau island. The plant is famous in Fiji for its fragrant flowers praised in a popular sentimental song. Extremely few Fijians have ever seen or smelled the plant. It does not grow wild and is rarely cultivated. One plant has been grown by Asena Liga at Toorak, and took seven years to flower. The plant somewhat resembles a pandanus shrub, with long sharp leaves with tiny thorns at the edge. Flowers are in a whitish sprig that becomes fragrant at dusk. The plant used to grow famously at Lasakau on Bau but there is none there today. The Lasakau were naval warriors with early Tongan affiliations. The Tongan woven cummerbund (*taufala* in Fijian) was often traditionally made of the leaves of *kukuwalu*, and the flowers used for chiefly Tongan *salusalu*. Commonly used today as Lauan *taufala* is the more accessible *voivoi* pandanus. John Parham does not list *kukuwalu* in his *Plants of the Fiji Islands*, and nor does A. C. Smith in *Flora Nova Vitiensis*. In Tonga the plant is known as *kukuvalu* and in Samoa as *uuwalu*.

kula (Polyn.) **1.** endemic small bird with bright red feathers, the Collared Lory, Phygis solitarius, feeds on nectar and pollen, favouring *drala* Erythrina sp., notably in August, September, moving quickly in groups, also favouring the flowering *vuga* trees. Tongans came to Fiji to barter for the red feathers, highly prized especially by Samoan chiefs. Tongans traded them to Samoa, a very significant commerce that existed long before the arrival of Europeans. The more ancient, indigenous Fijian name for this bird is *drisi* or *drusi* according to Geraghty.

kula (Polyn.) 2. highly coloured (red, blue) wool edging on the borders of some mats, a modern, less costly version of early Tongan mats that used red parrot feathers as an edging. *e dua na ibe vakula* a mat with an edging of highly coloured wool. *kulata* (or) *va-kulataka* v. to put a woolen *kula* fringe on a mat.

kula lailai n. Red-Headed Parrot Finch, Erythrura sp. Small bright green bird with red rump and tail and head. Found on the larger islands and in the Yasawas. Often seen on lawns, two or three of them, hopping about and fluttering away, very cute.

kuli-na n. skin (human, animal), bark (tree). *cecega na kulina* pull off the skin.

kuli, kulia, kuliraka v. to remove the skin, usually of a fibre plant such as *vau*, or barkcloth *masi* or a food such as taro.

kulikuli adj., adv. as in cooking food, to keep the skin on, especially root crops. *saqa kulikuli* v. to cook with the skins on.

kulina n. young boy before puberty, sometimes used facetiously to refer to young men. Implied is the notion that the boy is not circumcised.

kuli ni boci n. foreskin of the uncircumcised penis.

kuli ni tabua (Lau) n. barkcloth surrounding the grave of a chiefly corpse at burial. Only certain people may penetrate this symbolic barrier. May refer to the chiefly corpse itself in a rather pedantic expression. Syn. *kolo*.

kulu (West) n. breadfruit, totemic is some parts of the west and thus a word that is best not pronounced at Viseisei, for example.

kulu, kuluca v. to slip off, as of the skin of *dawa* fruit, or some root crops that have been cooked with the skin on, done under water to make the task easier. *nona itavi na kulukulu* his/her job is to slip off the skins.

kulumaca adj. damp, musty, usually of cloth, barkcloth. See *luma, tarasua*.

kuluta n., (Eng.) ("coal-tar") hard-top road, macadam road surface. Syn. *kolota*.

kuluva n. a well known, common, very fast-growing bush and timer tree, to 20 meters, with very large leaves that have a winged petiole, Dillenia biflora, Dilleniaceae. Used as a living fence. Once cut, the young stems and branches rot quickly because the centre is of soft wood; to endure they must be planted. They will then sprout promptly, sometimes becoming a nuisance, difficult to eradicate. Slash is red with red sap and pinkish brown wood. In Tailevu Province, *kuluva* is totemic for tribe Daviko and tribe Vugalei. An earlier location of village Nayavu was called Navunikuluva ("The *Kuluva* Tree"). Syn. (Ba, Bua, Macuata) *kulukulu*.

kuluvotu n. bird, Many-Coloured Fruit Dove, Ptilinopus perousii, favours fruiting banyan trees, common in forests.

kumala (Polyn.) n. sweet potato. This word and the plant have their origins in South America, proving very early contact with Polynesians. Cognates of this name occur throughout the Pacific islands. Syn. *dabici*, a much less common name.

kumakumare v. to flirt, or show off in front of the opposite sex. Syn. *wa-cece. wa-calacala*. See *wedewede*.

kumete (Polyn.) n. wooden bowl. This word extends to eastern Polynesia.

kumi-na n. beard, chin. *vakumi* bearded.

kumuna v. to gather together, people, things. *na kumuni sede* the collection (funding, as for school, church). Syn. *sokumuna*.

Kuna n. (Nadro.) form of address for chiefly man or woman, followed by their name, equiv. of Adi or Ratu is some other areas of Fiji, or for a woman, *Bulou* in Nadroga and Kadavu.

kuna, kunata v. strangle with a rope around the neck. This was the common way of killing wives and female attendants to be buried with a dead paramount chief, especially at Bau and Cakaudrove. Elderly people were often strangled when they became infirm. Fijians believed they were already effectively dead very soon after becoming incapacitated. *dau veikuna* n. hangman. The concept of hanging is not Fijian but was used as early as 1859 on Bau by Cakobau when he betrayed Mara Kapawai after assuring his immunity from any revenge for rebellion. Hanging as a legal punishment for serious crime was maintained during most of the colonial years and there was one official hangman.

kune, kunea v. to find. *kunekune* finding.

Idiom: *kunekune na yaloka ni dilio* impossible to find, does not exist, just as the eggs of the shore-bird *dilio* are never found in Fiji. (It breeds in Alaska or Siberia and migrates to Fiji seasonally.)

kune visible. *E kune na waqa*. The boat is visible.

kunekune v. to conceive (a child). *vakunekune-taka* v. to make (a woman) pregnant. *kunekune dredre* having difficulty conceiving, as of a woman wanting to have a child. *kunekune-ca* morning sickness. See *bukete* pregnant.

kune-ka adj. to be miserable.

kura n. small coastal tree, Morinda citrifola, Rubiaceae, edible but bitter fruit is a knobby oval, eaten ceremonially as an act of cleansing by grave tenders after the burial of a Bauan Vunivalu. The fruit is passed from one man to another, passed behind their backs, for each man to take a bite. (They then jump into the sea to bathe, all part of the cleansing ceremony.) When ripe the fruit is white with curious, distinctive taste liked by only a few people. It is normally eaten by virtually nobody. The root produces a yellow dye, reddish when mixed with lime. The bark makes a red dye. P. Geraghty suggests that the name derives from *kula*, proto-Polynesian version of *kurati* ("turmeric", and much later, "metallic gold") in the Moluccas). Called *hura* in parts of Vanua Levu. The old, ripe fruits become quite smelly as they rot. In the marketing of commercial herbal medicine this fruit is promoted as useful in the treatment of cancer and other ailments. The fruit is antiseptic but other medical properties are unproven. Polynesian names are variants of *noni*.

kurabui adj. surprised, amazed. *veika veiva-kurabuitaki* amazing things. *kurabuitaka* to be amazed at it.

kurabui, kurabuitaka v. to be surprised at something. *Sega ni kurabuitaki na nomu digitaki.* Not surprising that you have been chosen.

veivakakurabui-taki adj. surprising. *Cava e veivakakurabuitaki kina oqo?* What is surprising about this? *E dua na ka veivaka-kurabuitaki duadua.* Something extremely surprising.

kurau, kurauta v., adj. to be garrulous, speaking out forcefully, or even shouting as if to scare people or attract their attention suddenly.

ikurau n. exclamation, a modern word invented by language teachers.

kure, kurea, kuretaka v. to shake. *kure, kurea* may refer to shaking of branches to bring down fruit, or shaking a small tree to cause a fruit-bat to fall and be caught. Syn. *ure, urea*. *kurekure* to shake, usually the head, implying a negative response. Nodding an affirmative response would be done by a slight raising of the chin or eyebrows (*deguvacu*). *sautakurekure* v. to vibrate. See *sakure*.

kurei, kurei-taka v. to sprinkle some liquid, fine powder (flour, pepper), or sand. May have the implication of shaking it, even shaking it off the hands.

kureu startled.

kuri, kuria v. to add to, augment, to follow. *na kena ikuri* the supplement, *na ikuri ni itukutuku* the continuation of the report, (as in the next issue of a weekly newspaper.) *Me ikuri ni vakamacala, veitaratara kei iratou na qase ni vuli.* For further information, get in touch with the teachers. *E na qai kuri tale yani.* To be continued (as an ending of one part in a series of stories or articles published.) *na ikuriliu* n. the prefix to a root-word, as in *laukana*, the prefix *lau* attached as a prefix to the root-word *kana*. *ikuri-i-muri* n. suffix, as with *taka* in the transitive verb *kure-taka*. These grammatical terms are of course invented modernisms. Some school-teachers think it necessary to create Fijian words for these concepts.

vakuria v. to continue. *vakuria na noqu ilakolako.* continue on my trip.

kuro n. cooking pot, trad. only in clay, made only in a few coastal villages of Fiji, mainly by Tongan immigrants and their descendants in Nadroga Province (villages Nakabuta, Lewai), Rewa Province (Nasilai), Kadavu (Yawe), and in Ra Province, formerly also at village Levuka on Lakeba. Firing of pots is done in outdoor fires, not kilns. (Only at Noikoro, Navosa are pots cured in the sun, without fire). While pottery for cooking and water storage has been retained in Polynesian areas of Fiji, that practice was abandoned in Samoa, and was never a significant feature of Tonga. It is curious then, that pot-making in Fiji began only as an influence from Tongan immigrants. Large pots for storing water were known as *saqa*. Two basic types of cooking pot are the large, tall one for steaming food and a smaller, wide short, virtually round pot (*ivakariri*) for boiling fish. The base for all pots was always round, never flat, so props (*isue*) of clay or stones could keep the pot a sloping angle during cooking. The pot opening was plugged with a lid improvised from leaves. Pots were traded up into the interior highlands where they were very rare. They were imported there, usually in exchange for *yaqona* that thrives in many inland places. Curiously, pottery was never one of the goods used in traditional exchanges known as *solevu* which involved ceremonial and social interaction as well as exchange of goods. Highlanders used bamboo tubes for water storage and as cooking pots, and they grilled much of their food without the use of clay pots. The only highlanders who made clay pots were in Navosa where Tongans penetrated in the 1700s, introducing the making of pots and also of barkcloth (*masi*) from the mulberry tree.

In Kadavu, southwest and southeast Viti Levu, and also among the Levuka people in Lau, clay was formed in slabs, beaten together with a paddle. In Ra and LomaiViti, coils or rings were used. On the Vanua Levu coast, and at Yanuya in Mamanuca, there was a basal slab to which rings were added. After sun-drying, pots are fired on open ground with burning grass or bamboo, never fired in any sort of kiln. In a few places fire-pits are used. Cooking pots were never glazed and rarely had any decoration at all. When used for water pots, glaze has been made of resin *makadre,* from the *dakua* tree, though for tourist, store-bought varnish in now more common. Many of the clay pots made for tourists now are insufficiently fired to be strong enough to contain water. Some water pots were not glazed, to allow evaporation that kept the water cool. The only fanciful pots have been small water pots for direct drinking. They had one or more spouts, the water being poured into the mouth from several inches away. Cups were never used except until later, when folded leaves and then half coconut shells were adopted for drinking *yaqona.* Coconut shell cups came with the serving bowl (*tanoa*) that Tongans introduced with the Samoan custom of drinking kava in hierarchical groups, ceremoniously in an ordered circle, in the latter part of the 1700s. The adopted word for "cup" (*bilo*) comes from the word for the similarly shaped knee-cap. Previously, Fijians had no cups.

Sherd are still found of pre-Fijian pots dating to 1600 B.C., known as Lapita pottery, named for the place in New Caledonia where these type of pots were first found. Lapita pots often had simple markings as decoration. These were made by a seafaring people who settled only by the shore, e.g. Ba (at Natunuku) and Sigatoka, Nananu-i-ra Island. They are believed to be proto central Polynesians. By about 500 A.D. pottery was no longer made in Samoa or Tonga for reasons that are unexplained. Tongan pottery did continue in Fiji in a few isolated places, though it is now made only for tourists. The notion of minature pots for tourists originated with the author of this dictionary who made the very first ones at Wainadoi, Namosi for domestically grown spices to be sold in gift shops. *kuro ni ti* tea pot. *kuro ti* pot of tea. *kuro kava* metal pot. *kuro ni Bobei* Bombay pot, aluminium, with straight sides and flat lid, available inexpensively in many different sizes. *kuro vakasucuna* heavy, black cast-iron pot with round bottom but three "legs" to stand it up, for cooking large food over an open fire.

kurokatikatia n. heartburn, or gastric reflux of partially digested food.
kurosusunu n, chicken pox, an illness, usually of children. Syn. *susuna.*
kuru v. to fall, as of leaves from a tree. *E dau vakuru na drauna.* It is deciduous.
kuru v. to thunder (weather). *Sa kuru na vanua.* It is thundering.
   Idiom: *rogo ikuru.* to intrude into an event or feast without being invited, but just hearing about it. To "crash" a party.
   Idiom: *kurusiga* to grumble without doing anything about one's complaint. Lit. daylight thunder (without the rain.)
kuruseta v. to spread, of news, gossip, or a noise, around a place. *Sa kuruseta na koro na itukutuku.* The news spread throughout the village.
kuruvaka v. to resound, thunder out a noise, or information. *Sa kuruvaki na keni irogorogo ena veivanua.* Their fame resounded throughout the land. Syn. *rogovaki.*
kusa, kusa, kusava, kusata v. to hurry, to hasten. *Kusa mai!* Hurry here! *vakusakusa* hurriedly or to be in a hurry. *kusava na cakacaka.* hurry up with the work. *vakusa-taka* to hurry it up.
kusima, kusimataka v. to desire, to relish the thought of, usually some food.
kuta n. sedge, Eleocharis sp., Cyperaceae, the plant but also a mat woven of sedge, the specialty of Bua. The plant grows in water, in soggy land. These mats are fine, soft and white but do not withstand washing as well as mats made of Pandanus. Evidence of sedge mats dating 2,000 years ago have been found at the Sigatoka sand dunes, apparently used by the Lapita people.
kutari (Hindi "kudari") n. hoe. *kutaritaka* v. to hoe. The concept is novel to Fijians. They used only a pointed stick (*doko*) to assist in planting and that is often still the case.
kutu n. flea, louse (lice), bug. Fijians quite often pick over the heads of children for human head-louse, Pediculus humanus capitis. It moves about mostly at night and lives for four to six weeks. Custom has been for parents to eat the nits and head-lice, cracking them between the teeth. Head scratchers were formerly common, kept stuck in the hair. By ext., *kutu* may refer to person who is considered a parasite on society. Idiom: *kutu ni qele* farmer, lit. louse of the soil.
kutua-venuvenu v. to wriggle about.
kutu ni tana n. bedbug. This word seems to imply that Fijians think bedbugs were introduced from Vanuatu, the island of Tanna. Cimicidae family, several genera, active at night especially, feeding on blood.

kutu sebe n. "crab", body louse, *sebe* implying running around in a scattered way. Pediculus humanus, body lice are separate sub-species from head lice. Body lice are a little larger, with more stubby body. Pubic lice are Pthirus pubis.

kuturi n. worm-like creature found sometimes embedded in eyelids of village children, usually removed carefully with a needle.

kuveti n. board on which barkcloth (*masi*) is marked (*kesa*) with patterns, brown or black. Syn. *kupeti*.

kuvu, kuvuca 1. v. to cure (barkcloth, fish) by applying smoke (*kubou*) to barkcloth, which would then be called *masi kuvui,* barkcloth coloured dull yellow from being smoked; often used formerly for chiefs' shoulder band and turban (*isala*). *Masi kuvui* takes on a slightly greenish or pink hue when light mould forms in a humid environment. On Vatulele the barkcloth is first soaked in an infusion of the root-bark of the trees *kura* (Morinda citrifolia), and *gadoa* (Macaranga sp., Euphorbiaceae). The latter has a red sap. Curiously, some of the Vatulele people use indiscriminately the terms *masi kuvui* and *masi toni*, which is more usually used for the rich brown that results from being soaked in an infusion of the bark of the mangrove tree (*dogo*). Both are soaked (*toni*) in vegetable dye.

kuvu, kuvuca 2. v, to smoke, to create smoke (usually marijuana, less frequently referring to tobacco) but also a wood-fire. *Sa kuvu tiko na buka.* The wood-fire is smoking. To remove insects, this was sometimes done deliberately.

kuvu n. dust, smoke or steam, fine spray.

kuvui, kuvuya v. to smoke out a newly built thatched house before it is occupied, to remove insects and to "cure" the green thatching. Also to smoke a whale-tooth to give it a favoured yellowish-brown colour that implies venerable age.

kuvui 1. adj. smoked (fish usually). Syn. *ika vesa.* (Macuata) *koli ra'i.*

kuvui 2. v., n. to give hot steam treatment to clear the air passages when suffering from a head-cold. To boiling, steaming water, leaves are added for penetrating fragrance, usually leaves of citrus or *uci* (Evodia hortensis).

kuvui 3. adj. of *masi* bark-cloth, dyed yellow, to have a smoked appearance. Some is actually smoked.

kuvui ni namu n. mosquito-coil, a modern notion of course.

ikuvukuvu n. chimney, outlet for smoke to escape from a residential house or a cook-house (*vale ni kana*). The chimney is a modern concept to Fijians, introduced by Europeans. In older times, cooking was done within the house and and at night fires might be lit for warmth, so the discomfort of a smoke-filled atmosphere indoors was common.

kuvu-se v. of a boat, to skim through the water causing a wave of spray.

L

la 1. (West) v. to go. *la ma* come here. Syn. *lako, la'o.*
Idiom: *na tata ga me la* a regionalism of the West, meaning many words but little content, too much talk but nothing of consequence. lit. this is only muttering, and then one goes. Yatter a while and then take off.

la 2. (Colo East) n. an edible vegetable of the highlands, old withered leaves of almost any variety of taro when the tuber is rather overly mature. The leaf-ribs are all stripped out carefully, and the leaf is mashed and cooked. Flavour and texture differ considerably from the more customary *rourou*, taro-leaf that is taken from younger plants. *La* is preferred by many highlanders and is sold in the Suva public market.

la 3. n. the letter "l" as pronounced by a Fijian in spelling out each letter of a word or reciting the alphabet. Also the note *la* on the musical scale.

la 4. n. small edible univalve mollusc, its shell often used as house by hermit crab (*kasikasi*) that changes the shell (*na qa-na*) for a larger one as it grows.

ila n. boundary, border, as marked out in games, marbles, tennis, etc.

laba, labata v. to murder. *na laba* the murder. *daulaba* murderer. *beitaki ena laba* accused of murder. *cagilaba* n. hurricane. *cagi* wind.

labakara, labakarataka v. to attempt to murder (but fail).

Labasa! (Slang) as an exclamation, a mocking reprimand for any revealing absence of clothing or disarray of clothing near the genitals. The implication is "hot stuff!", from the fact that Labasa town has a hot climate.

labaseu n., v. of fish, to flap about, especially when caught. The noise attracts sharks. To catch sharks, Tongans mimic this sound by rattling a set of coconut shells to attract them.

ilabi n. wrist.

ilabi ni ika 1. n. wrist. Syn. *labeniika.*

ilabi (ni ika) 2. n. side-fins of a fish.

ilabi ika (or) **ilabilabi ika** n. (Islands) parcel of small fish wrapped in leaves before cooking. Syn. *ikovu ika.*

labo, laboca, labota, laboraka v. to apply leverage to raise up, push up, uproot, the suffixes indicating generally increased degrees of force applied. *ilabo* stick or implement used as a lever. *na ilabolaboti* the leveraging.

vakalaboca to apply pressure (on a person), "leverage" in a figurative sense, to forcibly obtain what one wants, often by trickery. *Me ilutua ni nodratou veivakalaboci ratou qai . . . .* As consequence of their deception they (several), will then . . .

labolabo kanace v., n. leap-frog, as a children's game. While in the English version, the kids bend over while standing, in the old Fijian version, the passive person is lying down. *kanace* mullet, that jumps over predators. Syn. *ladelade kanace.*

labue v. to bubble up, ripple, of water disturbed. *bue* to bubble, of water boiling..

laburabura n. acne, pimples (containing pus), often considered a malady of youngsters.

laca n. sail, canvas. *waqa laca* sailboat. *vale laca* tent. Fijian sails were formerly made of Pandanus leaves, and were a specialty of the Yasawa islands. They were a key reason for Bau's interest in control of the northern Yasawas. *ivava laca* canvas shoes. Kaba promontory of southeastern Viti Levu had the responsibility of maintaining the sails of Bauan canoes.

Laca n. the star-constellation Taurus, lit. Sail (as of a boat). Names of most constellations have been known only to Polynesian sea-faring specialists.

lade, ladeva, ladevaka v. to jump, jump up jump over (with the implication of then coming down). *ladevaka* v. to jump with something being held. May be used figuratively, as in *Ena macawa oqo eda sa na ladeva mada yani ki* (a different topic). This week we jump over to (a different topic). *ladekoso, ladekosova* v. to jump across. *lade-balavu* v., n. broad jump (in track sport). *lade cere* (or) *lade ova* v., n. high jump. *ladebai* v., n. to hurdle (track). *ladekau* v., n. to pole-jump, to vault. Syn. *rikava* or *rikata*, which refers to jumping down or down onto something. It does not refer to jumping up and then coming down, as is the case of *lade, ladeva*. (Colo East) *labo, laboca.*

ladelade kanace n,, v. to play "leap-frog" as a children's game. *kanace* mullet, that skims and jumps to evade the larger, predator fish. Syn. *labolabo kanace.*

ladi (Eng.) n. launch, motorised boat, usually with inboard engine.

lafu (Tonga, Lau) seabird, usually Pterodroma spp., various species of petrel.

laga, lagata. 1. v. to sing, lead off a song, before others who will follow (*camana*), to intone. *na laga sere* the singing. *na lagalaga sere* the continued singing of songs. *Sa lagati oti na sere.* The song has already been sung. *ilagalaga* n. tune or pitch, set of the lead for a song or *meke*. Syn. (Samoa) langi). 2. (Archaic) v. to wave a war club assertively, threateningly.

lagalagawa adj. assertive, demonstatively manly.

lagakali n. fragrant shrub or tree 5 to 10 meters tall, Aglaia saltatorum especially but other species are closely related, Meliaceae, famous in romantic (modern) Fijian song, a style Polynesian in origin. Endemic to Lau and Tonga, grown only at very low elevations. All Fijians have heard the name but very few would recognize the plant. J. Parham says it is common in Nadroga, flowering in June, July, with long flowers, bright red. Gov. Arthur Gordon remarks in his 1876 diary that he saw *lagakali* with small, orange-coloured flowers on Nairai Island in November. While *lagakali* is the name in Lau and Bau, other local names are *kautoa, misi, cavucavu,* and *kula*.

lagasai v. to fall backwards. Syn. *dalasai*.

lagi 1. (Rewa, Kadavu) n., v. rain. Syn. (Bau) *uca*.

lagi 2. (Polyn., Lau) n. sky. Syn. (Bau) *lomalagi*.

lagilagi adj. glorious.

vakalagilagi v. to praise, glorify, as in *Me vakalagilagi na Kalou.* May God be praised.

lago (Polyn.) n. fly (the insect).

lagokata n. stinging horse fly, stinging hornet, wasp. It is not always clear to which creature the word refers.

lago-ta-voivoi n. large biting bottle-fly.

ilago n. threshhold at entrance to a building. It has been considered presumptuous or impolite to sit on or at the threshold of a house. A rather formal word, perhaps now archaic, used mainly for chiefly houses and temples that were raised on a high base of rocks and earth. See *lagona*.

lagona v. to put wooden poles under the hull of a boat ashore, to be able to move it by rolling, or to put blocks of wood under something to keep it off the ground, as for a wooden drum *lali*, or a water tank. *na ilago* the wooden support as used in this way. In ancient times, live human bodies were put under large boats being launched at the seashore.

lai v. abbrev. of *lako ki* go to, sometimes spelled *la'i.* or also *la* or *laki*.
  Idiom: *Lai volo!* (Taveuni) Get lost! Make yourself scarce!, usually said to a naughty child. Literally, this implies to go looking for wild yams in the bush. In other words, get out of the way; go do something useful that does not bother people.

lailai 1. adj. small, little (singular), few. *lalai* (plural) n. often itself an abbrev. for *gone lalai* n. children. Syn. (Nadro.) *hewa*. (West) *sewa*.

lailai 2. n. (Ba, Nadroga) mangrove tree. Syn. *dogo*.

vakalailai-taka v. to reduce, make smaller, to abbreviate.

laialaia (or) **layalaya** n. small semi-cultivated plant, the liquid expressed from the corm is used commonly for coughs, colds, Zingiber zerumbet, probably aboriginal introduction. Syn. *cagolaya*.

laimi n. (Eng.) lime, an introduced plant grown mostly by non-Fijians. Two main varieties, one seedless, one with seeds, main fruiting season begins late June. In Fiji, most "limes" sold are actually the quite large Meyer lemons with the skin green in colour.

laino n. linoleum, "lino", a relatively inexpensive plastic floor covering. Syn. *ibe ni vavalagi*.

lairo n. edible land crab found close to the shore, Cardisoma sp., sold at the market in season, November to March in Suva area. In contrast to the seashore crab (*qari*), the *lairo* does not swim. Both are popular foods, sold in strings with the largest on the bottom of the string. *Lairo* are found walking about, or are dislodged from their burrows in sand or mud. The burrow is identified by many thin, tall piles of sand, often eight inches in height. Once a year in around November to January, at night the *lairo* make a mass migration to the sea to breed. The season varies with locality. Syn. (Rewa) *tuba*. *tara lairo* to catch land crabs. *una, unaka na lairo* to kill land crab with sharp stick. *kasi, kasina na lairo* to bind land crabs on a string. *ikasi lairo* n. string of land crabs. *cina lairo* to catch *lairo* by hand at night with the aid of a torch *cina*, especially as they move seasonally in mass to the sea. *yaya* of many *lairo,* move about audibly. *vula i yaya* n. lunar month around November, when *lairo* begin to move.

lairo-damu n. edible land crab, Cardisoma rotunda, with claws of equal length, unlike the "white" land crab, C. carnifex, *lairovula*, which can have one claw much larger than the other. Syn. *lairotui*, with equal claws.

lairo-vula n. edible "white" land crab, Cardisoma carnifex.

laiseni (Eng.) n. licence. *vakalaiseni* adj. licenced.

laiva v. to leave, let it be (only in certain senses). *Dou laiva vei au.* You (few) leave it to me. *Laiva meu cakava.* Let me do it.

laivi as in *biuta laivi* throw it out, discard.

lakaba n. a common bird, the White-rumped Swiftlet, Collocalia spodiopygia, often seen at the end of the day, never comes to land outside its nesting area in caves. Easily identified by its small size, white rump and erratic flight, darting here and there, not close to people. Syn. *kakaba*, not to be confused with *kakabe*, Pacific Swallow that has smoother flight and no white rump and is found further afield from the main Fiji islands, extending into Lau and on to Tonga.

lakaca n. medical problem of cracks on the underside of the foot.

lakalaka (Tonga, Lau) n. type of dance, standing up in lines, men and women together. In the original Tongan version, the women are seated and the men stomp, shout, and leap about. In Fiji, it is usually a women's exhibition dance, and according to Hocart, means "swift walk". The name refers to the manner of stepping.

laki v. to go to, usual abbrev. of *lako ki*, sometimes written *la'i*. To go and (do something): *Era laki gunu ti.* They (many) go and have breakfast. To go to do (something): *Erau laki moce.* They go to sleep.

-laki (or) **-raki** n. suffix added to a verb to indicate forcefulness. *buturaki* beaten up badly, of a person, usually done by several people. *butulaki* trodden down repeatedly. *Era butulaka na dalo na bulumakau.* The cattle walked all over the taro.

lako, lakova v. to go, go for (something). Syn. *lai*. (West) *la*. (Rewa) *qai, qaiva*. (Colo East) *bau*. See *lai, laki*.

Idiom: (Anglicism) *lako tiko* "going with", as in English, John is "going with" Suzie, implying a relationship. *lakokosova, lakokosovataka* v. to cross over, to go across (road, river, piece of land).

Idiom: *Kana, kana! Ka o lakova mai.* "Eat, eat! That's what you came for." Teasing a friend who passes by during a meal, invited to join in.

veilakoyaki n. transport, travel back and forth, here and there. *Minisita ni Veilakoyaki* Minister for Transport.

ilakolako n. trip, voyage.

lakolako Idiom: after a time, *ena lakokalo* in the passage of time. Syn. *Tikotiko kina . . .* Once upon a time . . . (as in story-books).

ilakovi n. ceremony to recognise the transfer of persons to identify themselves officially with another social group. Children may thus often become identified with their mother's clan (*mataqali*) rather than the father's. A Fijian "belongs" to one village and to one clan within that village. A person is supposed to be "written down" to a clan in the official registry *iVola ni Kawa Bula*. (The N.L.C. has estimated for me that about one tenth of all Fijians remain unregistered.) This system of transfer may be used to supply a chieftain where none was born to that role. This was the case with Ratu Josefa Iloilo, being re-registered at village Viseisei late in life to become Tui Vuda, when village Viseisei need a chiefly candidate, long after his initial registration to his mother's people on Taveuni.

lala adj. empty (container), depopulated (village), unoccupied (chiefly title). *lala didi* adj. completely empty of people, of a place, such as an old village, or a school-house during holidays.

Idiom: *ulu lala* ignorant, empty-headed.

Idiom: *Sa lala tu na koro*, lit., the village is empty of people, but in the case of a chiefly village may mean the chief is absent or that there is no chief. Quite a few titles are vacant due to internal disputes or complexities and delays in selecting a chief. In Rewa, chiefly village Lomanikoro was often said to be "empty" because the late chiefly Roko Tui Dreketi rarely visited the village.

Idiom: *vaka-tu-lala* to stay alone, when others have gone.

vakalala v. to vacate, leave empty (house, parliamentary seat etc.)

vakalala sitoa (Anglicism) n. store clearance (sale). *na lutu sobu ni vakalala sitoa* the store-clearance sale. A person going shopping, spending a lot of money, may be teased as if clearing out the store.

lala (Archaic) n. obligatory labour, usually farm labour, traditionally provided to a chief by the commoners, but might include other community labour such as house-building, road-building. The earlier right of chieftains to impose this duty was officially abolished by the colonial administration due to abuses by the chieftains who used it only to their own advantage. Abolition of such chiefly rights made a serious problem for those chiefs who had no salary from a government position or from income from leased land. Only the salaried provincial admininistrators (*Roko Tui*), and under them the Fijian District Officers (*Buli*), were allowed to impose *lala*.

ilala n. gang (usually of people), a cohesive group of followers attached to a leader (not necessarily related in the traditional social network). *na vaka-ilala* the member(s) of a group, gang, work-crew, those who belong to the group. *lala* v. to go along together, of two or more people.

lalabi (or) **lalabe** n. species of small, broad-leaf terrestrial fern, cooked leaves eaten as a green vegetable, Diplazium proliferum. Such edible ferns are generally referred to as *ota* and are semi-cultivated. Sold in the Suva market. Syn. *labe*.

lalaga 1. n. wall (of a building). *Lalaga Vesi* honorific reference to the Tui Cakau at village Somosomo, Taveuni.

lalaga 2. n., adj. spacious(ness), uncrowded, free(dom) from restriction or constraint.

lalaga 3. n. (Tonga "lagaga") traditional section of Tongan-style tapa cloth *gatu,* made in Lau. Each section is marked with a sequential number. 100 such sections make up one *lautefui*.

lalai adj., n. small (plural). Only very few Fijian adjectives have a plural form. *gone lailai* small child, *na gone lalai* the small children (often abbreviated as *na lalai*). See *leka* short, *levu* big, *balavu* long (or) tall.

lalakai n. a common weed, sp. of small plant boiled in water to give the finest shiny black appearance (*somosomo*) to leaves of *voivoi* (Pandanus sp), for decorative interweaving in the plaiting of mats, after the Pandanus has been left buried in mud (*soso*) for a time. This gives a shinier finish than an alternative plant, *wa damu*.

ilalakai n. small and very simple rectangular plaited mat, usually of coconut leaf, used traditionally as a kind of dish for serving food to a chief, though not for any flesh food for which green leaves or a wooden platter (*dari*) might be used. These are now sometimes sold as tourist souvenirs. Adopted as the name (*Nai Lalakai*) of a Fijian language weekly newspaper.

Idiom: *kana e bele ni ilalakai* lit. eat at the edge (*bele*) of the chiefly food-tray. Said of a dependent person who pretentiously tries to act as if properly a member of the important household.

lalama adj. translucent, as of very thin barkcloth (or cotton cloth), but modernly may mean virtually transparent, perhaps even like clear glass.

lalata v. usually of a sound, voices, to fill or dominate some place like a room.

lalau, lalautaka v. (of pregnant women) to crave some special food or beverage.

lalawa, lalawataka v. to plan, have an objective or goal for something. Syn. *navunavuci*.

lalawa n. sinnet lashings, often decorative, as in binding rafters of a traditional Fijian house, especially in Lau.

lalawa ni mate n. life-size or larger effigy of a dead chief erected ceremonially at the end of mourning period, when mourning clothes are removed. It is made of coir sinnet and dressed in *masi* barkcloth. Mourners bring gifts to lay at its feet, whaleteeth (called *vatu ni sulu,* in this context), or other ceremonial goods. This is strictly a Lauan concept, but adopted for Ratu Lala Sukuna in 1962, then for Ratu Penaia Ganilau in 1995 and later for Ratu Mara Kapaiwai after his death. People of Cicia Island are skilled at making the *lalawa ni mate*.

lali n. wooden gong or drum, or modernly, a metal bell. Today the large ones serve mostly to call village Fijians to church, or children to school. Very small ones with a high-pitched tone may be used at a traditional dance (*meke*), a custom introduced from Tonga. To beat the drum, or sound the drum, Fijians use the verb *qiri, qirita,* to ring, the same verb used to ringing a phone or playing a guitar. Formerly, signals were transmitted by various rhythmic beatings of the *lali* but now all such rhythms are forgotten.

lali, lalita v. to trip, to trip up, stumble especially in running. *lalita* refers to the legs.

lali, lalia v. to fib (to someone), usually not as any accusation that would have serious consequences, but more often as a joke.

veilali adj. duplicitous, deceptive.

laloi, laloya v. to cover and protect food in the earth-oven with small sticks or other vegetation, placed above. *ilaloi* plant material such as sticks used for this purpose.

lamalama adj. clear, translucent, transparent, usually said of water. See *lalama*.

lamasa adj. lacking in fortitude, insubstantial.

lamata v. to break through to the surface of the water, as a diver or a turtle comes up for breath.

lamawa n. v., yawn. Syn. *lamoa*.

lamea 1. n. mucus, usually from the mouth. Syn. *luka* which applies specifically and only to mucus of the nose.

lamea 2. n. painful, infective sores (probably fungal) in the mouths of children, usually. Fijian treatment sometimes calls for applications of macerated leaves of a fern called *vativati*. This malady is probably what is called "thrush" in English. See *macake*.

lami, lamitaka (Tonga "to conceal") v., n. to fib, to lie (about), falsehood. *Mai lami!* that's a fib! Syn. *lasu, lasutaka.*

lamoa n., v. to yawn. Syn. *lamawa.*

lamu adj. of a container or vessel, pipe or tube, has one or more holes, leaky. As an idiom applied to people, *lamu* (or) *lamulamu* means cowardly, fearful. It refers to involuntary urinating and defecation of a terrified person. A slang synonym is "fifty cents", suggesting a round and open rectum. The English words are spoken within the Fijian sentence, or used as an exclamation on their own.

lamu, lamuta v. to push or knock one or more holes in a vessel.

Lapita n. place-name in New Caledonia where there was discovered evidence of Proto-Polynesians who were the first, original settlers of these central South Pacific islands. The word now refers to those people who arrived in Fiji some 3,000 years ago. They were sailors who made pottery, the main artefacts of their settlements, and they usually remained near the coast. Many who came to Fiji moved on to settle Samoa, Tonga and the islands of eastern Polynesia. Skeletons has been found and shell middens and pottery sherds, but little else. It is possible that some Melanesians preceded the Lapita people but there are only legends and no archeological evidence.

laqa n. adj. slightly open, of a crack, gap, chink (of a container, boat, door, window, or a garment that remains somewhat open). The word may be used as a reproach to a girl who is not sitting properly, having her panties exposed.

larakini (Eng.) n. larakin, irresponsible young man.

lasa, lasata 1. v. to have fun, be happy. *vulagi lasa dina* truly happy visitor or stranger (words from the farewell song *Isa Lei*). *lasata* v. to please someone, some people. *na lasa vakavuravura* (Anglicism) the worldly pleasures.

lasa, lasava 2. v. to have an affair. *Erau a lasa tiko.* They (2) were having an affair. *lasa e tuba* to have an affair outside of marriage. *lasavi koya* having an affair with him/her. *na lasaituba* the infidelity, intercourse outside of marriage.

lasa, lasava 3. to enjoy. *Au lasava na danisi.* I enjoy dancing.

vaka-lasalasa (Anglicism) n. entertainment, concert, show. *dau-vaka-lasalasa* n. entertainer. Syn. *vaka-ta-suasua.*

Lasakau n. a tribe of naval warriors of Bau, considered traditional "fishermen" (*Gonedau*) but actually, brutal killers of Tongan origin from Beqa, men who supplied bodies for Bau's cannibalism. They were brought to Bau by the *Vunivalu* Banuve, father of Tanoa, grandfather of Cakobau. (Banuve died in the first decade of the 1800s.) Their descendants remain in a village of that name at Bau island. Others have settled in various parts of Fiji, such as Yale, Kadavu Island and at village Nuku (formerly Muaikacuni), Moala Island. Bau placed some Lasakau on Moala in the futile hope of forestalling the incursions of Ma'afu and his Tongan warriors.

laqara adj. tall and notably handsome, of a man, having a noble appearance.

laqere n. gravel. Place-name of a village near Suva that is rich in gravel. Syn. *qereqere.*

lasaqa n. frigate bird, Fregata spp. (two species), usually within 75 miles of shore, and is thus an indication of a nearby island. It can plunge into the sea catching food but cannot rest on the surface. Glides frequently, alert to steal food from the beaks of other seabirds. Distinctive sharp long wings and deeply forked tail. Syn. *kasaga, manu ni cagi.*

lase n. coral, coral sand. Burned, it is used to treat the hair as lime. Burning place known as *lovo ni lase*. A former *lovonilase* was located in the western part of Suva, and gives the name to the old Fijian cemetary by the Queens Road.

laselase n. sand, as from a beach.

lasu n., adj. false, lie, falsehood, liar. *lasulasu* n. lying. *lasulasu* adj. fake. *parofita vakailasu* false prophet.

lasu, lasutaka v. to lie, to lie (about something) or to lie (to someone). *Kua ni lasutaki au!* Don't lie to me! *na ilavo lasutaki* the counterfeit money. *lasulasu* adj. for a person who is a liar.

lata n. herbaceous plant, Solenostemon scutellarioides, Lamiaceae, commonly refered to as Coleus, various colours, red, green, yellow, some variegated, used now as decorative outdoor plants. The juice of deep red Coleus is taken internally with the rather naive notion that this will induce menstruation. *Lata* is also used for earache. Effectiveness remains unproven. Syn. *beta.*

lati, latia v. to form a screen, wall or barrier. *ilati kau* n. wooden screen. *Nailatikau* is a name that reverberates through Fijian history.

ilatilati 1. n. curtain, screen, as for a sleeping enclosure, formerly of barkcloth.

latilati 2. n. tonsils.

latui n. Fiji Goshawk, Accipiter rufitorques., endemic. Syn. *tuitui, waituitui*. (West, Namosi, Colo East) *reba*. Pink collar and breast; juveniles with speckled, streaked white breasts. Docile disposition except when defending nest.

lau, lauta 1. v. to pierce, to prick deeply with something that is sharp, pointed, a spear, a needle.
Idiom: *lauti koya na sui ni kena* he got caught in his own trap, he did it to himself. lit. the fish-bone from his own food pierced him. (*sui* bone)

lau, lauta 2. v. to strike with the fist, a club, stick, stone that is thrown. Can have figurative meaning, something that is striking, as words, a realisation, a vision, an appearance, something that is very affecting.

laulau v. used in the idiom *lai laulau* go plant taro.

lau- as a prefix followed by a verb. 1. indicates the sudden violence of striking an object. *lauvana mate* shot dead. *lauviri* stoned (struck by thrown stone or similar object), *lausua* stabbed. *laucoka* speared. *laucala* missed, of a sudden thrust or throw of a missile. (*laucala* is also a place-name.)

lau- as a prefix followed by a verb 2. indicates that something can be done or is done. *laurai* visible, within view. *laukana* edible, or is eaten by people.

laubu n. timber tree of dense forest, usually near water, Garcinia myrtiflora, Clusiaceae. Yellowish bark, yellow or brown latex, greenish white flowers, fruit red to purple from one to two inches in length.

laucala v. to miss the target. This is the name of a island, now freehold, formerly an empire of very considerable significance around Vanua Levu. Laucala was one of the very first states (*matanitu*) to have an extensive system of collecting tribute. Its decline came before the arrival of Europeans in the early 1800s. Around Vanua Levu Island, Laucala was ultimately over-shadowed by Verata and by super-tribe A i Sokula, an off-shoot of Verata that came to dominate Cakaudrove.

lauci n. candlenut tree, Aleurites moluccana, Euphorbiaceae, very likely an early aboriginal introduction, established throughout the Pacific. The oily nuts are flammable, formerly used, after drying, for lamps by coastal Fijians (not highlanders). Some 24 nuts were extracted from the shell, skewered, and placed over a bowl. One nut burned at a time, lasting only for a few minutes, with ashes knocked off as the next nut is lit. Soot used for tattoo and black colouring for barkcloth. Nuts used modernly in Polynesia, especially in Hawaii, for necklaces when the nut is polished to a shiny black but this was never done in Fiji. Roots supplied a reddish dye for bark-cloth. Bark is light grey. Slash of inner bark is white sap developing distinctive red colour. Oil, with coconut oil, used as skin lotion, and as a base for fragrant oil. Common around the coast, especially damp places, beside rivers, not reaching elevations above 2,000 feet. Can grow to 90 feet, often with no branches in the lower forty feet of smooth trunk, but more usually half that height. Timber soft, virtually useless for building, used only for case timber. Leaves light green on top, powdery silver below; young lves deeply 3-lobed. Flowers, cream coloured (male and female separate on the same tree), and fruits all year. Nuts are globose, fleshy drupes, 4 cm diam., never a staple food, nuts edible after roasting, rarely eaten and not agreeable to all. Syn. (Vanua Levu, Lau) *sikeci*. (Bua) *laci*. (Nadro., Serua, Ba) *toto*. (Vuda, Kadavu) *qereqere*. (Polyn.) *tuitui, kukui*.

lava v. as a surprise, to give a "start", be shocked, as in *lava na yatena*. (*yate* liver, the seat of courage)

ilava (Lau) n. garnish for a meal, accompaniment to the starch-food that is the "true food" *kakana dina*. Syn. *icoi*. (In the Colo East highlands *ilava* means fish *ika*.)

lavaka v. to exact or impose a requirement (usually something to be given). Also to suggest, or put forward an idea.

lave, laveta v. to raise, raise something up (not used for nets, fishing lines). *lave liga* raise the hand (as in school, or in voting by a show of hands). It is a modernism, an Anglicism, to use the word for raising the hand, though the expression is now in common use. In traditional Fiji, raising the hand would be an impolite, possibly even a threatening gesture.
Idiom: *laveta na vosa ni turaga* to carry out instructions of the chief.
Idiom: *lave na rara* the visiting team has won, lit. lifted up the playing field, an Anglicism.
Idiom: *laveliga* surrender, obviously an Anglicism, from raising the hands, as one surrenders by European custom. Fijians would *soro*.
Idiom: (Vulgar) *lavesaga* n., adj. prostitute, lit. raising the thighs *saga*, but may also apply to a woman giving birth. *Ivei o Mere? Sa baci lavesaga tu i Suva*. Where is Mere? She is a prostitute in Suva.
Idiom: *lave maca* drink excessively (alcohol). *maca* dry.

lave-ka-bi (Anglicism) n., v. weightlifting, to lift weights, as the modern sport. Such a word is a modern invention. Usually written as one word.

ilavelave 1. (Anglicism) n. copy, reprint, photocopy. *laveta, lavetaka* to make a copy, by writing out, or photocopy. *lavelavetaki* copying, making of copies.

ilavelave 2. (Anglicism) n. stretcher, to carry an invalid.

lavi, lavia, lavita v. to give a light (flame), as in bringing a burning ember to light another fire, or lighting a match for a smoker. Syn. *yala, yalaca*.

lavi, lavia (Archaic) v. of one person or immediate family, to request assistance from community for some heavy task, such as gardening, house-building. *veilavi* such community work. Some reciprocity was expected. Such custom has fallen into disuse in many places. Syn. *dele, delea*.

lavo n. form of address, and term referring to a person of opposite segment (moitié) of highlanders (*kai-Colo*). (Pronounced as *lavo* with emphasis on last syllable.) Every person is *lavo* or *tako*, alternating with the generations. This social system of the highlands persists in parts of Naitasiri, Ra, Namosi, Navosa, and former provinces of Colo North and Colo West, and around the coast, at Nakorotubu, and Ba, where highlanders have descended to the coast. (It is not customary in major parts of Colo East.) A person might be addressed as *Lavo* or *Tako*. Formerly it was normal for a *Lavo* to marry a *Tako*. Curiously, they have even had different totems in some parts of the western highlands. Normally, if a father is *tako* all his children will be *lavo*, and visa versa.

ilavo (Tonga via Lau) n. money. *ilavo bula* (or) *ilavo qaqa* cash money. *E sega na nona ilavo.* He/she has no money. *sauma na ilavo* pay the money. *Matailavo* adj. lit. "money-face", greedy for money, motivated mainly for money. The word *lavo* (from the Tongan "lafo") originally applied only to the round, flat brown seed of *walai* vine that is in the general shape of a very large coin. *ilavo ni veibiu* n. maintenance money from a divorced husband to his former wife. *ilavo musuki* n. money deducted from wages for income tax, agreed-upon contributions, or other extractions.

vakailavo-taka v. to finance, to provide funds for (some purpose). *na vakailavotaki* the financing.

lawa n. net, almost always these days for fishing. Anciently, birds were also caught in nets fixed in position. Birds were caught mainly for their red feathers (for Tongans, who would trade them to Samoa) but in the highlands especially, Fijians ate birds when they could catch them.

lawa ni yavi n. serving as a type of fish scare-line serviced by a whole community of villagers at the shore working together, about 100 meters in length, this is "rope" of vegetation floating mostly at the surface of shallow water. Villagers surround the floating scare-line, splashing, making noise to keep fish within the enclosure, finally hauling *yavi* them to the shore. The catch is shared widely within the community. *yavirau* n. this type of fishing. *yavi* to haul, *rau* grass or reeds.

lawa (Eng.) n. law. *vakalawa-taka* to legislate, pass a law (concerning something). *basu lawa* n. law breaker, criminal, crime. *lawa-tu* n. constitution (of an organisation, association, or government). *lawa vakaturi* n. proposed law. *Bose Lawa* Parliament. *Bose Lawa i Cake* Senate.

lawa, lawaca 1. v. to begin to weave, usually pandanus *voivoi* leaves, for mats. *na lawaci ni ibe* the beginning of a mat to be woven. *na ilawalawa* (or) *na kena ilawa* the long pandanus leaves for beginning a mat to be woven.

lawa, lawaca 2. v. to plait and wrap coconut-fibre sinnet (*magimagi*) around something firmly, house posts or rafters, warclubs, usually for decoration.

lawa, lawana v. to imagine, as in catching a thought or idea. The root-word *lawa* suggests catching, binding or encircling something in a mesh, as with a fish-net or a military ambush.

lawaki, lawakitaka n., v., adj. to trick, deceive, to ambush, deception. *na veilawakitaki* the trickery. Lawaki is the name of several villages in Fiji. *lawaki ca* really evil deception.

lawalawa 1. n. colander, for kitchen use, to drain wet food, or sieve with a fine mesh for smoothing flour. *lawalawa ni tenisi* tennis net. *lawalawa ni katuba* gauze-wire to keep out mosquitos and other insects from a house.

lawalawa 2. n. gang, group of people going together. Syn. *ilala*.

lawa-tu n. highest law, supreme decree, in normal times referring to the Constitution. See *Yavu ni vakavulewa*.

lawe-na n. bird feather(s), not usually including the small and light fluffy feathers.
  Idiom: *cavu lawe* lit. pluck out feathers, referring to a pretentious person who would show off by wearing a feather in the hair, acting inappropriately as if a chieftain. This idiom may mock any pretentious dress or demeanor.

lawedua n. White-tailed Tropic Bird, *Phaethon* sp. The Red-Tailed Tropic Bird is a vagrant, much rarer, and does not breed in Fiji.

laya (West) n. sail, Bauan *laca*. Used in the word *sakulaya* sailfish.

le 1. abbrev. for *lewe* people, used in compound expressions such as *rakavi le yavitu* rugby sevens, where there are seven people per team. *le levu* many people. *na le rua* the couple (of people). *na le tolu* the threesome (three people). *Au le dua ga. Eratou le vica.* I am only one person. They are several.

le 2. n. abbrev. for lesbian. Syn. *panikeke* (pancake).

ile n. purpose, point, motive. *na nona ile* his particular purpose, motive, the main point he is making. *na nona ile vuni* his hidden motive.

leba 1. n. indigenous forest tree, three to nine meters high, at low elevations, Syzygium neurocalyx, Myrtaceae, white flowers, highly scented ribbed fruit, deep purple when fully ripe, used as a dye. Women use scented fruit in a garland around the neck. Fruits to be found in the latter seven months of the year.
Idiom: *Sa dreu na kena leba.* Everything is perfect, and very timely. Lit. the *leba* fruit is ripe.

leba 2. n. (Archaic) female attendant for a high-born lady. Leba is also a personal female name.

leca Caution: *leca* and words compounded from *leca* are quite varied in their meaning, which may differ with the context and tone of voice.

leca (Eng.) n. leather.

leca (Rewa) absent, lost, disappeared. *Sa leca.* He/She/It is gone, lost, missing. Syn. (Bau) *yali*.

leca, lecava 1. v. to fail to recognize, fail to remember, do not know, be uncertain. *Au lecavi koya.* I don't know him. *kilaleca, kilaleca-taka* mistakenly think one recognizes (someone or something). *leca qalo* not to know how to swim. *leca tali* does not know how to weave.

lecava 2. v. to faint, lose consiousness *Au a lecavi au.* I had fainted, lost consciousness. Also *Sa lecalecavi koya.* He fainted, "passed out".

leca, lecava 3. v. to wonder, to be confused about. *Au se lecavi iko makawa tiko.* I was wondering for a long time who you are. *kila leca* mistaken identity.

lecava 4. v. to contradict, disagree. *Au lecava na ka o tukuna.* I disagree with what you are telling. *vakaleca* v. to contradict (someone).

leca-i-ka adj. lacking individual motivation; unthinking, forgetful; lacking knowledge.

lecalecavi forgetful.

veilecayaki adj. unsettled (of the mind, the situation, the weather), unsure, undecided, confused, mixed up.

vakaleca v. to lose (usually money, or a thing)

vakalecaleca-taka v. to ignore (a person or thing) deliberately, or fail to recognize. *ovisa vakalecaleca* plain-clothes policeman, undercover policeman.

vakaleca v. to cause someone to get mixed up. *Kua ni vakalecai au.* Don't get me mixed up (as when someone is trying to talk to a person who is doing sums or concentrating on something else).

veilecaleca, vakalecalecava v. to ignore (someone).

veilecalecava v. not to know (certain people) *Eratou veilecalecavi iratou.* They (few) do not know each other.

leca-taka (Rewa) v. to lose (something).

leka n. a legendary harmless and good-natured people of very short stature, said to have lived in western Viti Levu, and also at Vugalei, Tailevu, and around the Medrausucu mountains of Colo East, since before the arrival of Fijians. Similar stories of a short people are heard at Nacula Island in the Yasawa Group. No physical remains have been found. *Na Leka* may actually have been real people, earlier immigrants who were pygmy-size. There is no fantasy associated with them. They are distinct from the fabled gnomes or gremlins (*na iveli*) who are fantastic in their abilities and behaviour, though very real to some Fijians still today. *Na iveli* are centred in Waimaro country around Serea. They have been reportedly clearly sighted by Fijians at Wainadoi, at the Namosi coast. Waimaro people from the Waidina River area migrated south near to this part of the Namosi coast. The early existence of *na Leka* is quite plausible though they have never been seen. Earliest migrations of proto-island people came from southeast Asia, through what is now Indonesia, to settle in the Pacific. A tiny species of the Homo genus, Homo floresiensis, is well recorded as living in Indonesia, from 74,000 to 12,000 years ago, with skeletons found at Flores Island. (See article by Adam Brumm, Australian National University, et al, *Nature,* June 1, 2006.) This species of man was half-size to present-day humans, Homo sapiens. (See also *Science News*, vol. 269, 3 June, 2006, p. 341.)

lekaleka adj. short, brief. *vaka-lekalekataka* to shorten. *bati leka*, a formal term for clans of personal guards who fought as a last defence, protecting the chieftain. At Bau, the Masau were such warrior guardians for the Roko Tui Bau. *leleka* is the plural form. Only a very few Fijian words take a different form in the plural.

vaka-lekaleka adv. briefly.

ivaka-lekaleka n. (or) **ivakaleka** (both modern usage) abbreviation, short version, summary.

lekapai or **lekapone** (Slang) n., adj. person of short stature, usually said with a smile.

ilekau n. first fruits a fruit-tree ever yields, as it comes of age to bear. *na kena ilekau* such first fruiting of a tree.

lele, leleca 1. v. to lean. bend down, as a tree in the wind, a man reaching to pick up something, the Tower of Pisa in Italy.

lele 2. n. (Archaic) dirge, chanting for the dead, an ancient form of seated *meke*. *na lele kei Ratu Mara*. the dirge chanted for the death of Ratu Mara.

lele 3. v. to ferry, usually in a punt, raft or fiber-glass boat across a river, or from shore to a tiny offshore island, like Qoma Islands off the Tailevu coast. May also refer to fishing for *ta* (unicorn fish) in Vanua Levu, according to Joe Hewson.

ilele n. ferry, in Fiji normally these days a punt with an outboard engine.

vakalele n. the ferrying.

valele, valeleca v. to ferry (people, things) across a small body of water, usually a river.

leleka adj. short (plural form), applied to more than one person or thing. *leka* is the singular form of the adjective.

lelevu adj. big, large amount of, in the plural form. See the singular form, *levu*. *levu* big. *levulevu* fat (of a person). *lelevu* n. many people. (*lerua* two people. *letolu* three people), where the prefix *"le"* is an an abbreviation for *lewe* n. people. *lelevu* is a term adopted by language teachers to indicate a plurality of people in grammatical structures.

dau lelewa adj. of a person, very judgmental, overly critical.

lepo (or) **lepona** (Lau) n. earth oven made on the surface of the ground, not dug in. It is covered with sacks, vegetation and dirt or sand.

"leptospirosis" (Eng.) a potentially fatal bacterial infection of humans usually transmitted through contact with water that has been contaminated with animal urine.

leqa n., v. trouble, difficulty, needfulness, inoperative (motor, machine), dead (respectfully, of person). Idiomatically, *leqa* may refer to burdensome social obligations to provide money, mats, or goods for some ceremonial collection for family, clan, church, school or village, or to pay off a loan. The demands put a strain on a Fijian's resources. To fulfill his obligations he may be pressed to ask for money or "loans" from others around him, loans which might be difficult to repay. With a twist of irony, it is said that a Fijian's life is full of *leqa* -- until he himself becomes the *leqa*, by dying.
Idiom: *Kua ni leqa*. Not to worry. Don't worry about it.

leqa, leqataka v. to worry about it. *leqataki* troubled. *Kua ni leqataka*. Don't worry about it, do not go to any trouble.

vakaleqa, vakaleqa v. to cause trouble to (someone). *Me kua ni vakaleqai au*. Do not be a problem to me, make problems for me.

lera n. Red-bead Tree, Adenanthera pavonina, Mimosaceae, possibly an aboriginal introduction with red seeds commonly made into necklaces.

leredamu n. a fairly common seashore vine, Abrus precatorius, easily recognised by the small seeds starkly coloured a brilliant red with a shiny black spot, that were used in souvenir necklaces, but that is now discouraged as extremely dangerous. The seeds are deadly poisonous from cyanide that can be dissipated by boiling. The seeds were formerly used as a means of assassination. Flowers rose-coloured, pods 1.5 inches long with three or four seeds. Syn. *diridamu*.

leru (Lau) n. Trochus, edible shellfish but more important for its commercially valuable shell exported for manufacture of buttons. Syn. *sici*.

lesa v. to be distressed, crying, of a child.

lesi, lesia v. to choose, elect (person, people), appoint as a delegate or envoy.

lesi 1. chosen, elected (person). *ilesilesi* selection, (of a person) to some function. *Vakailesilesi* n. delegate, appointee, official representative.

lesi 2. n. Kingfisher, Halcyon chloris, bright blue bird, which – despite its name -- does not eat fish, but eats insects, lizards, young birds, crabs. It is often seen alone or with one companion, motionless, squatting on phone lines. Long pointed black bill. Syn. (Viti Levu) *sesi*, (Lau, Kadavu) *secala*, (Vanua Levu) *seasea, lelewai* (West) *lele*.

lesoni (Eng.) n. lesson.

lesu, lesuya v. to return, to return it, return to it or from it, to have been to some place. *Lesu!* Go back! Return! (to where you came from). *O lesu maivei?* Where have you been? *O sa lesu mai Labasa?* Have you been to Labasa? *na ilakolako lesu* the return trip, the trip back. *sauma lesu* to pay back (money). *taro lesu* to question back, respond with a question. *Solia lesu* to give back. Syn. (Lau) *suka*.

lesuva v. to review (and sometimes to correct), to re-read, to have repeated (story, presentation). *Me da lesuva na italanoa*. Let us go over the story again.. *raica lesu* look back, review.

ilesulesu n. return trip. *ilakolako* trip.

lesu tale v. to return (of a person).
Idiom: *lesu tale na koli i na nona lua* return to the scene of the crime, desire what has been previously rejected, lit. the dog returns to its vomit.

leti, letitaka v. to dispute, argue (about it). *na veileti* the argument, the dispute.

leu, leuta v. to remove (splinter, thorn, etc.) by a sharp instrument or pincers, tweezers.
Idiom: *Me ra leuta mada na malamala mai na matadra*. They should look at themselves first before judging someone else. Lit. They should remove the obstruction from their eyes, i.e, see things more clearly, take off their blinders.

ileu 1. n. small sharp instrument as for removing splinters. *ileu ni bati* toothpick.

ileu 2. n. horn (of cattle, goats, certain beetles), an extension of the the original meaning. The only horned animals were introduced by Europeans. Formerly the word applied to a sharp protusion on a war club.

leva, levaca v. to resent a person's presumption in failing to show proper respect or deference, most especially for causing a loss of face. *E dau levaleva o koya*. He/she is "touchy", tends to resent being told off or being corrected. *levataka* v. to be angry about it (the disrespectful action).

leve, levea v. to dodge. *levea na saumi vakacavacava* dodge the payment of taxes. Dodging was a useful movement to avoid spears and war clubs, a greatly developed skill of Fijians. That traditional skill has become useful in rugby and in boxing. *levedro* v. to dodge by running away.

le vica in a question, how many people? *le tolu* three people.

levu 1. big, large. *lelevu* is the plural form of *levu*. *vakalevutaka* to enlarge, make bigger. *vakalevulevuya* to aggrandize, make someone or something appear big or important. *levu cake* bigger, larger. *levulevu* adj. fat (usually of a person).

levu 2. much, a large amount. *E levu na nona ilavo* he has a lot of money.

levu 3. many. *lewe levu* many people.

levu 4. n. amount, size. *na kena levu* the amount of it, the size. *E vica na kena levu?* How big is it? (usually a number indicating size) *Vakacava na kena levu?* How big is it? May also apply to counting, the total.
Idiom: *Sa kena levu*. at the conclusion of a speech, report or declaration, these words indicate the end.
Idiom: *Levu la!* Teasing call to a person who is trying to show off to attract attention. Or as an adj. *levu la* means pretentious.

levu-i-vosa adj. a person who only talks but accomplishes very little.

levu la adj., n. aloof, proud (in a bad sense), pretentious.

levulevu adj. fat, stout (of person, animal). To Fijians, a stout body may indicate good health. A thin person may be thought to be unwell or weak.

lewa, lewa (or) **vakalewa, vakalewa** v. to decide, judge. *mataveilewai* court (law). *Turaga ni lewa* magistrate. *Lewa o iko*. You decide (the matter in question). *vakalelewa* adj., n. criticism, critical of mind, judgemental, criticizing. *dau lelewa* adj. highly judgemental (of others). *na vakataulewa* the judgement (court).

vakatulewa (or) **vakataulewa** v. to offer an opinion, judgement, to decide. *O Losana na qai vakatulewa*. Losana will decide.

Vakavulewa (Anglicism) n. as in *Yavu ni Vakavulewa*, Constitution (of government).

Lewa! informal form of address used by older person to a woman (*yalewa*) or girl (*gone yalewa*). It is often used affectionately. *vakasalewalewa* effeminate, of a man with homosexuality often implied.

lewamatua n, Stonefish, dangerously spiny bottom fish, by the shore, often concealed. Poison can be lethal, Synanceichthys verrucosa. Edible when handled carefully.

lewa-ninini n. Lycopodium spp., lit. "trembling woman", a large species sometimes used as head ornament for dances but a smaller species, L. cernuum, is used modernly in floral arrangements. This attractive plant grows wild.

lewe n. people. *lewenivanua* people, commoners, ordinary people (not chiefs). or population (of village, city, nation). *lewe vica?* how many people? *lewe lima* five people. Sometimes abbreviated as *le*: *le levu vei keimami e sa raici koya*. Many (people) among us have seen him. *lewenivale* members of a household but also traditional role of some kin groups to provide services in the household of a high chief; in turn, they enjoy some intimacy within the chief's household. *lewe ni waqa* n. crew members of a boat or ship. *lewe-vinaka* n. qorum, sufficient people for what is required.

lewe-na n. flesh (of human, animal, fish), contents (food in earth oven, contents of a book, contents of a basket). *na lewena* the basal stem (rhizome) of *yaqona*. *lewe ni lovo* food in the earth oven. *lewe ni manumanu* n. meat. See *lewena*, below.
  Idiom: *dro na lewe ni yavana* leg cramp from the cold. Syn. *cuqa*. *Sa cuqa na yavaqu*. I have a leg cramp.
vakalewena v. to fill out (a form, with information). *vakalewena na fomu* fill out the form.
lewena n. the basal stem (rhizome) of *yaqona*, which makes a milder drink than the root (*waka*). Islanders of Polynesian background (Lau, Cakaudrove, Kadavu) remove the skin of *lewena* before drying it. This yields a beverage lighter in colour and much less harsh. Highlanders never remove the skin, and traditionally did not dry it, but drank it "green", which has a much stronger effect of the drug. Rewans of Lomanikoro drink only *waka*, never *lewena*; their soggy land makes it almost impossible to grow *yaqona* there.
li a particle giving emphasis to a question or statement, sometimes with rhetorical implications. "really" might be one translation. It cannot always be translated as a separate word. *Na cava li o via kainaka?* What is it you really want to say?
lialia adj., n. crazy, foolish. Syn. (Colo East) *sauvou*. (Lau, West) *riva*.
liaca 1. v. to examine, take a close look, keep an eye on. *Me liaci koya*. Take a close look at him/her.
liaca 2. v. to fail to recognise, fail to remember.
lico n. very young sprout of a plant.
lidi (Eng.) n. lint, as for dressing wounds.
lidi, lidika v. to strike (of lightning), crack, crackle (rifle shot, spark). *E calidi na livaliva*. There is a strike of lightning.
liga-na n. hand (person), sleeve (shirt, coat). *liga ni wau* certain trad. warriors for a chief, now sometimes used honorifically for army soldiers. *liga ni lovo* men who cook the chief's food in an earth-oven. *liga bula* "green thumb". *liga mate* hopeless gardner of no ability, lit. "dead hand". *liga matau* capable, effective, of a person. *liga lala* n. poor person ("empty-handed"). *ligatawa* person with great wealth. *cakacaka ni liga* n. handicraft(s). *lave liga* raise the hand (as in a classroom), a modernism. *dodo liga* extend a hand, reach out to help. *qumi, qumia na liga-na* to close the hand. *daku ni liga* back of the hand. *buku ni liga-na* knucke(s). *qeteqete ni liga-na* palm(s) of the hand(s). *gau ni liga-na* forearm(s).
Ligadua n. a one-armed (implied in the name) giant spirit in human form, not malicious (in my experience) but people are frightened by him at night. He is still often seen and is well known at Wainadoi, Namosi and elewhere. Physical descriptions of him vary widely among Fijians who claim to have seen him.
ligaleka 1. (Ang.) n. shorthand (writing).
  Idiom: *ligaleka* steal, thief. *ligaleka-taka* to steal it.
ligaleka 2. (Ang.) adj. short-sleeve (as of a shirt).
ligaliga ca n., adj. person who performs witchcraft.
ligamamada adj. very strong (of a warrior), implying things are light (*mamada*) to his hand *ligana*. Also a secondary name of the soldier-commoner who led the 1987 military coup, and his namesake, a former Dewala chief at village Nagigi, Vanua Levu who had been a driver for the Agriculture Department.
ligamudu n., adj. person with a crippled hand, usually curled back in appearance, or amputated. *mudu* cut short. Tradition was to cut off finger at the death of a high chief as a sign of mourning. In principle, it was sometimes recompensed by a gift of land in usufruct. That land would be referred to as *iligamudu*.
ligatawa adj. very strong (of a warrior), a person of many resources, much wealth.
liku n. skirt; Formerly, all adults wore a skirt of sorts, usually made of leaves. The loincloth (*malo*), usually of bark-cloth (*masi*), was an early innovation from Tonga, used mostly by chiefly men, and by warriors as a war-time uniform, especially when serving as mercenaries for Tongans. Allies wore the same *malo* to recognise each other. Highlanders of Colo East had crude indigenous loincloth made of barkcloth other than the mulberry *masi*, which hardly existed there (only at Navosa, introduced by early Tongan settlers). The *liku* was of longer length for men but for women was a two to nine-inch band of fibre strings covering the loins when she reached puberty. Mature, married women wore the longer skirts. *Liku* may be used as a woman's personal name. *liku-i-loma* petticoat, *liku refia* skirt made of raffia, for exhibition dancing, often for tourists (raffia is not Fijian; most comes from China). *liku vasili* skirt made of *vasili* leaves, formerly common in the highlands. *liku voivoi* skirt make of *voivoi* leaves. *liku wadrega* European-style body-hugging tight skirt. *liku kidikidi* pleated skirt. Here

is a summary of comments by Seemann writing in the very early 1860s: Temporary *liku* might be made of leaves of plantain, coconut, or the climbing, vine *vono* (Alyxia spp., Apocynaceae), the stems partially broken to release the natural perfume. Permanent *liku* were often made of *sausauwai*, the threads of a vine called *waloa*, said by Seemann to be a species of Rhizomorpha, a creeper that grows on dead wood in swampy ground. The revised edition of Capell's dictionary names this as Armilaria sp., Agaricaceae. The stems are thin threads buried in mud for few days before being made into a black skirt. Women's skirts were often made of the inner bark of hibiscus, left in natural white colour, or dyed. Turmeric gave yellow, mud and leaves of Polynesian Almond (*tavola*) gave black dye, and red was derived from the bark of bush or small tree *kura* Morinda citrifolia, and the bark of the mangrove tree. Except in the case of very high chiefs on ceremonial occasions, Fijians normally wore nothing on the torso above the *liku*.

lila adj., n. thin.

lila balavu (Archaic) n. historic infectious disease that devastated the Fijian population. Apparent source was the schooner Argo, out of China, shipwrecked around 1800 at Bukatatanoa Reef eleven miles east of Lakeba. Survivors settled at Oneata, with a few going to Tongatapu, some to Lakeba and beyond at later times. Missionary John Hunt suggested the cause was probably cholera or dysentery according to Derrick.

lila waso adj. skinny (derogative, disparaging).

lili, liliga (or) **lilica** v. to hang up, suspend in the air. *Me lili na isulu.* Hang up the laundry. For retirement from a vocation, Fijians use the Anglicism of boxers "hanging up" their gloves, runners hanging up their shoes. *E a vakaliliga na nona ivava.* He/she has retired from track. The transitive verb *liliva* is used for hanging people. Anciently, Fijians sometime hung up corpses; they never had a person hang as punishment until Cakobau hanged his cousin Mara Kapaiwai in 1859. *wa-lili-caka na liga* to swing the arms, as in soldiers marching.

Idiom: (Vulgar) *polo lili* (or) *vakalili soresore* ineffectual man or boy, lit. balls (testicles) drooping down, sometimes called out in teasing *Lako tu o polo lili!* There goes Hanging Balls!

ililili 1. n. (Archaic) wooden hook for hanging oil or baskets of food with protective ridge as a guard against rats. Some are now carved for the tourist trade. *Naililili* is a place in Rewa, location of an important historic Roman Catholic church, formerly a place where corpses were hung up (as implied in the name) prior to cannibal feasts.

ililili 2. n. clothes line or clothes hanger, which are modern artefacts. Previously, clothing of barkcloth or leaves was laid out to dry in the sun.

liliwa adj., n. cold (temperature). See *liwa*. Syn. *batabata*. (Colo East) *kudukudua*, and of a person being cold, *drika*. *Sa vikadrikai au na cagi.* The wind has given me a chill. Syn. (Rewa) *drika*.

lima five. *tini ka lima* fifteen. *limasagavulu* fifty. *e lima na drau* five hundred. This word occurs widely throughout the Pacific, even to Indonesia and Malaysia and in some places can refer to the human hand.

liqaru adj. insulting term: man who lives off a woman, doing nothing, depending on the woman for everything.

liso v. n. gleam, gleaming, shine brightly, glisten.

Idiom: *mata liso* n., adj. having bright, attentive eyes.

lise n. nits, lice, a common pest in Fijian hair, particularly of children, picked out by hand, and usually cracked between the teeth to kill it, and then swallowed to dispose of it. Mothers occasionally check their children. See *kutu*.

Idiom: *Misika nona lise!* gross insult, implying a person is full of lice.

liti n. (Arch.) vegetable dye from the candlenut tree (*sikeci*, *lauci*), brown or black, formerly used to colour the hair by Fijians of the coast and small islands. The tree is not usually found in the highlands.

Idiom: *mai kere liti, moto kei na waiwai* come asking for this, then that, then another thing, imposing one's many demands as one sees things available -- in this idiom the objects mentioned are *liti* dye, *moto* spear, and *waiwai* body-oil.

liu, liutaka v. to lead, go first, lead out. *ena gauna iliu* in earlier times. *Liu!* You take the lead, go on ahead! *Au sa liu* I will take the lead (and you may follow). *Evei? Iliu.* Where? On ahead (of us), or as a Fijian would often say in English, "In front". *gone liu* head-boy (school). *na toso ki liu* the progress (the forward movement). *Yavu-tu ni Toso ki Liu* so-called Peoples' Charter as established under Interim PM Voreqe Bainimarama.

Idiom: *o ira sa liu yani* those who have already died (gone on before us).

lito v. to gleam, of direct or reflected light, a firebrand at night, or the eyes of a cow or dog at night, reflecting the light of a torch.

iliuliu n. leader, head (of a group).

vakaliu, vakaliuca v. to lead, as in to lead a clean life *me vakaliuci na tiko savasava.*

vakaliuliu v. to anticipate.

liu muri 1. adj. two-faced, duplicitous. This is a frequently mentioned characteristic.

liu muri 2. v. to betray. Lit. to lead from behind. A very common expression. Many Fijian wars and battles were won by betrayal rather than actual combat.

veiliutaki n. leadership.

liva (Eng.) n. lever. *livataka* v. to lever (something). Syn. *labo, laboca.*

liva (or) **livaliva** n. lightning. *tibi ni livaliva* lightning flash. See *lidi, lidika.*

livaliva 1. n. electricity. *wa ni livaliva* electric line. *ivaro livaliva* electric saw. *na veivakalivalivataki* the electrification (usually of rural area). *bera na liva* quicker than lightning. *Bera-na-Liva* Fijian name of the Phantom, comic-book character.

livaliva 2. (Lau) n. semi-ripe papaya cooked and served with coconut cream.

livi (Eng.) n. leave, vacation from a job.

livi, livia v. to pour, usually a liquid from a container, small amounts, as from a teapot, a cup of tea, from a bottle, a glass of wine, carefully. Some Fijian water-pots had spouts from which water was poured into the mouth without the mouth touching the pot. The spout could be several inches distant from the mouth. *livilivi* v. to do the pouring, as of tea. *liviraka* v. to do such pouring roughly, carelessly.

liwa, liwava v. to blow (of the wind), to blow at or over. *na vanua e liwa mai kina na cagi* where the wind comes from. *liwavi* blown over or at something. *liliwa* cold. *wasaliwa* ocean, sea (Syn. *wasawasa*).

liwa adj. as in *wasa liwa* open ocean, far at sea.

lo adj. silent, silently, secretly (of people's actions). *Tiko lo!* Shut up! Be silent! *koto lo* v. to lie low, identical to the English expression, implying secrecy. *tukuna lo* v. to relate something secretively, surreptitiously.

Idiom: *kana lo* eat secretly, by oneself, without sharing, very reprehensible by Fijian custom. It implies a greedy, selfish person.

vakalo adv. secretly, not openly. *Era tu vakalo.* They (many) stay secretly.

lo n. (Lau) ant. Syn. *kasivi* (or) *qasivi.*

loa 1. adj., n.. dark-coloured, black. *yaqona loa* dark-skinned kava variety. *na loa ni kuita* the black liquid ejected by octopus when disturbed. *Mata loa!* (Slang): You nigger! Lit. black face, an expression I have heard exclaimed by a (black) mother to her own child who was misbehaving.

loa 2. v. to throw, chuck, heave, toss, as in *loa vata*, throw together, sometimes implying indiscriminately, or with force. No separate transitive form for this verb.

loa 3. adj. (Lau) mature, ready to cut, of Pandanus leaves used in mat-weaving.

loaloa adj., n. black, dark-coloured. Can refer to soot or black dye or clouds (n. or adj). *tamata loaloa* (or) *loaloa* black people. *loaloa* may also refer to the bêche-de-mer species Microthele nobilis, a valuable item of trade to China, though not a usual food for Fijians themselves. It is known as *tavunia* in Macuata.

loba, lobaka v. to squeeze tightly, as with kava in extracting liquid from the fibre at the serving bowl, or coconut flesh to extract the "cream", or washed clothes to remove water. Also to milk a cow. *dau loba sucu* dairyman. The dairy industry was launched in Tailevu and Naitasiri for servicemen returning from World War I, becoming a cooperative called Rewa Dairy, though all dairy farmers now are Indians, Fijians and part-Fijians.

vakalobaloba v. to squeeze gently. See above, *loba.*

lobau n. intoxicating, poisonous shrub, Brugmansia suaveolens, formerly classified as Datura candida and closely related to Jimson weed. It has huge white flowers (some varieties yellowish or pinkish) that are trumpet-shaped (thus the common name *davui*, "trumpet") that bloom around April through September, and become fragrant only at night. Formerly it was planted near the house-sites of highland chiefs, and it may still be found by the ruined house-foundations at old villages such as Waikalou (near present-day village Serea). The plant has intoxicating properties, said to be like *yaqona* but vastly more potent, dangerously intoxicating and even poisonous, but not usually fatally so for adults. It was formerly used by highlanders as a secret drug to serve in *yaqona* presented to disable their enemy while pretending to talk peace. It served to knock out the enemy so he could be clubbed to death without resisting. How the plant reached the central Pacific is a mystery. Its origin is in South America.

Formerly *lobau* had mystical significance in the eastern highlands of Viti Levu. Trive Lobau is the branch of the Roko Tui Bau's people (super-tribe Vusaratu) that remained on mainland Tailevu Province at Nausori. The Roko Tui Bau moved on to Ovea and Kubuna at the coast, then invaded and settled Bau Island, possibly around 1760. The Lobau people at Nausori served as intermediaries in the Roko Tui Bau's communications with the Waimaro highlanders, by way of village (and District) Matailobau, and chiefly village Nairukuruku. This traditional path of communications was broken after the Vunivalu of the Tui Kaba people of Bau overthrew the Roko Tui Bau. While the highland Waimaro had been warriors and allies of the Roko Tui Bau, they long resisted the Vunivalu, whose communications to the highlands came via Sawakasa in Tailevu, by way of the Waimaro-i-wai. The significance of the *lobau* shrub is a rather forgotten aspect of Fijians' old traditions.

The word *lobau* is also noted widely throughout Fiji as the adopted name of an introduced plant Wedellia, useful only as a low-growing ground-cover that requires no care. It has small yellow flowers.

lobetubetu adj. soaking wet. Abbrev. *lubetu.*

lobi, lobia v. to fold, to bend. *lobia na isulu* fold up the clothes. *na idabedabe lobi* the folding chair. *kalobi* bent forcefully like the tines of a digging fork *mataiva* when they strike a stone. *sasa-lobilobi* very wrinkled.

lobo, lobora v. to strike with something pointed (spear, nail, fencepost), penetrating deeply or even completely. See *cobo, cobora.*

lobo (ena soso) v. of the feet, to be stuck deep when one walks in the mud. *lobolobo* n. swamp.

loga-na n. bed (sleeping place, garden bed). *na loga ni dalo* the taro bed (in the garden). *na veiloga ni dalo* the *dalo* garden beds where it is cultivated.

loga (West) n. woven mat, usually of pandanus. Syn. *ibe.*

logologo n. a slow-growing palm-like tree, Cycad, Cycas rumphii, a Gymnosperm. The pith provided a food for chiefs in Macuata. The fruits with poisonous seeds, edible when mashed and fermented, were a famine food on Koro island and Nairai island, perhaps also elsewhere. The cycad grows naturally in drier areas but can be planted and survive in the wet zone. Syn. *roro, wairoa.*

loka n. huge, of a wave hitting the shore. *ua loka* tidal wave, tsunami. By ext., may refer to a flooded area due to very heavy rain.

Idiom: *vaka tale na ua ni loka* lit., recede like a tidal wave, i.e., when departing after a visit, the visitor takes everything with him that he can take.

loka (Eng.) n. lock. *lokataka na katuba.* to lock the door.

loka v. to fall down, of many things in large numbers, leaves from a tree, papers from a desk. *veilokayaki* of many such things, to fall here and there. Syn. *qera.*

lokaloka adj., n. mauve colour, light purple, (as of clothes) also a var. of yam of that colour.

lokamu (Eng.) n. gaol ("lock-up"), an old slang word.

loki, lokia v. to bend, fold, as of a limb, arm, leg. (But note, to close the hand is *qumia na liga-na.*) *isele loki* pocket knife, jack-knife. *loki buina* tail between the legs, as of a dog in fear.

ilokiloki n. movable joint (human, animal, or mechanical).

lokiloki adj. crippled, lame, handicapped, disabled. *e dua na gone lokiloki* a crippled child. *ilokiloki* crippled person(s). *ulubale lokiloki* (Anglicism) n. lame excuse.

lokini 1. v. to curl up one's body, usually when cold, sleeping. *Sa lokini koto na caura vou. Me tatuvitaki koya.* The youth is sleeping curled up. Cover him with a blanket.

lokini 2. v. to curl up in a coil, as of a long rope.

ilokoloko n. soft pillow, a concept formerly quite foreign to mainland Melanesian Fijians. Modernly, as a gift at births or marriages, pillows may be presented with elaborate coloured patterns sewn on, or religious, homely slogans.

Idiom: *vuli ilokoloko* to learn (usually a language) from sleeping with one who can teach it. Implied is the notion that it is easy to learn fast from a bed partner. This is said with a smile.

loku, lokuca v. to arrange, set, as of an appointment to meet someone, or hold a conference. *na veiloku* the people with appointments. *Sa lokuci tiko na siga.* The day is set (agreed upon). *iloku* n. appointment, the date set for some occasion. *lokuyara-taka* v. to defer (a previously determined appointment or date). *loku-moce* to defer (meeting, some work) to the next day.

lokumi adj. as in *yalo lokumi* humble, unassertive, dis-spirited, depressed, discouraged.

loli 1. n. native fig, quite edible but small fruit, never cultivated for food.

loli 2. (Eng.) lolly. *loli ni vu* cough-drop. Idiom: *Memu loli!* You got what you had coming, got what punishment you deserved! (Childrens' talk.)

loli 3. n. black type of bêche de mer, sea cucumber *dri*, Halodeima atra, found close to shore, partly edible. Scraped, the surface yields a fish-poison. It is rubbed between the hands (*qilia*) and placed in shallow pools where it will stun small fish. Syn. (West) *loliloli.*

lolo 1. n. coconut cream, expressed from the mature nut. *lolo buta* caramelised coconut cream for use in Fijian puddings. *lolo droka* coconut cream heated with red-hot stones, and after cooling, poured over *vakalolo* pudding. *vakatoka lolo* to make *lolo*.

vakalolo a. adj. of a food (often fish), simmered in coconut cream sauce, as in *ika vakalolo*, a favourite Fijian dish of coastal people.

vakalolo b. n. Fijian pudding made of starchy root-crop (but not yams) or Polynesian chestnut *ivi*, with grated coconut, usually sweet, eaten as a heavy snack, not with meals. A basic distinction is whether they are made with caramelised coconut cream *lolo buta*, or with ordinary coconut cream *lolo droka*. Various type of pudding are: *darai, sivaro* or *sivaro maca, sivaro vula* (both from cassava, formerly taro), *sakosako, yakiyaki* and *tukivatu* (both usually of breadfruit), *vakalavalava* (of cassava), *bokoi* (cassava), *malimali* (Lau, Batiki, Vatulele, of *yabia*, or more modernly, cassava, with ripe plantain), *waiaua* (of baked banana), *vakasoso* (stuffed banana), *lote* (banana and arrowroot *yabia*, or pumpkin with cassava flour in a mash, with sugar), *tololo kumala* (Lau, sweet potato and *lolo*), *koko* (Polynesian chestnut *ivi*).

lolo 2. n. shin (human).

lolo 3. n, native fig, Ficus vitiensis. Edible fruit, appreciated by some Fijians, mainly youngsters, but it is never cultivated. Syn. *loselose, loli*. Other fig species are *loroloro* and *nunu* or *masimasi*.

lolo 4. v. to fast, abstain (from food, meat, smoking, sex), most often as a religious observance (Christians, Muslims, Hindus), sometimes for health reasons. Fijians may make such a sacrifice with the notion that they will be rewarded with success in something they wish for. Such fasting is a modern concept for Fijians.

lolo 5. v. *Sa lolo cake na ua*. The tide has risen.

lolo 6. v. to howl, as a dog howls at the moon.

loloa adj., n. sea-sick, sea-sickness.

lolobo n. soft black mud, such as used for dyeing pandanus leaves black by burying them in the mud. *vanua lolobo* n. swampy land.

loloku n. grief, grieving, in mourning. *iloloku ni mate* (Archaic) wives strangled at chiefly husband's death. Also the little finger, formerly cut off when a chief dies, a sign of loyalty in grief though the person expects a reward.

loloku, lolokutaka v. to mourn (normally a person).

lololo n. storage hut for yams in the garden area.

ilololo n. place of death, where a person or animal died.

loloma n. affection, caring. In ending informal letters: *Loloma vei Kesa* Give my love to Kesa. *Loloma bibi* Much love. *Loloma tu yani* We (or I) send our (my) love.

iloloma n. gift.

vakaloloma-taka v. to make someone miserable.

vakaloloma adj. pitiful, in a sorry state.

Lolopeau n. name of great historic ocean-going canoe in early Fiji and Tongan legend.

lolosi, lolositaka v. to grieve over the absence or loss of someone, something.

lolou 1. v. to bow the head, as from respect (as in the presence of a chief), or shame, or in grief.

lolou 2. (Archaic) v. to dig.

lolovira adj. 1. despicable, low or base, of behaviour.

lolovira adj. 2. low-lying, of land.

loma-na 1. n. inside, middle, centre. *ena loma ni koro* within the village. *ena loma ni rara* in the village square (or sports field). *e loma ni vale* inside the house. *e loma ni veikau* out in the bush. *sulu-i-loma* n. underwear. *ena loma ni macawa* in the middle of the week. *ena loma ni bogi* in the middle of the night. *e lomaloma ni bogi* in the very middle of the night, the dead of night. *loma donu* exactly in the middle. *kailoma* part-Fijian (person). *LomaiViti* Central Fiji (name of a Province).

loma-na 2. n. wish, desire. *A cava na lomamu?* What is your wish? *Sa loma i Vani me lako*. It is Vani's wish to go, Vani wants to go.

loma-na 3. n. spirit, will, atttude, mind (of a person, animal or a god). *lomaloma-rua* undecided, hesitant, "double-minded". *lomaloma ca* has qualms. *dau-muri-lomana* self-willed. *veilomalomayaki* fickle, capricious

loma prefix to a multitude number of words that indicate one's state of mind or personality. A prefix with similar meaning is *yalo* (spirit or mind), used in the same way.

lomabibi serious, grave, sorrowful, with heavy heart.

lomabutobuto ignorant, unenlightened, uneducated.

lomaca wrong-minded, bad-spirited.

lomadei firm in one's convictions, steady.
lomadina sincere, truthful.
lomadonu fair-minded, straight-thinking.
lomakasa firm in one's convictions, knowledge.
lomakatakata quick to anger.
lomaqa sturdy of spirit, self-willed, stubborn.
lomararama enlightened.
lomarerere fearful.
lomasoli generous, giving person.
lomatarotaro of questioning mind.
lomavata cooperative, in agreement together.
lomavou of modern ways, of fashionable mind.
lomawai weak-spirited, of little resolve.

vaka-loma-vinaka-taka v. to make someone (some people) feel good.

ivakaloma vinaka n. refreshing food such as fruit, sweet pudding, custard, served at the end of a meal; dessert. The concept of a dessert is not indigenous. Indigenous sweet puddings were substantial snacks, not usually a feature of a formal meal.

lomadonu n. dead centre, very centre of a place or thing.

lomalagi n. sky, heavens. *na Tamada Vakalomalagi* our Heavenly Father (a Christianism). *Lomalagi* Christian Heaven. Idiom: *ketekete ni bici na lomalagi* of clouds in the sky, whispy and streaked like the belly of the *bici* (bird), indicating fair weather.

lomaloma n. the area inside a reef. Name of a large village on Vanua Balavu Island.

lomana v. to love in the sense of caring for, feel for. *E lomani keda na Kalou.* God cares for us, loves us. *lomani* beloved. *Erau veilomani.* They (two) love each other.

lomanikoro n. inner section of the village, by the chief's house, where respectful decorum is essential. This word has become a village name in a few places, such as in Rewa.

"Lomipeau" n. legendary ship of Tonga and Uvea legend, associated with Tele'a, the 29th Tu'i Tonga, and father of Sinaitakala i Lagileka, who married the legendary Fijian Kubuanavanua, who took her to Muala Island. Her brother married a sister of Ngata, who founded the Tu'i Kanakupolu, ruler of Tonga in the very early 1600s.

lomo, lomoca v. to immerse, dip and soak in liquid. Of human hair: to dip the head to steep in coral lime (*lase*), ashes, or hair-dye (*ibena*). The purpose is to kill hair-nits (*lise, kutu*), and/or colour the hair. To soak, as in dyeing bark-cloth. *bolomo* n. a starch-food such as grilled breadfruit that has been kneaded in water (*lomo ena wai*).

lomolomora (Archaic) unsettled, in a disturbed state, usually said of a place.

loqa, loqata (Archaic) v. to draw (a bow, *dakai titi*). The word today is little known. The only bows now used are in archery as a minor, emergent sport.

loqi n. traditionally, the upper, private, sleeping area of a house but may refer to formal sitting area of a house, equivalent of "sitting room".

loqi tabu n. upper end of a house, sectioned off for privacy.

loru v. to shrivel, deflate, as of a swelling, a boil that has been released of pus, or a flat tyre or deflated balloon. *vakaloruya* v. to deflate it, to release the pressure of inflation.

lose, losea v. to mix, especially *yaqona*, preparing it for drinking by making an infusion with water. The transitive form *losea* is used but rarely. *na dau lose yaqona* the person who sits behind the *yaqona* bowl and prepares the infusion with appropriate ceremony, or the action of making the beverage.

lotari (Eng.) n. lottery. *winitaka ena lotari* win at the lottery.

lote n. a sweet, soft mash of pumpkin or papaya cooked with cassava starch, often served these days cold, as a dessert, plain, or with coconut cream or even ice cream. More traditionally, plantain or banana was used with arrowroot starch. (Banana, pumpkin and papaya were introduced by Europeans, the plantain by early Fijians.)

loto adj. free. *vodo loto* to go aboard, as on a bus or boat, without paying. *kana loto* eat free, without reciprocating or paying, "sponging" off other people.

lotu 1. (Tonga) n. religion, sect of religion *matalotu*, often referring to a Christian sect, or to Christianity itself. *na Lotu Vakaristo* the Christian religion. *Lotu Vakajiu* Jewish religion. *Lotu Musulamani* Muslim religion. *na Lotu Wesele* the Wesley (Methodist) Church. *Lotu Katolika* Roman Catholic Church. *Lotu Jaji* Anglican Church. *Lotu Kavitu* 7th Day Adventist church, *Lotu Tagitagi* (or) *Lotu Qiriqiri* Assemblies of God. *Lotu Momani* Mormon Church. *kau lotu* n., v. missionary, to missionise. *tawa lotu* n., adj. agnostic, not adhering to any religious sect. *tamata tabu lotu* n. heathen, pagan, atheist, non-theist. *daulotu* m. church-goer, religious person. Methodists dominate with some three quarters of the indigenous Fijians population. Roman Catholics dominate in Namosi Province and much of Rewa Province. Anglicans claim most of the Solomon Islanders in Fiji, and some of the upper-class aristocratic chiefs, following the colonial tradition of the British. Increasingly, Fijians have been turning to the more recently introduced sects from the U.S.A., Seventh Day Adventists, Mormons, Assemblies of God, various splinter groups of evangelicals as well as some indigenous inventions such the Church of the Poor. Pentacostals, inspired by Acts (of the Apostles) in the New Testament, take literally the Holy Ghost possessing the disciples so they would speak in "other tongues" and auditors would understand that in their own languages. Congregations participate with rapidly voiced emotion. Virtually no Fijians are agnostic or atheist though outside of the villages, a certain number no longer attend Christian services. Indigenous spirits and religious notions co-exist with Fijian versions of Christianity.

lotu 2. (Tonga) v. to hold or attend church service. *vale ni lotu* church bldg.

vakalotutaka v. to convert (religion), to evangelise.

Lotulevu (Eng.) n. Thursday. Syn. (Lau) *Dakuna*.

lou v. of certain root crops (taro, yam etc.) having thriving green leaves, sprouts.

loulala adj. of root crops, appearing to thrive with robust green leaves but lacking much substance in their starchy corms.

ilou n. leaves used to cover and protect food being cooked, as in an earth oven, or used to close off the mouth of cooking pots.

loulou n. edible fish, Lycodontis sp., the annual "*balolo*" at village Waitabu, Lakeba Island. Syn, *boila*.

loupulu (Tonga) n. food made as a package of cooked taro leaf containing coconut cream, usually also with tinned meat. Syn. *palusami*.

lova, lovara v. to pour out in quantity. Syn. *sova*.

love, loveca v. to bend, to make a curve, as of a bamboo, a fishing pole, usually something long. *kalove* bent. *lovelove* bendable. Syn. *lolo*.

lovo n. earth oven, prepared by men, usually now on Sundays. The concept was unknown to Melanesian highlanders of Viti Levu, but has become established throughout Fiji. *lewe ni lovo* food contents of the oven. *turaga ni lovo* man in charge of the oven at any one occasion. *bulu, buluta na lovo* cover up the oven. *cele, celeva na lovo* carefully part and open up the cover-leaves. *qe, qeva na lovo* remove contents of *lovo*. *kili, kilica* open up the *lovo* and remove cooked food. *Sa buta sau* The oven-contents are undercooked due to a witchcraft spell. *buta droka* undercooked. *qulali* over-cooked, root-crops baked too hard. Syn. (Rewa, Beqa, Kadavu) *irevo*.

Idiom: *cara lovo e macawa* bald on the crown of the head.

lovo ni lase n. place or oven where coral is burned to make lime for treatment of the hair. The main old Fijian cemetary in Suva bears the name Lovonilase from having been such a place in earlier times. See *lase*.

lovo ni mua n, feast given to farewell an important person who is departing. *mua* implies heading off.

lovo sa (Archaic) n. man-trap, a deep hole dug in a path, covered and concealed with vegetation where a man might fall in. In the hole there were pointed stakes or sharp bamboo sticks to wound or kill. The same type of trap is made to capture wild pigs. (I came close to falling into such a trap at Wainadoi in the 1980s.)

lova, lovara v. to pour out, usually a liquid, as from a bucket or pot, but may apply to a number of loose things from a box. Syn. *sova, sova, sovara*.

loya (Eng.) n. lawyer.

lu v. to be leaking, of a boat. May apply to urinary incontinence. Syn. *mimi*.

lua n. vomit. *lua, luaca* v. to vomit, to vomit on. *luacaka, luaraka* to vomit up (something that was eaten). *via lua* v. to feel nauseous.

Idiom: *lesu na koli ki na nona lua* lit., the dog returns to his own vomit, i.e., the criminal returns to his crime.

luba, lubata, lubalaka v. to gulp, to gobble.

lubetu adj. soggy wet, of clothes or mats, or some absorbent thing that has been rained on. *lulu betubetu* totally drenched, extremely wet, soggy.

luca adj. of fruit, overly ripe and soft and so not usable.

"lucky" v. (Pronounced *laki*). Idiom: to "make out", succeed with sexual partner. "*lucky*" *koya* to manage to have sex with him/her. Idiom: *Mo "lucky"?* What makes you think you can "make out" with me/her/him? (joking remark). Speaking English, Fijians use the term "to fix" someone. In Fijian they might say *fix-taka*.

luka n. mucus of the nose. *ucu luka* drippy nose, also *ucu vakadro*. Syn. (Kadavu, Nadroga) *drigo*.

luku, lukuta v. to gather up, hold, grasp (rice stalks, bunch of flowers or other things), scoop up with both hands, even with the forearm (earth to mound up plants, gravel to make a path, gathering abundant fruit on the ground). Although large shells were used for scooping in some places, Fijians in general had no regular tool such as a spade or shovel. All tools were disposable until stone axes were introduced from Polynesia. *lukuluku* n. holding of things in the hand(s).

iluku n. handful (of small things, sand, pebbles, rice, small fruits).

lulu n. barn owl, Tyto alba. Usually seen at dusk or early morning, swooping down after field mice. The owl is reported to be an iconic animal of the Vunivalu of Bau. Syn. (West) *vevewa*. *luluve* day-feeding owl, possibly extinct. Syn. (Namosi) *lulunisiga*. (Nadroga) *sego* (or) *tego* according to *Na iVolavosa VakaViti*. Watling mentions the barn owl probably has the widest distribution of any land bird.
  Idiom: *mata lulu* attentive in watching, literally "owl-faced".
  Idiom: *tokalulu* peeping Tom.

lululu (Tonga) v. n. shake hands, an introduced custom. Until the 1970s this European form of greeting was performed at each meeting and farewell, with a limp hand, often for a prolonged time. In recent years Fijian men shake hands more firmly and less often, more like Europeans of today.

luluqa v. to loosen, weaken, become unattached or slack, usually of a rope or cord, but also of human and social relationships. *vakaluluqa-taka* to slack off or loosen some cord or binding.

luluvu, luluvu-taka v. to be saddened, to cause (someone, some people) to be sad. Syn. *yaloluluvu*. *luvu* sink under water, drown.

lumaluma adj, n. clammy, cold and dank, usually of evening conditions. May by extension refer to the state of a person declining in condition or particularly, behaviour, a person on the decline.

lumi n. seaweed. *lumi cubi* gelatin seaweed, Maidenhair seaweed, Hypnea nidifica. *lumi cevata* cooked seaweed that congeals when it cools, a food made from *lumi cubi*, though these days the seaweed itself can be called *lumi cevata*. *lumi karo* prickly seaweed, always cooked. *lumi damu* reddish-brown seaweed eaten raw or cooked. *lidi* seaweed with crisp texture with snapping sound as it breaks, eaten raw or cooked. *nama* sea grapes, Caulerpa racemosa, bright green branching marine plant with nodules, usually eaten raw, sometimes steamed lightly, served as salad or with seafood, sometimes with lemon or chilli, occasionally with coconut cream. *lumi boso* type of seaweed, thin crisp, boiled, water discarded, strands are chopped, eaten often with *miti sauce*. People of Gau may be jocularly called *Lumi boso!* or other reference to their being associated with seaweed.

lumisa adj. shiny, relecting light.

lumu, lumuta v. to anoint, rub the body, with vegetable oil, usually coconut oil around the coast, or oil of *dilo* nuts. (Viti Levu highlanders never extracted any form of vegetable oil.) *lumudrodro* oil the body to the degree that coconut oil drips from the body, done sometimes just prior to marriage among coastal Fijians. *lumudara* oil the body prior to performing in a dance. *lumu drali* to grease the hair excessively, usually with petroleum jelly, to control it. *ilumu* oil used for anointing, sometimes scented.
  Idiom: *lumuta na moivi* tell a story already known, relate stale news. (*Moivi* was a type of warclub made from the *moivi* tree according to Capell.)

lupu (Eng.) n. contraceptive metal loop, a word understood only in context.

lusi (Eng.) v. to lose, lost. Syn. *druka* (of games, sports, battles).

vakalusi, vakalusia (Eng.) v. to waste. *vakalusia na gauna* waste the time. *vakalusia na ilavo*. waste the money, lose the money.

lutu, lutuka v. to fall, fail (in some competition or exam), to fade (of the wind). *lutuka* to fall on (something or someone). *vakalutu, vakalutuma* to cause (something) to fall. *moce lutu* fallen fast asleep. *lutu dole* death from premature birth (*sucu dole*). *Ni bera ni lutu na buto*. Before darkness falls.
  Idiom: *lutu na niu, lutu i vuna*. "a chip off the old block", the child resembles the parent. Literally: When the coconut falls (to sprout anew), it falls to the base of the parent palm-tree.

vakalutu v., n. abortion, miscarriage, more generally to cause something to fall. Traditionally, attempted abortions have been very common Sticks were used, as well as various herbal "medicines", which continue in use today. Virtually all techniques are ineffective or dangerous, and at least one is a deadly cyanide poison, such as the pretty, brilliant black-and-red seeds of *diridamu*, Abrus precatorius, a seaside vine.

vakalutu-bose v., n. to miss attendance at a meeting, absence from a meeting.

vakalutu buto ni gone (Archaic) n. ceremony after an eldest child's umbilical cord falls; the lady towards whom the cord falls was supposed to provide a feast by old tradition.

vakalutu cakacaka v., n. to be absent from work without valid excuse.
vakalutu-dromu-taka v. to cause to sink down, as of a ship by torpedo, or to scuttle (a ship or boat).
VakalutuiVoce n. a set of awards that have been voted annually for Fiji musicians, a modernly invented term, derived from an ancient expression for the lyrics of a *meke* as sung by two male voices.
vei-lutui (ni domo) v., n. of multiple singing voices, to harmonise, respond, and interact, complementing each other.
vakalutu lo v., n. to drop out unobserved, sneak out (of some function or meeting).
Lutunasobasoba n. name of legendary chief who led a migration to Fiji perhaps in the 1500s, landing at Vuda, a story often touted as the First Landing. In fact he was long preceded by Melanesians from the Solomons and Vanuatu. Stories differ, whether he remained there, died there, or travelled on to Nakauvadra Range, or even went on to Verata before dying. He was accompanied by Degei who settled at Nakauvadra. This whole movement introduced the notions of aristocratic chiefs, a foreign notion to earlier immigrants.
vakalutu vuli n., v. truancy, to skip school.
lutu sobu 1. v., n. to decline, literally to fall down. the decline.
lutu sobu 2. (Ang.) n., v. special "sale" in the context of retail shopping.
lutu-vaka-tagane (Archaic) n. game of young men, two teams, lined up facing each other. Each throws a bush orange at a person of the opposing line. If hit, he is "out". *veimoli* was another game played with oranges.
vakalutu yaloka v. to lay eggs.
ilutua n. what is left over, the remains or remainder, as food (and rubbish) from a feast. By extension, the consequence, results, what happens afterwards, what remains.
luva, luvata v. to remove, strip off, strip bare (clothing, hat, tree-bark), take off or take down (something hanging up, clothes from a line). *luva wale* naked.
luvaluva v., n. to undress, the removal of clothing.
luvaisulu adj. retired from uniformed service, as in *sotia luvaisulu* returned serviceman.
vakaluva isulu n. Christian ceremony of removing mourning clothes after 100 nights, a custom imposed by missionaries. Also called *vakatara-isulu*.
iluva-ni-vesa (Archaic) n. whaletooth presented in appreciation for an exhibition group-dance (*meke*). Dancers are dressed with leaf decorations (*vesa*), to be removed (*luva*) and discarded after the dance.
luvawale (or **luvaiwale**) adj. naked. Syn. *luvawaca*. Syn. (Lau) *telefua*.
luve-na n. offspring, son, daughter. *na luvei Pita* (or) *na luve i Pita* the child of Peter.
luvea v. to give birth (of women or animals).
vakaluveni adj. having borne offspring, children. *O sa vakawati, vakaluveni?* You are married, have children?
luve ni sala n. bastard, illegitimate child, an insulting term. *sala* n. path.
Luve ni wai n. a former indigenous cult, once a powerful movement of protest against government administration, enforced Christianity, and the hegemony of Bau.
luve ni yali n. orphan, child of a single parent. Such children may be raised by grandparents or aunties.
Luvequ my child, an affectionate way of addressing a child.
luvu, luvuca v. to sink in water, drown, flood. *na waluvu* the flood. *Taukei ni Waluvu* specific chiefly title of Waimaro highlands; that chief is supposed to have to ability at will to flood the Wailevu (Rewa River). This common version of the title is in Bauan language. The proper highland title -- which means exactly the same thing -- is *Taukei ni Wai Bureburg*. *ualuvu* tidal wave, though there is some confusion with the word *waluvu* flood. *Sa luvu na vanua* the place is flooded. The word *luvu* may be used somewhat figuratively, that is, to be drowned or flooded under things on the mind, worries, debts, sorrow, this being an Anglicism. *vanua luvuluvu* place that tends to frequent flooding, as of a low-lying location.

M

maba n. small, slender timber tree used for general construction, Diospyros major, Ebenaceae, appreciated for hairy fruit, yellow to brown, highly fragrant. Bark is dark grey to black while wood is white. *Kauloa* is the trade-name for all seven species of the ebony family. Syn. *bama*.
maca (or **mamaca**) adj., adv. dry. *gunuva maca* to drink it all, drink it dry. *Sa maca na taqe.* The tank is empty. *Sa mamaca na isulu.* The laundry is dry. Idiom: *Maca na nona wai.* He is finished, powerless.

maca v. to be empty, make dry, to dry out (as in drinking the whole amount of *yaqona* in the cup). *Sa maca na waiwai.* There is no more oil. In a *yaqona* ceremony, after an important person drinks his cup, the assembled people will usually clap *cobo* and cry out *Maca!* **vakamamaca-taka** v. to dry it.

vakamamaca n. one of the series of ceremonies of formal marriage symbolising arrival and reception for the marriage party. Symbolically, this implies a ceremonial drying off as people arrive at the shore though modernly people are likely to arrive in a car or bus.

imacamaca n. scab or scar that remains after a cut or wound has healed.

macake n. thrush (Med.), common in Fiji, especially among children, as an oral problem, and a problem on babies' bottoms, even into folds of the skin. The cause is a yeast, Candida, which can also irritate the vagina, especially modernly when tight nylon underwear is often worn. In the mouth there are white spots that cover red, inflamed points. The tongue is also affected. Current treatment for oral thrush is gentian violet or nystatin. Fijians have the curious belief that *macake* is caused by eating too many sweets.

Idiom: *macake na beka* something is much too sweet, lit. it would even cause bats to be afflicted with *macake*.

macala adj. clear, understood, obvious. *vakamacalataka* v. to explain, clarify. As a modernism, one may hear this word use for "clear", applied to coconut oil that is not cloudy.

ivakamacala n. explanation, clarification (of an issue).

macawa 1. n. space, air. *Mataivalu e macawa* Air Force.

macawa 2. n. week (an introduced concept). *na mua ni macawa* the weekend. *macawa-rua* fortnight. Fijians never divided their lunar month into parts, and never counted time in any number of units.

macawa! 1. interjection, indicating astonishment, implying that something is hard to believe, or that it is unimportant, nonsense.

macawa 2. adj. useless, futile, good-for-nothing person.

macawa 3. adj. of evil spirits, despicable

macedru n., v. hiccough, hiccup.

macou n. native species of Cinnamomum genus, bark of the trees used to scent coconut oil but never used in food by Fijians. Cinnamomum zeylanicum is commercial cinnamon, introduced, and having sweeter taste, is cultivated by one plantation on Viti Levu; it is best referred to as *sinamoni dina*. Some commercial bakers in Fiji use *macou* in their baking rather than the more expensive sweet-scented commercial cinnamon. Syn. *macovu*.

mada 1. little word that softens an assertion, rendering it more polite. *kua mada* no thanks, please don't. *Au sa kua mada* I won't have any (food, drink offered), thanks. I'd rather not participate. *Lako mada mai.* Please come here.

mada 2. (Rewa) adj. light in weight. Syn. *mamada*.

mada 3. (Rewa) n. warclub.

maderini (Eng.) n. mandarin fruit, introduced, now common.

madigi n. destiny, fate, luck, chance (in certain contexts), offering (as to the ancient gods). *vakawiri madigi* an Archaic practice of making a decision by spinning a coconut on the ground and seeing what person it points to, as the person chosen. These days it may simply refer to a person to be chosen, where the question is still in process.

madila n. special skill of a person, something at which one is adept, has a knack for, especially speaking. Has a gift for speaking. May apply to a child who begins speaking very young. *E madila ena vosa o koya.* He/she is adept at speaking. See *mesamesa*.

madra (or) **madramadra** adj. worn-out (of clothes, mats), decayed. This is the root-word for *madrai*, the fermented starch-food.

madrai n. baked bread, an introduced food, the term adopted from Fijian *madrai*, a traditional chewy, fermented but unleavened starch food. *e dua na buli madrai* a loaf of bread.

Idiom: *susu madrai* desc. someone raised in town, without a knowledge of their village environment and customs, lit., raised eating baked bread (instead of Fijian village food). In modern times, this is extremely common.

madrai (ni Viti) n. traditional starch-food fermented and stored in pits (*davuke*), dug in the ground. The *ni Viti* is added only if there might be confusion with modern baked bread. The starch-foods may be breadfruit, taro, *kawai*, arrowroot, Polynesian chestnut *ivi*, plantain *vudi*, sweet potato *kumala*, cassava, or *via*. Fruits used may be those of Malay Apple *kavika*, or even the mangrove *dogo kana* (especially on Fulaga island, and at Bureta on Ovalau). At Lovoni, Ovalau, there is a specialty of *madrai* made from the kernels of the *dawa* fruit (Pometia pinnata). The pit is usually lined and covered with plantain leaves and weighted down with stones. The storage period is normally six months to a year but the pit may be replenished occasionally to become virtually perpetual. The technique of food storage is particularly useful in areas that may lack regular, year-round crops. *waki, wakia na madrai* mix together the *madrai* ingredients. *cuvi, cuvia na madrai* place *madrai* in a ground-pit to ferment there in storage.

madrai vudi n. traditional Fijian "pudding" made of plantain, a specialty of Nabukelevu, Kadavu Island.

madrali n. small, delicious saltwater univalve shellfish, smooth, shiny and white, Nerita polita. Syn. (West) *weimami*.

imadrali n. offering to the gods in advance, when praying for special favour (not just regular presentation of "first fruits" and not as penance or thanksgiving). Traditionally, the priests benefitted. Modernly, the Christian churches benefit. *madralitaka* to make such offerings. In the 1940s off Waya Island I have seen such offerings made to the shark god Dakuwaqa, asking pardon for diving and requesting protection from shark attack.

madua n., adj. shame, ashamed, be embarrassed in front of people and thus lose face. *mamadua* shy, bashful, prone to inappropriate fear or shame.

maduataka v. to be ashamed (of something). *Sa maduataka na kena irairai.* He/She is ashamed of his/her appearance.

vakamadua-taka (or) **vakamadualaka** v. to shame someone. *vakamadualaki* shamed.

maga-na n. vagina, a word not used in polite company. The word *maga* is sometimes used as an interjection of negative surprise. *Magamu!* Your vagina! is an insult, usually joking in vulgar fashion. A synonym, even more common or vulgar is *pasa*, with the insult, *Pasa levu!* referring to a large vagina, usually jocular. *Maga-i-tinamu!* Your mothers' vagina! is sometimes heard. One may just hear *Tinamu!* The word *maga* is unknown in the eastern highlands; there, the proper and correct term for male or female genitals is *mata-na* or one uses the name of the social-group's totem (where it is not forbidden to pronounce the name of the totem). Syn. *subu-na, manene* (applied only to a young girl). (Lau) *ribi*.

magimagi 1. n. sinnet, coir, made by men of plaited coconut fibre. *niu magimagi* var. of elongated coconut with long fibre ideal for sinnet, a long thin nut with very little flesh.

Idiom: *tali magimagi* gossip, yarn, from the fact that men usually sit and chat together while rubbing coir against their thighs, and plaiting; tell a story at length.

magimagi 2. (Archaic) n. allotment of land on Vanua Balavu Island, assigned by Ma'afu on condition of tax payment in kind. These sections were in principle 100 fathoms wide at the shore and continued indefinitely inland. Inland border of any piece of land was defined only as far as the planter cleared and planted the land. The man who set out these sections was known as *Soveya* ("Surveyor"), a personal or family name that continues today. Earlier Fijian claimants to the land were displaced.

magiti n. ceremonial feast-food presentation. *kana magiti* n. feast where people actually eat the food at the ceremonial presentation. *magiti ni bili muana* feast to farewell a departing person.

"mahimahi" (Hawaii) n. a fish, with bright colours against a silver background when first caught, dolphin (not to be confused with the mammal dolphin), Coryphaena hippurus, caught by trolling, somewhat offshore, and thus unfamiliar to early Fijians who fished only close to shore and did not know trolling, a skill learned from Samoa via Tonga. Syn. (English) *dolofini*.

mai 1. toward the speaker(or) from, indicating a direction toward the speaker. *lako mai* come here (to where the speaker is). *Mai!* Come! *Solia mai!* Give it here (to me)! *yani* away from the speaker.

mai 2. from (a place) *O sa lako maivei?* Where did you come from? In Cakaudrove some chiefly titles pose "Mai" before a place-name, as in Mai Mataikoro. *mai* is a suffix on the minor title *Komai,* followed by a place-name.

mai 3. at, in (a place other than where the speaker is located). *mai Suva* in Suva (when the speaker is not in Suva). *mai vanua tani* overseas

mai 4. by, in such phrases as *Sa dola na soqo mai vua na vulagi dokai.* The function was opened by the distinguished guest. It is customary for the guest to present a financial gift (*idola*) for the occasion.

mai 5. in the expression *mai oqo* and *mai muri*, to indicate a future time. *ena macawa (vula) mai oqo* in the coming week (month). *ena macawa ka tu mai.* during the coming week. *na noda kawa mai muri* our future generations.

maiau (or) **mayau** (Lau) Set! Everything is in order, ready to go.

Maikoronisia (Anglicism) n. Micronesia, including the Gilbert Islands, Nauru, Marshall Islands, Caroline Islands (Yap, Pohnpei, Koshae), islands similar in culture and language.

maile (Eng.) n. mile. *e lima na maile* five miles.

maina n. (Eng.) mynah bird, Acridotheres spp., introduced unfortunately, the Common Mynah (especially around houses, nesting in the eves, distinguished by yellow patch behind the eye) and the Jungle Mynah, common in pastures, parks and gardens, often seen near feeding cattle, foraging for insects disturbed by them, distinguished by a tuft of hair bristles at the top of the beak, both species only on the major big islands. The Common Mynah is an aggressive bird, chasing away endemic species, a considerable nuisance and its nests are often infested with lice.

Maji (Eng.) n. March (the month of). Syn. *Mati*.

maji (Eng.) n. v., march (as in a parade). See *tayabe*.

maka n. type of cricket (insect) or the Green cicada (cicada that does not disappear, then re-appear years later). *Sa tagi tiko na maka*. The cricket is singing.

maka (Eng.) n. marks or grade in school exams.

makataka (Eng.) v. to mark, leave a mark, as in leaving a check-mark, or to assign a mark or grade, as for school exams.

makadre n. resin from the trunk of the timber tree *dakua*, Fiji Pine, Agathis vitiensis, Pinaceae. Resin used as fuel for lamps in the highlands, though it gives a very smoky flame. Also melted by women for glazing clay pots. No glaze was applied to pots used for cooking or for storage of drinking water. The absence of glaze allows some evaporation that keeps the water cooler. *makadretaka* v. to apply *makadre* glaze. For the tourist trade, commercial varnish often replaces *makadre* as a glaze.

makawa 1. old (referring to time or to things but not to people), long ago. *Sa yali makawa*. It was lost long ago. *koro makawa* former village location, abandoned. (Most Fijian villages have re-located since Cession. The reasons are many: the Pax Brittanica relieved villagers of the need for isolated and fortified locations. New locations near beaches, rivers or roads offered better access to markets for produce, schools and clinics, and towns where jobs might be available. Sometimes hurricanes or floods prompted re-location of villages, or this was done to separate and consolidate the various Christian sects. Idiom: *toa makawa* unkind reference to a woman who is trying to act like a very young woman when in fact she is middle-aged. This may be said jokingly, or may be serious and unkind. Lit. old hen (not a young chick!). In referring to people as old one would use the adjective or noun *qase*.

makawa 2. former. *ena gauna makawa* in former times, in olden times.

makete (Eng.) n. public market, centralised in towns though today there is much farm produce sold at little, improvised markets and even by individuals by the roadside. More generally, *makete* may refer to an outlet, a market for one's products.

makete-taka v. to market (as in modern business). *na kena maketetaki na weleti* the marketing of papaya.

makimaki (Lau) adj. slow. *dau vakamakimaki* habitually slow, late (of a person). *E makimaki na nona cakacaka*. His work is slow. *makimakitaka* to do things slowly.

makita n. a well known tree on the main islands, can grow to 65 feet but is so useful, many are cut much younger and shorter, Atuna racemosa, Chrysobalanaceae. previously listed by John Parham as Parinari glaberrima, Rosaceae, small white flowers tinged with purple, useful for its straight trunk; young trees are often used for house rafters and temporary sheds but not posts in the ground. Formerly used as spars for canoe sails and also as poles (*ikara*) for poling boats because they are strong and bend without breaking. Twigs of *makita* leaves are often used for thatching of house sidewalls because they are so durable. The twigs thrust into the house walls, that are often made of plaited bamboo strips these days. (That flexible bamboo was intro. by Europeans.) Small *makita* branches, leaves attached, were used as brooms in the Eastern highlands of Viti Levu where there were no coconut palms to make *sasa* brooms. Fragrant kernel of the nut is grated and used by lowlanders to scent coconut oil for body application, and after adding sour citrus juice, used by highlanders of Viti Levu when they treat their hair. The fruit is not eaten but was used for making a kind of putty for plugging the seams of boats. Syn. (Bua, Macuata) *mala*.

mako n. a common tree, Trichospermum richii, Tiliaceae, timber useful as casewood. Formerly, in the Viti Levu highlands, the inner, bast fibre of young *mako* was used to make womens' skirts, and as a binding cord. Gelatinous inner bark is used to arrest diarrhea. (It is more traditional than the now commonly used leaves of guava, which is an introduced tree.) The tree was formerly used for black face-paint. There are two types, *mako loa* (T. calycatum) and *mako vula*. *Mako vula* has a very light coloured trunk that rises high before branching. Flowers are cream coloured. Fijians might perceive some resemblance to the fragrant *makosoi* (or) *mokosoi*.

makosoi n. fragrant-flowered tree. See *mokosoi*.

makua-liliva v., n. to glisten, glistening, as of reflections of the sun on the sea, on shiny leaves, metal or glass. Syn. *makaliliva*.

makubu-na (Polyn.) n. grandchild. *O Masinawa, na makubui Rokomoutu vakavica* Masinawa, the several generation grandchild of Rokomoutu. Syn. (Tonga) *mokopuna*.

makutu adj. keen, diligent, applies oneself to tasks. *mamakutu* very diligent.
Idiom: *makutu i siga dua* lit. diligent for one day only, implying that the diligence soon lags. *makututaka* v. to do something diligently.

mala n. small part of something. *mala ni vosa* part of a speech or utterance. This gives rise to the personal name, now a family name Malani(vosa) in Lau originally, but now famously at Nakorotubu, Ra. *Ulu-mala-i-dua* name of legendary giant who (as implied in the name) had only one hair on his head. *vaka-riba-malamala* is an idiom, to make an allusion or play on words. Applied to physical objects, *mala* may be used for strands of fibre, such as sinnet *magimagi*, human hair, chips of wood. *malamala* is used for many chips of wood.

maladroka adj. of firewood, too green or wet inside to be useful. May apply to things that are not sufficiently dried, and need more exposure to the sun, such as pandanus leaves *voivoi* to be used for weaving.

mala ni meke n. words of a group dance-song. The words are often difficult to understand for outsiders. Local language is used and references, usually to some ancient occasion, are oblique and archaic.

malai 1. adj. faded, withered, drooping, usually of flowers or green vegetation, usually from lack of water.

malai 2. adj. feeble, enfeebled, weakened, of a person.

mala-malawa n. crack of dawn as light appears faintly.

malasese (Eng.) n. molasses (produced by Fiji Sugar Corp.).

mala-ude n. excitement, becoming absorbed in feeling with emotion, involvement in arousal, as with music, or the emotion and feeling of a group of people. This may be reflected in body movement.

malawaci n. As reported by Berthold Seemann (1825-1871), this is a Fijian name for the medium sized tree Strebus anthropophagorum, Moraceae, leaves with tenderising qualities, wrapped around human corpses before cooking, and then eaten as a vegetable with the cannibal meat. Botanist John Parham in *Plants of the Fiji Islands*, and Capell in his Dictionary are copying Seemann when they list the name *malawaci* for this plant. Botanist Al Smith reports this as a mistake but the few names he lists are not commonly known. Nonetheless, the plant was used for this purpose. Its watery or white latex is believed to have tenderised the meat (as the latex of papaya does). Another such plant mentioned by Seemann was *tudano*, now classified as Omalanthus nutans, also has a corrosive sap and has had the same use. Another vegetable also wrapped around corpses to be cooked and then eaten with the meat were the leaves of *boro dina*, Solanum uporu.

male n. native wild nutmeg, three species of Myristica, the forest hardwood timber used by Fijians but not the fruit. On Viti Levu more commonly called *kau damu* from the reddish colour of the sap and wood. Also the aril, a gelatenous, brilliant red covering of the nut, inside the yellowish husk. One of the species closely resembles the commercial nutmeg species, but it lacks fine fragrance and taste. The introduced true nutmeg is planted as a commercial crop only at Wainadoi, Namosi.

maleka 1. (Rewa) adj. very good, delightful, nifty, delicious.

maleka! 2. (sarcastic Slang) Serves you (him, her, them) right! *Maleka sara!* is a more extreme expression, often used in joking with an acid edge.

malele adj. concentrated, absorbed, focussed (of the mind, thoughts, conversation), of one mind (as of several people), agreed (among people). *Sa malele na nona vakasama.* His mind is focussed on one thing. By extension this may imply an attraction to someone or some thing

malevu n. pocket of a fish fence *ba ni ika* where the fish are collected.

malewa 1. v. to criticise, find fault with, used mostly in the idiom *E sega ni dua na ka me malewa kina.* There is/was absolutely nothing to find fault with it. (That is a common expression.)

malewa 2. adj. gauche, inappropriate, not suitable, discomforting, lacking in respect. *E malewa na veimaliwai mai Valelevu.* The ambiance around the chief is not appropriate.

mali-e! (Tongan, Lau) Thank you!

malimali 1. n. chip (usually of wood being chopped).

malimali 2. n. pudding made of *yabia* or modernly, cassava, with ripe plantain, especially in Lau, Batiki, and Vatulele, made traditionally with caramelised coconut cream (*lolo buta*).

malimali 3. grinning, to grin, low-key smile.

maliwa n. middle. *na yabaki ni bula mai na maliwa ni 20 kei na 19.* between 19 and 20 years old. *ena kena maliwa* in the middle of it. *ena kedrau maliwa o Suva kei Deuba.* In the middle between Suva and Deuba.

maliwai amidst, midst, among, amongst. *bula maliwai keda* live among us.

veimaliwai n. ambiance, social atmosphere, quality of relationship. This is an important Fijian concept, to have an absence of social discord though discontented feelings are often repressed. *veimaliwai vinaka* good ambiance.

Malo n. chiefly title in a few areas of early Polynesian influence, such as Kaba at the Tailevu coast, and also at Vatoa Island.

Malo! (Lau) Greetings! or Good! or Thanks! or Good-bye! Receiving such a greeting, one reponds with the same word.

malo 1. (Polyn.) n. Polynesian loincloth made of barkcloth (*masi*). As regular clothing this was adopted around the coastal areas of Fiji. The *malo* was adopted by some Fiji Melanesians, even in the highlands, most especially when serving as mercenaries for warring Polynesians. *malo* or *maro* is a Polynesian word for barkcloth and loincloth.

malo 2. (Colo East) n. ally in wars of eastern highlanders *kaiColo* when two or more allied peoples would wear the same style of loincloth (*malo*), to recognize each other in battle, usually as mercenaries for Tongans. *Malo* can be the form of address between people of two such Fijian villages. These former allies are said to be *malo vata*. An example is tribe Nadakuni at village Nasele on the Waidina River, related as *malo vata* to village Lutu-Wainibuka. The *malo* loincloth itself was an introduction to the highlands, probably from Tonga via Verata, and was made of barkcloth *masi* that was not grown and made at the higher elevations (except at Navosa, after being introduced by early Tongan settlers there). As mercenary warriors Fiji's Melanesian highlanders served Tongan leaders, even in Tonga itself.

maloku adj. reliable, obliging, steady, quiet in nature. *gone maloku* quiet child.

malolo (Samoa, Tonga) a word that appears in *vakamalolo*, dance in sitting position now danced in many places, originally (by legend) from Cakauyawa off the western coast of Viti Levu. It was adopted in Waya Island before spreading widely. Malolo also an island name in the Mamanuca Group. As a Samoan word "malolo" can mean to submit, implying some ancient defeat and submission, or simply a word implying a resting place, including even death itself. *Malolo* is also an expression heard in Lau when a person retires from a kava-drinking circle, to move back and take a rest.

Idiom: *dre ko Malolo* toward sunset, literally, Malolo island is pulling, Malolo being in the far west of Fiji islands. This idiom is typical of old Fijian language, speaking through allusions, hardly ever directly, bluntly or simply.

malu (Lau) adj. sheltered from penetatration by weather (rain or sun), of a place or an object, such as a box or some food.

malua slow, in a while. *Malua!* Take it easy! Not so fast! *vakamalua* slowly. *vakamaluataka* slow (it) down. *malua mai* in a while, after a time (unhurried). *vuki malua* adj. gentle and slow, even-tempered, of a person.

Idiom: "malua fever" refers to a slow pace of life, laziness, that is considered typical in the islands. "Fiji time" is a related saying, frequently heard.

vakamalua-taka 1. to slow it down.

vakamalua-taka 2. in Fijian ceremony, to express formal recognition and gratitude, expressing thanks. This is done, for example after "touching" *tara* and accepting a whale-tooth. It is often spoken supportively by a senior aide to the person accepting the presentation. In situations other than receiving a whale-tooth, the recipient may kneel or bow down and and clap the hands (*cobo*) several times. It is a modernism to follow the English custom, simply saying the words "thanks" or "thank you very much" *vinaka* or *vinaka vakalevu*.

ivakamalua n. gift made in payment for some service, as a way of thanking.

vakamamaka (Lau) adj. choosy, "difficult", very particular about what one likes, or does not like.

malugu (Lau) n. warclub.

malumalu v., n. to shelter. Syn. *rurugu*.

malumu 1. (Vanua Levu) n. warclub.

malumu 2. adj. weak, soft, not well (health).

malumalumu adj. or n. very weak (of person, things), soft (things), very gentle, weakness. *vakamalumulumu-taka* to weaken, to soften the way.

Idiom: *mata malumu* gentle, soft and gentle face (usually or a girl or young woman, or baby), sweet-faced.

mama, mama 1. v. to chew. May have an implication of mumbled speech.

mama 2. (Rewa) adj. light. Syn. *mamada*.

mama 3. n. ring (for the finger). *mama ni vakamau* wedding ring. In early times such rings were never worn by Fijians.

mamaca 1. adj. dry.
mamaca 2. adj. definite, effective(ly).
mamada (Polyn.) adj. light, as opposed to heavy (*bibi*). May imply something that is ineffective, lacking in some essential element.
Idiom: *mamada* (of a woman) has just given birth.
vakamamada-taka v. to lighten up, make lighter, less heavy. *na kerei ni vakamamadataki ni totogi.* the request for leniency in a court sentence.
mamadua adj. shy.
mamakeukeu n. or v. to sob, whimper. *me tarovi na nodra mamakeukeu* put a stop to their whimpering.
mamarau adj. very joyful. *marau* joyful, happy.
mamare 1. adj. translucent, virtually transparent (cloth, liquid). See *makare*.
mamare 2. adj. thin, cloth, of sliced bread, delicatessen meats, applied to virtually anything flat and very thin. Syn. *maremare*.
mamaqi adj. stingy, mean (a despised characteristic). See *maqi, maqitaka*.
mamau adj. sated, eaten one's fill, had enough to eat. Syn. (Lau, Kadavu) *bula*. (Rewa, Naitasiri, Natewa) *macu*.
mamavoavoa adj. very badly wounded. *mavoa* wound, wounded.
mami adj. perfectly ripe for eating, of breadfruit. Syn. (Lau) *moemoe*.
mana 1. n. personal power, prestige and effectiveness as recognized by others. This derives from a person's status and prestige, from his or her station in life (chief, priest, high official), or from some remarkable acts performed. One's *mana* pervades the body and even one's possessions, but is centred in the head, which formerly was never to be touched. The *mana* of a coastal, paramount Fijian chief was dangerous. *cakamana* miracle.
mana 2. v. to come about, good result or good fortune, fulfillment, usually from some action or some thing that can happen. There is an implication of magic or supernatural effect. For example, some Fijian villages have destroyed or turned over to the Methodist Church their old Fijian artefacts (clubs, spears, *yaqona* bowls) that pre-dated Christianity. They expect or hope that some good will come from that, such as, perhaps, better success for their children in school, or more good fortune for their village. *E sega ni mana na vuaviri.* No good will come from the (military) coup. *Era sa sega ni tokona na Charter e na sega ni mana na kena cakacakataki.* They (many) do not support the Charter since no good will come about from putting it into effect. This concept of *mana* is very "Fijian", and also typical throughout many South Pacific cultures.
mana! v. n. exclamation paronounced alone toward the end of ceremonies, indicating a wish of empowerment, a pre-Christian Fijian verson of "Amen", meaning "So be it!".
mana n. mud lobster, a much favoured delicacy at the shores of SE Viti Levu, but common from SW Asia through Australasia, Thalassina anomala, breeds Sept-Nov., heavy with eggs at that time. They emerge at night or on overcast days. Sold in the market at least through April, May. *Mana* have special significance in the history of the Roko Tui Dreketi. Syn. *tola*. *butu mana* press foot near *mana* hole to catch it. *la'i tavitavi* go snaring mud lobster. *kuco, kucora* v. to plug up mud lobster holes to catch it elsewhere. *cevucevu* n. mud lobster's burrow entrance in sand, mud. *daba* edible red egg sac of mud lobster. *Sa daba na mana* (or, in Rewa) *Sa sike na mana.* The land lobsters are bearing eggs, full. (*idaba* parcel, fascicle). *Sa draudrau na mana.* The *mana* are out of season, not in good condition for eating.
manamana 1. v. to become committed, determined, really want to do something, set one's mind to (a course of action, something). *manamana lako* determine to go. *manamana ivalu* decide to go to war.
manamana 2. v., n. to have a great liking for (an object or an action, to really enjoy doing something. *E nona manamana na tei vuanikau.* He has a great fondness for planting fruits. *E manamana gunu yaqona.* He loves to drink *yaqona*.
manamana 3. adj. show-off.
manamana 4. n. crown of the head, soft spot of a baby's skull.
manata 1. v. to affect as with sleepiness, or to afflict, as with a sickness, disease or crippling condition or influence that is not good. *Sa manati koya na vu.* He/she has a fit of coughing. *Sa manati au na mo.* I caught the mumps. *Au sega ni kila na cava e manati iko tiko!* I do not know what is getting into you! -- what is affecting you!
manata 2. v., adj. to be acting silly.
manawi 1. n. common coastal tree growing to 100 feet, Koelreuteria elegans, Sapindaceae, yellow flowers with red marks, leaves are cooked to make black hair-dye (*ibena*). Lvs bipinnate, with small

toothed leaflets. Though little known now, this was probably the most common hair-dye in coastal areas, used by men and women. Syn. (Ba, Vuda) *wiwi*.

manawi 2. n. common forest and coastal tree from Malesia east to Tonga, growing to 30 meters, to altitude 1000 meters, Pleiogynium timorense, Anacardiaceae, fls white to yellow, frts brown, distinctive scone-shaped capsule with ridges on upper surface found at base of tree all year round. As with *manawi 1*, leaves are cooked for black hair dye. Also useful timber tree.

manene n. female private parts of the body, a word perhaps most often applied to children by caring adults, suggesting that the girl wash herself properly. Derivation of the word may be from a shellfish that has a shape suggestive of that part of the female body.

mani particle sometimes adequately translated as "thus", or "then", as an unexpected consequence. It precedes a verbal form. *Kauta mai e rua na kilo suka ke mani vo na ilavo, qai dua na uma sovu*. Bring two kilos of sugar and then if there is money left, one bar of soap.

manidia (Eng.) n. manager.

manileda (Eng.) n. money-lender. Some urban Fijians use moneylenders, who exact high rates of interest though legally they are not supposed to exceed 12%. Most borrowers are Fijian civil servants and people with a steady job. Although lenders are required to be registered by government, such activities are not monitored. Many of the lenders are Fijians themselves. Their means of collection can include violence, as in the overseas underworld.

manini, maninitaka v. to conserve one's resources, to use them wisely, sparingly.

manioke (Lau) n. cassava, manioc, from an American Indian name introduced by Europeans, now the major starch-food staple, along with rice. More commonly called *tavioka* in Fiji. In Fiji the cultivars are non-toxic. Overseas some are toxic.

manipusi (Eng.) n. mongoose, introduced to the larger islands (not Taveuni or Lau). It had devastated the population of birds that nest on the ground and is always a threat to domestic chickens. Fijian supersitition may believe in good luck if a mongoose runs across the road from left to right in front of a person or a vehicle, and bad luck if it crosses from right to left.

maniwa (Eng.) n. manure. *vakamaniwa-taka* to manure (it), put manure on .

manulevu n. Swamp Harrier, Pacific Harrier, Circus approximans. Common, now extended to Tonga, bird of prey mostly hovering over open ground, large wide wings in conspicuous V shape, very long tail. Eats rats, snakes, lizards, large insects, occasionally fish, and carrion. Nests well hidden on the ground, surviving the threat of the mongoose. Syn. (West) *takubu*. (Nadro., Kadavu, Ra) *reba*. (Namosi) *tuivucilevu*. (Rewa) *tivuci*. (Tonga) *taiseni*.

manumanu n. animal (normally referring to a bird unless the context suggests another type of animal, such as iguana or snake). *manumanu vuka* lit. flying animal, i.e., specifically a bird. *manumanu dolo* crawling creature, snake, worm. When associated with a clan or tribe, *manumanu* means their symbolic animal or totem. *Na neitou manumanu na reba*. Our symbolic animal is the hawk. As an insult *Manumanu!* Beast! Fijians do not normally refer to fish as being animals. The official Fijian dictionary Na iVolavosa ni Viti (2007, p. 358) states that animals (*manumanu* have no spirit or soul (*yalo*), which sounds rather dogmatic to an animal lover. *manumanu lailai* (singular) or *manumanu lalai* (plural) usually refer to insects. *manumanu midimidi* microbes, germs, bacteria, lit. tiny animals. *lewe ni manumanu* meat.

manumanu n. frill, as on a dress, other clothing, or a mat.

manumanu ni cagi n. Frigate Bird, two species, the much more common Fregata ariel, Lesser Frigate Bird, with white patch on each side, and F. minor, Great Frigate Bird, that is all black in colour. These are coastal birds that rob other sea birds of their catch. They may be seen as far as 75 miles from shore, more commonly within 50 miles and is thus a sign of impending landfall for Polynesian seafarers. To highlanders in the mountains, appearance of these birds indicates the coming of storm winds, when the frigate bird takes refuge in the interior. In courting, a red chin-pouch may billow out conspicuously. Syn. *kasaqa*.

manumanu ni meke n. A comic who livens up a group-dance (*meke*) of men. He is a funny, very skilled dancer, very adroit, agile, active, spoofing the other dancers to have them perform at their peak. Without such a comic, men's dances can become tiresome and boring to watch.

manumanu soni n. epilepsy.

manumanu tabu n. totemic animal, bird or insect. (There can also be totemic plants *kau tabu*, and totemic aquatic creatures *ika tabu*.) Sacred totems are a feature of some Melanesian Fijians of Viti Levu, especially in the highlands. They are a symbol of reproductive ability, fertility, and survival. There are no totems in the more Polynesian kin-groups of the coast and smaller islands but there is sometimes a plant or creature, bird, fish, plant, insect, of object that has local significance that may be iconic if not totemic. (The spirit god of a tribe may take the form of an animal or object.) One adds the word *tabu* only if necessary to make the context clear that one is talking of a sacred totem. In most cases one must not pronounce the name of the totem, be it animal, plant, aquatic creature or, in some cases, an inanimate object such as a stone or piece of driftwood.

manumanu vuka n. bird. The adj. *vuka* flying is added only if necessary for clarity. Normally the word *manumanu* refers to birds but may refer to other animals, especially now that so many exist, imported (cats, horses, cattle, goats, mongoose, toads). Formerly there were few land animals other than iguanas and geckoes, frogs and salamanders. Fijians do not usually talk of fish as being animals.

manuwa (Eng.) n. man-of-war, warship.

maoli (Lau, Rewa, Vuda, Nadroga, Serua, Naitasiri) n. papaya, an introduced fruit that thrives best in calcareous soil, often near concrete foundations of houses. Male and female flowers on different plants with just a few hermaphrodites. Lauans eat the cooked green fruit as a vegetable, and may be referred to jocularly as *bati maoli* "papaya-eaters". The sap and leaves are sometimes used to tenderise meat. More common name in Fiji is *weleti*, in Lau *leweti* (pronounced "leweji") in an interesting reversal of syllables.
Idiom: *Maoli dada*: (Insulting): referring to a person from Lau, meaning lit. "soft papaya".

maopo (Lau) adj. sensible and careful, of a person.

maoqani (Eng.) n. large-leafed mahogany, Swietenia macrophylla, Central and South America, timber tree planted by Government in plantations on native land. While Government paid all the costs of planting, this has led to disputes as to ownership of the timber. Landowners are claiming the timber should belong to them. Another species, S. mahogoni, with smaller leaves, has also been planted in Fiji.

mape (Eng.) n. map.

mapolo (Eng.) n. marble(s). Village children often use the white seeds of the *soni* shrub as marbles. The game is introduced. Syn. *mavolo*.

maqa (Vanua Levu, specifically Bua) no, not.
Idiom: *Maqa na leqa! Matua na raisi*. No problem! Don't worry! There is rice at hand.

maqamaqa n. shorefront that are tidal flats. At the Nadogra shore, sea salt is extracted at such locations.

maqemaqe (Eng., monkey) adj. agile in quick movement, usually of a child or sportsman, physically evasive, difficult to catch.

maqi, maqitaka v. to conserve, to be very sparing in sharing, usually of something in short supply. *mamaqi* adj. selfish, stingy. Sharing is an important notion to Fijians.

maqo (Eng.) n. mango, an introduced fruit from India. Fruits seasonally from around November into March, earlier in the West. Mango fruits grow more successfully and earlier in the dry zones (Nadi, Labasa). In wet areas such as Suva, pounding rain often dislodges the flowers and tiny fruit, so that in most years the trees are barren of fruit. In wet climate an anthracnose fungus also causes flowers to drop. Like most fruits, the mango is often eaten by Fijians when it is hard and semi-ripe. With a ripe mango, Fijians will usually bit a hole at one end and suck out the fruit. They refer to drinking such fruit, not eating it. They never peel a mango the way Europeans do. Varieties: *tabua* a large, curved fruit with distinctive red colouring. *maqo loa* a superb var. of finest flavour, brilliant green when unripe, turning darker and dusky when fully ripe. Indians have special varieties for making pickles. For the Gujerati, mango leaves have symbolic, religious significance. At any new enterprise the leaves would be hung about for a benign ambiance.

maqosa adj. diligent and skilled. Syn. (Kadavu) *masokoi*. (Cakau.) *masomasoko*.

maquru adj. of Fijan hair, naturally frizzled with stiffly compact coils, distinguishing characteristic of Viti Levu highlanders (*kaiColo*). Sometimes laughingly compared to steel wool. The typical hair of coastal Fijians is softer, known as *ulu dina* "true" hair. In areas of greatest Polynesian or Micronesian influence, in Lau and parts of Cakaudrove, Fijian hair can be softer yet, some being wavy and flatter, known as *ulu wai* or if more extremely soft and long, *ulu waiwaiya*, like the hair of eastern Polynesians, long and flowing.

mara (Archaic) n. stench of a decaying chiefly corpse, and by ext. refers to a place for keeping or buying the body. The word does not have the unpleasant connotation of the English equivalent. It has been used as a name for a chief.

marama n. lady, and by ext., queen, in playing cards, contrasted with *turaga* (king), as in queen of spades.

marau adj. happy, delighted. *mamarau* emphatically happy.

marau, marautaka v. to enjoy, to be happy about (something).

veivaka-marau-taka v. to entertain.

veivakamarautaki n. entertainment, show.
maravu adj. calm, peaceful, of the sea.
mareqeta v. to treasure or keep protectively, as something beloved.
maresa n., adj. slender, usually of the female body, particularly the waist.
marimari v. to attempt to gain a person's favour by sweet talk, to cajole. *vosa marimari* "sweet talk". *mari, maria* (or) *marica* v. to sweet talk for some favour. Marica can be a girl's name. Cf. *tabetabe*. These are common concepts.
mariwana (Eng.) marihuana, Cannabis sp., the drug plant, strictly forbidden in Fiji, with prison sentences for possession of even minute quantities of a few grams. Sometimes referred to as *waigaga*, a general word for illicit drugs. Grown especially at remote locations in Navosa by farmers who have few commercial alternatives. For the usual Fijian root crops, transport to market is difficult from these isolated places.
maroroi, maroroya v. to keep, preserve, retain. *Baqe ni iLavo Maroroi nei Viti* Fiji Reserve Bank. *Vale ni iYaya Maroroi nei Viti* Fiji Museum.
marusa as in the idiom: *malua marusa*. delay means destruction. i.e., act promptly. *rusa* destroy.
masa 1. v., n. the background sound of continued laughter,
masa 2. n. unsettled, restless condition, anxious. *tauvi e na masa* in an anxious, unsettled, uncomfortable state, ill at ease. *Sa masa na yago-qu*. My body feels out of sorts, ill at ease, queasy.
masamasa adj. has a gritty, sandpaper-type surface, as of some forest tree-leaves, the *bokasi* variety of breadfruit, the skin of sharks and some fish such as *tabace*.
masake ni vosa adj. crafty in speech, not to be relied upon.
Masau n. on Bau island, a clan of household guards and protocol officers who serve the Roko Tui Bau's clan Vusaratu but later also for a time asserted influence in relation to the Tui Kaba. When the Vusaratu were overthrown, the Masau switched primary allegiance to the Tui Kaba though they retained ceremonial function for the Vusaratu. They are of Samoan origin, previously carpenters called *matasau*, or *mataisau*, connected with Tonga, and now a people of mixed race. Their influence has sharply declined in recent years.
masawe n. plant, Cordyline terminalis (or) fruticosa, Agavaceae, wild, green-leaved native varieties formerly used for extraction of sweet liquid solution from the tuber after baking for a few days, then shredded, and squeezed. It was formerly used in Fijian puddings only, not for sweetening anything else. *soko, sokota na masawe* v. to shred the *masawe* root. Other, coloured-leaf varieties have been introduced and are planted as ornamentals, know by the Hawaiian name *ti*. Leaves of native variety formerly used in making "skirts" for men and women, and still now used for dressing dancers for exhibition dances (*meke*). Leaves still used for wrapping food parcels. Syn. (Colo East) *vasili*, (Lau, Vanua Levu, Vuda, Nadroga) *qai*. (Vuda, Ba) *qolo*. (Rewa, Namosi) *tekula* for the introduced, reddish-leaved ornamental variety.
masei n. a sp. of palm, Pritchardia pacifica, edible seeds, leaves formerly used for fans that were for chieftains only. Grows only near habitations, present or past. Syn. *saqiwa*. Another, rarer species, P. thurstonii, is to be found on islets at Fulaga, Ogea, and on some islets at Vanua Balavu. The fan palm is called *sakiki*, in parts of Vanua Levu and northern Lau, but elsewhere, *sakiki* can also refer to Veitchia sp. Syn. (Nadro.) *roro*. (Parts of Lau) *iviu*, related to the Polynesian name "piu".
Masela (Eng.) n. *Yatu Masela* Marshall Islands, in the Micronesian sector of the Pacific.
masese (Eng.) n. matches.
masi, masia 1. v. to rub briskly, usually with a brush (*barasi*) or coconut husk (*qa ni bulu*). *masi-vava* n., v. shoe-shine, shoe-shine boy. *masia na batina* v. to brush the teeth.
masi, masia 2. v. to massage, rub with the hands, especially to relax muscles of the body. See *bobo*. Idiom: *masi polo* n., v. (Vulgar) apple polisher, ass-kisser, a schoolboy expression that sounds less vulgar in Fijian than its literal translation in English.
Masi n. title of a local chief in certain places on Vanua Levu Island, namely Seaqaqa, Wailevu and Udu. Ra Masi is a local title to be found in Lau.
masi n. bark cloth of Mulberry shrub, *vunimasi*, Broussonetia papyrifera, eight to fifteen feet high, which grows almost exclusively in coastal areas, near streams usually, in open places, often near cultivated land, and never in the bush. It is cultivated by suckers because the stems are cut before the shrub comes to seed. The stems are soaked in water, the inner bark (*lewena*) removed and pounded with a wooden mallet (*ike*). Sections are modernly pasted together with sticky arrowroot (*yabia*), cassava, or taro, formerly simply pounded together. Decorative local patterns are painted on, often with stencils. Colorants are made from charred candlenut *lauci* (black), puzzlenut *dabi* rind (black) or outer bark (red), *kura* Morinda citrifolia root (yellow) or bark (red), Malay Apple (*kavika*) inner bark with sea

water and lime (crimson) which is one I have not actually seen done. Authoress Gale Trexler also mentions the Upright Banana (*soaqa*), young shoots of this plantain as a purple dye. In Lau, red ochre (*umea*), formed into spindle-shaped blocks is famously obtained from Komo Island, which itself does not produce *masi*. Several varieties of the *masi* shrub are recognized: *masi dina*, with the thickest and thus the best inner bark, *masi damu*, with an outer bark that is somewhat auburn instead of grey, *masi vutu* the tallest *masi*, *masi kau* the most common variety. This was virtually the only cloth known to Fijians before the advent of Manchester cotton. There was little or none that grew in upper highlands, with the single exception of one place in Navosa, introduced by Tongans who penetrated up the Sigatoka River. Some Fijians used the bark of the breadfruit tree as cloth, but many Fijians used no cloth at all. Cotton is apparently an indigenous introduction but there are no records of Fijians using it for cloth. How or why cotton reached Fiji is a mystery.

masi toni brown barkcloth from dipping (*toni*) in an infusion of mangrove bark, often used for burials.

masi kesa barkcloth with coloured patterns in some local style, e.g. Vatulele, Moce, usually in browns and black, often via stencils, but from Lau can be free-form in more Tongan style. *kesa* v. to apply such colorant.

masi kuvui smoked *masi*, a chiefly product, formerly used for fine turbans and shoulder-bands, usually of a dull yellowish colour. On Vatulele, the *masi kuvui* is actually not usually smoked but derives the yellowish colour from being soaked in an infusion of the bark of the *kura* tree and bark of the *doi* shrub. The islands of Vatulele and Moce are well known for their *masi*, with distinctive designs, Moce using more detailed design and darker colours. On Vatulele, the brown colour is from mangrove bark, and the black is now made from the carbon residue of diesel oil. For commercial purposes, standard sheets are made 12 feet x 2 feet.

masi ni vanua (Archaic) n. man of chiefly rank in coastal areas; as formal dress he might wear a barkcloth train behind his loincloth, and/or a covering (*wabale*) up to his lower chest or to one shoulder.

masilini (Eng.). muslin (cloth).

masima n. salt. Available formerly only by trade from several locations around the coast, at Tavua, Ba and Tailevu, but most famously at Wai District, Nadroga: Made by evaporation on tidal flats (*maqamaqa*), and then boiling over an open fire in clay pots imported from Tavua, Malolo Group, formed into blocks in cylindrical packages (*na taba ni masima*) of mangrove *tiri* bark, ready for transport or trade but meanwhile kept above a fireplace to dry out. By ultimate user, the block was scraped with the scrapings added into water before use, so that chunks of hand-held food might be dipped (*toni, tonia*) in the saline solution. No one sprinkled salt. Only a few decades ago, such blocks (*taba ni masima*) were sold in the Suva Public Market. They were sold wrapped around in a package (*iolo ni masima*). In ceremonial presentations, ten *taba ni masima* would be referred to as one *wai*. In Lau, seawater was used to flavour food, and was kept in coconut shells (*pupu*) as containers. Salt was rarely available in the highlands but there a substitute, sometimes said to be superior to salt, was a terrestrial fern called *waruta*. Syn. (Tonga) *masima*.

Idiom: *Bau masimataka na nomu vosa* lit. salt your speech, implying that it should be made sweeter, more favourably interesting.

Idiom: *Masima!* Salt! a call to someone who coughs or clears the throat noisily. The one who coughs will reply *Karia!* Scrape it! (referring to the use of salt by scraping it from the block).

masiratu n. uncommon tall (to 90 feet) endemic timber tree on large islands, Degeneria vitiensis, Degeneriaceae, a plant family unique to Fiji with only one other species D. roseiflora, known as *karawa*, also a good forest tree. Curiously shaped, creamy, fragrant flower, 6 cm diam., spirally arranged, blooms November, December, apparently fertilised by a beetle. The fruit, 11x5 cm, from pink to purple to black when ripe, is a fat sausage-shape with seeds having bright orange fleshy testa in green pulp. Lvs large, leathery, alternate, with conspicuous yellow midrib and very long yellow petiole. Branches horizontal, emerging on all sides at the same height. Syn. *vavaloa* (a name also applied to Litsea magnifolia, which has similar fragrance from its cut bark.)

masiwala (Archaic) v., n. cummerbund of barkcloth wrapped around upper waist and to the chest by coastal chiefly warriors, often in a challenging mode.

masiyara (or) **tiniyara** (Archaic) n. part of high chiefly barkcloth clothing that falls as a tail, behing the back, reaching the ground, worn only on ceremonial occasions by Fijians where the coastal influence was strong.

masu, masuta, masulaka v. to pray. *masuta* v. to pray (to the Christian God, or to a person), to beg someone to oblige, to implore. *masulaka* v. to pray for (something). *Au masuti iko mo kua ni lako.* I implore you not to go. *masulaki ni kakana* n. grace said before a meal. Fijians offer a prayer on a very great many different occasions, certainly before any official meeting or function, and often also afterwards. They bless houses, boats and people in abundance. The prayers are usually rather extensive, verbose, elaborate and inclusive.

mata 1. n. official representative or spokesman, ambassador. *matanivanua* traditional spokesman for chief. *Mata nei Viti ki Japani* Fijian Ambassador to Japan. *Vale ni Mata* House of Representatives (Legislature).

mata 2. n. team or group, as in *matasere* choir. *mataqali* clan. *mataniveicaqe* football team. *caqe* v. to kick forewards.

matadravu n. fireplace, formerly in a corner at the "lower" end of the house (near the common entrance), used only for steaming foods in clay pots. *dravu* ashes. Because of the fire hazard in traditional houses, colonial authorities enforced the idea of a separate structure for a cook-house (*vale ni kuro*) that had never previously existed in Fiji. *mata dravu* may also refer to someone whose physical features indicate excessive drinking of kava, with dry, grey skin.

Idiom: *moce i dravu na koli.* No cooked food on hand, lit. the dog sleeps in the ashes (where food is cooked).

mata-na 1. n. face, and by ext. the appearance, type or inclination of a person. *wai ni mata* tears. *yaloka ni mata* eyeball(s). *bekabeka ni mata* eyelids, eyelashes. *Mata* is a prefix for many of people's characteristics, and a limited selection is shown below. When the prefix is repeated as in *matamatailavo,* instead of simply *matailavo,* lit. "money-faced", the characteristiic is more emphatic.

matabalavu daydreaming person.

mataboko blind.

mataburoro pimply faced, usually said of a youngster.

mataboto face with bulging, frog-like eyes, insulting reference to Tongans, perceived as having this facial feature.

matabuto fainted, to faint, unconcious, dizzy.

mataceba looking out of the corner of one's eye, squinting, sometimes implying a person may need glasses.

mata cigogo or *sigogo* squinting.

matacika conjunctivitis.

mataciri dreamy-eyed. *ciri* drift.

mata cucula pock-marked face.

matacudrucudru has an angry face.

matadamudamu person of white race.

matadre "Chink" (Oriental person having megalanthic fold in the eyes).

mata dredredre smile, smiling.

mata drisi blood-shot eyes.

matadrokadroka (Anglicism) queasy, sickly faced, "green" looking.

mata dua one-eyed.

mata-ganoganoa has a lovely, enticing face.

mata gonegone baby-faced.

mata-i-lavo "money face", stingy and overly concerned about making and keeping money.

matakani having a grog-doped face.

mata kanikani freckle-faced.

mata-kaukauwa stern faced.

matakibo having a swollen face.

mata lala empty-handed (when gifts are expected).

mata lasa "funny face".

matalau smiling, happy.

matalia transformed.

matalila thin-faced, haggard..

mata liso has facial expression with glistening, attentive eyes.

mataloaloa person of black race.

mata meli sweet faced.

mata momoto peaked or pinch-faced.

matapula (Lau only) having big, bright eyes, a woman usually, or facial expression with expressive, dominant eyes.

mata qiqo thin-faced.

mata rabaraba flat-faced (usually Oriental, some Gilbertese).

mata rai has good vision.
mata rarawa with a sad look.
mata reva cross-eyed.
matasara blind but with open eyes.
mata savasava having a clean look.
mataseila cataract.
mata siga dazzled by the sun, squinting in the sun.
mata sigogo (or) *cigogo* squinting.
mata sorokididiki wrinked face.
mata sukusukura rugged, rough hewn face.
mata tagitagi tearful.
mata tetedre broadfaced.
mata vakavula pleasant, moon-shaped face.
mata vulaci pale faced, washed out, colourless.
matavulavula albino. Syn. *rea. vulavula* white.
mata wanono staring, vacant look.
mata waqawaqa wide-eyed, bright, open eyed. Syn. *matawidriwidri*.
mata widriwidri wide-eyed look showing surprise, anticipation.
matayalewa girl-chaser.

mata-na 2. n. genitals. *vunitaka na matamu!* cover your genitals! (said when genitals are not properly concealed by clothes, typically when a man is seated, wearing a *isulu* but no underpants).

mata-na 3. n. front. *ena matamu* just in front of you. *na matanivale* front yard, of house. *mata va* glasses, or a person who wears spectacles. *mata-i-va* digging fork (implying four prongs). *matanalevu* openly, candid, without secrecy or hidden meaning.
Idiom: *Sa tawa na matana.* She is pregnant.

vakamata n., v. traditional greeting pronounced outside a house to announce one's presence. Formerly, it was extremely impolite and dangerous to approach a house silently. Even today it is extremely bad manners. *Sa rogo na vakamata ena mata ni katuba e Vale Levu.* The greeting was called out in front of the door at the chief's house. The greeting may vary in different localities. A common greeting is *Dua, O!* A verbal response will invite the visitor to enter.

vakamatana adj. conspicuous, striking, stands out, as with striking colours on certain clothing.

matabani (Ang.) n. band, orchestra.

matabose n. council. *Matabose Levu Vakaturaga* Great Council of Chiefs. See *bose* v., n. to confer in a group, conference.

Matabose kei Vuravura n. United Nations.

Matabose ni Qele Maroroi n. Native Land Trust Board.

mata-ceba adj. squint-eyed, cross-eyed.

mata-dra n. shrub six to eight feet tall, leaves that have a white underside are used as tea. Leukosyke corymbulosa, Urticaceae. Syn. *dra ni gata*.

Matagi (Tonga & Samoa "strong wind") Name of a resort island off Taveuni.

mata iloilo n. spectacles, glasses, or person who wears them. *matailoilo ni nunu* diving goggles. *iloilo* originally referred to a reflected image, as from a pond.

matai adj. adroit, skilled. *matai na tuli kuro* skilled in making pottery. *matai na tara vale.* skilled at building houses.

matai n. boat-builder with carpentry skills. These often formed clans (*mataqali*) attached to Fijian tribes (*yavusa*), especially in coastal areas and the smaller islands of Lau and Cakaudrove. Most were of Tongan origin known as Mataisau, having that as a function, and even their clan name. The most significant boatbuilders were Samoans who came by way of Tonga, serving the Tui Nayau, and settled at Kabara island.

A iMatai n. First Batallion, Fiji Infantry Regiment, known for combat in Malaya against communist forces.

imatai first. First, as in some sport competition, or first student in class. See also *isevu*, the very first of an occurence, such as the fruiting of a tree, first fruits, or the first time something has ever happened. See also *ikadua*.

matailalai adj. detailed and fine (of a work done), done with attention to fine detail.

vakamatailailai n., v., adv. fine work, as in weaving very finely.

matailelevu adj. sloppy, coarse (as contrasted to *matailalai* fine, in reference to mat-weaving). *Kua ni matailelevutaka na nomu cakacaka.* Don't be sloppy in your work

matai-via-kanavuaka n. Idiom: person who talks big but cannot perform, not skilled or motivated. He undertakes work only for the pay. In earlier times, village workers building a house would be thanked with a feast, including pork (*vuaka*).

mata-i-va (Anglicism) n. steel digging fork, usually with four prongs.

mataivalu n. army. *mataivalu-i-wai* navy. *mataivalu curu lo* commando. *mataivalu cola dakai* infantry. *mataivalu-i-macawa* air force.

mataka 1. n. morning. *ena mataka cake* morning of tomorrow, morning of the next day. *ena mataka lailai* early morning. *mataka-caca* extremely early in the morning. *ena kida ni mataka* at the break of dawn. *vakamataka* early (that is, morning-time). *ena veimataka* every morning.

mataka 2. n. as in *ena mataka* (or) *ni mataka* tomorrow. *ena mataka ni mataka* tomorrow morning.

matakarawa 1. (Archaic) n. ceremonial presentation of goods, food, in appreciation for some kindness.

matakarawa 2. (Archaic) customary ceremony in western Viti Levu, presentation of plantain, coconuts at arrival of high chief, before the *qaloqalovi* ceremony.

matakarawa 3. n. edible univalve shellfish, cat's-eye, Turbo petholatus. Syn. (Kadavu) *la*.

matakau 1. (modernism) n. doll as a child's plaything.

matakau 2. n. carved human figure or wood or whale-tooth; traditionally a female fertility image of an ancestral spirit, always kept wrapped and hidden in barkcloth. All or virtually all were made by Polynesians in Fiji. Only a few carved figures still exist, including a couple of wooden ones in the Fiji Museum. The Museum also has a colour photo of another one that was for sale in the U.S.A., a photo donated by Ronald Gatty. There have been two carved of whaletooth called the Drua Tabua, or Radini Waimaro. One, sometimes referred to as the Tui Waimaro, remains at village Nadakuni, Waidina District, Colo East. The other, was retained by tribe Siko at village Taulevu (formerly village Vuniduba), Matailobau District, both being people of super-tribe Waimaro. The *matakau* at Taulevu was declared missing in 2006, after being photographed by a foreigner. The chiefly family around that time became considerably wealthy. One has to assume the *matakau* was sold away. Another *matakau* was named Nalilavatu, and kept by the Tui Sabeto. Ultimately, in 1876, it was given to Governor Arthur Gordon. Fijians themselves made no carvings of people, or any other natural images. Modernly, the word *matakau* now include carved images, such as Roman Catholic statuettes and the Hindu gods.

matakau ceuceu n. statue, carved bust or figure, referring to a modern representation. Fijians themselves did practically no carving besides making clubs and spears and some rather plain bowls, neck-rests, and oil dishes for priests. The carvers of wood or whaletooth in Fiji were generally Tongan, Samoan or Maori, and later, certain Fijians in Lau.

mataki n. official representative from one village or one Territory to another. *Mataki Burebesaga* local representative who receives visitors from Burebesaga and acts as a go-between in any communications. The people are said to be *veimataki*.

mata-ki-lagi (Archaic) n. staff borne by chiefs or elders, longer than a walking stick (*i titoko*). Being left by the entrance of a house would indicate the presence of that significant person.

mata-lala (Naitasiri) adj. n. "black face", an unkind insult, sometimes said jocularly. Syn. *mataloa* (or) *mataloaloa*.

matalevu 1. adj. wide-eyed with desire.

matalevu 2. adj. "bug-eyed", having large protruding eyeballs, an unkind reference to a distinctive feature of many Tongans of mature age. Syn. *mataboto* (Insulting) "face like a toad".

matalevu 3. n. an edible river fish, to three inches in length, with very large eyes.

mata loaloa 1. n. black race, literally "black face". Fijians sometimes insult other Fijians by calling them *mataloa*. Some Fijians are colour-conscious, a characteristic that long preceded the arrival of Europeans. Young urban women frequently use modern cosmetic creams to bleach their face to a lighter colour. Fair-skinned children are often favoured.

mata loaloa 2. n. black eye (injury).

mata malumu adj. sweet, gentle-faced, lovely, pretty (girl, woman).

matamata 1. n. gate, main entrance. Prior to Cession, all villages were fortified and fenced.

matamata 2. n. goal-posts (as in football).

matamata 3. (Slang) n. messenger.

matameke n. dance-group that performs a traditional exhibition type of dance *meke*.

mata-mocemoce n., adj. sleepy-faced, sleepy head.

matamosimosi n., adj. pretty-face, gorgeously beautiful, of a person. Syn. *matavutu*.

matana-levu adj. haughty.

mata-ni-cagi n. direction from which the wind is blowing.

mata-ni-cina (Anglicism) n. electric light bulb, light bulb for an electric torch.

mata-ni-civa n. pearl. Fiji has only black pearl, not gold-lip pearl. It is extremely rare to find any natural pearl of much value. Some pearls now cultivated in Fiji around Nasavusavu. Traditionally Fijians placed no value on pearls.
mata-ni-cula n. eye of the needle.
mata-ni-da (Insult) n., adj. face like human excrement. May refer to the rectum *icici* itself. One does not normally pronounce these words.
mata-ni-demu (Insult) n., adj. person with a face like a rectum.
mata-ni-fika n. (Lau) Idiom: idea (in the sense of intention).
mata-ni-vika n. digit(s) 0, 1, 2, 3, 4, 5, 6, 7, 8, or 9, of a number, numerals.
mata-ni-gasau n. ceremonial presentation of a formal apology, accompanied by the gift of *tabua* whaleteeth. Lit. presentation of a reed (*gasau*). Ro Lala Mara had such a presentation made at village Lomanikoro, Rewa, as an apology for her absence from the chiefly village while she retained a firm claim to the title of Roko Tui Dreketi. She lived away from the village and devoted little time to chiefly duties associated with the title. In fact, she had "married away" to Lau, which by custom should have released her from an attachment to her father's village in Rewa.
mata ni katuba n. door-face (outside surface of the door), as in *tukituki ena matanikatuba* knock at the outside of the door, a modern custom, to gain admittance. Formerly one would cry out a *tama* and there were no wooden doors and certainly no swinging doors of any kind.
mata-ni-sere (Anglicism) n. choir, chorus (of people).
matanisiga 1. n. sun.
matanisiga 2. adj. eastern (of a province or territory), as in *Tailevu matanisiga* eastern Tailevu. Also Tonga Matanisiga, referring to the Kingdom of Tonga, as distinct from places in Fiji that bear the name Toga.
mata-ni-sucu n. nipple. May refer to rubber nipples as well as part of the human body.
mata ni ta-kunea adj. Idiom, referring to a person, usually a child, who so relishes some food that he/she cleans up every scrap of food on a plate, licks the plate or spoon, or keeps the spoon in the mouth after eating. Can also refer to someone, not used to good things, who obtains something good, tries to show off with it.
matanitu n. Since Cession, at Cakobau's suggestion (according to A. B. Brewster) this word has taken the meaning of "state" or Government, now implying a nation such as Fiji. Previously *matanitu* referred to an extensive Fijian territory *vanua* that exacted tribute though it could not govern directly. Prior to Cession in 1874 a sequence of such extensive territories each endured not much longer than fifty years. Laucala was one of the earliest known such territories, then Verata, Lau, Cakaudrove and, of course, Bau. In their early creation, they depended on sea-power. For Bau, there was early acquisition of European mercenaries who had guns and could use them effectively. Historically, the concept of *matanitu* is fairly recent, within the last couple of hundred years.
mata-ni-uca n. rain-drop. *uca* rain.
matanivanua n. herald, protocol officer, who handles formalities for the chief, and is normally chosen from a clan *mataqali* that has that express function. He is a spokesman for the chief.
mata ni vola (Anglicism) n. letter (of the alphabet). *matanivola kala* italics. *matanivola levu* capital letter. *matanivola lailai* lower-case letter. Words all created by teachers of Fijian language who feel a necessity for such words in Fijian.
mata ni wai n. water well, spring, source of water, pond. Syn. *vure*.
matapule (Tonga) n. 1. In Tonga, a traditional social and kin-group who served the chief as heralds, protocol officers, and in some cases had specialised functions such as navigation. 2. In Fiji, there are clans bearing the name Matapule, descendants of matapule who migrated from Tonga. 3. title for head of clan Welitoa at village Dreketi, Taveuni.
mataqali 1. n. type, class, kind. *na veimataqali tamata* the various types of people. *na noda veimataqali kakana.* our (many of us) kinds of food. *na mataqali tei* the type or species of plantings.
mataqali 2. n. clan, more inclusive than the extended family (*itokatoka*, or in parts of the West *bito,* or in Lau, *bati ni lovo*) and less inclusive than the tribe (*yavusa*). Mataqali have a definite kin-group origin whereas the *yavusa* are often the result of political aggregation, only sometimes (as with super-tribe Nabukebuke in Namosi, or super-tribe Waimaro in the Viti Levu highlands) related by kinship. The distinction is often blurred in Fijian society. Historically, Native Land Commissioner Maxwell attempted to define and standardise these groupings for the purpose of assigning title to native lands. In fact, Fijians do not much use these terms in identifying the level of their own social group. In eastern coastal areas, *mataqali* usually serve definite roles and functions in the larger society of the village and the Territory. One *mataqali* may serve as chiefs (*mataqali vakaturaga*), another clan serve as elders

who empower the chiefs (*na sau*). Other functions are as protocol officers and emissaries (*matani-vanua*), warriors (*bati*), priests (*bete*), fishermen (*gonedau*), boat builders (*matai* or *mataisau*), commoners (*lewe-ni-vanua*). There are far fewer different functions in the highlands where the "men's house" (*bure*) was the basic social group and there were not necessarily any tribes (*yavusa*) as such, and no use of the word *mataqali* for clans. Highlander men of the *bure* all slept together, side by side, in that *bure*. Women and children slept in separate houses. Missionaries later required men to live with their wives and children.

One or more of the clans may be original settlers and landowners (*itaukei ni qele*) who then accepted later immigrants as chiefs, as warriors, or merely as dependents.. Fijians usually feel a closer attachment to their clan, rather than the tribe but they do not often differentiate these social divisions. When they say "We" (*Keitou*, referring to themselves, their own people) they are usually speaking of their clan. Clans by the same name exist in various parts of Fiji. They may not be functionally related any more, having split off some of their family groups who moved away due to internicine disputes or in a search for more land. Many clans have become extinct. Others have been functionally merged into larger clans though land records may record them as distinct.

mataqali 3. n. relationship of two regions where the people may refer to people of the other region as *Mata* or *Mataqali* and address them as such. Implied is a common origin. Today these relationships, formerly specific, have now become generalised between to whole provinces, for example Ra Province and Naitasiri Province.

mata qaseqase adj. cunning look.

mataqiriqiri n. band, orchestra.

mataqito n. team (sports). *qito* play. Syn. *timi*.

matareva adj. cross-eyed, eyes with a squint.

matasawa n. beach landing, shore.

mata sigogo adj., n. squint, squinting.

matataka v. to represent (as an ambassador represents a nation, or sportspeople represent their country).

mata tamata n. race (of humans). *veimata tamata* n. various races of mankind. *na idabedabe vakamata-tamata* communal (i.e. racial) seat, in political elections. This is in contrast to the "open" seats (open to any race) *idabedabe veicurumaki*.

matatea adj. unable to cope well, unfortunate, a failure, of a person.

mata vaka-soresore-ni-vuaka adj. extremely insulting term, usually referring to a white man, lit. with a face like a boar's testicles.

matata adj. clear (statement, question, attitude -- not a liquid or other object). *vakamatata-taka* v. to clarify (a matter).

matau 1. on the right-hand side. *ki matau* to the right. *ki mawi* to the left.

matau 2. adj. adroit, adept, experienced, capable, accustomed to something. *matau ena vosa* adept at speaking. *ena vanua e dau mamatau kina* in the place he is accustomed to be.

Idiom: *O sa matau tiko?* jocular, rhetorical question, You think you can carry that off? What makes you think you can do that?

matau 3. n. axe, a Polynesian or Proto-Polynesian development, only as specialised adzes, used mainly for boat-building. Viti Levu highlanders never had any form of axe, and no stone implements other than stone sinkers (*vatu-kata-i-lawa*) for river nets to catch the fish *ika loa* (Cestraeus pliatilis) as communal efforts. Metal axes came via Tonga, from Tongans and early European traders who were the source. In converting to Methodist Christianity, Fijians were often given a metal axe (and a piece of cloth for clothing) as an incentive.

Idiom: *e voleka na vanua e buli tiko kina na matau.* remote, very far away; lit. near where axes are made.

matau vatu n. stone-axe, today also an idiom for a person, old-fashioned, ignorant , "stone age"; Fijian youth use the term, referring to parents and elders who remain in the villages and do not adjust to modern times, modern values. Some of the earliest Fijian settlers of the highlands did not have stone-axes or any chisels. These so-called *kaiColo* were a pre-Stone Age, more Melanesian culture.

mata-va (Slang) n. person who wears glasses ("four eyes"), an unkind reference.

mata vasona (Insult) refers to a person as an asshole; lit. with a face like a rectum *sona*.

mataveilewai n. court of law. *Mataveilewai e Cake* High Court.

Mata-veitarogi-vanua (Anglicism) n. Native Lands Commission, which investigates matters of native land rights and chiefly titles. Its decisions are definitive and authoritatively binding though disputes over titles may be referred to a Tribunal. Necessarily, much of the formal investigations (*Veitarogi*

Vakavanua) is incomplete, contains errors and omissions, and has included a great deal of biased, self-interested testimony from only some of the relevant elders who were present at the hearings. Elders were asked to record and swear to their testimony of land ownership and history in what is referred to as the *iTukutuku Raraba* for each tribe or clan. Deliberations have been difficult and sometimes quite arbitrary in the face of conflicting versions of oral history, complexity of the issues involved, and limited time for deliberation. In some case the N.L.C. staff have not had the local knowledge to make proper determinations. In earlier times the power of the club was the main determinant of chiefly titles and land usage rights. Decisions of the Commission have sometimes become influenced by political considerations. Beyond summary Reports published during the colonial era, records are now closed, unavailable for study. Pandora's box awaits being open for study and criticism. At the present time, only elders of a specific social group may gain access to records of their own group. Because knowledgable elders are now long dead, there is really no hope for easy clarity. Part of the problem lies in the fact that Governor Gordon established the inflexible legal notion that all land had originally belonged to some Fijian social group which is very far from the actual fact. Fijian settlements moved about considerably and most of the land was a vast no-man's land, too dangerous to be habitable. Pressed to make a decision, Commissioner Maxwell defined the primary landholding unit to be the clan (*mataqali*) and that simplification has caused problems. Social divisions and the names for them differed considerably around Fiji but smaller family units would have been more appropriately listed as custodians of the land. There was no permanent ownership in the sense that Europeans understand, only usufruct, a right to use the land. It is a further complication in that many chiefs and elders considered that they alone had total control of the land, including the right to sell it, give it, or assign it to whomever they liked. It has been a fabrication to impose the notion that the land belonged to the people. Curiously also, the notion persists, even today, that native land is to remain native land, forever held in common. In fact the original Land Ordinance of 1880 stipulates that communal land rights would be "desirable until the native race be ripe for a division of such community rights among individuals . . ." Governor Arthur Gordon never intended that native land should remain forever communal property.

Mata-veitokani n. Methodist group of youngsters who plan some activities together. The purpose is religious and social, involving girls and boys.

matavulo n. mask for the face. Very anciently crude masks were occasionally made of vegetation, sticks and leaves, sometimes with added human hair, used by men in some ceremonial dances. Some served to conceal one's identity in combat.

matavura n. shore, place where boats approach and anchor. *na matavura kei Suva.* the shore of Suva.

matavutu n., adj. beauty, beautiful (usually referring to a woman's face). *vakamatavutu* adv. beautifully (in this sense).

mate n. death, sickness, disease. v. to die. *Sa mate o koya* He/she is dead. *mate ni veiyacovi* venereal disease. *mate ni suka* diabetes. *mate ni uto* heart disease. *mate ni vakasama* mental illness. *na mate na AIDS* the AIDS disease. *Siga ni Mate* Good Friday. *tauvimate* adj., n. sick, sickness. Sickness often meant death to early Fijians. They did not always draw a sharp distinction. People aged or very ill, no longer productive in society, were often left to die in a remote place, or buried alive. *Vale ni mate* hospital, more modernly called *Vale ni bula*. Syn. *bale* to die, of a chief. By ext., *mate* may mean exhausted, dead tired, finished, about to give up, as from great effort, usually work or even love-making when a person is sated. Syn. (Respectful) *toki yani*.

Idiom: *mate vakabalabala* to die without progeny. lit. die like a fern-tree (*balabala*). Fijians knew that a tree-fern has no seeds, and has no suckers for propagation. They did not know of propagation by spores.

Idiom: *Mate na toa, kena isau na bici.* The exchange is not equal., lit. the chicken is dead, (given away or stolen), and all that is given in return is a *bici* (small bird).

Idiom: *Sa mate vakadua!* He/she was completely won over, fell for it hook, line and sinker, did not stand a chance, had to give in completely.

Idiom: *Mate o vale dua ka bula ko vale rua.* said good naturedly to someone invited to join in eating a meal at someone else's house, who declines with natural politeness. The jocular implication is that one lives well who can eat at two different houses but might die of hunger if one eats only at one's own family house.

vakamate, vakamatea v. to cause death, to kill. *E rawa ni veivakamatei.* It is possible to die from it. *Au a tovolea meu vakamatei au.* I tried to kill myself. (Suicide has been traditionally very rare among Fijians.)

veivakamatei n., v. killing(s), manslaughter, to die from some deadly cause. *beitaki ena cala ni veivakamatei* accused of the the crime of manslaughter.

mateca v. to desire, lit. to be dying for (something desired, such as a food, some object, an experience). Usually it refers to a loved one that (figuratively) one would die for. *mateci koya* die for him/her. In the highlands of Waimaro this word becomes *matece*. On seeing a girl of his desire, a Fijian youth may pass his hand in a slice across his own neck; the girl will understand that he pretends he will kill himself if she does not yield to his affections. There are the usual accompanying smiles and laughter.

matedewa n. infectious disease (as a generality). *dewa* transfer.

matemate adj. sickly.

matemate n. weakness. *Au kila na nomu matemate.* I know your weaknesses (I know how to appeal to you.)

mateni 1. adj. drunk, inebriated (from alcohol, or excessive *yaqona*). The term is indigenous and formerly applied only to *yaqona*. (Formerly, Fijians had no alcohol and no other intoxicants.) *Yaqona* intoxication can occur only with considerable consumption of the beverage in fairly strong form. It affects physical coordination but not mental acuity. Some people become addicted to *yaqona* with resulting social irresponsibility and affliction of a skin condition called *kanikani*.

mateni 2. n. (Eng.) mutton. Low-grade, fatty mutton from New Zealand has been one of the common foods bought by urban Fijians.

matenikete n. stomach ache. Syn. *mosi ni kete*.

mateniulu n. headache. Syn. *mosi ni ulu*.

mate ni vula n. (of women) menstruation, monthly period. Formerly, women used moss or barkcloth as menstrual pads.

matetaka v. sick with infectious malady (flu, cold, viral infection etc.) *veitauvi ena matetaka.* afflicted with *matetaka*. Syn. (Lau, Rewa) *bacataka*.

mate vou adj. of fruit usually, dropped prematurely before ripe, unusable.

matewale adj. useless, futile effort, usually to arrange for something that does not happen.

mati n. low tide, tide that has ebbed. Used only in certain expressions: *Sa di na mati.* The tide is out. *mati donu* very low tide. *mati ruku* n. morning low tide. *mati yakavi* n. evening low tide. *Sa mati na vanua.* It is low tide. *Sa ua levu.* It is high tide. References to an incoming tide (*so na ua*) may imply a local craziness, a daffy mind, associated with some people of Nasavusavu District, Cakaudrove Province, villages Vivili, Wainivunia, but also Naidi and Savudrodro.. See *matiruku*, below.

matia n., adj. low water, shallow.

matiruku adj. crazy, mad (related to the tide being out). *ruku* underneath. Syn. *lialia*.

matosi adj. scratched, and thus damaged, of a thing (pot, glassware), a person or animal, such as a horse on barbed wire.

matu (or) **matumatu** n. a common small silver fish to ten inches by the shore caught on 5 lb line with 18-20 size hook with bait of *kasikasi* or prawn, Gerres macrosoma or G. oyena, Gerridae, Silver biddy. *matumatu* is a small form of this fish. *matu-sa* is larger, to 15 inches, around reef, or in lagoons at clear patches, caught by net, or or two at a time from small boat.

matua adj. mature, of fruit, crops, fully developed but not yet fully ripe. *Yalo matua* responsible, no longer childishly irresponsible. *gu-matua* earnest. *ulumatua* eldest child.

    Idiom (Vanua Levu): *Sa ma'ua na raisi.* No problem, nothing to worry about, everything is "set", lit. the rice (*raisi*) crop is mature (*ma'ua*) so there will be plenty of food.

matuavosa (Anglicism) n. script, lettering, alphabet. Both Fijian and English languages are written in Roman script, that is, using a version of Roman lettering. A different script would be Hindi script for the Hindi language. *matuavosa* is a word invented by schoolroom teachers.

mau v. to gamble, to contest, match up, to take a position (as in making a decision), to confirm: *Sa mau na nona lewa.* His/her decision is confirmed. *Sa mau na veivosaki* It was confirmed in discussion. Syn. *dei* (implying being fixed, firm.).

imau n. "pieces" of a game, such as cards, or domino pieces, or the "men" on a chessboard.

veimau v. to play some game (not an active, physical sport), such as cards, typically *tarabu* or *warotu*, versions of "trump", played with two or four people. *vota yalima* deal out five cards each. *esi* ace. *joka* or *tevoro* joker. *turaga* king. *marama* queen. *jeke* jack. *daimani* diamond. *kalavo* club. *siveti* spade. *yate* heart (*yate* is literally "liver", the centre of courage for Fijians.)

veimau-ilavo (Anglicism) n., v. to gamble for money. This is a formal, stilted expression. The notion is foreign but a major lottery has become established that attracts poor people with dreams, especially in urban areas.

vakamau (Tonga, "fakamau") n., v. formal and official marriage, to marry. The suffix *mau* might imply an affirmation in Fijian but the concept and this word were introduced from Tonga, where the word originally referred to some sort of inquiry and became adapted for this use in Christianity. In Fiji the older, more traditional word is *veitube*, and also *vakawati*. Anciently there were no great formal marriage ceremonies, though there might be a feast when a chief took an important woman into his household. Formerly, the main point was for the man to provide housing for the woman and the children she might then have. The word for this is *vaka-vale-taka*, to provide housing. Custom evolved to bring a whaletooth to request the woman, or after an elopement, to bring one in a ceremony of informing the woman's parents, and another, later, begging forgiveness *bulubulu*. Rejection of the suitor is indicated by the return of another whaletooth. Many arrangements today are informal, outside the authority of a church, and referred to as *vakawati*. *o rau na vakamau* the newlywed couple (formally married). *o rau na veiwatini* the husband and wife (formally married or just living together).

Idiom: *tiko vakaSuva* (or) *tiko vakaSamoa* living together, of man and woman, without a formal arrangement. Certain liberties are possible in the city that would not be allowed in the village.

maucokona adj. rich in the sense of being ample, meaningful, elaborate, as of a speech.

maumau adj. spoiled, wasted (as of food, fuel, or some work).

maumi refers to a hilltop that is dry, barren. Name of a village near Bau Island. People of Maumi were early settlers on Nayau Island, Lau Province.

mautubu v. to sulk, pout.

mauwe (or) **maue** adj. noisy, of a crowd.

ma-uvu adj., n. constipated, constipation, bloated, flatulence. See *guguraki*.

mavo adj., v. healed, to heal, of a cut, wound. *mavomavo dredre* difficult healing. *imavomavo* scar.

mavoa n., adj. injured, wounded (person), damaged (goods). *mamavoavoa* very badly injured. *vakamavoa-taka* to injure (someone).

mavolo (Eng.) n. marble(s). *veimavolo* n. boys' game of marbles. Two types: in one there is a circle marked on the ground, in the other, there is a central pit that is dug that is called a "pillow". *toa* n. large marble used for shooting; smallest marbes are referred to as *de ni me* (goat droppings, from their physical shape and size) or "kind one" while middle sized marbles are "kind two". *vana na mavolo* shoot the marble; this is done with a thumb on the ground, forefinger against the marble, flicking that forefinger with the other hand. (It is not done by holding the hand as a fist and flicking with the thumb as might be more common with European children.) While it is normal for the thumb to be on the ground ("clean down"), one may by announcing it in advance, shoot from the knee or stooping posture ("five-eighth", so called), or from a standing position (*tu cake*). Rules are to be followed strictly and violations may well lead to a scuffle.

mavota n. timber tree endemic to Fiji, only known on southern coast of Viti Levu, Gonystylus punctatus A.C. Smith, Gonystylaceae. Globose woody fruit, 5-8 cm diam., 3-4 segments with smooth seeds, white fls clustered at the end of branches, thick shiny, simple, alternate leaves.

mavu n. the pounded mash of cooked starch-foods (taro, breadfruit, cassava, plantain), used to make Fijian puddings (*vakalolo*). *waki, wakia na mavu* mix the *mavu* with a stick *iwaki*. *Sa wakiwaki na mavu* The *mavu* is sticky, gummy. *Sa tata-ciqiciqi na mavu* The *mavu* is lumpy. *mono, monoka na mavu* form balls of the *mavu*. *kini, kinita na mavu* pinch off the *mavu* into balls. The cultivated root-crop yam *uvi* is never used for Fijian puddings. In coastal areas and some small islands, *uvi* is the most noble of the "true foods" *kakana dina*.

mavu ni Toga n. poisonous plant, Antiaris toxicaria var. macrophylla, shrub or tree in lowland rain forest areas, the latex used for arrows but mostly for food poison, especially by priestly castes in coastal areas (such as Tailevu) where the tree was often to be found growing around temples and in villages in the 1860s, according to Seemann. This poison was introduced from Tonga though Tongans never used it on arrows. (And Tongans never used bows and arrows in war.) The more potent variety toxicaria of this species has been widely used as poison in Southeast Asia. In Fiji, a more common poison used by super-tribe Waimaro was the shrub *lobau*, formerly mixed with kava to be consumed unwittingly by the victim. It is an introduced plant related to Datura. It disables a man. He would then be killed with a club. The Fijian Dictionary Na iVolavosa VakaViti lists Macaranga vitiensis, Euphorbiaceae, as having the name *mavu ni Toga*; I have been unaware of that as a fact, and it is not so listed as such in A. C. Smith *Flora Vitiensis*. Nonetheless, it may be correct.

mawa v., n., adj. stink, off-flavour, spoiled (of food). Idiom: (Vulgar) *Gusu mawa!* stink mouth!

mawe-na n. tracks, trace, as of an animal, or human, as in footprint. Syn. *we ni yava-na*. May refer scars or residual effects of strong winds or even fire.

imawe ni liga n. (Anglicism) fingerprints. Syn. *we ni liga-na*.

mawi left, on the left-hand side. *ki mawi* to the left. As a n. may refer to a left-handed person, sometimes with the implication that they are different, doing things "opposite", in a different and sometimes difficult way. Left-handed people were regarded with suspicion, often avoided as somewhat dangerous. *e dua na imawi* in a fight, a "left", a left-handed punch.

Me (Eng.) n. May (month). *na vula o Me* the month of May.

me 1. preceding a pronoun (not "you"), *me* indicates a suggestion, polite request or implicit command: *Me daru lako.* Let's go (us two). *Meu lako?* Should I go?

me 2. indicates an obligation, something that should be done, something that should be. *Meu* (or *Me'u*) *lako.* I should go. *Na cava meu cakava?* What should I do? *Me vakasakei na Minisita* The Minister should be sacked. *O cei me toboka rawa?* Who can (should) catch him? *Tukuna vua me kana.* Tell him/her to eat. *Me rua ga.* Only two (in response to a question as to how many of something are needed or desired).

me 3. particle between an adjective and a verb. *dredre me cakava.* difficult to do..

me 4. before a noun, for the purpose of, to serve as. *Solia vei koya me kena.* Give it to him/her, as food to eat.

me 5. n. (Onomatopoeic) n. goat. There are wild goats on some islands such as Cikobia, in Lau Province. Kadavu is usually associated with goats, which are joked about.
Idiom: *luve ni me* lit. son of a goat, a derogatory but usually jocular way of addressing a person from Kadavu. Also *Me damu!* the *damu* implies brown or auburn colour, from heavy Tongan influence in Kadavu.

me-- prefix indicating a beverage to be consumed. The suffix serves as a possessive pronoun indicating who will consumer the beverage. The possessive pronoun may stand alone without naming the actual beverage, or the beverage may be named after the pronoun. For Fijians, beverages include fruits such as mango, melon, citrus, pineapple, and ice cream. (They often tend to suck fruits, rather than treat them as a solid food.)
mequ my beverage, for me to consume.
medaru our (two) beverage for us two to consume.
medatou our (three or so) beverage for us to consumer.
meda our (many) beverage for us to consume.
memu your beverage etc.
memudrau your (2) beverage etc.
memudou your (3 or so) beverage etc.
memuni your (many) beverage etc.
mena his/her beverage etc.
medrau their (2) beverage etc.
medratou their (3 or so) beverage etc.
medra their (many) beverage for them to consume.

me baleta 1. concerning, as in *me baleta na ivalu* concerning the war. *na lewa me baleti koya* the decision concerning him.

me baleta 2. for (the purpose of), concerning (a given subject, or person). *na misini me baleta na nomu cakacaka* the machine for your work.

me vaka according to, as: *Me vaka sa tukuni* . . . As has been foretold . . . *Me vaka na nodra vosa* According to their words . .

me vaka ni since, because (or) as, at the beginning of an expression: *Ia me vaka ni 80 pasede na levu ni iTaukei era lewe ni Lotu Wesele, sa cala me laveti na vakatatabu ni Siga Tabu.* Since 80 percent of the Fijians are members of the Wesley Church, it is wrong to lift the Sunday prohibition.

meba (Eng.) n. member (association, club, parliament).

meca 1. n. enemy. *Era sa veimecaki kei na kaiColo.* They are enemies of the highlanders. *Nodra meca na kaiColo.* Their (many) enemies are the highlanders.

meca 2. (Lau) thing, often heard in the Lauan idiom *Meca i a fika ga* The thing is to figure it out (and then do it), in other words Be smart! Syn. *ka.*

medra possessive pronoun, their (many persons, beverage) for them to drink.

medratou possessive pronoun, their (several, beverage) for them to drink.

medrau possessive pronoun, their (two persons, beverage) for them to drink.

medre 1. n. ulcerous sores in the mouth, or at the rectum.

medre 2. (or) **medremedre** v. to tangle, tangled (fishing line, story-line, vegetation in the bush), matted, uncombed (human hair); incoherent or confused of speech (as of a person drunk). *Sa medre na gusuna.* His/Her speech is incoherent. *medre vakalailai ena liga ni lawa* somewhat caught up in contra-

vening the law. (This word can often have figurative meaning.) *tamedre* badly tangled, usually inadvertently, as of string or rope.
vakamedro or **vakamemedro** v. to masturbate (of men). Syn. (Lau) *vakatamemeno* (or) *vakamemeno*.
mei possessive pronoun: of (person who will consume the beverage). *Taloca yani na yaqona mei tamaqu.* Pour my father's *yaqona* (for him to drink). In the case of foods (or something integral to the person) this would be *kei*. For other possessives (neither food nor drink), "of" is *nei*. *na vale nei tamaqu.* my father's house.
mei, mea v. to look after a baby or very young child, being responsible for its comfort and safety.
meimei n. baby-sitter, housegirl, nursemaid.
meke n. Fijian form of exhibition dancing, usually by men or by women, with movements that act out the formal words of song and chanting. They celebrate historic of legendary events, or act out indigenous activities, including household tasks or war-like posturing. Rhymes of *meke* are simple, little more than couplets, often with forced final syllables to match the rhyme. Geraghty reports the Lauan word for rhyme is *veikapakapa* but that would be unknown to almost all Fijians. *Meke* are composed, and the dancers trained, by a dance-master composer (*daunivucu*), who is greatly respected and rewarded for his services. Some words and verses of ancient *meke* are no longer understood. And virtually no one knows any longer the meaning of some of the physical movements or gestures of the dancers. The *meke* "belongs" to the people who commission it from the composer and others may not perform it without permission. *mata-ni-meke* dance team. *ibola ni meke* n. leader of the dance group. *bola na meke* v. to lead the dance. *qaqa ni meke* n. verse(s) of a *meke*. *meke i wau* war-club dance by men. *wesi* dance with spear and fan (Vanua Levu). *meke-iri* fan-dance of men. *meketaka* v. to dance it, to dance about it (an occasion memorialized in a *meke*). *vakamalolo* women's sitting *meke*. Other *meke* are the *lakalaka*, and *seasea*, of Tongan origin. The social dances, locally invented, Anglicised shuffle-dance *taralala* and modern dancing are not considered *meke*. Fijians never had social dances, only group exhibition dances, the *meke,* and the unique single dance to an evil spirit *meke vula*.
meke-vula n. dance usually by a lone person, privately at night in the moonlight, often naked, dancing to a devil as a form of witchcraft. This is a reasonably common occurrence. Such a person is serving a devil, a rather Faustian concept.
mekesini (Eng.) magazine.
melaca v. to sing, usually sweetly. Syn. *tagica*.
meleia (or) **maleya** (or) **malea** (Eng. "Malaya") n. Tilapia, a common small edible freshwater fish, Oreochromis mossambica, originally from Africa, introduced in 1949 at the Sigatoka Agricultural Station for food for pigs though now used as human food. Has spiny fins. Parents incubate eggs in their mouths. Commonly produced in fish ponds but has taken over most of Fiji's wetlands and penetrated all the major river basins. The *maleya* has displaced indigenous fish, including the gudgeon (*vo*) and many of the sensitive goby species.
vakamelea v. to criticize, find fault, mostly used in the idiom: *E sega ni dua na ka me vakamelei kina.* There is nothing at all to be criticised about it. In other words, it is perfect just as it is.
meleni (Eng.) n. watermelon, introduced species. One "drinks" a melon. It is talked of as a beverage, as is an orange, mango, pineapple and ice cream as well a medicinal pills.
meli (Eng.) n. mail, postal service. *curu yani ena meli* sent off in the mail. *daukaumeli* postman (they do not wear uniforms in Fiji). *kato ni meli* post-box. Sometimes used as an abbrev. for *melisitima* (ship bringing mail), as in *meli ni saravanua* (tourist ship) that now frequent the ports.
melisitima (Eng.) n. mailboat, steam ship, a rather archaic word.
melo 1. v. to over-cook, especially of root-crops left too long in the earth-oven (*lovo*). Syn. *buta mate,* lit. cooked to death.
melo 2. going fine, as in *Sa melo na soko.* The sailing is going smoothly. *Sa melo!* Everything is going along nicely!
melo 3. fine-sounding, of a high ringing tone, as of a soprano or, in fact, the ringing sound of a fine steel knife such as the English brand Trumpet, when it is struck with the knuckles.
meme-na n. crumb, tiny part. *meme ni kakana* tiny bit of food. *meme ni madrai* breadcrumb.
memela adj. sweet-sounding, mellifluous, dulcet, usually of a singing voice or choir. *domo memela* sweet-sounding voice.
memu your (singular, beverage). *na memu* your beverage (for you to consume). *na memu ti* your tea (for you to drink).
Idiom: *memu sici!* (Slang): teasing a youngster who is being punished.
Idiom: *memu loli!* (Slang): That's what you deserve! Teasing.
memudrau your (2, beverage) to drink.

memudou your (3 or so, beverage) to drink.
mena possessive pronoun, his/her/its (beverage) to drink.
menemene v. to behave childishly.
menuke adj. portly, corpulent, plump (of person).
Mereke (Eng.) America, U.S.A.
merelesita n. well known var. of cassava. Also a woman's name.
meremerea adj. strong, stout, of a person.
mesamesa n. special skill or aptitude of a person. *Na nona mesamesa na tuli kuro.* Her special skill is in making pots. Syn. (Slang) *loga ni tavioka; bila.*
metereni (Eng.) n. matron (as at a hospital or boarding school).
meteresi (Eng.) n. mattress.
metia n. (Eng.) n. major, as a military rank.
meto n. (Archaic) protuberance, as on a warclub
meu abbrev. of *me au* (followed by a verb), often seen as *me'u* ... Let me ... (or) I should ...
vakameyautaka v. to resolve, settle it (problem, dispute), to arbitrate. *veivakameyautaki* settlement (of differences, disagreements). Also spelled *vakameautaka*. *Dau-vakameautaki* n. Arbitrator.
mi (or) **mimi, mica** n., v. urine, to urinate. *mica na meteresi* urinate on the mattress. *mi moce* of a child, adults sometimes, to urinate during sleep. *micaka na dra* to have blood in the urine. *misuqa* n. urinary infection (or) in the case of men, difficulties urinating as a result of enlarged prostate gland. Cf. *suasua*, a more polite word.
micini n. meat accompaniment eaten with "true food" *kakana dina* (traditional starch food, taro, yam, etc.) Syn. *icoi*, though *icoi* can apply to almost any garnish that accompanies the main thing consumed. (Could be biscuits with tea). In Lau the term is *tokai*.
midi adj. small, as in *e dua na gone midi* a small child. *midimidi* tiny. This is sometimes pronounced *minjiminji*. *manumanu midimidi* n. germ(s), tiny insect(s), virus.
midra adj. rotten, decomposed.
midre (or) **midri** as in *wa midre*, a vine used in building fish-fences, Stenochloena palustris, Blechnaceae. Immersed in water, the vine becomes stronger, used to bind straight, old vertically set reeds as a wall for the fence. Village Daku at the Tailevu coast is known for such fences, called *ba kalou* which they use seasonally to catch the yellow-striped goatfish *ki*.
mila v. to scratch with the fingernails to ease an itch. *Kerekere, me mila na dakuqu* Please scratch my back. *kadru, kadruva* v. to scratch, doing harm, by a person being aggressive, or by something sharp such as barbed wire or a cat with its claws.
mila (or) **milamila** v., n., adj. itch, itchy.
milamila (Slang) v., n. As in English, longing urgently for some thing desired, as for a person of the opposite sex, "itching" for something or someone.
imilamila n. (Archaic) head scratcher, long and thin, often kept stuck in the hair of men especially. It was used to dislodge lice or nits when they irritated the scalp. They were usually made of tree fern, turtle shell, or sometimes, a sliver of human shin bone.
mileniemu n. (Eng.) millenium.
mimimata n. stick insect or leaf insect that reportedly ejects poison that can blind the eyes of a person. Implied in the word is the action of pissing (*mimi*) in the face (*mata*). Three species of stick insects in Fiji, Hermarchus spp. The "leaf insects" in Fiji are of family Phylidae. Rarely every seen. They remain immobile, camouflaged as natural vegetation. Watling mentions the species Cotylosoma dipneusitcum.
mimisi v., n. nibble, of a fish starting to take a bait.
mina n. spleen.
mini, minika v. to pinch off with the fingernails, as one may pick off leaves from a plant, vegetables such as *rourou, bele* or medicinal plants.
minimini as in *vosa minimini*, to form words with the lips, barely pronouncing them.
Minisita (Eng.) n. Government Minisiter. One does not hear the third "i", though Fijian spelling requires the separation of these consonants.
miniti (Eng.) n. minute (of time).
mino 1. (Kadavu) no. Syn. *sega, warai, jikai, hikai*.
mino 2. adj. terrified, in a panic of fear.
miqa (Archaic) n. old-style fireplace for cooking in a corner of Fijian house, made obsolete by British regulations for separate cook-houses because of danger of fire. Before motorised boats become com-

mon, cutters sailing among the islands had *miqa* made of 44 gallon drums cut in half for wood fires to do the cooking.

mira (or) **miramira, mirica, mirika** v. of very small things, seeds, leaves, dust particles, to fall gently in a scattered fashion. See *miri, mirica*.

mira adj. faded, withered, usually of flowers.

mira, miraca, miraka v. to sprinkle (of pepper or salt, for example, though salt was never spinkled formerly, and pepper was unknown), sow (seeds, again a modern practise), to scatter (powder, fine grain). Also *vakamira, vakamiraca*.

"mirchaa" (Hindi) n. chilli pepper, originally a Central American plant, introduced by Europeans and/or Indians, now very widely used by Fijians. Often pronounced as a Fijian word *mirija*. Syn. *boro gaga, rokete*. A related Hindi word is *golmirch* black pepper which is the "true" pepper, Piper nigrum, grown commercially at Wainadoi, Namosi. Chilli pepper has no scent but is much cheaper than black pepper which was the original "hot" ingredient of curry.

Idiom: *tamata mirija* hurtful person, one whose words are biting, deceptive.

miri, mirica, mirika v. to fall off or out, of many very small things (flowers from stem, fur from animal, hair from human head, light sprinkle of rain). *Sa miri tu na uluna.* His/her hair has fallen out. *Sa miri tiko na vuti ni koli.* The dog is shedding its coat. *na mirimiri* the shedding of hairs or drizzling of rain. *mirika* to fall on (something, someone). As compared to *mira, miraca,* the word *miri* applies more generally to drip or drizzle, as of light rain

mirimiri v., n. to drizzle, usually of rain.

misi (Slang) v. smack (with the hand). *Sa misi nikua o Mere vei na qasenivuli.* Mere got smacked by the teacher today. *Sa misi!* That hurt!

misi (Eng. "miss") to feel pain, regret, at something unpleasant, something lost. *Sa misi o Seru ena sau ni ivodovodo ni basi.* Seru is upset at the cost of the bus-fare.

misila (Eng.) measles, a highly infection disease that can be transmitted without direct contact even before the rash appears. Symptoms are acute fever and rash and may be fatal. Ideally, babies should be vaccinated after they become one year old. The disease was introduced by Cakobau's party when it returned from a visit to Australia. In January 1875, a meeting with highland chiefs at Navuso was held to explain the colonial order and encourage their cooperation. Cakobau's own sons unintentionally spread the infection that killed off most of those highland chiefs. Though inadvertant, this devastating infection broke the spirit of the feisty highlanders. *misila ni jamani* German measles.

misimisi 1. n. shrub, Ximenia americana, Olacaceae, known best for its highly scented, oblong, reddish or orange-coloured fruit, used for floral necklaces in season, and to scent oil as a perfume. The ripe fruit happens to be edible and is eaten by pigeons, and the wood was formerly used for making Fijian neck-rests *kali* (according to J. Parham). I have noticed flower buds forming in September. The thin bark is a conspicuous pinkish tan colour, the tender leaves pinnate. A few quite different Fijian plants are known as *misimisi*.

misimisi 2. n. plant commonly growing in coastal swampy areas, leaves used as sturdy, durable thatch material. The material is hard to handle due to strips of tiny thorns on the edges of the long leaves. Hypolytrum nemorum, Cyperaceae.

misimisi 2. n. epiphytic plant of the high hills, noticed by Seemann as a useful, natural source of drinking water, from the rain. Collospermum montanum, Liliaceae.

misini (or) **masini** (Eng.) n. machine. *misini ni cula* sewing machine. *misini butu* sewing machine with foot-pedal power. *misini ni ilovi* x-ray machine (a rather artificial word).

misinare (Eng.) n. missionary. Syn. *dau kaulotu*.

vakamisinari (Eng.) n. collection of money for the Methodist church, to support church officials, such as ministers (*italatala*) and wardens (*ivakatawa*). Names are called out, announcing the amount given by each person.

misuqa (or) **micuqa** v. to have difficulty of urination, a frequent problem with age.

miti 1. n. (Polyn.) n. liquid condiment, sauce for fish or yams, made of lemon juice, salt water, squeezed grated coconut, and usually, chopped onion and chilli, many minor variations, always made at home, not a commercial product. To some coastal Fijians *miti* is an essential condiment for seafood.

miti 2. n. terrestrial fern, sold in Suva market, succulent stems and bundles of young shoots barely formed. The colour tends to be brown, especially when cooked.

"mix"-taka (Eng.) v. to mix.

mo n., v. mumps, swollen glands of the throat. *O koya e mo.* He/she has mumps. *E tauvi koya na mo.* He/she has a case of mumps.

mo particle implying "should" or "must" referring to some action by "you" (one or many). *Na cava mo cakava.* What you should do. *Mo dou cakava vakatotolo.* You (several) should do it quickly. For another form of imperative, not referring to any specific number of people, is given by the word *me*. That implies one should let something happen, or make that something happen. *Me moku!* Club (kill) him/her/them!

Idiom: *Mo ni kila* . . . Public Notice, i.e., Be it known to you (many) that . . .

moce, mocera 1. v., n. sleep. *mocera na ibe* sleep on the mat. *moce lutu* fast asleep, sleep soundly, or sleep in late. *moce-i-ca* (or) *moce vakaca* sleep poorly, badly. *vuanikau ni moce* sleeping pills. *moce-yadrayadra* v. to be half-asleep (often from worry, concerns on the mind). *ulumoce* or *mocemoce* n., adj. sleepy-head. *moce vata* v. sleep together, usually with sexual involvement. *imocemoce* n. bed, place to sleep. Syn. (Tonga) *mohe*.

Idiom: *kana moce* just eat and fall asleep immediately, which may imply a
life of leisure, depending on context. It can also be the result of a very hard day of work.

Idiom: *moce vakaura* : pretend to be asleep, lit. sleep like a prawn (*ura*) which may be very still, and suddenly move with alacrity.

Idiom: *moce vakasiga* sleep in the day-time.

Idiom: *moce i dravu na koli* there is no food in the house, lit. the dog can
sleep in the fireplace because there is no food to cook.

moce! 2. farewell!, good-bye!, good night! *Sa moce* (or, more respectfully) *Ni moce!* Good-bye (or) Good night. *Ni moce toka mada* Good night (good-bye) for now. *Drau moce* good bye (or good night) you two.

vakamoce n., v. farewell, to farewell.

vakamoce, vakamocera v. to put to sleep, put to bed (as a child).

veimoce, veimocera v. to sleep with (sometime person of opposite sex). *na nodrau veimoceri kei na dua na goneyalewa* his sleeping with a girl. *e rau veimoceri vata* they (two) slept together. (*moce vata* would be the more normal expression.) May refer simply to several or many people sleeping next to each other on the floor, as sometimes occurs when there are visitors.

mocelolo n. tree, 5 to 20 meters tall, Dendrocnide vitiense, Urticeae, fragrant flowers honoured in romantic songs. Flowers November to April, fruiting February to March. Closely related to the noxious *salato* D. harveyi which has stinging hairs on flowers and leaves, and irritating sap that becomes more irritating if washed in water. Idiom: *mocelolo* (Lau): go to sleep without having dinner or sex.

mocemata v. to nod off to sleep, usually while seated.

imocemoce n. bed. Syn. *loga* (in a traditional Fijian house).

moci n. tiny edible prawn, Palaemon concimus., P. debilis, or Macrobrachium sp., a specialty of the river deltas such as Rewa. Great skill is needed to shell the tiny prawns. Some Fijians catch them with a fast sweeping motion of the hand, throwing them onto the riverbank. This is said to be the aquatic symbol of a few clans but it may be rather an iconic animal. *mumukasi-taka na moci* to remove head and shell of *moci* by squeezing between the fingers. Syn. *ura-ura*.

modro, modrolaka v. to throttle, wring the neck, especially to kill a chicken. By extension, to bully, mistreat by harsh domination (people, animals). By further extension, in slang, for an older person to have a sexual/romantic relationship with a much younger person of opposite sex.

modri n., adj. lacking pubic hair, of a girl or boy, being young. While this is a "proper" word, it may be used facetiously, even meanly, to imply immature, childish behaviour. *Sa modrimodri na nodra wede.* It is childish, the (many) girls showing off (to the opposite sex). Syn. *drolua*. By ext., *ulu modri* bald head.

moi, moica v. to turn with a twisting motion, person in a dance, model on a catwalk, person wanting to show a scar on their back, key in a lock, pencil in a pencil-sharpener.

imoimoi n. style, clarity and precision of dance movements especially, best with a snapping turn, clean sharp movements, not sloppy. May also apply to a person's behaviour, attitude when it is clear, clean and snappy sharp, alert.

moimalua adj. slow of movement. *moitotolo* quick, smart in movement, often referring to dance movements.

moka n. stone enclosure put together as part of a fish trap at a stony coast. At low tide the fish may be collected from this part of the fish fence. *tuva moka* set up stone fish-fence. There is a *moka ni gata* stone enclosure for snakes (used previously for food) at village Noikorokoro, Kadavu.

Idiom: *qalova uaua na moka* to be obstreperous, of children. lit. to swim at high tide, harvesting from the stone fish-fence. Usually said of a child who tries inappropriately to act like an adult, or to anyone who tries to do something prematurely, such as harvesting a crop not yet fully mature. Harvesting the *moka* should wait till the tide is receding.

mokimokiti (or) **momokiti** adj. round, rounded.

mokiti-taka (Eng.) v. to mortgage.

moko n. gecko. There are a few species. Inside houses one finds the indigenous Mourning Gecko and the larger, vocal House Gecko. They are harmless, even helpful in killing insects, but their excrement is visible. Their round white eggs, in pairs, may be found in secluded nooks. They take on the colour of the background. (I have tested this on a Scottish tartan!) The word *vokai* is commonly used for the larger Polynesian Gecko and much larger Forest Gecko (to 12 inches) that live in trees. These larger *vokai* are roasted over a fire and eaten, especially by highlanders of Viti Levu.

moko, mokota v. to hug. *mokolaka* to hug very hard, grip a person tightly with arms around them. *vei-mokomoko* hugging.

Idiom: *moko kabi* clinging, of a child.

ivakamoko n. brassiere, a garment now very widely adopted. The implication is of a garment that hugs the body. Syn. *taganisucu*.

mokomoko 1. adj., adv. hugging, as in *danisi mokomoko* cheek-to-cheek dancing in close, gripping contact.

mokomoko 2. (Medical) pneumonia.

mokosoi n. fragrant-flowered tree, the Malaysian ylang-ylang, Cananga odorata, Annonaceae, traditionally used in floral necklaces, and personal adornment in the hair, flowers year-round but most heavily in January-February, origin in S.E. Asia and western Pacific, an aboriginal introduction to the central and eastern Pacific. Most fragrant in the morning. Reproduced by seed only, much loved by large parrots. Macassar oil is made of the floral scent in an oil base. Syn. *makosoi, makohoi,* (Labasa) *masoi*. (Tonga) *mohokoi;* (Samoa) *moso'oi;* (French Polynesia *moto'i*. Horizontal branches help identify the tree from afar, and the year-round flowers are quite distinctive, six unequal linear petals, yellow-green, with 3 sepals. Frts obovoid, 3 cm in diam, black at maturity hanging in clusters.

moku, mokuta, mokulaka v. to strike, hit, kill (traditionally, usually with a club). The word is sometimes used humorously for someone who should be punished. *Me moku* Kill him! lit. have him killed. Syn. (Nadro) *hakwa*.

Idiom: *Hakwa!* Kill! war cry challenge of Nadroga people, often heard at sports events, especially football which is a passion with those people. Syn. (Lau, Kadavu) *motu*)

imoku n. violent blow (club, broken bottle, fist).

moku siga Idiom: waste time, pass the time of day, laze about. Lit., to strike a blow at the day, a futile pastime.

molau tagane n. "Male *molau*", small tree to 8 m., Glochidion vitiense, Euphorbiaceae, hairy, rounded leaves with blunt apex, whitish grey on underside, with reddish stem covered in fine hair. Syn. (West) *qalo*.

Idiom: *qase molau* n. man who is no longer young but acts as if younger than his years, particularly in relation to women, an expression used in humour. The *molau* tree has young-looking heartwood though the outside wood and bark look aged.

molau yalewa n. "Female *molau*", small tree to 15 m., Glochidion seemanii, Euphorbiaceae, endemic to Fiji, distinguished by fine-pointed, spirally arranged leaves that distinguish it from *molau tagane*. Slash is red covering white to pinkish wood, while *tagane* slash is light brown with cream-coloured wood.

moli thanking, now used mostly as part of a ceremonial exchange. When a person sneezes -- a previously socially undesirable act that formerly deserved death if in the presence of high-ranking person -- a senior person these days says *Bula!* (Live!). The appropriate response is *Moli!* as a remark of polite gratitude. This exchange may be repeated a couple of times. If the sneezing continues, the host may jocularly respond to the sneeze with *Mate!* (Kill him!)

vakamolimoli v., n. (Lau) to thank, to express thanks, Bauan *vakavinavinaka*.

moli n. citrus. Syn. (Namosi) *soco*.

molijamu n. a sour orange, suited best for jam. Citrus aurantium. Botanist Seemann suggested this as indigenous, but more likely a very early introduction. Origin is Southeast Asia.

moli karo or **moli karokaro** n. very widespread bush lemon, with bumpy skin (which gives it its name), now used as hardy rootstock for grafting commercial citrus though shoots of that rootstock must be cut back regularly or it will over-power what has been grafted to it. In the highlands, the leaves are burned on wood coals to smoke mosquitos out of houses, then doors are closed and the fire discarded. Many Fijians use lemon leaves *drau ni moli* as a substitute for tea, especially when they have no money to buy tea. Citrus limon. Flowers and fruits February through April, perhaps May. It is vaguely possible (but not likely) that lemons were an aboriginal introduction; the species is indigenous to Southeast Asia. Lemons (and the Tahiti sweet orange) were introduced in 1832 by Vanderford as mentioned by John Parham. Vanderford was an American officer on the brig Niagara, out of Salem, (later a pilot on the Wilkes expedition of 1840), according to W. Lawry in his book *Visit to the Friendly and Feejee Islands*, 1850, as mentioned by R. A. Derrick in this *A History of Fiji*. Also known as *moli karokaro* is the introduced citron, C. medica, with a rough skin, as indicated by the Fijian name. This citron is a small fruit two to four inches in diameter, with a very sour pulp that tends to have a greenish colour.

moli taiti (or) **moli dawa** (or) **moli sere** n. Tahiti orange, a sweet orange, C. sinensis.

moli kana n. shaddock, pomelo, Citrus maxima (= C. grandis), Rutaceae, semi-cultivated around old settlement sites, two types, one with very large fruit, white flesh, (almost certainly an aboriginal introduction) and the other with grapefruit-sized fruit and pinkish flesh. The pith around the fruit is a quite bitter, and absolutely all of the skin and fibre around the segments should be completely removed before eating. Fijians used to peel the large fruit, keeping it whole, and pass a twine through the centre, hanging it over a fireplace for a few days. This facilitates removing the skin, and may sweeten the fruit. Fijians used juice from the leaves to treat external infections and indeed, the plant has been found to have anti-microbial properties. The grapefruit, C. x paradisi, is apparently a hybrid between the shaddock and C. sinensis, the sweet orange, grown privately in Fiji but not commonly planted or used by Fijians, and having no particular Fijian name. John Parham mentions it is very vulnerable to Citrus canker.

moli kini n. kumquat, introduced, Fortunella japonica with round fruit, and F. margarita with the fruit more oval. F. japonica is commonly grown.

moli laimi n. lime, C. aurantifolia, introduced 1823. Origin Malesia.

moli ni Batiri n. Valencia-type juice-orange grown commercially at Batiri, Vanua Levu. This has been a government project with a troubled history of mismanagement. The Valencia orange is sweetest in dry areas, but rather sour in the wet zone. C. sinensis.

moli maderini (Eng.) mandarin, well liked by Fijians. C. reticulata.

moli kurukuru n. inedible, C. macroptera, size of an orange, fruit and leaves can form a froth, sometimes used by Fijians in washing their hair. The fruit, rather hard, formerly used as a ball in traditional Fijian games.

veimoli (Archaic) n. young man's game, two opposing lines of men throwing oranges at individuals on the other side. When hit, a man is "out". By contrast, *vaqiqimoli* was a match-making game with a line of girls on one side and young men on the other. They rolled oranges on the ground, aiming toward the desired potential partner. Modernly, young Fijians choose other means of finding partners.

Momani (Eng.) Mormon. *Na Lotu Momani* The Church of Latter Day Saints. They are very active in Fiji and in Tonga, proselytising with youths from the U.S.A. Scholarships are offered to some converts. There is a major temple in Suva, closed to all but members of that church.

momo n. mother's brother. *noqu momo* my maternal uncle. Such an uncle has serious obligations to the niece or nephew who is said to be "*vasu*" to him, and make demands of him. The mother's village has such obligations in the case of chiefly status. These days the relationship tends to be reversed as villages ask for contributions from their *vasu*. A person should treat the *momo* with respect and a degree of reserve. The importance of the mother's village stems possibly from earlier, matrilineal Melanesian society such as still exists in Macuata. See *gadi-na*.

momo (West) daddy.

Momo n. title of chiefly position in western Viti Levu, such as Ba Province. The implication is that of a chief having been an elder, a fatherly figure, not an aristocratic, authoritarian chief as in Polynesia.

momona 1. adj. full, rich in significance, usually said of someone's speech at a formal occasion.

momona 2. adj. full, rich in flesh, of crabs, prawns, crayfish, usually October through December.

momo i valu adj. valliant in war.

momoqaqa adj. valliant, strong and victorious.

momoto adj. sharp, pointed. See *moto* spear.

vaka-momoto-taka v. to sharpen a pointed object such as a spear (*moto*).

mona n. brain. *na noqu mona* my brain. The brain was never considered a specially important feature of personality, intelligence, or body function. It was eaten by cannibals. *mona-taka* v. to think up a plan, project. This is a modernism, as is *mona livaliva* n. computer, though a Fijian is more likely simply to say the English word "computer" with Fijian pronounciation.

Idiom: *Vesu mona!* exclamatory humorous rejoinder in response to someone's excessive flattery or gripping story that has the listeners entranced. Implication is that you are being taken over and will be under their control. *vesu* – bound up, in the sense of being tied up.

Moniti (Eng.) n. Monday. Syn. (Lau, Kadavu, Nadro) *Monite*.

moqe, moqeta, moqetaka v. to writhe, struggle, twist and turn one's body forcefully, as in trying to escape, or as men might do in a forceful exhibition dance (*meke*), or as a person might do in great pain. *moqeta na dali* struggle against the rope. By ext., to make a big effort, as in meeting some deadline.

moqimoqili adj. round (shape), circular, spherical.

Morisi n, informal name for Morris Hedstrom Ltd., department store and supermarket chain, now part of the Carpenters group, owned by overseas Asians and now marketing many Asian products.

Moro name of an ancestral male spirit-god known for licentious and incestuous behaviour, especially on Kadavu and Beqa. *Moro Loa* is a particularly dangerous form of this spirit. He is thought to be active still today taking advantage of women. There is similarity and perhaps connectiveness with the legendary spirit Daucina.

moro 1. n. smelly slime of uncircumsized penis or women's genitals. A word not normally to be pronounced.

moro 2. n. sperm. Syn. *wai*, in context. (*wai* has several meanings.)
Idiom: (Vulgar) *moro kabi!* usually said by a woman to a man or of a man, implying he is disgusting, and has sticky sperm. Expression used for a man who lacks really warm, compassionate and intimate feelings.

mosa v. to finish off, beat up totally.

mosi (Western Colo) fertile, precious, as in *qele mosi*, especially treasured soil in Navosa highlands and also Namosi. This reference to a kind of land that gives rise to the name of Namosi Province. At Nokoro, pottery made (from a very early Tongan influence), using this soil, by custom may not be sold because the soil is precious and is to be honoured. *Era vakatoka na qele oqo me qele mosi.* They (many) refer to this soil as "*qele mosi*" (at village Nakoro, Navosa).

mosi, mosita v. to hurt, be painful. *Sa mosi na uluqu* I have a headache. *na mosi ni ulu* the headache. *mosi ni kete* stomache ache. *Kua ni mositi au.* Do not hurt my feelings. Jocularly, *mosi* may refer to the pain of forlorn love.

mosimosi adj., n. hurt, painfulness, hurtful, physical pain but also said of a person who uses caustic words that hurt.

mosita (Lau) n. type of Fiji cabbage, green vegetable, mustard cabbage with flowers, Brassica juncea, of Chinese origin, sold in the Suva market.

mosoi, mosoya v. to do something with haste that may be impetuous, in sudden action, such as resuscitating a drowning person, bringing clothes in before the rain, or of bats crowding around a fruit, pecking at it impetuously.

mosoni (Eng.) n. motion (in committee, parliament). *vakatura na mosoni* propose the motion.

motopai (or) **motovai** n. (Eng.) n. motorbike.

moto n. spear (for human combat, not usually for spear-fishing). *moto mataidua* single-pronged spear. *momoto* adj. sharp, pointed, having a point (pencil sharpened, spear). As weapons, some spears were made of Balaka palm, some of woody bamboo. That carving, as with clubs, was often elaborate.

motoka (Eng.) n. motor car. *motoka redetaki* rental car. *draivataka na motoka* drive the car. *vodo ena motoka* get in the car. *kelea na motoka* park the car.

moumouta adj. round in cross-section, cylindrical as with a pole, post, spear or tree trunk.

mua v. to head for (place, direction) in travelling. *muadonu* v. to head in the right direction. *muacala* v. to head in the wrong direction. *Sa mua ivei o Viti?* Where is Fiji headed?

vakamua v. to steer (usually a boat), take the helm.

mua-na n. end (as of a boat, or piece of land, a rope, a week, month). *ena mua ni macawa.* at the weekend. *ena mua ni vula* at the end of the month. *ena muaimuri* at the back end, such as the boot of a car, stern of a boat.

mua i cake n. the end of the land that faces the prevailing southeasterly wind, the front-end.

mua i ra n. the end of the land that faces away from the prevailing southeasterly wind, thus the western point. With a capital first letter this can be a place-name or name of a clan. *Muaira kei Viti Levu* the western side of Viti Levu (formal expression).

mucu adj. blunt (of a blade, knife, axe, etc.) *gata* sharp, of a blade (not a spear).

mudre adj., v., n. gentle, cooling, of a breeze. *cagi mudre ni wasawasa* gentle sea breeze.

mudrimudri adj. completely bald.

mudrau n. a form of respectful address for certain related people. It has not been respectful at any time to address a person by their name, though custom is changing. This is abbrev. of *kemudrau*.

mudu, muduka v. to end, cut short. *E a muduki vakasauri.* It was suddenly ended. *tawa mudu* without end, forever. *Me sa mudu na ivalu.* The war should be ended.
Idiom: *mudu ka vosa* incessant talker.

muduọ (or) **a muduọ** n., v. ancient, traditional exclamation of acceptance, thanks, appreciation, usually used only in formal ceremony, often repeated consecutively, accompanied by resonant clapping *cobo*, hands at 90 degrees to one another, at the end of the acknowledgment. Syn. (West) *rewa*.

vakamuduo adj., v. formally thankful, grateful, to give formal, ceremonial thanks.

mule (Samoa) n. buttocks, bum, rump (person's backside). See *mu-na*.

mulo, muloca v. to twist, spin. *muloca na dali* to twist the rope.

mulo (ni kete) n. stomach pain, indigestion.

mulomulo n. seaside tree, Thespesia populnea, Malvaceae, the fruits used by children as toy tops to spin by hand, hence the name. Wood is durable under water, formerly used for outriggers but also axe handles. Flowers hibiscus-like, light yellow with maroon centre, all year round. Widely known in the West Indies as the Bendy tree or umbrella tree, the seeds used there as a dye. No such use in known in Fiji. Syn. *wiriwiri*, which is also a name of the introduced Physic nut.

muloni swirled.

mu-na n. buttocks, rump, backside, bum (U.K.), ass (U.S.A.) of a person. *vaka-na-mu̱* v. to turn one's buttocks in someone's direction. This can be a gesture of disrespect, but also applies to exposing the bottom for a nurse's injection. Syn. (Colo East) *buli-na*.

mumu n. old, traditional var. of taro, moderately sized, yellowish flesh, delicious taste.

mumu (Hawaii) n. long frock that covers the woman's body from neck to ankles, imposed by missionaries in Hawaii, then adopted elsewhere, as in Fiji.

munemuneke adj. plump, fat, of people, plantains, bananas.

munu, munuka, munulaka v. to squeeze off, or pinch off with the fingers, pieces of something like clay for pots, to work it and mix in sand, or squeeze off with the hand a piece of pounded, uncooked rootcrop (*taro* etc) to work it or shape it, to pinch off the shell of tiny prawns (*moci*).

muri 1. behind, as in *e muri* (located behind, in the rear) *ki muri* backwards, *mai muri* (from behind). *i muri tale* further behind, further to the rear.
Idiom: *liu-muri* to deceive, deceiver, deceiving, lit. "to lead from behind", a very common expression in Fiji.

muri 2. *mai muri* can refer to a future time, as in *ena gauna mai muri* in future, in later times. *ena gauna e liu* in former times. *ena macawa mai muri* next week (not this current week).

muri, muria v. to follow. *soko vakamuria na baravi* to sail following the coast. *O sa liu, au na qai muri yani.* You go ahead; I will follow. *cemuria to* chase, run after. *murimuri yalewa* skirt-chaser. *murimuri tagane* woman who pursues men. *murimuri* especially bad. Taking the cue from English usage, *muri, muria* can also refer to following instructions or advice.

muria mai v. to follow as a result. *Na leqa e rawa ni muria mai na matenisuka.* Problems may result from diabetes.

veimuri n., v. to imitate, follow in the way of another's behaviour, imitation (of a person by another). *dau veimurimuri* weak-willed, imitative, unthinkingly following others like a sheep. Meaning of *veimuri* may simply be to follow behind someone or some people.

muriloma-na adj. self-willed, insensitive to others' wishes or advice.

vakatotomuria 1. v. to follow, as fans follow news of their idol, or football enthusiasts follow the activities of their favourite team.

vakatotomuria 2. v. to mime, as children might do, in acting out some biblical stories.

musa adj. virtually inedible, waxy and tasteless, somewhat hard with slippery surface, usually of taro corm, due to improper cooking, or cutting of leaves as a vegetable before the plant is fully mature. It is sometimes hard to know how this condition comes about. Cassava may be *musa*, as when cooked it becomes hard, waxy, like a candle, not really edible.

musu, musuka, musulaka 1. v. to cut (across) usually something long, a tree-branch, stem of a plant, piece of meat, loaf of bread, fishing bait). Can refer to a monetary deduction (sales price, wages). *musurua* v. to cut in two.

musu, musuka 2. v. to cut cleanly, body movements in an exhibition dance (*meke*). *musu donu* good clean dance movements.

musudomo v., n. as a jocular gesture, a young man might with his hand make the gesture of slitting his own throat, implying he will kill himself if the women witnessing this will refuse him. *musu* v. to cut. *domo* n. throat.

N

na 1. the (referring to specific things or a specific thing). *na vale* the house (a specific house). *na le va* the four people. *Na* may be replaced by *a* at the beginning of a sentence, as is *A cava na leqa?* What is the matter? "The House" as a general term, the concept, would be *A Vale*. *A iValu* War (as a concept in itself), not referring to a specific war. *na ivalu* the (specific) war.

na 2. particle following numbers of things: *e dua na dola* one dollar. *e rua na bilo* two cups. *e vuqa na tamata* many people.

na 3. particle indicating future tense. *Au na lako ena mataka lailai.* I will go in the morning.

na 4. in the form *sa na* may imply "would probably" or "have probably", as in *O sa na kana oti.* You have probably already eaten.

Na n. Mom, Mummy, familiar form of address for one's mother. Syn. *Nana, Nau.*

naba (Eng.) n. number.
Idiom: *Naba!* After someone sneezes, this exclamation calls them to name a number between one and twenty six. For example, a "four" would mean the letter "E", suggesting that one is to think of a person whose name begins with an "E". There is really no point to this game of children.

Naboro n. place-name some 17 km west of Suva, referring to Fiji's main prison compound of about 400 acres inside the Queens Road. Three main divisions are minimum, medium, and maximum security. Three menus are available to prisoners: Fijian, Indian and Other. This is in Naboro Valley where there is a river by that name.

nabu (Archaic) n. gift brought to a teller of tales, ancient stories, usually by appreciative youngsters, though such gifts were a requirement, demanded by the teller of tales. Gifts might include tobacco, a small kava root, a piece of food or anything useful. Radio and television have brought an end to many such occasions of story-telling. Syn. (Lau) *imanai.*

naga (Archaic) n. stone-rimmed compound for very secret indigenous religious observance, especially around the upper Wainimala River in the Viti Levu highlands. Some remnants may still be seen. Very little is known of the ceremonies associated with them. Some of the ceremonies had to do with boys' rite of passage to adulthood.

nagai n. edible nut, Canarium spp., tall forest trees. This is the name in areas of Austronesian language, especially in Vanuatu, southern Solomon Islands, and in parts of Fiji. In Fiji it is also called *yagai*, though most Fijians know no name for it. The Fijian varieties have quite small nuts that are little used; greatly superior varieties are to be found west of Fiji. The nut is difficult to crack without smashing the kernel. Known as galip nut (Papua New Guinea), kanari nut (Indonesia), pili nut (southeast Asia). In some areas of Melanesia (P.N.G., for example, but not Fiji) this nut was a starch-food staple before the introduction of cassava. There have been modern efforts to develop it commercially, especially in the Solomons and Vanuatu. without success so far. It is very rich in oil but the flavour of the nut is distinctive only if the kernel is toasted.

naica as in *e naica?* when? Used only in the form of a question. Also *ni naica* when the event referred to has not yet occured. *O na lako ni naica?* When will you go?

nailoni (Eng.) n. nylon.

Naita n. mutual form of address to a certain group of people, a relationship known as *veitabani*, traditionally mutual branches or close allies. The origin is theoretically based on their ancestral spirits having been cross-cousins *veitavaleni*. One may refer to someone as being *"na noqu naita"*. Two such related groups are the people of Kadavu and LomaiViti, and also Kubuna and Burebesaga. (A different interpretation is given by *Nai Volavosa VakaViti*, p. 858; there, the origin is said to have been between to peoples who were formerly at war with each other.) Today, these relationships are generalized between two regions. In earlier times, the two places were more limited to specific, smaller locations. There may be a hard joking relationship between the two groups.

inaki n. intention, purpose, plan.

nakinaki v., n. to plan to, intend to; intentions. *Era nakinaki mera lai qoli.* They (many) planned to go fishing. *na nona nakinaki me sa vakamau.* his/her intention to be married. *nakinaki lo* secret intentions, ulterior motive.

naki, nakita v. to intend, to mean (to do something). *Au nakita meu vakamatei koya.* I intend(ed) to kill him. *na laba sega ni nakiti* manslaughter (not murder), unintentional killing.

veinaki v. to mutually intend or agree to (do something).

naki ca, nakica-taka v. to have an evil purpose, intend to do evil (often associated with witchcraft). Most illness has been attributed to such witchcraft, and this is still a common belief. It may end in death.

nama n. sea grapes, a seaweed (*lumi*), Caulerpa racemosa, common food found at the seashore, rich in iron, low in other nutrients. Specialties at Ucunivanua, Verata, Koro island, and Nabukelevu-ira in Kadavu. Sold at the Suva markets, usually with a large red chilli (an introduced condiment) and a fermented coconut seasoning called *kora* or *kota*. Delicious eaten raw, sometimes served with *miti* or lemon juice, which is a Tongan introduction. Commonly it is accompanied by fish or shellfish. It should be washed in fresh water to remove any excessive salty taste and any sand. Another species of Caulerpa is *nama drau-ni-ivi* or *nama-kei-belo,* also edible.

nama, namata v. to consider, think over, think about (something).

Na Mata n. monthly magazine published by Fijian Affairs, 1876 to 1971, intelligent with useful historical information in its early editions. Resumed in 1989, becoming a mouthpiece for Government, with little information of lasting importance.

vakanamata v. head for, go in the direction of. *Vakanamata ki vanua.* Head for land. Syn. *namata. Namata sobu ki bulu.* Head down to the depths (as in talking to a diver).

namaka v. to look forward to something, or some occasion. *na olodei namaki* the happily anticipated holiday.

namu n. mosquito. *taunamu* n. mosquito net, in coastal areas only. These were formerly made from barkcloth, not usually available in the highlands. In the highlands the only preventative measure was smoke. There are 24 mosquito species in Fiji, some active at night, some only in daytime. Fiji has no malaria but has two viral diseases resulting from a female mosquito bite (*e dua ni ikati ni namu*), dengue fever (*deqe,* indigenous) and Ross River fever (introduced inadvertantly from Australia). Only one bite is required. The disease filariasis (*waqaqa*) is caused by a nematode transmitted by three Aedes species and one Culex species; continued biting over some ten years can result in elephantiasis (*tauna*).

Idiom: *namu* person who persistently begs and "borrows". Like the mosquito, they are a pest. See *namu, namuta*.

namu, namuta v. to bite hard, chew fast. and consume. To gobble (as of food). By extension, cunningly to use someone else's money, be exploitive of others, to impose one's demands on another person. *namunamu* v. to chew and swallowing noisily.

namuraka v. to strike, destroy, defeat, beat, beat up (persons, team). Syn. *buturaka.*

nana 1. n. sandfly, gnat. 2. n. pus, that exudes from an infection.

Nana 1. n. Mummy, Mum. Syn. *Nau. Nana levu* Auntie, elder sister of mother. *Nana lailai* Auntie, younger sister of mother. For Fijians such aunts are virtually as close a relative as the mother herself. This provides a wide emotional support for a child, not to be emotionally dependent solely on the mother. Syn. (Rewa) *Qei.* (Nadro.) *Namu.*

nanai n. locust, cicada, scientific name Raeateana knowlesi (or Tibicen knowlesi), that as nymphs live underground 30 cm to 2.5 m deep, feeding on root juices, for 8 years, lacking wings and reproductive parts. They emerge from the ground en masse around September, climbing trees, moulting (shed their hard skin) and develop wings. They live only two to three weeks, the female laying hundreds of eggs on plant leaves. Shells of dead cicadas remain on the plants. The whole season lasts no more than two months with cicadas singing. Their appearance is noted especially in certain parts of Navosa and in Nuku District of Serua Province (though Serua may have a different taxon; there are some 20 endemic species in Fiji). They are legendary to the Noemalu people. Up the Sigatoka valley, people collect *nanai* as they are drying their newly formed wings and tie them in a long strings, often presented to neighbouring villages. Cooked, they are considered a delicacy that signals a season or year of abundance (*yabaki ni sautu*). *Nanai* may be cooked in bamboo stems and served with coconut cream, though in early days there were no coconuts in the highlands. Women may also use them for bait when fishing. The *nanai* is closely related to the cicada *maka,* the Green Cicada, that does not disappear.

inanai n. small sticks and vegetation laid on top of the heated stones in the earth oven (*lovo*) to protect the food from burning during the cooking process.

nanamaki expected. *E nanamaki o Tailevu me na tarovi Nadroga.* Tailevu is expected to stop Nadroga (football). *na nanamaki* the expectation.

vakanananu n. memories.

vakananu adj. homesick, full of memories, missing a person or place.

vaka-nananu-ca-taka v. to think ill of (someone, something).

nanava n. gnats, sand-flies, tiny flying insects that bite, appearing at dusk, low to the ground. Some types can penetrate mosquito screens. Syn. *navanava.*

nani, nania, nanilaka (or) **naniraka** v. to beat, give a beating to, usually a person. Syn. *buturaka.*

nanoa as in *ena noa* yesterday.

nanuma v. to think, consider, remember, remind. *Nanumi au*. Think of me, remember me. *vakananumi au* remind me. *Au nanuma ka sa dina*. I believe that is true.

nanuma n. thought. *A cava na nomu nanuma kina?* What are your thoughts about that?

ivakananumi n. memento, memorial, souvenir.

vaka-nanu-taka v. to ponder it, think it over, keep it in mind.

veinanumi adj. considerate of others, thoughtful.

veinanuyaka n., v. of thought, going here and there, thinking of this and that, random scattered thought.

nara adj. too soft of fish flesh, often from over-cooking, or not cooked fresh. Some Fijian fishermen believe that when fish are caught at night, they should not be exposed to moonlight. They believe moonlight makes the flesh become soft.

nasi (Eng.) n. nurse. *nasi ni koro* village nurse. The training of Fiji nurses is readily accepted in some overseas countries, giving them good employment opportunities in migrating.

Idiom: *kana vakanasi* eats delicately with overly refined, very careful manners. This comes from the notion that nurses are very careful in measuring out doses of medicine, and meticulous in their way of working.

NaTo n. form of address between people of Lau, Cakaudrove, Macuata, and Bua, an abbrev. of *Na Tovata*, their former Confederacy of North and East Fiji (*Na Tovata ko Natokalau kei Viti*) formed in 1867 at the instigation of Ma'afu.

natu, natuka v. to crush, grind or mash, usually with a stone, food items, herbal medicine, small crabs to be used as bait. To knead with the hands, as with dough to make bread, would be *bali, balia*.

Na Tu-i-cake n. an honorific way of referring to the Lau Province. It implies "windward archipelago". *Na Tu* is abbrev. of *Na Yatu,* archipelago, in this case.

navanava n. sandfly, gnat. Syn. *nana, nanava*.

Nau n. familiar: Mom, Ma, mother, the most often used form of address though this varies regionally. Syn. *nana* (or) *na*. An aunt is also considered "mother" if she is the sister of one's mother. If older than the mother, such an aunt may be referred to as *nana levu*, and if younger, *nana lailai*. *Na lutu sobu baleta na Siga ni Tina*. The Mother's Day sale.

navu, navuca 1. v. to straighten up, usually a long thing such as a spear, using heat from a fire or steam, and hammering it. By ext., to have an intention, a plan.

navu, navuca 2. v. to steam certain foods, cooking them.

navunavu n. plan, intention.

navunavuci v., n. to plan out; planning.

nawa, nawaca v. to float on water (of an object, usually a boat).

nawanawa n. seaside tree to 15 meters, branching low, near the ground, Cordia subcordata, from Africa east throughout the Pacific. The relatively soft wood is of starkly variegated colour, white with brown heartwood, and is often used for tourist articles such as "native" bowls or carved wooden masks, not really authentic since this wood was not formerly used for carving because there never were any such masks in Fiji. Fiji Indians do much of the carving and commerce. Fibre soaked in seawater for making baskets and a base for garlands. Showy fls wrinkled, yellowish orange, 4 cm diam. Both fruit (a drupe) and seeds are edible. Fruit globose with longitudinal ridges, brown at maturity. *se ni nawanawa* a kind of orange colour (like the flowers of *nawanawa*). (Polyn.) *tou* or *kou*.

Idiom (Slang): *se ni nawanawa* five-dollar bill because of the colour. Similarly, *se ni kavika* can refer to a ten-dollar bill (though in fact, the *kavika* fruit varies in colour according to the variety).

ne 1. a particle that modifies an expression, usually an assertion, and may often be translated as "really" or "exactly". *E dua na nona taro ka vaka koto oqo ne*: One of his questions that is exactly this:

ne 2. a word that stands alone at the end of sentence, meaning "Don't you agree?", "Isn't it so?". It is equivalent of the French "n'est-ce pas?", or German "nicht war?"

nei 1. n. paternal aunt, i.e., sister of one's father, the familiar form of address and reference. *na noqu nei* my aunt (on father's side). *Nei* may be a form of address. It is sometimes used by a youngster for a woman who helped raise her/him. Today, in English, "Uncle" and "Auntie" may be used for older people who are close friends and almost part of the household.

nei 2. possessive "of", meaning his, hers. *na mate nei Seru* Seru's death. *na vale nei Seru* Seru's house. *na ivola nei Inoke* Inoke's letter (that he wrote). *na vale nei cei?* whose house? *Nei Suva na qaqa*. The victory is Suva's. i.e., Suva won the game (as written for a newspaper headline). This possessive pronoun becomes *kei* in the case of foods that person will consume, and *mei* for beverages they will consume. *kei* may replace the *nei* when the object is an integral part of the owner

nei becomes a prefix for possessive pronouns that directly refer to the people concerned, as follows:
neimami our (many, exc.).
neirau our (two, exc.).
neitou our (few, exc.)

neketai (Eng.) n. necktie, worn often at Church, and some other formal occasions. A bowtie is rarely worn, most markedly by the colourful character and politician of the people, the late Sakiasi Butadroka, an outspoken indigenist from Rewa who opposed Ratu Mara Kapaiwai. A red bowtie was his trademark.

nene, neneta v. to be sullen, angry, disturbed, upset; angry about something or someone. Syn. *cudru, cudruvaka, cudrutaka.*

nene n., adj. (Namosi, Tailevu, lowland Naitasiri) anger, angry.

neqe, neqeta v. to push together in the physical motion of sexual union, usually said of two people but could be applied to animals.

neto or **netoneto** interjection, "So there!" indicating some reproval.

neu interjection of disapproval.

ni 1. of (in certain contexts): *vunikau* tree ("plant of wood"). *na mata ni siga* the sun ("eye of the day"). Sometimes abbreviated from *ni* to *i*. For a number of words, the abbreviation is standardised, as with the names for lunar months, for example: *vulaidoi* (month of *doi,* when the *doi* tree flowers, approximately the month of May),

ni 2. for (in certain contexts), as in *bilo ni ti* tea-cup (cup for tea) as contrasted to *bilo ti* cup of tea. *tavaya ni bia* beer-bottle, bottle for beer, as contrasted to *tayava bia* bottle of beer.

ni 3. that (in certain contexts, following a verb): *E kaya ni tayabe oqo e baleta na lotu.* He says that this march is for the church. *Au kila ni sa cala ko koya.* I know that he/she is wrong.

ni 4. because, for or since (in the sense of because). *Keimami na sega ni vukei iko ni keimami kusa tiko.* We will not help you because we are in a hurry. *Au sa malumalumu mai, niu sa qase.* I have become weak because I am old.

ni 5. particle following the word *sega* not. *E sega ni rawa.* It is not possible. *E sega ni cakava.* He/she did not do it.

ni 6. when (in certain contexts): *Ni sa caka oti, tukuna vei au.* When it is done, tell me. *Ni bera ni oti.* Before it is finished. *Au wilivola tiko me yacova niu*

ni 7. pronoun, you (plural for many, or honorific for one or more, as subject of the verb). *Ni bula saka!* Good day sir/madame! *Ni vosota* forgive me, excuse me. *Ko ni* or *O ni* may begin a sentence. As the object of a verb this becomes *kemuni.*

nikua today, in recent times, these days. Syn. *edaidai.*
Idiom: *Ki Namuka vata ga nikua.* we will all get there at the same time, lit. we will all reach Namuka today. It makes no difference if one travels one way or another. The result is the same.

nima, nimata v. to bail (water from a boat). *inima* n. bailer, bailing cup or bucket.
Idiom: *Tu na inima, ka luvu na waqa.* The solution (to a problem) was at hand but nobody thought of it, lit. the bailer was there but the boat sank.
Idiom: *waqa nimanima* n., adj. an enfeebled person, lit. a leaking boat that requires constant bailing, thus feeble, ineffectual.

nimataka (or) **ni mataka** often written as one word. *ena mataka (lailai) ni mataka* tomorrow morning.

nini 1. v. to shake, tremble. *lewaninini* a plant, Lycopodium cernuum, lit. "trembling woman", from its shaking motion in the wind. The plant, growing wild, is used for festive body-decoration and floral arrangements. *sautaninini* v. to shiver, tremble.

nini 2. n. anger. *Au a tagi ena levu ni noqu nini.* I cried from the enormity of my anger.

nini, niniva, ninivaka 3. (Rewa) v. to be angry. Syn. *cudru, cudruva.*

nini, ninica, ninicaka 4. v. to delight in (something, someone), to desire, as of a person, or some particular food.

veivakanini v., n. to tease.

nino, ninova v. to peer, peep.

nita v. to make fire by rubbing pieces of dry wood. *nita buka* v. to light firewood this way. Hardwood is rubbed against soft wood. In the eastern highlands, dead wood *doa* was favoured but a great variety of woods could be used. Ignition can occur within a couple of minutes for an experienced Fijian. *kau ni nita* larger of two pieces of wood used to make fire. *iluveluve* (or) *isulu ni nita* smaller of the two pieces.

niti, nitiva v. to lop off the top of the taro corm in preparation for cooking.

niu n. mature coconut, copra (at any stage of preparation). Originally there were no coconuts in the highlands, none in the diet of the highlanders. Today there are few there. *vu ni niu* coconut palm. There are many var. of coconut and several stages of development:
- Fiji Tall, classic traditional plantation nut.
- Malayan dwarf, short, low yielding, intro. in 1920s.
- Hybrid, supposed to yield in 3 years instead of seven.
- *niu magimagi*, long thin nut, used for sinnet, not food because of shape.
- *niu ni Rotuma*, tall, few large nuts.
- *niu ni Toga* , very large, light brown nut.
- *niu yabia* very tall, drooping leaves, clustered leaflets.
- *bu drau* or *bulu drau*, tall with tiny nuts (yet rich and full).
- *niu damu*, large orange nuts, legendary tall var. obtained from Burotu, the spirit-island associated with Matuku Island.
- *sula,* nut too young to be drinkable.
- *bu sosou* young nut, gelatinous flesh starting to form, still very thin, but water drinkable.
- *bu dina* perfect nut for drinking, flesh can be scooped out easily.
- *drokai* flesh can be scooped out with thumb.
- *kade* nut with good edible white flesh to be scooped out with a knife or perhaps a spoon but the water may have a slightly gassy or musty taste.
- *niu madu* very mature firm white flesh with little water, ideal for copra. The water is somewhat laxative. The nut falls when mature.
- *mataloa* nut at mature stage when the three eyes have become hardened and dark in colour. The *vara* will begin to form inside, replacing the firm white flesh.
- *niu vara* coconut starting to sprout. *niu buta* copra. *iqali niu* bunch of *niu* tied together by a strip from each husk. *vida, vidaka na niu* (or) *kola na niu* to split open the coconut. *cici, cicia na lewena* to prise out the flesh. *sua, suaka na niu* to remove the coconut husk with a *isua* spike. *kari, karia na niu* to grate the coconut flesh. *vaka-vidika na bu* to tap the *bu* with the fingers to test it by sound. *beti, betia na niu* to twist off the coconut from the tree.

Idiom (Archaic): *niu ga kei madrai* just the same, six of one, half a dozen of the other, no difference, nothing much to choose between them, nothing special, just routine (of people), comparing two things that are of equal value.

Idiom: *Na niu a lutu ga i vuna.* A chip off the old block, offspring resembles the parent (often in behaviour); lit. the coconut falls the the base of the palm, sprouting and forming a new palm just like its parent.

Idiom: *vinaka vaka na niu.* Like the coconut, this (other thing) has a very great many uses, is useful in many ways.

niuniu n. generic name for several slender Veitchia and Neoveitchia palm species, and also Physokentia petiolatus and P. thurstonii, both with shiny black fruits. One called *niuniu* is Neoveitchia storckii, often found in rain forest, only along the upper Rewa delta. When young, leaves are rather like banana leaves, but more like coconut leaves in the mature plant. Egg-size red fruits in very compact bunch, edible, with curious tassles dangling from the centre of the bunch. Syn. *vilaito*. Another is V. vitiensis, in eastern Viti Levu and asociated larger islands, most common palm in the bush; Fruit red at maturity, long reins dangling. Syn. *sakiki, kaivatu*. V. joannis is widespread in Fiji, very tall to 35 meters with distinctive spear leaf pointed up. Syn. *niusawa, sakiki*. V. filifera is limited to Vanua Levu. Reference should be made to the excellent book *Palms of the Fiji Islands* by Dick Watling with splendid colour illustrations by George Bennett.

niu sawa n. slender palm, Veitchia sp., leaves used for thatch. Syn. *saqiwa*. See *niuniu,* above.

niu (or) **n'iu** abbrev. of *ni au* (that I), as in *Au nanuma niu na lako nikua* I think I will go today. Despite common usage to the contrary, official government grammarians insist on spelling this without the apostrophe.

niukila (Eng.) n. nuclear.

Niu Kini (Eng., "New Guinea") n. older var. of cassava, semi-cultivated, growing usually in the bush, up to 20 feet high or more, above the nearby grass or bush. Brown stem. Purplish skin to the corm. Matures in 9 months, still good to eat to 18 months or more (other vars. become woody). Occasionally still planted in gardens, where it grows to a normal height.

niumonia (Eng.) pneumonia. Bacterial pneumonia is most common, then viral pneumonia but mycoplasma seems to be a third, dangerous form.

niuniu n. white of an egg. *dromodromo* n. yellow (of an egg).

niusere (or) **niuse** n. affliction of a woman's breast; the nipple is very painful when suckled by the newborn baby.

niusiveva (Eng.) n. newspaper.

no 1. (West) v. to stay, be. Syn. (Bau) *toka*.

no 2. auxiliary verb sometimes used with *koto* v. to lie, to stay, to indicate a usual place of staying. *dau koto no eke ena qara na kuita* the octopus usually stays here in the hole. *E sa davoca no na buturara mai na dua na ivacu.* He remains lying down on the floor from a punch. *E tauvimate no.* He/she lies sick, is presently sick. (In this latter case, *no* replaces the more usual and more mundane *toka*, indicating a present condition. See *inono*.

noa as in *ena noa* yesterday.

noca (Eng.) n. north. Syn. *vualiku*. *tokalau* northeast or northerly.

noda (or) **na noda** our (many). *eso na noda*. some of our people.

nodaru our (two of us).

nodatou our (few of us).

nodra (or) **na nodra 1.** their, theirs (many).

nodra (or) **na nodra 2.** his/hers (in the case of a paramount chief).

nodratou (or) **na nodratou** their (few).

nodrau (or) **na nodrau** their (two).

noka, nokata v. to tie up, make fast, a boat from going adrift, an animal (pig, dog, horse, cow) from wandering loose.

noka (Eng.) knock-out, knocked out, and by ext. extremely tired, exhausted, dead asleep.

noke n. women's basket of woven leaves, usually used for collecting seafood.
   Idiom: *Sinai na noqu noke*. I have a lot of gossip/stories to tell.
   Idiom: *Sa lili toka na noke*. Don't talk about about what will be accomplished till the work is underway. Lit. the seafood basket is still hanging up (and you have not yet gone fishing).

nokonoko n. ironwood, tree, Casuarina equisitifolia, from SE Asia to South Pacific, possibly an aboriginal introduction, below 475 m. Groves of ironwood were considered the abode of spirits, possibly due to the sound of the wind in a grove of such trees and also the red sap. In Verata by village Ucunivanua there is a grove of *nokokono* that is believed by locals to be the burial site of Lutunasobasoba, legendary immigrant, ancestral super-spirit of the so-called First Landing at Vuda. Wood used for house-posts but in cutting, a blunt axe or machete simply bounces off the very hard wood. Formerly used for war clubs. Branches droop. Bark grey with longitudinal fissures that peel off. Lvs tiny, scale-like in whorls. Second sp., C. nodifloria is *velau*, or *cau*. Syn. (Nadi, Nadro, Serua) *qaro*. (Ba, Vuda) *velau*. (Rewa, Vanua Levu, Lau) *cau*. (Polyn.) *toa*.

nomodi n. silence (to describe an environment).

vakanomodi silent(ly). *Sa vakanomodi tu na koro ni vuli.* There is silence in the school.

nomu your (one person). *na nomu* yours (one person's).

nomudou (or) **na nomudou** yours (few).

nomudrau (or) **na nomudrau** yours (two).

nomuni your (many, or one or few honorifically).

nona his/her.

nono, nonova v. to stare fixedly.

inono n. location, place where something is put or found.

noqo 1. v. to proceed leaning forward with the head bent down, usually from respect or fear.

noqu 2. (or) **na noqu** my. *na noqu*. mine. See *kequ* (and) *mequ*.
   Idiom: *E sega ni noqu/nomu*. It is not mine/yours (so let's not worry about it). *E sega na noqu/nomu*. I/you have none. Note the distinctive difference in meaning when *ni* or *na* precedes the *noqu* or *nomu*.

nota 1. (Eng.) n. knot, nautical miles per hour. *ena lima na nota* at five knots.

noti 2. (Eng.) note (of cash currency).

notisi (Eng.) n. notice.

notisi, notisitaka (Eng.) v. to give formal notice, usually legal notice.

Noveba (Eng.) n. November.

novu n. stone fish, Synanceichthys verrucosa (Rob Wright says Synanceja verrucosa), usually immobile, very well camouflaged, very dangerous spines. The sting may justify hospital treatment. Syn. *lewamatua*. Occasionally eaten. *Sa lauti au na novu.* I was pricked by the stonefish.

nubu n. deepwater, of a pool, a bay, or the sea. *vodea* shallow.

nuenue adj. tired, overworked.

nui, nuitaka 1. v. to hope, to hope for, to yearn for it. *Nuitaka!* Let us hope so! *nui dei* firmly hopeful. *nui ca* (or) *nuinui ca* anxious and discouraged. *inuinui* n. thing or person hoped for, on whom hope depends.

nui, nuitaka 2. v. to rely, depend. *Ko rawa ni nuitaka na nona cakacaka.* You can depend on his work. *na cauravou nuitaki* the dependable youths. *Era dau nuitaki ira vakataki ira.* They (many) depend on themselves by themselves. *nuitaki* as in *na waqea nuitaki* the best boat one could hope for.

nuidei v. to believe firmly, to be convinced.

inuinui n. hope. *O koya na noda inuinui duadua.* He/she is our special hope.

vakanuinui adj. hopeful. *Au tiko vakanuinui.* I remain hopeful.
   Idiom: *vakanuinui e na bilo cicila.* depend on an undependable person (a "leaky cup").

vakanuinui n. wishes, as in *Vakanuinui vinaka.* Best wishes.

nuiqawaqawa n., adj. anxiety, anxious.

nuitaki adj. hoped-for, greatly desired, as good as one might desire.

nuki, nukia, nukilaka v. to crinkle or wrinkle or crumple (paper, clothing) usually by clenching in the hand.

nuku n. sand. *matasawa veinukunuku* (or) *matasawa nukunuku* sandy shore (also usually a boat-landing). *nuku balavu* long beach. *nuku loa* black sand. *nukuvula* white sand. By ext., powder, especially referring to gunpowder. (Fijians had no word for powder.) Syn. (Colo East) *lase*.

nukurama n., adj. clear sand shining brightly through clear water, reflecting the sunlight.

nunu tingling, as a human limb feeling numb and "asleep".

nunu n. sp. of fig tree, endemic to Fiji, Ficus pritchardii, Moraceae, fruits grow attached to tree trunk, edible, mostly used in famine times, smooth leaves. Also F. smithii, with figs normally borne among the leaves, edible, and distinguished by leaves with rough surface used as sandpaper. Syn. *losilosi*.

nunu, nunuva, nunuvaka v. to dive, to swim underwater, to dive for (something). *nunuva na sici* to dive for Trochus shell. *nunuvaka e dua na moto.* to dive with a spear. *waqanunu* n. submarine (boat). *daunu* diver. Syn. (Rewa) *kilu, kiluva*.

nuqa n. rabbit fish, Siganus vermiculatus, swarms close to shore beginning at the lunar month *vulainuqa lailai* (roughly December), increasing during the next lunar month *vulainuqa levu,* around January, when it is caught easily in very large numbers, usually with hook and line. Greatly prized seafood. Dorsal spines suggest caution in handling; a prick can be very painful. Other species of Siganus go by this name. There are mainly three different types, the largest growing to 30 cm is *nuqa ni dogo,* the mangrove rabbit fish, S. vermiculatus. Its marking tend to be circular and black. The *nuqa ni cakau* (or) *nuqanuqa,* S. spinus is somewhat smaller, with tan markings in more flowing lines. A tiny rabbit fish, called *nuqanuqa,* barely more than an inch in length, is the annual *"balolo"* of village Waitabu, at Bouma, Taveuni Island. Nasavusavu is known for the huge annual influx of *nuqa* Local tradition there forbids any of the *nuqa* to be sold. Syn. *rusarusa, volaca*.

nuqanuqa (or) **nuqa** n. Fiji Christmas tree, Decaspermum fruticosum (or) D. vitiense, Myrtaceae, a shrub of the bush, with fragrant white petals that lie back, exposing pink anthers and stigma. The plant is common in areas of moderate rainfall but found also in the wet forest. It has scented tiny white flowers in the *vulainuqa* time (approx. December through January), when the *nuqa* fish is abundant, hence the name. The totem plant of certain inland tribes. *Veinuqa* is the name of a tribe on the upper reaches of the Wainimala River, a tribe now largely dispersed. Leaves opposite, small, very smooth and fine, with only the central vein clearly visible. Leaves scented when crushed in the hand. Leafy twigs often bifurcate at the tip. Tiny leaves are interspersed with regular leaves. Highlanders have frequently used branches of this shrub as a broom (and branches of the *makita* tree also), even when the leaves are quite dried out, because leaves stay affixed to the twigs. Highlanders did not have coconut palms for the customary *sasa* brooms of coastal areas and small islands. *vakasenuqanuqa* n. (Archaic) n. local ceremony, still celebrated in some areas, welcoming the return of a chieftain who has been away for a time, visiting elsewhere. Name of the ceremony refers to the December flowering of the *nuqanuqa* tree, but an explanation for that name of the ceremony is elusive.

John Parham's *Plants of the Fiji Islands* also lists *nuqa* as the name of a moderately common small forest tree, Citronella vitiensis, with greenish-yellow flowers.

O

This letter is pronounced like **aw** in **awful**. Mispronounciation of this letter (and the trilled Fijian **r**) are common errors of foreigners trying to pronounce Fijian words.

O 1. as a lone, single capital letter, O (or *Ko*) may precede a proper name of a person or and place, as in *O Viti* (or) *Ko Viti*. Fiji *O Taiti* Tahiti. *O Pita* Peter, when that name is the subject of the sentence. Thus *O Pita a solia vei au* Peter gave it to me, but *Au a solia vei Pita*. The capital O is not used when Pita is the object. The use of *O* instead of *Ko* is a Polynesian influence.

O 2. The single capital letter "O" is also used as a response when one is being called. It is "correct" usage, rather than the now common *Na cava?* What? (What do you want?) which is an Anglicism and sounds impolite in Fijian.

O 3. you, as a subject. (*ko iko* or *iko* in the objective sense). *O via kana?* Would you like to eat? (Are you hungry?) *O kila vakavinaka.* You know it very well. The honorific, polite form (and also the plural) is *o ni*. *O iko* or *iko* you, as the object of a sentence. *O cei?* Who? *O iko* You.

o 4. n. cloud.
Idiom: *Sa sega sara ga ni ra bau raica na kena o.* They simply could find no trace of him/her at all. Lit., They could see nothing at all of his cloud (a cloud hovers over every island, and is a distant indicator of an island's location beyond the horizon). Alternatively: *E sega ni raici na o kei Seru.* There was no trace of Seru.

obasimani (Eng.) ombudsman. There is one appointed in Fiji. Syn. *obatisimani*.

oba, obata v. to pounce onto, as a cat might pounce on a mouse, or a male animal mount a female. See *kaba, kabata*.

O cei? who (as the subject of a question). *O cei a cakava?* Who did it? *vei cei?* to whom? *nei cei* whose? *O cei na yacamu?* What is your name? -- as asked of a child. (It would be rude to speak to an adult in that blunt way.)

o iko you, personal pronoun as an object of a sentence, spoken or implied. This form is used only for people with whom one is very familiar.

o ira (or) **o iratou** they (many, several), when the subject of the sentence.

o ni you (many, or honorific for one or more people), as the subject of a sentence.

O so! exclamation of reproach, often in response to an unreasonable request. *So* is a drawn-out sound, implying a reproach. It may be said in humour.

obo (Colo) Bauan *cobo*, v., n. to express thanks by clapping, resoundingly with hands cupped, not parallel. In the eastern highlands *cobo* refers to the rectum, a word that is not to be pronounced.

oburu (Eng.) n. homebrew alcohol for personal consumption.

oca adj., n. tired, tired of. *Au sa oca.* I am tired. *Au sa oca na tara vale.* I am tired of house-building. *loma ocaoca* in a disturbed state of generalised worry. *oca wale* laboured in vain, worked for no result. *cegu oca* out of breath. *veivaka-ocai* tiresome. *vakaoca, vakaocataka* v. to make a person tired,

vakacau-oca v. to become tired of, to give up on (some effort).

oco n. trad. food brought for villagers who are helping with a communal project (housebuilding, establishing a food-garden), provided by the one who benefits.

odo v. to emerge suddenly, burst forth, as a snake disturbed, or a ripe fruit burst open. By ext., for a person's eyes protruding suddenly showing wide-eyed surprise or fear.

odro, odrova v. with the arms, to clasp against the chest, as the tree-trunk, in climbing a coconut palm tree.

oga n. traditional duty, responsibilities, obligations under the Fijian social system, still exacted of Fijians who retain close association with their village. Many of the obligations are concerned with rites of passage: marriage, birth, coming of age, a first presentation of children in the mother's village, death. Obligations extend to villagers and relatives far outside the immediate household. The extended family (*itokatoka*) itself may include more than fifty people, and the clan (*mataqali*) many more. They are all required to participate and contribute. *E sivia na oga mai na koro.* There are too many social obligations in the village. These can be heavy burdens on many Fijians that make it difficult for them to accumulate capital.

ogataka v. to be busy, to be busy (with something).

ogaoga adj. busy.

vakaoga v. to bother someone who is busy, take up someone's time.

ogo n. barracuda, Sphyraena spp. Two main species, the larger (to one meter) *ogo levu* (S. barracuda), and the yellow-tailed, *ogo buidromo* (S. jello), to 80 cm. Though pelagic, they may be found near reefs. They may remain very still, motionless in the water, sometimes in small numbers. When attacked, the barracuda is extremely fast and dangerous. It would be dangerous to try to spear one. Young barracuda may be referred to as *silasila*, or *duluToga*.

Oi! exclamation of surprise or sudden understanding.

oi au I, the personal pronoun as the subject of the sentence, where the rest of the sentence is implied. One may see this spelled *o yau*. *O cei oqori?* Who is there? *Oi au.* I (am there). *Oi au, au nanuma ni sa cala.* As for me, I think it is wrong. Fijians are less inclined to begin a sentence with a personal pronoun or a person's name than in the case in English.

Oiauwe! emotional exclamation of amazement, sorrow, regret, great fatigue. See *iauwe*.

oilei! common interjection with many meanings, surprise, regret, frustration, depending on the context and tone of voice.

oisou very near, very nearly, come close. Often said of something thrown, slightly missing its target. *Oisou sara me keitou okati kina.* We came very close to being included. Perhaps more properly *waisou.* Syn. *isou.*

oka, okata v. to include (in counting, listing). *na veika ka oka kina* the things that are included. *O Viti, okati kina O Rotuma* Fiji, including Rotuma. See *wili.*

okani (vaivo) (Eng) n. pipe organ as a musical instrument in some Christian churches.

oki 1. n. plant formerly used for hair-dye (*bena*). Shrub to small tree 1 to 6 meters high, with spines, introduced prior to 1860 for its fragrant golden yellow flowers, appearing all year round, now a noxious weed in Fiji, Acacia farnesiana, Mimosaceae. Flowers known internationallty as Cassie, used commercially in southern France for perfume. Syn. Ellington curse. See other plants used for hair treatment: *manawi* and *makita*.

oki 2. (Eng.) n. hockey, a game recently adopted in Fiji.

oko, okota v. to cause to be ripened, of bananas, plantain, usually by covering them so that their own ethylene gas will hasten the ripening process.

Okosita (Eng.) August.

Okotova (Eng.) October.

ole, oleva, olevaka v. to howl in pain or great anguish. One may hear the scream *ole ole*. See *osi*.

olive n. wolf. There are no wolves in Fiji. The word becomes relevant only in children's stories based on English tradition.

olo (Eng.) n. hall. *tauna olo* town hall.

olo, ologa v. to wrap. as in a parcel. *kaveti olo* English cabbage. *Me olo?* Wrap it up? *na iolo* the parcel or package itself. *na ioloolo* n. the wrapped parcel.

iolo n. leaves, paper or plastic used as a wrapper of a parcel.

olo (Rewa) n. food speciality of Dreketi people (villages Nakorolevu and Nadoria), cooked taro leaves (*rourou*) with cooked taro (*dalo*) packed inside a wrapping (*iolo*) of *via* leaf, traditionally presented to the Roko Tui Dreketi.

olodei (Eng.) n. public holiday (not school holidays).

one (Central Polynesia) n. sand. In Fiji, *one* appears only in place-names such as village Vione, Gau island, village Uruone, on Vanua Balavu Island. It is a Proto-Central Polynesian root-word. Syn. *nuku, lase.*

omuburu (Eng.) "home-brew" alcohol. Syn. *uburu, oburu.*

oni (Eng.) n. honey-bee, yellow bumble-bee. The sting is not as severe as that of the hornet (*pi*). Honey itself is called *de ni oni*. Europeans in the 1960s brought in bees, mostly to Muanikau and the Domain areas. Mass migration to new hives happens when the old queens make room for the new queen bees. The old queen flies to find a new location and thousands of her bees follow. One finds new hives between March and June. One hive may accommodate 20 to 30,000 bees. There is small but active been industry developing in Fiji, especially around Rakiraki and in Nadroga.

onisi (Eng.) n. ounce. Now replaced by metric measures.

ono six. *na kaono* the sixth. *tini ka ono* sixteen. *onosagavulu* sixty. *ono na drau* six hundred.

oqo 1. now. *Cakava sara ga oqo.* Do it right now. The initial "o" is dropped when the word begins a sentence.

oqo 2. here, where I am (we are). See synonym *eke* (or) *e ke*.

oqo 3. this. *ena vula oqo*. this month. *ena vula mai oqo* next month (after this current month). *Oqo na motoka nei tamaqu.* This is my father's car.

oqori 1. over there, where you are. Syn. *ikeri* (or) *e keri*. In Lau this becomes *ka ya*.

Oqori! (or) **'Qori! 2.** Idiom: There, that's it! You've got it! You understand correctly! You got it right! The initial "o" tends to be dropped at the beginning of sentence.

ora v. to choke (something in the throat, or emotion). *Sa ora ena sui ni ika* The fish bone is stuck in the throat. *vakaora* to choke on something physical or over something emotional.

iore n. penalty for some offense against traditional manners. It is an offense, for example, to pronounce the name of the local totem in some Viti Levu villages, especially in the highlands. These days the usual punishment is to be splashed with a bucket of water, or be made to drink a huge cup of *yaqona*. *Sa nomu iore e dua na tabua.* Your (traditional) penalty is to give a whale-tooth.

vakaorei, vakaorea v. to exact a penalty for an infringement of traditional custom. *Au sa vakaorei iko.* I exact a penalty of you. Today this is said mostly in good humour. *na vakaorei* the imposition of such punishment. *Sa ore o koya.* He/she is under traditional penalty (for some infraction of custom).

ori, oria v. to slit lengthwise as in preparing pandanus leaf for weaving, or making a natural pandanus fringe of the edge of a mat. This is done with thorn, a sharp piece of shell, or a nail. *orilaka* v. to do this grossly, too crudely, without proper care. *na oriori* the stripping, slitting, of pandanus leaf.

oriori adj. striped. *na sote oriori* the striped shirt. *oriori vulavula* white-striped. Could apply modernly to a zebra, or a tiger though there are none in Fiji.

oro, orota v. to bundle up, to wrap around the body (cotton cloth, towel, barkcloth as formal dress) with some notion of it being tied or fastened. Or similarly, to bundle up, as with pieces of kindling or firewood.

ioro n. decorative wrap around arm, neck or body, sometimes for warmth. A traditional and old expression formerly applied usually to thin bark-cloth, most often as a sort of scarf. *ioro ni liga* arm bracelet (usually plant-material).

oru n., adj., v. mud, muddied, usually of the feet from walking in soggy ground. As a verb, to stick in the mud or be stuck in the mud. *Sa oru na lori.* The truck is stuck in the mud. *oruoru* v. muddied, of the feet.

osana (Eng.) hosanna.

ose (Eng.) n. horse. *vodoka na ose* v. to mount the horse. *idabedabe ni ose* n. saddle. *varaile* n. bridle. Horses are used as farm transport mostly in Navosa and the West. Horse races take place in the West. Idiom: *ose masi* n. key person, a mainstay, power-house, strong worker.

osepawa (Eng.) n. horsepower. Syn. *osivawa*.

osi, osiva v. to cry verbally over some drama, often death. *osiva* to cry for something, someone. *osivaka* to cry about something. See *ole*.

Ositerelia (Eng.) n. Australia.

oso, osova, osovaka v. to bark (of a dog). *osova* to bark at it. *osovaka* to bark because of it. *na iosooso* the barking. Syn. *kodro, kodrova*.

oso, osota v. to crowd in, as of people in a place. *osota na loma ni vale* fill the house (with people). May also refer to a person who does not fit into clothes that are too small a size.

oso drigi very crowded (with people).

osooso adj., n. busy, busyness. *Sa rui levu na nomu osooso* you are very busy, too busy. *vaka-osooso* v. to cause someone to be busy.

ota 1. edible fern-plant, common vegetable, semi-cultivated, relatively prestigious as a feast-food, leaves eaten after light steaming although they are edible raw. The stems are stripped off before cooking. Sold in the markets. Various types: *ota dina* or *ota vulu* (Athyrium esculentum), *ota loa* (Athyrium melanocaulon and Tectania latifolia), *lalabi*, which has a broad leaf, *ota mila* which is often eaten raw.

ota 2. (Eng.) n. order (usually commercial).

ota, otataka (Eng.) v. to order. *E a otataki Seru na ovisa me tiko lo.* The policemen ordered Seru to be quiet.

otela (Eng.) n. hotel. *cili ena otela* stay at a hotel.

oti, otiva v. to finish, to finish it off. *Sa oti.* It is finished (there is no more). *Sa caka oti.* It is already done. *ena vula sa oti* last month (before the current month). *ena macawa tolu sa oti* three weeks ago. Syn. (Kadavu) *kora*.

vakaoti, vakaotia v. to cause it to be finished (off). Idiom: *vakaoti gauna* waste time.

oti afterwards, as in *Oti, e a laki Suva*. Afterwards, he/she went to Suva.

iotioti n. end, last. *na iotioti ni gauna* the very last time.

vakaoti absolutely. *Sa totoka vakaoti.* He/she/it is absolutely beautiful.

ova, ovaca 1. v. to lean, or lean against, as a shed might be leaning against a house.

ova, ovaca 2. v. (Rewa) to swim, swim over to. *ovataka* swim with something, taking something. This is said to be the origin of the island name Ovalau, from a chief swimming there with such an aid, as an early settler.

iova n. a flotation aid, such as a piece of wood, or bundle of coconuts, for help in swimming long distances. In legend, Tui Boti, Waimaro chief, used such an aid in swimming from Verata to tiny NaWi Island in Nasavusavu harbour. His was some bamboo that afterwards began to grow on the island, according to legend. Reputedly, it is still there today.

ovi, ovica v. to brood (female birds, usually), take under the wing. It is perhaps by ext., that this may refer to covering up a child to keep it warm.
Idiom: *viavia ka-ovi* (Lau) to posture pretentiously, as an older man who pretends to be attractive to young girls, or a person who shows off (wealth, respected position) that is clearly pretense.

ovisa (Eng.) n. policeman, constable. *sitiseni ni ovisa* police station. *turaga ni ovisa* policeman (polite term). *ovisa vakalecaleca* plain-clothes policeman, undercover agent.

o ya that is (or) that, as in *Oti o ya, . . .* After that . . .(something happened). *Sa dina sara oya* That is very true. May be seen written as one or two words. Syn. *aya*.

P

P is a letter not used by Fijians except for words introduced from other languages, such as English and Tongan. Where Tongan influence is considerable, **p** often replaces the Fijian **v** or **b**. For example Fijian *valagi* becomes *palagi*. Fijian *balolo* can become *palolo*. These days the Fijian man's name Eveli (Abel) is perhaps more commonly heard as Epeli. The letter **p** itself is pronounced as **pa** when spelling a word in Fijian.

paikaleti (Eng.) n. pikelet, a fried food, flour with leavening, sugar and milk.
pailate (Eng.) n. pilot.
paileve n. a traditional food of ancient Laucala Territory, rarely made today, a kind of fermented pudding *madrai*, or more specifically, *bila*. People from Laucala Island (now living on Qamea Island) are sometimes jokingly referred to as *bati paileve*, people who like to eat *paileve*, a friendly "insult" mostly by people of Yacata Island and Korocau.
paini (Eng.) n. pine (tree, timber). This usually refers to the introduced, fast-growing Caribbean pine, Pinus caribaea, now the basis of a major export industry in Fiji.
"paidar" (Hindi) v. to walk. This is used especially by Tailevu people who say (mixing English, Fijian and Hindi): "Tailevu no *leqa*, no *basi*, paidar". This means that in Tailevu one can get around on foot when there is no bus. (The land is not mountainous.)
"paisa" (Hindi) n. money, a word well known to almost all Fijians.
"pakapaka" (Hawaii) n. toothless fish, Pristipomoides sp., some five species, distinctive yellow dorsal fins, highly prized by Europeans and Japanese, but as a deep-sea fish caught on line to depths of 400 meters, unknown to early Fijians. Length < 50 cm. The French of Vanuatu refer to the fish as "poulet".
pakete (Eng.) packet (as of biscuits).
pakia n. (Lau) edible taro leaves. Syn. *rourou*.
palagi n. (Lau) abbrev. of *kai vavalagi*, stranger, foreigner, now only used for Europeans (white people). Syn. *valagi*.
palasita (Eng.) "plaster" (usually refers to adhesive tape to cover minor cuts)..
palasita-taka (Eng.) to apply a "plaster".
palasita simede (Eng.) plaster that hardens (used to protect bone fractures, or as outside covering for buildings). *simede* n. cement.
palasitika (Eng.) n. plastic, plastic bag may be implied.
palimedi (Eng.) n. parliament.
palusami (Samoa) n. food of wrapped package of cooked taro leaf enclosing coconut cream, sometimes including tinned meat.
pama (Eng.) oil palm, Elaeis spp., and date palm, Phoenix spp., introduced but uncommon and little known, probably never utilized.
panikeke 1. (Eng.) pancake, various versions of fried flour and water with sugar, some with only the vaguest resemblance to pancakes. Often a breakfast food. Without baking powder (*vakatubu*) is may be called *parile* (or) *parale* and *saparaki*. Similar are the *babakau*, the *paikaleti* and the *panikeke waicala*.
panikeke 2. (Eng., Slang) n. lesbian.
"panja" n., v. (Eng.) puncture.
"panpan" v. to sniff petrol for self-intoxication, an extremely dangerous practice of some youths. Some have also been sniffing glue, usually the glue used for shoe-repair.
paodi n. (Eng.) pound (weight or Brtish money).
papau n. (Slang, origin uncertain) penis.
papitaiso, papitaiso-taka (Eng.) n., v. to baptise. *na veipapitaisotaki* n. the ceremony of baptism.
"Papua" n., adj. mat-weaving design of a style thought to have been imported from

Melanesia, incl. Papua New Guinea.

paraiminisita (Eng.) prime minister. Pronounced much as in English, but with rolled "r", and the last syllable stressed, pronounced "stah".

paraimiri (or) **paraimari** (Eng.) n. primary, primary school.

paraivate (Eng.) n. private, as an army rank.

parokaramu (Eng.) n. programme.

parakaravu (Eng.) n. paragraph.

paralase or **paralasi** (Eng.) n., adj., v. paralysis, paralyzed, paralytic.

parile n. type of unleavened, flour-based pancake, usually eaten for breakfast or as a snack. Syn. *saparaki*.

parisi (Roman Catholic & Anglican) n. parish.

parofesa (Eng.) n. professor.

parofita (Eng.) n. prophet. Syn. *varovita* (R. Cath.) *parofeta, voroveta*. Fiji has had a few of its own prophets who presaged radical developments for Fijians but all have led an eccentric existence with flamboyant life-style.

ipasa (Lau) n. digging stick as an garden implement, preparing ground for planting. Syn. *isau, saupa, doko*.

pasede (Eng.) percent. *e lima na pasede*. five percent.

pasi, pasi-taka (Eng.) to pass, as at an exam; *pasi, pasitaka na volo* to pass the ball.

pasidia (Eng.) passenger.

pasipote (Eng.) passport.

pata n. introduced cultivar of plantain, short plump fruit, grey skin, edible raw or cooked. Mostly in Lau and southeastern Viti Levu. Syn. *jamani* (in Rewa), *paka*.

pata v. (Slang) have sexual intercourse, a word used by young people.

pati (Eng.) v., n. party. *pati vakapolitiki* political party.

patuni (Eng.) n. platoon (military). Syn. *palatuni*.

pauta (or) **pouta** (Eng.) n. powder, usually talcum powder. In Lauan custom called *fakawela*, spectators of a dance may powder the performers, especially the women, as a sign of favour and admiration. In Slang among young people, *pouta* can refer to someone who enlivens a grog session (social drinking of *yaqona*).

pea (Eng.) avocado pear, introduced in 1880s. Fruits mainly February, March. Thrives on Taveuni. Not commonly eaten by Fijians.

pediki (Eng.) appendix (of human body).

peipei (Eng.) baby, a word used in Lau.

peke, pekea (Lau) v. to grease a pan, or apply butter.

pekepeke (Lau) v. dipping of food in salt before each bite. Also said of dipping in coconut cream, usually when eating sweet yam.

peni (Eng.) 1. n. penny. 2. n. pen (or) pencil. *peniwai* pen (for writing).

penikau (Ang.) n. pencil.

penikuini (Eng.) n. penguin.

penilamu (Ang.) penny coin during colonial era, that had a hole in the centre. Introduced October 1935. The thought was that since at that time most Fijians had no pockets or purses, they would string the coins through the hole. In fact, Fijians never did that. Quite sensibly they keep their cash concealed.

peniseni (Eng.) n. pension.

penisilini (Eng.) n. penicillin.

peniwai (Ang.) pen (writing instrument), including ballpoint pens.

pepa (Eng.) n. paper. *pepa ni valenivo* toilet paper.

peresitedi (Eng.) n. president.

Peritania (Eng.) n. Britain. See *Bolatagane*, an old reference.

pi (Eng. bee, but the honey bee is called *oni*), n. the inadvertantly introduced yellow-jacket hornet, Polistes olivaceus, with painful bite, flocks in season, July-August, often around houses. They do not attack but will bite if molested. They stay quiet in the cold months to emerge in October to build nests. Large nests in the vegetation are a occasional nuisance in gardening. The hornets can be smoked out. Provoked, they may attack in swarms. Pain is alleviated by applying mud. *sova ni pi* hornets' nest. *vaka e kati na pi* sting like a hornet.

pikini (Eng. "napkin") n. diaper for babies. (*bikini* n. bikini bathing suit). Syn. *navukini*.

pinati (Eng.) n. peanut(s), commonly sold in the city streets, mostly by Indians.

pini 1. (Eng.) green beans (or) green peas. *pini balavu* is long bean, Vigna sesquipedalis, commonly sold in the market, mostly by Indians.

pini 2. (Eng.) clothes pin or other clip, such as paper clips in an office. May apply to almost anything that in English is called a pin.

pi ni qele black mud-wasp, builds nests of mud (*qele*) under leaves, or against windows or screens. There are two types: The bite of the larger one is extremely painful and results in severe lasting swelling. Some people are allergic to the bite and suffer greatly. The wasp does not bite unless inadvertantly provoked. The smaller black mud-wasp has a much less painful sting but will tickle and itch for a day or so afterwards.

pipi n. private parts of a person, in vulgar or childish slang, a vagina or penis.

piqi (Eng.) pink.

pisipisi 1. (Eng. piss) n. African tulip tree, introduced, rarely above 300 meters. Conspicuous, large orange to red flowers used by children as miniature water pistols, hence the name. The timber is useless for building and the tree is a fast-growing nuisance, almost impossible to eradicate. After being cut down the tree can rise again from the roots. Elongate brown capsules to 20 cm long, with hundreds of small seeds having plastic-like wings. Syn. sometime incorrectly referred to as *sekoula*, confusing it with the flamboyant tree.

pisipisi 2. (Slang) v. to spray perfume from an atomiser or hand-spray.

pito (Tonga "pito") belly-button, navel.

po (Eng. Slang) potty, for toilet-training a toddler.

vakapogipogi (Tonga) n. ceremony of four days (nights) of relative isolation of a chief being installed, especially in Taveuni, where Tongan influence is considerable. He stays only with elders and intimates.

poidi (Eng.) n. point(s), goal(s), score. *toqa e dua na poidi* to score a point. *tini poidi tolu* ten point three (as a decimal).

politiki (Eng.) n. politics. *daunipolitiki* politician.

polo (Eng.) **1.** n. ball (cricket, football, tennis). Syn. *volo*.

polo (Eng.) **2.** n. testicle(s). In Fijian this word does not have the vulgar connotation of "balls" in English. Idiom: *masi polo* "brown-nose", usually students in relation to a teacher, or employees with employer. This again does not sound as vulgar in Fijian as it would in English.

polo kani(kani) adj., n., very vulgar slang, a would-be humorous put-down, usually said by a girl to a boy, referring to his testicles as suffering from *kanikani*, a dry and scaly skin condition that results from excessive drinking of *yaqona*. The girl is usually responding to some taunting remark of the boy.

polotu (Tonga) n., v. Christian worship (*sokalou*) among Methodists of Lau, the singing of hymns by men and women and church service.

pono, ponoka (Lau) v. to catch and hold, capture (person, animal). Syn. *tobo, toboka*.

popotu adj. of a person, somewhat overly rounded body. May refer specifically to protruding buttocks.

poreti (Eng.) n. porridge.

pori as in *ulu pori* bald (of the human head). *ulu tasi* bald shave head.

porokaramu (Eng.) n. programme (schedule of events).

porosi (Eng. "prostitute") n. prostitute.

posi(tovesi) (Eng.) n. post-office. Syn. *meli*.

pota n. a food specialty of Vuna, Taveuni Island, leaves of taro cooked in earth oven without the addition of any coconut cream *lolo*; sometimes generally referring to greens.

pote (Slang) adj. humiliated, as a child reprimanded, or rejected. One hears young children unkindly mock another child who has been found out doing something naughty, calling out *"Pote!"* Syn. *sima*.

pouta (Eng.) n. powder.

"puja" (Hindi) n. Hindu worship, prayer.

pulea (Lau) v. to criticize, judge.

pupule (Lau) adj. overly critical, too judgemental (of a person).

pupusia (Taveuni) n. blowhole, high-flung spray that surges high into the air through old volcanic holes in the rock formations along the coast. The word is from Tonga, where this rare phenomenon also occurs along the coast of Tongatapu Island. In Fiji it occurs on Taveuni Island at Vuna, at Bouma and, a very small one, at Soqulu. There is another at Naidi, by Nasavusavu. This word is not generally known.

purini (Eng.) n. classical very heavy, brown Fijian pudding-cake, made by steaming or boiling in a cloth, made of flour, water, coconut cream, caramelised sugar. Sold in the Suva City market.

pusi (Eng.) n. cat, often pronounced *vusi* or *vosi*. Some are feral, a threat to birds that lay eggs on the ground.

Q

The letter **q** is pronounced **ng** as in "finger". (The letter **g** is always pronounced as a soft **ng** as in **song**.) In reciting the alphabet, one pronounces the **q** as **qa**.

qa v. to firm up, lock up, to secure, as in closing a door securely.
qa-na n. shell, husk. *qa ni vivili* shellfish shell; *qa ni niu* coconut husk. *qa ni bilo* coconut shell. *qa vunu* cleaned husk fibres for use in laundry scrubbing or ready for plaiting. *qa ni yaloka* eggshell. *Qa-na* may also refer to the shell or exo-skeleton of a crab. *manumanu vaqaqa* (Anglicism) n. crustacean, animal with outer shell, such as crab, crayfish.
qa ni bulu n. coconut husk used as a scrubber for cleaning (the body when bathing, dishes being washed). Syn. *qa vunuvunu*.
qa ni liga n. (Anglicism) glove. *liga* hand. *Mo vaqaniliga me taqomaki kina na ligamu.* Do wear gloves to protect your hands.
qa ni niu n. shell of a coconut. After smoothing, the dark shell of the mature nut may be used as a cup, as for drinking kava. White shell of immature nut may be smoothed to use as a soup bowl. Both are introduced concepts, probably from Tonga.
qa ni tavaya n. broken bottle-glass; Idiom: sharply cutting, insidiously destructive, of a person. Syn. *bati ni toro* n. razor blade. (Broken glass has previously been commonly used as a razor.) Disposable razor blades were sharpened by rubbing inside a porcelain cup.
qacaru adj. empty-handed, "broke". Syn. (Anglicism) *ligalala*, (Eng.) *nomani*.
qaciqacia adj. overly proud, full of oneself, arrogant, conceited, egotistical. *qaciqacia-taka* to be proud of it (in a bad sense). In English, Fijians talk about someone going about "collar up", full of arrogant pride. In old Fijian villages no one but a high chief would wear anything above the navel. It would be seen as arrogance.
qaco, va-qaco-taka v. to bind tightly, such as a bandage on a leg, waistband *ioro* around the waist.
qacoya v. to apply oneself diligently, dedicated, heavily committed, intent.
qaco (ni kete) (Obsolete) v., n. to be constipated, an old term now little known.
qai particle modifying a verb, an action next in a sequence of events. The meaning may vary a little in context. *se qai* usually implies a somewhat recent action. *sa qai* usually implies a more strongly definite action that has ultimately taken place. *Oti, qai laki Suva* Afterwards, then go to Suva. *Oti, sa qai laki Suva.* Afterwards, he/she finally went to Suva. *Au se qai sili oti.* I've just had a bath. *Sa dede daru qai sota.* It has been a long time since we two met.
qai (West, Lau, Cakau.) tall green plant growing wild, the corm formerly baked for a few days before the extraction of sweet liquid used to flavour puddings. Leaves commonly used to wrap parcels of food to be cooked in earth oven. Cordyline terminalis or C. fruticosa. Introduced red-coloured and variegated leaf varieties are planted as ornamentals. Syn. *vasili, masawe*.
qai, qaiva (Rewa) v. to go. *iqaiqai* trip. Syn. (Bau) *lako*.
qala-na n. male genitals. *sore ni qala* (or) *soresore* testicles (now more commonly called *polo*, even by doctors). *qala qaqa* n. castrated animal, steer or male horse. *ceke* fallen testicles, from hernia or from elephantiasis.
qala mate n., adj. impotence, impotent, erectile dysfunction. Syn. *uti mate*.
qali, qalia v. to twist or roll together, as with coir fibre in forming sinnet (*magimagi*), rolling it on the thigh, or in curling a person's hair. Rubbing between the hands or fingers is *qili, qilica* or *mulo, muloca*, which implies a twisting motion. Both *qilia* and *qalia* may apply to rubbing the head as in a shampoo, working the hair with the fingers.
qali adj. tributary, of one traditional territory to another. Failure to pay tribute in goods would result in murderous reprisal. There is an implication of being "bound" to the senior territory. Bau, having few resources itself on that island, depended on subject territories to supply food and services. *Qali vakaBau* territory of people who are subject to Bau, but they were often ready to rebel against their masters. The relationship is referred to as *veiqali*. The concept is foreign to Melanesian Fijians and was introduced under Tongan influence.
iqali (Archaic) n. bunch of ten mature coconut tied together by torn pieces of their husks to be carried more easily.
veiqali sominiwai n.,v. "stand-off" confrontation. neck-and-neck competition. *sominiwai* moustache.
qaliki (Eng.) n. garlic.

qalita n. natural buttressing of the basal trunk of some trees such as the *ivi* (Polynesian chestnut) or the *dawa*. These buttesses formerly served as an improvised drum for signaling that can be heard four kilometers away.
Idiom: *Qiri qalita qai kara na kaka* Boast about oneself. Lit. Beat the buttress (as a drum), then cry out like a parrot.

qalo, qalova v. to swim, to swim to (some place). *qalovaka* or *qalotaka* swim carrying (something). *qalo vakoli* (Anglicism) v. to dog-paddle. *Qalo* implies there is some purpose in mind or going somewhere or getting something. Simply to go bathing or swimming for pleasure is referred to as *sili*. But *vaka-ta-qaqalo* v. to "horse around" in the water, swimming for pleasure.
Idiom: *qalo mai* v., n. insulting reference to a Fijian from another island who has come to live on Viti Levu, home of the "real Fijians", *kaiViti dina,* the hill tribes of the interior who were the earlier immigrants. These hill tribes often see immigrant Fijians and Tongans as presumptuous and "pushy". Syn. *ciri mai,* implying the person just drifted to Viti Levu.

iqaloqalo n. life preserver, any floating support used by a swimmer.

iqaloqalovi n. ceremony of welcome for high chiefs (or officials), sometimes abbrev. as *iqalovi*. It implies a swimming out to the arriving boat but the ceremony can be done on land when the chief arrives by car. A whale-tooth is usually presented and is called the *iqalovi*.

qalo-na n. arm or tentacle of an octopus (*kuita*), leg of a crab.

qaloka-na n. toe. Also the legs of a land crab *lairo*.

qalolo (Colo East) n. yam storage house located in the garden, usually distant from a village. The house might serve as shelter for the night if the gardener stayed out. Some were provided with an inside fireplace *matadravu* for cooking. Such houses are rare now. There is less of a need to store yams and these days there is a danger of theft. In very early history, few yams were grown by highlanders of eastern Viti Levu; for the most part they planted only taro and relied on wild yams. In the interior of Viti Levu, cultivated yams never took on the noble connotation they have in Lau. Syn. *lololo*.

qalu n. a Fijian sweet pudding *vakalolo*. Idiom: (Lau) *qalu kania* a common humorous idiom, referring to a person who has married someone from their own village or people (implying a pudding already tasted).

qalu yaca (Lau) n. type of Fijian pudding. *yaca* grated.

qami, qamita v. to hold, squeezed underneath the arm or legs.

qamiqami n. sanitary napkin for menstrual periods. Moss was commonly used in early days, and bark-cloth. Cotton cloth is used in rural villages. Syn. *qamuqamu*.

qamu (Eng.) liquid gum for gluing paper.

iqamu 1. n. tweezers, pincers, pliers.

iqamu 2. n. handcuffs, as used by police. Syn. *qato sitila,* a rather forced expression. Modern handcuffs are often made of plastic.

qamu, qamuta v. to close or clamp shut (usually the mouth), to squeeze or hold with pincers.
Idiom: *qamu gusu kina*: keep quiet about it, "clam up" about it.

qanuya or **qanu** n. rattan cane palm, Calamus vitiensis, Arecaceae, thin stems, very hard when mature, difficult to cut. Very long leaves, white flowers and scaly, round, tough fruit. Used in making round baskets (*sova*), often used for food presentations (*magiti*). School-teachers have used it for canes in disciplining children. Also uaws for walking sticks, and formerly, especially in the eastern highlands, for bows (as for shooting arrows) for combat. Around the coast, Fijians more commonly used mangrove aerial roots (*tiri*) for bows, but that was not available to highlanders. Syn. *qanu*.

qaqa 1. n. lyrics, of songs or the words of *serekali* verses. verse of a song or *meke*. *ena ikatolu ni qaqa ni meke* in the third verse of the *meke*.

qaqa 2. adj., n. victorious, victory, warrior, strong and bold. *Yaloqaqa* brave (when sure of success), high-spirited with confidence. *ilavo qaqa* cash.
Idiom: *Sa evei o qaqa? Sa laki yara.*
    Where is the champion? He is gone to his death.
Sa evei na datuvu? Sa lai tukutuku.
    What of the coward? Lived to tell the story.

qaqa 3. v. to win (in war, sports competition). *Qaqa vei Toga o Viti ena 21:18.* Fiji won over Tonga 21:18.

qaqa 4. adj. as in *ilavo qaqa* cash money.

vaqaqa (or) **qaqa** v. to investigate, question in detail, search. *vaqaqai* investigated. *na veivaqaqai* the investigation. *na dau veivaqaqai* the investigators, the people searching, the explorers.

vaqaqalo or **vaka-ta-qaqalo** v. to play around, swimming.

vaqaqa-taka v. to strengthen, to encourage, give confidence.

iqaqalo n. finger(s), toe(s). *iqaqalo ni liga* finger, *iqaqalo-ni-ligaqu* my finger(s). *qaqalo ni yava* toe. *iqaqalo levu* thumb (or) big toe. *vuso ni iqaqalo* fingertip (or) tip of the toe. *iqaqalo-ni-liga-mu kava* n. your third finger (ring finger) but fourth finger by Fijian counting. *kava* fourth. Most Fijians use specific names only for the thumb (*idovidovi-ni-kakana*), the index finger (*idusidusi-ni-turaga*). In olden times the other fingers in turn were referred to as the *tubu-siviti-ira*, the *drogadroga-wale*, *iloloku-ni-mate* and as suggested by that name for the little finger, that was chopped off in grief at the death of someone important such as a chief (and one would expect to be rewarded for showing such extreme grief).

qaqau-raka v. to destroy, crush violently. Syn. *samuraka*.

qaqawe (or) **qaweqawe** n. edible, very long-legged red-coloured land crab found on smaller islands. It has special significance at village Narocivo on Nayau Island, treated as an annual feast food when it moves en masse to the sea when the moon is full, on two consecutive months.

qaqi, qaqia v. to crush, grind; by ext. to beat up a person.

iqaqi n. mill (sugar, flour, pepper, timber), grinder. A famous part of old Suva is Na iQaqi, the location of a former sugar mill, at Carnavon Street, near the old U.S. Embassy and the Old Mill Cottage restaurant. *iqaqi ni suka* sugar mill. *iqaqi ni kauvaro* sawmill. *iqaqi ni vatu* n. stone-crusher. *iqaqi ni pepa* n. pepper grinder. *iqaqi ni falawa* n. flour mill. *na qaqaqi* the milling.

qaqo, qaqota v. to covet, to be greedy to take, others' share of some (usually food) distribution. There are many village occasions for collection and re-distribution of foods.

qara 1. n. hole *qara ena gaunisala* n. pot-hole in the road. *qaraqara* full of holes, potted (road). *qara ni ucuna* n. nostril. *qara ni benu* n. garbage pit (an introduced concept).

qara (or) **qaravatu 2.** n. cave. Some caves are sacred and in some, offerings were made. In a few places, caves were used for burials. Some were used to leave old people or sick people when they were no longer useful in the community. In Lau, some caves serve as a source of fresh water, as at Katafaga Island. Before the Pax Brittanica caves often served as part of protective fortresses for the village.

qara 3. n. cavity (dental). *Buluta na qara* to fill the cavity.

qara 4. (Anglicism) n. mine. *qara ni koula* n. gold mine.

qara (or) **vaqara, vaqara** v. search for. *qara vala* v. to look for a fight. s
  Idiom: *vaqara bitu* of a a woman, go look for a man to make love to. (Young sprouts at the base of a bamboo plant are thought to look like an erect penis.)
  Idiom: *qara ilavo* v. to raise money, seek funding, as for a charity, or a school. Such fund-raising is a frequent activity in Fiji.

qaramu (Eng.) n. gram (weight).

qarati (Eng.) garage.

qarauna v. to look after, watch over, take care of, be careful. *Qarauni iko!* Look out! Beware! *Me qarauni na coka.* Be careful about (Look out for) diarrhea. *Moni dau qaqarauni vinaka.* Always be very careful. *na qaqarauni* the carefulness.

qarava v. look after, take care of, attend to, treat (medically). *Mo qaravi iko.* Do look after yourself. Fijians speak of a wife taking care of her husband or people taking care of a chief, or a sick person. There is a very firm notion that a man should be looked after by a woman. Only a few decades ago, one or several women in the village would be assigned to "look after" a visitor. They attended to his every need or desire.

veiqaravi (Medical) n. treatment, medical care. *na nona itovo ni veiqaravi* his/her manner of treatment, his/her way of taking care of someone, something.

veiqaravi vakavanua n. traditional ceremony (a general term). These ceremonies usually require presentation of *yaqona*, whale teeth, woven mats, bark-cloth, traditional foods and/or more modern goods such as kerosene, cloth, tinned meat, biscuits. Implicitly, all ceremonies reaffirm social relations and assert a hierarchy of status.

qaravaki with head bowed down (usually from respect or fear).

qari n. Mangrove Crab, rock crab of the mangroves that swims, a favoured food, Scylla paramamosain or S. serrata, Portunidae. Commonly sold at the Suva market and by the side of the Queens Road usually tied in stacks of about five crabs in ascending order of size from top to the bottom of the string. In ceremonial food presentations ten *qari* might be referred to as one *vatu*. *ciriciri* immature, of sea crabs. *vacu-na* claw (or a crab), or fist of a person, or eyebrow of a person. *Sa momona na qari.* The sea crab is "full", in season. *Sa tawa na qari.* The sea crab is full of flesh. *Sa lala na qari.* The sea crab is empty of flesh. *Leuta mai na lewena.* Hook out the flesh. *lawasua* (or) *lawaicua* trap for sea crab. *vakasoso* n. sea crab flesh removed, then replaced in crab shell, cooked with coconut cream, a specialty of Lakeba Island (not to be confused with *vakasoso* pudding that is a sweet starch-food.) Syn.

qari vatu n. a rock crab, Swimmer Crab, Thalamita crenata or Calappa spp.

qari, qaria v. to graze, glance off, to brush against, as a boat against a wharf, one car against another.

qarikau adj. of a man, well built, huge in stature and girth, lit. graze the trees.

qaro, qarota, qarolaka v. to pierce, to prick, usually of a thorn, needle. Syn. *gadrota*. *qaroqaroa* (or) *gadrogadroa* adj. prickly.

qaru, qaruta v. to scratch (either gently, as for an itch, or harshly, like a cat).

qaru n. (Slang) self-interested chief or leader from the privileged upper classes who exploits his position for personal gain.

qaruqaru v., n. raking, to rake (leaves, cut grass). Fijians sometimes rake up rolls of cut grass with their hands to clear it away. Wire-grass lends itself to gathering up by rolling as if it were a very thick mat.

qase v, n. or adj. to age, aged, old, older person, elder (of the kin-group). *qase vei au* older than me. Age is relative, not absolute. Fijians never counted the years. In a village it is the elders (*na qase*) who advise the chief and help make decisions. People of Ra Province are sometimes respectfully referred to as *Na Qase* by Fijians of other areas, when they consider they themselves had originally come from Nakauvadra, Ra. *Qase makawa* person who has been around for a very long time. *Qase yalobula* elderly person who is lively, spirited, youthful in behaviour, attitude. *Sa qase mai o koya.* He/she has aged. Respectfully, children may refer to their parents as their *qase*.

Idiom: *Qase raqaraqa* elderly person who seeks our much younger partners, often with sexual implications.

Idiom: *Qase molau* in outward appearance elderly but inwardly youthful, and lustful with strong sexual interest. (The *molau* tree has youthful-looking heartwood),

qase ni vuli n. school teacher. *qasenivuli i liu* headmaster/headmistress of a school.

dau veivaqaseni n. person of mature or older age who takes advantage of young children, tricking them or exploiting them. Modernly the word is used for paedophiles, for adults who desire sex with under-age youngsters. Statutory rape in Fiji includes youngsters below 18 years of age.

qaseqase 1. adj. of a person growing to maturity, looks at first appearance as younger than he/she is, usually meaning small for his/her age.

qaseqase 2. sensible, careful, cautious, experienced in taking some responsibility (looking after a child, ensuring that food is properly divided up at a distribution of feast-food).

qaseqase 3. adj. diplomatic, crafty, cunning, experienced in judging and handling people.

qaseqasea adj. of a child, trying to act like a grown-up, somewhat inappropriately.

qaseta v. to be experienced, adept and responsible at something.

qasi, qasiva, qasitaka v. to crawl (child, crab). *qasiva* to crawl for or towards something or someone. *qasitaka* to crawl with something. *gone qasiqasi* n. child who has learned to crawl around. *qasi i duruduru kei na ligana* to crawl on hands and knees. See *kasi*.

qasikalolo n. ant.

qasivi n. very small type of ant. An influx of *qasivi* signal rainy weather to Fijians. Syn. *kasivi*.

iqaso n. claw (as of a crab, bat or cat), hook or clasp, latch (of a door), metal hook for taking in fish caught on a line; Wooden hook (*kau vakaiqaso*) used to gather cut grass (*co*) into rolls. Large hook to bring in a fish on a line beside a boat.

qaso, qasota v. to catch, clutch with the claw(s), to hook down and grasp, as of picking breadfruit, using a wooden hook *iqila*. See *qila, qilata* v. to use such a wooden hook (usually improvised hook from a broken or chopped branch).

qata, qatava v. to enclose, secure within a fence, as of animals in a compound, pigs in a pig-pen.

veiqati adj. envious, aggressively competitive, determined to win. *na veiqati* n. the envy, the rivalry, the competitiveness.

qatia v. to strive earnestly, to vie for, compete for.

qatima n. very small shrub, Urena lobata, Malvaceae, now a common weed, but introduced by aboriginal Fijians, probably because of its usefulness for the hibiscus-like fibre of the stem. The three-lobed, toothed leaves are lightly furry and grainy, used still for cleaning pots, rather like a scrubbing pad. The young leaves are sometimes chewed and swallowed to relieve diarrhoea. Also the stems are chewed and used as a probe to clean one's teeth. This use of young leaves and stems are customs shared with Fiji Indians. Flowers are pink and small. Prickly capsules of five seeds stick to clothes and animal fur, and are difficult to remove. Syn. *qatika*.

qato n. **1.** bracelet, arm-band or anklet, usually of leaves (as at a dance exhibition *meke*), discarded after the occasion. Also a bracelet of shell, such as Trochus, and modernly any bracelet. See *vesa*.

qato n. 2. bracken. May refer to the edible Pteridium esculentum, often growing on dry barren soils, especially Macuata and Ba, along with Dicranopteris linearis, a fern that is not eaten.

qatu-na n. vagina. Syn. *maga-na*. Words not used in proper company.

qau 1. n. possessive pronoun/noun for things that become an integral part of oneself. *na qau ibulubulu* my grave (where I will be buried). *na qau itukutuku* the report about me. *na qau* my (food, tobacco) that is mine in the sense that I will consume it. *Mequ* would apply to liquids, mine to consume (inc. ice cream, melons, oranges). *au kere qau* I request food (for me to eat). *e dua na qau pakete tavako* my package of cigarettes (for me to consume). Syn. *na kequ*.

qau 2. n. (Ra, Eastern Colo North) taro (*dalo*).

qauri (Hindi) n. male homosexual. The word is sometimes used mockingly. *Qauri qase* (Slang) old poofter. Syn. *vakasalewalewa* effeminate, of a man, often implying homosexuality.

qava, qavaraka v. to dodge, duck down, in hiding or in dodging some missile such as a spear, or a stone.

qava, qavata v. to dig, as in digging out soil for a ditch or grave, or in digging at the surface to remove weeds, as one might do modernly with a hoe. *na qavaqava* the digging. *iqava* implement used to dig. *kutari* hoe. *na isivi* the spade, shovel. In early days coastal Fijians might use a large shell; highlanders had only a digging stick (*doko*). See *keli, kelia* v. to dig (as of a hole in the ground, or a ditch for drainage, or as to dig up a wild yam).

iqavi (Archaic) special kind of package, wrapping up traditional blocks of sea salt at the coastal village Lomaniwai, Nadroga. The wrapping is made with strips of thin, sturdy bark from aerial shoots of mangrove. *iqavi masima* n. wrapped block of salt. In traditional exchanges, ten such blocks would be referred to as one *wai*. The same word *wai* refers to ten packages of Fijian pudding *vakalolo* or traditional *madrai* as made at village Naila, near Suva.

qavi, qavia (VanuaLevu) v. to weed. Syn. *were, wereca*.

qavokavoka n. skull. Syn. *qa*.

qavu-na n. small remaining portion, the very little that is left, the very few that remain. *na qavu ni waiwai* the very small amount of oil remaining. *na qavu ni turaga dina* one (or very few) remaining true chieftains. *qavu e dua ga na nona isulu*. He/she has only one piece of clothing.

Idiom: (Slang) "No *qavuna*" No money. I am broke.

qawe-na n. leg(s) of a crab.

qe, qeva v. to scoop out, dig out earth, sand (of a person with the hands or a dog with the paws), or as scooping up shellfish in the hands.

qeavu v., adj. destroyed, disappeared, exterminated. Examples: village or jetty or garden by a hurricane, a city by bombs, an old village abandoned, overgrown.

vakaqeavu-taka v. to destroy (it).

qei (Rewa) mum, mummy. Syn. *nana, na*.

qele 1. n. land, soil, earth, clay. *qele bulabula* fertile land. *qele matemate* infertile land. *qele damudamu* latersol, infertile acid soil, red from iron compounds (and useful only for growing pineapple). *qelekuro* soil for making clay pots. *qele lisi* lease-land. *qele voli vakadua* freehold land, held in fee simple. and can be sold (foreigners buying need ministerial approval). *na kena volitaki na qele* the sale of land. *Qele Maroroi* Native Land (owned by Fijian kin-groups and cannot be sold). *Qele Kovu* or, more fully, *Qele Kovuti Maroroi* Native Land Reserve, assigned to clans or tribes for their own use (not to be leased to others). *Qele boro damudamu* land belonging to the government (state land, formerly crown land). *itaukei ni qele* native landowners. In ancient tradition this referred only to the first settlers who remained on the land. Later accretions to the settlement were often given land which in many cases then became registered as belonging to the new settlers. Politically, *itaukei ni qele* now refers to all those Fijians registered as owning native land as recorded by the Native Lands Commission.

qele 2. n. flock (as with sheep, an expression often used in church) or school (as with fish). *na qele ni ika* the school of fish. *na qele ni yatu* the school of tuna. *e dua na ika ka dau qeleqeleni vata tu* a (type of) fish that schools together. *qeleni* flocked together, gathered together as fish in a fish-trap or net, herded together (cattle or sheep).

qeleqelea adj. soiled with dirt, as of clothes or the hands after gardening.

qelo n., adj. club-foot.

qeqe n. a small shellfish at the shore, Gafrarium turridum, but several edible species resembling the larger, better known *kai koso*, Anadara cornea.

qera, qeqera v. drop down (leaves, seed capsules, light fruit, usually many of them). *qeqera* implies many leaves, seeds, fruit. *vaqera, vakavaqerataka* to make such things fall. For some fruits Fijians may beat the tree branches for the ripe fruits to fall. *bita, bitalaka na tabana* to beat the branches in this way. *Sa-*

kurea na taba ni maqo e na qai qera na vuana. Shake the branch of the mango tree so that the fruit will fall down.

Idiom: *qera* v. to lose, in sport such as football.

qeremavu v., n. to belch or burp. This was formerly polite custom for a guest to burp when eating, as a compliment to the host, for the satisfying food. This is hardly done in modern times. The custom was fading by the mid 1900s. See *dorokona, derekona, todoge.*

qereqere n. gravel. *vaqereqeretaka* to lay down gravel (on road, path). *na gaunisala qereqere* the gravel road.

Idiom: (Vulgar Slang) *sova qereqere* to vomit after drinking too much *yaqona* or alcohol.

qesa 1. adj. somewhat charred by fire, usually of food such as root crops. *qulali* charred seriously and dried out from over-cooking.

qesa 2. n. Lipstick tree, introduced, Bixa orellana, usually cultivated. Seeds formerly used for brilliant red face-paint in the last decades of the 1800s.

qeteqete (ni liga-na) n. palm (of the hand). Syn. *ketekete.*

qeteqete (ni yava-na) n. sole of the foot.

qeu, qeuta 1. v. to draw out the coils of Fijian hair, to straighten and extend them from their normal compact condition. This is traditional custom, formerly done with a single-pronged probe *iqeu.* Paramount chiefs had specialists (*dauniulu*) who trimmed, dyed and extended their hair.

qeu, qeuta 2. v. scrape up, dig up with the hands, usually in soft earth or sand (as in gathering some shellfish).

qia, qia (or) **qiava** v. to tattoo, traditionally only women, around the mouth, and private parts and upper thighs, often a necessary ritual before marriage. In nearby Polynesia, to the east, only men had a tattoo; there has been much masculine prestige associated with the tattoo. Commonly Fijian youngsters, girls and boys, now have a crude tattoo, school initials, names, simple markings made by amateurs. *veiqia* n. tattooing. *iqia* (or) *bati ni veiqiiia* n. thorn used to prick tattoo into the skin. *samuqawe, samuqawe-taka* v. to tattoo, more usually refers modernly (not old custom) to this done on a man or to youngsters, just for fun.

qila, qilata v. to hook down (as of fruit from a tree); to hook long, thick grass for cutting or rolling into a large roll, for burning. This is done with a stick that has a crotch or hook at the end, from a lopped off branchlet.

iqilai n. wooden crook used to pull and gather grass to be cut when clearing land, or used to roll up a carpet of grass after it is cut loose with the knife. Another use is to pull down branches to reach fruit to be picked. The tool is improvised from a small tree-branch and is usually discarded after its immediate use.

Idiom: *leka na noqu iqilai* lit., my *iqilai* is too short, i.e., I do not have the power or authority to do that. That is beyond my reach. I cannot do that.

qilaiso n. wood coals, especially as used for earth oven. *qilaiso boko* extinguished coals.

qili, qilia v. to rub, as between the hands, or with hand against thigh, as in rolling sinnet (*magimagi*), or in softening medicinal leaves before applying to a wound. Also applies to a child's top, to set it spinning. *qilia na matana* to rub one's eyes, as in waking. *qiliraka* break up forcefully in the hands, as with some tree-bark in preparating of native medicine.

qiliqili 1. adj. smooth.

qiliqili 2. n. cooked balls of dough with leavening, a breakfast food. Often grated cassava, finely grated coconut, with cassava starch that has been prepared in advance. The balls are boiled in water. Syn. *yaloka ni vonu.*

qiliqilica adj. entangled, unkempt, uncombed, of the hair.

qima 1. (Colo East, Rewa) finished.

qima 2. (Archaic) a word spoken in challenge, offering a riddle. The response is "*qama*".

qimaqima (Archaic) n. riddle. Syn. *vatavata-i-ra-lago.*

qina n. edible sea urchin, echinus, similar to *cawaki* but shorter spines. Echinometra sp. Syn. (Nadro.) *qinaqina.*

qio n. shark. Fijians of Tongan origin, from Benau or Kadavu Island, have little fear of sharks. Dakuwaqa is a widely recognised shark-god who can be protective of people, especially if a libation of kava is poured for him. Sharks are symbolic for the Tui Cakau at Taveuni Island. One is supposed to appear at the shore when a Tui Cakau is being installed. Unlike Samoans and Tongans, Fijians have not usually fished for sharks. (Samoans and Tongans have done it from a small canoe, with a noose and a knife, sometimes a fishing line.) At Vatoa Island and at Waya Island there has been a custom of burying gutted sharks to preserve them for food. Despite the extremely strong foetid smell, the taste is considered excellent by locals. For food, Fijians have more commonly caught seasonal baby sharks near the beach, by spearing. Most adult shark meat is soft and relatively tasteless, except for the mako shark where the flesh is firm and white, rather like the swordfish. Shark flesh has been reported as occasionally poisonous but more often, shark liver can be deadly poisonous. It is mainly, if not only, Gilbertese who relish shark liver, usually made into a sort of sausage with shark intestine as a casing.

Idiom: *vakania na qio* vomit (usually from sea-sickness), lit. "feed the sharks".

Idiom: *Leqa ga na qio qai kata.* lit. The shark only bites when in trouble, said of a person who did something wrong only because they were in trouble.

qiovuki v. sprained, of the ankle.

qiqi 1. n. wagon, trailer, cart. *qiqi ukutaki* n. decorated "float" (as in a parade, such as Suva City's Hibiscus Festival). *qiqi vakaivalu* military tank. *vaqiqi, vaqiqica* to roll something. to cause something to be rolled along. *yava ni qiqi* wagon wheel(s). *yava ni motoka* motor-car wheel(s). Ancient Fijians used rollers only for moving boats to water; there were no carts or wheels as such.

qiqi 2. n. Layard's White Eye, or the more common Grey-Backed White Eye, Zosterops spp., a small endemic bird with conspiuous white ring around the eye. It tolerates the close presence of a human, and may be regular visitors to a verandah. Often flies in flocks. The Grey-Backed White Eye has a more distinct yellow breast and underparts.

qiqi, qiqica v. to roll (ball, metal drum, boat on rollers). *qiqica na taya* to roll the tyre (as children might do). Fijians had no concept of wheels.

Idiom: *qiqi cabe* to move by rolling over in pretended sleep, with the purpose of making love to someone lying nearby. This is similar to the idiom *kedru toso* to pretend to be sleeping (snoring lightly), while moving closer to a prospective lover who is lying nearby. (The visitation is usually not at all welcome.)

Qiqi mai, Qiqi yani (Ang.) n Ro-Ro boat, "Roll-on-- Roll-off".

vakaqiqiqi v. to roll over and over, keep rolling.

qiqo adj. narrow (as of a road or path). By ext., the Anglicism, to be narrow in one's thinking.

qiri, qiria 1. v. to beat (traditional wooden gong, *lali*).

qiri, qiria (or) **qirita 2.** v. to ring (bell, telephone). *Qiria na* crime-stoppers ring up the crime-stoppers. *qiriqiri ki na naba* 336 2888. Phone the number 336 2888. Phone numbers are spoken with a series of single digits: *tolu, tolu, ono . . .* etc.

qiri, qiria 3. v. to play (instrument such as guitar). *dauqiriqiri* instrumentalist (for Fijians, usually a guitar or ukelele but also electonic keyboard). *Lotu qiriqiri* Assemblies of God, a Protestant evangelical sect that emphasizes emotive singing with guitars as a principal instrument. *na mataqiriqiri* (or) *na qiriqiri* n. the band (musical). *na qiriqiri* the ringing (of bell), the sounding (of a drum *lali*), the playing or strumming (of guitar, ukelele).

Idiom: *qiri kava*: beating on tins, usually by youngsters, at occasions such as New Years Eve, as a means of celebrating, often walking about. Where they visit they may expect some food or gifts, candy or cash on the occasion. It is custom to splash them with water but then one should give them some dry clothes, a custom called *vakamamaca,* a drying off. To some extent, such behaviour continues in rural areas.

Qirimiti (Hindi) n. Girmit, indentured labour from India.

qirinami (Eng.) n. "green army", gang of no-account unemployed youngsters who cause trouble in town. They hang out together.

qirisi (Eng.) n. grease. *dakai ni qirisi* grease-gun.

iqisa ni veiqia n. tattoo "ink", trad. made from candlenut in coastal areas, *makadre* (burnt resin from the *dakua* tree in the highlands), charred coals or modernly, plain black soot. The blackening was usually mixed in vegetable oil, mostly coconut oil along the coast. The highlanders never had any kind of body oil.

qisa, qisa v. to paint the face (formerly usually with war-paint). *iqisa* face-paint. *iqisaqisa* face-painting. Syn. *qumu*. Putting on war-paint or removing it is a symbolic act of importance, beyond its practical significance.

qisa n. introduced annato, "lipstick" tree, Bixa orellana, mature seeds brilliant red, may be applied directly. Used as face-paint in latter half of 1800s. Syn. *qesa*.

qisi, qisia 1. v. to appoint (person) to some position or task.

qisi, qisia 2. v. to stir in, mix in, with a stick or heavy spoon, as with heavy ingredients for a pudding (*vakalolo*) or cake. *iqisi* stick used to stir forcefully.

qisi, qisia 3. v. to quick-fry. (Nothing was fried in ancient Fiji; there was no cooking oil). Street vendors of BBQ foods are now common in the larger towns.

qiso, qisora v. to stir up a fire, by re-arranging the burning wood using a stick, especially for earth-oven (*lovo*) stones. *iqiso* n. stick used as a poker.

qita (Eng.) n. guitar. *qita livaliva* electric guitar.

qitawa n. edible fish, tiger fish, crescent perch, Therapon jarbua, that schools close to shore, often caught in nets by groups of women together, standing waist-deep in the water with a long nets. Grunts when caught or handled. A scavenger, it eats all sorts of garbage including human excrement at the seashore. The tiny baby fish appear in March. Syn. *qiawa, kabarara, ovisa ni baravi.*
qito n. game, sport(s). *rara ni qito* playing field.
dauqito n. sportsman, sportswoman.
qito, qitora v. to play, play with (person, people).
qitoca v. to contravene the rules of a sport or game.
veiqitori v., n. play around, fool around.
qitotaka v. to play, play with (an object). *qitotaka na polo* to play with the ball. *na qitoqito* the playing.
qiva, qiva v. to drill a hole, to bore a hole.
qivoqivora adj. short, thick-set, stocky and hardy, usually of a man.
qo here, now, this. Common abbrev. of *oqo* when it begins a sentence or follows a word ending in a vowel. *Na tamata qo* This (or these) person (people).
qo, qota (na uluna) v. to "dong" (someone's head) with one's knuckles, to flash (as a cat's paw).
qoca n. stones used in earth oven (*lovo*), to be heated and cook the food. A household keeps the location and stones for re-use. Appropriate stones are not available in many places. *Sa dravu* (or) *rarasea na qoca* The stones are hot enough.
qoka that's it. here it is. More of less the equiv. of the French expression "Voici!".
qoli, qoliva v. to fish, to fish for (marine animal). Usually this is done with nets. This term did not traditionally include hook and line fishing and definitely excludes trawling which was not a technique known to Fijians. *na qolivi ni vonu* the fishing for turtle. *qoliva na balolo* v. to fish for *balolo. Tabana ni Qoliqoli* Fisheries Department.
iqoliqoli n. traditional fishing grounds reserved by law for one or more Fijian clans. There are somewhat more than 400 such reserves. It is a subject of many disputes. Within lagoons one may not fish without permission of the clan or tribe that owns the fishing rights there. Poaching can be a serious problem.
qolo-na n. grass or shrub having internodes *vakatagona,* such as bamboo, *yaqona,* sugar cane, *duruka.* See *tagau, tago-na.*
qolou , qolouvaka v., n. to shout out, scream or shriek in sudden response, surprise, alarm, fear, sudden shock, to shout about something. *qoqolou* v. to scream very strongly. See *kaila* v. to shout.
qolua (Colo) n. river fish-trap made of bamboo (*bitu dina*) or the hollow trunk of a fern tree (*balabala*). Eels (*duna*), prawns (*ura*) or fish find refuge in the trap. Nothing prevents them from escaping, but Fijians lift up the trap suddenly and often thus capture what creatures are hiding there.
qonini v. to shiver from the cold, especially when wet. *sautaninini* v. to tremble, shiver and shake.
qoqo, qoqona (or) **qoqota** v. to take up in the arms (e.g. pile of clothes, leaves that have been raked), by extension to carry off a prize (sports, school). A fish with a mouth that gathers its food is said to have a *gusu qoqo* a mouth that gathers up its food. This contrasts with predator fish such as the barracuda or shark that attacks its prey.
qoqori v., n. to mutter, murmur indistinguishably, as in one's sleep or trance, as when possessed by a devil.
qori there (where you are), abbrev. of *oqori,* especially when used as an expression alone, or at the beginning of a sentence, or following some words ending in a vowel. As an exclamation by itself, it can variously mean "That's it!", "Right, you are correct", "You got what you deserved!" (implying the person was warned). *Qori gona na vuna!* There, that is thus the cause! *Qori kina!* Idiom: There!, that's what you deserve!
qoro, qoroya (or) **qorotaka** v. to be amazed at (something), to admire greatly., to stare at and marvel at.
qoroi adj. amazing, admirable. *E qoroi o Tukana.* Tukana is amazing. *na iqoroi* the thing that amazes; the thing causing amazement.
qoroqoro n. amazement. *ena qoroqoro* in amazement.
qoroqoroya v. to be proud, boastful, of something as if it were amazing.
qoru adj. as in *bati qoru* gap-toothed (of visibly missing teeth). Syn. *bati lutu.*
qou, qouta v. to strike (usually the head of a child) with the middle knuckles of the fist (not the whole fist). This is a brutal punishment for children. *iqou* n. such a blow, usually to the head. *lauqou* n., v., give such a blow very hard.
qua, qua or **quata, quaraka** v. to wipe hard, rub hard (or even scrub hard). *na iqua* the scrubber (the thing one scrubs with or rubs hard with). *quata na gone lailai.* wipe the baby's bottom.

quava (or) **quwawa** (Eng.) n. guava, an introduced weed tree that is most difficult to eradicate because the roots persist and give rise to new shrubs. The mature leaves are chewed as an effective cure for diarrhoea. The fruit is relished though fruit fly does great damage.

qulali adj. charred and dried out, of food burnt accidentally in earth oven. See *qesa*.

qulaqulau 1. v., n., adj. proud in the sense of being vain, showing off. *vaqulaqulau-taka* v. to show off about something.

qulaqulau 2. adj. of work, performance, undependable, erratic.

qumi, qumia (or) **qumita** v. to clench or clutch in the hand. *qumia na liga-na*.

iqumi n. fist.

qumi-ivacu v. to form a fist with the hand, as if ready to strike. Syn. *bulivacu*.

vaqumi, vaqumia (Slang) v. to bribe.

veivaqumi n. bribe, bribery, corruption "pay-off".

vaqumia-i-ligana v. to pass off something to someone secretly, putting it in their hand inconspicuously.

qumu n. large tree to 20 m., Acacia richii, Mimosaceae, endemic to Fiji on the two major islands, small, pale yellow flowers in fluffy, globose heads and fruit (linear pods to 12 cm) May to December. Bark provides a blackening used formerly as war paint for the face. Botantist Degener mentions that it was its charcoal that was used to blacken the face as war "paint". Timber for building.

qumu, qumuta v. to paint the face (formerly with war paint). Applying war paint is an idiom used figuratively, to indicate preparation for a serious confrontation. Application and removal of war-paint were both highly symbolic actions. Warrior mercenaries expect to be rewarded before they remove war-paint. *qusini-loa* n. to wipe off war-paint. Syn. *qisa, qisa*.

iqumu n. facial paint (as for a warrior), using the plant-dye *qumu*.

quralasawa (ni liga) n. wrist. See *quraqura ni yava*.

qurulasawa (ni yava) n. ankle.

quraqura (ni yava) n. hoof of cattle or of horse. Syn. *ququ-na*.

ququ v. to drag, of an anchor. *Sa ququ na ikelekele*. The anchor is dragging.

ququ-na n. hoof of animal, base of the human foot.

ququ adj. fixedly curled in, as of an arthritic hand.

ququ, ququca v. to close the hand, to clasp in the hand, to clutch.

ququ ni pusi (Archaic) n. a punishment for young school children, having them hold out the hands and striking the ends of their fingers with a ruler. From idle curiosity, I have had this demonstrated on my hand by none less than the late Semesa Sikivou, former headmaster of Queen Victoria School, later Minister for Education. It is indeed very painful.

quru, quruta, qurulaka v. to crunch, as in eating.
  Idiom: *quruta na uluna* "eat his head" by crunching it with the teeth, threatening words about someone one hates, but not to be taken literally these days. The head was considered sacred as a receptacle for a person's personal power (*mana*). *caca-quruquru* adj. crunchy, crackly as with a crisp piece of toast, or some snack foods. See *raqosa* crackle, crispy, rustle.
  Idiom: *Laki quru rokete* lit. go crunch hot chilli, i.e., gone to gaol.

veiquru biting, usually with a grinding action of the teeth, often done when people are grappling in a fight. Serious wounds can be inflicted. This is usually done along with forceful kicking and punching.

qurulasawa n. ankle bone.

quruquru ni liga n. knuckles (of the hand).

quruveibati v. to grind the teeth together. *E quruveibati na batina*. He ground his teeth (with emotion, anxiety). Some people do this in their sleep.

qusi, qusia, qusiraka v. to wipe, wipe up (table, floor), rub out or off (blackboard, warpaint from the face), to wipe dry. *tata qusiqusi* partly erased, faint, unclear. *iqusiqusi* n. towel for drying dishes, or hands and mouth after using a finger-bowl at the end of a meal. *iqusi ni liga* n. hand towel.

iqusi ni loaloa n. ceremonial presentation of goods, food, in appreciation for warrior service of suborned allies or mercenaries for their aid. Literally, the wiping off of warpaint. Only after being rewarded would warriors remove the war-paint. Fijians now speak of this figuratively, bringing an end to hostilities.

R

The Fijian **r** is very strongly rolled, or trilled. In reciting the Fijian alphabet, **r** is pronounced as **ra**.

Ra 1. (followed by the name of an animal). In stories for children, as in Fijian or European fables, animals may be referred to as *Ra Vonu* Sir Turtle, *Ra Qio* Sir Shark, and so on, for other animals.

Ra 2. n. name of a Fijian Province.

Ra 3. or **E ra** or **Era** they (many people, more than four), as subject of sentence.

ira them (many people), as the object of a sentence.

i ra or **e ra** 1. below. *E vei? I ra, ena ruku ni teveli.* Where? Down below, underneath the table. The opposite "up" is *e cake, ena dela ni teveli*, above, on top of the table.

i ra or **e ra** 2. downwind, which usually means in a westward direction. The opposite "upwind" *e cake*. The prevailing tradewind in the southern hemisphere comes from the southeast. In the northern hemisphere it comes from the northeast. In between, in the central tropics, are the doldrums.

vakara westerly. *ena Yasayasa vakaRa* in the Western Division (administrative area of Fiji). Originally, the closest Fijian equivalent of the west was in fact the northwest, downwind of the tradewind that comes from the southeast. Fijians now modify their naming of directions to match the European names of compass directions.

raba n. width. *rabalailai* not wide enough. *E vica na kena raba?* How wide is it? *raba levu* too wide. *raraba* adj. wide. *vaka-raba-levu-taka* or *vakararaba-taka* v. to make it wider. *Rabailevu na vakacaca ni cagilaba.* Damage of the hurricane is widespread. Syn. *raraba*.

rabe, rabeta 1. to kick with forward motion, usually with the side of the foot, as often done in soccer. *rabelaka* kick with full force. *caqe, caqeta* v. to kick forward, as in football, in a drop-kick, using the front of the foot. *teke, tekea* v. to kick with backward motion, as a horse does.

rabe, rabeta 2. to trip up a person, usually with the foot.

rabe, rabeta 3. to drink a cup of *yaqona* after a chief (or person of high status) as a symbol of being a "second" to him. For a chief, this is usually his *matanivuanua* who drinks after him. The order in which individuals are served is a silent statement of hierarchy. Outside of highly ceremonial occasions, the senior person may defer to someone else as an indication of proper humility. *Au rabeti koya.* I follow him/her (in order of being served). Such ceremonial drinking of *yaqona* that re-affirms the social hierarchy is of Tongan innovation, now adopted throughout Fiji, but in earlier times, quite foreign to highlanders and other indigenous Melanesian Fijians.

raberabe n. a painful malady of the finger or toe with some swelling. The skin becomes separated, rather like a blister and pus (*nana*) may emerge. This, and a very few other real physical ailments are known as "Fijian ailments" (*tauvimate vakaViti*) that are not readily distinguished in Western medicine by having their own name. See *baubau, drimi*. Some Fijians believe witchcraft is the cause of *raberabe*, but this is a very common belief for virtually all illness or afflictions.

rabo, rabota v. to lash, as in the act of whipping, or firing off a sling. *Sa raboti koya na vai.* The stingray lashed him. *veirabo* lashing. *vakarabota na laca* flush out the sail (with the wind).

raborabo-caka n., v. to punch out forcefully.

irabo n. sling, a weapon formerly used in war, especially by Melanesian Fijians for hurling stones quite accurately. The ancient skill is lost. These days little use is made of slings, only rarely by children at play.

radini(vale) n. housewife. *radini sotia* soldier's wife.

Radini (followed by place-name). In some places, such as Levuka, on Lakeba Island, this is the title of the chief's wife, as in Radini Levuka, wife of the Tui Levuka. Radini Waimaro has been a leading chiefly designation in the highlands of Viti Levu, only known by the name of a sacred wooden figurine of super-tribe Waimaro. With elaborate respect some prominent positions might justify courtesy such as *Radi ni talatala* wife of the preacher.

rafolo (Eng.) n. raffle, a very common way of raising money in Fiji.

Ragone a friendly term of address to a group of young people by someone senior. For youths, *Ra cauravou*.

rai, raica v. to see, view, look (at). *rai mai!* look here! *e na noqu rai* in my view (opinion), as I see it. *rai lesu* look back, review. *raici lesu* reviewed. Syn. (Kadavu) *gaca*.

Idiom: *Rai ira me dua na kemu da!* It's right there in front of you, what you are looking for! Lit. Look down to find your own excrement!

rai n. opinion, personal view. *Na cava na nomu rai me baleta na Yavutu.* What is your opinion of the Constitution?

veirai v. to look at each other, see each other. *Erau sega tale ni veirai.* They (2) never saw each other again.

raibasika, raibasika-taka v. to see through, as very thin clothing, or figuratively, to see through some devious scheme.

rairai 1. v., n. to seem, appears that. *rairai tauvimate* to appear to be ill. *E rairai ni sega ni rawa.* It seems it is not possible. *Eratou sa rairai kila e dua na ka.* They (few) seem to know something. *E rairai vinaka.* It looks good.

rairai 2. (Ang.) v. to appear, as in *rairai ki na Mataveilewa* to appear before the court. to put in an appearance.

rairai 3. v. to foresee what is unknown to others, as by a seer (*dau rai*), usually accompanied by drinking of *yaqona* and shamanistic trance, still done today.

irairai n. appearance. *na kequ irairai* my appearance, my looks, how I look or seem. *e rairai kilikili ka rakorako* has a fitting and tasteful appearance. *na kena irairai* its appearance in the sense of what it looks like or figuratively, the way it seems.

dau rairai or **dau rai** n. soothsayer who speaks from an emotive trance after a special *yaqona* ceremony (and Christian prayer these days). Given a question, he/she is supposed to reveal the truth of past or future. This is not a full-time occupation but rather a sideline of gifted people. The questioner brings *yaqona* but normally pays nothing.

rairai rua v. to see double, as with troubled vision, or intoxication.

veiraiyaki v. n. looking about here and there.

vakaraica v. to watch, to look for something or someone.

raica sobu v. (Anglicism) to look down on, despise.

vakarai-taka to show, reveal, demonstrate.

ivakaraitaki n. demonstration, example (to illustrate a point). *E dua na kena ivakaraitaki* An example of it.

raici lesu reviewed, looked back upon.

raikivi, raikivita v. to glance briefly over the shoulder, look back over the shoulder (at something). *raikivita* may imply a more studied look.

Railevu n. title of territorial chief of Burenitu, Serua Province.

railo, railotaka v. to take a secret look, sneaky look. *lo* silent.

raimate v., n. (Anglicism) medical rounds of doctor at hospital. *mate* illness.

raimuri, raimuria v. to look back at (something), as in looking over the shoulder but also to look following something in action that is moving, as an aeroplane coming in to land, or a bird in the sky. *muri* can mean "back" or behind, or it can mean to follow.

rairai-rua (Angicism) v. to see "double", as with impaired vision.

raisara v. to stare blankly, eyes remaining open (lit. "just look'), gaze unfocussed, seeing nothing, which may continue a long time. The mind is vacant, quite blank.

raisi (Eng.) rice. This non-traditional starch food is very commonly eaten because it has been cheaper than traditional root starches (taro, yam), and is not so perishable. Unfortunately, it lacks the nutrition of traditional starch-foods. Rice is always purchased, never grown by Fijians in their food gardens, so Fijians must earn money to buy it. In Fiji, rice is labour-intensive, not an economic crop except for poor farmers who have no alternative. *raisi ni veikau* a small, useless weed with tiny white flowers; the seeds resemble miniature rice and the roots have a pungent, pleasant smell.

Idiom: *kana raisi* to be in prison (where rice is a common food).

Idiom: *Maqa na leqa, sa matua na raisi.* (Macuata): Nor to worry, there's rice we can eat (even if nothing else).

raitayaloyalo-taka v. to illustrate, to show or make apparent, bring to mind, to imagine.

raivakababa, raivakababa-taka v. to look from the corner of the eye.

Raitena n. chiefly title, for example at Nasaga, Bureta.

raivotu, raivotutaka v. to envision.

raivotu 1. n, apparition, to appear as a spirit, as the Virgin Mary, for example, or as an indigenous spirit *kalou*.

raivotu 2. n. (Modernism) foresight or vision of or for the future.

rai vou n. (Ang.) "new look", of something revised, more fashionable.

raivuki, raivukica v. to look in turning back, to turn back and look.

raivuli n., v. school inspection. *dau raivuli* school inspector.

raiyawa n., adj. far-sighted, literally or figuratively; visionary who forsees future developments.

rakavi (Eng.) rugby. The second "a" is hardly pronounced. *rakavi saumi* rugby league (professional rugby). *rakavi le yavitu* rugby sevens. *rakavi liki* rugby league. Rugby is virtually an obsession of some Fijian men. It is a useful sublimation of the earlier Fijian's combative warrior culture.

rakorako adj. appropriate, suitable, in terms of fitting into a context, as one piece of clothing matching another.

Raluve n. princess (of European aristocracy), or daughter of a paramount chief in Polynesian areas, where such hierarchies have some relevance. In Fijian culture today these terms appear only in children's stories or in relation to the English Crown. *Ravovou* prince, similarly, non-existent in Fiji.

rama ca faint, dim, inadequate light, as from a lamp lacking fuel. Syn. *ramalailai*.

Ramacake n. legendary man at Makogai Island, an origin spirit of the super-tribe Mataisau, canoe builders and carpenters from early central Polynesia who settled in various places of eastern Fiji. He was famous for his lilting, romantic music played on his nose-flute. This music was heard by ladies at Bau Island who were attracted to search him out. Thinking himself ugly – it is speculated he may have had leprosy - he diverted them to search elsewhere while he remained alone and shy.

rama levu bright, of a light. See *ramase*.

Ra Malo n. chiefly title at Dravuni (Ono Island, Kadavu Province), Nacavanadi (Gau Island), and Ketei (Totoya Island).

Ra Marama 1. archaic title, no longer used, for a very high-born lady.

Ra Marama 2. name of famous double canoe, a *drua*, built at Somosomo in mid or early 1840s by Tongans, given to Cakobau by Tui Cakau, who then gave it to the Tui Tonga (Nov., 1853) in anticipation of military help that defeated Rewa and Bau rebels at Kaba in 1855. The ship made three trips to Tonga. After Cakobau's death in 1883 it was returned to Taveuni, where it was left to rot. Length 102 feet (*Rusa-i-vanua* was 118 feet.), beam 18 feet, mast 68 feet, crew of 140 men. Men clubbed at keel-laying but prevented by missionaries at launching. Lasakau provided 21 bodies at Bau to compensate for that omission. (See Derrick's *History of Fiji*).

ramarama (Archaic) n. oil lamp, usually coconut oil in a simple clay dish, made only around the coasts. Highlanders had no oil lamps but used wood fires and burning resin (*makadre*) of the *dakua* tree as a light in the evening. Sleep usually came early.

ramase v., n., adj. very bright, of a lamp light. Syn. *ramalevu*.

Ra Masi n. chiefly title at Natokalau and Navatu, Kubulau (Vanua Levu Island), at Qalikarua (Matuku Island), and Nasaqalau (Lakeba Island), and Moce Island.

ramu (Eng.) n. rum, manufactured in Fiji from local sugar cane.

ramusu adj. broken (limb of person or tree, axe-handle). See *musu, musuka*.

vaka-ramusu (Slang) v., adj. to act the fool by body posture or facial grimace as a youngster might do when a photo is being taken.

ranadi lady of very high chiefly rank. Applied to the U.K. this word means Queen. Capitalised, and followed by a place-name, as in Ranadi ni Narauyabe, this is a proper way of referring to the wife of certain chieftains. This may be abbreviated as Radi Narauyabe.

rapa (Eng.) n. rubber. May refer to a condom.

raqa, raqataka v. to show off (something).

raqa, raqataka v. of a boar, to lash out with his tusks, as in fighting off dogs.

iraqa (ni vuaka) n. boar's tusks, sometimes worn around a warrior's neck.

raqaraqa adj., n. self-consciously assertive, putting oneself up in a showy way, show off.

raqosa 1. adj. dry and crisp (as leaves might be, or potato chips, or toast).

raqosa 2. v. to rustle, sizzle, make a noise like stepping on crisp dry leaves.

rara 1. n. village "square", an open field, usually in the centre of the village, by ext., playing field (sports), aeroplane field for take-off and landing. Anciently, there was no established custom of a village square. *tuirara* church warden. *rara ni waqavuka* n. airfield. *rara ni qito* sports field. *rara ni veivacu* boxing ring. *Raralevu* Albert Park in Suva, where some sports are played. *rara ni ivalu* battlefied. *buturara* n. floor.
Idiom: *lave, laveta na rara* win the game (of visiting team). The term is adapted from English, to "raise" the field. Syn. *cola na rara*.

rara 2. n. (Archaic) ten pigs for ceremonial presentation.

rara 3. smarting, as from sunburn, or from a smack of a hand-slap.

rara, raraga v. to warm up something by the fire, usually plantain leaves used for wrapping food. Heat makes them more readily flexible or pliant and less inclined to split or tear. Also applies to warm one's body by a fire, formerly often done by highland men of Viti Levu in the evening.

irara (Archaic) n. indoor fire used for human warmth (rather than cooking). *tatalai* v. to warm oneself in this way. Formerly, in a men's house, there might be a fire for each sleeping section for one or two men, especiall in the highlands.

vakarara v. to warm oneself by a fire made for that purpose.

ivakarara (Archaic) n. frame, usually of bamboo, formerly used by men as a prop for their legs, to warm them beside a fire in the evening. This was a custom mainly in the highlands of Viti Levu, where the mountain air and icy streams can be very chilling. (Temperatures down to 40 degrees F. may occur and icy hail is common.) The eastern highland term is *iragiti*. *lai vakarara* go prop up one's legs by the fire to warm them. The custom has fallen into disuse because of the availability of clothes, but also the disappearance of men's houses and their indoor, bedside fires. *raraga* v. to warm one's body in this way.

raraba (or) **raba** n., adj. width, breadth, the totality of an area; common or widely accepted. *Evica na kena raba* (or) *raraba?* How wide is it? *raba-i-levu* very wide. *na kena rabailevu* its width. *Na cagi laba a ravuti Viti raraba.* The hurricane struck a killing blow to the whole of Fiji. *na yacana raraba* the common name (as for a group of things, places).

raradamu n., adj. dull red, like the dead leaves of some deciduous trees.

rarakaka smarting painfully, as from sunburn, scorching. Syn. *rara*.

rarama n., v. to be lit up. light (as opposed to darkness of the surroundings).

vakararavi adj., n. dependent (person, people, clans). Clans that settled later at a village (i.e., not the original settlers there) have often been accepted, and permitted to use land, while remaining in a somewhat subservient, dependent role. Similarly children or adults may be accepted into a household and supported. While this is often a healthy relationship, there are instances of exploitation of individuals who become unpaid servants. *vakararavi vei au* dependent on me.

raravisa, raravisa v., n., adj., n. to be cutting, strident, domineering, hurtful and harsh in behaviour, especially in words.

raravu adj. of *lovo* stones, properly hot, by visual evidence. Syn. *qoca*.

rarawa n. sorrow, sadness.

rarawataka v. to regret, be sorry about (something).

rasarasa v., n., adj. gleaming, glistening, shining, as the sun on the sea.

Ra Sau (Tongan "Hau") n. title of chief of tribe Buca, village Lomaloma, Vanua Balavu. There are a few other *Sau* titles in Fiji, as at Vuna, Lau, and at Ra , the Gonesau.

rasiti (Eng.) receipt. Syn. *risiti, resiti*.

"rasta" (Jamaica) n. rastafarian hair arrangement with dangling curls deliberately formed, as a symbol of rebellion, individual assertion for some men of the common classes. Some think of this as being chic.

ratou (pronoun) they, them (three, or just a very few). May appear as *eratou* at the beginning of a sentence and *iratou* as the object of a sentence.

Ratu chiefly title for men used alone as a form of address, or in front of the chief's name, only in certain places The source of the Fijian title is Verata, and it has spread throughout Fiji during the past century, now applied to many local, minor chiefs as well as the major ones. The concept of his type of title is from Tonga. Strictly speaking, the title belongs only in Verata. In their time, Cakobau or Tanoa, his father, never themselves used the title of Ratu. It does not appear with Cakobau's name or any other chief's name in the Deed of Cession of 1874. (Exceptionally, in the 1850s, Ratu Mara Kapaiwai was one of the few who did use the word Ratu, though that may have been a name rather than a title.) It has been affixed to the names of Tanoa and Cakobau by later Fijians, retroactively. The Cakobau Memorial Church on Bau Island is now referred to as the Ratu Cakobau Church. Ratu may also be used as a personal first name or second name. The title may be acquired as part of a chiefly name, by a namesake. In such cases, it does not imply chiefly status. Adi is the female equivalent, sometimes heard as Yadi in Lau.

Ratu-mai-Bulu (Archaic) n. a principal legendary spirit mainly in Tailevu, Wainibuka, LomaiViti area, residing in the after-world until rising temporarily at annual harvest time (*yabaki*) around December. He was not worshipped but his imagined return to the underword was celebrated with joy and a great deal of noise (drums, shouting, *davui* trumpets). *Bulu* implies an after-death nether world. This spirit has been known as Latu-ni-pulu in Tonga.

rau 1. (pronoun) they, them (two of them). At the beginning of a sentence *rau* may seen as *E rau* or *Erau*. May mean "he" or "she" along with another person.

rau 2. to fit, suffice, be adequate. *rau, rauta*.

rau 3. as in *yavi rau* n., v. community fishing at the shore with a "net" of simple rope with attached leaves, a scare-line for scaring the fish toward the shore, enclosed within, surrounded by people in the water whose presence and activity keep most of the fish inside. In some places the scare-line get the fish to move inside a stone enclosure (*moka*) at the reef. These community efforts are less common than in earlier times.

rau 4. type of grass or other plant used in thatch walls of a house, or plants used in making a fishing dragline. *vale rau* n. thatched house, cottage. See *rausina,* below.

rauni, raunitaka (Eng.) v. to go around. Syn. *wavokita.*

veiraurau matched together, proportional, of two things, appropriate, well suited to each other. See *rau, rauta.*

rausiga n. (Colo East) a thin-stemmed shrub of the bush, leaves entire, with veins parallel, like cinnamon leaves. After removal of outer bark, the thin stems may be eaten raw, as a bush food.

rausina n. house in style of western Viti Levu with outside appearing to have rounded ends rather than rectangular appearance. *rau* grass usually, sometimes referring to reeds used in thatching. *rau* grass. *sina* (West) reeds.

rauta 1. enough, adequate. *Sa rauta.* That's enough. That will do.

rauta 2. suitable, appropriate. *Sa rauti au.* That suits me (or) that's enough for me (or) It fits me (shoes, clothing).

rauta 3. ought to, should. *Sa rauta me marau o Saki.* Saki ought to be pleased, can well feel pleased.

rauta 4. approximate(ly). *E rauta ni $40 na kena levu.* It amounts to about $40.

rauta 5. just as well, as in *Sa rauta me solia.* It is just as well to give it.

veirauti appropriate, suitable, as in *e veirauti na totogi kei na cala.* The punishment fits the crime.

rauva n. var. of wild or semi-cultivated yam, Dioscorea nummularia, with huge tubers, up to six feet long, that in nature grow straight down and deep. Sections of corm are sometimes planted so the tubers will grow horizontally, for easier harvest. This food is best known to highlanders and Rewa Province where some highlanders migrated. Cooking was usually done by steaming in green bamboo tubes laid over fiery coals and turned to prevent burning of the bamboo, a technique called *vuki* (*vuki, vukica* to turn over). Formerly, there were no clay pots or earth-ovens in the highlands.

rava adj. snub-nosed, flared flat, of the human nose.

rava, ravataka v. to be extremely fearful. *rava* n. great fear.

ravarava adj. cowardly, fearful.

ravete (Eng.) n. rabbit, existing only in children's stories.

ravi, ravita v. to lean against.

iraviravi n. something to lean against, support.

iraviti n. someone or something one can depend on, such as a reliable person who can stand in for someone else.

ravidi v. to snap, make a snapping or cracking sound, like something breaking off. such as a piece of bamboo, section of *duruka,* branch of a tree.

ravisi (Eng.) rubbish, literally as garbage, or figuratively, as nonsense. Of a thing such as clothing, shoes, may mean old and worn-out.

vakararavi adj. dependent. *vakararavi vei au* dependent on me, trusting in me to take care of (person). Within a village one clan may be dependent on another, having no land of its own. Within families, poor relatives of outsiders may be adopted informally as dependents, sometimes treated as servants.

ravo, ravoca v. to warm up already cooked food over the burning coals of a fire.

ravolo (Eng.) raffle. *ravolotaka na motoka* raffle off the motor car.

Ravouvou n. prince, youth of the nobility. The word appears mostly in children's stories and in references to the British royal family. This word is a way of politely referring to the chiefly son. In Fijian culture it is not a formal title and not a form of address, and is not attached to the name of the person. *na Ravouvou, o Prince Charles.* Prince Charles. The female equiv. is *Raluve.*

ravu, ravuta, ravulaka v. to knock down forcefully, strike as with a warclub, to destroy. *ravu lesu* knocked back (figuratively or literally).

iravu (Nadroga) n. warclub. Syn. *iwau.*

ravu-i-gusu adj. rough-spoken, loud-spoken, but ineffectual, of a person.

ravulesu v. to take violent revenge.

ravuravu n. destruction, devastation, as of hurricane or tidal wave, knocking down houses, trees, gardens.

rawa, rawata v. to be possible, to be able to, can, to achieve, to earn. *Sa rawa.* It can be done, it is possible. *O na cakava rawa.* You can do it. *rawata e dua na ilavo.* to earn some money.

rawai v. to overcome. *rawai koya* overcome him. *rawai ena ivalu.* defeated in battle.

rawa-i-lavo adj. profitable. n. *na rawa-i-lavo* the earning of money.

rawa-ka n., adj. capability, capable (person), achievements, achieving.

rawarawa easy. *vakarawarawa* easily.
rawata v. to defeat, win over (a competitive team).
rawataki v. to be obtained by chance, get a lucky break.
rawati koya to be successful, achiever, a "doer", influential.
re (Bua, Wailevu) good (Bauan *vinaka*), as in: *Bula re!* = *Bula vinaka!* Good day to you!
rea n. albino.
reareata greyish in colour, faded white, often applied to sky colour, overcast.
reba n. Fiji Goshawk, Accipiter sp., fairly docile, and less common than the larger Swamp Harrier *manulevu*. Most Fijians make no distinction between the two species. Syn. (Vanua Levu) *tuitui*. (Lau) *latui*.
rebo v. to feel dizzy, to have the head spin, to faint. Syn. *matabuto*.
rede, rede-taka (Eng.) v. to rent (it). *rede* rent.
redeu v. to shock, to startle.
referi (Eng.) n. referee. Syn. *raivari*.
regu, reguca v. to kiss. European-style kissing was unknown to Fijians, but is now very widely done to babies who are often fawned over. Young urban Fijians have adopted romantic kissing but there is never any public demonstration of romantic affection. Social kissing as a greeting or farewell has been copied from Europeans by some Fijians. *regulaka* is a rather modern verb for stongly emotional kissing; one even hears a syn. *kisilaka* from the English kiss. Traditionally, the Fijian "kiss" was a sniffing with the nose against the cheek, still practiced with family members, at greetings and farewells, and symbolically to a corpse at death. *iregu* n. kiss. Syn. (Lau) *uma, umaca*. Idiom: *regu iloilo* "window shopping".
reguregu n. a ceremony, the ceremonial "kissing" (actually sniffing) of dead person. Gifts (*ireguregu*) are brought by the visitors. Men are supposed to bring a whale tooth (*tabua*) but these days one whale tooth might serve for a group of men, or some men may bring some root of *yaqona*. Women might be expected to bring a mat each but these days a mat might serve for a group of women. The actual sniffing of a corpse is falling into disuse, but the ceremony persists as a first step in the sequence of ceremonies at a death. It is followed by the *somate* (burial ceremony), and finally, the *burua*, reciprocal ceremony, food presentation of a butchered cow and other uncooked food that is taken home by visitors. These days the ceremonies are usually compressed and all completed at the single visit of the guests if they come from far away.
regua n. edible fish, type of snapper, Lutjanus rivullatus, often toxic October-November, during *balolo* season.
rejisitataka (Eng.) v. to register.
reki (Eng.) n. rake (for gardening).
reki n. joy. *rekireki* joyfulness. *rereki* joyful nature.
reki, rekitaka v. to rejoice (over it). *vakarekitaka* to make a person joyful.
  Idiom: *rekirekitaki waqa vou* thrill over some transient novelty (an emotion that will soon pass), such as a child with a new toy.
remoremo v. to be dazzled by the light (the sun or a lamp), impeding the vision. May imply a scintillating light.
rere n. fear. *rerevaki* frightful.
rere (Archaic) n. legendary spirit folk of Beqa Island who bestowed the gift of firewalking in return for release from capture.
rere, rerevaka v. to fear (someone, something). *Na cava o rerevaka kina?* What are you afraid of? Idiom (Ang.): *rerevaka ni mate* frightened to death of it. *viarere* fearful, inclined to be afraid, timorous.
vakarerea v. to frighten. *vakarerea na vusi* frighten the cat. *ivakarere* n. frightening thing, something that causes fear (such as a ghost or spirit or shark in agonistic posture). Fijians are often frightened of dogs.
rerevaki adj. fearful, dangerous.
rerega n. turmeric, natively introduced from Southeast Asia, now growing semi-cultivated, formerly used on mothers and babies in Fiji but also in India. It is in fact a proven antiseptic. Grown commercially at Wainadoi, Namosi, as an ingredient of locally produced curry powder, mainly for export. Fijians have never consumed turmeric except in purchased curry powder. Syn. *cago* (*ni Viti*). The "*ni Viti*" is a modern addition because commercial ginger, a more modernly introduced plant, has taken on the name *cago*. Both are of the genus Zingiber. Syn. (West) *reregwa*.
resiti (Eng.) n. receipt. Syn. *risiti*.

reterete (Roman Catholic) n. retreat, religious and/or meditative.
retio (Eng.) n. radio. *kaburaka* to broadcast.
retio yaloyalo (Eng.) n. television but a Fijian is more likely simply to use the English word TV.
reu v. to burrow in the sand as a stingray or some fishes may do. Syn. *revo*.
reva adj. as in *mata reva* cross-eyed.
reve n. sp of edible riverine fish that tolerates brackish water.
reveni 1. (Eng.) n. ribbon. The cutting of ribbons at the opening of some institution or event has become a very common new tradition in Fiji.
reveni 2. (Eng.) n. Plimsoll mark on sea-going ship.
reveni 3. (Eng.). n. edible fish, Flame snapper, red-coloured, Etelis coruscans, to 50 cm in length, depths 90 to 400 meters, tail long and sharply forked. Syn. *onaga*.
revereve n., v. to wash a starch-food in fresh water to remove poisonous elements, said of wild yam (*kaile gaga*). The yams are first cut finely or mashed.
reveri (Eng.) n. referee. There are various spellings of this word. Syn. *referi*.
revo v. to burrow in the sand as a stingray may do, or some fishes. Syn. *reu*.
irevo n. (Beqa, Rewa, Kadavu, Namosi) earth oven. *vilairevo* firewalking. Syn. *lovo*.
revurevu 1. n. var. of inedible taro that grows with a very small corm (root, in common parlance), in swampy places. The leaves are embedded with poisonous, extremely irritating oxalate crystals. It is one of the two types of *dalo ni wai* (water taro). Leaves of the other var. can be eaten. One highland tribe makes a specialty of eating the poisonous variety after heat treatment.
revurevu 2. n., adj. poison, poisonous nature (usually unsuspected), as when speaking of say, the *revurevu* taro, or of the drug marihuana (*mariwana*) which in Fiji is considered to be dangerous and is strictly illegal even in minute quantities.
revurevu 3. n. devastation, as after-effects of hurricane or of war, or calamitous results of fast-spreading disease. *na revurevu ni cava*. the after-effects of the hurricane or gale wind.
rewa 1. v. raised up (sail, house structure, pole).
rewa 2. n. coconut oil with leaves of medicinal herbs for applying to the skin for what is thought to be a curative effect.
rewavaki adj. raised up high, often said of a pile of food at a ceremonial feast-food presentation *magiti*.
rewana (Archaic) v. to pile up high, of foods or traditional goods (such as barkcloth) to be offered at a ceremonial presentation (*magiti*).
rewa ira v. to set up something at an elevation that is too low.
vakarewa, vakarewa-taka v. to raise up (flag, sail). *E rewa i cake e dua na yasana.* One side is raised up. *vakarewaicake-taka* v. to raise up on high.
rewai n. (Rewa) eel. Syn. *duna*, (West) *tuna*.
  Idiom: *Vakavuti sara ga na rewai, qai vuku na kai Viti.* As soon as the eel develops fur, then the Fijian will become wise (i.e., never).
ria n. love potion, thought to have come from the Solomon Islands. It involves the use of leaves crushed in vegetable oil, to anoint a prospective lover.
riba v. **1.** to jump, spring up or out (typically fish from water, chip from chopped wood), give a startled response (as with the heart, at some shock). See *cariba*. **2.** v. to move out of the way, to one side, as in *riba tani*.
  Idiom: *ribaki koya na sui ni kena* caught up in one's own trap, lit., to be stuck with a bone in one's own throat from one's own food.
ribariba v. to jump about, spring up, dance about (typically a school of little fish, or a stingray, or fish caught and flapping about in the boat). *na ivaka-sa-ribariba* the trigger (of gun).
ribi n. shin, sharp edge of the shin-bone. *sui ni ribi* n. shin-bone. See *saulaca*.
rideu n., v. (Lau) to shudder. *E rideu na yaloqu.* I shuddered (with emotion such as fear).
rido v. to hop, skip, usually of children but also of a hobbled cripple. By extension, to leave out or skip something.
rika, rikava, rikata v. to jump down. *rikava* jump down for (something) or jump down to (place). *rikata* jump down onto (something). Syn. *lade, ladeva*, properly to jumping up, but now one sometimes hears *rika* and *lade* used inter-changeably. *lade* seems to be the more general word for "jump", with *rika* implying a downward movement.
--riki Old Polynesian of proto-Polynesian meaning "small", appearing in place-names such as Moturiki, literally "small island", or Wairiki "small river". Alternative spelling is *driki*, as in the name Ogea driki, "small Ogea", an islet off Ogea Island in Lau Province. *sewa* is another ancient synonym, as in the name of the island Waya Sewa.

rikou n. sudden shock (from fear), that may paralyse a person's actions.
rio v., n. to descend quietly, of dusk and then darkness that comes very quickly in the tropics. There is a very brief twilight. *Sa rio mai na vanua.* Night is falling silently, quickly. See *karabo* n. dusk, twilight.
ripabuliki (or) **ripapuliki** (Eng.) n. republic.
ripea, ripeataka (Eng.) v. to repair, to fix.
ripote (Eng.) n. report. *ripotetaka* v. to report.
riri 1. (or) **vakariri** hasty, quickly. *moce riri* fall asleep suddenly. *Vakariri!* Hurry it up! Be quick! Syn. *kusa, totolo.*
riri 2. n. temporary shelter improvised for sleeping over in the bush, as when far from home.
riri, ririga v. to boil (only certain foods such as broth, or fish), formerly in a round clay pot with no permanent lid. This method of cooking existed only on the coast, not in the highlands where virtually no pots existed. Highlanders never boiled food; they used bamboo containers to steam it, or they simply grilled it.
vakariri, vakaririga v. to cause certain foods to be boiled in water, formerly in a clay pot *ivakariri.* In Lau, cook (in a pot or pan), not necessarily boiling.
ririko, ririko-taka v. to be apprehensive or anxious about (something), fear what may happen.
ririkotaki apprehensive.
vakarise-yate or **vakarise-kete** v. to startle, to shock.
risiti n. (Eng.) receipt. Syn. *rasiti, resiti.*
veiriti adj. suited, well matched, appropriate in relation to one another by custom or good taste.
riva (Lau, West) adj. dumb, crazy, of a person. *mata-vakariva* look stupid.
rivariva-bitaki adj. worried, frightened, disconcerted, anxious.
rivirivi square (as a modern term, not traditional); an older meaning would refer to something that is humped or arched, not round. The concept of something being square did not exist. Syn. (Eng.) *sukuea.*
Ro n. chiefly title that precedes the name, man or woman in Rewa, Nadroga, Serua, Namosi, Colo East. Ro Muakalou of the Wainimala, for example was a famous warrior chief of Colo East, ultimately betrayed by his own people.
ro, roya v. to fan away flying insects, flies, mosquitos. *iroi* n. such a fly-whisk. The concept and practice is Polynesian and aristocratic.
ivakaro, n. advice (from someone with authority), instruction.
vakaro, vakarota v. to give instructions, advice (from someone with power, influence).
roba, roba (or) **robaka, robalaka** v. to slap, implying some hurt. *iroba* n. slap. May refer to the sharp slapping of waves. *roba* is a harder slapping than expressed by *sabi, sabica.*
robaka v. to slap (him, her, it) violently. Cf. *vacu, vacuka* to punch.
robaroba v. to flap, flutter (the wings), of a bird ready to fly.
robo v. to lie flat, hidden or half hidden, like a flat fish such as a stingray, or a *davilai.*
iroborobo n. the hiding place. See *robo* v. to lie hidden.
robo, robota v. to spread, spread out (disease, rumour, people, branches of a tree, icing on a cake), resound (noise, news, joy), disseminate widely. *na iroborobo* n. the spreading around.
rodu adj. curved, bent. *daku rodu* n. hunchback.
roga (Archaic) n. small plant, Pipturus argenteus, Urticaceae, bast fibre used especially by Tongans to bind together parts of breastplates (*civavonovono*) they made of pearlshell and carved pieces of whale-teeth. These Tongans were in the service especially of Bau. Stem fibre also used for fish nets, and by Tongans for fishing lines.
rogo, rogoca 1. to hear, listen. *rogo levu* famous. *rogo ca* of bad reputation. *Rogoca!* Listen here! *na rorogo* the sound. *rogoca na kisi* (Anglicism) to hear the case (in court).
Idiom: *E sega ni rogo mai na toa mai na nomu koro* However important you may be in your Territory, it means nothing here, lit. "The fowl crying from your village is not heard here." (The jungle fowl is symbolic of a warrior). At home in his own village or Territory (*vanua*), the Fijian may feel quite independent of any outside authority, though that is not always the case.
rogo, rogoca 2. to listen and obey. One "listens" to his chief or to his employer, to do what he is instructed to do. *Au rogoci koya.* I do what he wants, what he says. I serve under him.
vakarogoca v. to listen, as in *vakarogoca na vunau* listen to the sermon. This implies paying attention. *vakarogoca na veivosaki* listen to the conversation.
rogo lailai soft (of sound).
rogo levu 1. loud (of sound.

rogo levu 2. famous.
rogomi n. water cress, common wild plant in wet places around habitations, used mostly medicinally, not usually as a food, Rorippa sarmentosa, probably an aboriginal introduction. Syn. *waciwaci,* which just might be the origin of the name for the Waciwaci people of Lau, though *waciwaci* is also a name of a tree.
rogo rivata v. to hear partially, incompletely some conversation, some account.
irogorogo 1. n. fame. *na irogorogo kei Cakobau.* the fame of Cakobau.
irogorogo 2. n. hearing-aid for deafness.
irogorogo 3. n. stethoscope, earphones as for music.
vakarogoya 1. v. to make (someone, something) famous. *E vakarogoya na yaca i Viti ko Manu.* Manu made famous the name of Fiji. *E vakarogoi Viti ko Serevi.* Serevi made Fiji famous.
vakarogoya 2. v. to announce, make known, let it be heard.
vakarogorogo-cataka v. to defame.
vakairogorogo adj. made famous, much heard about.
veirogorogoci n. 1. hearing, as in some public investigation or court case.
veirogorogoci n. 2. obedience, as in paying attention to social protocol.
rorogo v. to sound, as in *rorogo vata* to sound the same. *vaka-di rorogo* silent, as of a house.
vakarorogo v. adj. listen to, accept advice or orders, obey; obedient. *tawa vakarorogo* disobedient.
vakarogo-taka v. 1. to publicise, advertise (a person, action or thing).
vakarogo-taka v. 2. to inform someone.
rogoseva, rogosevata v. to mis-hear, to hear something incorrectly.
rogotalanoa-taka v. to hear the story of . . .
rogovaki rumoured. *E rogovaki tiko ni ra vakamuri Kuli.* It is being rumoured that they follow Kuli. *Na kena rogovaki ni a bukete tiko.* It is rumoured that she is pregnant.
Rogovoka (Archaic) n. Fijian name of a legendary ship that brought some chiefly immigrants to Fiji, supposedly the same as the *Lolopeau* by its earlier name. *Lolopeau* corresponds to *lolovira na biau* meaning "the waves are beneath its dignity". (Spellings of that name vary slighty.) The *Rogovoka* is also said to have brought from Uvea Island stones for the tomb of the Tui Tonga. Idiom: *vaka na ivana ni Rogovoka* very tall. straight and strong, literally like the mast of the legendary ship Rogovoka.
rogo-vukavuka v. to hear on the fly, unverified rumours.
iroi n. whisk, for brushing away flies, mosquitos, used by chiefs. Syn. (Lau) *fue.*
iroiroi n. pectoral fins, fins on both sides of fish, for propulsion.
roka-na n. colour. Anciently Fijians divided the colour spectrum at different frequencies than Europeans do. There has thus been some confusion in translating colour-names though Fijians now tend to follow the European system. Formerly, Fijians' naming of colours was based on the colour of known objects, not by frequencies on the physical colour spectrum. *duiroka* of various colours. *dua roka* of a single, uniform colour. *roka-ca* off-colour, faded. *oriori* striped. *tavu-tonotono* speckled, spotted.
rokete 1. n. (Eng.) chilli pepper, ("rocket"), a plant introduced by Indians and, probably earlier, by Europeans. *kana rokete* a punishment of children, to eat chilli pepper. Formerly, a chilli might be placed in the rectum of a naughty child. Hot chilli, so popular among Fijians today, originated from the Americas; it was unknown in India as well as Fiji. Chilli has become an essential ingredient of the ever popular Tongan sauce *miti,* with coconut cream and onion, served with fish.
Idiom: *quru rokete* be in prison, lit. crunch chilli.
rokete 2. n. (Eng.) fireworks.
Roko n. abbrev. of Roko Tui, the salaried, administrative head of a Province.
Rokola (Archaic) n. name of a legendary master boat-builder and carpenter with home village of Narauyabe at the western end of the Nakauvadra Range in Ra Province. He gave protection to the Ciri Twins who angered Degei, the Snake God, by their having killed his favoured pet fowl Turukawa at Conua, Nakauvadra. These acts initiated the famous Nakauvadra Wars. Rokola is thought to be of Tongan extraction, founder of the carpenter clans *mataisau* in Fiji. Along with the Ciri Twins, he was banished by Degei. His adze was stolen along the Wainibuka River and he died en route in southerly travel. Historian Derrick wrote that he was supposedly a son of Degei.
Rokotakala n. chiefly title in Ono (Kadavu), Namuka (Tailevu), and Ovalau.
rokova v. to show respect by one's behaviour and attitude. Idiom: *rokoroko va-kanace* showing disrespect, as mullet leaps up avoiding predators.
Rokovaka n. very minor territorial title, as at village Nabouwalu, Ono Island, Kadavu.
rokovi n. respect. *na rokovi ni lawa* respect for the law.

vakarokoroko v. to show respect (more emphatic than *roko*). *na nodra vakarokoroko vua na tamata.* their respect for the people.
Idiom: *vakarokoroko vakanace* pretentious and disrespectful behaviour in the presence of one's superiors, or elders, lit. respectful like a mullet (which jumps and splashes high out of the water over the heads of its predators).

roko n. persistent muscular pain deep inside the back or torso, rather like in twisted, knotted muscle. alleviated by specialists of massage.

Roko-- n. Prefix of traditional chiefly title that varies from one locality to another. Most widely recognised is the *Roko Tui Bau* of super-tribe Kubuna at Bau.
RokoTui (or) *Rokotui* is a title also at Cautata, Namata, Namara (Roko Tui Veikau), Viwa, Kiuva, in Kadavu and also Nakelo (Tailevu) and Ovalau.
Rokotuni (or) *Rokotui-na-mata* at Vukavu in Naceva, Kadavu, also at Nacokoni in Burebesaga, and in Noco, Rewa.
Rokosau is a title on Totoya Island, Lau Province.
Rokoji is a title on Kadavu.
Rokodurucoko is a title at Naqarani and at Naselai (Tongan origin)
Rokovaka is a title at Nabouwalu, Ono Island, Kadavu Province.
Roko Takala at Naqara (Ono, Kadavu), Namaka (Bau) and Daku, Nasinu, at Ovalau.
Rokotuni equivalent of *Rokotuinimata*.
Rokotunimata at Vukavu, Naceva, in Kadavu, and Nacokoni and Noco in Rewa Province.
Similarly, *Rokisi* is a title at Nabouciwa and Naselai. Some of these examples were published in the Fijian Dictionary *Na iVolavosa VakaViti*, 2007.

Roko part of a personal name indicating high social rank for a man or woman in some parts of Lau Province. *Roko* may also be a personal name with no implication of social rank.

Roko Tui (followed by name of a Province) top Fijian administrative officer appointed to a Province. (In normal speech locally, this administrator can be referred to politely as "the Roko".) For most provinces this salaried Fijian is a native of the province he administers. Exceptions are provinces of Ra and Ba, where a high Bauan chief has often been appointed. Roko Tui Bau is the traditional high chief of super-tribe Vusaratu, originally the highest chief on Bau Island and super-tribe Kubuna.

roko-tu-i-kete n. gastritis, persistent stomach pains. One Fijian remedy is to make an infusion from the inner bark of the *yalu* tree. Sometimes abbreviated as *roko* or *koro*.

roloka (Eng.) n. rowlock for rowing a small boat, and at the stern, serve to hold an oar for sculling.

roqoroqo n. v., ceremony for mother and newborn, bringing them gifts and, usually, holding the child in the arms (*roqota*). Syn. (Lau) *kevekeve*.

iroqoroqo n. gift that is brought for newborn child.

roqo, roqota v. to hold, clasp in the arms, against the chest. One might hold a baby this way, or firewood, or a bundle of clothes.

roqoliga v., adj. to cross one's arms, clasp one's arms in front, folded on the chest.

ro (or) **roro, rova** v. to approach, usually a bird, airplane, come in to land, or approach in time of some occasion. *vakaroro na waqavuka* v, to land the plane.

iroro n. perch, as of a bird, a place where it lands, a place for landing. *iroro ni waqavuka* aeroport, landing place for an aeroplane.

roro n. (Nadroga) the fan palm, Pritchardia pacifica, more widely called *masei* in Fiji. Leaves were used for fans and/or umbrellas for chiefs. Elsewhere in Fiji, *roro* may refer to the Cycad, Cycas spp., which provided a food for chiefs in Macuata but was used as a famine food in Koro island. The nut is edible only after treatment. It can be poisonous.

roroi, roroya v. to close off a fish net or fish fence (as of reeds) by attaching the final closure. *iroroi* n. seam or attachment where net or fish fence is closed off.

rosi (Eng.) rose (flower), introduced, mentioned in modern native romantic songs which are themselves Polynesian in origin. Rosi is also a female name.

rosi ni bogi (Anglicism) n. edible fish, Malabar blood snapper, Lutjanus malabaricus, to 100 meters. Syn. *su (ni Radini ni Bau)*. Very similar to *rosi loa,* Timor snapper, L. timorensis, which has slightly darker red back and fins.

roso, rosova v. to squat on one's haunches, sit on one's heels, for convenience or from respect for the presence of important people.

rotaka or **vakarota** v. to order, give orders for things to be done. *ivakaro* n. order(s).

roto v. to fart inadvertantly.

rotu, rotuka, rotulaka v. to beat up (a person) usually with sticks or fists. A common revenge or punishment is a physical beating, usually with the victim taken by surprise, attacked by several men. *roturotu* beating.

rourou n. leaves of the taro plant that are to be used as green vegetable. Certain varieties of taro are best for this and are grown in damp ground under cultivation specifically for that purpose. Thorough cooking is necessary to avoid the itchy effect of oxalic acid crystals in the plant. In coastal areas and smaller islands, *rourou* may be served in coconut cream, or used as wrapping in preparing *palusami*, often including tinned fish or canned corned beef. *rourou vaka-utona* "stuffed" *rourou*, as the leaves are used as an edible wrap, enclosing some other food. *rourou vaka-taci-rua* taro leaves wrapping *kora* (grated coconut that has been lightly fermented in saltwater) with coconut cream *lolo*. *rourou karakara* taro leaf simply boiled, without coconut cream. *gutu-va na rourou* to cut off the leaves of *rourou*. *sagi-ta na rourou* to pluck, pick *rourou* leaves. Syn. (Lau) *pakia*. (Kadavu) *ivuso*. (Colo East) *sovu* and *la*.

rove, rovea v. to cut up in small pieces, a root crop such as taro or yam, preparatory to cooking.

rovu v. to sprout (teeth of baby, buds on a plant). *na rovurovu* the sprouting.
Idiom: *Vosa o iko, sa rovu e liu na batimu.* You speak first, you are older than me (and thus I defer to you), lit. your teeth sprouted first. (This is said in humour, especially when two people begin speaking at the same time.)

ru (or) **ruka, rukaka, rulaka** v. to curse, swear. *ena voso ni veiru* in swear-words. *iruka* n. curse. Between certain related peoples (*veitabani* or *veitavu dredre*) liberties may be taken, including swearing. Syn. *borata*.

rua two, as in *e rua*. *ruasagavulu* twenty. *e rua na drau* two hundred. *na ikarua* the second. Syn. (Tonga) *ua*.
Idiom: *Karua* now used mostly humorously, as a term of relationship or form of address, joking with a person of the same sex. It indicates that the person addressed (or referred to) is intimate with the same spouse or sex-partner, a rival for the affections of the same mate. Among intimate friends it may only imply jokingly that one admires the other's spouse.

ruarua both. *ena yasa ruarua ni gaunisala.* on both sides of the road. Similarly, *tolu* three, and *tolutolu* all three.

vakarua-taka v. to repeat, to copy, to replicate, double up.

rube, rubeca 1. v. to suspend, hang up. *vakarubeci e domona* hung around his neck. *rube ena kauveilati* v. to crucify, hang on the cross. See *lili, liliva*.

rube, rubeca 2. v. to delay or defer (as in a case pending in court).

rubi, rubica v. to beat or flog, as one beats an octopus *kuita* with a stone to prepare it for cooking.

rubu 1. v. to pout. *vakaruburubu* sullen, pouting.

rubu 2. n. type of handbasket woven of *voivoi* pandanus leaves.

rugua (or) **rugurugua** adj. in the shade, sheltered from the sun, as in *sa rugurugua na vanua nikua* It is cloudy today. *vakarurugua-taka* v. to shelter from the sun, to put (something, someone) in the shade.

rui very, excessive(ly). *Sa rui sau levu.* It is too expensive.

ruku, rukuta 1. to leave early in the morning. *rukuta na basi* take the bus early in the morning. Syn. *sou, souta*.

ruku, rukuta 2. (Rewa) v. to enter. *Drau ruku sara mai!* You two come right in!

ruku-na under, underneath. *ena ruku ni teveli* underneath the table. *vakaruru ena ruku ni vunikau* to shelter under the tree. *ena rukuna* underneath it.
Idiom: (Ang.) *ena ruku ni matanisiga* everywhere, lit. under the sun.
Idiom: (Ang.) *ena ruku ni kuila* in colonial times, under the British flag.

rumu (Eng.) room (as part of a building). *rumu ni moce* bedroom. *rumu ni kana* dining room. *rumu ni wawa* waiting room. *rumu ni vuli* schoolroom. *rumu ni gade* living room, sitting room.

ruru adj. calm, peaceful (sea, wind), eased (of pain, sickness).

vakaruru v. to take shelter (usually from rain or sun), often heard as *va-ruru*.

ivaka-vakaruru (or) **ivakaruru** n. sheltering place, from rain or sun, or safe and protected anchorage.

rurugu adj. sheltered, overcast, of the sky. Syn. *rugua*.

vakaruruga v., adj. to shelter, overcast (sky).

rusa, vakarusa v. to destroy, *Lasarusa* is a man's name, implying he enjoys destroying. *Sa rusa ena cagilaba.* It was destroyed in the hurricane.

Rusa-i-vanua n. famous ship built 1842 by Tongans at Fulaga for the Tui Nayau, the largest one recorded in Fiji, length 118 ft., deck 50 x 20 feet, deck to keel 6 ft. Critics argued it would never be floated because of its size; in response the ship was named "Destroyed on land".

ruve (Tonga lupe) n. pigeon, Columbia spp., White-throated pigeon is native, C. vitiensis. Feral pigeon in towns, introduced, C. livia. Syn. *soqe,* but *soqe* mainly refers to the two barking pigeons, Ducula spp.

Ruve n. association of women founded by Mrs. Derrick supporting women's interests, sewing, cooking, Methodist activities, later re-named *iSoqosoqo vakaMarama*.

S

S is pronounced as an almost hissing sound. In speaking English, a Fijian would normally pronounce the word **boys** as if it were **boyce**. In western Fiji languages and dialects it is common for the letter **s** of standard Fijian to be replaced with a **c**, as in *sici*, Trochus shellfish, to be heard as *cici*, and *sucu*, breast or born, as *cucu*. In most areas of Nadroga, the **s** may be replaced by an **h** which is an influence from Tonga; village Sanasana would be pronounced Hanahana, for example.

sa 1. particle modifying verbs to indicate definiteness, emphasis, having happened or sure to happen, or already happened, something changed or activated. *Sa oti.* It is finished. *Au sa lako.* I'm going now. *Sa lako ko koya.* He/she has gone already. *Sa kana?* Have you already eaten? *Sa lako?* Are you going (just now)? This particle stands in contrast to the particle *se* which can indicate present and continuing action, something that may happen or is likely to happen.

Sa! 2. interjection of surprise, shock, disapproval, an expression often over-used by people learning the language. This same expression exists also in Tonga.

sa 3. n. spear, usually now referring specifically to a multi-pronged spear for fish. The chiefly titles Vunisa and Tunisa imply a warlord, from the use of spears (as told to me by the late Vunisa at village Weilagi, Taveuni). *dau vakasasa* pig-hunter who uses spears (and dogs).

sa 4. n. a sp. of tree, Parinara insularum, Chrysobalanaceae. *na vunisa* the *sa* tree. Red sap. This large tree usually grows on poor soil, and itself is of little use as a timber, except for house-posts. The wood is very hard to cut when dry, so for firewood Fijians will chop it up soon after felling the tree. In season, the fruit falls to the ground, and the crisp flesh may be eaten raw though it is tough to chew. Kernel of the nut is not eaten. Bats are attracted to the sweet-smelling fruit flesh after it has softened. Syn. *sea*.

isa 1. n. a sudden frightening wind that strikes from one side, usually around September-October, near the sea on the main islands. Blasts can recur or continue for several hours. In English this type of wind is sometimes called a cat's paw from its dangerous speed and power.

isa 2. n. partner (marriage, tennis, business), mate, a necessary second of two things (one shoe out a pair of shoes), a gift made in exchange for another, a necessary opposite of two things, as with a rafter of a house (matching a rafter on the other side of the house).

isa 3. n. wooden rafter(s) supporting the ceiling of a house.

veisa 1. (Archaic) n. game of skill using four white cowry shells, rarely played today.

veisa 2. n., v. women's exchange of traditional goods (mats, pots, etc.) for modern goods such as cutlery, kitchen equipment. This reaffirms social relationships and allows village women (who might have little cash) to acquire some household goods that otherwise must be bought for money. See *solevu*.

veisa-vosa n. verbal exchange, discussion in which there are opposing sides as in a debate.

sababa adj. flat in shape, as of some fish (sole, flounder), pancake; deflated, as of a balloon or tyre. *ulu sababa* flat-faced.

sabaka, sabalaka v. to smack, slap hard with the open hand. *sabalaka* indicating greater degree or duration. *isaba* n. slap. See *sabi, sabica*.

sabalia or **vakasabalia** v. to wander about pointlessly (people, cattle, dogs in the village). *vakasabalia na bula* to waste one's life. *vaka-sabalia na kakana* to waste the food. adj. careless, inappropriate in behaviour.

sabaya v. to block, as in fending off a blow, oppose some action, take an opposing position, to be contrary, to ward off something impending. *sabaya na inaki ca* to ward of the evil intention. By ext., to bat (in cricket).

sabe v. to walk without ability to put a foot flat on the ground. One either drags a foot, or raises it stiffly, planting it down at each step. This is due to a birth defect or to a leg injury.

sabe, sabeta v. to kick with one side of the foot, not the toes. Syn. *rabe*.

sabe sala Idiom: to walk around doing nothing, wasting time, wander about.

sabi, sabica v. to slap lightly, as with the open hand, to pat. *ivava sabisabi* (or) *sabisabi* "flip-flops" (rubber sandals). See *sabaka*, more forcefully.

sabolo (Eng.) n. sample.

sabu! (or) **sabusabu!** interjection showing disapproval, reproach, disbelief.

vakasabusabu-taka v. to abuse, misuse carelessly, wastefully (tools, equipment, supplies), to "spoil".

sabutu n. snapper, Emperor fish, one of the finer edible fish, Lethrinus mahsena or L. obsoletus (longitudinal yellow stripe along each side of belly), L. atkinsoni (yellow-tail emperor, brown patch on forehead). When small it may be called *vuruvuru*, when very large *babaloa*. Same genus as *kawago* (L. nebulosis, large yellow stripes on face, radiating from eyes). Syn. *cabutu*. (Lakeba) *ika dina*.

sacasaca n. sweet smelling shrub, florets often placed behind the ear, in the hair, Evodia hortensis. Syn. *uci*, the much more widely known name. More commonly, the name *sacasaca* applies to an ornamental closely related to the crotons, Codiaeum variegatum, Euphorbiaceae, noted for its highly coloured leaves.

sacau n. a very well known tree, endemic to Fiji, growing to 24 meters, not above 600 meters in altitude, Palaquium hornei, Sapotaceae, durable hardwood timber for house-posts. White latex. Late tage of growth is indicated by loss of leaves, and greying bark. Logging has taken a heavy toll of their existence. Other timber trees in this genus are *bau* and *bauvudi*, all endemic to Fiji.

saga-na n. thigh. *vu ni saga-na* thigh-joint. *saga ni sipi* leg of lamb (or mutton). The original notion has been that of a crotch.

Idiom: (Vulgar) *cabola ni sagana* to fart explosively.

saga, sagava (or) **saga** v. to strive, struggle to overcome. *isasaga* n. striving, directed effort. *na nona saga* his/her effort. *tamata sasaga* n. striving person, person who tries hard.

saga, vakasaga v. to tease, harass, persecute, cause trouble for someone. *vakasagai* teased, harassed, persecuted.

saga-ca-taka v. to molest, harass; there can be sometimes an implication of witchcraft.

sagale n. common at mangrove edge and coastal strand, Lumnitzera littorea, Combretaceae, often used for firewood, sometimes for building. Bark mud-grey, fissured, peeling in thick flakes, revealing light grey patches. Slash orange, then yellow wood. The timber is superior to the common mangrove trees *tiri* or *dogo*. It endures water better than most timbers, so is used for posts and piles for jetties. Tongans in Fiji fashioned it for fishhooks. Clusters of bright red flowers at tips of branches, all year. Lvs narrow, tough, dark green, spirally arranged. Syn. *sagali*.

sagavulu (Polyn.) n. as in *rua sagavulu* twenty. *sagavulu* is an ancient Proto-Polynesian word for "ten", now changed in Fiji to *tini* from the English word for ten. Sagavulu was the name of a son of Lutunasobasoba, one who remained behind at Vuda. Syn. (Tonga) *hongofule*.

sagi, sagita v. to pluck off, usually leaves.

sai 1. n. amount of a bid or wager in gambling, card-playing.

sai 2. n. arrow, usually made from a hardened reed, to be shot from a bow (*dakai titi*), used in ancient warfare as a defensive weapon, by Melanesian women or men. Arrows also formerly used to shoot down bats for food. (Tongans used bow and arrow only for chiefly sport.)

sai 3. n. see *saisaia*.

"saijan" (Hindi) n. drumstick tree, Moringa oleifera, Moringaceae, introduced. Leaves and fruit used as cooked vegetables, and as folk medicine, by Indians. The drum-stick shaped fruit is often sold in the market. Excessive rain reduces fruit-set. Extracts from the plant have effects that are anti-microbial, ease muscle spasms, and reduce blood pressure in experimental animals.

saini, sainitaka (Eng.) v. to sign (it).

vaka-isaisa v. to cry *isa!* with disappointment, regret, sorrow, as at departure of a loved one, or on hearing of someone's death.

Sainiai (Eng.) Sinai (peninsula).

saisai n. multi-pronged spear, now used for fishing spears. Such fishing spears never existed in the Viti Levu highlands. In early times *saisai* could refer to a multi-pronged spear used in war.

saisaia adj. very thin, of a person. *sai* n. smallest animal in a litter, often thin and under-nourished, usually referring to piglets.

saiva (Eng. cipher) zero, naught. (Vulgar Slang) asshole, as an insult.

Saka Sir (or) Madam, polite form of address in speech or writing. *I'Saka* form of address used in correspondence, equiv. of Dear Sir (or) Dear Madam. *sakava* v. to say *"Saka"* in addressing some significant person.

sakaramede (Eng.) n. sacrament.

sakasaka adj. clumsy, inappropriate in behaviour.

sake (Eng.) v. to sack, to dismiss from employment.

sakelo n. small edible freshwater fish, Kuhlia marginatus.

vakasakera (Lau) n. meal of chinese cabbage or mustard cabbage (*mosita*, Lauan word for Brassica juncea) cooked in coconut milk (*lolo*) with pieces of fish, and/or shellfish such as *kaikoso* clams, or Trochus shellfish, with condiment of fermented coconut condiment known as *kora*.

saki, sakita v. to marvel (at). *isakisaki* n. marvel, glory.

sakitaka (or) **vaka-sakita** v. to take great personal pride in (something, someone). *sakitaki koya* boastful, vain, conceited.

sakiki n. more than one species of palm, usually Veitchia spp. Trunk is tall and thin.
Idiom: *vakavu ni sakiki* marvelous something greatly admired.

isakisaki n. object of admiration, usually a person, a favoured child or benificent leader or role-model; something or someone to be proud of.

sako, sakoca v. to whack with a stick, usually the mash (*mavu*) of cooked taro held in the hand. This is preparation of making pudding (*vakalolo*). *sakosako* n. type of Fijian pudding made this way. *na sakosako* may refer to the whacking. *sako* may apply to whacking a person, or even a ball, *sakolaka* when it is done forcefully. *sako-i-drauna* Fijian pudding of grated taro in caramelised coconut cream (*lolo buta*), a specialty for the Tui Nayau as made by the people of Natokalau, Matuku Island, and Waitabu and Yadrana on Lakeba Island.

sakosako n. type of Fijian pudding made usually with mashed taro and either regular coconut cream (*lolo droka*), or caramelised coconut cream (*lolo buta*).

saku 1. n. edible garfish, Tylosurus crocodilis, which skims on the surface of lagoons. Not highly preferred as a food. It has a pointed nose.
Idiom: *vaka e siri na saku* fast (just as the *saku* skims on the surface).

saku 2. n. any of the large billfish. May refer to a swordfish (*saku vorowaqa*). Also sailfish, sawfish (*sakulaya*), and/or one of the three species of marlin: Blue marlin (Makaira nigricans), Black marlin (M. indica), Striped marlin (Tetrapturus audax). Billfish not often caught by Fijians who rarely fished beyond the reef so there is some confusion as to specific names of the various billfish.

saku beta adj. mucky, as with rotten fruit, disgusting. *saku betabeta,* more so.

saku ca adj. clumsy, ineffectual (person), badly done (of work)

saku, sakuta v. to club a person forcefully on the head.
Idiom: *Saku vakaNamara* lit., club someone in Namara fashion, that is forcefully, effectively. (Capell reports that this expression implies scalping the head of the victim as done formerly by Namara people.) Namara warriors of Tailevu have been famous for their expert clubbing. The implication is to do a job efficiently, expertly, expeditiously.

sakuku (West) n. leper, afflicted with leprosy, Hansen's disease. There were in several places on Viti Levu Island special stones (*vatu ni sakuku*), the property of certain clans (*mataqali*). Through these stones, heads of the clans claimed they could transmit leprosy when compensated to do so; this was a way of disposing of unwanted people, mafia style. Ref.: D. W. Beckett, *Trans. Fiji Society*, 1966. Syn. *vukavuka*.

saku-loa n. black marlin, Makaira indica, with dark upper body. There are two other spp. of marlin, M. nigricans the blue marlin and the somewhat more slender Tertapturus audax, striped marlin, both quite similar with blue upper bodies; there is no tradition or consistency in their specific Fijian names. Marlin have often been caught inadvertently by net fishermen; others are caught by game fishermen. They are sold as the fish in fish and chips, only sometimes identified as marlin.

saku-saisai n. swordfish, Xiphias gladius, not trad. caught by Fijians, and not common. In the deep sea, swordfish are sometimes seen lying on their sides, sunning themselves on the surface. They are not dangerous unless attacked or caught on a fishing line. Caught only by gamefishers, as are marlins. Some people (including this author) have more sympathy for these noble fish than for the game fishermen.

saku-voro-waqa n. sailfish, Istiophorus platypterus, to 140 cm, not favoured as a food by Europeans. Flesh is often riddled with the holes of parasites. The name refers to its capability of breaking up (*voro*) a boat (*waqa*). The name *saku* is sometimes used. Sailfish has a huge blue-coloured dorsal fin extending along the back. It eats sardine-type fish, encircling schools of them, keeping them close-in together, then plunging into their midst, swinging their beak like a sword. Sailfish are caught only by game fishermen. Syn. *sakulaya*. *laya* is a noun and means "sail" in western Fiji.
Specific Fijian names of sailfish, swordfish, marlin all have the prefix *saku*—but any full name of each one would be known to extremely few Fijians and there is little consistency of names, some being modernisms decided by Fisheries Dept. Reason is that Fijians were not deep-sea fishermen and virtually never caught these fish. They rarely, in fact, ever saw them. They are not usually at the surface of the sea.

sakure v. to shake, rumble, tremble, shudder, as a stomach might, or an earthquake, or a motor car out of fuel, or a house in very strong gusts of wind. See *kure, kuretaka*.

sakulevu, sakulevutaka v. to be careless, neglectful in responsibilities.

sala 1. v., n. path. *gaunisala* road, trunk road. *salatu* highway, main road. *salavata* v. to go together, taking the same path. Every part of Fiji is criss-crossed with old paths, though they may be difficult to discern today. *salawai* of a village, reachable only by boat. *sala vaka-vanua* traditional path for communications between two places or people, and extremely important concept to Fijian traditionalists.

Idiom: *E tubua na sala ki na nona koro* He/she has lost connection to his village, never visits it (lit. the path to his/her village is overgrown). For a person living away, it is sometimes a burden to maintain relations with the village, with various demands from relatives. And these days, the village may not be so relevant as many Fijians are pre-occupied with their lives in towns or other distant places of employment. To renew relations to one's village is *cara sala* to "clear or sweep the path" to the village. It can be an expensive process, requiring gifts of goods, and time spent. A Fijian's village is almost always demanding support.

sala 2. n. By extension, *sala* may mean figuratively, the way or means (the path) to accomplish something, or may mean to extend, as in extending the hand or leg.

salabogi v. set out on a trip in the afternoon, and thus travel or arrive at night. The personal name Meli Salabogi is well known in the lineage of the chiefly Gonesau at Nokorotubu, Ra Province.

sala ni cagi n. windpipe but more generally, throat and bronchial tubes, lit. path of the breath.

sala ni dra n. vein or artery (human or animal body). *dra* blood. Fijians made no distinction between a vein (for blood returning to the heart) and an artery (for blood leaving the heart).

sala ni ke-na n. digestive track (human or animal body).

sala-ni-mi n. urinary tract, a newly created word.

sala ni valelailai n. colon (human or animal body). *valelailai* n. toilet, a concept introduced by Europeans.

sala ni ivalu n. lit. path of war, meaning the specific social connections between two or more places in preparation for making war. Formal communications should pass through various specific kin-groups, tribes or villages. See also *sala ni vanua*.

sala ni vanua n. traditional approach in communicating formally with another tribe or kin-group on matters other than war. Communications should pass through certain specific people as a matter of formality.

sala ni volivoli n. ancient term for a traditional route whereby goods passed in tribute, and perhaps also in a form of exchange that by-passed the formal, highly social and ceremonial exchanges of the traditional *solevu*. From this activity, there are some places named *Volivoli*. Laucala and then Verata were a couple of the first major territories to establish such a system over an extensive area that included parts of Vanua Levu. Bau later established such a system, as did Burebesaga.

salawai n., adj. reached by water, usually of an isolated village with no good access by road. An example is village Qoma, formerly turtle fishermen for Verata, located on two very small islands off the northern coast of Tailevu.

Sala ni Yalo n. "Path of Spirits", a legendary and real path of early migration on Viti Levu. It was supposed that after death spirits would return on this same path. On Viti Levu, one established formal path led southward down from Ra and the eastern highlands to the coast around Veisari. This mountain range down the eastern coast of Viti Levu was called Tualeita. Some would claim it begins not far from Vuda, far in the west of Viti Levu, and passed through the Nakauvadra mountain range.

sala, salaga v. to wrap around, as leaves, vines or creepers, or paper, in making a parcel, or (formerly) to wrap a chiefly turban (*isala*) of barkcloth on the head.

isala head-covering, hat, formerly wrapped around the head as a type of men's turban made of fine, thin barkcloth *masi*, in coastal and small island areas, worn only by chiefs. Missionaries caused the custom to be discontinued. The use of such hats or turbans occurs these days only at the installation of certain chiefs. Today, rain-hats may be improvised with plastic bags, towels, cardboard cartons, the leaves of plaintain.

isalasala n. wrapped parcel of leaves containing food such as fish to be cooked in the earth oven. *isalasala ika* n. long, leaf-wrapped parcel of fish. Syn. *ikovu*, though this is a round, bud-shaped parcel.

vakasala-taka v. to advise. *ivakasala* advice. *daunivakasala* advisor. *Daunivakasala Levu ni Veika Vakalawa* Solicitor General.

salala 1. n. fish, long-jawed mackerel, Rastrelliger kanagurta, edible but not greatly appreciated because of the lack of meat in the head. Fijians appreciate the head of the fish as having more flavour than the other flesh; the head will often be offered to a guest. This seasonal silver fish lives close to shore and travels in fairly fast-moving schools.

Idiom: *ulu salala* empty-headed, stupid.

salala 2. n. cultivar of *voivoi* pandanus leaf that has long leaves and no thorns along the edge of the leaf. Much easier to handle than the regular, prickly *voivoi* but the quality of the leaf is not as good, so it does not displace the regular cultivar. Syn. *voivoi ni Rotuma*.

salato 1. n. a harmful wild shrub or tree of the central South Seas, 10 to 15 meters high, Dendrocnide harveyi, Urticaceae, with stinging hairs on the margins of the leaves and sap that stings very irritatingly. The irritation is aggravated by water. The itching burn occurs within half a minute but the after-burn may recur for months. Veins on underside of young lvs are purple or reddish. The totem plant of some highlanders where the name must not be mentioned. Thrives best in secondary vegetation, identified by heart-shaped leaves with finely serrated edges, and white to cream coloured flowers, small (under 5 cm) forming white, thin-skinned single-seeded fruit. Formerly planted deliberately at perimeter of some fortified villages as defensive device.

salato 2. n. edible small coloured jellyfish with long stinging thread, Physalia physalis.

salavata v. to go along together. *vata* together.

sala waqa v. to go by boat.

salayame v. to have to tongue hanging out, as a dog does when too hot. (Dogs cannot perspire; cooling is done by keeping the mouth open and by drinking water.) By comparison, *darayame* usually just refers to sticking out the tongue, as a child might do in teasing. *yame* tongue.

salayava v. to extend the leg(s). *yava* leg(s). This may be done as a person excuses himself after a meal and shifts where his back will be against the wall, relaxing. Syn. *dodoyava*.

sali, salia (or) **saliva** v. to flow down (current of water), or flow through as of a narrow channel, or opening of a reef, where the tidal current flows through. Also to droop down (thatching from the roof of a Fijian house). Salia can be the name of a village.

salisali n. opening through the reef of a lagoon, that serves a path or channel for the passage of boats, or for the movement of fish with the tide.

isalisali-ni-wai n. gutter, or drain as passage for water flow. This is a fairly modern word.

salu n. traditional specialty food; for people of the warrior castes, usually inland, this is mainly pork since they are considered to have wild pig easily accessible; for coastal people it is mainly seafood, and coconut dishes. One must offer one's *salu* to visitors who have a different *salu*, and one may not eat one's own *salu* in their presence. The rule is still fairly strictly maintained even by urban Fijians and even if the Fijians live overseas. Nothing need be said, and the foreigner will probably notice nothing. Curiously, as people have so often moved and resettled, the traditional warriors may actually reside near the sea, the coastal people moved inland; they nonetheless retain the old customs. *isasalu* delicacy. *veisasalu ni wai tui* seafood delicacies.

saluaki adj. scented. *isaluaki* scent used to perfume oil. A popular Fijian scent is *mokosoi* flowers but there are many others. Crushed nuts of *makita* tree are also traditional.

isaluaki 1. n. scent, fragrance; this now includes commercial perfume.

isaluaki 2. n. condiment, spice, added to food. This is modern usage. Fijians anciently used virtually no condiments other than salt or a sweetener (such as sugar cane or *masawe*). In the highlands the terrestrial fern *waruta* was used and often preferred to salt that was rarely available to them. Modernly, Fijians use cane sugar, chilli pepper, salt and pepper but few other condiments.

saluka v. to blow the nose Fijian-style, without the benefit of a handkerchief, holding a finger against one nostril. For young children, the snot (*luka*) will be wiped away onto the child's clothing. Adults sometimes do the same, using the shirt or T-shirt. The handkerchief is an introduced concept. Syn. *wadruluka*.

salulu adj. wrinkled, loose, drooping, of human skin and flesh, usually from aging. *wa-salulu* extremely wrinkled. See *sanuki*.

salusalu n. massive and heavy garland of flowers and sweet-scented leaves, framed in woven fibre of pandanus and/or hibiscus, presented to distinguished guests at formal occasions. The flowers often include *bua ni Viti*. *cori salusalu* to string a garland. *Era vakasalusalu kece.* They (many) all wore floral garlands.

Idiom: *vakaciri salusalu* v. to throw flowers onto the sea for loved ones departing in a boat. This custom is not truly Fijian in origin. It was perhaps introduced from Polynesia. As a practice, it probably reached its peak with commercial steamships, especially the Matson Line, in the 1930s with the Mariposa and Monterey sailing through the South Pacific.

saluma (Lau) v. to wear something around the neck, usually a garland. Syn. *taubena*. *vakasaluma* v. to place something around a person's neck, usually a garland.

salutu, salutu-taka (Eng.) n., v. to salute. (Military).

sama n. small tree, Commersonia bartramia, Sterculiaceae, wood soft like *vau* (hibiscus shrub), but brown colour. Flowers are white, begin blooming in early December through early June. There are two varieties, *sama ni vanua*, and *sama ni wai*.

samaka v. to clean garden of weeds, or clean house, especially by sweeping. *samaka na vale* sweep out the house.

samani 1. (Eng.) n. "salmon", actually mackerel, processed and packed in tins, salmon style; this is a rather oily and salty, imported fish, packed in Fiji as an inexpensive food, much used by those Fijians who have a modest cash income.

samani 2. (Eng.) n. summons, from police, or the courts. *waradi* n. warrant.

samarini (Eng. submarine) n. diving goggles, by ext. one who at a meal has eyes only for meat or fish (*na kena icoi*), rather than rice, bread, or the starch-food that is considered "true food" (*kakana dina*). Syn. *vakakilivati, savumarini*.

same (Eng.) psalm. Fijian church women have developed a custom of singing the psalms in rhythm and tone adapted from ancient chants.

veisamei n., v. to flirt.

samila v., n. to lisp, to stutter; speech defect.

samu, samuta, samulaka v. to strike down with a stick, as in knocking down fruit such as *dawa*, mango, citrus, often with long heavy sticks. May also apply to the beating of barkcloth (*masi*), and beating of the surface of the water when driving fish into a net or into a fish fence.

Idiom: *samu ni dawa*. get the consequences, as with *dawa* falling on the person below though the striking may be by someone else. One version of the idiom is *samuti koya na isamu ni dawa*. Lit. to be struck by the falling *dawa* as a result of one's actions.

samusamu n. beating with a stick in preparation of barkcloth, or beating other thing as mentioned above. See *samu, samuta, samulaka*. Women's beating of barkcloth is a frequent if not constant sound in some villages of Lau and a few other places.

samuraka v. to destroy, exterminate.

samuqawe, samuqawetaka v. to tattoo, mostly on men as a modern custom. Young men and women often have a crude tattoo, with their own initials or initials of their school. In ancient times in Fiji only women had tattoo, elaborately done around the mouth, upper thighs, rump and genitals, preparatory to marriage.

sanasanaita adj. thin and small, frail (person usually). Syn. *lila*.

sani, sania (or) **saniva** v. to pick (usually edible vegetable leaf) by pulling. *sani ota* (or) *bele*. pick *ota* leaves (or) *bele* leaves for eating. *sani rourou* cut off leaves of *rourou* (*dalo* leaves). Syn. (West) *sagi, sagia*.

sani, saniva v. to cross though an area where there is no path, through the grasslands, reeds or bush.

sa ni balolo n. gusty wind and bad weather that often occurs presaging the rise of the *balolo* (edible marine annelid), in certain locations only, away from Viti Levu.

sanisovu (Eng.) n. sandsoap. *sovu* n. soap.

saniveva (Eng.) n. sandpaper.

saniwiti (Eng.) n. sandwich. Named from Lord Sandwich, who popularised this novelty in his time. He ate them at the gaming table.

sanuki, sanukia v. to crumple, crush or cause creases or wrinkles, usually of clothes, mats, pandanus leaves *voivoi* for weaving, paper to be discarded. *sanuki* wrinkled. May apply to wrinkles of elderly people. *sasa nukinuki* all crumpled up. Syn. *saloki*.

saparaki 1. (Lau) n. flat pancake made of flour, water, sugar. Syn. *topai*.

saparaki 2. (Lau) adj. disorderly, untidy (clothes, household, things strewn about).

sapo (Eng. Slang) "supporter", underpants, especially men's. *sapo ni yasana* extra large underwear. *isulu i loma* underwear.

saqa n. edible fish, crevally, with delicious flesh, in some places formerly reserved for the chieftain. There is more than one genus and several species.

saqa n. large traditional clay pot for storing water. Such artifacts were known only around the coast, virtually all of Polynesian or Proto-Polynesian origin. Highland girls used bamboo tubes to carry water from the river, and to store it.

saqamoli n. small clay water pot made in Rewa, usually in three round sections, like three oranges (*moli*) with a small spout. Now it is mainly a tourist item. This pot is featured on the one dollar coin, initiated in 1996, so in slang *saqamoli* may refer to one dollar.

saqa, saqa (or) **saqava** v. to cook (of the food), traditionally by steaming in huge clay pots. Now the word is more inclusive and refers to any type of cooking in a pot, including metal pots. *Saqa* does not refer to grilling (*tavu*) on a fire or cooking in an earth oven (*vavi ena lovo*). Cooking in clay pots was unknown among Fijians of the highlands of Viti Levu. **saqamoce** v. to cook overnight, to be ready for eating the next morning, often done for cassava, *via*, or *ivi* that can be hard, almost woody.

vakasaqa, vakasaqa v. to cook. *na dau ni vakasaqa* the cook. *na vakasaqa nei Losana* Losana's cooking.

saqa, saqata 1. v. to bump into, collide with.
  Idiom: *saqamua* prostitute (insulting term), woman of loose morals. *mua* bum.

saqa, saqata 2. v. to oppose, go against. *saqata na nona vakatutu* oppose his/her proposal. Verb normally used the transitive form *saqata*.

saqata 1. n. a space little used (part of a room, house, village, nearby bush).

saqata 2. n. space in between two things. Internode (of a plant with nodes, such as bamboo, *yaqona*. Syn. *tagau, tagona*.

saqata 3. n. road.

saqiwa 1. n. slender palm tree sp., Pritchardia pacifica, red fruit, common around November, is not eaten, and nor is the kernel. The palm resembles *sokiki* which has edible seeds, when the seeds are young and crisp, not too hard, but the tree trunk is much thicker.

saqiwa 2. n. by extension, the similar Areca palm nut ("Betel" nut), introduced to Fiji. Fijians do not chew betel nut. That is a custom of some western Melanesians, mainly Solomon islanders and some Indians in Fiji. Betel is actually the name of the pepper (Piper betle) leaf that is chewed with lime powder and the Areca nut.

saqoqo adj. withered, shrivelled, of vegetation, cloth, person's features.

saquma v. to grab.

sara 1. just, which can imply "at once", immediately, when it follows a verb. *lako sara mada* just go (at once). *vodo sara ena waqa* get on board the boat right away. *nanuma sara tiko* just thinking about it.

sara 2. following an adjective, *sara* means "very". *levu sara* very big. *totolo sara* very fast. *na ka sara ga au nanuma* the very thing I am thinking

sara 3. absolutely, thoroughly. *E sega sara ni dua e namaka*. Absolutely no one expected it. *Sa mate sara.* He/she/it is quite dead.

sara n. boar, i.e., a male pig.

sara, saramaka v. go through and under (as in the bush), push something under and through. In Colo East this become *saramake*. *wa sara* a wild starch-food tuber usually eaten raw. It has a furry stem that penetrates the underbrush, growing close to the ground. This is almost certainly the same as *yaka* or *wa yaka,* Pueraria lobata, Fabaceae

sara n. small silver edible fish, Atheridinae sp., that schools seasonally close to shore, often used as bait by commercial fishermen. Schools scatter when disturbed and may regroup elsewhere. Levuka people are sometimes jokingly referred to as *bati sara*, intimating that *sara* is one of their favourite foods.

sara, sarava v. to look, to gaze at. *sarasara ga* just looking (with no other intention), browsing (shopping). *vale ni sarasara* n. stadium for spectators (for sports functions). *Siga ni sarasara* Open Day, for the public to visit, as at some public institutions, university, mental hospital.

saravanua n. tourist, tourism, a modernism of course.

sarau n. edible reef fish, small, yellow with markings on the sides. Lutjanus kasmira. Syn. *danabe, tanabe*. (Lau) *takabe*.

sari-na (or) **sarisari-na** n. rib-cage, ribs (person, animal). Syn. *saresare-na*.

sarisari adj. thin, with ribs evident (person, animal).

saro, saroya v. to arrange for and set up small sticks, as for supports to yam vines, or small sticks for a fire. This word has a confusing array of meaning but all involve thin sticks.

sasa 1. n. coconut-leaf midribs, or a broom made of that. Fijians normally prefer the *sasa* broom to European-style brooms. Since coconut did not exist in the highlands, for brooms the people there used branches of *makita* in Colo East, and *nuqanuqa* or *de ni ose* at Korolevu, Navosa. In traditional exchanges between two *villages*, ten *sasa* were referred to as one *ibe* (woven pandanus mat).

sasa 2. n. young barracuda that school near the shore. The school may appear almost stationary but can in an instant move very fast. Sphyraena sp.

sasa 3. n. ten woven mats as displayed to be given at ceremonial occasion.

sasa 4. adj. erect or extended to full length or height. *tu cake sasa* stand up rigidly straight.

sasa 5 (Eng.) n. saucer.

sasa 6. v. to sting, as from a sharp smack, insect bite, a minor burn.

sasa 7. n. main long section of fish fence by the shore.

vakasasa v., n. to hunt (usually pigs), with dogs, spears, knife; *na vakasasa* the pursuit (animal or man) with intent to capture or kill.

sasabai v. to bat (as in cricket).

isasabai n. anything that serves as protective device: savings account as "nest egg", insurance policy, safety helmet, bullet-proof vest, cricket bat, good-luck charm. See *saba, sabaya*.

sasaga n. effort, attempt.

vakasasaga-taka v. to make a considerable effort (to achieve or obtain something).

sasamaki n. cleaning-up, usually a house, mostly sweeping with the *sasa* broom but may apply to cleaning up a village. *na sasamaki e loma ni vale* the sweeping within the house.

sasala n. rheumatism. *sasala* might also imply arthritis since it implies painful joints of the human body.

sasalu n. food delicacy, as in *sasalu ni waitui* seafood delicacies. Certain regions are known for their food specialties, village Naila, in Tailevu, for example, for its *bila*, Kaba in Tailevu for the stingray (*vai*), Rewa for its tiny prawns (*moci*).

vakasasa n. pursuit (of person).

vakasasataka v. to pursue (person, animal) in order to capture.

sasau n. fern growing at river banks, thin black stem, edible raw, a delicacy served with prawns. There are two varieties that differ in eating quality.

sasau (ni wai) n. broad category that includes all ferns and fern-like plants, mostly edible, including *vuti*, *balabala* (tree-fern), *ota* (small edible ferns, cultivated and marketed).

sasauni, sasauni-taka v. to do one's personal toilet, apply cosmetics, primp. Syn. *sauni. E sauni koya tiko*. She is putting on her make-up (doing her personal toilet). Hairdressing and oiling the body were formerly the only type of personal toilet.

isasauni n. cosmetics, toilet articles.

isasavu n. territorial dependency, This word has been used to refer to the Yasayasa vakaRa, not yet recognized as a separate confederacy (*matanitu*), but dependent on Kubuna or Burebesaga. *Lakeba kei na kena isasavu* Lakeba and its territorial dependencies (vastly expanded since the time of Ma'afu).

sasivani (Eng.) saucepan.

satini (Eng.) n. sergeant. *satini metia* sergeant-major.

vakasauri adv. suddenly. *Sa vuki vakasauri*. It changed suddenly.

sau 1. (Tonga "hau") n. traditional social power, as *nasau* or *sauturaga* the clan of a tribe that empowers the chief, as elders and protectors of the chief. They can play a role in the selection of the chief. Also *na Turaga Sau* the chief in power, the empowered chief. *cola sau* of a clan, to bear responsibility for empowering a chief. *wa ni sau* (or) *wa tabu* sinnet cord extended from serving bowl *tanoa*, pointed to person(s) of highest status, seated at *yaqona* ceremony. One must never cross in front of that cord except at very informal occasions and even then, one must touch the *tanoa* with the hand in passing, as a mark of respect. The notion of social ceremony serving and drinking *yaqona* comes from Tonga. The specifics are Fijian. Curiously, in Cakaudrove, the nubbin and cord of the *tanoa* are placed to face into the server of the *yaqona*.

Sau 2. n. originating from Tonga via Lau and Taveuni, a chiefly title in a very few places such as Vuna and Kabara Island. Questionably, the title Sau has been taken by the Tui Nayau at Lakeba when it might more properly have remained at Kabara. *Sau* corresponds to the Tongan Hau. *Roko Sau* chiefly title at Totoya Island. *Gonesau* chiefly title in Ra Province (though referred to as *Nasau* in Boyd's 1927 Native Lands Commission report that includes Ra Province). *Sauvou* chiefly title at village Vunikodi, Udu, Macuata Province.

sau 3. n. a set of specific Fijian maladies, unknown to foreigners; one example involves very bad breath with the gums growing over the teeth. There are at least five Fijian maladies thought to be strictly Fijian and unresponsive to any European medication.

sau 4. n., prefix. limit, at the end or back. *sauka-na* n. outskirts, of village, town, garden. *saula* n. outside the village, in the bush. *na sauloa* n. the deep sea, outside the lagoon.

sau 5. v. to clap the hands, as for example, a teacher to get attention, or as part of their act, performers clap their hands at a *meke* exhibition dance. *na isausau* the clapping. This was never done as a form of applause.

isau 1. n. response, reciprocal action in response or in reaction.
   Idiom: *kemu isau, sa vuni tu.* your reward (success) will come in time (though not now apparent), lit. your reward remains concealed.

isau 2. n. price. *E vica na kena isau?* What is the price? *sau levu* (or) *sau dredre* expensive. *sau rawarawa* inexpensive. *Sa lutu sobu na kena isau.* The price has been reduced. The commercial notion of price derives from *isau* 1, above, meaning a reciprocal action.

sau ni daliga n. earring. Formerly, all adults had their ears pierced, often with enlarged holes plugged by a piece of wood or other objects. More specifically this archaic practice would now be referred to as *sauciqi*. Missionaries eliminated the custom. Modern fashions for women copy Europeans: *saulili* n. earing(s) for pierced ears. *saukabi* n. earing(s) attached by a clasp.

sau, sauca 1. v. to pierce. *sauca na bu* pierce the young coconut for drinking.

sau, sauca 2. v. to prick, as in a tattoo, with a tattoo needle *iqia*.

sau, sauca 3. v. to attempt an abortion by inserting a sharp stick into the uterus. *vakalutu gone* n. abortion. Attempted abortions have been very common in Fiji, some by consuming herbal medicines, some by physical means. Most of the herbal concoctions are ineffectual or dangerous. Collected by the present author, they have been submitted to scientific research by a major pharmaceutical company in the 1960s. Certainly the use of the stick is extremely dangerous.

saubulu, saubuluta v. to caulk (a boat). This has been done with fibre of coconut husk (*bulu*), with some glue such as the white sap of the breadfruit tree. *na isaubulu* the stuff used in caulking.

sauca (Eng.) south. "Sauca" may be an informal form of address referring to a native of Kadavu, a direct translation of Naceva, a region of Kadavu but also a way of referring to Kadavu Island which lies to the south of Viti Levu.

sau dredre adj. expensive. *sau rawarawa* inexpensive.

sauka n. outskirts (of village, town). *ena sauka kei Suva*. in the suburbs of Suva.

saulaca n. (Archaic) needle for stitching sails, formerly often made of human shin bone.

sauloa n. deep sea, open ocean. Syn. *wasawasa*.

sauloki n. hank or skein of sinnet. For formal presentation or sale such skeins of sinnet (*magimagi*) may be rolled into balls. *kava, kavana na magimagi*.

sauma 1. to answer (question, letter). *na saumi taro* the answering of questions. *na sasaumi taro* the anwering of continued questions.

sauma 2. to respond, as with revenge or reciprocal act of kindness.

sauma 3. to pay (in reciprocity for something), pay with money. *sauma lesu* (Ang.) to pay back (money usually). *na itavi era saumi kina* the job they are paid for (paid to do). *na sausaumi vakalalai vakadinau* installment payments. *na matai ni veisaumi* n. the first payment of wages (or other incoming money). *na siga ni veisaumi* n. payday. *na veisaumi* n. the pay, payment. *na imatai ni sausaumi* n. the first payment (outgoing payment, as in hire-purchase). *na saumi rumu* the room-rent.

saumaka 1. v. flip lengthwise, turn end over end, somersault. *na isausaumaki* the short pandanus leaves used for finishing the weaving of a mat, turning them end-for-end.

saumaka 2. v. to convert to religion. *tamata saumaki* n. people converted to religion.

saumamu v. to chew or crunch noisily. Syn. *namunamu*.

saumidinau v. to pay off a loan.

saumure n. iguana. Two species in Fiji, the Banded Iguana (Brachylophus fasciatus) and the Crested Iguana (B. vitiensis), though the two species may yet be recombined. Among the Banded Iguana, only the male is banded, with green and grey bands, while the female is totally green. The species exists only in Fiji and Tonga and the early origin of any iguana is certainly from the very distant continent of America. The Crested Iguana was discovered by John Gibbons in 1979. Both species eat plants, including fruit and flowers, as well as insects. Eggs are laid in damp ground usually at the base of trees, where they spend much of their time. Iguanas are found in Yasawa and Mamanuca islands and rarely on Viti Levu. (In the Namosi jungle at Wainadoi I have observed a major breeding place but have only ever seen the iguanas there twice.) They are often immobile, camouflaged, and may be high up in forest vegetation. A wildlife sanctuary has been established for the Crested Iguana on the 70 ha island Yadua Taba located 21 km west of Naicobocobo, Vanua Levu. It has been necessary to pay the chief of the native landowners, the Buli Raviravi, a "goodwill" and informal lease payment of F$1500 a year, which was increased to $2,500 in 1990 and formalized as a contract with the National Trust. A final lease was formalized after a further necessary $50,000 payment was made to the landowning unit in the year 2000. Syn. *vokai*, as used by some Fijians, but *vokai* properly refers only to the forest gecko, much more commonly seen in the bush than iguanas are. Forest geckos are a smaller reptile of which there are several species in Fiji, some as long as seven inches. Most were commonly eaten by Viti Levu highlanders. The two common household lizards are generally referred to as *moko*. Few Fijians are familiar with the word *saumure*. Fewer have ever seen one.

saumi paid. *saumi oti* already paid. *na rakavi saumi* professional rugby. *na veivacu sega ni saumi* amateur boxing. *na veika sega ni saumi* free things. *na icurucuru e sega ni saumi* the entrance is free. See *sauma*.

sausaumi n. payment(s), as in making payments for hire-purchase goods. *vakadei ni sausaumi* deposit on payment.

veisaumi n. the payment, payroll, giving of wages.

sauna v. to put on cosmetics, lipstick, comb the hair, use hair dye, hair grease, face powder, body oil, perfume. *E sauni koya tiko*. She is putting on her make-up, putting the finishing touches in her personal toilet. *na sasauni* the cosmetics, toilet article. In early times cosmetic attention was only even given to the hair with dyes, bleaches and attention to lice. In areas of Polynesian influence, scented coconut oil might be applied to a woman's face and body as a cosmetic for special occasions. Syn, *sasauni-taka*.

sauni see *sauna*.

vakasaurara-taka v. to oppress, to force (someone).

vakasauri adv. suddenly.

sauriva v. to blink (eyes), twinkle (stars), flicker (lamp).

sausau n. physical limit or border of almost any kind, garden, compound, path.

isausau n. record (athletics), formerly a spot where a reed might be stuck into the ground indicating the distance a sporting javelin *itiqa* was thrown. It indicates a limit. *cavu isausau* v. to beat the record.

vakasausau-taka v. to clap, applaud. This is an introduced custom.

sausau vuki v. to flip over, tumble over.

sausauwai (Archaic) n. vine, Rhizomorpha, formerly used for making skirts for men or women, as mentioned by botanist Seemann. Before the introduction of cotton cloth, *sausauwai* and pieces of plantain leaf were the commonest clothing for adults. There were no undergarments. Syn. *waloa*.

sauta prefix implying continued motion, often from sudden energy, as in *sauta-kurekure* vibration (from *kure* to shake), *sauta-ninini* and *sauta-ribariba*.

sautabu n. chiefly graveyard. In pre-Colonial times there were no graveyards or burial sites except in areas of strong Polynesian influence. Bodies of important men were often buried within their own house-site for fear of body parts being taken for witchcraft. Sometimes bodies were hidden away in caves. There were no elaborate funeral actions except for chiefs, when it was mainly a matter of strangling of wives and chopping of little fingers. For most Fijians there was no such thing as a formal funeral ceremony. Elderly people, disabled people, no longer productive in society were often secluded in some remote place and left to die.

veisau, veisautaka v. to change, to exchange. *veisau* n. change, as of clothes. *Sa veisau na gauna*. Times have changed.

veisau n. change (as of clothes); change (in coins or bills) after a purchase.

veisau-vosa v. to answer back, especially as of a child, impolitely, after being scolded.

saute (Eng.) n., v. shout (drinks). A word used only in town.

sautu n. peace, prosperity. *na veisaututaki* the pacification, bringing about peace and prosperity.

sauturaga n. functional role of certain clans to empower and protect the chief. These are elders of the clan or tribe who have a senior function in choosing the chief and installing the chief. *sau* implies chiefly power. *cola sau* to be responsible for carrying on duties in support of the chiefly power.

sauva v. to stake out some limit or boundary, as in the archaic sport *veitiqa*, or in gardening.

Sauvou n. chiefly title at village Vunikodi, Udu, Macuata.

sauvou (Colo East) adj. crazy. Syn. *lialia*.

sava, savata v. to wash it. *sovu ni savasava* laundry soap. *sovu ni sili* bath soap. *na sava isulu* the laundry. *vunisava* functional duty of certain clans to be custodians of chiefly burials, especially the wake of four nights (*bogi va*) in the house of the deceased. Within that house they are in charge, drink *yaqona* even before the chieftain. Food, plates, blankets brought to them during this time remains their property.

savasava n. laundry, washing (clothes, things) *sovu ni savasava* laundry soap. *misini ni savasava* washing machine.

savasava adj. clean. The word now also applies to moral conduct.

veivaka-savasava-taki n. cleansing, referring to conduct that Fijians often believe will gain them favour from God, bringing them good fortune. This may include fasting, removal of pre-Christian artefacts (spears, clubs), wearing of proper clothes on Sunday, restraint of sports, music other than hymns, and refusal to travel. It may also curb all smoking and drinking of *yaqona*. See *Nai Lalakai,* 28 April, 2005, p. 7.

savavuka adj. extremely clean, already well cleaned, village compound, clothes washed, teeth brushed.

veivakasavasava-taki n. a Methodist notion of cleansing old devil influences by means of religious services, and yielding up of all old Fijian artefacts, clubs, spears, *tanoa* bowls, wooden food bowls, old barkcloth, whale teeth that might have been related to devilish practises. Some Fijians believe such a cleansing improves the school performance of their children and many other aspects of their village life, bringing them good fortune, bringing them into God's good graces. Wainibuka went through such a cleansing in the year 2001. Preacher Jokatama Rabukuivalu has been a leader of this movement.

save n. weak child when a second child has been born too soon after the other. Fijians have believed there should be a gap of at least two years between children to allow for adequate breast feeding.

savu 1. v. to hang down, as of a rope or vine, to drip, flow down of water or other liquid, oil, mucus from the nose.

savu 2. n. waterfall. *savusavu* set of waterfalls. *bari ni savu* cliff or edge of a waterfall.

savu 3. (in measurement or counting) "and then some". *Na vale oqo sa katu lima ka savu na kena balavu ka katu tolu ka savu na kena kubu.* This house is five fathoms long and a little more, with a gable that is a little more than three fathoms. *savu* is an unspecified remainder, or an additional amount.

savu, savuya 4. v. to rinse, splash water on (some part of the body, something) usually to clean it, using the hands. *savuya na yavana.* wash the feet. *sasavui* wash the feet. See *sevu, sevuya, sevuka.*

Idiom: *vakasavu liga* (Anglicism) uninvolved, ineffectual, idle, wash one's hands of any responsibility.

Idiom: *vakasavu itukutuku* pour out a story, give a verbal report.

savumarini 1. (Eng.) submarine. Syn. *waqanunu, samarini.*

savumarini 2. (Eng.) diving goggles. Syn. *savumarini.*

sawana n. sandy shore, usually where boats are beached. Sawana is a place-name of a Tongan village next to Lomaloma, Vanua Balavu Island. Ratu Sukuna decided to incorporate these Tongans as a Fijian tribe, officially registered as Fijians with claims for the land they occupied. By 1980 they had all adopted Fijian language of Lau. They are descendants of the Ma'afu retinue that simply expropriated the land. Some of their land claims are disputed by Fijians. Sawani is a place-name on the Waimanu River, location of Adi Cakobau School.

saweka adj. handsome.

sawelu adj. soaking wet, drenched, as of fur or hair, leaves and other vegetation, woven mat, mattress and perhaps clothes.

sawena n. natural fringe, of a woven mat, with the edging shredded into thin slices of the pandanus leaf. Such a mat is said to be *vakasavusavu.*

se- (root-word) bright, as in *serau.*

se- (root-word) v. to flee, go astray. *ise ni ivalu* refugees of war. See *sese, sesewa, sevaki.*

se 1. verbal particle that occurs only immediately before a verb, indicating a natural continuity of unchanged action or state of being, present tense, or something that may continue. *Eratou se moce tiko.* They (few) are sleeping. *Au se tabu tiko na tavako.* I am abstaining from smoking.

se 2. or. *seu lako se sega.* if I go or not. *seu* is sometimes written *se'u.*

se 3. whether, as in *Au sega ni kila se vinaka se ca.* I don't know if it is good or bad. *Na nomu lako se sega e vakatau vei iko.* Whether you go or not is up to you.

se 4. particle preceding *cava*, "what", in certain contexts. *se cava?* is it not so? (lit. or what?). *E sega ni kila o Seru se cava me cakava.* Seru did not know what to do.

se 5. v. to flee. *seba* would apply usually to a group of people fleeing off in various directions.

se 6. v. to stand on end, as in *se na votona* to have one's body-hair stand on end, as in shock or fear.

se, seva v. to foam, or spray, as the top of waves or wavelets.

sedre n. (Archaic) bowl of wood or clay, usually used by priests for kava or for oil. See *dari.*

se, sei v. to flower (of plants). *senikau* n. flower.

seile (or) seila (ni mata-na) n. cataract of the eye, glaucoma.

se-na n. flower. *se ni kau* n. flower. *sei* n. flower of the pandanus palm, which happens to be the sacred plant totem of some highland tribes in Viti Levu.

sea (Eng.) share(s), as in shares of a corporation, or co-op, owned by shareholders.

seasea n. fan-dance by women, standing, originating from Tonga.

seasea n. pinkish edible worm thought to be found only at village Tiliva, Nakasaleka, Kadavu, at damp places on sandy beach, cooked with taro leaves as a local delicacy.

seavu 1. faded, of colour usually. *Sa seavu na buto*. The darkness is "fading", i.e., dawn is approaching. Syn. *siawa, seawa*.

seavu 2. relieved, dissipated, of emotion or concern such as anger or sorrow, fog or mist. *E seavu nona vakatitiqa*. His doubts were relieved.

vakaseavu-taka v. to cause to fade away, alleviate.

seawa n. saltwater mist or light spray.

vaka se bati v. to smile openly (showing the teeth).

seba v. to come apart, separate, split, go their separate ways (people). *Erau dui seba*. They (2) went their separate ways; they parted, separated. *Era veisebayaki*. They all scattered, went off in various directions.

vakaseba, vakaseba v. to separate, take apart.

secala n. a bird, Kingfisher. Syn. *lesi*. (West) *lele*. (Rewa) *semoli*.

sede 1. (Eng. cent) cent, and by ext. money, wages. The one-cent and two-cent coins were dropped from circulation beginning in late 2008. *e lima na sede.* five cents.
  Idiom: *gunu sede* social gathering for a money-making purpose with sale of cups of *yaqona*. A person pays and names who must drink. If they do not wish to drink, they must pay. This "forces" people to drink too much *yaqona* and/or give money for the cause at hand.
  Idiom: *Adi sede* modern community festival of competitive giving to raise money among groups, each represented by a "Queen". Distinguished guests are invited who will presumably make substantial contributions.

sede 2. (Eng. scent) perfume, as used by women.

sedimita (Eng.) n. centimeter.

sedre (Archaic) n. traditional clay bowl used in certain coastal areas where clay was available and potters had the skill. Virtually all of Fiji pottery was inspired or made by people of Tongan origin. In various areas, *sedre* referred to a wooden bowl. See *dari* traditional bowl, usually of wood.

sega 1. no, not. *au sega ni kila* I do not know. *sega sega sara ga* most certainly not. *sega vakadua* never. *Warai* or *wara* are common regional synonyms. (Kadavu) *mino*. (Rewa) *segai* or *sigai*. (Nadro.) *hikai*. (Navosa) *jikai*.

sega 2. Well, . . . (an introductory word at the beginning of a sentence before expressing a thoughtful comment, usually in response to a question).

segai emphatically no, no, on the contrary.

sei, seia (or) **seya** v. to tear something lengthwise, such as cloth.

sekavula adj. bright, clean stark white (colour), shiny, lustrous. Applies to cloth, barkcloth, plastic, seafoam, some woven articles, teeth, the moon itself at times, and snow (if a Fijian were to talk about snow). The colour *vulavula*, usually translated as "white", can include off-white and even a slightly yellowish white like the moon, *vula*.

vakasekavula-taka v. to make shiny, glossy (as of the hair, with glycerine).

sekaseka (Archaic) skirt (*liku*) made of split leaves of plantain (*vudi*) as used formerly by men and women before the advent of cotton cloth.

sekederi (Eng.) adj. secondary (of school). Syn. *sekedri*.

sekereteri (Eng.) n. secretary.

sekeseni (Eng.) n. section.

sekodi n. second (of time).

sekoula n. lit. "Golden Flower", flamboyant tree, poinciana, Delonix regia, Caesalpinaceae, that flowers brilliant red in December. This in not to be confused with the introduced African tulip tree (*pisipisi*) that has reddish flowers throughout the year and has become a great nuisance, hard to eradicate. *se* flower. *koula* gold.

se-kutukutu v. to have "goose pimples", especially when one senses a spirit around, to have a tingling of the nerves, perhaps to the hair stand on end, to have an erie feeling. *kutu* bug.

sele, seleta (or) **seleva** v. to cut (with a sharp instrument, formerly usually a sharp strip of bamboo or sharp shell, then a razor blade), to circumcise young boys, to operate surgically, or modernly, to castrate animals. *na sele* n. the steer (castrated bull), or other castrated animal. *sele gutuva* v. to cut off short(er), usually of a rope or vine. See *sili, teve* for circumcise.

veisele vakavuniwai n. surgery (medical).

seleseleta v. cut it up finely.

isele n. knife. This often means a cane knife, as used in gardening. *iseleloki* pocket knife. *isele cariba* n. jack-knife, switch-blade knife. *isele ni cici-niu* n. knife for cutting copra. *isele ni ta raisi* n. sickle, knife with curved blade to cut rice stalks. Aboriginal Fijians had no knives other than shells or slivers of bamboo. Fijians have had a great preference for the English made steel knives that bear the Trumpet insignia. They test it by knocking it with their knuckes to hear it ring. They speak of that ringing sound being *melo,* sweet-sounding at a high pitch. Syn. (Tonga) *hele.*

iselewau (Anglicism) n. sword, lit. "knife used as a club". The wooden "swords" sold to tourists are a commercial invention that have nothing to do with Fijian tradition. Tourists are harrassed to buy this trash. *itawatawa* n. sheath (as for a sword or a sheath-knife). *iwau* war club.

Selekomu n. Sherlock Holmes, implying a smart detective. One Fijian detective, adopted this name and in 1990 published a very boastful story of his experiences in the police force. Ratu Leone Lautabui of Nakorovatu, Naitasiri, born 1912, considered himself the Fijian equivalent of Sherlock Holmes. Syn. *Selokomo, Selakomu.*

Selo! (Eng. Sail!) cry shouted out at the sight of a boat arriving at remote location. This is a somewhat archaic expression. *vakaselo* to greet the arrival of a boat.

sema, sema, semata v. to patch up, patch together, to join and seal together.

isema 1. n. patch (for joining things, parts of boat, house, clothing).

isema 2. n. joint or seam where two thing are joined, as in carpentry, clothing, human/animal body. By extension, connection between two or more events or things, people or places. *isema ni sala* junction (of road or path). *na isemasema* n. the joining. See *bota-na* patch. *Keda isema kei Rotuma.* Our (many) connection(s) with Rotuma.

isemaleka n. conjunction in Fijian grammar: *kei* and, *ia ka* but, *ni* of, etc. This word was invented by schoolteachers who teach Fijian grammar using only the Fijian language.

semasema adj. patched-up in many places. *vale semasema* patchwork house, made of pieces put together.

semi-fainala n. semi-finals of some sport tournament, such as rugby.

semikoloni (Eng.) semi-colon ";", as used in punctuation.

seneti or **senati** (Eng.) n. senate. *seneta* n. senator.

senijiuri (Eng.) n. century. Syn. *seniteneri.*

senikau n. flower.

se ni loli n., adj. pink (colour), colour of the *loli* fig tree flowers.

se ni nawanawa n., adj. dark yellow or orange (colour), like the flowers of the *nawanawa* tree that grows around the coast and thus a word not used by highlanders.

seniteneri (Eng.) n. centenary. *Na Seniteneri* refers to the Centenary Methodist church in Suva. Syn. *senitenari, senijiuri.*

senitoa n. Hibiscus rosasinensis, Malvaceae, decorative flower-bush, European introduction, many hybrids developed, some with double or triple blooms. The hybrids are much more difficult to propagate. At the annual Hibiscus Festival in Suva during August, a "Queen" is selected, named as Adi Senitoa. Crushed leaves are used as a gelatinous hair conditioner.

se ni wadro-wadrovi n. edible seaweed that looks like noodles.

sepuni (Eng.) n. spoon. Anciently, Fijians had the concept of ladles but not of spoons. No utensils were normally used for eating. Syn. *itaki.*

serau adj., v. to gleam, to shine brightly, bright, gleaming (stars, reflection, lamp, but not the sun).

sere, sereva, serevaka v. to sing. *sere* n. song. *seretaka* (or) *serevaka* v. to sing about (some person or occasion, or topic). *serevi ira na saravanua* sing for the tourists. *sere ni meimei* song to pacify a baby. *sere ni moce* lullaby. *sere ni lotu* church hymn. *sere ni cumu* singing of a group of men sitting in a circle, facing inward toward each other, face lowered, typical in the village. *na dau ni sere* the singer (usually the person who leads the singing), or conductor. *matasere* choir. *ivola ni sere* hymnbook. *sere ni matanitu* national anthem. *same* psalm(s).

serekali (Archaic) n. Fijian type of verse usually commemorating some occasion or offering praise. Formally composed, in rhyming couplets, Fiji-fashion of rhyming, in simplest form, in verses now normally written in four to six lines each. Traditionally recited at home, at rest, sometimes to keep children quiet for rest and sleep. *kali* refers to the wooden neck-rest that formerly served as a pillow for the head. The listeners are presumably relaxing. (Source: S. T. Bulicokocoko.) See *serevasi* with which *serekali* is often confused.

sere, sereka 1. v. to untie (rope), to release, to let free (prisoner), unleash (dog, cow), to retrieve from a pawn shop, to divorce (of married couples). *na veisere* n. the divorce (of a married couple). *viebiu* v. to be separated (of a couple). n. former spouse. *sere dali* v., n. to let go the mooring (usually of a boat).

Idiom: *Sa sere na koli.* Literally, the dog is let go (off the leash), but by extension referring to people suddenly freed from restriction or discipline who may act a little wild.

sere, sereka, serelaka 2. v. to reveal in detail, set out the details in an explanation, to explicate.

sereki (ni vuli) n. school holiday(s). *sereki vakayabaki* annual holidays. *sereki ni Siganisucu* Christmas holiday(s). *sereki macawa rua* two-weeks holiday.

seremaia (Eng.) n. soursop, Annona muricata, Annonaceae, introduced fruit tree, seldom eaten by Fijians

sere-na n. breast, chest.

Serene (Eng. Sydney) the city of Sydney but also several varieties of pineapple of the Smooth Cayenne type, larger than the older, more familiar Ripley Queen types, and with fewer prickles on the leaves (and thus easier to handle). There are about three types of *Serene* pineapple differing in size, colour of fruit at maturity, and the presence or absence of tiny seeds.

serevasi (Archaic) n, traditional form of singing chant, now long forgotten by virtually all Fijians. Formerly, usually performed by one man in a relaxed position, even lying down, sometimes joined by a second man who may intone a wordless accompaniment. The words come from a sort of trance, spontaneous and unique to that occasion, thoughts that pass throught the performer's mind, with no rhyming necessary. There may be tacit messages in the content but nothing will be discussed later by the performer. (There might be an analogy with the concept of modern-day "rap" by predominantly black American performers, though *serevasi* is not performed in an excited state.) The occurence of *serevasi* is after some task that required exertion, such as weeding, or digging a drainage ditch. It is done at a period of relaxation. An audience of sorts might gather around and listen, silently. The old word *vasi* implies a cleaning off, or peeling off the surface or skin of some food, and is thus used figuratively or symbolically in the word *serevasi*. It is also used for removal of fish flesh from the bones. Solo Bulicokooko discusses *serevasi* at length with me. He wrote a small book *Serekali and Serevasi*, Lotu Pacifica, 1988, 81 pp., illustrating both concepts. Semiti Kaisau wrote briefly about *serevasi* in *Essays on Pacific Literature*, Fiji Museum, 1978, p. 29. But Kaisau speaks of the *serevasi* as being sacred which is probably not at all a necessary component.

seru, seruta (Polynesia) v. to comb. Syn. *kava* (an earlier Fijian word). *serutavi, serutavia* comb and pat into shape (head of hair). *tavi, tavia* to pat with the hand. *ulu medre* entangled hair (that needs combing). Syn. (Rewa, Kadavu) *vani, vania*.

iseru (Polynesia) n. comb. Formerly, keeping a comb in the hair was a mark of chiefly rank or warrior prowess. Originally this was a single spike, partly as a head-scratcher, and means of loosening tight coils of hair. Syn. *ikava*. *iserukau* n. wooden comb Fiji style with long prongs, a concept introduced only in the 1830s, according to Fergus Clunie. *iserutaku* tortoise-shell comb (lit. turtle-shell), European style for soft hair, these days made of plastic. The honorific name Seru was granted to warriors of distinction. Now it is a common first name as most Fijians have adopted the English system of a first name and a surname. *na iseruseru* the combing, manner or style of combing. Syn. (Rewa, Kadavu) *ivani*.

sese v. to go astray, to be lost (person).

sese adj. foolish, scatter-brained, of a person.

sese n. a common coastal bird, the kingfisher, more commonly known as *lesi*.

sesewa adj. n. scatter-brained, unthinking, weak-willed, stupid, going astray. *Au sa sesewa sara koi au* I have been stupid, made a bad mistake.

"Set!" (Eng.) Set! Everything is ready, everything is okay. It is as good as done. I understand what is to be done and will do it. Often heard as "Set *tiko*!" Everything okay, ready. A very modern (early 2009), and perhaps fleeting expression is "I'm set with Digicel!", parroting a Digicel commercial slogan. This is said within the context of youngsters' Fijian speech.

Setani (Eng.) n. Satan. *Pielisipupi* Beelzebub. Syn. (R. Catholic) *Satani*.

Seti! exclamation of mild reproach.

seu if I, a contraction of *se au*, as in a statement *seu lako se sega*. Commonly seen as *se'u*.

seu, seuta v. to scratch, as a hen does, or a dog pawing the ground for a resting place. Also, to scoop, as one might scoop sand with the hand. *seseu* such action emphatic or continued.

vaseu v. to walk hurriedly, in great haste. There is an implication of kicking up sand or dust with fast steps.

seuta v. to scamper, run off, run away. *E ra seuta ni ra sa raica na ovisa*. They ran away as soon as they saw the police officer.

seuseua adj. choppy (of the sea), a word often heard in nautical weather forecasts.

seuvou-taka v. to found, establish for the first time, initiate, as in founding a new village. New villages are sometimes named Seuvou, or similarly, Korovou.

seva v., adj. to err, to be wrong, incorrect, tangled up. *rogoseva, rogosevata* to mishear. *wiliseva, wilisevata* to miscount, misread. *Sa seva na noqu wiliwili.* I lost count (perhaps interrupted by something). *Sa seva na noqu wa ni siwa.* my fishing line is tangled.

vakasevaseva-taka v. to mislead or fool someone.

seva, sevaka v. to hate, despise, reject totally, expel, send away. *sevaki* n., adj. outcast, exile.

vasevaki v. to banish, banished, to avoid, as of an objectionable person.

Seviteba (Eng.) n. September.

isevu 1. n. the first time something has happened.

isevu 2. n. first-fruits, presented to the chief, formerly to priests, but modernly to the church. *vula isevu* month (lunar) of first fruits, around February.

sevu, sevutaka v. to "break in", to do something or use something for the first time.

isevusevu n. presentation of *yaqona* root (*waka*) or rhizome (*lewena*) in a ceremony of introduction or greeting by a visitor. The root is stronger in lactones, more expensive, and much more prestigious. In Rewa especially, where very little *yaqona* is grown, it is unacceptable to present *lewena*. *sevusevu dredre* v. to arrive without bringing a *isevusevu* of kava.

sevu, sevuya (or) **sevuka** v. to splash water (on something), often the face, to refresh.
  Idiom: *gunu sevusevu* drink from the hands by splashing water up to the face.

sevuga n. pectoral fin(s) of a fish.

vaka-sewasewa-taka or **vakasewasewana** v. to belittle, to demean. (from the Western word for "little" *sewa*.)

si 1. as in *E si*. I do not know (in answer to a question of fact).

si 2. n. semen, male sperm. *kaisi* low-class commoner, an insult. Syn. *wai* (*ni tagane*).

siawa v., adj. to fade in colour, faded, light in colour.

sibiboti n. elephantiasis of the thigh and female genital area.

sici 1. n. Trochus niloticus, edible, univalve marine shellfish, conical in shape, the shell gathered commercially for export, used in manufacture of buttons. Locally used to make bracelets. A similar, smaller Trochus is the *tovu*, T. pyramsis. The name *sici* applies to at least a couple of edible freshwater univalve shellfish. In freshwater is the small, edible *sicimoto*, Melanoides sp. small in long sharp shape. Syn. (Lau) *vilivili, leru*, (Vuda, Nadro.) *tebetebe*. (West) *cici*. Idiom (Children): *Memu sici!* You got what you deserved! Syn. *Kemu maleka!*

sici 2. n. whistle (sports, police), horn (motor vehicle). *uvu, uvuca na sici* blow the whistle. *bitu sici* n. a var. of bamboo, with very thin stem, from which children might make a whistle. In western Viti Levu, worn by chiefs, there existed some whistles (*ikalu*) made of miniature coconut shell blown from the end, with a hole on the side. See photo, F. Clunie, *Yalo ni Viti*, Fiji Museum, page 46, item 75.

ivakasici n. roll of *voivoi* (Pandanus sp.), some 30 leaves, that is sold in the market. It is used for weaving mats. Best to check inside the roll for consistent quality.

sicini n. piles (malady), painful sores at the rectum.

sicini(dakai) n. bullet, shotgun cartridge.

siga n.,v. day, to be shiny or lit with the sun, sunshine, sunlight. *e na siga cava?* on what day? *E na siga Moniti.* On Monday. *ena siga ka tarava* on the following day. *mata ni siga* n. sun. *dausiga* drought, lit. continual sunshine. *dravusiga* drought, parched (land). *Siga ni Lewa* Judgement Day. *Siga Tabu* Sunday, Sabbath. *Siga Tabu ni Gone* Palm Sunday. *Siga ni Mate* Good Friday. *Siga ni Tu Cake* Easter Sunday. *Siga ni Sucu* Christmas day. *vanua sigasiga* sunny place. *Siga dakuna* (Lau) Thursday. *Siga vakaoti vola* (Lau) Friday. *Siga cokonaki* (Lau) Saturday. *Na nodratou vakanuinui vinaka ni Siganisucu* Their (several) best wishes for Xmas.
  Idiom: *mokusiga* kill time by doing nothing, waste time.

Siga cokonaki (Lau, Tonga) Saturday. *cokonaki* refers to gathering food for Sunday.

sigalaka to continue till daylight. *E sigalaka na noqu cakacaka.* My work continued until daylight. Syn. *sigavaka*.

sigalevu n. noon, but in "Fiji time", extending from late morning to to mid-afternoon. *sigalevu tutu* high noon. *sigalevu tutu donu* exactly high noon.
  Idiom: *kila vakasigalevu* know very clearly.

vakasigalevu (Anglicism) n. lunch. Fijians formerly ate only two meals a day, one in the morning (*katalau*), and one at dusk (*vakayakavi*). There was no formal midday meal. Working in their gardens, people might take snacks from garden food.

vakasiga, vakasigana v. to sun out (something), set out to dry in the sun. *me vakasigani* sun it out.

vakasigasiga Idiom: when it is raining, to take shelter and wait for the sun. *Ena uca, au a laki vakasigasiga ena vale.* In the rain I took shelter in the house. To continue doing something till daylight.

sigasiga v., adj. to shine very brightly, of the sun. *ulu sigasiga* blond hair. *mata sigasiga* dazzled by bright light, either the sun, when emerging from a dark place, or by a bright torch shining in one's eyes at night.

Siga Tabu n. Sunday. *Sigatabu ni Gone* Palm Sunday. *Siga ni Tucake Tale* Easter Sunday.

siga-tara n. weekday, including Saturday, when Methodists allow work (excluding Sunday).

sigavaka v. begin something in the night and continue through till daytime (dancing, work).

Siga vunau (Lau) Wednesday.

sigawale n. very small, edible marine bivalve shellfish found in the shallows at sunny, sandy beaches, eaten especially by children. Atactodea sp. or Donax. Syn. *qeqe*.

sigege facial features showing the teeth, such as smiling or grimacing. Could apply to a person, dog or other animal with the teeth exposed. May even apply to a corpse. The word can refer to the vagina and because of this double meaning the word is best avoided. There is some sort of twisted joke in very bad taste referring to the vagina as having teeth or rather, not having teeth.

sika (Eng.) n. cigar, usually hand-made by the smoker just before smoking it, though the custom is giving way to commercial cigarettes (in town), and thin, rolled cigarettes of native tobacco with a newspaper wrapper (in the villages). The tobacco *tavako ni Viti* is very strong, locally grown. *tibi, tibika na sika* v. to roll the cigar. Tobacco and the notion of smoking anything was introduced by Europeans and very quickly adopted especially by men. In the Solomons adult women also smoked, particularly using pipes. Fijians never adapted to pipes.

sika 1. adj. protruding, sticks out (only in certain contexts). *bati sika* has teeth that stick out, *gusu sika* has protruding mouth, and by extension an insult for a person who cannot keep a secret.
Idiom: *maga sika!* very vulgar insult, "protruding female genitals!"

sika 2. v. a root word meaning to appear, become visible as in *Sa basika na waqa* The boat has come into sight.

sika 3. n. grey, of hair. *Sa sika na ulu-qu.* My hair is grey. *sika droka* prematurely grey-haired.
Idiom: *sika vakabeka.* old, but young in spirit.

sika, sikava 4 v. to splash, to spurt, of a liquid (water, oil, blood). *tasika* to spurt abruptly, suddenly, forcefully, as of a bursting water pipe.

vakasikasika formal traditional presentation of newborn eldest child to relatives, usually four nights after birth.

sika, sikava v. to spew out, spray, splash. *sikavi au mai na wai* splash water on me. *na sisika* the splashing. *na sikasika* the spray (seaspray, rain, farm spray).
Idiom: *gusu sikataka* (or) *dau gusu sika* loudmouth, gossip, spread rumours.
Idiom: *Sa sikava na waitui* Idiom about the people at Levuka, Lakeba, as they formerly helped themselves to others' goods; as saltwater sailors they were figuratively spraying their salt water on landlubbers' goods.

sikalutu v. to slip, stumble and fall down suddenly. *lutu* to fall.

sikaramu (Eng.) scrum (rugby).

sikeci n. (Lau, Vanua Levu) candlenut fruit of coastal tree, Aleurites moluccana, dried nuts formerly strung on a coconut-leaf midrib, used as lamps by Fijians around the coast and on some of the islands, but not interior highlanders of Vit Levu. Syn. *lauci*. Polynesians introduced the notion of making lamp-oil from the nut, and of eating the nut after cutting up and thorough cooking, particularly used as a condiment in the small islands. Uncooked, the nut is highly purgative. The dried nuts are polished to a shiny black, strung as a necklace for sale to tourists, an idea adapted from Hawaii's tourist trade.

sikele to be sleepy during daytime, usually from failing to sleep at night.

sikereti (Eng.) cigarette, a very formal word, written but hardly ever spoken. Normally one would say "roll", using that English word, or the Fiians version *itibi tavako* or some variation of that. *tibi, tibika* v. to roll a cigarette or cigar from pandanus-palm (*balawa*) leaf or plaintain leaf as *suluka*. *koula* refers to Benson & Hedges cigarettes because of the gold (*koula*) package.

siki adj. of bivalve shellfish, full of good edible meat.

siki, sikira, sikiraka v. to shift (usually something heavy, or oneself). *na sikisiki* the shifting, of heavy things such as furniture, cases or boxes of food, sacks of goods. Syn. *kisi*.

siki, sikita v. to slip, perhaps by stepping on something squishy (mud, fruit), usually accidentaly. *sikisikidara* slippery (ground, path, road). *sikiti* trodden upon and squashed.

siki-dara v. to slip up, to slip down. Syn. *tidara*.
sikimu (Eng.) n. scheme, plan, project.
sikinala (Eng.) n., v. signal. For Fijians this can be a discreet, private signal indicated with the eyes, a slight word, a seemingly casual touch. Such secretive, personal signals are common.
sikiviro n. type of Fijian puddin of grated *ivi* nut, Polynesian chestnut. Syn. *koko*.
siko v. to look, as in checking on people.
sikoa n., adj. grey (of the hair).
siko, sikova v. to visit someone or (less commonly) some place. *siko vanua* visit (a place). *veisiko* visiting. *sikova na dai* visit the trap(s) to check and see if something has been caught. *na siko dai* the checking of traps.
  Idiom: *A siko!* Ah, a visitor! (*A tiko!* used when discovering that someone is already here).
  Idiom: *Sa vaka na siko dai.* Just like checking the (animal) trap, with frequent regular visits, implying that the visitor is perhaps too pressing, too frequent.
veisiko n., v. to visit, to go visiting, usually unannounced. *na noqu veisiko ki Japani.* My visit to Japan. *na noqu sikovi Japani.* My visiting Japan.
sikolasivi (Eng.) n. scholarship.
sila 1. n. jawbone. *sila ecake* upper jaw. *sila era* lower jaw.
sila 2. n. sheet, of a sail. *sorosila* (or) *soro, sorova na sila* v. to let out the sheet (to sail before the wind).
sila, silava v. to sheet in the sail, to haul it in. *Sila mai!* Sheet in!
sila n. maize. Originally this word referred to Job's Tears, Coix lacryma-jobi, aboriginally introduced natural edible grain with a hard shell, used as a snack by Fijians, and modernly strung as necklaces, mostly for tourists. No food grain was ever used as a staple by Fijians. Sweet corn is virtually unknown in Fiji because it requires the purchase of imported seed for each planting. Introduced by Europeans, field maize is used as animal feed, but also sold boiled, unhusked as a snack food at the market or at sporting events. Idiom: *voci vaka-sila.* to understand something by taking one step at a time, as in peeling off the skin of a cob of maize to reach the kernels.
sili, silima 1. v. to bathe in shallow water, gather from shallow water. *sili kai* mussel-gathering. *silima na kai* to gather the mussels. *sili dri* to gather, dive for *dri*. *sisili* bathing. *Era sa sisili tiko na gone.* The children are bathing. *veisilimi* swimming for fun (*qalo* swim with a purpose). *wai ni sili* n. bathing-water. *wai ni sili* n. creek used mainly for bathing. *silivata* to swim with (clothing worn, knife, warclub, other person). *laki sisili ki na savu* to go swimming at the waterfall. *lai sili* to go swimming (for fun, not purposeful swimming). Purposeful swimming would be *qalo*.
  Idiom: *silima na gau ni dali.* to interfere, to butt into a conversation.
  Idiom: *sili vakaivavalagi* to bathe by rubbing the body with a wet towel rather than bathing in the water. This may be done in cold weather or when the water is very cold.
sili 2. v. to treat a woman as for fallen womb, by feeling with the hand, usually of an older woman, for a woman who is seated in a stream.
sili 3. v. to circumcise (males). Syn. *teve, sele.* Female circumcision is unknown. Male circumcision is thought necessary.
siligi (Eng.) n. ceiling (of a building).
silika (Eng.) n. silk. May be a woman's name.
silikaya (Archaic) n. type of warclub that can be hidden in the loincloth when swimming, used to fight while standing in the water.
silini (Eng. shilling) (Obsolete) n. money. Since metric money has been adopted, the term has become *sede* (cent), meaning money or wages in an informal sense, as with casual workers.
siliva (Eng.) n. silver. By ext. may refer to silver medals in athletics.
sima adj. ashamed of wrong-doing, or failure. Syn. *madua, vela, dranu*.
simasima n. plaited coconut or other leaves serving to block a doorway, or other purposes of shelter or cover. Fijians had no attached, swinging doors.
simede (Eng.) n. cement, cement block. *vale simede* cement-block house. *simedetaka* v. to cement it.
  Idiom: *simede balavu* n., adj. person who has not had sex for a long time. The implication is that one feels heavy, and needs to unload the burden that feels like cement.
  Idiom: *lai tala na simede* to go have sex (after long abstinence). Literal meaning refers to unloading of cement. Used for men or women.
sina (or) **hina** n. (Nadro, West) reed. Syn. *gasau*.
sinai adj. quite full (of a container). *sisinai* absolutely filled to the brim. *E sinai vutucoqa na loma ni rumu.* The room is packed (with people).
vakasinai, vakasinaita v. to fill it completely full.

vakasinoi (Bau, now rare) n. dissension.

sinu dina n. "true" *sinu*, Phaleria disperma, Thymelaceceae, coastal shrub to 25 feet, terminal fls, usually solitary, fruit to 1 inch x .5 inches, two seeded.

sinu gaga n. poisonous *sinu*, Excoecaria agallocha, Euphorbiaceae, coastal tree to 50 feet with white latex that irritates the skin and may cause blindness. Often grows around mangroves. Syn. (Ba) *sota*. (Vuda) *toca*.

siosio adj. cheeky, naughty, interfering or speaking up in matters that are not one's own concern, acting out of turn. Mostly refers to children or people of junior status. See *siova*. Syn. *ciocio, ciqobaca*. (Lau) *ciobilo*. (Rewa) *qalisua*.

siova v. to interfere in or with, to meddle in. *Kua ni siova na politiki*. Don't meddle in politics.

sipi (Eng.) n. sheep, mutton. Urban Fijians today eat a great deal of N.Z. mutton, tinned or frozen, usually lamb neck and lamb chops. A local breed of sheep has been developed but is not common and the meat is expensive.

Sipika (Eng.) n. Speaker (of legislative body). Syn. *sivika*.

siqeleti (Eng.) n. singlet, men's undershirt. *siqeleti domo coko* turtle-neck or high neck singlet.

siri v. to disappear suddenly. *Sa siri oti*. It/he/she has already disappeared.
  Idiom: *vaka e siri na saku* suddenly, lit. the way the *saku*, Tom fish, Tylosurus crocodilis, disappears.

siri (Wainimala) v. to slip down, come apart.
  Idiom *sa na siri na duamu* "your legs will get knocked out from under you", said to a man attracted to a highland girl, meaning he will fall hopelessly in love.

sirita v. to avoid someone, from dislike. Syn. *calata*.

siro, sirova v. to go down, get down from a higher place to a lower place, such as from a tree, roof, from a porch to the ground, or down a slope, often meaning to go down to the sea-front, to the water. *Siro mai!* Come down! Syn. To clamber down, perhaps implying more agility, would be *kevu, kevuta*. Idiom: *siro mai* n., v. refers jocularly and impolitely to a highlander of Viti Levu who is in town, probably Suva, having literally come down from the hills.

isirovi n. beverage such as soup or tea drunk after *yaqona*. Modernly, young people are more likely to speak of a "washdown", meaning alcohol such as beer or spirits drunk after drinking *yaqona*. *sirovi* v. to drink soup or tea after drinking *yaqona*.

sisa (Eng. Caesar) v. do a Caesarian surgical operation for a mother to give birth.

sisi n. (Lakeba, from Tonga) garland (*salusalu*) of flowers and scented leaves attached to an hibiscus-fibre base, worn around the neck, various forms, types. Syn. *itaube* as a general term for necklace.

sisi, sisiva v. to slip (on or because of something), slide, skid, ski (as on snow). *sisi-buluta* v. to bury in a landslide. *Sa sisibuluta na vale e na uneune*. The house was buried under a landslide in the earthquake.

sisi (Slang) v. to over-stay illegally in overseas country, usually for employment opportunities.

sisi ni qele n. landslide, common on the large volcanic islands especially when the soil is soaked by rain. The common reddish latersols (lateritic soils) lack internal structure that might keep them in place. They are inherently unstable. Landslides are a real danger in some areas. Houses have been buried. Great gashes may be seen in the hilly rainforest where the soil structure has collapsed. Landslides are prompted by heavy rain or earthquakes. They have caused human casualties.

vakasisi v., n. to bribe.

vakasisi n. v. private and usually very discrete signal between the sexes, indicating attraction and interest.

vakasisi, vakasisia v. to cause something to slide.

vakasisila adj. abominable, as in *itovo vakasisila* abominable behaviour.

sisili (or) sili v. to bathe. bathing. *vale ni sili* bathroom, shower-room.

sisili-dravu (Archaic) v., n. for a new mother, to daub the hair with ashes and then go down to the sea to bathe four nights (*bogi-va*) after the birth of her child. Syn. *sisili e wailevu*.

sisinai as full as can be. See *sinai* full.

Sisita (Eng.) n. Sister, of some Christian sect, or senior nurse at a hospital or regional clinic.

sisiva, sisivataka v. to be jealous. See *vuvu*.

sisivo, as in *dau sisivo* competitive, envious by nature. Syn. *vuvu*.

sitaba (Eng.) n. stamp (postage, Customs). *Kasitaba* Customs. *vakabira na sitaba* stick on the stamp. Also rubber stamp.

sitarake (Eng.) v., n. to strike (of labour). Syn. *vakabesebese*. (*bese* refuse).

sitavu (Eng.) n. staff, sometimes referring to officials, as with qualified nurses *sitavu-nasi* at hospitals and health clinics.

siteki (Eng.) steak, as a cut of beef.

siteseni (Eng.) station (police). Might apply to a petrol station.
siti 1. (Eng.) n. bedsheet.
siti 1. (Eng.) n. city.
sitila (Eng.) n. steel. *sitili ulu* n. steel wool. *sitili qita* n. steel guitar.
sitima (Eng.) n. steamship. *sitima ni vanua* train (locomotive)
sitoa (Eng.) n. store, shop.
sitokini (Eng.) n. stocking, socks.
sitolo (Eng.) n. stall, as at the market, selling vegetables, fruit.
sitovu (Eng.) n. stove. *Me waqa na sitovu.* Light the stove. *Me boko.* Turn it off. Many Fijians use an inexpensive Chinese-made kerosene stove.
Siu! an interjection of reproach or outright rejection.
siu, siuva, vakasiuva v. to hiss (steam, owl, cat), hiss at. *Sa siusiu na vaivo.* The pipe is hissing (as with steam).
sivala (Eng.) n. shovel. See *isivi*, a more common expression. See *siveti*.
sivaro n. types of Fijian sweet pudding made usually from cassava (formerly taro) and coconut. *sivaro vula* and *sivaro maca* are the two types.
siveti (Eng.) n. spade, shovel. Also applies to spades, as in suite of playing cards.
isivi n. spade, shovel, spade, formerly an adze (only known at the coast, not in the highlands). The cutting edge was a shell such as the giant clam *vasua*. The large bivalve shell Pinna swamosa was used as shovel. *na i siviyara* the plough. is
sivi, sivita 1. to carve (usually wood). *na dau sivisivi* the woodcarver. This is a Polynesian rather than Fijian skill. Fijians' woodcarving was mostly for clubs and spears and wooden bowls for food or oil. Souvenir woodcarving is a modern trade. Some warclubs for tourists are faithful copies, as are some oil dishes and neck-rests. Many other tourist carvings, such as masks, are non-traditional. *na isivisivi* the wood-chip but also anciently, the adze.
sivi, sivita (or **sivia**) 2. to go beyond, pass beyond, surpass, exceed. *tu sivia* n. or v. overstayers, to overstay (usually referring to a visitor's visa). *Ni sivi ga e rua na siga. . .* When only two days had passed . . . *sivita na isausau* beat the record, as in athletics. *lako sivia* v. to go past, go too far, go beyond. *uasivi* special. *veisivi* v. to compete. *na veisivisivi* the competition.
Idiom: *Sivi na koro qai kalu.* Do not boast or claim success until you have actually accomplished what you set out to do. Lit. do not whistle till you have passed the village.
sivi, sivita 3. to fart. *sivi lo* n. quiet fart. Syn. *ci*.
sivia too much, too far. *rui sivia* far too much, much too far. *gunu yaqona sivia.* drink too much yaqona. *vakasivia* excessive, excessively. *katataka vakasivia* excessive heat.
veisivisivi v., n. to compete, competition. Competitiveness is a strong Fijian characteristic, especially in sports. cf. *dau sisivo* competitive (of a person's character).
sivirigi (Eng.) n. spring.
isiviyara n. plough, a modern concept to Fijians who formerly used only a digging stick. The word implies a shovel *isivi* being hauled along (*yara*). Usually a bullock does the pulling. *siviyarataka* v. to plough (the field).
siviyau v. to take inventory, properly *sivi iyau*.
sivo v. to dismiss, sack, fire, expel, demote (a person) from a position, rank or job. *vaka-sivoya* v. to dismiss (someone). See *sake*.
vakasivoi dismissed, sent away, expelled, as of a person from a job, a government from office at a coup, schoolchild for serious misbehaviour.
sivisivi n. wood chips from chopping or carving.
isivisivi 1. n. adze, used with a chopping motion, a shell serving as a blade. The use of stone blades and then metal blades was introduced from Polynesia, mainly Tonga but also, especially later, Samoa, with boatbuilders coming from both places.
isivisivi 2. n. style or design, especially of wood carving.
siwa, siwata (or **siwava**) v. to fish with a line, to fish for (a kind of fish). *siwa yatu* fish for tuna with hook and line, trolling. *siwa toni* still-fishing, often leaving the line overnight, as for eels and river fish. *tonia na siwa* to leave the fishing line overnight. *siwa bogi* fish at night. *siwa cavocavo* to fish with fishing rod. *bati ni siwa* fish-hook. *wa ni siwa* fishing line. *siwa kolokolo* v., n. to fish with a thown line. *uma-ni-siwa* sinker, lead weight for fishing line. *baca* bait. *yavi mai* haul in. *isiwasiwa* fishing grounds (for line fishing and trolling). *qoliqoli* traditional fishing grounds owned by one tribe or clan, registered by the Native Lands Commission but often subject to dispute. *qoli, qoliva* v. to go fishing. *qolilawa* v. to fish with a net. The concept of hook and line was

introduced by Polynesians. Trolling was a specialty of early Samoans and Gilbertese. Fishing rods and nets thrown from the shoulder were unknown to Fijians. *boi sisiwa* to smell "fishy", like stale fish. Virtually all Fijian fishing was inside the lagoon or rivers, by traps, spears, fish poison, or scare-lines.

"Snake grouper" (Eng.) n. Syn. *kuli-ni-dovu, votoqaninubu,* Comet grouper, edible fish, Epinephelus morrhua, with dark streaks, longitudinally along a dull greenish and white background, supposedly snake-like markings, to 50 cm in length, depths 89 to 370 meters, a large, deep fish caught on line in modern times, not anciently.

O so! interjection of usually mild reproach, reproval, often in response to some unreasonable request or statement. Probably a variation of *Sobu!*

so v. to simmer (of water, soup), as in *me so na wai* instructions to simmer the water.

so very, as in not very: *sega so ni totolo* not very fast.

so v. to be abundant in clustered amounts, as of certain fruit or nuts in a heavily laden, fruiting tree (mango, *dawa, ivi, tarawau*). *Sa so na dawa.* The *dawa* tree is bearing heavily. *isoso dawa* cluster of *dawa* fruit.

so some (or) some more, as in *eso tale* some more. *eso na tamata* some people. *eso vei ira* some among them. *ena so na gauna* sometimes.

ivakaso n. as in *na ivakaso ni wai* the reservoir of water.

soana (Lau) v. to be apprehensive.

so sa v. to be fed up, tired (of hearing), as in *Au sa so sa na rogoca na ulubale.* I am tired of hearing excuses. Also written as one word *sosa*.

soaqa n. species of plantain, the "upright banana", Musa fehi or M. trodlogytarum, unique in having fruit that grows on an upright stalk, not a pendant stalk as with the plantain or banana. Aboriginal introduction throughout many islands from the coast of Papua New Guinea to Melanesia and Polynesia. The fruit is used more by Polynesians (such as Rotumans), rather than Melanesians. It was formerly a staple in Tahiti where it is known as "fe'i". There are many varieties, many of them with pinkish flesh. They are normally cooked before eating. Syn. *dra i Turukawa*.

soata n. pumice, occasionally found at sea and on beaches after underwater earthquakes. At times there are massive amounts. Fijians use it for scaping and cleaning as in cleaning cooking pots at the shore. It has also been used in upper layers of house foundations, above the stones and below the fern and mats.

soba n. the bulbous, purple flower shoot that hangs down on the plantain and banana tree, and remains as the fruit is forming. Fijians often cut it off from the maturing fruit, believing that this helps prevent disease on the fruit. Used by highlanders for black hair-dye (*bena*). Cooked, it is edible, but not used as a regular food.

sobe, sobeta v. to hang securely. *sobeta na siti me kua ni lutu.* hang up the sheet(s) so as not to fall.

sobi (or) **so bi** adj. very plentiful, of fruit on a tree or vine. Applies to any fruit that is heavily laden on the tree.

sobu down, downwards. *muria sobu na uciwai.* follow down the river. *toro sobu* get worse, decline.

sobu, sobura v. get down, get off (vehicle, aeroplane, boat). *sobu e tauni* get off in town.

vakasobu 1. n. formal ceremony receiving a chief who has come some distance.

vakasobu 2. v. to lay down, as in *me vakasobu na duru* lay down the housepost. *vakasobu na bila* lay down the *bila* (a form of Fijian *madrai* "bread") to ferment in food-storage pits (*davuke*) dug in the ground.

vakasobura 1. v. to unload (truck, boat), discharge (cargo).

vakasobura 2. v. to get off (or) to let off or to "land" passengers (from boat, plane, motor vehicle). *Me vakasoburi koya.* Let him/her off.

Sobu! Sobu! interjection of reproach, disbelief, regret.

sobusobu n. cold wind that blows to sea off the highland hills in the very early morning. See *caucau*.

sodo, sodomaka v. to insert, as into a sheath, or a socket, as a knife, electrical plug, or a key in a lock. Syn. *codo, codomaka, vakacodo*.

sodrega v. to squeak, creak, a board under heavy weight, a door opening.

sodro adj. disorderly, confused, mixed up. *qaqa sodrosodro* foolhardy.

soga n. sago palm, endemic Metroxylon vitiense, growing wild in swampy places, mainly around the Navua River, noted as endangered species in 1993, cut out mainly by Fiji Indians for the edible heart, sold by the side of the road. Fijians have never eaten it. Locally in Serua and Rewa, they used the leaves as an excellent, durable thatch. No one makes a sage starch powder, or pudding, as in done in Papua New Guinea and Solomon Islands and northern Vanuatu (of related species). This palm matures around fifteen years of age, producing a huge terminal flowering panicle some 12 feet in height, with 20 or more branchlets. The round fruit is almost 4 inches long and two inches wide, with shiny brown scales. The tree dies after fruiting, after some twenty years of age. Syn. (Ovalau) *niu soria*. (John Parham has the name listed as *sogo*.) There is a similar, introduced species, M. warburgii that grows mainly on Vanua Levu Island, distinguished with erectly held pear-shaped fruit on a three-branched stalk.

sogo, sogota, sogolaka v. to close (it), as of a door, turn it off, as of a tap, or an engine, plug up (clay cooking pot, jar, bottle), closed in (or out, of people or animals), to stop up (liquid flowing). *Era a sogoti tu i tuba na tamata cakacaka maivei ira na nodra manidia.* The workers (many) were locked out by the managers.

isogo n. 1. plug used to close a container, such as a plug of leaves to close a clay cooking-pot, or cork or cap to close a bottle. 2. door. Syn. *katuba* (or) *darava*. There were formerly no hinged doors in Fijian houses. Entrances were closed off with various plant materials. 3. closure, the means of closing off something that can be opened and closed, a clasp, a lid of a pot or jar.

sogo butu adj., v. to close up tight, as a house might be closed up.

sogolati, sogolatia, sogolatitaka v. to close off (an area, a room, a flow of water), to enclose.

sogosala v. to close of a road or path. This is done fairly often by clansmen who feel they have been mistreated by outsiders who have leased some of their land, or by the Native Land Trust Board that makes lease arrangements and collects payment. *sala* path, road. See *suguvanua*.

soi, soiya v. to scrape off, usually the skin of some root crop before cooking (taro, yam) or fibre-plant such as *voivoi*, or barkcloth. Formerly this was most often done with a sharp shell (at places around the shore), or a sharp edge of bamboo (in the highlands). *na soisoi* the scraping (of this sort).

soi, soilaka v. to scratch or prick deeply, as of coral, thorny bushes, a needle, or tip of a knife.

sokalou n. worship, religious session, meeting for Christian worship.

soke-na n. crotch, knot (wood), node (on stem or branch of plant such as bamboo, *yaqona*, cassava). See *tagau, tago-na*.

soki v., n. to scream, shriek, squeal loudly as warriors with war cry, people in terror, bat making bat noises, rats squeaking, pig squealing in terror, child squealing with tears. *sosokiki* lots of shrieking, squealing.
Idiom: *qitoqito vakoli, vuki ga, soki* said of children, begin playing like puppies but soon there are tears (squeals) when one has been hurt.

soki n. a man-hole trap dug in olden days, covered lightly with leaves; sharp stakes in the pit will injure the victim. The same technique is still used to trap wild pigs. They can be dangerous to the stranger walking inattentively on a pig trail in the bush.

sokisoki n. porcupine fish, Diodon hystrix, named for the shriek of pain (*soki*) from being pricked by the spines. Length to 45 cm, body grey back, speckled with spots, rounded fins. Fish eaten by Fijians but ovaries dangerously toxic and rarely if ever by Gilbertese who believe they may die from a single broken egg. Syn. (Tonga) *sokisoki*.

soki, sokia v. to pick by breaking off with a twisting motion (ripe breadfruit for food). The essential notion is that of twisting, often done with a pronged stick to reach the height of the fruit. *soki uto* pick breadfruit. *yava soki* lame twisted leg (person).

sokidi v., n,. adj. wrinkled (clothes, *voivoi* leaves, barkcloth, human brow), wavy, choppy (sea). *sosokidikidi* very wrinkled, etc.

sokiki n. a distinctive, tall palm of the rainforest, with a very slender trunk and hard wood, formerly used for spears. The tiny seasonal nuts are easy to open and are edible when young and crisp, before they become hard. Usually only children eat them. Watling's *Palms of the Fiji Islands* lists only *sakiki*, not *sokiki*. Sakiki is said to apply to Veitchia joannis, V. vitiensis, and Pritchardia pacifica (the fan palm). There are many regional differences of names for the Fiji palms.

soko, sokota v. to sail (to direct a boat). *sokota na matasawa*. sail toward or up to the landing. *sokota i Levuka* sail to Levuka. *soko kosova na toba* sail across the bay. *soko muria na baravi* to sail along the coast. *soko ravita* to sail right up to, next to (some place). *soko-taka na iyaya* to ship the gear by boat. *sokovoli* (or) *soko volita* (or) *soko wavoli* (or) *soko wavoki* to sail around (some area or place).

sokobale, sokobaleta v. to sail beyond, or sail past the place intended.

sokobale n. a large cultivar of cassava that can be left in ground for up to a year, growing larger, a much longer time than most cassava.

sokonu v. to shiver, shake, tremble, to quake (of the body, as from cold or fear).

sole, solega v. to wrap, often inside a mat or cloth, such as a sheet. Also wrap, as with insulating tape or plumber's tape. The implication is of wrapping around, as a mat is rolled. This wrapping is most often done for clothes, cloth, barkcloth, but also a human body, especially for burial. *isole* n. shroud, wrapper (usually in cloth or blanket). *sole itutuvi* to wrap up in a blanket. *isolesole* n. mat containing items rolled up inside.

solesolevaki v., n. community effort, house-building, planting crops, collecting money, often on a wide and large scale. The word may apply to small group efforts where many hands make light work. The beneficiary at any one time can be one nuclear family. The group may take turns helping individual families. This is probably one of the finest features of Fijian culture, when the people can work together at a task that might otherwise be onerous. Such occasions are now becoming fewer as three-quarters of the Fijian population lives in towns, cities, or suburbs Syn. (Lau) *balebale*.

solevaka v. to work together on a project as a community. See *solesolevaki, sosolevaki*, synonyms or closely related concepts.

solevu 1. n. traditional exchange of goods between two villages. People in the highlands might acquire clay pots and mats, or salt, while those in the lowlands receive *yaqona*. Today the custom is much less common and its purpose is now almost exclusively social, with festivities, dancing, feasting, to reassert community relations. These events have been very important in re-affirming peaceful relations among different rural communities.

solevu 2. n. presentation of goods at traditional ceremony

soli, solia v. to give. *Solia mai!* Give it here! *Solia vei iratou* Give it to them (few). *solia na veivakadonui* give permission (such usage is direct translation of the English, not traditional usage). *solia vakailoloma* give it as a gift. *solia na matana ca* to give a bad look. *solia na liga-na me lululu.* give the hand to shake (hands). *soli bula* v. to be ready to give one's life to some cause. *vaka-solisolia* v. to pretend to give.

Idiom: *solisoli vakatoa* give and then take back, "Indian giver", lit. give like a rooster who offers the female some food in the beak and then grabs it back. Syn. (Lau) *solisoli vakapoipoi*.

Idiom: *solia na kesu-na* to turn one's back (in disdain), to reject an approach or request.

Idiom: *mana soli* gifted (as splendid singing voice, a special intelligence or ability that one may be inborn.)

soli n. gift, periodic contribution (money, goods), usually a payment required of each villager for some common purpose, such as repairing the village church. Even when living away from the village, Fijians are told how much money they must give. Solicitation is made as well to those who have married someone from the village. Collection procedures are often relentless. If a Fijian fails to pay, he or she could become estranged from the village. *na isolisoli mai vua na Kalou* the gift from God. *isolesole* n. something that is given. *soli ni yasana* n. tax exacted by the Province of people aged 21 to 60.

veisoli 1. giving. **2.** specifically, village collection, calling upon members and relatives to contribute for some common cause. These days it is customary also to call for contributions from families of women who have married away from the village, a class of people now referred to as *vasu*. Formerly, only the children of such a marriage were *vasu* to the village, and they could demand privileges and goods (except not from Bau), but the role is now reversed. The *vasu* may be expected to give rather than take from the village.

soli dre n., v. professional, registered moneylender, limited legally to 12 percent interest, serving mainly civil servants, and employees of established companies.

veisolisoli n. exchange of goods, repeated giving.

solimaka (Slang) n., v., adj. to "sweet talk", use duplicitous behavior, trying to win favours ("marks" as from a teacher) from a superior by flattering, catering to whims, preferences. Syn. *tabetabe*. . Syn. (very vulgar) *masi polo*.

solimu, solimu-na v. to turn one's backside to someone in contempt. Syn. *cu, cucu, vakacucu*.

solipasi (Anglicism) v. to direct traffic at busy street corners, of policeman.

isoli ni yaca n. whale-tooth given to father of a child, asking that the child be named after the donor of the tooth.

soliwai v. to administer herbal medicine.

soliwale adj. free, normally of goods given by a merchant at no extra charge, usually on condition of some purchase.

soliyate v., n. to give emotional support, as fans do in sports, cheering on their champion(s) or their team. *yate-na* liver, for Fijians the source of courage, as the heart might be to Europeans.

solo (Kadavu) n. rock. Syn. *vatu*.

solo, soloya (or) **solota 1.** (Lau) v. to scrape, rasp, grate, light (a match). Syn. *yaca, yacaraka*. **2.** to wipe, usually plates, to dry, or the body after bathing. *isolo* n. cloth used for drying what is wet.

vakasolo-kakana-taka v. to whisper.

vakasosolo-taka v. to pack up (for travel), to wrap up (clothes, goods, baggage), to gather up one's things

isolosolo n. people added to a clan (*mataqali*) or tribe (*yavusa*) as a matter of permanent accommodation, rather than kinship or related origin. Such people may have been given land to use but may never become elders or chiefs at their new location. Informally, may refer to the many children of a couple. (Formerly it was cause for ridicule to have a great number of children.)

solopuli (Lau) n. pudding made of grated *ivi* (Polynesian chestnut) and coconut cream, wrapped and cooked, usually in leaves of *qai* (Cordyline terminalis, a plant also called *masawe*, or *vasili*, or in Hawaii, *ti*). *Solo* suggests the grating, *puli* means *buli*, shaped or formed.

solovatu n. ankle. Syn. *qurulasawa*.

somate n. funeral ceremony. Visitors gather, bringing gifts (*ireguregu*) such as *tabua*, mats, barkcloth, in the first phase of ceremony that is called *reguregu*. Syn. (Lau) *soputu*.

somidi adj. tiny. *manumanu somidi* tiny "animals" (e.g. bacteria).

isominiwai (or) **sominiwai** n. moustache.

somisisi (or) **somisise** adj. impudent, mostly of children.

somo, somota v. to soak (*tonia*) in mud (*lolobo*) to dye black, of pandanus leaves (*voivoi*) used in weaving, or of sinnet (*magimagi*), used in decorative bindings of house-timbers, or wooden clubs. After then being rinsed in fresh water, the material is cooked with certain leaves, candlenut (*lauci*), *tavola, koka, kalabuci*, to fix the colour, then washed again and dried by hanging up outdoors. There are alternative ways of blackening. See below *somo*.

vakasomo-taka v. to weave blackened *voivoi* into a mat or basket.

somo n. pandanus leaf (*voivoi*, P. caricosus) that has been dyed black for weaving patterns into mats. The dried leaf is sometimes boiled with the leaves of a wild herb called *lalakai* (not be be confused with *ilalakai*, which is a very small, woven mat used a plate for a chief's food). Today, *voivoi* is instead often soaked for a few days in water that has been boiled with a few old batteries from an electric torch. The resultant black colour is not the fine shiny black of the traditional technique. In the Suva market *somo* is usually sold as bunches of individual, dried leaves, or as a small roll. The rolls often conceal inferior leaves inside. *ibe vakasomo* (or) *ibe somo* woven pandanus mat with some leaves dyed black. *butu somo* v. to soak the *somo*. *vakacabe somo* v. to dig out, bring out the *somo* from the mud.

somuna 1. n. wart, mole. Syn. (Lau) *sonusonukuita*.

somuna 2. n. sucker(s) on the arms (*na qalona*) of the octopus (*kuita*).

sona n. rectum. Syn. *icici, ivekaveka, mata ni da*. (Colo East) *cobo*.

so na ua 1. daffy, said of a person who by nature responds in unexpected ways that amuse others. Literally, in Vanua Levu, *so na ua* means the tide is full. *Sa so mai na ua*. The tide is rising. In Tailevu, *mati ruku* means low tide (usually referring to the early morning), which has taken on the same meaning of daffy, when speaking about an odd person. It is believed that some people's behaviour changes with the tide, be it full or low. One may ask then, when someone acts crazily, if it is low tide or high tide. The effect of the tide on people is remarked upon particularly in Vanua Levu, Nasavusavu District, especially villages Vivili and Waivunia. Those locals have a reputation of being daffy in relation to the tide. This is the source of many jokes and funny stories. Syn. (Colo East) *dale, sauvou*. **2.** not commonly, but *sonaua* can occasionally have vulgar connotations when referring to a person, simply because of the coincidence that the *sona* part of the word means rectum. Vulgarity will be indicated by context and tone of voice.

soni, sonita v. to pierce or to prick with a sharp object, usually a knife or a needle in these modern times. In earlier times a piece of broken glass might be used, and before that, a sharp piece of seashell. Also to remove the tiny thorns from edges of pandanus *voivoi* leaf in preparation for stretching it, prior to weaving mats (*ibe*). Traditionally the tiny thorns were slit off using the shell of mussel *qa ni kai*. *na sonisoni* the removal of tiny thorns from edges of *voivoi* leaf.

soni n. common climbing coastal shrub, Caesalpinia spp., yellow flowers and seeds, thorns and prickles on the seed-pods are implied in the name. Also Solanum torvum, spiny shrub that has become a noxious weed on Viti Levu and many of the small islands.

soniwai n. rivulet, tiny stream.

sonosono-ua n. wrinkled, furrowed (of the brow), having many folds, especially of the face, in anger or sorrow.

soporano (Eng.) n. soprano.

soqe n. Peale's pigeon, the "barking pigeon" that barks like a dog, endemic, Ducula latrans, often shot for food by Fiji Indians. The hunting season is set during the last two weeks of May or a few days in very early June, when hunting is done openly. Same name for Pacific Pigeon, Dacula pacifica, which extends to Samoa, Tonga, known there as *lupe* (equivalent of Fijian *ruve*). In Fiji the fairly common White Throated Pigeon, Columba vitiensis, is known as *ruve* or *soqe loa*. The introduced Feral Pigeon Columba livia lives only in larger towns and has no distinctive, separate Fijian name.

soqo n. meeting (of many people). *e dua na soqo siga rua* a two-day meeting. *vale ni soqo* n. meeting house.

soqo, soqova v. to meet and discuss or celebrate something. *Na cava o ni soqova?* What are you (many) meeting about?

soqona 1. v. to gather together, of things or people. *na isoqosoqoni* the gathering together.

soqona 2. v. to sum up, to summarise. *na isoqoni* the total.

soqoni n., adj. assembly. assembled.

soqorasa v. jumbled together, of things; mingled together, of people.

isoqosoqo n. association, club, group of people meeting together.

iSoqosoqo Vakamarama n. Womens' Association of the Methodist church, founded by Mrs. Derrick who gave it the name *na Ruve*.

soqosoqo n. trash, rubbish. *tomika na soqosoqo* pick up the rubbish.

soraka make something sprout up, grow rapidly, as in building up the flame of a fire.

sore-na n. seed(s). In former times, only some fruit trees were planted by seed.

sorevuce n. elephantiasis of the testicles. *vuce* swollen.

soresore n. testicles. Syn. *polo, sore ni qala-na, vua ni soresore*.

Sori! (Eng.) Sorry!

soro, sorova, sorovaka 1. v. to surrender, give up, submit, or apologise. Traditionally, make a formal offering of submission or or surrender, usually to a chief, to humble oneself, worship. After defeat in battle, a surrender offering was sometimes a basket of earth as a symbol of surrendered territory. Women were a frequent gift, some of them chiefly. By extension, the word may be used to say that one has eaten enough, or had enough to drink, and quits eating/drinking. Or, similarly quitting a game, having had enough. *na isoro* the thing(s) one gives when surrendering or asking forgiveness, such as whaletooth, or ceremonially, a reed in a ceremony called *matanigasau*. *sorovaka* to *soro* because of . . . (whatever wrong).

Idiom: *Tabu soro!* Never give up!

Idiom: *sorosoro wale* give up easily without a struggle.

soro, sorova 2. v. (of a rope or fishing line) to slack off, let go, let it out, of a tide to slacken.

sorosoro v., n. to serve a devil, wanting his service to perform evil, by presenting a gift, usually pouring *yaqona* for the devil. *Me qarava na tevoro.* Look after the devil.

sorosoro adj. unreliable, untrustworthy, person who should atone (*soro*) for unfulfilled promises or duties.

isorosoro n. gaggle of young chickens, ducks, who follow their mother as a troop.

sorokicididiki v., n., adj. wrinkled (of skin, as in old age), to ripple (as of water in a lagoon). Syn. *sosokidikidi*. See *sokidi*.

sosa to be irritated, bothered, by something or someone.

vakasosa-taka v. to bother (someone), take up their time. See *so sa*.

soseti (Eng.) n. sausage. *soseti rolo* n. sausage roll.

sosipani (Eng.) n. saucepan, pot.

soso 1. n., adj. mud, muddy. By extension, in ceremonial speech, *soso* refers very modestly to one's own land. Even in ordinary speech to an outsider, a Fijian will speak modestly of his own garden-land, as if it were of little value. In the Bible, *soso* means earth, as in the burial service. *Sa soso na nomu isulu.* Your clothes are muddy.

isoso 2. n. cluster (fruit, nuts such as *wi, tarawau, dawa, tavola*), shoal or school (of fish). Syn. *tausoso*.

soso 3. n. (Medical) carbuncle, one or more very deep, painful boils that begin with a cluster of pimples. Some Fijians believe this occurs most commonly on the back and neck.

soso 4. adj. stuffed as in *tiaina soso*, "stuffed" bananas, as a snack or (modernly a dessert), sliced down the middle lengthwise, stuffed with grated coconut and perhaps coconut cream. Sweet plaintains, an aboriginal introduction, may be used as a substitute for bananas, a European introduction. Syn. *vakasoso*. Type of pudding.

soso dregadrega v. of tree branches or bamboo stems, to make a sound as wind blows through and rubs them against each other. This sound of bamboo has been noted at NaWi Island in Nasavusavu harbour, and also at Qoma Island off the north Tailevu coast. Such a sound has been thought to be significant, involving spirits.

isoso ni tavaya n. bottle-stopper, cork, often improvised with a shaped piece of coconut husk

isoso ni waqa (Archaic) n, food and gifts put aboard a new boat being launched. Syn. *ivakasoso ni waqa*.

soso, sosoga v. to plug up an opening, as of a bottle, with a stopper, plug or cap. *sosoga na gusu ni tavaya* to close up the mouth of the bottle. *isoso ni tavaya* n bottle-stopper, often improvised with a carved piece of coconut husk or a rag. See *sogo, sogota*.

sosoko adj. concentrated, of a beverage (*yaqona*, coffee, tea), the opposite of *waicala* dilute. *rui sosoko* too concentrated, too "strong". Syn. *soko*.

sosolevaki n. work done together as a group, housebuilding, gardening, etc. See *solevaka* v. to work together as a group, helping each other in sequence. Traditionally a very important Fijian concept based on the notion that many hands make light work of a task. Syn. *sosovaki, solesolevaki*.

sosomaka v. to push into, through a crowd, to stuff.

sosomi-taka v. to substitute, replace. *E sosomitaki Jone o Seru*. Seru replaces Jone.

isosomi n. the substitute, person or thing, deputy serving in an acting capacity. *na kemu isosomi* the substitute for you, your replacement.

sosova v. to go in a very large group or crowd of people.

sosovaki n., v. work all together first on one man's garden, then another man's. Working together gets the job done fast, This is easier and more pleasant than each man working alone on his own garden. *Sosovaki* has been an extemely important custom in village life and still is to some extent.

sosovi lago v. for flies, to cluster about, usually food. *Sa sosovilago na kakana* The flies are flocking over the food.

sosovu adj. sleepy, drowsy, head nodding with sleep. Syn. *damule*.

sota, sotava v. to meet (person, people), to encounter. *sota vata* meet together. *Au a sotavi koya* I met him. *isotasota* n. meeting, meeting place. By ext., may mean to encounter some situation: *Keimami sotava ruarua eke, na draki katakata kei na draki batabata*. We (many) encounter both hot weather and cold weather here.

sotasota n. match(es), usually in sports such as boxing, rugby.

sote (Eng.) n. shirt. In the late 1940s, British regulations required Fijian men to wear shirts in Suva. At that time a fair number of men owned no shirt and no sandals and most men wore a *isulu* rather than trousers.

soti a particle, not directly translatable, used to modify expressions to make them more emphatic, assertive and clear, usually in the negative, as in not at all: *Kua soti ni dede mai*. Do not then be very long in coming. *E rau sega soti ni veiyaloni kei Seru, o Manu*. Manu and Seru are not so much in agreement (not of the same mind). *O cei soti?* Who then? Who then might that be? *O cei soti o iko?* Who do you think you are? *Sega soti* Not at all! A virtual synonym is *so*.

sotia n. (Eng.) n. soldier. Sotia is used also as a personal name, usually female, to commemorate a relative who served in the military services.

sou, souta v. to go in the early morning. In early custom, Fijians left home for garden work or for fishing very early in the morning, coming back much later for a late breakfast (*katalau*). Their second, final meal would be taken toward the end of the daylight, just before nightfall. *sou i wai* go down to the water (river, lagoon) very early in the morning. *souta na motoka* go early in the morning in the car.

isou very near(ly), almost, of some occurence. *isou sara* extremely close.

souru pleated, usually of cloth or barkcloth, usually of a woman's dress, causing a frilled effect.

sova n. practical, utility-basket woven of coconut-frond leaves or more carefully from *vilawa*, usually for carrying food, cooked or raw. By extension, a bird nest.

sova v. to flock about, as with flies, bees, children. *Sa sovi koya na namu*. The mosquitos flocked about him.

sova, sova (or) **sovara** v. to pour out, dump out, usually with brusk motion, quantities of liquid, or rubbish, or things that occupy a container. *sovara na simede* pour out, dump out the cement. *Sa tasova* (or *kasova*) *na sucu* The milk is spilt. (*kasova* may also imply the milk is poured out quickly or forcefully.) *sova yaqona* pour out (on the ground) *yaqona* as tribute to one's devil, said of people who are *vakatevoro*, who have a devil they serve, in return for favours that are usually evil. *sova yaqona* may also refer to pouring out *yaqona* into the sea as an offering to Dakuwaqa, the shark god. Such an offering by divers is intended to retain Dakuwaqa's protection from shark attack, though to gain that protection, divers must also have restrained from recent amorous adventures. I have a scar on my leg from a shark nibble that my diver friends insist, resulted from my having violated that rule. Idiom: *sova wai* v. to urinate (a rather coarse expression).

isovasova ni benu n. rubbish dump.

sovea, soveataka (Eng.) v. to survey (piece of land).

veisovia (Archaic) v., n. competitive game of two teams on a field with a sort of goal-post at each end. To score, one had to touch the opponents' post. Syn. *veibuka*.

sovivi n. common coastal twining vine with edible leaves, mostly eaten in Lau, Ipomea gracilis, Convulvaceae. A Lauan dish of such greens is called *borovasi*, often served with seafood.

sovu (Eng.) n. soap. *sovu ni sili* toilet soap. *sovu ni savasava* laundry soap. *sanisovu* n. sandsoap. *sovu ni torotoro* shaving soap. *sovu pouta* soap powder. *vakasovusovu-taka* to soap (clothing usually). Fijians formerly had no knowledge of soap (and nor did the ancient Greeks). Fijians cleaned with sand, fine gravel, and sometimes with body oil (as did the ancient Greeks), though highlanders of Viti Levu never had any body oil. Fijians sometimes used the leaves of a moderately common shrub *vere* (= *vusolevu*), Colubrina asiatica, as noted by Father Neyret, and also by Berthold Seemann, who specifies its use for washing the hair. Later, they have used leaves of the small woody introduced weed, Koster's Curse, Clidemia hirta, that has several Fijian names not widely known. A froth can be raised by rubbing the leaves of either species. The tiny purple fruits of Koster's Curse happen also to be tasty and edible. Crushed leaves of the introduced *senitoa* hibiscus are used currently in hair treatment.

sovusovua adj. soapy, frothy.

sovu, sovuta v. to wash something by soaping.

su 1. n. soup, as in *wai ni su*, fish soup, though in Kadavu *su* refers to ripe bananas in coconut cream (*lolo*) sauce. Fijians made no soup except with fish.

su 2. n. dry, soft grass, fern, or leaves used to create a soft floor under the floor mats (*icoco*) of the traditional Fijian house. *Vakasu vinaka na buturara ni nona vale*. The floor of his house is softly padded. Frequently used have been the ferns *koukou, karuka, qato,*

isu n. fresh coconut-leaf basket, quickly made and disposable, made usually by men and used by both men and women, for food, garden produce such as *tavioka*. *isu weleti* basket containing papaya. *isu sei* n. such a basket made of young shoots of screw pine pandanus (*vadra*). Idiom: *tube isu* to be an unimportant person, a simple carrier, carrying things to accompany an important person.

sua, suaka, sualaka v. to spike, to stab (with spear, knife, sharp stake), by ext. to remove husk of coconut. *isua* n. spike of wood or metal stuck in the ground, used for husking coconuts (or) modernly, a dagger or sheath-knife.

sua, suataka v. to scull (boat, with one oar from the stern, an introduced custom). Idiom: *sua mai, sua yani* rock-and-roll dancing.

suaigelegele v. to wobble, stagger of an infirm or drunk person, or a boat in troubled water, a tree under the weight of the wind.

isuai n. work-clothes. The implication is that the work-clothes get wet *suasua*, either from sweat and/or rain. *vakaisuai* to dress or be dressed in work-clothes. Also *suwai*.

suasua adj., n. wet, humid. *via suasua* adj. still damp (usually of clothes), slightly damp. Idiom: *Sa suasua na yava-na*. He/she is a newcomer, just arrived, not a knowledgable local. literally, His/her feet are still wet (from coming ashore from a boat is implied).

suasua (or) **laki suasua** v., n. to urinate (polite term). *via suasua* to want to urinate. *Sa dau dra na nona suasua*. There is usually blood in his/her urine.

vakasuasua-taka v. to wet, throw water on, to water (garden).

vakata-suasua, vakasuasuataka v. to entertain. *dau vakatasuasua* entertainer(s). *vakatasuasua* n. entertainment to an audience. Can be music, dance, or a short skit. This term is a modernism. Origin probably lies with old custom that one hears about, sprinkling of water to make people laugh, done by elderly women, pretending to urinate like men, with a coconut shell full of water between their legs.

subu-na n. mons veneris, woman's genital mound, vagina. Syn. *maga-na* (specifically vagina). Words not to be pronounced. *subu-na* is not a well known word.

sucu 1. v. to be born. *vakasucu* to give birth. *na isucusucu* the birth. *sucu dole* born prematurely. *sucu saumaki* breech birth. *vale ni vakasucu* n. maternity clinic. *siga ni sucu* birthday. Siga ni Sucu Xmas Day. Traditionally, Fijians never counted or remembered the day or even the year of their birth. Only the relative age of siblings was relevant. Today many Fijians celebrate children's birthdays, order birthday cakes, and even place elaborate notices in classified ads of newspapers, replete with a photo of the child. A trad. ceremony four days after birth (*bogi va*) is a feast celebrating the probable future survival of the baby. *turaga sucu* born a chieftain, in contrast to the more Melanesian practice of choosing a chief on his qualities rather more than just lineage. Fiji has had both systems.

Birth-right now tends to predominate though there are many disputes over that right and many vacant titles because the matter cannot no longer be settled by violence.

sucu, sucuma 2. v. to suckle the nipple, the mother's or the bottle's. *sucuma na tavaya* to suck from the bottle. *na sucu vei tina-na* the suckling from the mother.

vakasucu, vakasucuma v. to give birth (to offspring).

sucu n. milk. *ti vakasucu* tea with milk. *sucu mamaca* n. dry milk (powder). *sucu sosoko* n. evaporated milk.

sucu dole v., adj. born prematurely. *gone sucudole.* premature baby.

sucu dudu n. protruding breasts.

sucumate adj., v. still-born.

sucu-na n. breast (male or female). *mata ni sucu-na* nipple. *sucu lodo* breast with insufficient milk.

sucuwalu n. large type of commercially very valuable bêche de mer, dark brown, greyish brown, creamy white in colour, sometimes with blotches, with eight "breasts" (*sucu*) on each side, as suggested by the Fijian name. Holothuria fuscogilva or Microthele nobilis. Syn. *loaloa*, (Macuata) *tavunia*. The names *sucuwalu*, *loaloa* and *dri loa* are also used for different species.

sudra, sudra v. to shift a little to one side, of a person or an object. *Sudra yani meu dabe.* Shift over a little to make room for me to sit.

isue n. prop(s) for supporting Fijian traditional clay cooking pots, usually three of them, often made of clay. Syn. *sori.* *katuba-i-sue* n. doorway at the end of the Fijian thatched house, near the cooking area, used by family and people of no particular distinction. The side door was reserved for elders and important guests. In the west, *sue* can refer to a house (*vale*). Prior to Cession, most Fijian houses had only one doorway. Having two doors, and windows, was a post-European development.

sugu, suguta v. to snatch away, to take sudden control of (usually unfairly or inconsiderately), to "hog" some place or facility, to block off (in the case of roads), In modern times, villagers sometimes block roads as a form of protest over land disputes. Syn. *usu, usuta*.

suguvanua n., v. incursion, taking control of a territory, closing off or blocking roads, commonly done by Fijian clans making monetary demands for the use of their native land for roads, electricity, schools, water-pipes, et cetera.

sui, suiva (or) **suiya, suilaka** v. to splash, sprinkle or spray water (watering flowers etc.). *na veisui* the splashing, watering. At certain occasions, celebrations, it has become custom, especially for children, to splash a bucket of water on friends or relatives. New Years eve is one such occasion that may extend for a number of days (until village elders call for a halt). Another is at the annual Hindu festival of Holi, around April, when the splashed water is often red coloured. Fijians sometimes participate in splashing, though rarely understand the symbolism and religious significance. They are just having fun.

sui-na n. bone. *sui tu* n. backbone, spine. There is no separate word for "skeleton"; one would say simply *na sui ni tamata* (human bones, skeleton). *ora ena sui ni ika.* to choke on the fishbone. *suisuia* adj. very skinny (person), bony, lots of bones (of a fish). By ext., midrib of a leaf of frond (palm, fern). Syn. (Tonga) *hui*.
   Idiom: *Sa lauti koya ena sui ni kena.* He/she got caught in his/her own trap, lit. the (fish) bone in his/her food got caught in his/her own throat.

vaka-suina barbed, as of speech with bitter remarks, that may be half-concealed.

suidromo adj. of a person, animal, too thin, or not filled out appropriately, considering the age or stage of growth.

sui ni gata n. lit. "snake-bones", very large Lycopodium spp. that resemble the skeleton of a snake. L. foliosum and L. phlegmaria, decorative foliage.

suiti or **suwiti** (Eng.) n. switch.

sui tu n. backbone. Also, by extension, an Anglicism, the plot, as of a story, a word invented by Fiji's Education Dept.

suivotu adj. very skinny, of a person, suggestive of bones showing.

suka (Eng.) sugar. *vakasuka* v. or adj. to add sugar (to tea, food), sugared. Previously, only Fijian puddings were sweetened, using the expressed juice from corms of *masawe*, after extended baking in earth oven, a practice known only around the coast. There were no earth ovens in the highlands.

suka, sukava v. to return. *Me suka mai na noqu isele* (Please) return my knive. *suka bera mai* come back late. *suka mai na valeniveivesu.* get out of prison. *suka mai vuli* get out of school. *sukanaivalu* returned serviceman. *sukava tale na noqu ivakamacala* to turn back again to my explanation.

vakasuka v. to resign (from a job or position). *Sa mai vakasuka na turaga mai na pati ni politiki.* The gentleman resigned from the political party.

vakasuka, vakasuka-taka v., adj. to sugar (tea, coffee etc.) sugared (as a cup of tea), containing sugar.
vakasuka, vakasuka 1. v. to return (an object).
vakasuka, vakasuka 2. v. to dismiss or "send down" (a person).
vakasukasuka v. to retreat, move back.
sukanaivalu n. returned soldier.
sukau (or) **sikau** small wild tree of the forests, to 15 m., a lowland evergreen, grows at altitudes below 250 m., Gnetum gnemon, Gnetaceae, a gymnosperm. The young pink or green leaves were often steamed and eaten as a vegetable on the major islands and Koro Island. The seeds, 3 cm diam, fleshy covering, ripening yellow to orange to red, and are occasionally eaten. Fls and frts October, November. In swampy lowlands such as Rewa the tree is unknown. Syn. *bele sukau*.
"suki" (Hindi) Fijian tobacco, cured leaf twisted into a rope, rolled into a large ball of some 8 to 9 kilos, sold at the market by length or weight. Fijians roll a smoke with it. They may use the expression *kana suki* to smoke (Fijian tobacco). Much of the Fiji tobacco has been grown in Nadroga, famously at Qalimare. It is very strong.
suku-na n. knot (in wood), node (bamboo, *yaqona* plant, sugar cane, *duruka*). An internode is *tagau* or *tago-na*.
sukuna (Eng.) n. schooner. Adopted as a name for Ratu Sukuna, after Cakobau's schooner, captained by Madraiwiwi, Ratu Sukuna's father. The name was held previously by one of Cakobau's sons by a secondary wife.
sukuru (Eng.) n. screw (as for carpentry).
sukusukura adj. knotty (of wood), rough or bumpy (of a road), and by extension, untidy (of a person).
sula n. green coconut having no flesh and too young to be drinkable.
isulasu n. palm fronds woven to carry various large foods. See *isu sei*.
suli n. 1. n (regional) *dalo*, taro, Colocasia esculenta.
suli n. 2. n chunks of *dalo*, taro, Colocasia esculenta, sometimes sold at the market, cut usually to take out damage such as that of the taro beetle.
sulisuli n. suckers, usually for planting (taro, banana, pineapple), sometimes abbrev. as *suli*. Suckers grow up around the mother plant.
isulu n. cloth, clothing. *isulu tavoi* simple cotton wrap-around clothing. *isulu vakaToga* long, ankle-length wrap-around, a style introduced from Tonga, first to Lau, but not common around Fiji till after mid 1900s. *isulu vakataga* man's tailored *isulu* with pockets (invented by Ratu Sukuna). *isulu i loma* underclothes (a very modern concept). *isulu ni yaqona* cloth used to strain pounded *yaqona* in the *tanoa* (bowl for mixing and serving *yaqona*). Early Methodist converts were given an *isulu* of Manchester cotton cloth (and sometimes a metal axe) as an incentive to convert. Previously coastal men might wear a loincloth of barkcloth, but often a skirt of split plantain leaves, or *waloa*. Women wore a very brief fringed skirt *liku*. Highland men and some mature women wore a skirt of leaves, usually *vava* or *masawe*, sometimes plantain. No underclothes were ever worn. *vakatara isulu* removal of black mourning clothes (or symbolic black ribbon) 100 nights (*bogi drau*) after the death of a close relative. Such use of black mourning clothes comes from missionaries as do virtually all funeral customs. Early Fijians did not perform elaborate funeral ceremonies except for the strangling of widows at the death of high chiefs.
vakaisulu, vakaisuluma (or) **suluma** v. to clothe, dress in clothes. *vakasuluma na gone* to dress the child.
vakaisulu adj. clothed. *vakaisulu-taki* to have been dressed up.
sulu, suluma v. to grope with the hand into some covered place, blanket, basket, mud-hole of eel (to catch eel). By extension, penetrate female genitalia with the hand. *Wainisulubonu* name of a creek at Wainadoi where mud-eels (*bonu*) are caught by hand in their mud-holes.
sulua n. octopus or squid. Octopus is more commonly called *kuita*, except in the West, Rewa, Kadavu and a few other places where the word *sulua* is used. There are regional variants of the names and species. Octopi are normally caught with a spear. Squid is rarely caught by Fijians. Near the shore small squid travel in large schools, stay still for a while but move suddenly with great speed, caught only with nets and only with difficulty. They have excellent eyesight. Squid have 8 arms and two tentacles. Giant squid, to 15 feet in length, half a tonne in weight, are a favoured food of the Sperm whale. Scars on those whales indicate momentous battles at great depths, never witnessed by humans. The squids themselves eat fish especially and are also cannibals.
suluka n. heat-cured leaves of Pandanus tree (*vadra* or *balawa*) or plantain (*vudi*) used as a wrapper for hand-rolled cigars and cigarettes, and by ext., may refer to newspaper used for the same purpose.

These hand-made smokes are sometimes called *suki*. Most young Fijian smokers today demand ready-made cigarettes.

suluma, sulumaka v. to put on clothes, to get dressed.

sumusumu n. puffer fish, Tetraodon sp., edible if the poison sacs are removed, but fatal if not. Numbness, dis-coordination of limbs are early symptoms, then difficulty of breathing. Death may occur within 24 hours. Fish is skinned and gutted immediately because toxin is in mucus of the skin and viscera, all to be done with very exact knowledge and care. In Japan chefs must be licenced to prepare this fish.

"sunfish" giant edible, deep-sea sunfish, Mola sp., unknown to most ancient Fijians, now sold in Suva market, brought in by the modern deep-sea fishing boats. The Mola is common in the tropics and subtropics, sometimes seen lying on its side, basking in the sun (just as a swordfish does). It may weigh more than two tonnes. Inoffensive, and unafraid of humans, the sunfish has a diet of kelp, algae and plankton, small fish and crustaceans. The flesh tends to be very white or pink, but tough and lacking texture. The skin is very tough.

suni, sunia v. to scald, of shellfish, by soaking in a cloth or sieve in very hot water.

sunisuni n. sugary, fibreless residue of coconut, light brown in colour, eaten as a candy by children, and also rubbed on the hair of bride and groom as glittery decoration.

sunuka (Eng.) snooker.

sure, sureta v. to implore, invite, request. *sureti au* invite me. *O ni sa sureti tu.* You are invited. *na veisureti* n. the invitation.

surevaka v. to persuade forcefully. *surevaka na veivukei* demand the help.

veisureti n. invitation (usually to attend some occasion).

suru, suruta v. to sneeze at or on, trad. in Fiji, a rejection, or an act that will bring misfortune to a prospective undertaking (fishing, going to war). To sneeze in the presence of a chief could be a mortal offense. Sneezing is still somewhat impolite, but is now perfunctorily excused by the exclamation *Bula!*. (Live!). One replies *Moli!* to express gratitude that one's life is spared. The verbal exchange is good natured. If the sneezing is repeated a few times, the humorous exclamation may be *Mate!* Die!

Idiom: *Sa suruta na vusi.* lit. The cat has sneezed on it, meaning that some plan went wrong by misfortune.

suruwa n. (Hindi) food (usually seafood, small fish), fried and curried, in coconut cream, a favoured food of Fijians and Indians. *suruwa-taka* to prepare food in this manner.

susu, susuga v. to nurse, raise a child or domestic animal. *Au a susugi e Viti.* I was raised in Fiji. The island Susui is named for being the place to raise a chiefly child safely, away from the dangers on Vanua Balavu.

veisusu n. up-bringing, raising, as of a child but by extension may apply to raising a young animal, such as a calf. *Vakilai na yaga ni veisusu vinaka.* The value of a proper upbringing is recognised.

dau ni veisusu n. guardian, caretaker for a youngster, nanny for a child.

susu manumanu n. animal husbandry. *susu toa* raising chickens. *susu bulumakau* raising cattle.

susuna n. an illness, usually of children, chicken pox. Syn. *korosusunu*.

susu yago v., n., adj. nicely plump and healthy, of a young child, implying the child is well fed. By extension, this word applied to adults can imply a person who stays around the house and does very little work.

sutu (Slang, Eng.) v., n. suit of clothes, and there can be an implication of getting all dressed up to impress others, particularly the opposite sex. *sutu vata* wearing matching clothes, such as people of a choir, or children in school uniform.

suva (or) **suvasuva** n. mound or pile of stones used to mark a place, particularly a boundary. The word was adopted as the name of a few villages, one in Ra, and one at what it now Suva City, now part of Rewa Province but formerly allied to Bau. It is also the name of the tribe of the Tui Taveuni.

suvania (Eng.) souvenir. Many of the Fiji souvenirs sold in tourist gift shops originate from Indonesia, the Philippines (examples are shell necklaces), or are manufactured in Australia. Modernly carved warclubs are one of the few types of souvenirs made in Fiji, some of them very well done by traditional woodcarvers but many are crudely made imitations. Carved wooden masks are fake souvenirs, not traditional in Fiji. Fans are often made at village Daku, and Fijian barkcloth, often from Vatulele, is sold for souvenirs.

suveia (or) **sueia** words spoken after drinking a cup of kava, preceding a wish that will be expressed. More commonly known is the term *vosa ni vakacivo* a wish expressed on such occasion, usually for fair weather, good crops, safe voyage, something benign. (The word *suveia* is new to me; it is taken from *Na iVolavosa Vakaviti*, p. 588. – R.G.) The custom is less common in modern times.

suvi, suvia (or) **suvisuvia** v. to cut into large pieces, usually a root-crop such as yam, sweet potato, breadfruit, potato, usually before cooking. *isuvisuvi* chunk, as potato cut up for a for a stew.

suvu (Eng.) soup. Soup is customarily slurped, even if a spoon is used. (Spoon is a modernism). As a separately cooked dish, soup was known only in coastal areas, not in the highlands where there were virtually no clay pots. The main soup was fish broth, usually called *wai buta* or *wai su*. Fish is the only food that was sometimes boiled. (The only exception is human bodies boiled in whalers' giant iron pots that had previously been used to reduce whale blubber.) In the lowlands, virtually all food was steamed in huge clay pots. It was not boiled. Or food was grilled over a fire, or cooked in the earth oven (*lovo*), though the earth oven was unknown in the highlands. In upper-class Fijian households it is now customary to serve soup in white half-shells of immature coconut (not the dark, mature shells used for *kava* cups). Soup is said to be drunk *gunu, gunuva*, not eaten *kana, kania*. Like taro leaf, meat, tea, soup is considered as a garnish (*na kena icoi*) for "true" food (*kakana dina*) such as taro or yam root crops.

suwai n. work-clothes. Syn. *suai*.

suwe (or) **sue** (Ba, Nadi) n. house. Syn. *vale*. (West) *were*. Tribe Suelevu settled into the Nadi area from Naviti Island, changing their tribal name to Vatulevu. Pushing aside the indigenous settlers, they assumed a new title they called the Tui Nadi. Their earlier origin was in Vanua Levu via Ba according to N. L. C. Commissioner David Wilkinson.

T

The Fijian **t** and **d** are in certain words pronounced as a hard **j** or **tch** in Lau. Examples are *itiToko = ijitoko* (walking stick) and *midimidi = minji-minji* (tiny). Kadavu Province may also use the **j** sound. In South Sea languages it is the vowels that anchor the meaning of word, not the consonants, so these differences are not confusing to us.

In western Viti Levu the letter **t** usually replaces the **d** of eastern Fijian when it is the first letter of the word. Thus *daniva* (sardine) becomes *taniva* in the west, and *duna* (eel) becomes *tuna*.

In Bua, the **t** is often replaced with a glottal stop which sounds a bit like a hiccup.

ta- prefix attached in front of a word, indicating a sudden, forceful action, usually unintentional. *tasere* suddenly let loose, come undone, separated, snapped (rope). *taqusi* suddenly smeared. *tasova* spilt abruptly. *tamusuka* cut off abruptly. *takoso* cross over abruptly. *takosova na ikawakawa* cross over the bridge. *tacaqe* to trip. *tace* torn in two. *tacece* to skip over the water (like a high-powered speedboat), or a stone thrown. *tacoka* gushing forth, as a watermain burst. *tacuqu* to butt into something unintentionally. *tadola* to burst open, of a door in the wind. *tadodo* to stretch out suddenly, as a rope under strain. *tagede* bob up and down, of a fishing-line float. (See *gede*)

In most cases, this dictionary lists words according to their root (as in *qusi, musu, sova, koso*) rather than alphabetically by the prefix. The prefix *tata* indicates a frequent, repetitive or greater, more forceful action that the simple prefix *ta*.

ta n. two species of unicorn fish, edible reef fish with a "horn". Largest is Naso unicornis. N. lituratus is more brightly yellowed. They feed on seaweed, algae.

ta (Lau) not. Bauan *sega*. *E ta lako ki Suva.* He/she did not go to Suva.

Ta (or) **Ta-ta** n. Dad, Daddy, as said by a child. See *tama-na* father.

ta, tavaka v. to wait for, to meet and greet (person).

ta, taya, talaka 1. v. to chop, cut forcibly. *laki ta buka* go chop firewood. *taya na buka* chop the firewood. *taya na gaunisala* cut the road. *taya na waqa* build the boat ("chop the canoe"). *na ta waqa* the ship-building, the building of ships. *tatalaka na nona meca* chop down his enemies. *na veita domo* the slitting of the throat(s). *na itata ni buka* the chopping of firewood. *e dua na ita* one chop. Idiom, rather obsolete: *Au mai taya nomu waqa.* I ask to share in what you are enjoying (usually food, some delicacy), a rather archaic expression, perhaps somewhat childish. Helping build someone's boat would normally call for some recompense.

ta, taya 2. v. to gather up with a quick, choppy action, as with sand in a shovel, or *balolo* (edible sea annelids) in a net or container. *ita nuku* shovel-full of sand. *e dua na ita balolo* one scoop of *balolo* worms.

ta, taya 3. (Anglicism) v. in cricket, to go to bat. *pate* (or) *sasabai* n. bat. *tavi, tavia na polo* v. to hit the ball. See *sabaya*.

Taba! (Slang) Agreed! From children especially one may hear *Sitaba!*

itaba 1. (Anglicism) n. photograph (or) camera. *veitaba Sitiveni Moce* photo by S. M. *dauveitaba* or *dauniveitaba* photographer.

itaba 2. (Anglicism) n. stamp, usually referring to a rubber stamp. *sitaba* postage stamp.

taba, tabaka 1. v. to press down with the hand and arm. *tabaka na kato me sogo vakavinaka.* press down on the box to close it well. *tabaka na bulukau* press the button.

taba, tabaka 2. v. to press on with, proceed with, as in *tabaka na vala* to press on with the fight.

taba, tabaka 3. v. to print, publish. *iyaloyalo tabaki* printed image, picture.

taba, tabaka 4. v. to play (musical instrument such as piano, organ, accordion).

taba, tabaka 5. v. to take a photograph. to make a film. *itaba* photo.

taba, tabaka 6. v. to say traditional words of acceptance and gratitude in receiving *isevusevu* of kava, or receiving a whaletooth or feast food at a formal ceremony.

tababoko, tababokoca v. to extinguish, of a law, regulation, or of a branch of government or business, organisation, or branch of people. Not a commonly used word. *boko* v. to extinguish.

taba-caca v. of a person, not yet matched with a partner, as in a sport like tennis. Implication is that that person is "left over" for the time being. May refer to things of uneven number, lacking a corresponding "match".

tabacakacaka n. ministry, branch or department, usually of government or a business. *T. ni Vanua* Home Affairs, *T. ni Vanua Tani* Foreign Affairs, *T. iTaukei* Fijian Affairs, *T. ni Teitei* Agriculture. *T. ni Vuli* Education.

tabace n. small edible fish at shore or reef, light-coloured body with vertical stripes, with thick, gritty skin, Acanthurus triostegus.

itaba-gauna n. epoch, period of time.

itaba-gone n. younger generation. *tabavata* of the same generation.

itaba-qase n. older generation.

itaba-tamata n. generation (of people, in time). Polynesian chiefs (such as Ratu Sir Kamisese Mara) have claimed to recite their lineage for up to 14 generations, using a generous imagination to fill in some gaps with illustrious names. For chiefs of Viti Levu, no records extend more than about 8 generations, usually fewer. The more purely Melanesian lineages are rarely remembered for more than just a very few generations.

taba-na 1. n. branch or limb (tree), wing (bird), upper arm (person), branch or "side" (of a family, as in the "woman's side" versus the "man's side" in a marriage). *vunitaba-na* shoulder (of person), branch as of a government department. *tabataba* shoulder-to-shoulder. *vatuvatu ni taba-na* shoulder blade.

Traditionally, "the side" of a family has been referred to as *na itaba*, a term heard less commonly today. This old term presumably gave rise to "*Na ita*", a form of address between people of various specific territories that became allied and bonded, different tribes but branches of the same people. Fijians today know with whom they have such a relationship referring to themselves as being *veitabani* with those people; they know how to behave in that relationship, but normally they have no idea of the historical facts that created the relationship.

Two kin-groups that are *veitabani* are in a fiercely competitive but friendly relationship. The relationship is traditionally said to be that the ancestral spirits (*vu*) of the two groups are related as cross-cousins *veitaveleni*. This is the case with Nakelo and Tokatoka in Tailevu Province. They may take extraordinary privileges with each other, friendly but forceful insults and even indecency. In effect it is somewhat like a *veitauvu dredre* relationship. See *tauvu*.

taba-na 2. n. storey (building). *vale taba tolu* three-storey building. *ena taba rua* on the second floor. *na vale tabavica* the house with multiple storeys.

taba-na 3. n. page (of a publication). *ena tabana e va kei na lima.* on pages four and five. Syn. *drau ni veva*.

tabana 4. n. department (of government), branch (of company). *Tabana ni Bula* Health Department. Syn. *Tabacakacaka*. *T. ni Vanua* Home Affairs (Police, Prisons, Military), *T. ni Cakacaka* Labour Department.

tabana 5. n. section (publication). *tabana ni qito* sports section (of newspaper).

veitabani see *taba-na*. This is a type of kinship relation for a whole community, now often generalised to regions. In earliest times, this was based on two sets of people having ancestral spirits that were cross-cousin. They may refer to each other as *Naita*. They make treat each other impudently, jokingly disrespectful, similarly to the *veitauvu dredre* relationship.

tabaikelekele v. to place hands on hips, both sides of the body.

tabailago-taka v. inquire informally of a young woman's family, as to the prospects of approaching with a formal marriage proposal (*duguca*). *vosa yalewa* ask for a woman's hand in marriage. In modern times these formal customs are often by-passed.

tabaleka adj. short-sleeve, of a shirt or blouse, vest. *e dua na sote tabaleka* a short-sleeved shirt.

tabaliga (Archaic) v. to make a thumbprint as a signature, for someone who cannot write, mostly relevant in early history of Fiji.

tabalili n. (Modernism) bibliography.

tabaivola v. to print (newspaper, pamphlet, book, etc.)

tabaiwalu n. leather-back turtle with relatively soft shell having seven longitudinal ridges, and thus eight plates of carapace, as implied in the name. It does not breed in Fiji and is not often seen. Dermochelys coriacea. Syn. *tuvonu*.

vakataba ni uto 1. v., n. Idiom: have an casual affair, lover. The implication is that the branch of breadfruit breaks easily; the relationship may not endure.

vakataba ni uto 2. Idiom: to be ineffective, unable to contribute and thus useless. A person who has no adequate presentation-goods to offer at a *magiti* is said to be *vakataba ni uto*. Such an expression might not be known to youngsters.

tabakau n. crude matting made of split coconut branches with leaves interwoven. These serve as temporary flooring or temporary walls for a shed. May refer simply to branches of the coconut palm. Idiom: *dabe ena ibe qai kisi ki na tabakau.* said about one who was riding high, and was then reduced to a lowered status. Lit. sit on a fine mat, and than shift to the crude matting of *tabakau*.

tabakidua adj., adv. self-reliant, acting independently, by oneself or themselves, alone. *tu tabakidua* to stand alone; of one kind only, as in *na nuqa me ra soqo vakatabakidua* implying only one kind of fish, the *nuqa*, collecting themselves together.

tabale v. to proceed, but staggering or wobbling this way and that, as if drunk. See *tataivatia*. Not to be confused with *taubale* to walk.

itabale n. mountain pass.

tabaluvu, tabaluvuca v. to push a person down beneath the surface of the water, as in some baptisms, or children playing in the water. See *taba, tabaka*.

tabe, tabea v. to hold or carry something with both hand supporting the burden from underneath, to support. *Eratou tabea toka na kumidra.* They (several) have their chins in their hands. *tabe ulu* to hold one's head in the hand, as in heavy thought, or perhaps having a headache. *tabe liga* to hold one's hands behind the back. (*roqo liga* to clasp one's hands in front of the body.)

itabe n. Fijian form of tray, made from leaves, carried with hands supporting it underneath, such as a *ilalakai*, food-mat for a chief, or a tray held in this way. *itabetabe* n. the thing(s) such as food that is brought this way.

tabekasere (Western highlands) n. woman's backpack basket, usually made of split bamboo.

tabetabe v., n. adj. to cater to (someone), play up to someone, flatter deceptively to gain favour, usually with a superior (chief, boss, teacher), to be supportive. As a noun, the word *itabetabe* has the prefix "*i*" attached.

Idiom: *tabetabe mai* bring food (especially of women, respectfully).

tabika 1. v. to press down on something, applying weight, as in pressing a rather full suitcase to close it. Syn. *danu, danuya, tatuva*.

tabika 2. v. to place some weight, such as a stone, to hold down say a mat, or *voivoi*, to keep it in place, as on a windy day. Syn. *danuya, tatuva*.

See *bika, bika* to press down.

tabikai n. weight used to hold something down, in the office a paperweight, in the village stones or heavy object to hold down a mat being aired in the sun, or to hold down *voivoi* that is being dried outdoors, not to be blown away.

tabilai (Archaic) n. blunt-ended Fijian war canoe use for ramming enemy canoes. Length about 60 feet, the hull of single-log length.

tabili 1. v. to move quickly, people rushing, pushing in a crowd. *Era tabili yani na laki volivoli.* They (many) moved quickly in a disorderly crowd in going shopping.

tabili 2. n. mortar for pounding *yaqona*. Present versions are made of wood or of metal, metal becoming more common. The concept and word were apparently introduced from the Solomon Islands, according to P. Geraghty. In earliest times, kava was grated on coral (at the coast) or stone such as *sule* in the Viti Levu highlands (*cule* in standard Fijian). The notion of having youngsters chew kava before mixing it was probably introduced from the central South Seas. It has not been a highland custom in Viti Levu among the "real" Fijians.

tabisa (Archaic) n. v. ceremony for a new event, usually concerned with the arrival of people, a boat, or other vehicle. Original concept concerned recognition of recent death of a chief ashore. An arriving boat's sail would be thrown in the water. Gifts are brought, historically hung around the boat. Hosts will compete for them. See *cere, cereva*.

tabogo v. disappeared, out of sight, not visible, from the view being blocked.

tabola v. to split suddenly, as accidentally in falling, as a melon might do. Syn. *kabola*.

tabonaka v. to conceal, cover up, something physical (a stolen object, or a gift), a light, a sound, an idea or a thought or a fact.

tabono v. to become blocked, closed off, as fallen leaves might block a drain. See *bono, bonota*.

tabu 1. adj. sacred and (modernly) holy. *Sautabu* village chiefly cemetery. *iVola Tabu* Holy Bible. *Yalo Tabu* Holy Ghost (Christian). *Siga Tabu* Sabbath. *Siga Tabu ni Tina* Mothers' Day. *Duatolu Tabu* Holy Trinity. *Tui Tabu* Pope. *vakatabui* sanctified, blessed. Syn. (Tonga) *tapu*.

tabu 2. specially reserved (as for chiefs, priests, any special people). *Sa vakatabui me nomu.* It has been reserved for you, for your use only.

tabu 3. adj., n. forbidden, prohibited, taboo. *Sa tabu na curu eke.* Trespassing forbidden. *Au sa tabu tu* (of Methodist Youth member). I am under promise not to do something (usually smoke, drink). *Sa tabu vei au.* That is forbidden to me. *Au se tabu tiko na kana tavako.* I am abstaining from smoking. *tabu kaisi* n. very fine pandanus mats woven at Ono-i-Lau, traditionally forbidden to commoners. *Sa tabu na ta niu.* Cutting copra is forbidden. *tabu dredre* strictly forbidden. *tabutabu* very strictly forbidden. In villages it it forbidden to eat certain seasonal food until they have been presented ceremonially to the chief, and modernly, also to the Church. This applies primarily to yams, both cultivated and wild, but also, in places, to breadfruit, and to some fruits such as *dawa*. Also, after the death of a chief, locally there may be a prohibition to fish or to harvest certain foods for a time.

tabu 4. n. person with whom one is *veitabui,* with whom one may not speak. For example, formerly a brother and sister were not permitted to talk together. Also the relationships such as the *vugona,* or *daku*.

tabu-- as a prefix, *tabu--* indicates that something that is not normally done: *tabusili* not bathing often. *tabutoro* often unshaven. *tabuvuli* often skipping school. *tabudredre* strictly forbidden. *tabudredre* unsmiling. *tabukana* eats very little. *tabugunu* doesn't drink. *tabuvosa* hardly speaks at all. *tabukoti* unkempt, usually needs a haircut. *tabulotu* not usually going to church. *tabusuka* does not use sugar. *tabuyaqona* do not drink *yaqona* (as is the case of some Christian sects of American origin, Mormons, Adventists etc.) More emphatic would be the prefix *tabutabu--*, as in *tabutabulotu* for many non-theists who might never go to church services.

veitabui (or) **veitabuki** in Fijian custom, forbidden to talk to each other, to communicate directly, or to eat certain food in each other's presence. Certain social groups may not associate directly with each other, such as Waimaro people and the people of Bau. There are also food prohibitions:- in having meals together, highland people may not eat pork in the presence of coastal people, and coastal people may not eat seafoods or coconut products in the presence of highlanders. The distinction is based on the notion that highlanders are traditional warriors for coastal people but in fact their geographical locations may have switched with time. Supposedly, highlanders have more ready access to wild pigs, and coastal people more ready access to seafood and coconuts. Within families there can be prohibitions (no contact, no conversation) between children and the maternal uncle, and also between brothers and sisters (as an incest prohibition, though no such prohibition in the west). *Keirau veitabui kei Seru.* Seru and I are *tabu* in relation to each other.(and I might therefore refer to him as my *tabu*.) Family relations that may be *veitabuki* are *ganena, vugona* and one's *daku*. In some areas, a son may not normally address his own father.

tabuisulu v. dress in mourning, black, for 100 days after a death in the family, a custom adopted from the missionaries. *vaka-tara-i-sulu* ceremony after 100 days when normal clothing may be resumed.

vakatabu, vakatabuya 1. v. to impose a *tabu*, a tradtional prohibition. In Fijian custom, village leaders place a *tabu* on something, as on coconuts or fishing grounds, preventing its use for a time, often six months. This is done ceremonially after the death of a chief or generally, to save up stocks of fish or crops for some special village purpose.

vakatabu, vakatabuya 2. v. to prohibit, forbid. *Au vakatabuyi iko mo curuma na vale oya.* I forbid you to enter that house. *E vakatabuya vei ira.* It is forbidden to them. *Sa vakatabui na kana tavako.* Smoking has been prohibited.

Idiom: *vakatabui cegu* hold the breath.

vakatabu, vakatabuya 3. (Modernism) v. to sanctify or bless (a church, building, boat), customs introduced by missionaries. *vakatabui ena masu* blessed with prayers, sanctified (as for a new church).

tabucagi n. hurricane lamp fueled by kerosene, a standard item in the village.

tabu-kaisi n. very finely woven mat from Ono-i-Lau, "forbidden to commoners".

tabu-kana v., adj. off one's food, not eating sufficiently, under-fed, anorectic.

tabu-kele n., adj. express, non-stop, as of a bus, this being a modernism.

tabu-lotu v., adj. does not usually attend church. Syn. *sega ni dau lotu*.

tabu-moce v., n., adj. sleeplessness, sleepless.

tabusiga adj. of a chiefly marriageable young woman, kept indoors, out of the sun, to maintain a fair skin to make her more attractive. The custom is more Polynesian than Melanesian. Many Fijians have been colour-conscious. Insults to other Fijians sometimes refer to them as being black. After circumcision young boys are kept out of the sun for few days. *Era tabusiga kece ka tiko e loma ni vale.* They are all kept out of the sun and stay inside the house.

tabu-sauriva unblinking, as of a steady staring, watchfulness.

tabu-sili v., n., adj. disinclined to bathe.

tabusoro Idiom: never give up, never surrender. This may be an exclamation.

vakatatabu 1. adj. (of a person) subject to a *tabu* (e.g. against a haircut or shave), usually after a death, usually for 100 nights, or one year. Former, men might forego shaving, or keep shaven part of their hair until they achieve revenge.

vakatatabu 2. n. prohibition, as in a *tabu* against fishing in a certain area after the death of a chief, or a prohibition against certain behaviour in the village, as carrying burdens on the shoulder, wearing a hat, or wearing immodest dress. Immodest dress is a missionary notion. In earlier times, men should wear nothing above the waist unless they had chiefly status. Women's dress barely covered the loins.

tabua n. whaletooth, from the lower jaw of sperm whales which have about 50 such teeth, about an inch apart embedded into a massive jawbone in a straight line; all but about ten of them seven or eight inches in length, suitable for Fijian ceremonial use. *Tabua* are the most valuable of ceremonial presentation goods for Fijians. Such goods are referred to as *kamunaga,* a Fijian version of wealth. In ceremonial presentations ten *tabua* were counted as one *vulo,* as a form of counting the wealth presented. Previously, *tabua* in Viti Levu were reportedly carved of wood, specifically of *bua,* in the approximate shape of a plantain. No such ancient artefact has been collected other than wooden ones in fairly modern times, substituted for the genuine article, to be placed in chiefly graves. Stories tell that the wooden *tabua* was polished, and coloured with sap from the fruit of candlewood tree (*lauci* or *sikeci*). Also formerly used as *tabua* on the coastal islands was a poisonous species of cone shell, up to nine inches in length, Conus marmoreus, known in Bau as *cava* but as *sauwaqa* in Vanua Levu. It is impossible to know much at all of these previous customs. Tongan themselves never used whaleteeth in any ceremonial function; they traded them in Fiji for sandalwood, used to scent their coconut oil. Tongans and commercial whalers introduced whaleteeth to Fiji, probably in the 1700s after whaling ships arrived in the South Seas hunting whales for whale oil to fuel lamps in the United States and Europe. That industry peaked around 1846 when there were 900 whaling ships active, four out five from the U.S.A. In 1853 some 8,000 whales were killed for oil but by the end of that decade the industry declined sharply, when whale oil began to be supplanted by kerosene for fueling lamps, an innovation from the United States. Whalers introduced a few huge walrus teeth which were used with the same purpose as sperm whale teeth. Some Tongans learned whaling from American whalers, and have done hand-harpooning of whales themselves from small boats for the meat sold at Nukualofa wharf until almost mid-century 1900s. Fijians have never caught whales. Some whales have been beached by themselves and Fijians have taken teeth that are to be found in the upper jaw. Most whale teeth have been obtained from whalers. Modernly there is a considerable shortage and extremely high price on whaleteeth. It is forbidden to take them out of the country but there are no effective controls to prevent that. The best teeth are oiled and polished, protected by wrapping, becoming an attractive yellow-brown in colour that is prized and referred to as *tabua damu.* Colouring has been effected with the root of *masawe,* or of turmeric, or of the fruit of the candlenut tree. *Tabua* are normally attached at both ends to a cord of plaited sinnet. Presentation is always done with fairly elaborate ceremony, holding the cord away from the tooth, and kneeling before the recipient. Acceptance calls for more ceremonial speech. The present-day scarcity of whaleteeth and extremely high cost causes diminished use in Fijian ceremonies. They are normally sold through pawn shops at prices exceeding F$500 in 2009. A large tooth can cost twice that price.

tabua damu n. whaletooth that is highly valued for being smoked to a deep tan colour (*damu*), a former practice of Tongans in Fiji. Smoke is from smouldering fire of native sugarcane or of sweet tubers of the indigenous *masawe* (= *vasili* = *qau,* Cordylene terminalis). To preserve the colour, the tooth was oiled with coconut oil and kept away from the sun, wrapped in barkcloth. *Tabua* may be boiled with roots of *kura* Morinda citrifolia, Rubiaceae, to give the desired rich tan colour. Turmeric (*cago* or *rerega* or *reregwa*), was also used for its yellowish colour.

tabu-cala adj. perfect, faultless, not likely to make mistakes.

tacaqe v. to stumble, stub the toe, to trip on something. *caqe, caqeta* to kick.

tacece v. to become separated, unsettled as the corner of a mat, or page of a book, blown by the wind. Virtual syn. *tacega.*

taceme v. to babble.

tacenu, tacenumaka v. to do something with vigour.

tacere v. to come undone, as of a parcel.

taci-na n. younger sibling of the same sex. A brother's younger brother, a sister's younger sister. *tuaka-na* refers to the older sibling of the same sex.

veitacini adj., n. siblings of the same sex. *na vertacini* the brothers or the sisters (one of them younger than the other(s).

Taciqu n. affectionate way of addressing a somewhat younger person of the same gender, ("My young brother" if the speaker is a man, "My younger sister" if the speaker is a woman). *na veitacini* the group of two or more siblings of the same sex. Modernly, and more vulgarly, one hears young men addressed as "*Bro*" or "*baraca*" (brother), mimicking the speech of some American blacks.

tacoka v., n. to burst forth in a rush or gush. May apply to a sailboat under a burst of wind, perhaps to a predator such as an owl pouncing on its prey, and perhaps even to a car in a drag-race. *na tacoka ni wai e na tolo ni uciwai na Sigatoka.* the gush of water in the Sigatoka River. See *dobui*.

tadodo v. to stretch out, extend, as an arm, leg, an implement or rope.

tadoka n., v., relapse (medical). Fijians had this concept prior to the advent of Europeans.

tadonu 1. adj., of conversation, flowing easily, comfortably with direct speech. *Tadonu vinaka na nodra veitalanoa.* Their conversation flowed easily and directly. Syn. *tadrodro*.

tadonu 2. v. to cut at the exact required location. *ta, taya* to chop.

tadra, tadrava v. to dream, dream of (usually in one's sleep). *tatadra, tatadrataka* to (day)-dream, often implying a desire, a longing for something or someone.

tadre n., adj. tug-of-war; tight, taut, as of a rope or binding. *dre* to pull.

vakatadraicake in a face-up position (person, plate, glass, any object that has an upper and lower side). *davo vakatadraicake* to lie down on one's back.

tadrua n. cleft (rocky terrain), deep gully, ditch, channel between two pieces of land. The middle area between two places. *na kedrau tadrua ko Suva kei Navua.* the area between Suva and Navua. The word can imply deeply cut (*ta, taya*), with two sides.

tadruku n. edible univalve shellfish, chiton, with eight segments of shell, clings firmly to rocks, Acanthozostera gemmata, Polyplacophora. Soaked in hot water to remove shell and hairs. Syn. (Kadavu) *kulisolo*.

tadu v. to arrive (a formal word, usually after long voyages), or to arrive at birth. *E a tadu lesu mai ki Viti ena 1995.* He/she arrived back in Fiji in 1995. *tadu lala* to arrive with nothing, no presentation, unceremonially. (Some children born out of wedlock have been given this as a name.) Syn. (Respectful) *toka-tu*.

vakatadumata (Archaic) v., n. for a chief, to send out his *matanivanua* (protocol officer) to pass on his instructions to heads of his tribes (*yavusa*) and clans (*mataqali*). Often this is an order to assemble for a formal conference to discuss or to decide on some community matters.

itafi (Lau) n. long-handled broom of coconut mid-ribs, much used outdoors. See *taufale*.

tafia (Lau) v. to sweep. *itafi* n. broom. Syn. *sasa, itavitaviraki*.

taga n. sack, bag or pocket (of pants, shirt, coat). Pants, shirts, coats and pockets are of course, modern concepts. *sulu vakataga* men's tailored skirt with pockets, invented by Ratu Sukuna. *taga pepa* paper bag. *taga niu* bag of coconuts (or copra). *taga ni niu* bag for copra. Indigenously, in earlier times, Fijian men used baskets but no bags or pockets. *tagana* v. to put things in a bag. *tawana ena taga* to fill a bag, put things in a bag.

taga-lala (Slang) v., adj. lit. having empty pockets, i.e., having no money. Syn. *nomani*, from the English "no money".

taga, tagava v. to use a hand-net to catch (it), usually prawns, small fish, crabs. Hand nets were not used in the highlands of Viti Levu. *tagava na balolo* to net the *balolo*. *itaga* n. hand-net. *lai taga ura* go netting prawn.

itagaga (Archaic) n. the "horned" masthead of early Fiji sailing canoes that could sail in only one direction. The halyard passed over this masthead.

tagaloa n. a Fijian infectious disease, thought mostly to affect children who have visited the house of a dead person, or an elderly person who has been bed-ridden for a long time. Symptoms are dark pimples on the body.

tagana v. to bag (something), put things in a bag. *na kena itagatagani* the bagging. Syn. *tawana ena taga*.

tagane n., adj. man, male (gender of human, animal or plant). *na gone tagane* the young man, the youth.

vakatagane like a man. *dabe vakatagane* sit with the legs crossed, as a man does. (A woman sits with the legs to one side *dabe vakayalewa*.)

taganimi n. urinary bladder. Syn. *bolanimi*.

vakatagataga sa v. of a place (house, school, playing field), to be empty of people, lacking the usual, familiar noise and movement.

tagau n. node or internode (as of bamboo, *yaqona* plant, sugar cane). The internode is *tago-na*. Idiom: *Tagau dua*, In brief, .. (to express something in few words).

tagava v. to remove the fibres *kosakosa* from *yaqona* when mixing it. This is done filtered through a cloth, or more traditionally, through a swatch of long fibres such as hibiscus or, in the highlands, fern leaves. *ibo* such a filter.

tagi, tagica, tagivaka v. to cry, *tagica* to cry for something or somebody. *tagivaka* to cry about (something). *kua ni tagi* don't cry. *tagi ivalu* call to arms (to an ally), declare war. The cry of certain animals is also indicated by this word. *tagica* n. soprano. *vakatagi sici* blow the horn (as of a car). *tagi* may imply a complaint, or appeal. *tagitagi* v., n., adj. crying
   Idiom: *Sega ni tagi na toa mai nomudou me rogo mai ki ke.* lit., the rooster that crows from your place is not heard here. Someone may be a powerful person in your village, but that means nothing in my village. *tagicaka* v. to cry (because of), to cry (for something). *tagitagi* n., v. continued crying, to continue crying. *gone dau tagitagi* "cry-baby. *tagitagi-ve* continual crying, cry-baby. Syn. *ole, oleva, olevaka* to cry out loudly as in sudden pain, or urgently, as in crying out for one's life. Syn. (Tonga) *tagi*.
   Idiom: *tagitagica na yaloka ni mata ni vonu.* lit., cry like the eyes of a turtle. When caught and beached the turtle's eyes exude tears, appearing to cry. Those tears are in vain. This applies to someone who yearns for what is impossible. (And in reality, it is a pathetic sight to see a turtle's tears.)
vakatagi v. to play (a musical instrument, music tape or compact disc). *na dau vakatagi piano* the piano player. *na dau vakatagi bitu* the player of the Fijian nose-flute (Polynesian introduction). To play a guitar would normally be *qiri, qiria* as for ringing a bell, or ringing of a telephone.
ivakatagi n. instrumental music. *dau ni vakatagi* n. musician.
tagica 1. v. to sing (a song, or traditional *meke*).
tagica 2. (Anglicism) n. soprano. *alto* alto. *tena* tenor. *besi* bass.
tagi-ivalu (Archaic) v., n. declaration of war, call to war. Modernly, may be used figuratively.
tagilitia n. medicinal annual herb growing wild, Vernonia cinerea, Compositae, small herb growing about two feet high, a weed used medicinally. The tiny flowers are light blue. The leaves are rubbed in the hands, then unfolded again and plastered flat over cuts. The notion is that it will stop bleeding and accelerate healing. Experience suggests this may be effective. Syn. *kaukamea*.
tagimaucia (or) **tagimoucia** n. distinctive climbing plant, often epiphytic, famous in Fiji for its white petals and brilliant red bracts, Medinilla waterhousei, Melastomataceae, endemic to Taveuni and Vanua Levu. It is the basis for several simple legends. Various species, with different colouring, are found on other Fiji islands, including Gau Island.
tagitagi adj. tearful, crying. *gone tagitagi* crying child, cry-baby.
itagitagi n. larynx, vocal chords, throat. *Lotu tagitagi* or *Lotu qiriqiri,* Assemblies of God church, a Protestant denomination from the U.S. that emphasises singing and playing of guitars, as well as speaking in (unknown) tongues.
tagitagikaua 1. v. to cry endlessly, unceasinglly.
tagitagikaua 2. n. lion-fish, small very graceful fluttering-finned reef fish, dark and white, or blond-brown, not eaten, spines are poisonous, very painful but not life-threatening. Supposedly more painful at low tide, hence the name.
tagitagi ivalu (Archaic) n. v. call to arms (or) war-cry. Tribes or kin-groups often had a specific war-cry, rallying their own forces, and intended to frighten the enemy.
tagi-yaso v. to cry by howling desperately, frantically over great fear or sorrow.
tago-na n. internode (on stem or branches: bamboo, kava plant, sugar cane, *duruka,* etc.) See *tagau* n. node or internode. The word *tagona* has been adapted by teachers of Fijian language to mean "syllable". Thus a two-syllable word might be referred to as *e dua na vosa tagoirua*. Outside of those specialised class-rooms, virtually no one would know this. *tago bi* n. stressed syllable (usually the second to last syllable of a Fijian word). *tago mamada* n. syllable that is not stressed when it is pronounced.
tagole v. to turn around by itself, as a wind-vane might do. *tagole na dakumu* twist your back painfully by a sudden turn.
tai 1. (Eng.) n., v. tie (sports), equal scores. *Erau sa tai tu ena 18 kei 18.* They (two) tied 18 to 18.
tai 2. n. coast, shore, river-bank. *na tai kadua* the other (opposite) shore. *Tailevu* name of a Province, lit. "Big Coast".
taielo (Lau, from Tahitian *taiero*) n. condiment made of crushed raw prawns fermented overnight in grated coconut, a specialty of Oneata Island. Syn. *taiyelo*.
taifote (Eng.) n. typhoid fever, a danger in some rural areas of Fiji where there is wet soil, infected water and unsanitary conditions. There are various spellings of this word. Causal agent Salmonella typhi passed in the stool and urine of infected people, transmitted often by sewage or infected food or water. Some people can be "carriers". Symptoms usually occur one to two weeks after exposure but can occur from three days to three months. Symptoms are very high fever, diarrhoea or constipation,

stomach pain, headache, slow heart rate, diminished appetite. As many a twenty percent of infected people may die if not treated with anti-biotics. Fijians had no word for typhoid fever.

taika (Eng., Slang) n. tiger, referring to a sports champion, especially in boxing.

taiki v. to turn the body sharply while sitting to face the audience. A particular case is in the movements often performed in the sedentary *meke* dances of women. The movement should be sharp and clean-cut.

tailevu n. mainland, coast (*tai*) of a large island, especially when it is across from a small island. Kadavu Island is *tailevu* in relation the small island Ono. Tailevu is a province of eastern Viti Levu Island.

taimi, taimitaka (Eng.) v. to time (an event, such as a boxing match, or a race).

taipa (Eng.) typewriter. *taipa, taipataka* v. to type. *dau ni taipa* n. typist.

taisau, taisau-taka v. to be assembled on opposite sides, lined up on each side (dancers at a performance, articles exhibited in a room.)

taitai n. grandfather, mother's father.

taiyelo (Lau) n. a condiment, see *taielo*.

taji (Eng. touch) n. touch football as a game.

taka (Archaic) n. a very uncommon musical instrument made of bamboo, a kind of jew's harp, resounding in the mouth when plucked with the fingers.

taka, takara (or) **takava** v. brought, to spread, originate. *vakataka* v. to spread, disseminate, to originate something. *E taka maivei na ka oqo?* Where did this thing come from? *Na mate oqo taka mai Vanuatu.* This illness spread from Vanuatu. *Sa takalevu e veiyasa i Viti.* It has spread out to all parts of Fiji. *takalailai* found in only a few places, as with a biological species, birds, plants.

Takala n. a minor chiefly title in some specific villages of the islands Vatulele, Kadavu, Gau, and Koro. In Kadavu and Lau, the title is also used for some of those who install a chief. In Gau the title is referred to as *Takalai Gau*, and pronounced that way, not Takala-i-Gau, as might be expected; he is responsible for communications from the *vunivalu* of Bau Island to people of Gau Island. In a sense, he is an interpreter of the chiefly will.

taka-lailai adj. as of a plant or animal species, of limited distribution. *takalevu* refers to something that is widespread.

takali 1. died (of a person, polite term), lost permanently.

takali 2. n. ocean, deep sea. *ua mai takali* wave from the ocean.

vakatakarakara n. image, representation, statue

takasa v. to drift ashore, as of a log or boat.s

itakataka 1. n. origin or source of something such as a word, a food, a disease that can be disseminated. *matetaka* sick, refers to an infectious disease, one that spreads from a source such as flu.

itakataka 2. n. a new usage of a word adapted by schoolteachers to indicate the correspondence of a Fijian spelling for a foreign word taken directly into Fijian language, such as *simede* for the English word cement.

takava v. to stain.

itakele n. centre-piece, central factor, keel (of a boat), originally referring only to part of a boat, but now generalised to be a central thing or central consideration, using the word figuratively.

takelo v., n., adj. crooked or bent, as of a long piece of timber, or winding of a path or road. *ikelo* n. turn or bend or branching, as of a road or branch of a river.

takete (Eng.) n. target, goal, aim. *yacova na takete* achieve the goal, reach the target. *taketetaka* v. to target, set a goal.

takeu v. bent over at the end as with a faucet at the end of a water pipe.

taki, takiva v. to dip (a container) into liquid. *Taki!* Serve a round of *yaqona!* a rather familiar idiom especially at grog sessions. *itaki* n. ladle, dipper, spoon. *na itakitaki* container for carrying water, usually, from a well or source, a pool. *takivaka* v. to use as a container to carry water, as one uses a bucket, or a length of bamboo (in the highlands, formerly, before the introduction of buckets.)

taki-na 1. n. part, as of part of the body. *Cava taki-mu e mosi?* What part of your body is in pain?

taki-na 2. n. social or family relationship. *Cava takimu o koya?* What relationship is he/she to you?

itakitaki n. cooked food supplied for important visitor such as a visiting preacher. In the village, one or more families will be assigned this obligation for any one occasion. Syn. *itabetabe*.

takia (Archaic) n. open outrigger canoe with no deck covering for short trips and river travel even in the Viti Levu highlands, along with dug-out canoes (*bavelo*) and bamboo rafts (*bilibili*). On larger ones, six to eight paddles might be used. Tippet (p. 86) reports the *takia* as coming from the hill counttry of the Rewa Valley, Naitasiri, and the tributary valleys, Waidina, Waimaro, and Wainibuka, and also the Waimaro and Suva. Deve Toganivalu records that the *takia* was developed by mountain people and later adapted by coastal Fijians to use for fishing. Around the shore, *takia* might have a sail or in shallows, be pushed along by poling.

takitua (Tonga, via Lau) in cricket, hit for a six.

takivei-- prefix meaning "of many different sorts. *takivei-roka* of many different colours. *E takivei-yaga na vu-ni-niu.* The coconut palm has many different uses.

tako̱ n. a dualistic "moitié" division of society that defined local potential marriage partners in the western highlands of Viti Levu, Colo North and Colo West, and parts of Colo East and Ra. A person is either *tako* or *lavo*. One did not marry within one's own group. If a father was born *tako,* all his children will be *lavo,* and if he is *lavo* they will be *tako.* The *tako* and *lavo* could have different totems. A person may be addressed by his/her classification *tako* or *lavo.* In a few locations Colo tribes have brought the custom down to the lowlands in Ba, for example, and in parts of Ra. The social custom has eroded in some areas, losing a little of its significance. No careful study has been made of this social division and its relevance or significance. The details differ from place to place and changes have come with time.

takona n. large wooden bowl trad. used for food preparation or presentation. See *sedre, dari*.

takoso, takosova v. to go directly across, cut across. *vosa takoso* interrupt (speaking). *Sega ni dede sa takosovi koya koso na tamana.* Before long his/her father interrupted him/her abruptly. *Sa tabu na curu takoso eke.* It is forbidden to enter and cross over this place. *na itatakoso* n. the crossing (as of a road).

taku 1. n. hawkbill sea-turtle, Eretmochelys imbricata, much smaller than the green sea turtle but feistier, less passive. Its shell-parts overlap and are very valuable in contrast to the less valuable contiguous, side-by-side shell sections of the green turtle. Food is mainly as a carnivore, eating jellyfish (*drose*), and crabs and shellfish. The hawkbill never attacks a person but defends itself with a dangerous beak. Traditionally, turtles were caught in nets by specialist clans (*gonedau*) who were mainly of Tongan origin. It used to be considered improper to spear a turtle. Now there are attempts to preserve turtles. See *vonu*.

taku 2. (Archaic) adj. plastic, as in *e dua na bilo taku* a plastic cup. This rather dated word comes from the time when turtleshell was used for making such things as combs. Turtles are now to some degree protected.

takulu v., adj. scratched, abraded, as one's arm or leg might be after a fall. Syn. *drakulu*.

tala up until a certain time or event: *E tala bogi na noqu cakacaka.* My work will go on till night-time.

tala̱ v. to send (someone), as on an errand. *talairawarawa* compliant, obedient, implying they can readily be sent on errands. *talaidre̱dre̱* disobedient. *vakatalai ki tuba* sent off (the field, in sports).
Idiom: *e dua na itala ni vulagi* a means of getting rid of a visitor, getting someone to leave.
Idiom: *talai vakatoa* child who is slow, unreliable when sent on an errand. (Like a chicken, the child is diverted, losing track of the purpose of the mission.)

talabiu n. deportee, someone sent away.

talabiu, talabiuta v. to dump, discard, or in some cases throw cargo overboard, for a ship in distress. See *biu, biuta*.

talabusese v. to scatter in all directions (of people, fish, birds), usually from some sudden fright. *Era talabusese na bose tiko ni sa kaila yani o Seru.* The people at the meeting scattered when Seru yelled at them. Syn. *cerebu*.

tala drodro v. to flow smoothly, together, as a swarm of fish, or water in a stream, people in a moving crowd, a story that flows along nicely, a speech that goes on and on.

Talai ni Kovana (Archaic) Secretary for Fijian Affairs during the colonial era. These were Europeans, the last one being A. C. Reid, before Ratu Sukuna took the post.

Talai Veivuke n. District Commissioner, for one of the three administrative divisions of Fiji, Central, Northern, and Western, concerned with Fijian Affairs.

italai n. messenger, emissary.

tala, talaca 1. v. to unload (truck, boat). Can also imply loading instead of discharging. *talaca na buka* reduce or extinguish a fire by removing firewood. *talaca mai na buka* bring up the firewood, implying it should be dumped by the fire. (*mai* implies bringing it.) *tala kako* unload cargo. Syn. (Cakau.) *ala, alaca* or *eli, elica*.
Idiom: *tala* or *tala simede* (unload cement) may refer to having sex after long abstinence. *vaqara tala* to go looking for sex. *Me laki rawataki ikeri na nomu tala?* You are going to try your luck there at getting sex?

tala, talaca 2. v. to throw into the water, fishing line (*wa ni siwa*), fish net (*lawa*), anchor (*ikelekele*).

tala, talaca 3. v. to transplant (a plant, flowers, shrub or food plant). *talacukicuki* widespread uprooting of plants/trees, as from a hurricane. See *vakadewataka*.

tala, talaca 4. v. to farewell, send off someone, which may involve a social gathering and taking the person to the boat or aeroport, their bus or car. It is custom to accompany someone departing as far as practicable. See *talatala*.

vakatala v. to send (someone) away. *Me vakatalai koya.* Send him away, have him sent away (from here).

talatala v. to say farewell. *veitalatala* v. to say good-bye to each other. *veitalayaka* v. to send off (people or things) in several directions

italatala n. Protestant preacher. *iTalatala Qase* Methodist leader. From the Tongan word *talatala* to inform, to contact.

italanoa n. yarn, story, fable, legend. (Anglicism) *italanoa buli* fiction story, novel. *Na italanoa kei Nayau* The story about Nayau. *Oya e dua tale na veitalanoa.* (Anglicism) That is a different story (matter). Syn. (Tonga) *talanoa*.

talanoa, talanoa-taka v. to yarn, chat, relate (a story), usually for entertainment, social amusement.

talasiga n., adj. dry land burnt by the sun, scorched earth with little but dry grass, often referred to in western Viti Levu. This land was mostly forested in early days, the trees burned off by early Fijian settlers looking for wild yams or clearing land for gardens. Grass replaced the trees.

talaucaka v. to empty out, unload (things from box, trunk, bag). *na italautalaucaki* the unpacking, emptying out. See *talaca*.

talavaka v. to send, as in *talavaka na ivola.* to send the letter.

talave 1. v. to rise up quickly (as of a person, alarmed or an aeroplane taking off); to raise up quickly. *E dau talave mai Nadi na waqavuka.* The aeroplane usually takes off from Nadi.

talave 2. v. tilted, in a tilting position. *vakatalave-taka* to tilt (something). There is an implication of rising up. Syn. *talaqa*.

talavo adj. quite sufficient, ample. *Sa talavo na kakana.* There is quite enough food.

talayavu v. to extinguish a fire completely, usually after cooking or camping.

tale 1. again *cakava tale* do it again. *tukuna tale* tell it again. *lesu tale* return. *italetale* n. chorus (of a song or *meke*). *tale ga* also. *taletale* repetitive.

tale 2. more. *eso tale.* some more. *e dua tale na ka* another (or) one more thing. *sega tale ni wawa* without waiting any further (any more). *kei na so tale* et cetera.

tale 3. other, as in: *E sega tale na sala.* There is no other way. *solia vei ira tale na so.* give to some others (many).

tale 4. else. *A cava tale?* What else?

tale 5. already, as in: *O sa oti tale?* You have finished already?

taledi (Eng.) n. talent.

taletale repetitive. *ua taletale* n. tsunami, tidal wave that comes in several surges.

italetale n. chorus (of a song). *na italetale ni sere* the chorus of the song.

tale, taleva 1. v. to visit (a place or person). *E mai talevu na noda vanua na Tui Tabu.* The Pope came to visit our country. *Au na talevi Levuka tale.* I will revisit Levuka. See *siko, sikova* to visit (persons) with express purpose to see them. Also *vakataleva*.

tale, taleva 2. v. to go over again, to repeat, review. *taleva tale na tepi.* go over the tape again. *na ikatolu ni noqu taleva na veika kece.* the third time of my going over everything. *taleva tale na nomu lesoni.* go over your lesson again.

talefoni or **talevoni** (Eng.) n. telephone. *qiri, qiria* to ring someone. Telephone numbers are spoken with each digit separate, as in 362 2504 spoken as *tolu ono rua, rua lima saiva va.* It is typical not readily to reveal one's name when phoning. Syn. *telefoni*.

talega also. Sometimes, perhaps more properly, written as *tale ga*.

talei 1. adj. delightful. **2.** adj. precious. *vatu talei* gemstone. Fijians had no notion of precious stones. Talei can now be a girl's name.

taleitaka v. to delight in . . , to enjoy.

talevaka v. to do something several times, or repeatedly.

talevoni (Eng.) n. telephone, various spellings. Syn. *televoni*

itale-vunau n. food provided for visiting Methodist preacher on Sundays. Villagers may take turns in providing this food. It is Methodist custom to have visiting preachers. Syn. *itale ni vunau*.

ta-lewe v. to chop off the husk and remove the flesh, of coconuts. *lewe-na* flesh. See *cici, cicia*.

tali, talia v. to weave (mats, sinnet). Plaiting of sinnet (*magimagi*) is usually done with three strands (*qamina*). Such plaiting of sinnet, or of a girl's hair may be referred to as *tobe, tobea.* A girl's plaited

locks (*itobe*) indicate that she is a virgin. (Fijians have no specific word for virgin.) In the Viti Levu highlands at Naboubuco the number of locks indicated the girl's age. *tali-sasa, talisasa-taka* v. to plait coconut leaves to contain fish or meat to be cooked in earth-oven.
Idiom: *tali magimagi* chat together, lit. to plait sinnet, because men often chat together when they plait sinnet, to tell a story or report in very great detail.

veitalia v. no matter, does not matter (May be said alone). *Sa veitalia vei au*. It is all the same to me, I do not care. Whether or not this is polite depends on context and tone of voice. Sometimes abbreviated as *talia*.

tali-sasa, talisasataka v. to weave coconut palm leaves to protect food to be cooked in earth oven.

vaka-talitalia falsely.

taliva v. to gleam, glisten, usually with reflected light. *talitaliva* to gleam very stongly. Syn. *caliva*.

talivi v. to be spilled out in a small stream. See *livi, livia*.

taliwa, taliwa-taka v. to stitch with a needle, to sew, usually cloth.

talo, talova v. to pour deliberately, controlling the liquid in small quantities as for *yaqona* or a cup of tea. *Talo!* Pour! Serve it! (usually of *yaqona*). *talotaloca* v. to go on pouring.

taluva v. to come undone, loose, let go, inadvertently, as a knot in a rope. See *luva*, also *tasere*.

tama, tamaka v. to call out formally, announcing one's intended visit to a Fijian house, a ritual call (that varies from region to region), that the host responds to, normally to welcome the approach.

tama 1. n. a call to announce one's presence outside a house. Exact words vary by region but a common version is *"Dua o!"* Properly, one waits for a response before coming closer or entering. Woman's greeting may differ from a man's.

tama-ni 2. huge, a great deal of, used only in context:- *tama ni ka levu* huge big thing. *tamani-ose* huge horse. Syn. *tamatama*. See *tinatina* mature female animal.

tama-ni 3. huge amount of: *Tama ni ilavo o a rawata!* Huge lot of money you have earned (obtained)!

tama-na n. father. *tamaqu* my father. *Tama i Seru* Father of Seru. Traditionally in Fiji it was impolite to mention a person by name. It is still better form to refer to a person by some term of family relationship or title. Paternal uncles (father's brothers) are considered fathers, just as cousins are considered as brothers. A person may be named Tamana if his namesake is a *tama-na*. *Erau veitamani* They (2) are father and son (or daughter). Abbrev. *ta, tata*. Syn. (Macuata) *maqu*. (Nadro) *vava*.

tama-na lailai n. uncle, younger brother of the father.

tama-na levu n. uncle, older brother of the father.

veitamani n., v. father(s) and child(ren).

tamata n. people. *mata tamata* race (of people). *na veimata tamata kece* all races of peeple). Traditionally, all but a chief should respectfully say *tamata, tabuyani*, not just *tamata* alone. *tamata bula* healthy person in the prime of life. *tamata cakacaka* n. workers. See *lewe*.

tamatama n. mature male, of an animal such as chicken (rooster), pig (boar), cattle (bull).

tamela v. to ring out, of a pleasant sound, a bell, or two bush knives clashing.

vakaitamera adj. enormous, awesome.

tamoi 1. v. to twist or turn sharply, revolve, turning on itself.

tamoi 2. n., v. to sprain, sprained, twisted (as of ankle). See *moi, moica*.

tamo-na n. mid-section of the body.

tamole n, See *damole*.

tamosa v. non-melodic noise, as of children unsupervised, clinking, scratching, May imply a continued ringing or rustling sound.

tamulo v. twisted unintentionally, as of a rope. By ext. may refer to stomach cramps.

tamure (Tahiti, Cook Islands "tamure") v., n. tamure, Polynesian dance by young women and men, emphasising fast hip movement of the girls, the rapid beat of the drums. Danced mainly as a tourist attraction, now widely performed in many of the Pacific Islands.

tamusu, tamusuka v. to cut off abruptly, sharply. See *musu*.

tanabe n. edible fish, close to shore, Lutjanus fulvus. Syn. *kake*.

tanene n. tiny fish, young Sicydiaphiinae, sub-family of Gobies, spawned in fresh water, develope in the sea, then migrate upstream annually in huge numbers, in the Navua River, for example. Caught in nets, eaten rather like the whitebait of New Zealand. Syn. *cigani*.

tanoa (Samoa - bowl) n, wooden bowl, usually made of *vesi* timber, for serving kava. On Viti Levu it has four legs and an abrupt lip; in Lau it has eight or even 12 legs and a smooth lip. Formally and properly, many *tanoa* have a frontal piece with two white cowries and a long, thick sinnet cord (*wa tabu*) laid out in the direction of the chief, with a single white cowrie attached at the end. This is apparently symbolic of a penis with the notion of fertility. It is forbidden for anyone to walk in front of the sinnet cord. An early form of kava bowl was a clay bowl (*sedre*) with no legs, though the concept of pottery was an introduction of Tongan settlers. (The earliest, Proto-Polynesian settlers made pottery but those pre-millenium Lapita people had no significant, continued existence in Fiji.) In some places a wooden bowl (*dari*) with legs was used. In the highlands of Viti Levu a bowl was improvised with leaves in a depression dug in the ground. The wooden *tanoa* was introduced via Tonga only in the latter half of the 1700s. Informally, these days, Fijians may use a simply enamel basin though still a few ceremonial words and gestures are made before serving. It is a rather firm custom that when a "mix" is made in the *tanoa*, it must be all consumed at that sitting. The *tanoa* is not washed; a prized patina forms on the surface after long use. The bowl should be hung against the wall when not in use, so that dust does not settle on it. Most *tanoa* are made at Kabara Island, centre of wood-carving in Fiji. Wood-working machinery is now used.

tani 1. particle placed after a verb indicating direction out and away (from some place). *lako tani!* get out! go away! *vakauta tani* export, send (something) away. *duatani* different, strange, unnatural, foreign.

tani 2. particle indicating a place away *mai vanua tani* overseas, in a foreign country. *vakawati tani* married away, away from home.

tani 3. n. foreigner, *kai tani*, one who is not a native Fijian, not a local person. *Vulagi* is a more polite term, implying a guest or visitor.

tani 4. (Eng.) ton or tonne (a measure of weight). *e lima na tani* five tonnes. As in English, there are various types of tons or tonnes, the old English ton, the metric tonne of 1,000 kilograms, and the maritime tonne.

tao v. to be caught, stuck, restrained or constrained, and by ext. can mean "tied up", being busy with someone and thus perhaps late for another appointment. *Au a calata na basi, au a tao vei Seru*. I missed the bus, I was tied up with Seru. *Sa tao na noqu wa ni siwa*. My fishing line got caught, stuck (as onto a rock).

vakatao-taka v. to stop, impede, restrain, constrain, to make something stuck or stopped, as a rope or line.

taoni (Eng.) town. *na taoni o Korovou* Korovou town. *vaka-taoni* urban. *tauni-olo* town hall. Syn. *tauni*.

ta'ovala (Tonga) n. woven pandanus deep cummerbund worn around the waist by men, women and youngsters in parts of Lau. This has been customary especially in the Tongan settlement Sawana, by Lomaloma, Vanua Balavu. Wherever there are Tongans, at formal occasions the *ta'ovala* will be worn. Held in place by a type of belt called a *kafa*, made of braided cord sinnet. Different styles of *ta'ovala* are used for different occasions, colourful for weddings, solemn ones for solemn occasions, tattered ones to show respect and humility. Instead of a *ta'avola*, women may wear a *kiekei*, a women pandanus belt with many strands dangling decoratively, reaching below the knees, woven in a fancy way, sometimes with shells or other ornaments attached. Syn. (Samoa & Lau) *gafegafe*.

tapisi (Anglicism) v. to spray out, as a water-pipe leaking under pressure.

taqa, taqara v. to lay down, stack (on the ground, on a shelf), yams, books, dishes, etc., placing one thing on top of another or on top of something (such as shelf). *taqairua* two layers (of things in a stack). *itaqataqa* place for putting somethings down.

taqari, taqarica or **taqaritaka** v. to wipe one's bottom (with something) after going to the toilet. *itaqari* n. toilet paper equivalent, such as leaves, newspaper. Syn. (Lau) *kavelu*. Cf. also *quata na gone lailai*. to wipe the bottom of the baby,

Taqa ni Qaqa n. Victory Parade (as after World War II). Formerly *taqa* referred to the assemby and exhibition of warriors, as a military review, only for coastal, paramount chiefs, before the combat of war. It was largely a boastful show.

taqaya, taqayataka v. to be anxious about usually (some specific danger for specific people or possible events). *taqataqaya* constant worrying.

taqe (Eng.) n. tank, as in fuel tank.

taqe, taqea v. to scoop up, as of ashes, sand, rice, money, nails, many small things.

taqo, taqomaka v. to protect, keep safely (things or people). *na tataqomaki* the protection, preservation, defence (emphatic). *na veitaqomaki* the protection (more generally).

taququ v. drift, of a boat when the anchor is not holding. *ququ* to drag, of an anchor.

taqusi 1. v. to be smeared, smudged. *tataqusiqusi* v. to scrape hard. See *qusia*.

taqusi 2. v. to be erased, wipe off. See *qusi*.

tara, tara v. to be permitted, allowed. *Sa tara na lako*. Going (there) is allowed. This is the opposite of *"tabu"*, forbidden, prohibited. *ivola tara* licence, permit.

vakatara, vakatarạ v. to permit (person or action). *E vakatarai vei au me'u lako* I am allowed to go. *Sa vakatarai na cakacaka e na Siga Tabu.* Work is permitted on Sundays.

vakatarai n. permission, the lifting of a prohibition, as in *na vakatarai ni Siga Tabu* the lifting of the Sunday prohibitions.

tara, tarạ 1. v. to touch, handle, to contact (person), undertake (begin doing something). *vuli tara* learn(ing) by experience, "hands-on" experience. *veitarai* children's game of "tag". *E qai tatara yani ki na taga* he/she groped, felt in (the: his/her) pocket. *veitaratara* touching each other. *veitaratarai* adjacent.
Idiom: *tara-koro* to gossip together, as an informal group, about people, relatives, news from the villages (*koro*).

tara, tarạ 2. v. to accept a presentation (usually a whale-tooth) by a ceremonial touching with the hand.
Idiom: *tara na kamunaga* in formal ceremony, reach out and touch the whale tooth offered, indicating acceptance. This will be followed by a speech of acknowledgment.
Idiom: *tara tabua* n. second oldest child. One's oldest child is referred to as the *ulumatua*.

tara, tarạ 3. v. to take in the hand, to catch in the hand (prawns for example). *tara ura* catch prawns by hand. *tara na bilo ena teveli* take the cup on the table.

tara, tarạ 4. v. to catch (usually fish, crustacea), taking by the hand. *tara nuqa* to catch rabbit-fish. *tara kuita* catch octopus. *tara qari* catch sea-crabs. *tara lairo* catch land crabs. *tara duna* catch eels. *tara kawakawa* catch rock cod. *Era dau tara ika ena duva.* They (many) usually catch fish with fish-poison. *Eratou a tara na ika ena loma ni bai.* They (few) caught the fish within the fish-fence (probably with the help of spears). *tara ba (ni ika)* to collect fish from the fish-fence. Syn. *tobo, toboka*.

tara, tarạ 5. v. to reach, to affect, to afflict. *na leqa ka tarai ira kece* the trouble that affected them all. *na HIV ka tarai iratou* the HIV that afflicted them (few).
Idiom: *tara reveni* reach the limit, accomplish the goal (sometimes said when drinking *yaqona*), come to the end. *raveni* ribbon.

tara, tarạ 6. v. to build, or make, as of a house, or a village (which can be done in a very few weeks).

tara adj. under-cooked, usually as of a root-crop in the earth oven, not cooked long enough, or located too far from the steam or hot rocks. May apply to other foods. Syn. *butadroka*.

veitara v., n. children's game of "tag".

tarabe v. to stumble, to trip up. *vakatarabe-taka* to case someone to trip. See *lalia*

tarabewa adj. very high, "touching the rafters" (within the house). *taratarabewa* extremely high (indoors).

tara-bi v. to be burdensome, difficult to undertake, or do, or perform, as a duty or task. *taratara-bi* to be very burdensome.

tara-ilavo v. to widthdraw money, as from a bank account.

itaraki n. hand-net, as used by one person, usually a woman, for catching small fish. Syn. *itaga*.

veitaratara v. to contact, get in touch with. *veitaratara kei Tukana* get in touch with Tukana.

veitarataravi adj., n. continuous, continual, consecutive or sequential order. sequence. *na vu veitarataravi* the continuous coughing. *tuvai vakamatua vosa ena veitarataravi* arranged in alphabetical order. *na veitarataravi ni veika e yaco*. the sequence of things that happen.

tarabu (Eng.) 1. trump, a card game commonly played by Fijians. *mata ni imau* cards. *daimani* diamonds. *kalavo* clubs. *sivi* (or) *siveti* spades. *yate* hearts. Note that in playing cards Fijians speak of the liver (*yate*) in place of the heart (*uto*). For Fijians, the liver, and not the heart, are the place of emotions or courage. 2. Trumpet brand of cane knife, English made, often preferred by Fijians though now expensive. Fijians call the brand *Biukila* for bugle. 3. *tarabu* may also refer figuratively to a trump card in an argument or negotiation, as a trick up the sleeve, a winning card, so to speak, a deciding point in one's favour.

vaka-taraisulu v., n. ceremony with a feast ending 100 days of wearing mourning clothes, after death in the family. Normal clothing is resumed.

tarakadru, tarakadruta v. to touch very briefly, usually very discreetly, another person as a secret, non-verbal signal with the hand, arm or foot. In mixed company such silent, secretive signals are common in interpersonal communications. Sometimes a glance with the eye may suffice. *kadru* to scratch.

tarakari n. (Hindi) v. to make a curry (fish, lamb, beef or vegetable).

taralalạ (Eng. "tra-la-la") n., v. simple, shuffling dance of man and woman, side by side with arms around each other's waist, quasi-traditional since early colonial times, invented at a school in the Ba area following an English tune. For a great many decades, this has been the only type of social dance performed in the rural villages. A guest will be invited to participate by a local woman. (She may be appointed to that task.) Slang terms *butu kai, taura tale*.

taralala-taka v. to dance the *taralala* with (person).

tarasea or **tarase** n. species of sea slug (*dri*), Actinopygia mauritana, Holothuriaceae, rigid body, reddish, rusty brown colour and white blotches; average 24 cm, found at 0-10 meters. Has commercial value, but much less valued than the black types (*loaloa*). Syn. (Kadavu) *togo*.

tarausese (or) **tarusese** (Eng., Tonga talausese) n. trousers.

tarasua adj. damp, usually clothing, the hands, feet. See *kulumaca*.

itara-tabua (Archaic) n. second child, after the eldest.

taratara v. to feel movement of an unborn baby, by the mother; that may involve early signs of on-coming labour.

tarava v. to follow in time (things or events), follow in order, follow in movement. *vakaveitarataravi* put in consecutive order, arranged in order. *ena vula ka tarava* in the month that follows. See *muri, muria*.

veitaravi consecutive, next. *e rua na yabaki veitaravi* two consecutive years. *ono na druka veitaravi* six consecutive losses. *vakaveitaravi* consecutively. *jabeni veitarataravi ena tolu na yabaki.* champion for three consecutive years. *veitarataravi-taka* to do something repeatedly, consecutively, as in catching fish one right after another.

tarawai adj. water-proof, as of a watch, a rather forced modernism, of course.

tarawau n. tree, Dracontomelon vitiense, wild or semi-cultivated small fruit, rather thin-fleshed and tasteless to non-Fijians. A common snack-food in season, around June, July. Legend speaks of it as a food of the gods, and hence the idiom *laki tei tarawau* to die, lit. go or gone planting *tarawau*. *isoso tarawau* cluster of *tarawau* fruit.

taro (Colo East) n. ceremonial presentation of goods to compensate for one's absence when a relative has died in the village. Syn. *boka*.

taro n. question. *na nomu taro* your question (the question you ask). Fijian are usually discouraged from asking too many questions. Mostly they are expected to learn by observing. *na biubiu ni taro* the putting of a question (questions). *loma tarotaro* questioning mind.

taro, taroga v. to ask a question. *me tarogi koya* ask him (the question). *na veitarogi* the questioning, exam. *Matabose ni Veitarogi Vanua* Native Land Commission (determines existent clans and assigns native land rights). *na vakatataro* n. the repetitive or continued questioning. *Taro ivakasala vei ira na qase ni vuli*. Ask advice from the (many) school teachers.

veitarogi n. exam, questioning. *Veitarogi vakavanua* n. official questioning Fijian village elders on land ownership by Native Lands Commission, usually resulting in legally binding decisions. Native land is usually assigned to individual clans *mataqali*.

tarosa adj. to rustle as paper may do or dried leaves, See *raqosa*.

taro, tarova v. to stop. *Sa tarovi koso na bose.* The conference was stopped abruptly. *na veitarovi* the stopping. *na itatarovi* n. obstacle, hindrance, the thing that causes stopping, as in the case of the contraceptive *na itatarovi ni vakaluveni*. *itatarovi ni cagi* windshield (of a car, boat).

tasala v. to cut a new path or road. *sala* path. *gaunisala* road.

taroro (Rotuma) n. specialty food, flesh of young coconut *bu* cut up and left to ferment for four days in the sun, often served with some garnish *na kena icoi*.

tase, tasea v. to split lengthwise, as of a log, to make planks, deliberately and more forcefully than *se, sea* to split or tear lengthwise. *tasei* split. *sei* torn, though the words are almost synonymous.

tasere v. to become untied (unexpectedly), as in *Sa tasere na buke*. The knot came undone.

tasi (Eng.) n. task, task-work, piece-work in labour agreements, in contrast to day-labour (*murisiga*). Fijian workers usually perform better with short-term, well defined tasks with immediate cash payment.

tasi n. very thin partial moon.

tasi, tasia 1. v. to peel (taro, yam, cassava).

tasi, tasia 2. v. to sharpen by scraping, shaving (spear, pencil).

tasi, tasia 3. v. remove the surface hair (pig, human head, body). *tasi* shaved (of the head), bald, as in *ulu tasi* shaved head.

tasili, tasili-taka (Eng.) v., adj. to tar-seal, tar-sealed. *gaunisala tasili* tar-sealed road.

tasina, tasinataka v. to paint design on barkcloth without the use of a stencil.

tasiri v. to spurt ahead, usually of a person or animal running, or of a boat. See *siri*.

tasoqo v. jetsam, flotsam washed ashore.

tasoro v. to become slack, as of a rope. See *soro, sorova*.

tasova spilt, usually water or milk. See *sova*.

tata n. dad, daddy, sometimes abbrev. as *ta*. The relationship includes the father's brothers. Such a paternal uncle is referred to as *tata levu* if older than the father, and *tata lailai* if younger. *Tata* or *ta* are affectionate abbrev. of *tama-na*, father. Syn. (Nadroga) *nahuna* (or) *nana, vavai*.

tata v. to spread, disseminate, be evident or known (usually news, stories, rumours). Often used in the causative form *vakatata. Sa noqu inaki me vakata-taki na vuna*. It is my intention to make known the cause. *Sa vakatata na we ni mauwena*. His footsteps are clearly visible.

itata n. crossroad, where two paths meet.

tata v. to stutter. Syn. *gusu-tata* n., v. *dau tata-cemeceme* n. stutterer.

tata-- prefix to a verb, implying repeated, vigorous or great amount of an activity. *tata-sei* to split. *tata-laka* to chop down. *tata-melamela na rorogo ni qiri kava*. noise of the banging on tins. *tata-gedegede* battered about, as a boat in heavy seas. *tata moce* to babble with sleep-talk. *tata-balebale* v. to fall here and there, staggering, as when drunk. *Era tata-mosamosa na lairo e loma ni dramu kava*. The mud crabs scratched around noisily inside the metal drum. *tata-qiriqiri* sound like chipping rust off metal.

tata, tatataka v. to rub the body vigorously with a wet cloth, especially the face. Syn. (Lau) *tatafi* (or) *tatavi*.

tatadra, tatadrataka v. to dream, to dream of while awake (often with a sense of longing). *tadra, tadrava* to dream (in one's sleep).

tatafi (Lau) v. to wash the face.

itata n. wooden paddle used by potters to shape pots. No pottery wheel has been used in Fiji.

tataba v. to press the arm against something, the wall, the floor, the table, perhaps for support. *taba-na* n. arm.

tata-balebale v. to stagger, falling here and there, usually of a drunk.

tataivatia v. to stagger. Syn. *tatabalebale*.

itataviraki n. broom. Syn. *sasa*, when made of coconut palm-leaf midribs.

tataka v. to chop with (something). *E tataka na matau*. He chopped with the axe.

tatalai v. to warm oneself by a fire.

tatalaka v. to chop repeatedly (big things usually, trees, people) with force, chop up (little things, though less commonly applied to little things). See *ta, taya*.

tatalo v. to be simulating, going through the motions, acting out, pretending to be doing something (children playing at adult activities like cooking, workers slacking off, idling at their work and accomplishing little). *Vakatatalo-taka na cakacaka* go through the motions of work. *dakai ni vakatatalo* toy gun. *iyaya ni vakatatalo* toys.

tata-melamela v. make a lot of noise, of many objects ringing out, such a tins being banged with a stick. (Children do this around New Year's Eve.)

tata-mosamosa v. to make a lot of repeated sounds, as in *Era tatamosamosa na lairo e loma ni dramu kava*. The land-crabs scratch about, making a continued or repetitive sound, in this case a rustling, inside the metal drum.

tatara v. to catch eel, prawn, crabs, octopus, fish, reaching, groping, snatching with the hand, often by women. *tara* implies some action of the hand by touching, catching hold of something.

tatara n. in an earth oven (*lovo*), a protective layer of vegetation between the hot rocks and the food to be cooked. This is often coconut leaf with midribs, or stems of banana or plantain.

itatara or **itaratara 1.** n. protective layer or cover generally, to prevent something from being damaged, such as food, or a book. This may be a form of bag, of woven material, cotton cloth, paper, sheet of plastic.

itatara 2. n. (Anglicism) lingerie, specifically a woman's slip or half-slip. (The implication is of a protective layer.) *sulu i loma* underwear. Syn. *liku e loma*

tataro v. to intercede, as in a dispute between others, and by ext., to flag down a passing vehicle, to hitch-hike or catch a bus. To stop a car or bus one pats the air with an extended and lowered arm, raising it no higher than the waist. (It would be rude or threatening to show a raised hand.) *tataro motoka* v. to wave down a car, to hitch-hike.

itatarovi n. obstacle, hindrance. See *tàrova* to stop, prevent.

itatarovi ni vakaluveni n. contraceptive. *luve* child.

tatau, tatautaka v. to request politely (for some permission, especially to take one's leave). *Au sa tatautaka mada meu lako* I request permission to leave, to go. *Au sa tatautaki au meu sa lesu ki na noqu vale*. I have asked permission to return to my house. Caution: this word is often confused with the similar word *tataunaka*. *tatautaka* is "correct" older usage but not commonly used these days. More commonly heard today might be: *Au sa tatau oti meu sa lesu ki na noqu vale*.

itatau n. formal polite request, almost invariably to take one's leave.

tataunaka v. to assign or give responsibility for the care of someone or something, often as a request. *Au tataunaka na cakacaka oqo vei Saba*. I give responsibility for this work to Saba. *Au tataunaki iko vei Seru*. I leave you in Seru's care. *O tataunaki tu vei cei?* Who is supposed to be looking after you? (to a child, often said reproachfully). *Au tataunaka vei Seru me kauta mai*. I ask (asked) Seru to bring it.

tatawai v., n. to babble or talk in one's sleep. See *tetewai*.

tatawasewase adj. fragmented in many pieces. *tawase* divided. See *wase, wasea*.

tateba n. crevice under a ledge, as at a coral reef. *teba* implies a spreading out above and undercut below. *ulu-teba* refers to hair that is long, combed to spread up and out.

tatiki v., adj. tilted, as in *Sa vaka-tatiki na vula*. The moon is tilted on its side. (For Fijians this may be a sign of impending rain.)

tatuki 1. v. inadvertently to bump the head on something hard or be struck on the head.

tatuki 2. v. to make a throbbing, drumming sound, as with a Fijian drum (*lali*).

tatuku n. swollen testicles, elephantiasis of the testicles (*ceke*). In the central and eastern Viti Levu highlands the word is *matuku*, a legendary power of super-tribe Waimaro, and source for the name of Matuku Island and some clans named Matuku. Huge testicles were prestigious symbol of strength and fertility for which the Waimaro highlanders were famous. *tuku* implies a lowering of something that hangs, as from a rope. See *ceke, tauna, waqaqa*.

tatuva v. to place some weight, such as a stone, to hold down say a mat, or voivoi, to keep it in place, as on a windy day. Syn. *danuya, tabika*.

tau-- prefix for numbers, as in *taudua* one alone, single, *taurua* two at a time, etc.

itau n. friend. Syn. *itokani*. *vakaitau* to have a friend, chum, boyfriend, girlfriend.

veitau 1. adj. to be or to have friends, chums, friendship. *Eratou veitau*. They (several) are friends. *Au sega ni veitau*. I have no boyfriend (girlfriend), with romantic implications, these days often said even by very young teenagers. *itau* n. friend.

veitau 2. v., n. competitive race. *veitau-cici* running race, track race. *veitau ose* horse-race.

Tau n. friendly form of address between people of certain different regions who are *veitauvu* (related anciently either by having the same ancestral spirit (*vu*), or by ancient chiefly marriage that united them). See *tauvu*.

tau, tauca 1. v. to fall, especially of rain. *Sa tau na uca*. It is raining. *Sa tau bi na uca*. It is raining hard (heavily). *Sa tau bi*. It fell (or falls) heavily (rain, heavy object). *Biuta na senikau ituba me tauca na uca*. Put the flowers outside so that the rain can fall on them. *Sa suasua na isulu ni tauca na uca*. The clothes got wet when the rain fell on them.

tau, tauca 2. to set down, to put down, to let fall. . *Tau!* Drop it! Let it fall! *Me tau na icolacola* drop (let fall, put down) the burden (that is carried on the shoulder). *Sa tau mai Nadi na waqavuka*. The aeroplane set down (landed) at Nadi.

tau, tauca 3. v. to speak, pronounce (words, speech), make a pronouncement or judgement, a set of traditional words such at at a *isevusevu* ceremony. *tauca na vosa* to speak the words, make the speech, pronounce the words; to pass, pronounce (judgement), pronounce, to impose (court sentence). *Me tau na itotogi* Impose the penalty. *itautau* n. pronouncement

tau, tauca 4. v. to pick (breadfruit, orange, mango, *tarawau*, etc.), cut and gather leaves such as *voivoi* for weaving. *Tauca mai!* Pick it!. *itautau* n. stem (of leaf, flower or fruit), the part of the plant where it is picked or plucked. By ext., may imply winning a prize.

tau, tauca 4. v. to obtain. *tauca na kakana* to obtain the food.

tau, tauca 5. v. in sailing, to turn into the wind, to luff.

itau 6. n. ends, fore and aft, of a boat. Syn. *mua-na*.

vakatau (Archaic) n., adj. type of boat like a *takia* but having both ends covered to impede the inflow of surging waves or spray, sometimes referred to as a *waqa vakatau*.

taubale, taubaletaka 1. v. to walk. to walk on (a path, road, beach). *itautaubale* n. walkway, path, and modernly a pavement or sidewalk.

taubale v. to eat starch-food (*kakana dina*) with no relish (*na kena icoi*). *Keitou taubale dalo tiko*. We (few) are just eating taro, with no garnish.

itaube n. necklace or garland hung around the neck. Some chiefly ones were made of shells, cowry, for example, as a fertility symbol, later, of pearlshell that was inlaid, some composed of fashioned pieces of whaletooth, made by Tongans. Traditional types of *itaube* made of sperm whaleteeth include the *sisi* and the *waseisei*. *Waseisei*, made of strips of whaletooth, were used by Bau to reward some

Waimaro highlanders for their cooperation (and betrayal of their fellow highlanders). The small white cowrie was traditionally worn around the neck only by a chiefly female. *taube civa* n. pearlshell necklace.

taubena v. to wear (necklace or garland, usually of fragrant leaves, flowers, or of shells). *vakataubena* put such a garland on (someone), as for a guest of honour at a ceremony. Distinguished guests are always so honoured at formal receptions.

tauca v. *tauca* to put down, let down, as of some burden.

taucoko 1. whole, all, entire, entirely, complete.

taucoko 2. jam-packed, full of people, as a meeting room might be.

taudaku (ni koro) n. outskirts (of town, village), outside. *vakawati ena taudaku ni lotu* married outside the church. *ena taudaku kei Ovalau* beyond Ovalau, on the other side of Ovalau (from Viti Levu).

taudonu timely, on time, at the right time, apt. appropriate at the occasion.

taudua alone. *taurua* only two, both, for both. *Au sa lako taudua ga.* I'm going quite alone. *tautolu* only three, for three people.

taufale (Tongan) n. whisk-broom of coconut-leaf ribs (*sasa*) bound to a wooden handle, usually with coconut-fibre sinnet cord. Formerly, most Fijian whisk-brooms (*sasa*) had no attached handle. Both types of broom are sold at the public market. *itafi* similar broom but with longer handle, more for outdoor use.

itauga n. (Archaic) wooden hook with rat-guard rail used for storing food, hung from house rafter, safe from rats, dogs, ants. Now seen only in Fiji Museum and sold as handicrafts in tourist shops.

itaukei adj. native Fijian, as in *sotia itaukei* native Fijian soldier.

itaukei n. owner of some thing, *itaukei ni motoka* owner of the motor car. *na kena itaukei* its owner. Originally, this word referred to a person who maintained usage rights over something, and might have rights concerning its disposal, not strictly speaking an "owner" in the European sense of that word.

itaukei n. Fijian native (of a place), these days often capitalised as *iTaukei*, referring to indigenous Fijians in general. The word has become a polite way of referring to Fijians as in *e dua ni cauravou iTaukei* a Fijian youth. *gone iTaukei* native Fijian. *turaga iTaukei* Fijian gentleman (polite term for mature adult Fijian man). The new term *iTaukei* may refer only to officially registered Fijians. *iTaukei dredre* hardline iTaukei, belligerent in politics, asserting rights of Fijians versus Indians, Europeans and other ethnic/racial groups. Traditionally the term *itaukei ni qele* refers only to original settlers of an area, not the clans or tribes that joined the settlement later (though, often the case, the later settlers force their way to takeover the chiefly position.) As a modernism, the word has come to include all native Fijians who own native land. *o ira na itaukei ni qele* the (many) landowners. In fact, some Fijian clans own very little land and some clans own none at all. These days quite a number of Fijians are not even registered as Fijians in records of the Native Lands Commission. The N.L.C. has estimated at least ten percent.

Taukei (followed by place-name) title of traditionally appointed chief in various places of western Viti Levu Island. the word Taukei being followed by the name of the people, Chief of . . ., as in the Taukei Nakelo, Chief of Nakelo people (as at village Viseisei), or the Taukei Sawaieke, Chief of Sawaieke, a form of title at Vuda for head of the tribe Tububere at village Viseisei, spokesman for the Tui Vuda. Other examples: Taukei Navo at Dratabu, Taukei Werenidri at Nasigatoka, and the Taukei Vidilo at Namoli.

taukena v. to own (something, house, boat, land); to have usage rights by traditional custom. Ownership as such might have a very different meaning to Fijians, as compared to European notions of ownership. Individual ownership is less common. *E rau taukena na sitoa.* They (two) own the store. *na kena itaukei* the owner (literally, its owner).

itaukuku n. nail, as in *itaukuku ni liga-na* fingernail, *itaukuku ni yava-na* toenail. Also hoof (horse, cow), trotter (pig), claw (bird, cat). *ivako* n. carpentry nail.

taulaka v. to give birth (a very respectful word), *taulaki* born. Syn. *vakasucu*.

taumada first (before something else in time), first in importance, firstly, first of all. *a vosa taumada* foreword (of book), prologue.

tauna n. elephantiasis, particularly the grotesque swelling of certain parts of the body (legs and arms especially but also testicles and scrotum), and sometimes causing blindness, that follows from filariasis infection (*waqaqa*), with symptoms of fever, fatigue, weakness and swollen lymph glands. *Waqaqa* is caused by any one of 9 thread-like nematodes in the lymph glands. Different vectors affect different parts of the body. Infection is transmitted from person to person usually by the bite of a mosquito, a Culex sp. (one species) or Aedes spp. (three species), or possibly, a fly. There was an infection rate almost 10% in the Fiji population in 2007. There is a national programme to provide free preventative annual pills (not advised for pregnant women and children under two years of age). Continuing, repeated infection over a ten-year period can bring about elephantiasis. Syn. (Lau) *fua*. See *tatuku*.

taunamu n. mosquito net. Originally, this was made of barkcloth (*masi*) but did not exist in the most of the Viti Levu highlands where there was no barkcloth (except in Navosa, brought by Tongans) and just smoke was used to avoid mosquitos (*namu*).

tauqeraqera v. scattered, to scatter in disorderly fashion, such as tools in a tool-room.

taura 1. v. to take, take hold, to hold in the hand, to accept. *Taura!* Take it! (Anglicisms) *taura vakamamada na ivakasala* take the advice lightly. *taura vakabibi* take it seriously.
Idiom: *taura tale* v., n. dance (man and woman as a pair), lit. "take again". Syn. n., v. *taralala* (a specific type of social dance, as a European influence).
Idiom: *tauri lisi* to receive lease money for native land leased to tenants.

taura 2. understand. *O taura na noqu vosa?* Do you understand what I am saying? *taura cala* to misunderstand.

taura-tale v., n. to dance with a partner, as at a village *taralala* dance, a dance derived from European custom, not indigenous.

veitauriliga v. to hold hands. Syn. *veiqumi liga*. *Rau veitauriliga ena sitoa na veitinani.* The mother and child held each other's hand in the store. By ext. to work together co-operatively, to help one another. *Me da veitauriliga ena cakacaka vakoro.* Let us (many) work together on the village work. Young men may walk together holding hands. There is no sexual implication to that. It would be thought improper for male and female Fijians to to be seen holding hands romantically.

tauri-itukutuku or **vola-itukutuku** (Anglicism) v. to take the minutes of a meeting.

tauri-uli v. to take the helm of a boat or wheel of a car. *uli* helm, rudder.

taurivaka v. to use. Syn. *vakayagataka*.

taurua alone, of two people together. *taudua* alone (one person). *tautolu* just three people, and so on for any number of people.

tausoli v., n. collection of money for community purpose.

tausoso n. bunch or cluster as of hanging fruit (such as mango or *wi*) or coconuts. Syn. *isoso* but *tausoso* implies hanging down of clusters of greater substance.

itautau 1. n. enunciation of rhythm (of music), of words (in speech), distinctiveness of movement (in gestures, motions of dance).

itautau 2. n. pronouncement.

itautau 3. n. implication, innuendo, of something said. *E veibeci dina na itautau ni nomu vosa.* Your words really have despicable innuendo.

itautau 4. n. stem (of leaf, flower or fruit), the place on the plant where it is picked or plucked.

tautaubale n. a very large grey-coloured freshwater river eel that nests in rocks and suns itself. When disturbed it can be aggressive and attack, and often goes on land, even flinging itself at an aggressor. It sometimes lies under leaves, giving rise to the false impression that it is a snake. This eel has ample fat and some of the flesh is brown and oily to the taste. The name derives from its ability to "walk" (*taubale*).

itautauri n. handle (as of basket, bucket, box, cup), not of a knife, axe or hand-tool where the proper word would be *dia-na*.

tautauvata 1. same, even (sporting score, level of ground). *tautauvata kei* same as, equal with, equivalent to.

tautauvata 2. level, smooth, physically even, flat.

vakatautauvata, vakatautauvatana v. to compare. *Sa mai 84 na iwiliwili ni vakatautauvatani kei na 90 ena yabaki sa oti.* The count has reached 84, compared with 90 last year. Syn. *vakatautauvatana*.

tautuba n. outside (of house, building).

tauva 1. v. to afflict by (usually some infectious illness). *Sa tauvi koya na mate.* He/she has been afflicted by a sickness. *rerevaki ke tauva na gone lalai* dangerous if it inflicts little children. *tauvimate* v., n., adj. sick. Syn. *taka, takava*.

tauva 2. v. to stain (a person, clothes, wood) as from a dye, paint, fruit juice). Syn. *taka, takava*.

tauvanua n. commoner, common people, usually with no specialized traditional function for their clan, such as priest, warriors, fishermen. Syn. *lewenivanua* implies simply that the people are not chiefly or significant elders.

vakatauvatani compared with, in comparison to, as in *ni vakatauvatani kei na . . .* as compared with the . . . Syn. *vakatautauvatana*. See above.

tauvica in a question, how many people? Also applies to fruit, asking how many. *Na kavika, tauvica qori?* How many *kavika* fruit are there there (where you are)? Syn. *le vica?* (how many people?).

tauvimate n., adj. sick. *tautauvimate* sickly. Syn. (Lau, Kadavu) *baca*.

tauvu n., adj. people of certain geographically separated tribes who in legend derive from the same ancestral spirit (*vu*), or have been united anciently by chiefly marriage. One says that the people are *veitauvu* (related in this way). One may address one's *tauvu* as "*Tau*". They are inclined to make jokes, play tricks against each other, playful insults, sometimes obnoxious. For relationships where the tricks can be extreme, they are *tauvu dredre*, "hard" *tauvu*. Similar mutual behaviour occurs in the *veitabani* relationship. These days this relationship may extend to whole Territories or even Provinces rather than specific localities or specific tribes that was the older tradition. Nayau Island in Lau and Noco Territory in Rewa are *veitauvu*, based on an ancient marriage of a Lauan lady into Noco. See *Tau. taba-na. veitabani*.

tauyavu, tauyavutaka v. to establish, to found, to lay the foundation for. *yavu* foundation, basis.

tava, tava v. to slice, cut off or cut into with a knife (formerly this was often a sharp strip of bamboo). May refer to cutting open a mature boil, castrating animals (not traditional), removing skin of cassava or *kawai* yam. Applied to a child, this means to punish by making about three slices in the flesh, usually on the upper arm. *tavatava* slicing, which may imply child punishment or bleeding for Fijian medical purposes. See *tavatava*.

tava-cicila having many tiny holes, as a mosquito screen does, or a sponge. This is very probably a modernism.

tavaka 1. v. to wait for (people). *Tavaki au*. Wait for me. Syn. *waraka*.

tavaka 2. v. to "possess" in the sense that a devil possesses a person.

tavaka 3. v. to yank, as in *Tavaka na wa ni siwa!* Jerk the fishing line! Yank it! This to ensure the fish is well hooked after it has bitten the bait.

tavako (Eng.) n. cigarette, tobacco. *kana tavako* (or) *vakatavako* to smoke (tobacco). *Sa tabu na vakatavako* Smoking is prohibited. *tavako ni Viti* is grown in Fiji, wrapped tightly in coils the size of a soccer ball, and sold in the market; it is a very strong, dark tobacco that elderly Fijians use to roll their own smokes. Covers (*suluka*), as for home-made cigars, are usually dried leaves of plantain or pandanus smoothed (*wadruca*) between the fingers.
Idiom: *itibi tavako* (or) *itibi* a "butt", literally a "roll", slang for a cigarette.

tavale-na n. cross-cousin, ie., child of one's father's sister or of one's mother's brother. *veitavaleni* adj. related as cross-cousins, or as n., the set of two or more cross-cousins. This is an extremely close relationship, very supportive and essentially members of the same family. Those of opposite sex are favoured candidates to marry each other in Fiji though first-cousin marriages are prohibited among Europeans. *Tavale* are usually addressed as "*tavale*", rather than *tavalequ*. These days one's *tavale* may be of the same or opposite sex. More traditionally, two *tavale* would both be male cross-cousins, and in English be referred to as "cousin-brother". Cross-cousins of different sex would be *veidavoleni. davola-na* is the "correct" term. When both cross-cousins are female the relationship is *vei-dauveni*, and they may refer to each other as *Dauve*. When two separate kin-groups have gods (*kalou*) that are *veitavaleni*, those two groups are said to be *vetabani* and they may address each other as *Naita*. In effect, this is similar to a *veitauvu* relationship, a close familiarity that allows hard joking, harder perhaps than that of two groups that are *veitauvu*. See *tauvu*.

tavali v. to pass before, or go across, one's field of vision. *vuki tavali* to go back and forth across one's field of vision. *Au a raici koya ni tavali ena noqu matanivale*. I saw him/her go past the front of my house.

tavasa n. unexpected sound, not always immediately identified, usually a rustling, cracking or crackling (twigs broken by a person walking, plastic being shuffled about, or being folded). *Au rogoca e dua na tavasa etuba*. I hear a strange noise outside. *Sa tavasa na veikau*. There's a strange sound in the bush.

tavatava 1. n., v. to punish a child by slicing parallel, superficial cuts on the back or arm. The scars may remain for life. See *tava* slice.

tavatava 2. n, v. as a native medical remedy, to apply a series of usually small cuts to a painful part of the body such as the back, arm, or leg, to bleed it with the notion that will cure the pain. A heated glass, sometimes filled with smoke is then applied over the wounds to draw out the blood, or over a boil to draw out the pus.

tava-tukituki (ni uto) v., n. rapid beating (of the heart), usually at some excitement.

tavaya n. bottle. *qa ni tavaya* chip or piece of broken glass, formerly used for cutting, and for shaving. Glass was introduced by Europeans. *tavaya bia* bottle of beer. Gourds (*vago*), Lagenaria siceraria (formerly L. vulgaris), aboriginally introduced vine, now naturalised, the fruit's wooden pericarp formerly used as bottles for water or coconut oil, only at lower elevation areas of Polynesian influence. Botanist Seemann noticed they were in widespread use in the 1860s. Glass and plastic replace them. Anciently in the Viti Levu highlands, the only liquid containers were segments of bamboo. Coastal people sometimes used shells of mature coconuts or clay pots.

tava-yaya adj. unsettled, confused, uncertain, anxious.

itavi n. task, duty, function.

vakaitavi v. to participate, serve, be occupied with or assigned to some task, involved. *era sa vakaitavi e na soli itukutuku* they are involved in the release of the report. *na nodra laki vakaitavi ena yadrava na veisautataki* their (many) going to serve in guarding for the pacification (as for the United Nations.)

tavi, tavia v. to hit, whack hard, usually a ball, as in tennis, cricket. *tavia na volo* hit the ball. *itavi* (or) *pate* n. bat (as in cricket). *itavi ni tenisi* n. tennis racquet.

tavia v. to slap or tap with the open hand.

tavitavitaka v. use the hand to pat, pet, (a cat, a baby).

tavilaka v. in forming clay pots, to whack to the outside with a paddle (*itata*) with a stone held inside the pot.

taviraka v. to sweep, sweep out (usually house). This is normally a vigorous work, using a traditional broom called a *sasa*, made of the mid-rib of coconut leaflets. Fijian women usually prefer this to European-style brooms. Formerly, highlanders had no *sasa;* they used branches of the *makita* tree that retain their leaves.

tavidi v. to proceed very quietly, with hardly any noise.
Idiom: *e tavidi na vusi* proceed quietly, as a cat moves. *E tavidi na vusi na nodra cakacaka*. They went about their work quietly

tavioka (Eng. tapioca) n. cassava, manioc, Manihot esculenta. Originally from tropical America, introduced by Europeans, it is now the most frequently eaten starchy root-crop. A reddish-skinned variety called New Hebrides is commonly exported. For ceremonial food presentations, cassava is not a prestigious root-crop like the traditional yam or taro. Eager for quick yields, Fijians sometimes talk of a variety called *Vula tolu*, that matures three months after planting, as suggested by the name. No such variety exists. Seven months is minimum time to maturity. *Sokobale* is a very slow maturing variety and need not be harvested promptly.

itavitaviraki n. broom. *sasa* usual Fijian broom of coconut-leaf midribs. Syn. (Lau) *taufale, itafi*, both types with wooden handles. Syn. *itataviraki*. See *taviraka*, above.

tavivi v. entangled, as in *E tavivi na me*. The goat is entangled (in its tether).

tavo, tavoca v. to beach a boat or to launch it into the water. By extension modernly it can mean to launch some new project. a public programme, a new product. *tavo ki wai* to launch a boat in the water. *tavo ki vanua* to beach a boat. *itavotavo* place at the shore for beaching a boat.

tavo, tavoraka v. work too hard, sweat for it, to over-work or over-use something.

tavo, tavoya, tavoitaka v. to wipe the face, especially when wet or damp. *me tavoi na matamu* wipe your face dry. *tavoya na wai ni matamu* wipe away your tears.

itavoi n. handkerchief (an introduced concept), or small cotton towel, mostly used for wiping the face. *sulu tavoi* cloth used to dry a person after bathing. Presumably, in lowlands, barkcloth (*masi*) was used as towelling before cotton cloth was introduced.

tavola n. Fiji almond, edible nut, like an almond, from a common coastal tree, Terminalia catappa, Combretaceae. It has conspicuouly horizontal branches with lvs spirally arranged at tips of branches, very large colourful red, leathery falling deciduously around the shore. Fls small, white, on racemes to 30 cm. The nut is difficult to crack. It is eaten mostly by children, or as a casual, occasional snack, not normally sold in the markets. The nuts (along with coconuts and fish) once helped this author stay alive when castaway on an atoll called Cakau ni Sici (lit. "Trochus Reef" but called Bird Island in English). Geraghty speculates that the name *tavola* is borrowed from a Solomon island language; the earlier Proto-Polynesian name was *talice* (Fijian *dalice*). Syn. (Nadro, Serua) *tivi* or *jivi*. *tivi* is also the common name for closely related coastal species T. litoralis but having smaller lvs and smaller fruits than the edible T. catappa. Well known is timber tree T. capitanea, called *tivi* or *tavola ni veikau* that has winged fruits. The several other Terminalia spp. have limited forest distribution. Syn. (Lau) *tatavola*.

tavu (Eng.) n. tub. *tavu ni sili* bathtub.

tavu, tavuna v. to grill, roast on embers. This was formerly the commonest way of cooking in the highlands of Vit Levu, where there were no clay pots (*kuro*), and the earth-oven (*lovo*) was unknown.

See *tavuteke* to fry, a relatively modern term, formerly unknown in Fiji. No cooking in oil or fat was used by Fijians. Idiom: *tavu vudi*. wishful thinking, as might be exclaimed by one boy to another who is looking wistfully at a desirable girl. The expression is heard mostly in that context.

tavude v. rise to the surface after sinking. See *vude*.

tavukadiridiri adj. spotted, speckled finely, freckled, mildew(ed).

tavuki v. overturn. The name of a few villages, memorialising the overthrow of an early chiefly lineage, a common occurence.

tavulaka v. to throw forcefully, as a stone, or in boxing, a hard punch.

tavulaki knocked down, dropped (a person dropped by a blow, a heavy parcel dropped hard, or a a boat knocked over (as in a storm). By ext., *veitavulaki ena rakavi* knocked down (defeated) at rugby (of a team). *tavutavulaki* more forceful knock-down.

tavuleni (Eng.) n. tarpaulin. Today these are commonly made of cheap blue plastic rather than canvas. Several spellings.

tavuloni v. to cover or wrap something with a piece of cloth or barkcloth. *Me tavuloni na wai ena dua na tiki ni isulu.* Cover the medicine with a piece of cloth.

tavusasa n., v. to make decorative marks burned onto a person's body, shoulder, chest, or the back, burning the central vein of a palm leaf (*sasa*) pricked into the skin. These are often short parallel lines with no special meaning, done to a child for punishment, or an adult as decoration. Syn. *tuboko*.

ta-vusoya v. to relate (a story) gushingly. *vuso* froth, foam.

tavuteke v. to fry, a method of cooking previously unkown to Fijians. *itavuteke* n. frying pan. In towns, lard is widely used because it is cheap. Popularity of frying is partly due to the speed of preparing fried foods, and the shortage of firewood, a severe problem in suburbs.

tavutoka n. Threespot Reef Crab that has three dark spots on its shell at back. Syn. *kavika*.

tavu-tonotono spotted. This applies to a rash on the human skin, fungal spots on a plant leaf, spotted or speckled design on a shirt, blouse or dress, or an animal. See *tono*.

tavuto (or) **tovuto** n. whale. Though this term has been mostly understood to mean the Sperm whale, it generally applies to both the major species. Seen most often is the Humpback whale (Megaptera nadosa) that migrates from Antarctic, past New Zealand, to Fiji and then Tonga in June, July, August, for breeding, the mother often swimming beside her baby, both returning then to the Antarctic. The Humpback is harmless, quite friendly and unafraid of humans or boats. It is possible to make eye-to-eye contact. The carniverous, dangerous, predatory Sperm whale, Pyseter catadon, is source of all Fijian whaleteeth (*tabua*), used as ceremonial gift *kamunaga* of great value. Fijian obtained the teeth only by trade, or from the lower jaw of the occasional dead whales found on the shores. (The upper jaw is virtually toothless.) This Fijian use of whale teeth is not much older than a couple of centuries, an innovation from Tonga after 1750, around the time of the earliest arrival of the whalers. Interestingly, Tongans themselves never used the whale tooth in any ceremonial function and never used any other such symbolic, ceremonial gift. Previously, mainland Fijians used wooden *tabua*, and the small islanders (Lauans) used a poisonous cone-shell (*cava*). Only stories remain of wooden *tabua*. There is not even a good description of what they looked like.

A major whaling industry flourished in Fiji waters from the 1700s to mid 1800s, with a peak from 1840s to the mid 1850s, when there were more than 700 whaling ships based out of northeastern U.S.A. By the early 1850s some 8,000 whales were killed for oil each year. By 1859, kerosene began to replace whale oil for lighting lamps. Ambergris ("grey amber") was not named or used by Fijians, though it has been used since ancient times in Malaysia and China for spicing wine. Its use in the European perfume industry is as a fixative, to prolong the fragrance, and a couple of the essential ingredients add their own perfume. The fine, sweet fragrance is obtained only after the very smelly, greasy, lumps of grey raw ambergris have been dissolved in cold ethyl alcohol. Ambergris is rare, with quantities up to 200 pounds found in the head of just a very few Sperm whales, but smaller amounts may be found floating at sea, or at the seaside strand. Fijans have been unaware of ambergris and never made use of it.

Uniquely there was a Tribe Ra Tavuto, as one of the five or perhaps eight social groups of the Butoni(vanua) fishermen who live on the flatlands of Bau Islands before the incursion of super-tribe Kubuna around 1760, an incursion that soon after, displaced the Butoni, as well as the Korolevu (Levuka) sailors and fishermen who lived on the hill. The Butoni then settled mainly in LomaiViti, especially on Koro Island but also elsewhere. On Bau Island the Butoni had constructed the council house called Naulunivuaka, with a separate door for each of their tribes.

tavutu v. describes a sharp, strong motion that comes to a sudden end, as in a boat striking a reef, or bumping one's head, usually inadvertantly, stub one's toe, push something hard as far as it will go (as a post in the ground). *Vutu* suggests banging, pounding, and "*ta*" suggests a sharp action.

tavuwai, tavuwai-taka v. to cook quickly by throwing into water that is already boiling, as one might do with shellfish. This is not traditional. Grilling was traditional.

tawa as a prefix, without, indicating an absence of something. *tawa mudu* infinite (without end). *bula-tawamudu* n. "live forever", name of a plant, Kalanchoe pinnata, Crassulaceae; the succulent leaves can form rootlets around the edges, and remain alive a long time. *tawayaga* useless. *tawa donu* without right, unrightful(ly). *tawa guilecavi* unforgettable. *na itovo tawa kilikili* improper behaviour. *vakatawa dodonu* unrightfully. *tawamalaca* uncertain, uncertainty.

vakatawa without, un- . *vakatawa dodonu* unrightfully.

tawa, tawana v. to fill (container), populated (land), loaded (gun) *vakatawana* fill it, populate it. *Sa tawa na taqe.* The tank is filled. *Sa tawa na vanua.* The country is populated. *tawana na koro* inhabit the village. *na tawaqele* the populace, inhabitants. *tawa-vanua* v., n. to populate, first immigrants, first settlers. For a place or territory, *tawa, tawana* may indicate that there is a presiding chief. *tawa* implies the process of being filled whereas *sinai* refers to the state of being completely full. Idiom: *Sa tawa na matana.* She is pregnant.

Idiom: *tamata tawa* n. person who has a devil, and serves that devil, a person "possessed", who must pour a *yaqona* to his devil and gains favours for that.

tawaitini adj. canned, as in *kakana tawaitini* canned food.

itawatawa (ni benisini) n. filling station, petrol station, bowser. Syn. *bausa* (Eng.) a much more commonly used word.

vakatawa, vakatawana 1. v. to fill (container). *tawaipakete-taka* to package (in packages, usually commercially).

vakatawa, vakatawana 2. v. to populate. *vakatawana na vanua vou.* populate the new land. Idiom: *vakatawana na bure* get married (move into a house of the husband).

vakatawa, vakatawana 3. v. to keep watch. *na ivakatawa* guard, person on watch, Wesley catechist. *Peresitedi Vakatawa* Acting President.

tawake (Archaic) n. pennant, small flag. Syn. *drotini*. *kuila* flag. *Vatanitawake* was a famous shed on Bau Island, conceptually and originally having shelves (*vata*) for the drying of the nautical pennants of the high chief, especially the Roko Tui Bau.

tawala n. (Lau, from Tongan "ta'ovala") traditional Tongan binding of sinnet that serves as a belt holding in the formal cummerbund (*gafigafi*) woven of Pandanus *voivoi* (called *kie* in Lau). It is worn at church, and at any ceremonial occasions.

tawa-nuitaki adj. undependable, untrustworthy.

tawase, tawasea v., n. split, torn apart, divided, separate. *E tawasei ira na kaiColo.* They are divided among themselves, the highlanders. *na yalayala ka tawasei rau na yasana o Tailevu kei Ra* the border that separates the two provinces of Tailevu and Ra. See *wase, wasea* to divide, often to share out. *na tawase ni yabaki vou* the New Years Day.

Vakatawase (Anglicism) n. New Years Eve and may imply New Years Day as well. *Siga ni Vakatawase* New Years Day.

tawa-vanua v., n. first immigrants or settlers to populate a place. *tawa* to fill.

tawayaga useless. *tawa* without. *yaga* useful, usefulness.

tawa-yalani limitless, infinite. boundless.

tayabe v. to march, as in a parade. *yabe* to walk about unencumbered.

tayana v. dis-arranged, scattered about carelessly.

te n. foamy scum found on the surface of coastal waters some days before the rising of the *balolo* seaworm (an annelid, Palolo viridis), which will be gathered as food. When the scum is sighted, locals stay alert to the arrival of the worm. The rising usually occurs twice a year, October (*balolo lailai*) and November (*balolo levu*), according to the phase of the moon, but only at certain places and not always regularly, and not at Viti Levu Island. See *balolo*.

tea v. to plant (to grow). *Sa tei oti.* It has already been planted. *teivaki* planted, as in *sa teivaki na qele* the land is planted; *na kena itei* the planting stock. After harvest of *yaqona*, some people do not discard the piece of old planting stock that remains; it can be used, making a much weaker beverage. Traditionally, in farming, Fijians planted only from corms, sprouted seedlings, and suckers. They never deliberately planted seeds except for a few fruit trees. Their only gardening tools were a club to knock down bush for clearing by burning, and also a digging stick (*doko*) that is still commonly used. *iteitei* food garden. Fijians planted some ornamentals but never had ornamental gardens.

tebara n. alluvial flatland, such as at Nakelo, Tokatoka, Noco, Rewa. The place-name Tebara is recent, a far-out suburb of Suva city.

tebe-na n. edge (thick), as in *tebe ni gusu* lip(s), *tebe ni maga-na* labia pudenda of a woman.

tebe, tebeka v. to chip, break off, of something brittle, such as pottery, plate or cup. *itebetebe* n. chip(s) off something brittle, sherds. *katebe* chipped.

teda (Eng.) n. tender (as in the commercial term, a formal offer to buy, or to carry out construction). *tedataka* to make a tender offer.

tegu n. dew. Syn. *bite*.

tei 1. verbal modifier adding the meaning of "first of all", "just", "just now", or "for just now". Offered more food one might say *sa tei rauta mada*, that's enough for now thanks, or *Au tei kua mada* I won't (take more) just now, thanks. *Ni sa tei moce toka mada* Good-bye for now. More elaborately, *Ni sa tei toka saka tale mada. Tou tei kana mada, qai lako.* Let's (several) eat first, then go.
Idiom: *Sega ni ura me sa tei damu.* Where there is smoke there is fire. There must be a cause for that to happen, and the cause is yet to be known. lit. no prawn just turns red (unless someone has cooked it) – there is a reason for it turning red.

tei 2. planted. See *tea*, to plant. *dau tei dovu* n. sugar-cane farmer.

itei 3. n. segment of a plant that is planted to propagate it, such as a section of yam tuber, or a section of *yaqona* stem that would include a node.

iteitei n. food garden. *dau teitei* farmer, planter. Around villages, food gardens are usually far away from the houses.

teivaka 1. v. to plant (the land). *teivaka na noqu qele.* to plant my land.

teivaka 2. v. (Modernism) to set, establish (as a new record, in sports). *E teivaki e dua na isausau vou.* A new record was established.

teimavi n. a sp. of freshwater crab, common on Viti Levu, usually no more than 2 inches across, a light brown colour. The left claw is large and orange-coloured. It may be caught in hand prawning nets. Grilled on an open fire, it is sucked on and chewed, and the shell-parts are spat out.

teivovo n., v. a specific, brief challenge enacted out and chanted by the Fiji national football team before a major match. Though now "traditional", the custom dates only from the late1930s. The custom was inspired by an abbreviated version of "haka" war-dance performed by N.Z. All Black rugby team. The Fijian version was composed by a Vusaradave chief at the request of the Vunivalu of Bau, Ratu George Cakobau. *teivovoi* is probably an abbrev. of *tei voavoa*, with *voavoa* referring to a field that is abandoned after use as a garden. (In early days, Fijian gardeners rotated the land, not the crops. Some still do that.) *tei* refers to something being planted or struck into the ground. Here the implication is a war-fence.

teke, tekea v. to kick backwards, as a horse does. By ext. refers to the "kick" of a handgun or rifle when fired. Idiom: *tekea na vokete* (Anglicism) to kick the bucket, to die. Interesting that Fijians have this as a backward kick, rather than a forward kick, as assumed by most Europeans.

tekesi (Eng.) n. taxi. Syn. *tekisi*.

itekiteki n. flower or other decoration stuck in hair, usually behind the ear, by women or men. A sprig of fragrant *uci* is commonly used. This is often a matter of whim rather than any special occasion. One hears that a flower behind both ears means you are married, a flower behing the right ear you have a romantic partner, and behind the left ear, you are looking. This was invented as tourist talk, and is not traditional. The usually red, ornamental hibiscus (*senitoa*) is introduced, not a traditional *tekiteki*. It is contrary to custom that a *itekiteki* be worn casually in a chiefly village area.

teki, tekia, tekilaka v. to stick a pole, post or stake, cricket wickets, into the ground. *tekiteki-vaka* to thrust hard, stick forcefully (something such as a stick), usually into the ground.

teki, tekina v. to stick a *itekiteki,* flower or scented plant, at the side of the head.

tekicuva v. to bow the head in a fixed position. *cuva* implies leaning forward.

tekiduru v. to kneel. *duru-na* knee.

tekisi (Eng.) n. taxi. Syn. *tekesi*.

itekivu n. beginning. *na itekitekivu* the very beginning.

tekivu, tekivuna v. to begin, to begin it.
Idiom: *Tekivu e Jerusalemi* (Biblical) Lit., Begin at Jerusalem, i.e., begin by making changes at home, oneself before trying to change others. By a curious twist this can imply doing favours for one's own people before anyone else, implying that nepotism is justified. Helping one's relatives is a firm custom in Fiji.

tekivu-taka v. to start it.

Vakatekivu n. Genesis.

vakatekivu mai ... beginning with, as in *vakatekivu mai na gauna* beginning with (or from) the time ...

televiseni (Eng.) n. television. Syn. *retio ni yaloyalo*. These days one is more likely to hear an exact copy of the English abbreviation TV.

temaka v. to tempt, entice. *Kua ni temaki au.* Don't tempt me. *na veitemaki nei Seru vei Vani* the tempting of Vani by Seru. That is a rather formal, archaic kind of expression.

itema n. enticement, lure, that which tempts someone. **veitemaki** n. temptation, enticement. See above.

temo n. calf of the leg. May sometimes refer to the forearm *temo ni liga-na*.

tena (Eng.) n. tenor.

tene, tenea v. to seat or set down on the lap, usually of a child. *na itenetene* the lap.

teniseni (Eng.) v. to stand at attention (military).

tenisi (Eng.) n. tennis.

tepi (Eng.) n. tape (as in recording tape). *na tepi ni lagasere* the tape(s) of recorded song. **katokatoni** n. recording (as of music).

teqa 1. adj. deformed, of a person's limb. *yava teqa* n. bow-legged. (Syn. *yava veqa*).

teqa 2. n. vanity. *teqa-taka* v. to be vain (about something).

vaka-teqateqa n. adj. posture or stance of a person showing off with proud bearing, often with new clothing.

tera (Eng. terror) n., adj. fearsome (person), formidable, domineering, brash, overly forceful and "pushy". *vakateratera* v. to try to appear tough.

teratera v. to show off.

tere, terega v. to touch lightly in passing, to graze by. Such a movement may be used by Fijians as a secret sign between two people.

terema v. to clear the throat, with a sort of cough. This may be a way of catching someone's attention.

tereni (Eng.) v. to train, physically by exercise, a custom adopted at advent of jogging, much spoken of in modern times.

teretere n. comb on the head of a chicken.

teri n. Purple Swamp Hen, Porphyrio porphyrio, on main islands virtually extinct due to mongoose and feral cats, but still reasonably common on some other Fiji islands and very common in New Zealand. The species also exists in Europe, Africa, Asia, Central America and Florida according to Paddy Ryan. Some live in social groups and may include two or three males, each mating with each female. The males help in incubation and feeding of the young. Partly nocturnal and not at all restricted to wet or swampy places. Watling says it may be a nuisance in some fruit and vegetable gardens, damaging bananas, plantain, taro. I have not observed that. Syn. (Lau, Kadavu, Nadro.) *kitu*. (Vanua Levu) *qala*.

teri (Rewa, Verata) no, not. *Au teri kila*. I do not know. Syn. *tara*.
Idiom: *Sa teri!* No way! Nothing doing!

teru adj. slack or loose, as of a rope, not taut. *vakateruya* v. to slack off, of a rope, cord, belt, or the sail of a boat, or by ext. to speak slowly and meaningfully.

tete, tetea (or) **teteva** v. spread out, disseminate (seeds, rumours, disease). *vakatetea na vosa* to spread the word. *teteva na vuravura* spread throughout the world. *na tete ni kama* the spread of fire (as through the dry bush). *Sa tete vakatotolo na mate*. The disease spread quickly. *gusu tete* wide-lipped (person). *tetela* spreading sore.

vakatetea v. to spread, disseminate, as with propaganda, or gossip.

tetewai v. adj. babbling, self-centred in speech. Syn. (Colo East) *tatawai*. Cf. *tatawai* to talk in one's sleep.

tevale or **tepali** (Eng., Lau "table") n. pulpit (often used figuratively).

teve, teveka v. to circumcise (males). *veiteve* circumcision. This takes place usually from age six to nine. The process is usually called *tiko e bure* and requires a few days of isolation. The coming-out feast is known as *bogi va* (four nights). *teve vakabeka* circumcision that involves only a slicing on top of the penis, not a complete removal of foreskin. Syn. *kana lekutu* (or) *cebe, cili*. Female circumcision is unknown in Fiji.

teveli (Eng.) n. table. *ena teveli* on the table.

tevoro (Tongan tevolo) Satan, the Devil, best perhaps capitalised as Tevoro; also dangerous indigenous spirit(s) which Fijians have commonly believed to be nearby, especially at night, formerly just known as *kalou* spirits. Spirits that came to be called the *tevoro* in Christian times often possess people and they may be exorcised by the victim being made to believe he or she is "eating" them. Some people are believed to have a *tevoro* do evil for them, by serving the *tevoro*, and pouring *yaqona* to honour it. If they cease to so honour the *tevoro*, they themselves may fall victim to it. This usually means seizure, illness and even death. There is analogy with the European legend of Faust. Belief in both Satan and in traditional Fijian spirits is quite current. *tevoro* may refer to the joker in a deck of cards.

vakatevoro adj. bewitched, possessed by a devil.

tevu, tevuka v. to lay out, spread out (usually mats, sheets, blankets), also open out (as a book).

tevutevu n. part of a marriage ceremony, formerly only for people of high rank, the presentation and symbolic laying out of mats where the marriage is to be consummated.

itevutevu n. mats or other gifts given to a newly married couple by the wife's side of the family. This custom is falling into disuse around urban areas. The word implies the laying out of mats.

ti (Eng.) n. tea. As a substitute, Fijians are often quite content to use mature leaves of lemon tree or other citrus leaves.

tiaina (or) **jaina** (Eng. "China") n. banana, introduced cultivars. *ikau tiaina* hand or small bunch of bananas. *ikaukau tiaina* whole stalk of bananas. Cf. *vudi* plantain. *liga ni marama* lady fingers (tiny) bananas. The plaintain *vudi* is an aboriginal introduction, as is the *soaqa*, the upright banana Musa fehi. The introduced "China" banana was brought to Fiji by Rev. George Pritchard in 1848, from Samoa by way of Tonga; the botanical classification was Musa Chinensis at the time. That particular cultivar was hardly six feet tall, and thus resistant to wind damage according to Seemann. Other varieties, introduced later, have been known as Cavendish and Sitivenu ("Stephen"). Bananas have been grown mostly in the eastern Viti Levu highlands and floated in bamboo rafts down the Rewa River. The commercial export industry was formidable in its day but came to an abrupt end when quality control was abandoned by Fijian growers after Fiji's independence from colonial government in 1974.

tiale (E. Polyn. "tiare") n. gardenia, the national flower of Tahiti. Fiji has some ten species of the genus Gardenia, nine of them probably native. Gardinia taitensis was most likely a Polynesian introduction, not common in Fiji. *tiare* is the general Maori word for flower.

tibi, tibika v. to flash, as of lightning. *Sa tibi na liva.* The lightning flashed. *tibika* v. to strike something or someone (of lightning).

Idiom: *Tibi na liva* Quick as lightning

tibi, tibika v. to roll (something). *tibika na sika.* roll the cigar.

itibi n. "roll", cigarette. More completely, *itibi tavako*.

Tibio! exclamation of child who opts out of a game such as "hide and seek" (*veivuni*) or a game of "tag" (*veitara*).

tibou n. fruit of the mangrove tree, an emergency food.

tidaloko n. small fish, mud flipper or skipper, 4 to 5 inches, of no economic use, dark coloured, lives in swampy places.

tidara v. to slip (of person or animal), in a slippery place, walking or running. *titidara* very slippery, as of a muddy path. Syn. (Colo East) *sikidara*.

taka-na n. kin relation, as in:- *A cava takamu o Seru?* What relationship is Seru to you?

tikau n. a common variety of edible wild yam, Dioscorea nummularia, sold in the market. This was a principal food of highlanders. Syn. (Colo East) *dasi*. Around the Nasavusavu area *tikau* may refer to any of the several types of wild yam.

tikidua n. leaflet, pamphlet, page.

tiki, tikica v. to separate apart, to cut off or break off a piece, often said of some food such as bread, or cooked root crop. *tu vakatikitiki* v. to stand next to something, to stand aside.

tiki-na 1. n. part, piece. *e dua na tiki ni keke* a piece of cake. *tiki-ni-siga* n. date of the month. *tiki ni yago* part of the body.

tiki-na 2. next to, beside. *dabe e tiki-mu* sit next to you. *ena tiki-na kadus* on the other side. Syn. *tikiva* v. to be next to. *tikiva na vale* next to the house.

tikina 3. n. subject matter. *na noqu vakasama ena tikina oqo* my thoughts on this matter (about this topic).

Tikina 4. n. administrative District of Fiji. *na Tikina o Noco* the District of Noco. To some extent Districts are designed to encompass traditional territories (*vanua*) but that goal is far from being achieved. The numbers of Districts and their boundaries have varied greatly through Fiji's modern history. At various times the administrative title *Buli* has been used for District administrators. In 1948 the Districts, called "Old Districts" (*Tikina Makawa*) were combined into larger groups called United Districts (*Tikina Cokovatai*). In 1987 the old system was restored. The old Districts of highlanders of Viti Levu, Colo East, Colo West, Colo North, were abolished and merged with other Districts to suppress the feisty, independent spirit of the highlanders, the *kaiColo*.

tikitiki partly. *tikitiki kai Viti* part-Fijian. *tikitiki Jaina* part-Chinese.

vakatikitiki apart, to one side. *biuta vakatikitiki e yasaqu.* put to one side, at my side. *tu vakatikitiki* stand aside.

tikite (or) **tikiti** (Eng.) n. ticket.

tikiva next to, alongside, to one side, adjacent to. *Na valelailai ka tikiva na makete.* The toilet next to the market. *E dua na yanuyanu lailai ka koto tikivi Ovalau.* A small island that lies next to Ovalau.

veitikivi to be next to each other. *Eratou toka veitikivi.* They (several) stay next to each other.

tikivili n. nectar-eating parrot, Red-Throated Lorikeet, Charmosyma amabilis, favours red-flowering *vuga* trees.

tiko 1. v. to be (but only used where necessary, much less often than in English, and only used in specific contexts). *Tiko lo!* Be quiet, shut up! (to a child). *E tiko eso na suka?* Is there any sugar? *Io, e tiko.* Yes, there is some.

tiko, tikora 2. v. to reside, to stay, to be (at some place). *E tiko mai Suva.* He/she is in Suva, stays in Suva. *itikotiko* n. residence. Syn. (West) *no.*

tiko 3. particle that follows a verb to indicate continuity of action. *Sa moce tiko.* He/she is sleeping. *Lako tiko! Lako tiko!* Keep going!

tiko 4. n. existence, or being, as in *tiko yavavala* disturbed existence, social unrest. *na tiko vinaka.* the well-being.

tiko, tikora 5. v. to set down, oneself, a person, an object such as a pot.

vakatiko, vakatikora v. to place (it). But note: *tikovata* to stay by someone, to remain with a person. *vata* together.

tikoga (or) **tiko ga** still, in the sense of a continuity of a condition or an action. *E cakacaka tikoga.* He/she is still working.

iTikoqe n. aide-de camp of Governor (prior to the 1987 military coup), or to the President of the Republic (since the military takeover).

Tikotiko kina . . . Idiom: Once upon a time (there lived, there was) . . . -- as said in beginning to tell a story.

itikotiko n. residence, place where one stays, address. (A relatively modern word.)

tikovata v. to stay by someone, remain with a person. The usual implication is that of a couple living together as partners in a quasi-married state. *vata* together.

tiko-vinaka v., n. well-being, a modernism.

tila, tila, tilaka v. to strike with a wooden club, the top of a stake, or the human head.

tilo, tiloma v. to swallow (food, beverage). (Anglicism) to "swallow" a tall story.

tilodru v. to gobble (food), to guzzle (beverage), swallow in haste.

tilomuri n. after-taste, as when tasting *yaqona*, one's first impression may be modified by a somewhat later taste-effect in the mouth.

tiloqa-taka v. to swallow whole, without chewing.

itilotilo n. Adam's apple, fore part of the throat, throat.

tilou (or) **tulou** excuse me (said when passing close beside, behind or above someone). Syn. *tulou.* The word is never modified (one cannot *tilou* "very much"). In Fiji it is bad manners to have one's head above a chief, or to walk or stand close behind a person of rank. *vakatilou* to make the gesture of saying *"tilou".* Syn. (Tonga) *tulou.*

tina-na n. mother or mother's sister, maternal aunt. Also father's brother's wife.

tinatina n. mature female animal.

tini (Eng.) ten. *vakatini* ten times. *tini ka dua* eleven ("ten plus one"), *tini ka rua* twelve, etc. *tini na kuro* ten pots. *tini na udolu* ten thousand. The thing counted is named with its definite article *na. tini vakacaca* a few more than ten. *na ikatini* one-tenth, tithe (as in some Christian sects). Legendary *Yavusa* (Tribe) Tinitini involved ten children (numbered and named *Dua, Rua, Tolu* etc.) of the ancestral spirit of village Nasilai in Tailevu Province, with a mother from Kaba.

In olden times *sagavulu* was one of the more common words for ten, as evidenced by the word for twenty, *ruasagavulu,* thirty *tolusagavulu,* etc. Anciently, counting systems differed considerably among the various tribes that migrated here from Vanuatu and the Solomons with their different languages.

tini (Eng.) n. tin (of food, such as canned beef). *vakatinitaka* to can (food). *kakana tawaitini* canned food. Syn. *kava.*

tini, tinia v. to end, to end up, conclude, terminate, finish. Used only in specific contexts, perhaps not used as often as *vakaotia* or *cava. E tinia ena nona kaya . . .* He/she concluded by saying . . . *tini koso* end abruptly. *tini dole* end prematurely, before its proper time. *tini botoilevu* to end abruptly (harsh implication).

itini 1. n. the end, the last (usually as an abrupt transition). A last child may be named iTini, and that name may be passed on to others though they themselves are not a last child. *itini yara* "train" of barkcloth that trails behind a man in traditional formal chiefly costume.

itinitini n. ending, as of a story or action completed.

itini 2. (Eng.) n. commercial agent.

tinimaka v. a transitive form of the verb *tini, tinia*, meaning to finish off, or put a stop to something. May include "tuck in" a *sulu* wrapped around one's waist.

tini-yara (Archaic) v., n. of a chief, to wear a barkcloth form of dress with a long trail behind. *yara* to drag.

itiqa n. sporting javelin formerly used seasonally in competitive games (*veitiqa*). The handle (*dia*) was made of a reed (*gasau*), the blunt head (*ulutoa*) usually of a very hard wood. The javelin skimmed and skittered to its final stopping place which was then marked by a reed stuck in the ground. The objective was distance, not accuracy of aim. There still remain remnants of old playing grounds marked with stones. *itiqatiqa* playing ground for *veitiqa*. *tiqa, tiqava* to throw the *itiqa*. Most commonly, competitions were between different villages. In May 1995 the sport was exhibited at Lakeba on the occasion of the birthday of Ratu Sir Kamisese Mara. Traditionally, women were attracted to the champion.

tiri, tirima v. to drip, as with a leaky roof or faulty faucet. Syn. *turu*.

tiri (or) **tiriwai** n. red mangrove, with red sap and creamy wood, Rhizophora mangle (= R. samoensis), growing half-submerged salt water marshes, vitally important breeding places for many species of fish, and home for crabs. Many drooping prop roots, long thin fruit, and flower calyx with four lobes. The stronger roots were formerly used to make bows used in war (not fishing or hunting) by coastal people. *tiri* means to drip, as of water (*wai*). The bark is rich in tannin, formerly boiled and then used to "cure" fishing nets before the days of nylon cord. *veitiri* grove of mangrove. A hybrid species with R. stylosa, (*tiritabua*) has no flowers and is known as *selala* ("empty of flowers"). Syn. (Nadroga) *kubala*.

tiri tabua n. tall mangrove tree growing on the sea side of *tiriwai*, and is distinguished by white flowers and leaf tips that do not curve down, Rhizophora stylosa.

tiri vanua n. an endemic sp., small tree of the bush, Crossostylis seemannii, Rhizophoraceae, deriving its name from similarity to mangrove *tiri* in its aerial roots as buttresses (though only at the base of the trunk) and bark. The timber is soft, hardly useful even as firewood. Fls white, tiny, 1 cm diam., finely hairy. Lvs opposite, brown hair on underside. The wood is orange. Bark and root used by women as an aid for conception. This "land mangrove" *tiri vanua*, usually grows in a damp place but may be well inland from the sea. All mangroves make long lasting, hot fires as excellent firewood.

tiro, tirova v. to look into a mirror (*iloilo*) or water, more traditionally, at a reflection, usually checking one's own appearance. *na titiro* n. the looking at a reflected image on the water or in a mirror. This is the origin of the name *iloilo* for Fiji's President; his mother in Taveuni used to see her reflection in a pool (by his own account).

tisaiveli (Eng.) n. disciple. Syn. *tisaipeli*.

Tiseba (Eng.) n. December. *ena i kalima ni Tiseba* on the fifth of December.

titeqe tip-toe. *vava titeqe* high-heel shoes.

titi as in *dakaititi*, bow (to be used with arrows), branch or bark of mangrove. Originally, the word for bow as simply *dakai*. With the introduction of guns being called *dakai*, the word for bow became *dakaititi* to make the distinction. The arrow is *sici*. Bow and arrow were used only in war (by men or women), never as a chiefly sport, as in Tonga, and never in fishing.

titi v. to ooze, squish out slowly, to seep out, as pus from a sore, resin from tree-bark, saliva from the mouth.

vakatitiqa-taka v. to doubt something or someone. *E a vakatitiqataka o Seru na isau ni taro nei Mela.* Seru doubted Mel's answer.

vakatitiweli adj. mouth-watering, flavorful. *weli* saliva.

titobu adj. deep (as of water, a pool or the sea, or a hole).

ititoko n. walking stick. fig. used for a last drink, customarily *yaqona*, before departure, "one for the road". Fijian walking sticks were never carved decoratively or elaborately, as they were in Vanuatu. *vakaititoko* v. to use a walking stick. Syn. *itoko*.

titolo n. bare branches (as of *vau*, or *masi*) after bark is stripped off for fibre or barkcloth (*masi*).

tiva v. to go off or turn aside suddenly, with alacrity, as an animal frightened, or a car swerving sharply on the road, a person ducking into the bush to avoid someone.

vaka-tivara (Slang) v. to change the subject of conversation.

tivi n. timber tree, Terminalia litoralis, Combretaceae, similar to T. catappa, but nuts not edible. Caution: *tivi* or variations of that name refers to T. catappa in parts of Vanua Levu, Rakiraki and the West.

tivitivi n. edible reef-fish, yellowish colour.

vakativitivi sideways.

tivoli n. wild or semi-cultivated variety of yam, Dioscorea nummularia, a common source of food available long after the regular yam harvest (February to March). An aboriginal introduction, as were virtually all the yam species. Smooth round stem, spiny near the base, not angled like the cultivated *uvi*, but like the *uvi*, the stem twines to the right, clockwise. Good-size tubers grow deep and take two or three years to develop. They are often sought by burning off the vegetation, which has caused depletion of the earlier forest in western Viti Levu. It has been good Fiji custom to replant a section or leave part in the ground to ensure continuance of supply, but these days that custom is often ignored. Unlike taro (*dalo*) and yam (*uvi*), *tivoli* plays no part in ceremonial food presentations. It is sometimes sold in the market. *tivoli ni Toga* a very large-rooted *tivoli*. *Tikau* and *rauva* are quite distinct, different varieties of this species. They also are sometimes sold at the public market. These wild varieties of yam, and to a less extent cultivated taro, were the staple root-crops of Viti Levu highlanders. Cultivated yam (*uvi*) was important as food and prestigious presentations only at the coast and on small islands where also, it marked the passage of the year with its annual harvest (*yabaki*).

tivote (Eng.) n. teapot. Syn. *tipote*. It is common custom to serve tea with sugar and milk already added with a considerable amount of both.

to, tovaka v. to contain liquid, as a water-well, a bucket or other container, a woman's breasts with milk). *Sa to na sucuna* her breasts are full of milk. *toevu* n. well (for water). *Sa to nawanawa na matana*. He/she has watery eyes (emotion, age, sickness). *E tovaki wai na matana*. His/her eyes are full of tears (but not falling much).

ito n. associate, peer, partisan, party (political). *na iTo ni Veisaqa* the Opposition Party. *au tovaki koya* I take the part of him (support him, defend him). *to vata* closely associated, as of partners, teammates, colleagues. *Tovata* n. confederacy of Lau and Vanua Levu, so named in the latter half of the 1800s, much under the influence of Ma'afu. See *totaka*.

toa 1. n. chicken, orig. the aboriginally introduced jungle fowl, Gallus gallus. A few still exist in remote areas. Most have now interbred with chickens introduced by Europeans. In olden days the eggs of the jungle fowl, very difficult to find and were not commonly eaten by Fijians. Some thought them disgusting, like mucus they would say, though some ate snake eggs and some Polynesians ate turtle eggs. Male jungle fowl have flamboyant colours. They were sometimes caught by tying up a female as an attractant. Genetic evidence with mitochondrial DNA seems now clearly to indicate the Proto-Polynesians brought jungle fowl to Chile in long-range voyages. (*Science News*, Vol. 207, 9 June 2007, p. 356.) They also brought back the sweet potato *kumala* and retained the name from the Americas.

Idiom: *kana yava ni toa* lit. eat chicken feet said to a child who is hyper-active, unable to sit still.

Idiom: *solisoli vakatoa* lit. giving like a rooster, that is, giving a gift and then taking it back, as a rooster gives grain to a hen and then pecks it back, what in the U.S.A. would be called "Indian-giving".

Idiom: *toa makawa*. impolitely refers to a woman, no longer young, who affects continued youth and thus makes a fool of herself. Lit. "old hen".

Idiom: *moce vata na toa* to be extremely tired and go to sleep early, lit. to go to sleep at the same time as the chickens.

toa 2. n. champion, warrior. *toa ni vala* champion (as in sports). *toa ni valu* champion warrior.

toa 3. as in *ulutoa* head of javelin used in the sport of *veitiqa*. It was usually made of very hard wood and attached to a shaft made of a reed stem.

toba n. bay (inlet of the sea), harbour. *Na toba o Laucala* Laucala Bay.

Idiom: *Sa dui cagi ni toba* lit. Each bay has its own different wind, i.e, Your authority is effective in your territory, but is irrelevant here in this territory. Each can be a chief in his own land.

tobe, tobea v. to plait (human hair, basket). Cf. *tali, talia* to weave (mat).

tobe 1. n. traditional "curls" of hair hanging down on one or both sides of the head as a sign of a virgin girl.

tobe 2. n. by extension, pigtail or ponytail as worn by man or woman.

tobo, toboka v. to catch, seize, capture (person, animal). *na lairo, tobotobo rawarawa ena bogi buto* the land-crab *lairo*, easily caught in the dark of night. As an Anglicism, one speaks of catching the bus.

Idiom: *tobo koki* try to "pick up" girls, lit. catch parrots.

vakatobo-i-cu, vakatoboicu-taka v. to turn upside down, bottom up, so to speak.

tobu n. pool, pond, bay. *torobu* very small pond or tidal lake. *tobu ni qalo* swimming pool, *tobu ni sisili* bathing pool, swimming pool. *titobu* deep.

toci, tocia v. to smooth off with sharp blade, as *tocia na voivoi* to cut off spines from the edges of Pandanus leaves preparatory to weaving, usually using a sharp shell such as *drivi* or *kuku*, referred to as *itoci*. The best *voivoi* for mats has such spines, while what is called Rotuman *voivoi* has none, but is only used for inferior mats, or baskets. By ext., *toci* refers in carpentry to plane some wood.

itoci n. plane (carpenter's tool), also the sharp shell used in stripping *voivoi* leaves of spines, preparing the leaves for weaving mats.

todi, todia, todilaka v. to squeeze, usually between the thumb and forefinger, as in squeezing a boil that is mature.

todra adj., v. extremely hot (weather), to scorch (of the hot sun).

todrou, todrova v. to lap up (liquid) without use of cup, bowl, as a man or dog might drink from a stream. This was the Fijian manner of drinking from a stream, without the use of one's hands. In rural areas this is still the custom. In the Viti Levu highlands, no cup of any form was ever used though leaves sometimes served as a temporary substitute to carry water a short distance. The *yaqona* cup (coconut shell) was introduced from the coastal areas.

toevu n. well (for water). *Sa to na toevu.* The well contains water.

togiaki (Archaic). n. Early large twin-hulled Proto-Polynesian sailing canoe with a huge deck, used for ocean voyages between Fiji, Tonga and Samoa. The outrigger side lay to starboard. It could not reverse direction of the sail and had very poor ability to sail to windward. This brought Tongans to Fiji with the southeast tradewind, but made Fiji to Tonga travel very difficult. It was displaced during the late 1700s by Tongan development of the *drua* or *kalia* ocean-going outrigger canoes which could beat to windward by interchanging of bow and stern. While the boat-building skill was Tongan and most particularly Samoan, the timber was more available in Fiji, where the boats were made. The sail-plan was probably inspired from Micronesian concepts according to Fergus Clunie.

togoraka v. to force. Tongans were considered a forceful people and the word Tonga was often transformed to *togo* as in *togoraka*, and in the place-name Korotogo.

toi n. clitoris. Syn. *toitoi, cui,* words not usually spoken.

toka 1. now, just for now, or at that particular time (indicating a change, or temporary situation, espec. in combination with a preceding *sa*). *Keitou sa lako toka.* We (few, exc.) are going now. *Sa vinaka toka.* It's good now (the way it is now). *Sa moce toka mada.* good-bye for now.

toka 2. v. n. to be (location, condition), location (at the time), in the sense of "staying" for a while. *Sa dede na noqu toka e Suva.* I have been staying in Suva a long time.

toka 3. v. to sit down, as on a mat, or the grass.

toka, vakatoka v. to proclaim, announce.

vakatoka, vakatoka or **vakatoka yaca** v. to name, give a name (to a person). This is a ceremonial matter for people, boats, buildings. Often the entire set of two or three personal names is passed on to a younger person, including even a title as part of the name. The resultant relation with one's namesake (*yaca*) is close. In older Fijian custom the namesake was hardly ever the direct parent of the child. Family names as surnames did not exist until recently adopted, following the European custom. Formerly, a person might be accorded a new name at a different stage of life, and even after death. In villages, the major house-sites (*yavu*) all have formal names. Properly, in referring to a family, one uses the name of their house-site, not their own name. Place-names have been ubiquitous in every part of Fiji, though many are lost to memory.

tokamoce refers to leftover cooked food to be eaten the next day.

vakatoka ua v., n. the action of surfing on a wave, a Polynesian recreation, especially anciently at Vuna, Taveuni. No ancient surfboard has been preserved. The custom is now a modern sport, mostly European. Some tourists come to Fiji for that purpose.

vaka-tokatoka Idiom: to practice songs or *meke*.

ivakatoka n. prop, something used to prop up another object.

tokatoka (ni gone) n. placenta.

itokatoka n. extended family within a clan (*mataqali*), type of kin-group in some parts of Fiji and now applied throughout Fiji by the Native Lands Commission. The word implies a place where the family is staying. Where the concept exists, this is usually the "true" occupant of the land, the people entitled to use the land. There was never any concept of land ownership in the European sense. Land was held in trust with usage rights. The Native Land Commission standardised the *mataqali* as a major landowning unit in official records, as if the clan were the owner. In Lau a rough equivalent of *itokatoka* is the *bati-ni-lovo*. In Nadroga/Navosa there are *bito* or *beto* and in Ba, *kete* or *nalewe*. On

Vanua Levu one sometimes hears *kausivi*, according to Roth. Members are always related by marriage or birth and adoption of individuals. In larger kin-groups, such as clans, some members may have joined in, coming from elsewhere. The *itokatoka* is literally a family, and is considered as such. All members are intimately related by birth and marriage. There can be fifty members or more of the family. The distinction of nuclear family was formerly less emphasized than the *itokatoka*.

tokaitua n. mountain ridge. As a formal name Tokaitua refers to an extension of the Nakauvadra range. Migrations from Ra down into Tailevu followed this ridge part of the way. On Vanua Levu Island a significant ridge extends out to Udu, separating out Macuata Province from Cakaudrove. Syn. *tuatua*.

tokalau n. northeast wind. Original Fijian names of directions were based on typical wind directions. There was no notion of North, East, South, West and, of course, no compass. Syn. *vualiku*. (Tonga) *tokelau* north.

tokalau cevaceva n. southeast (or) southeasterly wind, the prevailing trade wind. This is a modernism, adapting to European names of directions. Above the equator, above the doldrums, the tradewind is from the northeast.

Tokalau-i-loma n. Middle East (Lebanon, Sinai, Kuwait, etc.). *Tokalau* here implies an easterly direction but Fijians had no notion of an exact east.

tokalulu, tokalulu-taka v. to peer, as from a position of concealment. *lulu* owl.

toka, toka-vaka v. to proclaim, announce.

toka ivalu n. declaration of war. Syn. *tagi ivalu*.

itokani n. companion, chum, colleague. Implied is one who is protective, supportive. *Na nona itokani dredre*. His/her close friend.

tokara v. to put on (kettle on stove, pot on fire, clothes such as a coat). *tokara na vinivo* put on the dress. Also *vakatokara*. See *daramaka*.

tokatu v., n. to move or go (from one place of residence to another), (Resepctful) to arrive.

itoka ulu n. roof-thatch.

toka-ulu, tokaulu-taka v. to attach or fix thatching on a roof. Syn. *bevu, bevuya*.

tokavoki n. whirlwind, which is always extremely dangerous. Houses are swept away, boats lifted out of the water. Usually they have a narrow base, unlike the tornado so common in the U.S.A. that can often wipe out a town.

toki, tokia (or) **tokotaki** v. to shift a heavy object, or move, as people from one residence to another. *Sa toki na koroturaga ki Suva*. The captital city was shifted over to Suva. *tokitaki* shifted.
Idiom: *toki yani* has died, a euphemism, lit. shifted away.

itoki n. beak (bird, certain fish), hooked protuberance (warclub).

toki, tokia, tokilaka v. to peck. This may be very forceful, as by a hawk.

toko, tokona v. to prop up, support (a point of view, another person's cause), be protective toward.
Idiom: *gone ni toko* favourite child; "apple" of the parent's eye.

itoko n. prop or pole to hold something up or out (such as a sail). *ititoko* walking stick.

itokotoko n. bayonet (because it protrudes and protects).

toko, tokoca v. to steep or sop something in a liquid, usually a starch-food in tea, or Fijian pudding (*vakalolo*) in coconut cream. Cf. *toni, tonia* to dip, steep, soak. *bolomo, bolomona* to steep.

tola adj. hollow. *vaka-tola-taka* to hollow it out.

tolili n. vehicle, now almost any vehicle, but formerly, and to some extent still today, implies a new vehicle, one to be admired. Possibly this notion originates from weapons or articles of value hung about the house, to be admired.

tolo-na n. stem (plant, tree), trunk (tree, human). *tolonikau* tree trunk. See *gau*.

tolu three. *vakatolu* three times. *tolusagavulu* thirty. *tolutolu* all three. *tolu na drau* three hundred. *katolu* third. *e rua na ikatolu* two-thirds. Syn. (Tonga) *tolu*.

tolua (or) **toluwa** (or) **qolua** n. (Rare) bamboo water container, three to five feet long with leaf-plug, or fringe of leaves tied at top when used to add water to *yaqona* bowl. Used formerly to carry water, mainly in the highlands where pottery was unavailable. Girls normally fetched water.

toma, tomana 1. v. to accompany (person). *Keirau a vetomani tu kei Seru ki na koro*. I accompanied Seru to the village.

toma, tomana 2. v. to continue (story, report, letter, one's studies). *lai tomana na noqu vuli* go and continue my studies.

itoma n. the continuing part, sequel.

Tomanivei n. name of highest mountain in Fiji, 1300 m, near Nadarivatu in central Viti Levu, named Mt. Victoria by Adolph Brewster. Residing nearby at Nadarivatu for many years, he was one of the first persons known to climb to the top. Many people incorrectly believe the name is Tomanivi and think that is an adaption of Adam and Eve. Tomanivei actually means "bubbling and springing from where?" according to Brewster whose information came directly from locals. The mountain's name suggests the oddity that from different faces of the mountain flow sources to the major rivers Ruwailevu (Sigatoka River), the Wailevu (Rewa River) and the Ba River. Located in Naitasiri Province, it is near the borders of three other provinces: Nadroga/Navosa, Ba, and Ra. Nearby are villages Nasoqo and Navai. The mountain is home to two tree species, *vugayali* and *vugayalo*, not yet confirmed as to scientific name, though both are on exhibit at Wainadoi Gardens. *Vugayalo* is totemic to tribe Nacavodo. *Vugayali* was reported by Basil Thomson to figure large in the legendary Nakauvadra wars of Degei, the snake-god, and also in the origin of the Vugalei people of Tailevu Province. They are distinct from the well known *vuga*, usually said to be Metrosideros collina, though the name *vuga* also applies to two species of Geissois because the name suggests a tree with bright red blossoms.

Tomasi or **tomasi** (Biblical) n. doubting Thomas, as in the idiom: *Au Tomasi kina*. I doubt that is true, I wait to see concrete evidence. See *vakatitiqa* to doubt.

tomata (Eng.) n. tomato, an introduced plant.

tomi, tomika v. to pick up, gather up (many small, scattered things, fruits or flowers fallen from a tree, small bits of rubbish around a compound). *itukutuku tomiki* rumour. *na tomitomi* the task of picking up such things. *Na cava o cakava?* What are you doing? *Tomitomi*. Picking up things (from the ground).

itomitomi n. selection of scattered items, as with diverse essays or stories in a book, or things gathered up from a scattered condition.

tomo adj. dirty, usually said of a child, whose face or nose need wiping or washing.

tomole n. plant, leaves sweet smelling, Ocimum basilicum, Lamiaceae, florets white or purple, used in perfuming coconut oil. Syn. *domole, tamole* and other variations.

tona 1. n. sexually transmitted disease (STD), gonorrhoea. There has been no separate Fijian word for syphilis. The English word is used. Syn. *mate-ca*.

tona 2. (Lau) n. yaws, formerly a very common ulcerous disease among children throughout the South Pacific, caused by a spirochete very closely related to the spirochete that causes syphilis. Syn. *coko*.

tone (Eng.) n. metric tonne.

toni, tonia v. to dunk, steep. Fijians often dunk or sop their starch-foods in a liquid, especially biscuits in tea. Biscuits may thus be eaten without butter or jam, and are softened and easier on the teeth. *toni somo* soak in mud in process of dyeing black some Pandanus leaves for mat-weaving or sinnet cord for decorative binding. *toni moce* to soak overnight. See *bolomo*.

tono, tonoka, tonolaka v. to poke, as with the pointed fingers, or a sharp instrument. *itono* poker, stick or any long, pointed thing used to poke.

Idiom: *vosa tonotono mata* talk accusingly, poke one's nose in the affairs of others, or one's finger in another's face, direct talking, lecturing other people on their behaviour.

topito (Eng.) n. torpedo. *topito niukilia* nuclear torpedo.

topoi n. a type of Fijian pudding, boiled or fried, mostly just wheat flour, leavening and water, sometimes sugar and coconut cream (*lolo*). Common breakfast food.

toqa, toqa v. to cut with an incision as on wood, stone or metal, to pierce, to make a sharp marking, check-off as on a questionnaire form or to underline something written, as emphasis. *na vosa ka toqai na rukuna*. the words that are underlined. See *tosi, tosia*.

itoqa 1. n. (Anglicism) check-off, "tick", as on a questionnaire filled out, something checked.

itoqa 2. n. (Anglicism) a typographical accent associated with a vowel, as with *itoqa leka* hyphen. *itoqa-dela* macron. *itoqa-ruku* underline. *itoqa cabe* acute accent, and *itoqe siro* accent grave.

toqali-taka v. to carry something over the shoulder, hanging from a stick, as with a bunch of bananas. *itoqali* something carried in this manner.

toqi, toqina v. to coil up (rope, weaving material). *toqitoqini* coiled, plaited (of hair, usually considered a feature of Indian women).

itoqi 1. n. coil or roll. *itoqi ni dali* coil of rope. *itoqi ni filimu* roll of film.

itoqi 2. n. coil of woven pandanus leaf used as a prop or "seat" for Fijian clay pots which all have had only rounded bottoms.

Tora n. specific, rather minor title, of Dreketi (Tora Dreketi), and also LomaiViti (Tora i Bau at Batiki). The title originates from Verata. It implies a standard-bearer. The title has been used for the head of the *mataqali sauturaga*, the clan that empowers the chief. Also used as a man's personal name.

tori v. to prick up the ears, as of a dog alerted.

toro n. pig pen. Some Fijians keep a pig pen near their house where it is convenient to feed them and supply water, though it may not be very sanitary.

toro, toroya 1. v. to move, shift. *toro sobu* to decline, decrease, often in a critical sense, as in *Sa torosobu na nodra ivakarau.* Their (many) behaviour has taken a turn for the worse. *torocake* built up, increased, improved as with company profits or improved behaviour.
Idiom: *ivakarau toro sobu* despicable behaviour.

toro, toroya 2. v. to shave, person's beard or soft body hair. *yame ni toro* razor blade. *torotoro* shaving. To shave the head is *tasi, tasia na uluna*.

itoro 1. n. razor. In the highlands, early Fijians used the sharp edge of a bamboo sliver. In coastal areas they used a broken shell. Broken glass then became popular. Almost all now use razor blades. Village men have sometimes resharpened blades by rubbing inside a cup or glass. *itoro livaliva* n. electric shaver.

itoro 2. n. rasp (carpenter's tool) to smooth out wood. Formerly, Fiji boatbuilders used the tail of a stingray. *itoci* is a carpenter's plane, or formerly, a shell used as a plane for smoothing wood. See *varo* to saw (previously, to rasp, before introduction of saws.)

toro cake v. to move up, develop, increase, improve. *toro sobu* decrease, decline, shift downward. *na vuli torocake* higher education. See *toro, toroya,* above.

vakatorocake-taka (Anglicism) v. to develop (the economy, the land), a modern concept.

veivakatorocake-taki n. development (usually economic), a modern word.

tosi 1. (Eng.) n. toast, as served at an urban breakfast.

tosi, tosia 2. (Eng.) v. to toss, toss up, as of a coin, heads or tails winning.

tosi, tosia 3. v. to make a marking, scratch with pointed object; modernly, to check off, to "tick" as on a questionnaire. *tositosi vulavula* white marking(s). Syn. *toqa, toqa*.

itosi n. "tick" or check-off, mark or streak. *na tositosi* the checking off. Syn. *toqa* which is rather more forceful. Originally meaning was simply to mark distinctively.

toso, tosoya v. to shift along, move along (of things or people). *Toso!* Get moving! *toso tani mai!* come away (from there to here)! *na veitosoyaki* the moving about, the travel, getting around, the moving here and there.

toso, tosova v. of a person, to shift toward (someone, something)

totaka v., n. to give support to (another person's views or position, or an ideal), go along with. *na noqu totaka na dina* my sticking by the truth. See *to*.

vakatoto v. to turn away, in refusal or rejection.y

totobu n. small deep pool surrounded by shallows, at swampy land or reef. See *tobu*.

veitotoci n. feeling by touch, smoothing. See *toci*.

totodro n. well known, wild and common creeping herb with semi-circular leaves on erect stems, Centella asiatica, Umbelliferae, tends to grow in wet places, often around houses, probably aboriginal introduction to Fiji. In India, an Ayurvedic medicine, Brahmi (Brahma-manduki), and used medicinally in Tonga (called tono) and Samoa (called tongo). In Fiji, used externally on cuts, internally for aches of the joints, stomach ailments, general weakness. Some use the leaves to alleviate diarrhoea. Occasionally served as a vegetable.

itotogi n. penalty, fine, punishment. *totogi mate* n.,v., death sentence, sentenced to death, discontinued in Fiji. (There was formerly an official hangman.) Syn. (Tonga) *totongi*.

totogi-taka v. to penalise, punish, to fine.

totoka adj. beautiful.

totokia (Archaic) n. so-called pineapple war club, a beaked battle hammer with heavy swollen head and beak intended mostly for quick jab to the skull. This club did not require the wide sweeping blow of many other clubs. It was often intended for assassinations with one quick short blow but it was a large club, difficult to conceal, often used for display in ceremonial duties.

totolo quick. *Totolo!* Be quick! *lako vakatotolo* go quickly. *vakatotolotaka* to speed it up. *Me vakatotolotaki!* Speed it up! Syn. *kusa*. (Lau) *remo*.
Idiom: (Anglicism) *Na kena totolo na kena vinaka* The quicker the better.

vakatotomuri, vakatotomuria v. to imitate, follow the example of (someone). *muri, muria* v. to follow.

totowiwi n.plant, three-leafed shamrock, yellow flowers, Oxalis corniculata, Oxalaceae, grows in damp areas, near houses or wherever people urinate (*wiwi*), as implied in the name. Medicinal uses, unproven.

touva v. to glue together sections of barkcloth using a vegetable paste, a starchy product such as cooked taro (*dalo*), cassava (*tavioka*), or arrowroot (*yabia*). Properly, the use of such pastes should not be necessary.

tovaka v. to take the part of, support, defend. *E tovaki Seru o Tukana.* Tukana takes the part of Seru. *na veitovaki vakapolitiki* the political involvement.

tovisi n. Ribbon fish, Trichiurus haumela, edible, silver colour, seasonal. Syn. *tovici, beleti.*

itovo 1. n. customary behaviour (of person, animal), habit. *itovo vinaka* good behaviour. *itovo vakasisila* abominable behaviour. Syn. *ivalavala, ivakarau.*

itovo 2. n. manner, regular way (of doing something). *na itovo ni veiqaravi* the manner of treatment (as in medical care). *na itovo ni rai* attitude.

itovo 3. n ethnological custom(s). *itovo vakaViti* Fijian custom(s).

tovolea v. to try, to attempt.

vakatovolei n. testing, testing out. *na vakatovolei iyaragi* the testing of weapons.

veivaka-tovolei n. the testing period, trial run, practice trial.

vakatovotovo n. testing, practice.

vakatovotovo-taka v. to practice (for testing or to improve).

tovu 1. (Eng.) top, as a child's toy.

tovu 2. (Eng.) n. Top Shell, Trochus (or) Techtis pyramis. A smaller version of the commercial Trochus shell. See *sici.*

tovure v. to overflow. *tovure noqu bilo* my cup overflows (an Anglicism). See *vure.*

tovutovula adj. brackish, of water.

tu 1. to be, indicating a state of being, to exist, implying it has been that way for a while, or has been in that place for a while. *E lako tu.* He/she is gone. *tu vakai koya* independent. *E vinaka tu na waqa.* The boat is in good condition. *evica na vosa ka sega ni tu eliu* some words that did not exist before. *veituyaki* located here and there in a rather scattered fashion. Cf. *toka*, which indicates a changed condition or state of things. See also *tiko* that refers only to the present.

Idiom, exclaiming an announcement, surprise or discovery: *A tu!* There he/she/it is! *Sa ra tu na Turaga!* The chief has arrived!

tu 2. v. to have. *Sa tu vei au e dua.* I have one. *tu ga e lomana* have thoughts, feelings kept to oneself, unexpressed, where open expression of opinion would be considered intrusive or rude. It is not customary to express opinions in front of someone senior.

tu 3. v. to stand *Tu! Tu cake!* Stand! Stand up! *na Tucake Tale* the Resurrection (of Christ). *Matanitu Tu Vakawawa* Interim Government. *tu vakarau* be prepared, stand ready. *tu vakatikitiki* stand aside. Syn. *wavu = tu cake* stand up.

Tualeita n. See below, *tuatua.*

tuatua n. mountain ridge. *tokaitua* principal mountain range, usually referring to the one on eastern Viti Levu, course of the Spirit Path (*Sala ni Yalo*), and of many migratory travels south from Nakauvadra mountains, more specifically named the *Tualeita*. Also, the mountain chain along the length of Vanua Levu, separating Macuata from Cakaudrove.

tu lo v. to attack under cover of darkness. Fijian attacks are almost always unexpected. In combat, Fijians are direct and confrontational only as a last resort or when they are fairly certain of victory. They excel at making an ambush.

tuba (or) **e tuba** outside (usually of house, the immediate vicinity outside). *Tuba! Laki tuba!* Go outside! Get out (of the house)! *tautuba* completely outside (usually outside the house compound). *curu yani ki tautuba* go outside. *na daku ni tuba* n. outside the lagoon, outside the reef. *Gusu ni Tuba* n. local name for the lower reaches of the Ba River. (*gusu* mouth).

Idiom: *lasa e tuba* have an affair outside of marriage.

tube, tubea v. to hold in the hand, often said of offering a whaletooth.

Idiom: *tube tabua* to bring a presentation of whaletooth.

itubetube n. handle (as of a bag, basket). *kato vakatubetube* handbag.

tube, tubera 1. v. to lead, guide with the hand, as with a child, to take by the hand, and by ext., to guide in the sense of teaching. *veitube* hold each other by the hand. Acceptable behaviour for same-sex friends, especially young ones. Romantic couples or married couples do not normally hold hands in public.

tube, tubera 2. v. to hold by the handle (basket, handbag, bucket) or ceremonially, to hold a whaletooth when presenting it.

veitube (Archaic) n., v. formal marriage, to marry. This is an old, properly traditional word used mostly for chiefs and ladies. The currently used word for formal, ceremonial marriage *vakamau* was introduced with Christianity (Tongan fakamau) More traditionally, a man would formalise marriage by providing a house for the woman (*vakavaletaka na yalewa*). *lotu ni veitube* church marriage ceremony. Bride price, so important in parts of western Melanesia, was not common custom in Fiji.

Since the late 1700s, a whaletooth sufficed in many cases, several teeth in the case of important women. Wives and concubines were often given by a defeated tribe. Anciently, lower-class commoners had little if any ceremony in taking a wife. In many cases taking a woman for one night meant you had just taken her as a mate. Her relatives would normally enforce that.

"tubelight" (Eng. Slang) of a person, slow on the uptake, slow to react or understand, as with the hesitation of a fluorescent lamp to be lit.

tuboku (Archaic) v., n. *tono buka*, to burn scars on the human body, chest, shoulders or back, prodding it as with a burning coconut midrib *sasa*. This was done as body decoration or sometimes as punishment for a child. Syn. *tavusasa*.

tubu v. to grow in size or amount (plants, animals, people). *tubu ni dra* (Anglicism) n. high blood pressure, hypertension, formerly unknown to Fijians.

tubu n. interest (on money), profit (of business), growth.

tubu cake n., v. increase, to increase.

vakatubu, vakatubura v. to give rise to, to make grow, to cause, to set up *vakatubura na rere* to cause fear. *vakatubu leqa* v., n. to cause trouble. *Me vakatubu na lovo*. Set up the earth-oven (a request). See *tubu, tubura*.

ivakatubu (Anglicism) n. baking powder. Leavening was unknown to Fijians though European-style bread and cakes are now eaten frequently.

tubu koso sudden, suddenly.

tubua 1. n. edible vegetable plant, Amaranthus sp., probably an aboriginal introduction of Polynesians or Proto-Polynesians, semi-wild, a virtual weed, the leaves cooked and eaten by coastal Fijians (not highlanders), and also by Indians, who introduced their own varieties and cultivate them. Syn. *moca, driti*. (Hindi) chauraiya. Interestingly, some Amaranthus species yield edible seeds, a common food in Africa but no grain was every grown or eaten as a basic food by Fijians before the introduction of rice.

tubua 2. adj. overgrown with weeds, of a garden or path.
Idiom: *Sa tubua na sala ki na nona koro*. He/she no longer visits the village. i.e., has not maintained traditional relationships with village kinfolk, suggested by the path (*sala*) being overgrown by vegetation. Maintaining the relationship can be expensive for urban Fijians who may be expected to provide for their rural relatives. Also, some Fijians have left their village due to internal disputes, religious differenes, shortage of land or simply that their village is remote from their employment, their children's schooling or medical clinics and shops or markets for their farm produce.

tubu-na n. grandparent. *Tubu i Seru* Seru's grandparent, which may serve as a name.

tubu-da n. our forbears, our forefathers, our ancestors. *tubu-qu* my forbears.

tubu, tubura v. to grow upon or within, particularly an emotion. *E tuburi au e dua na cudru*. I am becoming angry.

itubutubu n. parents (as of schoolchildren).

tubutubu n. growth (usually of a plant or creature, but could apply to the economy).

tubusiviti-ira n. middle finger (of the hand).

Tu-cake-tale (Anglicism). Resurrection.

tudei permanent. *Vunivola tudei* Permanent Secretary. *dei* firm.

tudonu as in *tamata tudonu* adult person.

Tudrau n. chiefly title at village Dravo, Tailevu Province.

Tuei n. chiefly title at Wainikeli..

tuga, tugana v. to put away in its place, to put aside carefully, to place in memory, keep in mind.

tugalala (or **tu galala**) n. independence. Also refers to a Fijian who has formally arranged to live independently, usually on his own personal farm, separate from his clan, and not owing traditional obligations to his village community. This system was introduced by the British but opposed by Ratu Sukuna. He himself lived totally separate and independent of any clan or village but he believed that other Fijians were not ready for that type of freedom that he insisted to have for himself. This system could hardly succeed when the independent Fijian remained living close to his village, say as in leasing land from his own clan. Relatives are accustomed to impose traditional and family obligations that most Fijians could not bring themselves to refuse for fear of being socially ostracised and despised by their own kin.

tugadra n. small, silver, edible crevally-shaped fish, schooling seasonally around November, Selar crumenophthalmus. On Lakeba Island, village Yadrana, and at Fulaga Island, village Naividamu, the schooling of this fish is celebrated as an annual *"balolo"*, a festive occasion. Syn. (West, Kadavu, Rewa) *yatule,* (Nadro) *jule*.

tugavu n., adj. usually of a child, dirty face, runny nose, etc.

tui 1. (West) n. dog.

Tui 2. n. King or Chief, chiefly title followed usually by place-name or tribal name. *Tui Nawaka* Chief of Nawaka. *Roko Tui Bau* Chief of Bau. *Tui Sabeto* Chief of Sabeto. Many such titles were relatively modern adoptions, since Colonial times, inspired from Verata, adapted from Tongan titles. The Tui title has become very popular in usage, displacing many of the older, properly Fijian titles such as Vunivalu, Vunisa, Momo, or is added to them as an additional title. In formal ceremonies both types of titles may be cited. *tui* king. *vakatui* royal. *na matavuvale vakatui* the royal household. *Tuina* is a title at Nacamaki, Koro Island. Only in Cakobau's time did the newly invented Tui Viti title come to be used by Europeans. Cakobau conceded any claim to that title to Queen Victoria and her successors. *tui* also means dog around western Viti Levu.

itui n. string (of crabs, small fish etc., strung together). *tuitui* strung together (of crabs, fish, etc.) *na ituitui* the items (crabs, fish) hung in the string. Syn. *idoi*.

tui boto (Anglicism) n. lit. "king frog", referring to the European dance, the conga, often done for tourists, a long line of people each holding onto the one in front of them, the line weaving around the room with a sort of hopping motion, suddenly reversing direction. Lots of laughter.

Tui Tabu n. Pope (Roman Catholic). The Pope actually visited Fiji in 1986.

tuirara 1. n. village steward who apportions feast foods at food-presentation ceremonies. This is a delicate task with the recipients watching closely to see if they get their fair share. He will sometimes have assistants who help guide him in allocation acceptable portions.
Idiom: *Wasewase o Tuirara*. Said of one who keeps a large portion for himself when his duty was to divide the portions into fair shares. *wase* divide. Syn. *votavota vaka Tuirara*. *vota* v. to share out.

tuirara 2. n. local warden of the Methodist church.

tuitui n. (Polyn.) candlenut tree with useful oil nuts, Aleurites moluccana, formerly used for lamps and for hair dye in coastal areas. Syn. *lauci, sikeci*.

tuitui n. goshawk. Syn. *latui*.

tuituina adj. very salty (water, food). *rui tutuina* much too salty. *wai tui* saltwater. Syn. *konakona*.

tuka-na n. grandfather on the side of either father or mother. *na tukai Seru vakarua* Seru's great grandfather. *Tukai* is the usual abbreviation for grandfather, but may be applied respectfully in referring to other elderly gentleman. Like several other terms for family relationships, *Tukai* (or) *Tukana* may be used as a personal name if one has been named after a grandfather. *tukadra vakarua* their (many) great grandfather(s). *na tukaqu vakatolu* my great great grandfather. *na veitukani* n. the grandfather(s) and grandchild(ren) together.

tukai n. grandfather. Syn. (Lau) *tua*.

tukada n. our forebears, ancestors, always preceded by "the", as in *na tukada*.

tuki, tukia 1. v. to knock, to hammer. *tatuki, tatuki-taka na uluna* to strike (someone) on the head. *tukia ena mata ni katuba* knock on the door.

tuki, tukia 2. v. to punch. Syn. *vacu*.

tukiyadre n. Cape Gooseberry, Husk Tomato, Peruvian origin. Very small edible fruit. Children knock the ripe gooseberry against their forehead to make a popping sound, hence the Fijian name. *yadre-na* forehead. Many local names for this annual plant.

ituki n. hammer. *na itukituki* the hammering, knocking on something hard.

tukituki, tukitukia v. to hammer it.

itukituki toa (ni qio) n. dorsal fin of a shark that may appear above the surface of the water.

tuku, tukuca v. to lower something by loosening, usually something suspended by a rope. *tukuca na velovelo* lower the dory, rowboat.

tukuna v. to tell (it). *sa tukuni* it has been told (referring to legends, prophesies). *tukuna vei au* tell me. *Kua ni tukuni au*. Don't tell on me. *tukunataki* related, already told. Syn. (Nasavusavu) *avola*.

tukuni, tukunitaka v. to recount traditional folk stories, legends. (

itukuni n. traditional tale, folk story, legend.

itukutuku n. report. *itukutuku tomiki* rumour. *dau-vola-itukutuku* reporter for the news media, report-writer. *itukutuku raraba* official reports on tribal (*yavusa*) background, prepared for the Native Lands Commission from signed testimony of local elders known as the *Veitarogi vakavanua*. *itukutuku ni leqa* obituary, announcement of death(s). *itukutuku saumi* n. advertisement. *Tabana ni Vakau iTukutuku* Information Department (govt).

vakatukutuku adj. tells stories about others, gossipy.

vakau itukutuku n. communications.

tukutukuna v. to boast. *E tukutukuni koya tiko*. He/she is bragging.

vakatulewa v. to pass judgement, to judge, determine.

tuli, tulia na kuro v. to shape and make the clay pot. *qele ni tuli kuro* potting clay. *dau tuli kuro* n. potter. The potter's wheel is not known. Syn. (Nadro.) *voca*.

tulou (or) **tilou** (Tonga) interjection of apology for passing too close or above another person. It is considered rude to stand above a person of high status, or to pass the hand above their head. There is an implicit possible threat to such a position or motion.

"tulsi" (Hindi) n. basil, holy herb-plant grown around Indian houses, naturalised as a weed. This is the potherb basil, Ocimum basilicum, Labiatae, used as such by Europeans in Fiji. Similarly, sage grows virtually as a weed. Neither is normally used by Fijians.

tuna, tunaka v. to gut (fish, eel, chicken, pig) usually before cooking.

tuna (West, Kadavu) n. eel. Syn. *duna*.

tunatuna n. conger eel, Conger cenereus. Syn. *baku* (West).

Tu-ni-kalou n. a minor chiefly title at village Vanualevu, Tokatoka Territory. Culturally this is of Rewa, but is assigned politically to Tailevu Province.

Tunimata n. a minor chiefly title in Verata, village Navuruvuru, and in Bureta, at Tai.

Tunisa n. a minor chiefly title of tribe Dewala at villages Nagigi and Nacavanadi, near Nasavusavu, Cakaudrove. The origin is near Nakorotubu, Ra Province.

TuniToga n. title of the spokesman (*matanivanua*) of the chiefly Vunivalu, Tui Kaba at Bau Island. He heads clan Matanivanua with five extended families and some ten house-sites on Bau Island.

tunu, tunuga v. to warm up food that was previously cooked. *vakatuna* (causative) to make it warm.

vakatunudra (or) **tunudra** n. ceremony celebrating the fourth night after a birth. Formerly, at coastal locations, blood from the birth was washed off and excretia from the baby washed away in the sea. *dra* blood. Feast is prepared for the grandfather and relatives of the new baby who have attended the *roqoroqo* ceremony to which they brought gifts at the birth of a baby. The fourth night *tunudra* ceremony implies the baby will probably survive since it has lived through the first few days of life.

vakatunuloa n. temporary shed, usually erected for special occasions in the village and at suburban homes, often made for marriages, ceremonial feasts. Modernly, Fijians often rent the corrugated iron sheets used for temporary roofs. Supporting posts may be decorated with branches of coconut palm and flowers.

tunua n. open, outdoor fire-place for grass or bamboo fire that hardens pottery and makes it resistant to water. All firing of pots is done outdoors with no furnace. Pottery made for tourist trade is not always heated sufficiently for use as a water container, flower vase or cooking pot.

tunumaka adj., n. hot and humid (the air, the weather), humidity.

tupeni (Eng. Obsolete.) n. tuppence, two pence. (There used to be such a coin.) Occasionally used as a personal name Tupeni, the only way one hears the word today.

vakatura v. to propose, or move a motion in a meeting. *Au sa vakatura me sogo na bose*. I propose that the meeting be closed.

turaga n. gentleman, chief. Long ago adopted from coastal areas, *turaga* was anciently an unknown word among the indigenous Melanesians. (The same applies to *marama*, lady). *na turaga bale* the high chief. *na gone turaga* the high chief.

turaga ni cakacaka n. supervisor, man in charge of the work or task.

turaga ni koro n. village headman, an administrator, usually not of high rank, paid a small stipend. He manages government regulations in the village, and collections of money but has no chiefly status. Word and functions created by colonial officials.

turaga ni lewa n. judge, magistrate (of court).

turaga ni lovo n. man in charge of cooking a *lovo* earth oven.

turaga ni ovisa n. police officer (polite term).

turaga ni ivalu n. military officer, soldier (polite form).

turi, turia v. to prepare washed, starchy mash from grated roots of arrowroot *yabia* or some wild yams *kaile,* for food.

turu, turuma (or) **turuva** v. to drip, drip on (as rain through a roof, hair-dye on the face, tea from the spout of a teapot). *Sa turumi au na uca.* Rain is dripping on me. *e dua na ituruturu* one drop.

turu ni dra n. menstruation, menses.

turu (ni vale) n. eves (of a house).

vakaturu buto v. to become covered (of sun or moon) by sudden clouds, darkening the sky. *vale vakaturubuto* shade-house (nursery for young plants).

tusanaka v. to confess, to talk truly of important matters. *A lai tusanaki koya vua na bete*. He/she went to confess to the priest.

Tusiti (Eng.) Tuesday. Syn. *Tusite*.

tutaka v. to support, be supportive, as people may be to their elders, their chief.
tutu-na 1. n. corner (building, playing field), column (written by media correspondent). *Na tutuna nei Mesake* Mesake's Column (in the newspaper).
tutu-na 2. n. dorsal fin of a fish.
tutu 3. v. to beat bark-cloth in order to join the pieces and smooth out the texture.
tutu 4. exactly, as in *sigalevu tutu*, exactly midday, noon. *bogilevu tutu* midnight exactly.
itutu 1. n. title. *itutu vakaturaga* chiefly title(s). *na keni itutu* his/her title. Some tribes *yavusa* have no formal title for their chief and some do. Some require a formal installation ceremony, and some do not. Titles have varied considerably and some have changed with time. In the west, there are Momo or Momo Levu. Vunivalu and Vunisa are old titles concentrated perhaps on Viti Levu (there is also a Vunisa at Weilagi, Taveuni Island). Vunivalu is the classical title on most of Viti Levu. Sau exist at Vuna and Lakeba (or perhaps more properly, Kabara) and Ra, and a Roko Sau at Totoya, corresponding to the Tongan Hau. Other titles, outside Viti Levu, include Ra Malo, Ra Masi, and Takala.

The title Tui (followed by a place-name), usually gives a form of address "Ratu" to the chief, a custom that originated in Verata which had extremely early contact with Tonga. Many if not most other places in Fiji have adopted the Tui (with place name) and Ratu form of address. This dates only from colonial times. The widespread use of Ratu has no justification in tradition outside of Verata. The word Roko might precede the Tui, as in the RokoTui Bau, and there are RokoTui also at Cautata, Namata, Namara, Viwa, Kiuva, Kadavu, Nakelo, and Ovalau. Rokotuni is an alternative.
itutu 2. n. position, stance, as in *na itutu ni Lotu me baleta na Siga Tabu* the position of the Church on the issue of Sunday.
itutu 3. n. stand, where something is placed. *itutu ni TV* n. television stand.
vakatutu n. position or "stand" (on some issue), point of view expressed, proposal. *Na cava na nomu vakatutu?* What is your proposal, point of view?
vakatutu-taka v. to propose.
vakanatutu adv., adj. sideways (as a crab walks), on its side. *davo vakanatutu* lie down on one's side. Syn. *vakababa*.
tutu-balebale v., adj. to be unsteady on the feet, as a person dizzy or drunk.
tutuga v. to light (a fire, lantern, matches).
tutaka v. stand up for (someone, something). *tutaki koya* stand up for him/her *vaka-tutu-taki* proposed.
tutua (Colo) n. any family relative who is older than the person speaking. Term of reference or term of address. Most commonly used for one's father's father.
itutuvi n. blanket, a covering, modernly of cloth, formerly of barkcloth or woven matting. *iTutuvi kuta nei RadiniBau* name of Cakobau's warclub, lit. "Sedge-blanket of the Queen of Bau", sometimes rendered as *A i Tutuvi ni Ranadi i Bau"*, dropping the reference to sedge. Originally a Namosi club, it was given at Cession for Queen Victoria, and later returned to Fiji and used as mace for Legislative Council, more recently for Parliament. *tuvi, tuvia* v. to cover over.
tuva, tuva̱ (or) **tuvana** v., n. to arrange, arranged, array, to stack (boxes, stones for a fish fence). *tuvanaka* v. to arrange in detail, carefully.
ituvatuva n. arrangement, classification, array, programme.
iTuvatuva ni iLavo n. government Budget. *tuva-ilavo* v. to set out a financial plan, usually an annual budget for a company or organisation.
tuveitavaki v., n. have a fit, possessed (by a devil) usually, or having an epileptic fit, "interim, waiting state". The notion of a devil possessing a person for a while serves as an acceptable, understandable justification for temporary, erratic behaviour that would be otherwise reprehensible or socially unacceptable. It can be a kind of safety valve in an extremely closely controlled society.
tuva itutu (Anglcism) n. *na tuva itutu ni koro ni vuli* the school graduation ceremony, when degrees and prizes are handed out. *tuva* to arrange or stack. *itutu* title(s).
tuvakei n. plant, Tephrosia purperea, Leguminosae, formerly used as a fish poison in quiet ponds. Pounded, released underwater. Fish float to the surface, dead but edible. A totemic plant at village Naqara in the Colo East highlands, where the name is not to be mentioned. *duva, duva̱* v. to poison fish. *duva* n. Derris sp., another fish poison, two species.
ituvaki n. condition, state. *na ituvaki ni bula* the standard of living, conditions of life. *na ituvaki ni yagoqu* the condition of my body. *na ituvaki ni gaunisala* the condition of the road. *ituvaki ni draki* condition of the weather.
tuvi, tuvia v. to cover over, to conceal by placing something on top; of an earth oven *lovo*, to cover it with leaves. *ituvi* leaves used to cover a *lovo*. Syn. *icaqomi* or *itutu*. *Sa vakaituvi na lovo* The

earth oven is covered with leaves. Small stick to cover the *lovo* are called *isagoi* or *ilaloi*. *lalo, laloya* v. to put such sticks in place.

tuvonu n. leatherback, also known as *tabaiwalu,* largest of the sea turtles, often 250 kg but may attain 700 kg, one to two meters long, Dermochelys coriacea, uncommon in Fiji waters, seen mostly in open ocean, around shore only if deep water. Breeds at Australian north coast, Solomons, Papua and migrates to Indian Ocean. During five years of fishing and diving around Fiji I have seen it only once. Prevalent around Malaysia, Borneo, and visits but does not breed in Fiji. Back is leathery with seven long ridges, black spots with white blotches, without a shell, and the flippers are huge with no claws. Eats mostly jellyfish. Fast swimmer, to 30 mph according to the late Rob Wright, authority on Fiji fishing. Other sea turtles 15 mph. Leatherback can dive to almost 4,000 ft, deeper than other sea turtles. While most Fijians may have hear the word *tuvonu*, they have no knowledge of it. There is some confusion with the equally elusive loggerhead turtle, Ceretta carette gigas, the larger of two subspecies, the one that inhabits the Pacific. It is much smaller than the leatherback, weighing 115 kg to a a very rare maximum of 450 kg and differs also in frequenting lagoons and reefs. Food again is frequently jellyfish, but also clam and mussels, squid and flying fish. Unlike the leatherback the loggerhead has a massive head and very powerful jaws. Its carapace is reddish brown, formerly useful in commerce, as has been the shell from the hawkbill turtle, now however a forbidden trade.

tuvu n. freshwater spring that seeps up, as on a sandy beach.

tuvuka-na n. (Rare) very tip or top of a long object such as a tree trunk or ship's mast.

tuvu, tuvulaka v. to wash wet clothes by beating with a stick against rocks.

tuvutuvu-laka v. to keep beating (drum, laundry). *na katuvu ni lali* the beating of the drum.

tuwawa n. giant, man of giant size. Stories of Fijian gods and founding spirits often tell of giants. Some are still occasionally reported as seen. Today the term is used more figuratively, meaning a very big and powerful man. Formerly also referred to a very small, supernatural kind of being that inhabited *baka* trees in Vanua Levu. They killed their victims with bow and arrow. See Capell, p. 245.

U

u I, the personal pronoun, as an abbrev. of *au* when that pronoun follows a vowel, as in *E dina, seu lasu?* That is true, or am I wrong? (Commonly, one might see *seu* written as *se'u*.)

ua 1. n. wave, tide. *uaua* adj. slight, of the sea. *vakaua* adj. moderate, of the sea. *ua lokaloka* tidal wave, tsunami. See *sonaua*. *ua levu* high tide. *Sa lo na ua.* It has become the quiet period just before change in tidal flow.

vakatoka ua v. to ride the waves, to surf. Syn. *vakadavo-ua*. Surfing was a sport little known to Fijians except at Vuna, introduced by Polynesians but discontinued in the early 1900s. After mid-century surfing was re-introduced as a sport, from Hawaii. In Fiji most surfers now are Europeans or part-Europeans. *qalova uaua* swim with the tide, waves, or current.
  Idiom: *Kakua ni qalova uaua na moka.* Do not try to do something before you have the appropriate maturity or experience. This might be said to a child to discourage smoking, or pre-marital sex. *moka* stone fish-fence.

vakatulewa v. to make a judgement, decision. Syn. *vakataulewa*.

vakatulewa (Archaic) v., n. recitation of genealogy, mainly in areas of Polynesian influence, that may extend back 14 generations. A fair amount of the lineage is usually imaginative, of self-serving importance. There are often some gaps and discontinuities. In areas of Melanesian origin, recounted lineages would normally be limited to about four generations, not more than about eight.

ua 2. n. vein, muscle. *ua dradra*. n. varicose veins. *dra* blood.

iua n. paddle, stick used especially for laundry, beating wet clothes against a rock.

ua, uaca or **ua** v. to beat with stick, clothes in washing, mash of root crop for pudding, pandanus leaves for weaving. v. *uaraka* to beat forcefully

uabula adj. of people, in a productive, adult phase of life.

uabale to the extreme, to the fullest, a word rarely used. *vuabale* to overflow.

ua-dradra n. varicose veins. Syn. *uasala*.

ualagani swell (of the sea).

ualoka (or) **ualokaloka** n. tidal wave, tsunami. There is a famous *meke* in Rewa, celebrating a major *ualoka* that created great devastation. These are caused by an undersea volcano.

ualuvu n. flood. Syn. *waluvu*. See *luvu*.

uasivi special, exceptional. *sivi, sivita* v. to pass, to go beyond.

vaka-uasivi especially.

uasivi, uasivita v. to surpass, to excel. *O sa uasivi ganemu ena veitarogi.* You have done better than your sister in the exam. *O sa uasivita na nona na cakacaka na tuakamu.* You have done better than the work of your elder brother.

uaua choppy or rough of the sea.

iuaua n. drumsticks (formerly used only for signaling and for exhibition dancing).

uauana having prominent, bulging veins, of a person.

ubi, ubia v. to cover over, conceal by covering. *iubi* n. cover.
  Idiom: *were ubiubi* to pretend to work, literally to fake the work of cutting grass, weeds, by just knocking vegetation down to lie against the ground. By extension, this idiom may imply that someone is not telling the whole story, that they are concealing some truth.

iubi-ni-matana n. eyelid(s). Syn. *dakudaku ni mata-na*. eyelash(es) n. *bekabeka ni mata-na*. *yaloka ni mata-na* n. eyeball. *vacu-na* n. eyebrow.

uburu (Eng.) n. home-brew (alcohol). There are various spellings of this word.

uca n. rain. *sa tau na uca*. it is raining, rain is falling. *sa ucauca na draki*. it is rainy weather. *uca bi* heavy rain. *kote ni uca* raincoat. *uca tokavuki* rainy squall. *uca waicevata* n. hail, that does occur, especially at certain highland locations. The hailstones can be quite large and even somewhat dangerous to people. Syn. (Lau, Rewa, Kadavu) *lagi*.

uci n. small shrub, Evodia hortensis, Rutaceae, known to all Fijians, semi-cultivated, often growing near houses, leaves and flower shoots used as a fragrance, placed behind the ear by women or men. The white flowers themselves are not conspicuous. Seeds appear in July. The shrub grows best in partial shade and does not thrive standing alone in the full sun or in places where the roots remain in wet ground. The leaves are edible and tasty, but rarely eaten. Small shoots grow from fallen seeds around the plant, which are the best planting material. Syn. (Vanua Levu, Kadavu) *rauvula*. Elsewhere, *sacasaca*.
  Idiom: *veidau uci* adj. of a man who consorts with several different women, not faithful to one woman.

uciwai n. river or stream.

ucu-na 1. n. nose. *ucu gara* broad-nosed, of person. *ucu rava* has a flat nose, of person (those expressions not widely used). *ucu cega* turned–up nose. *dokaniucu* n. bridge of the nose. *qaraniucu* n. nostril(s). *ucu bi* n. blocked or stuffed nose, as from a cold.
Idiom: *ucuucu ni kalavo* or *ucukalavo* bloody nose, blobs of stringy congealed blood and mucus that emerge from the nose during a nose-bleed, and may be pulled out. They are preceded by fast dripping of blood. When the blobs pass, Fijians believe that the nose-bleed is coming to an end. My observation suggests they are correct.
Idiom: *"Ucui cei? Ucui lei."* "Chip off the old block", looks like the parent.
Idiom: *ucu mai duru* unbelievable "tall yarn", "if you believe that you will believe anything", lit. nose growing out of the knee.

ucu-na 2. n. protrusion, protuberance. *ucu ni vanua* n. cape, point of the lands-end, as in Suva Point, promintory (of land). Idiom: *dui mate ena noda ucu ni vatu.* each die defending our very own territory.

ucu, ucuya v. to resemble, have similar features, said of people, usually related as parent and child.

ucu v. to proceed out, come on the scene, as of dancers, or people making ceremonial presentations, proceeding out in a procession to the arena.

ucuna v. to draw out (knife from sheath, reed from within a stack of reeds, book from a shelf of books, etc.).

ucu ni vanua n. promintory (land).

udolu thousand. *e rua na udolu* two thousand.

udu v. to land, come ashore from a boat, to approach the shore and anchor. This can become a place-name.

uga n. hermit crab, often used as bait, common at the shore, edible but not commonly eaten. *kasikasi* smaller hermit crab, useful only as bait.

uga vule n. the very large coconut crab, Burgo latto, rare except on a few remote islands such as Katafaga. Easy to catch by hand though they have formidable pincers. They actually open coconuts with their pincers though this in not often observed since they are nocturnal feeders.

ukalele n. (Eng.) n. ukulele, introduced by Europeans, from Hawaii, via Portugese sailors. Fijians had three musical instruments: a nose flute, Polynesian in origin, rare in Fiji, a jew's harp of bamboo, also very rare, and a simple section of bamboo thumped against the ground for rhythm, which is still common. Wooden gongs or drums were used only for signals and communications. The use of small wooden gongs for music was introduced from Polynesia.

ukomu (Eng.) n. hookworm. (Slang) big eater, gourmand.

uku adj. of clouds, become black, heavy with rain about to fall.

iuku or **iukuuku** n. decoration, ornament, adornment.

uku, ukuta, uku-taka v. to decorate, add embellishments, to adorn, to dress grandly, as with special clothes, flowers.

vakaiukuuku adj. attractively dressed up , "all decked out".

ula, ulaca 1. v. to jump, jump over. Syn. *lade, rika. Sa ula tiko na kanace.* The mullet are jumping, skimming. *dau ula* n. jumper (sports, long jump, high jump).
Idiom: *sa ula!* fantastic! (food, dance, a delightful experience).

ula 2. (Hawaii) n., v. hula dance, modern introduction of Hawaiian hula, a sensual, undulating dance of women, formerly a quite different type of dance of men in old Hawaii.

ula! 3. Interjection of sudden delighted admiration

iula (Archaic) n. throwing club for use in fighting, often carried thrust through a man's waist-band.

ulaka (or) vaka-ulaka v. to hurl (something) at someone, something, or to somewhere. Syn. *kolo, kolotaka.*

ula 4. n. tiny jumping frog, the Fiji tree frog, barely more than two inches long, Platymantis vitiensis, which lives only in trees, usually in wet canopy forest, and thus rarely seen. No free-swimming tadpole phase. Sometimes found close to the ground in Pandanus palms, near streams or wet places. It is different from the much larger Fiji ground frog *boto* or *dreli* in having large, adhesive well padded feet and highly varied coloration. It can jump amazing distances. Highlanders *kaiColo* grilled the *ula* over embers of flame, and ate it whole with the intestines. See also *boto* Fiji ground frog, but also an adopted name for the toad, unfortunately introduced, now a pest.

ulabale, ulubaleta v. to over-step, figuratively, as in acting above one's station.

ulala! Interjection of surprise and admiration.

ula-sauvesu v. to somersault. Syn. *sausauvesu, ulu-sauvesu.*

ulavi n. parrot fish, mainly Scarus harid, dull reddish colour, but several species at the reef, edible. In various places, this name applies to Bolbometopon spp.

uli, ulia, uliraka 1. v. to stir, as of sugar in tea, milk powder and water. *uliraka* to stir fast, forcefully, as in whipping eggs. *na iuli* n. stick or spoon used to do the stirring.

uli, uliva 2. v. to comment on a speech when it is finished, often summarising and complimenting the speech in ceremonial reception of it. *uliva na noqu vosa* to receive respectfully and comment on my speech.

uli, ulia, uliva 3. v. to steer (a boat, vehicle). *uliva na waqa ki na matasawa* to steer the boat toward the shore. *ulia na motoka* to steer the motor car. *iuli* n. rudder, helm.

ulo n. maggot.

ulu (Colo East) n. ceremonial presentation to a village after a death of a woman or her offspring. The gift is made to the woman's people.

ulu-na (Polyn.) n. head, head of hair. Traditonally in Fiji the head has been sacred, not ever to be touched. A few decades ago this was strictly observed and in some situations still today. Formerly high chiefs had a special individul to trim their hair and colour it. Fijian hair is not naturally black; in ordinary situations it is often dyed black. In preparing for war, various colours were used. *ulumatua* eldest child. *ulu dina* "real" Fijian hair, crinkly. *ulu kabi* very tightly crinkled Fijian hair of the highlanders; sometimes laughingly compared to steel wool. Syn. *ulu manji* or *ulu maquru*. *ulu wai* soft hair. *ulu waiwaiya* very soft hair, usually falling down the back. *ulu damu* red-head, ginger-haired, a common natural occurence in Fiji, but may be simulated by bleaching or by dye. *ulu sigasiga* blond hair, light-coloured (no red). *ulu kaukauwa* intelligent. *ulu tawa* knowledgeable person. *ulu lala* ignorant ("empty-headed"), *ulukau* stupid ("wooden-head"). *ulu ca* wrong-headed. *ulu buki* with hair knotted, as in a bun. *ulu qali* with plaited hair (sometimes an indirect way of referring to an Indian woman.) *ulu balavu* having long hair. *ulu pori* or *ulu cou* or *ulu drika* bald. *ulu tasi* shaved head. *ulu maquru* short, tightly curled hair that cannot always grow long (it breaks). *ulu se* scattered spikey hair. *bui ni ga* "duck-tail" hair style. *ulu viro* long hair, curled. *ulu vula* white-haired. *drau ni uluna* hair. *mala ni uluna* single hair(s). Syn. (Tonga) *'ulu*.

ulu- or **ulu-ni-** prefix indicating the high part or upper part of something. *ulu-ni-vanua* high point of land, mountain. *ulu-toa* head of *tiqa* javelin.

ulu cavu (or) **ulu mate** n. wig, traditionally often made of human hair, later of horse hair after Europeans introduced horses. Fijian men sometimes wore wigs, in case of natural baldness, or hair removed as a sacrifice at the death of someone close or chiefly. Men were formerly proud of their head of hair, taking elaborate care of it as a main feature of male vanity. That was still quite common fifty years ago, but is now quite rare. Missionaries discouraged this. Military service also required shortened hair style. There are a couple of clans (*mataqali*) called *Ulucavu*, a major one at village Nakorosule, Colo East. Their ancestral spirit is a white man. When he removed his hat, Fijians considered he was removing his wig.

Ulu-ni-Vuaka (or **Naulunivuaka** n. an early place name of Bau Island, referring to the fishermen by that name who occupied the low flatlands that were also known as Butonivanua, and the people also as the Butoni who all later departed Bau for their own safety. The name Naulunivuaka also applied to their large tribal house (120' x 60') with five doors (some say eight), one for each clan: Tunidau ni Bau, Yavusa Ra Tavuto, Taurisau, Bale i Nasinu, and Sanisamu. It was used for church services 1854-1880, when the Methodist church was completed, later named Ratu Cakobau Church. The 5th Vunivalu of Bau, Penaia Kadavulevu, (died 1914) removed the building to make room for playing cricket. It was replaced by a public toilet.

ulu moce n., adj. sleepy-head.

vaka na ulu v. head for, head towards, go toward. *vakanaulu i baravi*. head for the coast.

ulubale, ulubaletaka v. to offer an excuse.

iulubale n. excuse. *iulubale lokiloki* lit. "lame excuse", an Anglicism.

uluteba n. head hair grown long and combed out straight, usually trimmed neatly, and under-cut sharply in men's tradition, common till the mid-1900s.

uluqa n. edible fish, also called "Bedford" because its face is shaped like the front of a Bedford truck, Saddleback snapper, Paracaesio kusakarii, with four dark yellow patch on its sides, against a sight silver background. There is a very similar species, somehat smaller, P. stonei, Cocoa snapper, that has three or four dark patches on each side, against a yellowish background.

ulurua n. an edible parrotfish, Chlorurus microrhinos, blue back, then pink and belly yellowish. Blunt head. Same genus as the *karakarawa* parrotfish.

ulu sauvesu v. to go head over heels, somersault. Syn. *sausauvesu*.

ulu sawelu n. damp hair, sodden with water or, in the case of men, sometimes vaseline or other hair ointment.

ulu sede (Slang) n. money-conscious, "tight" with money. Syn. *matailavo*.

ulu teba n. hair grown long, then undercut sharply.

ulu toa n. (Archaic) head of javelin for the competitive sport of *veitiqa*, Usually made of hard wood, attached to a reed shaft and thrown as far as possible on an established course devoted to that sport.

ulu vakaViti n. hair let grow out, dressed neatly in early Fiji-fashion, formerly proudly worn by Fijian, now only very rarely seen among men, and only occasionally among women. Men now crop their hair closely.

uluvatu n. promintory, rocky peak, literally rock-head. *Nauluvatu* is a major super-tribe from the Waidina highlands, now, widely dispersed.

ulu viro n. deliberately curled long hair, as some men do, rasta fashion.

uma n. 1. a body, lot, pile, or bar of something, soap, ingot, tobacco, brick, block (as of traditional sea salt *masima* or red ochre *umea* for colouring bark-cloth). *na veiuma qele* the parcels or lots of land. *uma tamata* n. bunch or group of people. *veivoli umauma* (Modernism) wholesale.

uma n. 2. lead (the metal).

uma n. 3. weighted ball used in the European game of bowls. *viritaka na uma* to hurl the weighted ball.

umea (Lau) **1.** red ochre pigment from a certain soil for staining bark-cloth, a specialty of Komo Island, Lau Province, which supplies the pigment but itself makes no bark-cloth. Made into spindle-shaped blocks that are given, traded or sold. Dry reddish powder is scraped from the block.

umea (Lau) **2.** n. rust. Syn. *veveka*.

uneune n. earthquake, tremor, common in Fiji, causing landslides (*sisi ni qele*), especially in the red latersols, acidic, infertile soils that are amorphous in structure, and thus unstable when soaked in rainwater. Landslides are visible in the hills and mountains as red gashes in the verdure. They can be quite dangerous, burying houses suddenly and leaving great gashes, crevices in the ground.

univesiti (Eng.) n. university. There are now two in Fiji.

uqe, uqeta v. to move swiftly the mid-section of one's body, mostly as a dance movement. This is rather a specialised word. By ext., to stir oneself, be in motion, moved to action. *vaka-uqeta na yalona* to motivate.

ura n. prawn, Macrobrachium lar, for "true prawn" (*ura dina*) and some other species, caught by hand or hand-net. Some live in fresh water, some in salt water. *ura ivi* (a very small prawn), *ura kei Ra saqa* also known as Tiger Prawn, Penaeus monodon, a brackish-water prawn that lives at river mouths and around mangrove swamps. It is believed that crevally (*saqa*) eat them. Prawns are the aquatic totem of several Fijian clans. *moci* is a tiny shrimp, a food specialty of Rewa. *ura tu* king-sized prawn. *yaci, yacia na ura* (or) *taga, tagava na ura* net the prawns with a hand-net. *Sa vidi na ura.* The prawns are jumping. (In rivers and streams they are often trying to escape the eels that feed on them.) Prawns are often sold by the roadside, but not always safe to eat, since some are killed with stolen, poisonous Paraquat. a weed-killer.

Idiom: *Sega ni ura me sa tei damu.* Where there is smoke there is fire. The truth will come out. i.e., there must be a cause for it to happen, and it will be known. lit. no prawn just turns red (unless someone has cooked it).

Idiom: *moce vakaura.* Lit. to sleep like a prawn, ready to rise to instant action from apparent sleep.

ura buta n. prawns that are naturally red; this requires a very specialised alkaline environment, with brackish water, connected underground with the tidal effects of the sea. At Vatulele Island the best known species is Parhyppolyte uveae, held sacred, and may respond to ceremonial calls. (They also respond to a simple stirring of the water but that is not traditional.) The same species is known at Naweni, Cakaudrove Province, and at a one-hectare limestone island in the Philippines where they are called pulang payasan. There are other species at Vatulele, smaller ones, that local Fijians assume are simply the young ones. In Fiji the red prawns are serving as a tourist attraction. At Naweni a fee is charged for sighting them and one is told of the prohibitions: no touching, taking, and no photographs. The ritual call: " *'eitou qo na marama ni Vuna, 'eitou mai via sara ura buta. E tuba, e tuba, e?"* This is said to recall that people here supported the Tui Wairuku in aiding the Tui Cakau and Dewala people to defeat the Tongan forces of Wainiqolo." It is unclear how those Fijian words reflect the military support but such is oral history. (Ifereimi Nadore, *"Na ura buto ni Naweni", Nai Lalakai,* 14 August, 2009, p. 13.)

urata n. Banded Prawnkiller, Slipper Lobster, Lysiosquille maculata.

urau n. large crayfish, "spiny lobster", Palinuri dae, most readily caught at night by torch-light, but now becoming more scarce. When the moon is shining they go into hiding and are harder to find. When trying to escape they dart backwards very quickly. Best and freshest when caught alive by hand, as done by Gilbertese and Tuvalu people, and cooked while alive. Fijians normally spear them and sell them dead to hotels, resorts, where often they become tasteless and rubbery. *iseru* (or) *lawe-na* antennae of crayfish. *tara urau* to catch crayfish by hand. Several type of crayfish: *urau dina* Panilirus versicolor, large, green with white and black markings. *urau bola* or *urau tamata*, P. ornatus, very large and greenish with markings. *urau vatu, urau kau* or *urau kula*, the Golden Rock lobster, P. pencillatus, short and dark. Quite different in appearance is the *vavaba*, Slipper crayfish, Parribacus caledonicus, flat and small, lacking antennae. Syn. (Lau) *ura*.

ure, urea v. to shake, as of a tree branch, to bring down fruit. Fruit bats are caught, especially by highlanders, shaking a tree where the bats are resting. The bats fall in their confusion and are easily picked up. Syn. *kure, kurea* or *sakurea*.

uro n. solid meat-fat (especially of pork, beef). Many Fijians are unaware of its dangers to health. Housewives boil down lard to use cooking fat because it is cheaper than commercial brands of vegetable cooking oil. (No such frying was ever done in early Fiji.) By 1997 it became common to hear *uro*, called out as a call of enticement to a sexually attractive person of the opposite sex. This was done in an innocent jocular manner. The expression is now rather dated.

uru, uruca v. to furl (sail) and figuratively, may imply arrival at destination; to lower (flag), to fold up (umbrella).

usa, usana v. to carry the cargo, freight.

iusausa (followed by name of things) n. cargo or load of (such things), as in *na iusausa waiwai* the cargo of oil.

usa bi v., adj. heavily laden, over-loaded (usually of boat, vehicle, horse).

uso, usora v. to poke, usually with a stick, usually speaking of stones in a fire for grilling food, or stones for an earth-oven, to arrange them. *usoraka* refers to the stick or other instrument used for poking.

usouso (Lau) adj. exacting, "difficult", demanding.

usu, usuta, usumaka (or) **usuraka** (or) **usulaka** v. to grab, to force (someone, to do something), obstruct the way, close off (as of a road), take away, to "hog" (some space, some thing). Syn. *sugu, suguta*. *vaka-sau-rara-taka*.

usutu n. theme, important issue, central point or idea.

uti-na n. (Archaic). circumcised penis. Listed in Capell, and known to some people, but the word seems obsolete, unknown to many people; it is more likely to be thought of as a version of *vuti-na* for pubic hair (though *vuti-na* can apply to other soft hair). For reasons that remain obscure, testicles (*soresore*, or more commonly, *polo*) may be mentioned unabashedly but the penis is less often mentioned directly. Perhaps the more common word for circumcised penis is now *qala-na*. Cf. *boci* n. refers to an uncircumsized penis, extremely shameful for a Fijian male of mature age. Fiji Indians are not normally circumcised. *Boci* may be an impolite, crude way of referring to an Indian man.

Idiom (Insult): *uti riva* suggests stupid, inappropriate conduct, referring literally to an impulsive penis.

uto n. breadfruit, Artocarpus altilis, Moraceae. There are some forty varieties which now extend the fruiting season much longer than the mainly two months of harvesting in early times, March and April. The tree is native to coastal Fiji which has had a large gene-pool of breadfruit. Some varieties have seeds, some none, and in certain areas the seeds are eaten. Fiji varieties were taken as far east as the Marquesas by early Polynesians. Caution: in Ba and Yasawa, *uto* refers to papaya, the *weleti*. Inner bark of *uto* was used for cloth in coastal areas if there was little *masi* barkcloth. (Neither was available in most of the Viti Levu highlands.) Leaves of *uto* formerly used as plates. The breadfruit is sacred, totemic at Vuda, not spoken of freely, though it is eaten there, which is unusual for a totemic plant. At Vuda one must eat it if it is presented at a meal, and should eat the skin as well as any seeds. There, it would never be cut with a knife. Syn. (West) *kulu. Kulu, kuru, 'ulu* or *'uru* are names that extend through Polynesia.

Idiom: *vakataba ni uto* n. or v. someone who is ineffectual or unreliable, dependant on others, not to be depended upon. Also to have a brief love affair that could not become a dependable, lasting relationship. (The branches of breadfruit tree are fragile and breakable).

Idiom: *drau ni uto lutu i wai.* useless (usually of a man).

Idiom. *vuki na uto.* sudden, unexpected change. When *uto* is roasted on a fire, it is turned around in a sudden action to avoid burning.

Cultivars:

uto dina, round, dark green fruit, smooth skin, no seeds.

balekana, excellent taste, small round fruit.

bokasi, early maturing. (Gives the name to Wainibokasi River.)

buco, long fruit, rough skin, excellent eating.

koqo, small fruit, rough skin, firm flesh, no seeds.

uto ni Idia n. jak fruit, Artocarpus heterophyllus, eaten mostly by Indians. The huge fruit grow directly from the tree trunk. Syn. (Hindi) *katari.*

uto-na n. heart. Modernly, the word is often used in direct translation from English as in: *uto kavoro* broken heart. Traditionally Fijians never thought of the heart in relation to emotions.

uto ni kau (Anglicism) n. heartwood, of a tree.

uto-uto 1. n. green jobfish, Aprion sp.

uto-uto 1. n. float, as used for fishing lines or nets.

utu, utura 1. v. to place end-to-end. *utu buka* v. to light a torch by touching it to a firebrand. *utu lacalaca* to furl sail.

Idiom: *utu boko* v. to chain-smoke, lit. lighting one cigarette from another, then extinguishing (*boko*) the butt.

utu, utura 2. v. to shift logs or branches in a fire, better located to burn well.

utu 3. n. path that pigs travel in the bush. These can be recognised, distinct from paths used by humans.

uvi n. cultivated yam, Dioscorea alata, a most noble starch-food for ceremonial food presentations in coastal areas. This is a strictly seasonal, annual crop planted in June or July, harvested when the vines die back, around March, the earliest ones in February. The only starch food that can be stored above ground for many months without fermentation. (Cassava can be kept in the ground for a time.) This has been mainly a food of the coastal areas and smaller islands and its harvest (*yabaki*) marked the end of the year, though years were never counted. Highlanders of Viti Levu, certainly in the eastern sector (*Colo Isiti*), have no great tradition for cultivation of yams though in modern times that is becoming more common. They much more often ate the wild species of yam, and *taro* that they cultivated and grows much more quickly. Popular early yam varieties are *vurai balavu* and *vurai dra.* Late maturing varieties are *uvi ni Futuna, Kivi, Taniela vulaleka.* Planting of yams requires more specialised knowledge than most other crops. The top section (*na uluna*) of the yam is cut off for planting. In a well matured yam, that can be quite thin, and it is often dried out by being placed on a bed of ashes before planting. The bottom part of the yam (*dromuna*) is cut off where it is soft, sometimes only one cm. section, when the yam is at the right stage, and that part will be for food. The middle section of the yam (*na kobena*) supplies planting material (*na vacina*) that is cut off in vertical sections to include a good layer of outer skin and those pieces may have a notch cut to indicate the bottom side that will be planted down. *Vacina* can be no thicker than an inch or so. The inside chunks of *kobena* will be eaten. Some farmers have the notion that a little salt on the planted mound (*buke*) may help the growth. Some sprinkle a handful of sand so that theft of the planting material will be revealed if the sand is disturbed (and the sand itself is thought to have salt). Theft can be a common problem since the planted *vacina* is perfectly edible. A hand can easily dip into soft earth of the planted mound. Without the disturbed sand, the farmer might wait in vain for his harvest from the empty mound.

uvu, uvuca v. to blow out air or tobacco smoke from the mouth or nose. *me uvu na sici!* Blow the whistle! (Whistles were known anciently in Colo West, now displayed in the Museum, though purpose or function is not known). *uvuca na biukila* to blow the bugle. *na dau uvu biukila* the bugler. *uvu bitu vakatagi* (Archaic) to play the nose-flute. *uvu davui* blow the Triton trumpet-shell horn. That horn is blown at the death of Polynesian chiefs, but also regularly, by fishermen returning with fish to sell. Formerly, in coastal areas, priests blew that Triton shell horn in celebration of the *yabaki* annual harvest year.

uvu-na n. newly sprouting leaf of coconut or plantain, not yet opened.

uvuuvu wai n. A word unfamiliar to most Fijians. Harmless, and even quite friendly, the humpback migrates from the Antarctic past New Zealand, through Fijian waters, then to Tonga, June through August, in breeding season, before returning to the Antarctic after the birth of their young in tropical waters. Fijians have seen it in coastal waters. It is capable of spectacular leaps out of the sea, presumably associated with giving birth to the young that may be a third the length of the mother. Most Fijians tend to use the word *tavuto,* referring to any kind of whale. Though few have seen the carniverous sperm whale, all know this as the source of the whaleteeth used as symbolic wealth for ceremonial gifts. There is no regularly used word for the pilot whales or blackfish, the much smaller whales that school in these waters but are usually seen only by sailors at sea.

uwea n. spindle-shaped fish trap usually made of mangrove roots, by the sea.

V

Where Polynesian influence is considerable, the **v** of Fijian is often pronounced and spelled as a **p** or an **f**. Thus *vuaka*, pig, may be heard as *puaka*. Fijian *vale* house, is *fale* in Tongan.

Our list here omits in most cases those many words with the prefix *vaka* (or its abbreviated form *va*), indicating an action, a verbal or adverbial form, or a similarity. Those words that begin with the prefix *vaka* are listed under their root-meaning. Thus *vakatotolo* adv., meaning fast, and *vakatotolotaka*, meaning hurry it up, are listed under *totolo* adj, fast.

Also, the many words beginning with *vei*, indicating plurality, or reciprocity, are in most cases listed under their root-word. Thus *veitalanoa*, to yarn together, is listed under *talanoa*. Some words combine both prefixes, as *veivaka*. Still, in this dictionary, the word would appear under its root, not the prefixes.

Similarly, names of plants are often preceded by *vu ni* as a prefix, such as *vunidakua* for the *dakua* tree, or *vuniboro* for the *boro* shrub. Names of plants are listed under the root-word. Fruits and nuts are also mostly named by adding a prefix *vua* in front of the root word for the plant. *vuanikau* fruit. *vuaniivi* nuts of the Polynesian Chestnut. In this dictionary they would be found under the root word, not the prefix.

va four. *ikava* fourth; *vasagavulu* forty; *e va na drau* four hundred; *vakava* four times. Syn. (Tonga) *fa*.

va- prefix, shorter version of the prefix *vaka*. *va oqo* like this. *va oqo-taka* do it like this.

vacea n. a large forest tree, usable as timber, bark boiled for medicine especially for colds and for a feeling of weakness, Neonauclea forsteri, Rubiaceae, native from Solomons through to Society Islands. Syn. *bo, vutoro*.

vaci, vacia v. to cut pieces of yam-root especially for planting. *na vacivaci* the cutting of yams for pieces to plant.

vaci n. piece of yam-root cut off to be used for planting. The other part, for eating, is the *kome*.

ivaci(ni taba-na) n. shoulder blade. Syn. *civa-ni-taba-na* or *civacivanitabana*.

ivacu n. fist; punch.

vacu, vacuka v. to punch with the fist.

vacu-na n. eyebrow. *na vacumu* your eyebrow. Contrast with *nomu ivacu* your fist. *vacu toso* waggling eyebrows. *deguvacu* to indicate agreement by raising both eyebrows slightly, usually with an expressionless face. Syn. *becuru*.

vada 1. n. age-group. *Kua ni dau veimaliwai kei ira e sega ni nomu vada*. Don't mix with people who are not of your age-group.

vada 2. n. (Archaic) concubine and maidservant of chief, a term only very rarely used today but understood by many Fijians. Can refer to an unmarried woman.

vadi, vadiga v. to pick with the fingers, as in picking a guitar or ukelele, or to check something like food, by squeezing it between the fingers. *Me vadigi na qita*. Play the guitar. *vadivadi* strumming (as of a guitar).

ivadi n. clever, ingenious act, usually *ivadi ca* devious act, trickery

vadra n. Pandanus pyriformis (or P. odoratissimus or P. verus) that grows in damp, coastal places, usually in poor soil. Fruit is edible, eaten mostly by Micronesians, who have varieties best suited to that. A flour can be made from the fruit, cooked as a mash. Edible nut inside very hard shell. Colourful ripe fruit used in floral garlands. Leaves used for weaving coarse mats. Dried leaves used as tobacco wrap (*suluka*). Syn. *balawa*. Historical significance in the famous "first landing" immigration of Lutunasobasoba at Vuda, their first sighting of mainland occupation was smoke arising from an area called Vadravadra, land of the original, indigenous *kaiNadi*, Melanesian people, earlier settlers here. Later, some of Lutu's people settled in what is now Ra Province, at the mountain range Nakauvadra, again named for the pandanus. Legend relates that after death a man wishing to reach the next world would have to throw a whaletooth and hit a Pandanus tree. The legend cannot precede the 1700s, with the introduction from Tonga of whaleteeth as a prestigious symbol. *na sei* the flowers of *vadra*.

ivadreti (Eng.) n. bandage. *vadretitaka* to bandage (it). *na vavadreti* the bandaging.

vadugu v., n. roaring (waves on reef), droning (sound of aeroplane), resounding, resonant or vibrating hum. *domo vadugu* bass voice.

va-gatara v. to sharpen (it). *gata* sharp.

vagauna only occasionally. *gauna* time.

vagenegene to be stubborn with a sullen attitute.

vago n. a vine, bottle gourd, Lagenaria siceraria (earlier known as L. vulgaris), young gourds edible, older gourds up to a meter long used by Polynesians as a bottle for water, oil, but never so used by highlanders of Viti Levu. Botanist B. Seemann said such bottle gourds were in common use in his time, the 1860s. Aboriginal intro., now naturalised. White petals and anthers, fruit green to yellowish. Syn. *daibe, dago. didi.* See *kitu.*

vagugu, vagugu-taka v. to hum, usually in rendering a tune without the words.

vai n. stingray, skate. Large ones may be seven feet across the wingspan, small ones just 18 inches. They nestle in the sand, almost invisible, and if stepped on, disturbed, or caught on a line, may be dangerous with the whipping tail and their spike. (A very large one almost killed this author. It had been caught on a shark line from a dory.) That tail was used formerly to shape wood because of its granulated skin, said to be *varovaroa.* The bony tail-spike (*irabo*) can be a lethal weapon. *sua vai* to catch stingray by spearing, a speciality of Nautodua people of Kaba, Tailevu, where this is a food specialty. Catching is done with five or six men from a boat, usually at high tide, their leader throwing the spear. *voto ni vai* n. spike of the stingray. Kaba people provide stingray to the Vunivalu of Bau as traditional food, when requested. If they have offended the Vunivalu, they may beg forgiveness with presentation of a stingray spike.

vaini 1. (Eng.) n. vine, sometimes spelled out as *vu ni vaini,* indicating that it refers to a plant that is a vine.

vaini 2. (Eng.) n. wine. Few Fijian ever drink wine and this word is hardly ever used outside of European hotels or restaurants. Beer is the common alcoholic beverage. Syn. *waini.*

vaivai n. several species of tree, Mimosaceae family, many introduced by Europeans for decorative flowers and urban planting, one species local, now called "bush *vaivai*" (*vaivai ni veikau*) or *vaivai ni Viti,* Serianthes melanesica. *Vaivai ni vavalagi* usually refers to the raintree (= monkeypod tree), Samanea saman, native to Central and South America, to 35 meters high, often planted at roadsides but invasive in dry, western parts of Viti Levu. Favoured for carving of handicraft bowls for tourists, but also as flooring. Fls white or cream to pale yellow in branched inflorescences, stamens very long and pink. Woody, flattened pod to 25 cm long with seeds embedded in pulp. Similar species, Albizia lebbeck, has yellow-green flowers and flat pods that lack pulp.

vai-vukivuki 1. n. giant Manta ray, harmless with no "sword", beautiful, graceful and unafraid of people. Fijians have no way of catching it. Syn. *vevewai.*

vaivukivuki 2. v., adj., n. show-off.

vaka 1. as, like, similar to, as if it were. *vaka na imatai ni gauna* as if it were the first time.
Idiom: *me vaka* just as. *me vaka e sa tukuna na Turaga* as the Chief told it.
Idiom: *me vaka ni:* since or because, as a result of: *Me vaka ni o ni a liutaka na mataivalu . .* Since you were leading the army . . . .
Idiom: *ka vaka* in this way, like this, as in *Sauma sara o Seru ka vaka "Io, baleta na cava?".* Seru promptly answered in this way "Yes, but for what reason?"

vaka 2. to say, as in *E vaka vei iratou "Bula!".* He said "Hello! to them (3). (The implication is to do like this.) In this vein, *vakabula* to say hello. *vakamoce* to say good-bye.

vaka vaka this way and that way. *Eratou taubale tiko vaka vaka.* They (few) are ambling this way and that way.

vaka- 1. often abbreviated to *va,* , a prefix that makes an adverb of an adjective or an adjective of a noun. *lako vakatotolo* to go fast. *vinaka vakalevu* (or) *vinaka valevu* thanks very much (a modernism). *vakalotu* religious.

vaka- 2. prefix in front of an adjective or noun to form a verb of causative action. *vaka-totolotaka* make it go fast. *vakalevutaka* make it bigger. *vakatubu, vakatubura na rere* give rise to fear, cause fear. *vakabukete-taka* v. to make pregnant.

vaka- 3. a word or prefix meaning according to, implying a similarity or comparison: *E vaka vei au . . .* It seems to me, in my opinion, according to me. *cakava vakaoqo* do it like this. *va-oqotaka* do it like this. *me vakataki* such as. *na veiyanuyanu me vakataki Ono, Vatoa* the various islands such as Ono, Vatoa.

vaka n. (Lau) trad. spokesman for a Lauan chief, chamberlain. Syn. *matanivanua.*

vaka-bai to be fenced off. *vaka-bai-taka* v. to fence off.

vakabau to be approved, supported.

vakabauta v., n. to believe; belief.

vaka-bibi especially.

vakabibi-taka v. to emphasise, to give weight to, make heavier.

vaka-be-gusu v. to show disapproval, disdain by protruding the lower lip.

vakacegu, vakaceguya 1. v. to relieve, to give rest to, to rest up.

vakacegu, vakaceguya 2. v. to retire.

vakacegu 3. (Respectful) dead. *vakacegu vakadua*, said for clarity of this meaning.
vaka-cavara v. to finish off (what one is doing).
vaka-ceva-ruru v. to continue to bluster, whir, flutter, throb, as sound of engine, or the wind in the trees, or a sail flapping in the wind.
vaka-ciri-loloma v., n., adj. emotionally touching, deeply affecting.
vakacivo (Archaic) v., n. to express briefly a wish at the drinking of a cup of kava, generally for fair weather, good crops, health, the well-being of current visitors. Most often done by chiefs, some still today.
vaka-curu-i-lavo (Anglicism) v. to deposit money, as to a financial account.
ivaka-dei (Anglicism) n. deposit, usually of money on account, as in hire-purchase.
vakadeuci v. transmit, pass along.
vakadre, vakadreta v. to pull tight. *Me vakadre na dali.* Pull the rope tight.
vakadre, vakadreta v. to caution, advise, beseech. *Au vakadreti iko mo ni toka dei toka.* I caution you to remain steady. The term is usually used when a senior person gives advice to a subordinate or junior person.
vakadrecike v. to be stubborn, recalcitrant.
vakadua once. *sega vakadua* never.
vaka-evei? how is it? How is it going? Syn. *vakacava?*
vakai- prefix to personal pronoun: *vakai-   koya* by himself (or herself, itself). *vakai-au* by myself, according to me.
vakaicili to shelter, be sheltered, housed temporarily. *icili* n. shelter.
vakaitovo well-mannered, of a person. Syn. *vakaivakarau.*
vakaiyanaqa adj. huge, tremendously big in size. Syn. *vakaitamera.*
vakaiyau well-off, wealthy in material goods.
vakalavalava n. a rather mundane starch-food as a snack, made of grated cassava, salted or sugared, baked or boiled in a leaf wrapping.
vakalolo 1. n. Fijian pudding made by men or women, using starchy root-crops or Polynesian chestnut *ivi,* and grated coconut, usually sweet, eaten as a snack, not with meals, not as a dessert. See *lolo.* There are perhaps twenty different names for the various sorts of these chewy puddings, depending on the region of Fiji, and the starch-food used, and the use of coconut cream, whether caramelised (*lolo buta*)or not (*lolo droka*). Never existed in the highlands of Viti Levu, where there were no coconuts.
vakalolo 2. adj. cooked in coconut cream, usually fish (*ika vakalolo*).
va-kalougata-taka (Anglicism) v. to bless, in Christian fashion. In full version, *vaka-kalougata-taka.*
vakalotu religious.
vakalusia 1. (Eng. lose) v. to waste, to cause a loss. *O Seru a vakalusia na timi.* Seru caused the loss of the team.
vakalusia 2. (Eng. lose) v., adj. of prawn, crab, crayfish, in a state of replacing the shell, to adjust for growth. At this stage, flesh is plump and soft-shelled; it may be cooked and eaten without removing the shell.
vaka-lutu-vuli (Anglicism) v. to be a truant from school.
vaka-luveni v. to have children (*luve-na*).
vaka-macala, vakamacalataka v. to explain. *macala* clear.
vaka-macawa (Anglicism) weekly, every week.
va-kamakama (Slang) v. to burble on, words with little content.
vaka-masima, vakamasimataka v. salted, to salt (it). Salt was always liquified before use. It was unavailable in the highlands except rarely, by trade.
vaka-meau, vakameautaka v. to mediate, arbitrate, bring about peace, compatability.
vaka-misinare (Anglicism) v., n. to give a major annual monetary levy to the Methodist Church.
ivakamoko (Anglicism) n. brassiere.
va-kana, vakania v. to feed (usually animals, pig, cat, dog, cattle, horse).
vaka-na-bi lop-sided, weighted too heavily on one side. *bi* implies heaviness.
vaka-na-daku, vakanadakuya v. to turn the back (toward something or some person). *daku-na* back.
vaka-na-mata v. to face (someone or something).
vaka-na-yava v. to extend one's legs, stretch out one's legs (*yava-na*).
vaka-nuinui v. to depend. Idiom: *vakanuinui ena bilo cicila.* to rely on someone who is undependable.
vakanuinui vinaka (Anglicism) best wishes, as for some anniversary.
vaka-oqo like this. Syn. *va-oqo.*
vaka-raica v. to look at carefully, to look for closely.

vakarai-taka v. to show, reveal, demonstrate.
ivakaraitaki n. demonstration, example
vakarau, vakarautaka 1. v. to prepare (it), to get ready, about to happen. *vakarau* prepared, ready. *tu vakarau* be prepared. *na vakarautaki ni lovo* the preparation for the earth oven. *Eda sa na vakarau galala.* We are about to be free.
vakarau, vakarautaka 2. v. to weigh, as on a scale; to measure (dimensions).
veivakarautaki n. training, preparation.
Idiom: *vanua ni veivakarautaki mai Nauluvatu* St. Giles mental hospital which happens to be located at the Nauluvatu section of Suva City.
vaka-vakarau n. training (as for sports), preparation.
ivakarau 1. n. conduct, behaviour, custom, manners. *vaka na ivakarau vakavanua* according to traditional custom. *A iVakarau vakaPasifika* The Pacific Way, implying good relations, mutual goodwill and sensible compromise, rather than confrontation and conflict. This is a relatively modern cultural myth.
ivakarau 2. n. weighing scale. *ivakarau wai* n. bubble-level, as used by a builder.
Vakaraubuka (Ang.) n. Friday, in early Christian times a day for gathering firewood, as implied in this word. Syn. (West) *Vakarau balavu.*
vakarau-ni-Siganisucu n. Christmas ever.
Vakarauwai (Ang.) n. Saturday, in early Christian times a day for Methodists to fetch water, in preparation for their Sunday sabbath. Syn. (Lau) *Cokonaki.* (Vuda) *Vakarauleke.* (Nadro.) *Vakarauleka.*
vakaravi n. temporary overnight shelter improvised, usually in the bush.
vaka-rawarawa-taka v. to facilitate.
ivakasala n advice. *taura vakamamada na ivakasala nei tinana* take his mother's advice lightly. *taura vakabibi na ivakasala.* take the advice seriously.
vakasala, vakasalataka v. to advise.
vaka-sisila adj. despicable, disgusting, disreputable, usually of behaviour
vaka-soso n. pudding made of plantain with grated coconut inserted into a slit. Formerly a snack but modernly a sweet dessert.
vakasuva of a couple, to be living together un-married. Syn. *vakaSamoa.*
ivakata – prefix to a verb indicating a playful action, or acting "as if".
ivaka-ta n. drainage ditch. Syn. *sala-ni-wai.*
vaka-tadu-mata v. for a chief, to send his herald (*matanivanua*) to pass a formal message along to the relevant people in traditional manner. Such formal channels of verbal communication have been very important in Fiji.
ivaka-tale n. farewell ceremony for visitor that usually includes serving kava and at important occasions, presentation of a whale-tooth.
vakata vuaka v. to hunt wild pigs, usually with dogs.
vakataki 1. (followed by pronoun) by oneself. *vakataki au* by myself. *vakataki koya* by himself/herself/itself. *Sa tadola na katuba vakataki koya.* The door got opened by itself. See *vakai au, vakai koya.*
vakataki 2. such as (when preceded by the particle *me*) *e levu na matanitu me vakataki Mereke, Jamani, Varanise* many governments such as America, Germany, France.
vaka-ta-medroka v. to masturbate (of males).
vakatau depend, in this sense only:-- *E na vakatau vei iko.* It will depend on you (on your behaviour, your reaction, your decision).
vakatoka v. to put, to put on, as in *Me vakatoka na kuro.* Put on the pot (put it on the stove or fire.) *Me vakatoka na wai.* Put on the water (put it on the stove or fire, as for making tea).
vakatoka, vakatoka v. to name, give a name to. *vakatokai* named.
vaka-totovo, vakatotovotaka v. to practice, to try out, to make a trial.
vakatubu- prefix; to cause, as in *vakatubu-leqa* v. to cause trouble. Syn. *vakavu-.*
vakatubu n. baking powder. Idiom: (Slang) *Kua ni vakatubutaka.* Don't exaggerate, be pretentious, blow things up out of proportion. Syn. "baking powder" as a verb; Syn: *vakayisi-taka. yisi* yeast.
vaka-vu, vakavuna v. to cause. *vu-na* n. cause, origin. *vu-vakavu* n. newly invented word by language teachers to signify causation, as by the prefix *vaka* or *va.*
ivako n. nail (carpentry), horn (cow, goat). Originally, I believe, the word applied to a sharp protuberance on a warclub. *ivako wiri* n. drill bit.
vako, vakota v. to nail (it), a modern concept, of course.

vala, valata, valataka v. to fight, fight for it. *Era a vala mai Bokanivili.* They fought at Bougainville. *valata na meca* fight the enemy. *valataka na yaca i Viti* compete, fighting for (or in) the name of Fiji. *na valataki ni bula galala* the fighting for freedom (which is a modernism, of course.) *valataki bilo* fighting for the cup.
Idiom: *na valataki vanua* fighting for the country, representing the nation (usually in team sports these days).

valagi (Tongan palagi) as in *kai valagi*, European. *valagi* is a common abbreviation for *vavalagi*, polite term for European.

valata (Lau) v. to do it, make it. Syn. *cakava*.

ivalavala n. conduct, behaviour, used today often in a negative sense. *ivalavala ca* bad behaviour, usually referring to some specific behaviour. *ivalavala kaukauwa* forceful behavious, violent behavious.

vale n. house. *vale vakaViti* Fijian thatched house. It is incorrect to refer to a Fijian house as a *bure*. *vale kau* wooden house. *vale vatu* (or) *vale simede* cement-block house. *vale tabatolu* three-storey building. *vale vakenani* lean-to, shack, camp-house, temporary house (Biblical, Canaan house, temporary shelter). *vale ni wawa basi* bus shelter. *Vale ni iTukutuku Maroroi* n. National Archives. *na veivaka-valetaki* the housing. Size of traditional houses is indicated by the number of fathoms of length, e.g., *e dua na vale katu rua* a house two-fathoms in length. The traditional Fijian measure *katu* is approx. one fathom (six feet), the span of a person's outstretched arms. In principal, a man provided a house for his wife, or one for each wife, where she would raise their children. Normally, in early days, the man did not regularly sleep in the house of a wife. A high chief would have his own house. In the highlands, men all slept in a large *bure*, a men's house. The women and children slept quite separately.
Idiom: *vale katu dua* burial grave, lit. house six-feet in length.
Idiom: *mate vale dua, bula vale rua.* literally, You might die if you eat at only one house but you can live if there are two houses where you can get food. The implication is that you should feel comfortable eating meals or staying at a relative's or friend's house. Often said in good humour to one who has declined a meal. Fact is, it is a social strength in Fiji that a person who does not feel well treated in one house of the extended family, may usually move in with an aunt or uncle or cousin where there is a more welcoming attitude.
Idiom: *vale drauna* fruit of the *ivi* tree, Polynesian chestnut, an edible starch-food (this preciosity derives from the fact that the fruit grows almost hidden in a small bower of leaves).

vale lailai n., v. toilet, to defecate (polite term).

valeni (or) **voleni** (Eng. fall in!) v., n. military: fall in!, also used as a noun for a parade formation. Often this word is pronounced just as in English.

vale ni bula n. hospital, formerly known as *vale ni mate*, "house of illness (or) death".

Vale ni iTukutuku Maroroi n. National Archives, an old building built in 1915 in Suva, originally for Government Printer, now with an extension. It houses old issues of newspapers and a substantial library composed of the libraries of Sir Alport Barker, Harold Gatty (including books of Dr. Ronald Gatty), and James Borron Snr.

vale ni veivesu (Anglicism) n. prison. Korovou is the holding prison in Suva as a convenience to the courts. (It is named after the earliest but temporary prison of Fiji, after Gordon's Little War.) At Naboro valley, 17 km west of Suva, is the largest prison of Fiji with some 400 acres of land.

vale ni vo n. lavatory, out-house. The concept is introduced. Fijians formerly went into the bushes or to the beach and used leaves or reeds *gasau* as toilet paper. Syn. *vale lailai*, *vale ni po*. Especially in mainland Fiji, human excrement was normally concealed to avoid witchcraft so no one identifiable place was used as a toilet. *valenivo dre* n. flush toilet. *valenivo keli* n. pit toilet.

Vale ni Yaya Makawa n. Fiji National Museum, located in Suva. The Museum benefitted from the early care of George Barker, and later, until 1987, the leadership of Fergus Clunie and Kate Hindle. Visiting research scholars are helped by the local staff who have field experience.

vali, valia v. to extract with the thumb, and by pulling and pushing as in removing a mussel from its shell, or fishhook from mouth of a fish.

ivalu n. war. *A ivalu!* It is war! War is begun! *na ikarua ni iValu Levu* the second World War. *buca ni ivalu* field of battle.
Idiom: *toa ni ivalu* warrior, champion. The concept of the rooster symbolising a warrior derives from Tonga.

valu, valuta v. to fight, wage war, fight for. *na veivaluvaluti* the fighting, battle(s), warring. *na valuti ni cakacaka vakailawaki* the combating of corruption.

valutu v. to have a miscarriage. *E a valutu o Mere* Mary has a miscarriage. *vakalutu yaloka* v. of a chicken, to lay eggs.

vana, vana v. to pierce, to shoot (arrow, gun) at it. *vanataka na dakai* to shoot the gun.

vanavana n., adj. piercing, pierced, pocked with small holes or depressions.

vavana v., n. shooting. *dau vavana* marksman, shooter.

ivana 1. (Tonga, fana) n. mast (of boat, ship). *vana-rua* two-masted. May also imply antenna, as for broadcasting or reception, radio, TV or mobile phones.

ivana 2. n. wooden shuttle used to pierce thatch of a house, when binding it in place.

ivana (ni namu) 3. (Modernism) n. mosquito spray. *vanataka* to spray (it).

vanini v. to vibrate or tremble with sound, to twang, tremulo. Could be the vocal chords, could be the rhythmic rumble of marching feet, or a wire strung tightly. *nini* suggests the notion of trembling.

ivani n. comb. This is a "true" Melanesian Fijian word, common in some regions as in Burebesaga.. The more usual word today is *iseru*, a word of Polynesian origin. *vani, vania* v. to comb. Syn. *seru, seruta*.

vanivani v., n. to comb (the hair), combing.

vanisi (Eng.) n. varnish.

vanua n. territory, land (but not soil itself or any specific piece of land), country, nation, place. *vanua tani* overseas. *tauvanua* (or) *lewenivanua* n. ordinary people, commoners, in contrast to chieftains or others of high function. *na vanua o tiko kina* the place where you are. *Na vanua cava e mosi vei iko?* Where do you feel pain? (i.e., in what place of your body?). *Na Vanua O Wailevu* The Territory of Wailevu. The concept of a large Territory (*Vanua*) under a paramount chief is an introduced Polynesian notion, first established in Fiji at Verata and perhaps Laucala and later, by the immigration of Lutunasobasoba and his people at Vuda. This imposed hierarchical system enabled indirect rule by the British and continues now under the Republic. The concept is Tongan and British and not Fijian but it is convenient for purposes of national administration. *Minisita ni Vanua* Minister for Home Affairs.

Idiom: *wai ni vanua* n. *yaqona* for drinking, a term of preciosity, used pompously in speeches.

vakavanua adj. traditional, customary. *veiqaravi vakavanua* traditional ceremony. The word can be used facetiously. Asked how or where he acquired something, a modern Fijian may reply *Vakavanua*. In other words, he simply took it. Fijians may take things freely from relatives especially but also from others if the person has such things in abundance and is not carefully on guard, or is not under the chief's protection. This may not be considered stealing.

vakavanua-taka v. to make a traditional approach, usually for something desired, as in *la'ki vakavanuataka na marama me la'ki watina* go make a traditional approach for the woman to become his wife.

ivaqa n. food supplies for a voyage, "viaticum" (in Latin terminology, as used in English). Christian preachers often speak of *ivaqa vakayalo*, their notion of inspirational quotations from the Bible. They see this as food for the soul.

ivaqakoro (Slang) to show off, put on airs impetuously.

vaqara n. search.

vaqara, vaqara v. to search for, investigate.

veivaqaqai n. investigation.

vaqe n. taro suckers that grow by the mother plant. These are better planting material than the cut tops of the taro corm, which yield a root that is truncated flat.

vaqo abbrev. of *vaka oqo*, like this.

vaqo-taka v. to do it like this.

vara n. young sprouting coconut. The spongy inside of the nut is a sweet delicious food eaten raw or grilled over a fire. That spongy material replaces the water and flesh inside the coconut as it starts to sprout and form roots.

vara adj. deaf. Syn. *didi vara, didi*.

varada (Eng.) n. verandah.

Varanise n., adj. France, french.

varasa 1. n. onion, an introduced vegetable, greatly liked by Fijians but almost all imported, not grown locally. There are also some unimportant indigenous plants bearing this name.

varasa 2. n., adj. (Eng.) brass. *vaivo varasa* brass pipe. *metali varasa* or *varasa* bronze medal (in competitive sports).

vari-na n. scale(s), of fish.

vari, varia v. to scale (a fish). *na varivari ika* the scaling of fish.

varivari n. ringworm, red fungal lesions on the body, usually of children. Pharmacists usually suggest tolnaftate cream. Some Fijians treat with external application of macerated papaya leaves, which are corrosive on skin (and can be used as a meat tenderiser.)

variivoce n. edible fish with delicious white flesh, humphead wrasse, giant wrasse, Cheilinus undulatus, having a heavy snout and a huge hump over the head, and very large, tough scales (hence the Fijian name), and sharp, powerful fused teeth. Though it is carniverous it has not been readily caught by hook and line, but by spear or fish poison. Usually found in reef passages and crevices but now rare. Can grow to seven feet in length, weighing several hundred pounds, body colour greenish. Range is from eastern Pacific through Papua New Guinea, Southeast Asia and northeastern coast of Africa. Everywhere the flesh is greatly prized, and in some places, Cook Islands, Palau, reserved for nobility. Overfished, this wrasse is an endangered species, since 2004 protected by Fiji law, a law that is impossible to impose. Syn. (Burebesaga) *dagava*; *ulurua* (a name shared with another species, a parrotfish Chlorurus microrhinos), *varevoce* (as listed by Rob Wright.)

varo, varota v. to saw. *kabani ni varovaro* lumber company, timber mill. *varovaroa* rough, unplaned, of wood, planks, bumpy of skin, as of some breadfruit. *de ni varo* n. sawdust. *varomusu, varomusuka* v. to saw across the grain (rather than with the grain) of the wood.

varota (or) **vakarota** v. to order, to command (that something be done). Direct orders bluntly stated are not characteristically Fijian unless the person in command is extremely angry.

ivaro (ni kau) n. saw. *ivaro gata* n. sharp saw.

varovaroa adj. rough to the touch, as of skin (shark, some breadfruit varieties), bark of a tree.

vasa 1. n. white muscle of the *vasua* giant clam, delicious raw. No point in cooking it. The black mantle is very tough and is best minced and heavily marinated if it is eaten at all.

vasa 2. (or) **vasa damu** n. small shrub, Euphorbia fidjiana, often planted at the border of gardens to protect it from spirits and from human theft. It is no longer very effective as protection against theft but it is still usually planted. Red purple stems and leaves, with bright pink flowers that begin blooming in early December. Syn. *vasa kinikini, rewa*.

vasa 3. n. medium-sized, soft-wood tree to 20 meters of the shore and bush, Cerbera manghas, Apocynaceae, leaves dark and glossy green, with white fragrant flowers (3 cm diam.), sometimes pinkish centre, growing at tip of branches, used for garlands. Fruits egg-shaped, reddish, dark purple or black when mature, 2 to 3 inches in diam. White poisonous latex. Syn. (Lau, West, Rakiraki) *rewa*. (Polyn.) *reva* or *leva*.

vasi, vasiga v. to scrape off, clean off the surface or skin of food, such a grilled starch-food. Can include skimming off slime from a seafood.

vasili (or) **masawe** (or) **qai** n. the "ti" plant (*ti* is a Polynesian name), Cordylene terminalis or C. fruticosa, Agavaceae. Now mainly a decorative garden plant. The corm of a tall indigenous, green-leafed wild var. was used as a source of sugar after being cooked in the earth oven for a few days. *Tikula* is a red-leafed ornamental variety with a Polynesian name. Syn. *masawe,* (Lau, Nadro, West) *qai.* (Kadavu) *kokoto* or *masawe*.

vasiri v. to take a step and slip down from slippery or unsteady footing. Syn. *tidara*.

vasu 1. (Modernism) n. a person from outside a village who has married a person of the village in question. In this modern sense, it usually refers to the person of outside origin who does not live in the village, but may include the spouse if the outsider is a man. Today such an outsider is expected periodically to contribute money and goods for village purposes. Formerly, a couple almost always settled in the village of the man.

vasu 2. n. Traditionally, in the mother's village of origin, it is the offspring who are called *vasu* and they could make demands for services or goods from the village, especially from their mother's brothers (*momo*), who might be addressed as *momo* or *mudrau* (abbrev. of *kemudrau* a polite form of "you".) Formerly, chiefs had extraordinary *vasu* powers to make demands. This custom of making such demands is falling into disuse To have his children recognized and accepted in their mother's village, a husband must bring goods (kerosene, food, mats) and whales' teeth for a ceremony called *kau na mata ni gone* ("bringing the children's face"). Today the tendency is to bring several siblings at the same time, often waiting for years till some of them are virtual adults. The children must not be seen at the village until the ceremony is performed. *Na cauravou oqo e vasu ki Bau.* This youth's mother is from Bau island. *E vasu ivei o iko?* To what place are you *vasu*? i.e., What village does your mother come from?

vasu, vasuta v. to ask for (something), as in the *kerekere* custom, where it is virtually impossible to be refused. A special form of demand is that of the traditional *vasu* (see above) who could in former times, take anything from the maternal uncle without even asking for it. A chiefly child might make very great demands. Remnants of this custom persist.

vasua or **vasua dina** n. giant clam, Tridacna derosa. *e dua na matau vasua* ten *vasua* clams offered at a ceremonial food presentation. *Sa dala tu na vasua.* The *vasua* is agape. *Qarauni iko de qamuti iko na vasua.* Be careful lest the *vasua* clamp on you. (It is a real danger. One came close to killing this author.) *vasa* muscle of the *vasua,* delicious part, usually eaten raw. The black mantle is very tough and should be very finely chopped if it is to be eaten at all. Syn. *matau.* Other Tridacna species include the *cega,* the Fluted giant clam, T. squamosa, and the *katavatu,* the Rugose giant clam, T. maxima.

vata 1. n. shelf (usually in a house, office or copra shed). *vatanivola* n. bookshelf.

vata 2. together. *lako vata* v. to go together; *salavata* v. to travel together. *kalavata* matching (in colour, as with clothes). *vata kei au* together with me.

vata 3. same, as in *kaivata* fellow countryman. *tautauvata* same, equal, flat, even.

Vata-ni-Tawake (Archaic) n. alternatively Navatanitawake, name of house-site (*yavu*) for a large building on Bau Island of early fame, reconstructed several times. After being successful in the Nakauvadra War, Vueti held the privilege of flying his personal banner (*tawake*) on the upper yard-arm of his ship(s). Name of this building means "Shelves for Drying Out the Flags". This was the temple (*Bure kalou*) of Ratu Mai Bulu, god of the Roko Tui Bau. Vueti, first Roko Tui Bau was also named Koroi Ratu Mai Bulu, as a human manifestation of this ancestral god. Vueti was also referred to as Ko Mai Vatanitawake. After the Tui Kaba became dominant, after over-throwing the Roko Tui Bau Raiwalui, the temple was also used to serve the Kaba god of war, Cagawalu. The Vatanitawake was destroyed in 1837 when Tanoa was being restored as Vunivalu. Tanoa replaced the building. Cakobau was installed at the Vatanitawake on 26 July 1853, and for the occasion 18 bodies were presented. It was again destroyed by fire in that same year. Calvert published an illustration of the temple drawn in the 1850s. In 1879 it became the Bau Council House. In 1968 Legislative Council voted funds to refurbish Bau, and specifically to rebuild a council house on this site. Lauan carpenters were brought from Namuka to do the job. Bodies were found buried in the two-tiered mound, or base. Local legend relates that these are mainly Tongans who fell at Kaba Point in 1855, when forces of the King of Tonga defeated Rewa and the Bauan dissidents.

vatavata ira lago-taka v. to imagine, to concentrate on or set one's mind to (something).

vatavatairalago n. riddle, puzzle.

vati, vatia v. to lash together, as of reeds for a fish-fence or wall of a Fijian house. The items so lashed are usually long and thin.

vativati n. small medicinal epiphyte, Phymatodes scolopendria, Polypodiaceae. In Lau and Cakaudrove the name also refers to a rather large, coarse fern Acrostichum aureum, more commonly known as *boresi* or *boreti*, which has edible young fronds and grows in brackish swamps according to J. Parham.

vatonaka n. blessing and good wishes, usually expressed by a host who is receiving a formal presentation of *yaqona* in an *isevusevu* ceremony that introduces the guest. Also *veivatonaki*. Before drinking, it has also been custom to express good wishes, as for a fair wind, for a guest's safe return. Spitting has been part of this formality, a custom now falling into disuse.

vatu 1. n. stone, rock. *veivatu* stony (of a piece of land). *vale vatu* concrete-block house. *matau vatu* stone-axe (adze was the only form of stone axe), as a n. or adj. today it usually refers impolitely to conservative villagers considered ignorant and backward by the younger generation. Stone axes were unknown to Viti Levu highlanders. *na uluvatu* the rock-face (cliff), or promintory. Bearing Nauluvatu as a name, there is a village in Waidina District, Naitasiri Province, and some tribes as in Suvavou and the islands Tuvuca, Cicia, and Vanua Vatu in Lau Province. There is an amazingly widely dispersed diaspora of Nauluvatu people. None remained at village Nauluvatu. Syn. (Kadavu) *solo*.

vatu(ni-yayani) 2. (Anglicism) n. iron for ironing clothes, sheets. *vatu livaliva* n. electric iron. *yayani-taka* to iron (clothes, sheet).

vatubu-ca v. to cause trouble, create bad feelings.

vatubu-cu v. to turn over (person being given massage, of some object to turn it over, to turn it upside down.) *cu* v. to show one's bottom.

vatuka, vatukana v. to shape, give form to, as in arranging the hair or setting the sail of a boat. *vatukaivinaka* adj. well shaped. *vatukaica* badly shaped. *vatukailailai* shaped small. *vatukailevu* of large form or shape, big in appearance.

vatukana n. form, outcome, appearance.

vakavatukana-taka v. to fulfill. *vakavatukanataka na nona gagadre.* to fulfill his/her wishes.

vatu-kata-i-lawa n. (Archaic) stone sinker perforated in the middle, used to weight down a drag net in highland river fishing. These are the only known stone artefacts of the Viti Levu highlanders, a people who were essentially pre-Stone Age in culture. Such fishing in the highlands was mostly for *ika loa* Cestraeus picatilis, and was a boisterous community effort that might involve more than one village. It is not known if these stones were ever made in pre-European times.

vatu ni ceva (Archaic) n. special stone that was used to call up a favourable wind, notably at Beqa Island, and Levuka. *vatu ni sakuku* stones used to transmit leprosy (*sakauku* in some Western speech),

vatuvatu adj. stony, of a piece of land or small island.

vakavatu adj. (Anglicism) rich, influental. This derives from a fanciful notion of wealthy people having jewels as precious stones *vatu talei*, a foreign concept to Fijians.

vatuvatu ni taba-na n. shoulder. *taba-na* arm, limb, of a person, wing of a bird or aeroplane.

vau n. native hibiscus shrub or small tree that grows near the shore, Hibiscus tiliaceus, Malvaceae, the bark used as a fibrous cord, and as a dye, and as a filtering sponge when mixing kava, and in coastal areas was formerly used for the brief fringe-skirt worn by women. Flowers are yellowish with maroon centre. In farming, this small tree is sometimes used as living fence or as a windbreak. There is a short variety, *vau leka*, that grows to only about 5 m. and has darker green, lobed leaves. The taller var., to 10 m. height, is called *vau balavu*. Upper leaves of the short var. are applied externally, shiny side down against the skin, to alleviate sprains and swelling of arms or legs. Leaves are often used as toilet paper. The wood is very light, burns easily, and used to be used as a base for making fire by friction. Syn. *fau* (Tonga, Samoa, Tahiti).

ivauvau n. (Archaic) turban of thin fine barkcloth formerly worn only by some chiefs. Missionaries eliminated the custom. *vakaivauvau* adj. wearing a turban. The custom has been revived only for the installation of a few high chiefs.

vauvau 1. n. cotton shrub, Gossypium hirsutum (one variety native to the South Pacific), or G. barbadense, two 26-chromosome American species. Cotton grows only around present or past human settlements. It is quite possible that some variant of cotton was an aboriginal introduction from America brought back by early Polynesians. It extends right up into the highlands of Viti Levu. The cotton is used by coastal Fijians (not Melanesian highlanders) for stuffing soft pillows (*lokoloko*), which is an introduced Polynesian concept, not known to early Fiji Melanesians. The chewed leaves are applied medicinally to wounds and sores. *Vauvau ni valagi* is the term often used for the commercial cotton varieties, Gossypium arboreum, a 13-chromosome species from Asia, was introduced by Europeans. Commercial growing of cotton in Fiji ceased by 1870 with revival of cotton production in the U.S.A., after the American civil war.

vauvau 2. (Rewa, Suva, Colo East, Namosi) n. regional syn. for *bele*, a common green cultivated vegetable, Abelmoschus manihot.

vauvau 3. n. introduced kapok tree and its "cotton", Ceiba pentandra, Bombacaceae that grows in coastal areas. Fijians never plant it but occasionally use the "cotton" to stuff pillows.

vauvau 4. n. cotton wick (for kerosene lamp or stove), mantle (Coleman lamp).

vava n. board, as in *vava ni yayani* n. ironing board, *vava ni savasava* n. washing board. Around Nasavusavu I heard this as *papa*.

ivava n. shoe(s). *ivava ni cici* n. track shoes. *ivava laca* n. canvas shoes.

vava n. a wild species of ginger family, Alpinia spp. Zingiberaceae, with broad leaves, to 20 feet height, the leaves sometimes used for wrapping. In early times, the leaves were often used to form a kilt, as the only clothing, especially for men, and especially in the highlands where there was no barkcloth until that was introduced by Tongans. Syn. *boiboia, boeboe*. The stalks are favorite food of wild pigs, the fruit a favoured food of pigeons and parrots. Flowers and fruiting clusters appear at the top of the plant near the leaves, above the tall bare stem.

ivava n. woman who is occasionally possessed by a spirit, and through whom the spirit speaks. This is still all quite real to some Fijians, and a common occurence.

veivava n., v. to carry piggyback. *Rau a veivava toka o Seru kei na buna.* Seru's grandmother was carrying Seru on her back. *Vava!* or *Vava mai!* Climb on (my back)! *vava, vava* v. to carry on one's back (especially babies).

vavaba n. slipper crayfish, rather flat, lacking antenae. Paribacus. There are many regional synonyms.

vavaca v. to reach a place. *E ratou sa vavaca yani na Sau Tabu.* They (few) have reached the Sau Tabu.

vavai n. cultivar of dalo, known and highly favoured from ancient times. It has small corms, divided in two. The colour is a little yellow, and the taste and texture magnificent. Young Fijians may not know of this.

ivavakoso n. congregation (church), gathering of people. For Fijians this is now a very major social grouping that involves strong allegiance to their denomination.

vavaku n., adj. thickness, thick, of solid things (timber, cardboard, metal sheet, etc.), not liquids.

vavalagi or **valagi** (Tongan palagi) n. European place overseas. *kaivalagi* white person.

vavaloaloa n. blackboard. Syn. *vavanivolavola*. *joke* n. chalk.

vavi, vavia v. to roast (formerly only in earth oven *lovo*), usually taro, yam, breadfruit, pork, chicken, fish, palusami. This is done by men, most often these days on the sabbath, or for some feast. Before modern times the earth oven was unknown in the highlands of Fiji. *vavi moce* bake overnight in the earth oven. *Eratou a vavavi.* They (few) did some baking. *na vavavi keke* cake-baking, the baking of cakes (not an early custom of Fiji). *vavi kulikuli* v. to bake (root crop) with the skin on. *kuli-na* n. skin.

vaya! (Slang) an interjection: yeah, maybe! Might happen! Could be! There may be an element of disbelief in this interjection.

vea adj. overly ripe and soft, of a breadfruit (*uto*).

veata or **kotia** n. sea-hare, an edible creature of the reef, seen on sale at the Suva market. Unsightly when cut open but exquisite in taste, usually eaten raw. Dolabella auricularia (D. auriculata?) and perhaps other species. The usual one is somewhat greenish in colour and another type is dark-coloured, called *veata-ika* or *kotia-ika*. Syn. (Nadro.) *baga, kosia*. (Kadavu) *samu*. (Lau) *mone*. (Nayau) *qaqawe*. At Nayau Island this is the seasonal, annually harvested "*balolo*" celebrated locally.

vecea v. to flatter, or "butter up" someone. There are several synonyms.

vecu. vecuka v. to kill an octopus (*kuita*) by turning its head inside out. Requires great experience, with medium-sized octopi to three feet in length. It can be dangerous. The octopus does not cooperate. It has a sharp beak.

veiba, veiba-taka v. to dispute, argue, oppose.

veibo v., n. to wrestle, wrestling, a very minor former Fijian sport, mostly Polynesian in origin, now forgotten. *veibo liga* "Indian" wrestling with the hand to contest strength of the arm.

vei 1. to or from, as in *solia vei au* give it to me.

vei 2. of (or) among (as of people), as in *e dua vei rau* one of the two of them.

vei- 1. as a prefix, indicating collectivity or plurality: *veikau* forest, bush. *ena veiloga ni dalo* in the taro beds (in the gardens).

vei- 2. prefix indicating all, each and every one: *ena veisiga* every day. *ena veigauna kece* at all times. *na veimotoka kece* all motor-cars. *na veikoronivuli kece* all the schools. A multiplicity may be indicated by repeating the *vei*, as in *ena vei-vei-gauna kece.* at all the many times.

vei- 3. prefix indicating interaction or reciprocity. *veivacu* boxing (punching). *veimaliwai* n. social ambiance, human environment. *veimau* v. play for stakes, as in gambling. *veicai* v. to have sex together, a blunt word, but perhaps socially acceptable in certain contexts. (*veicai* is a swear word). *Keirau sa veikilai.* We (two) are known to each other, know each other, have already met each other. *Erau veilomani.* They (2) love each other.

vei- 4. prefix indicating a relationship, such as family relation, as in *veitinani* mother and child(ren) *veitamani* father and child(ren) *veitacini* brothers or sisters, of the same sex. *veiwekani* related, relations (people). *na veiwatini* the married couple(s).

vei- 5. prefix, indicating a change. *veisau, veisautaka* v. to change. *noqu veisau* n. my change (usually of clothing). *veisau* n. change (small money). *na veiveisau* the series of changes, the changes in progress (and sometimes, implicitly the notion of reform).

-vei 1. where? *e vei?* where? (where is something, someone). *O lako maivei?* where do you come from? where have you been? *Kivei?* To where?
Idiom: *Mai vei!* No way! Out of the question!

-vei 2. whom (preceded by *ki -* or *mai-*, indicating a direction to or from, as in *kivei* to (person named) as in addressing a letter. *maivei* from (person), as on an envelope.

-vei 3. how (preceded by *e-*), as in *Vaka-evei?* How is it going? What about it? What's up? *Vakaivei na veidigidigi?* what about the election? How is the election going? (The prefix *vaka* is often abbreviated as *va*.)

vei-(verb)-yaki this way and that way, here and there, as in *veilakoyaki* to go here and there, *veiqaloyaki voli* swim around here and there. *vei-raiyaki* to look here and there.

veibasai opposite, across from (in location). *E toka veibasai kei na sitoa.* It is located opposite the store. *veibasai kei na cowiri ni liga ni kaloko.* counter-clockwise. *ibasa* n. may refer to a person holding a corresponding position on an opposing team.

veibiu v. to become separated, of a married couple. *veisere* v. to divorce.

veiciu (Archaic) n. cat's cradle, string figure made in the hands, a girl's game of yore.
veidonui opposite each other. See *donuya*.
vei-dresu-qa-ni-bulu v., n. Idiom: to compete fiercely. *dresu* to tear up. *qanibulu* coconut husk.
veilaroi brackish, of water. Syn. *tovutovula*.
veileti v., n. dispute. *veileti na Hindu kei ira na iTaukei.* dispute of the Hindu(s) with the (many) native Fijians.
veimama n., adj. half. *ena ikarua ni veimama* in the second half (sports). *veimama na lima* half past five (o'clock).
veimau n., v. game, as in playing cards such as poker, bridge, or for chess, checkers. *veimau(ilavo)* gambling for money, as with cards or games of chance.
veiqati v, n., adj. to be competitive, sometimes said in an unfavourable context. *Suva kei Nadi na veiqatitaka na bilo ni Farebrother.* Suva and Nadi will compete for the Farebrother cup.
veisau, veisautaka v. to change, exchange.
veisau n. change, exchange (often referring to a change of clothes, or change meaning money).
veisei v. divided, especially of people not in agreement.
veisere v. to divorce. *tasere* separated, of a couple (but also to come untied, of a cord or binding). *veibiu* v. to become separated, of a married couple. See *veibiu*.
veitalia no matter! It is a matter of no concern. Just as one wishes. *vakaveitalia* any way, any which way, casually, without due concern.
veitau v. to relate as friends (*itau*). The implication may be that of boyfriend or girlfriend in a romantic sense.
veitauvu see *tauvu*.
veiwa n. type of wild yam, often preferred.
veiwali n. v. joke. *au sega ni veiwali tiko ena tikina oqo* I am not joking about this matter. Joking is a strong characteristic of most Fijian conversation. No conversation proceeds long without some quip or witticism.

Idiom: *veiwali vakaNavaga* to fight instead of pleasantly joking with horse-play. Lit. to joke like the people of Navaga. Village Navaga in Magodro District, Ba Province is peopled by highlanders of Colo West, defeated by Bau's troops and exiled to Koro Island where they established a village also called Navaga. Like most Viti Levu highlanders they have been tough fighters.

veiyacovi n., v. sexual intercourse (correct and polite term). Lit., to come together.
veka! 1. (Vulgar) exclamation of surprise, usually pleasurable.
veka 2. n. excrement; disgusting mess. *veveka* rust. *ivekaveka* n. anus.

Idiom: *Vakamici na gone qai veka.* Treat someone nicely then they treat you badly. Lit. Have a child urinate then the child defecates.

veka 3. v. to defecate (ordinary term, polite enough).
vekabiu v. to leave a disgusting mess, specifically in failing to clean up and put things away after use.
vela (or) **vela vela** expression of surprise, mild disgust, or disbelief at what is asserted.
velavela 1. adj. tasteless, of food or of a person's behaviour.
velavela! 2. awful! (reproaching someone's behaviour, often jocularly), disgusting. Tone of voice indicates the degree of displeasure.
veleko n. hard, polished part of a tool or weapon, tradionally a stone or shell, modernly a metal surface or blade. (No such tools existed in the highlands.)
veleti (Eng.) n. plate. *veleti kava* tin plate (usually enameled metal, made in China). Syn. *disi* n. dish. *disi lase* n. porcelain dish.
veli n. type of Fijian forest gremlin, very short, and very strong, with long unkempt hair. They may play tricks on people but are never evil. Their *yaqona* is supposed to the the *yaqoyaqona* (in fact a virtually useless weedy shrub), and their coconut the *niu sawa*. To some Fijians they are quite real and are reported as still seen and encountered. They are associated particularly with highlanders of Colo East in Viti Levu, especially at Serea, Solo-ira. They have been reported around Wainadoi in recent years. Before clearing parts of the forest for planting, workers have called out to the *veli*, asking politely for their permission. See *leka*, a different kind of legendary dwarf in Fiji though not having extraordinary strength, eccentric features or any unusual behaviour. May refer to earlier memories of a pygmy people.
velovelo n. rowboat, dory. This may be propelled with a pole, or by sculling with one oar, a technique learned from Europeans.
veluvelu adv. as in *duka veluvelu* extremely dirty.
vakata-vevelo v. to play with sex organs. Lauan *vakatamemeno*.

veni (Eng.) van, now sometimes referring to almost any commercial vehicle (but not a bus). Small trucks may be called *veni*. Large trucks are called *lori* (lorry).

veno, venoka v. to bore a small hole, as on shells to string a necklace. See *qiva*.

venu, venuka v. to clear one's nose of mucus by squeezing with the fingers. Fijians did not use handkerchiefs of any sort. See *wadruca*.

vere n. trap, literally, but often referring to trickery.
Idiom: *vere vakaBau* typical Bauan trick of deception and treacherous behaviour for which they are infamous.

veretaka v. to deceive, trick, betray (people).

vereverea adj. complicated (any situation, problem), entwined or entangled (rope, cordage). Syn. (Lau) *fijia*.
Idiom: *lako vaka-vereverea* have affair(s) outside of marriage.

vesa n. decorative arm-band or ankle-band of vegetation worn by dancers, or by chiefs on ceremonial occasions. Made of barkcloth, the *vesa vakavanua* is in some places tied ceremonially on the arm of a chief being installed. For dancers, the *vesa* is often strung together or woven leaves, often of the *ti* plant Cordyline sp., discarded after the one-time use. Syn. (Tonga) *vesa*.

vesa, vesa or **vesana** v., adj. deliberately to expose to the sun, as in *ika vesa* fish that has been smoked slowly over a open fire; can apply to sunbathing, exposure of a person to the sun. Sun-dried fish is first salted before drying and has a lighter texture than smoked fish.

vesi n. noble tree-timber of the forest, Intsia bijuga, Caesalpinaceae, used for large boats, *yaqona* bowls, war clubs. The wood does not float. It is one of the useful plants with symbolic significance for some tribes especially of eastern Fiji. Many Tongans came to eastern Fiji to build boats with this timber. They introduced the arts of building ocean-going vessels. The tree grows at beach and coastal forests below 450 m. Fls white or yellow turning purple, to 2 cm diam., one showy petal, falling easily. Pods flat 20x5 cm, 3-7 seeds, orange, mealy inside.
Idiom: *Sa ciri saka na vesi!* Good night! said only to a paramount chief of eastern Fiji. The implication is that of the chief's canoe, made of *vesi* timber, would be drifting off from shore.

vesi wai n. seashore timber tree, Milleta pinnata, Fabaceae (formerly Pongamia pinnata, Papilionaceae), from Malesia east to Samoa, superficially similar to the *vesi* Intsia bijuga, though unrelated. *vesi wai* is a very dense wood. Pink fls, 1 cm diam., pods in clusters, peaked apices. Seasonally, may lose all its leaves. Syn. (Lau) *vesivesi*.

vesu, vesuka 1. v. to capture (escaped prisoner), tackle (rugby). *na veivesu* the tackling (rugby). *vale ni veivesu* n. prison. *kaivesu* n. prisoner.

vesu, vesuka 2. v. to bind, tie up firmly. *ivesu* n. bundle. *ivesu dalo* bundle of dalo.

veta n. as in *na veta icake* the upper hands of bananas in a bunch, which are the best ones. This can be applied to people *na veta icake* are the uppermost, influential or important people. *na veta ira* the lower ones, the lower classes of people.

vetao or **vetau** n. tree, Mammea odorata, Clusiaceae, Sap was used by Fijians to dye their hair an orange-brown colour. P. Geraghty says that *vetau* is an ancient word for the related *dilo* tree, Calophyllum inophyllum.

vetuna n. type of edible worm that lives in the sand, Siphonosoma spp. or Sipunculis spp. May be eaten raw. Syn. *vurai*. See *ibo*.

veve adj. crooked, bent. *A veiveveyaki na sala eratou muria.* The path they followed was winding and curved. *E veiveveyaki na kava ni vale ni oti na cagilaba.* After the hurrican, the corrugated roofing iron of the house was cooked and bent.

veveka n. rust (a concept unknown till the introduction of metal). A word derived from *veka* excrement. Syn. (Lau) *umea*.

veveku adj. sad-looking, sorrowful, close to tears. *vaka-mata-veveku* glum.

Veverueri (Eng.) February. Traditionally the first month of harvest for yams. First-fruit tribute (*isevu*) is offered to chief and church. Syn. (Archaic) *vula i isevu*.

vevewai n. Manta ray, huge and harmless, unafraid and beautiful in motion. The word may be unknown to many Fijians. Syn. *lelebo, vaivukivuki*.

via 1. v. to want (followed by a verb) *Au via lako.* I want to go. *Au via kana.* I want to eat. (But *au vinakata* I want it.) *viavia levu* pretentious, wanting to be important. Syn. (West) *mata*.

via 2. almost, nearly or tending to be, as in *via loaloa* almost black.

via 3. should be, or needs to be done. *Sa via bulu na benu.* The garbage should be buried.

via 4. n. Swamp Taro, very large edible plant with starchy corm, Cyrtosperma chamissonis, Araceae, growing in wet, lowlands areas, a specialty of Rewa but also in relatively dry areas like Vanua Balavu

Island, where it is a staple. Though not a prized food of most Fijians, this is a specialty of Rewa, where people know the right stage of harvest, and best cooking techniques – not a simple matter. It qualifies as a "true food" (*kakana dina*), but is not considered a prestigious presentation food for ceremonial feasts. Not widely sold at the markets. Syn. *via kana, via kau*.

via mila (or) **via gaga** n. Alocasia macrorrhiza, Araceae, plant with starchy corm, usually considered inedible except in times of extreme shortage, by islanders who know how to treat it to become edible. The stems also can be edible to the cognoscenti. Leaves have classically rounded valentine heart-shape. Below the leaf-stems, a rough "trunk" rises above the ground. Syn. (Polyn. *kape* or *'ape*.) The edible, tasty, *dalo ni Toga* (Xanthosoma sp.) with much smaller corms can have a similar "trunk" but it is a smaller plant and its leaves are pointed.

viavia 1. n. a small decorative plant in sandy, coastal areas, grown in lines near dwellings, Crinum asiaticum, Amarillidaceae. The long leaves are a shiny green on a stout stem, the flowers graceful and white. Shiny white sections of the leaves have been used by Europeans as trolling lures. Trolling is not a native practice of early Fijians. It was mostly a specialty of Samoa.

viavia 2. (before an adjective or noun) very nearly, almost, tending to be, wanting to be. *viavia loaloa* very nearly black. *viavia turaga* acts pretentiously like a chief (though he is not).

viavia levu adj. pretentious.

vica 1. how many, how much (in a question). Preceded by an "E" at the beginning of a sentence. *E vica na kena isau?* What is the price? *Lewe vica?* (or) *E vica na tamata?* How many people?

vica 2. a few, several (may appear as a separate word or as a suffix). *Me toni bogi vica ena wai.* Let it soak for a few days in water. *Eratou levica ga.* They are only a few people. *E vica ga.* Only a few. *na vale tabayavica* the house with serveral storeys.

vakavica a few times, several times. *Vakavica?* How many times?

viciko n. flesh, as of meat, in contrast to fat (*uro*). In early times this applied only to pigs, where the flesh is not usually marbled. Pork and fish were the only large mammals in the diet.

vico n. several species of large grass, especially Erianthus maximus. As a bush food, the small fruit may be eaten rather like a tiny *duruka* fruit ("Fijian asparagus"). Totemic plant of some of the Waimaro highland people and iconic name for some people of Dravo, Tailevu. *Vico* leaves have been commonly used as thatching for houses.

vicovico n. navel, belly-button. Syn. (Tonga) *pito*.

vida, vida, vidaka v. to split, split up, split apart (wood, coral, piece of food, marriages, partnerships), divide up (land sub-division, writing into sections). *Kua ni balata na ikelekele vakaveitalia de kavia na lase.* Don't throw the anchor any which way, lest the coral be broken up. *na vidavidai* the splitting up, the dividing up.

vidavidai split up. *Sa vidavidai tu na vanua* the territory is divided up (into many parts). The verb *wasea* would imply a deliberate division with a notion of sharing (though the shares might be quite unequal for some acceptable reason.)

vidi v. to spring out suddenly, water from a leak, blood from a wound, an animal from hiding. Jumping may be implied, and/or a sudden sound such as a clicking or ticking.
Idiom: *vaka e vidi na ura* conveys the notion of something that jumps suddenly into action, as the prawn does.

vaka-vidi-ulo n. feast on the fourth night after a burial. The implication is that by this time worms (*ulo*) will be jumping around the buried body. (This entry is suggested by Rosiana Lagi of Moala.)

vidi, vidika v. to flick with the fingers, finger pressured against the thumb, suddenly released, as against the ear of a child in punishment. May refer to snapping the fingers, as in getting someone's attention.
Idiom: *Vidika na yadremu!* Wake up your mind! (usually accompanied by a flicking gesture of the finger against one's own forehead), coming suddenly to a realisation.

vidividi 1. v. clicking or flicking noise, as in *Era vidividi na daniva*. The sardines are skipping at the surface, making a clicking noise as they try to evade their predators. Prawns also make such a clicking noise.

vidividi 2. n. common square board-game of wood with counters that are flicked. A women's game, traditional precursor of this modern game, often used segments of reed that were flicked to a distance. Syn. *veividi*.

vidikoso n. (Medical) ulcerous sore.

"vidio" (or) **"video"** (Eng.) n. video (pronounced just as in English). Rental of videotapes has been common among Fijians and a significant substitute for the cinema. Videotapes are usually referred to as *tepi*. DVD discs have largely replaced the tapes. Pirating has been prevalent.

vika (Eng.) n. arithmetic, calculation. *vika kau tani* subtraction. *vika soqoni* addition. *vika vakalevutaki* multiplication. *vika wase* division. *vika kakavorovoro* fractions.

viko n. whirlwind, whirlpool, a word now sometimes used figuratively. Whirlwind can destroy a boat or a village. Unlike a hurricane, it is quite specific. In my experience, a boat can avoid it by steering away in time. *na viko ni cagilaba.* The eye of the hurricane.

vilavila-irevo n., v. traditional fire-walking of Beqa island. Feet of locals are impervious to heat of the hot stones said to be recompense for sparing the life of a certain spirit *rere* that had been caught by their ancestors. Outsiders may be invited to join it, unharmed, but very few do so. This act is now largely paid entertainment for tourists. Science has not yet determined how it is that the firewalkers' feet are not burned when they walk on the stones. There is no good explanation for this phenomenon. When they stand still on the stones the feet are protected by a layer of green vegetation. These are special stones, considered sacred. One speculation is that a very thin layer of ash separates the stones from the feet, serving as a kind of insulation. Firewalkers freely invite foreigners to join them, holding their hands to prevent a fall. This author has not accepted the invitation.

vili, vilika v. to gather, of certain foods such as *wi* fruit, *dawa, ivi* (Polynesian chestnuts), mature coconuts, mango, and mussels or small clams. *Mai vilivili!* Come, pick them up!
Idiom: *vili wi vakaca* to be beaten by a large margin in some sport or game, lit. to gather *wi* fruit unsuccessfully.

vinaka good. *vinaka vakalevu* very good. It is a modernism that these words have also come to mean a simple thank you, and thank you very much, following European custom. In ceremonial speech, trad. Fijians do say words of praise and appreciation but traditionally they never said *vinaka* "thank you" in such a simple and direct manner, though *malo* might be said by a Lauan. Appreciation of a substantial act or a gift was, and still is, properly indicated by a few soft claps of the cupped hands, usually done from a seated position, or with a bowed back. Gifts may very often be taken for granted as if they were properly due so that gratitude would be superfluous. Verbal expression of appreciation or gratitude is not considered necessary for simple acts of giving. In some sense, the ceremonial words *a muduo* would indicate acceptance and appreciation in very formal circumstances. Syn. (Bua, VanuaLevuiloma) *re*, as in *bula re* (= *Bula vinaka*) Good day! Hello!

vina du (West) good, thank you. *vina du riki* thank you very much.

vaka-vinavinaka n. thanking, thanks.

vaka-vinavinaka-taka (Anglicism) v. to thank.

vinika (Eng.) n. vinegar.

vinakata v. to desire, wish for. Syn. *gadreva*.

vinivo (Eng. pinafore) n. dress (as female clothing).

viri, viria v. to tie up, set up, throw together, establish, as of a fence, bamboo raft, type of bridge-crossing, or a defence.

viri, virika, viritaka v. to throw (usually a stone) at person, animal, house. Fijians throw with great accuracy from long experience. Usually, stones are thrown from a position of concealment. Stones may be thrown at houses or cars of people with whom there is dispute. For the throwing of sticks or clubs, the word *kolotaka* applies, not *virika*. *virika na tamata* to throw at the person. *viritaka na vatu* to throw the stone. *viriviri* throwing (things, usually stones).

viriba, viribataka v. to set up fencing, as around a garden, to keep out pigs. Lit., throw up or tie up *viri* a fence *ba*.
Idiom: *viribai* v. to get ready for imminent war, setting up defenses, specifically war fences around a settlement.

virikotora v. to establish, enact, as in *Lawa Virikotori* Act of Parliament.

viritaka v. to throw it forcefully (stone, ball). *viritaki uma* shot-put (athletics).
Idiom: *Sa viritaki na kena vatu.* It is already decisively rejected, lit. a stone has already been thrown at it. Can also mean that the decision has been made to quit something, such as a game. A child may spit on a stone and throw the stone into the bushes to indicate that he is quitting a game. The notion is that if you found the stone he would be forced to stay. Actually, nobody much would try to find it.

viritalawalawa n. spider. *lawalawa* suggests the spider's web as netting.

visa, visa v. to burn hot, of a fire, cause the flame to rise, build up a fire by adding wood. Cakobau's father Tanoa earned the name Visawaqa for burning boats of the Roko Tui Bau Raiwalui at Vuna, Taveuni Island.

visako n. Mangrove Heron, small, dark, secretive, difficult to observe, common on most coastal areas of islands, excluding Yasawa archipelago and southern Lau. Solitary nests, 2 to 3 pale blue eggs. Syn. (Rewa, Kadavu) *sako*.

viti, vitika 1. v. to push apart (vegetation) to peer ahead, in the bush. This is sometimes said to be the origin of the Fijian name "Viti" for Fiji, "Fiji" being the English spelling for the Tongan pronounciation of Viti.
viti, vitika 2. v. to break something. *vitika na taba ni kau.* break the branch of the tree. *ka viti* broken.
vitu n. seven. Syn. (Tonga) *fitu. tini ka vitu* 17. *vitusagavulu ka dua* 71.
iviu n. umbrella. Original proto-Polynesian form of the word meant fan-palm, and *ipiu* still does mean that in parts of Lau. In much of Fiji the fan-palm is known as *masei*, and its use as a sun-shade or umbrella was reserved for chieftains. Syn. *ivakaruru*, implicitly a shelter.
vivi, viviga v. to roll, roll up, as a mat, roll of cloth, or bandage. *viviga na kequ itibi* roll myself a cigarette.
vivili n. shellfish. *qa ni vivili* shell of the shellfish. *la'ki vivili* go gather shellfish. *koda, koda na vivili* eat raw shellfish. *gunu, gunuva na vivili* eat cooked shellfish (*gunu* drink). Freshwater shellfish are not eaten raw. *vivili tebe i rua* bivalve shellfish (lit. "two-lips").
vivinaka good, better (plural or emphatic form) *e vica na ivacu vivinaka* a few very good (better) punches.
vo several sp. of edible river fish, mudfish, Eliotris spp. *vo loa* a somewhat darker coloured *vo*.
vo n., v. remainder, what is left over, to be left over. *na kena vo* what is left over. *Sa vo e dua.* There is still one more, one remaining. *na vovo ni yago-na* the remains of his/her body. *na ivovo* that which is left over, the remains. *vale ni vo* n. toilet, lavatory, out-house. The concept of an outhouse was introduced by Europeans. Fijians formerly used the bush and usually concealed their excrement, mostly from fear of witchcraft. Leaves or reeds were the only toilet paper.
voavoa (Archaic) n. field, usually abandoned that is held under certain property rights, that may now be forgotten, left aside.
vo ga except, except only, excepting, excluding. See *vo*.
vakavo v. leave some. *Me vakavo na sucu!* Leave some of the milk! (Don't drink it all!).
vakavo, vakavoca v. to exclude, to leave out. *Kau kece na ika lelevu vakavoca na ika lalai me baca.* Take all the big fish and leave the small fish as bait.
vobo n. wild and semi-cultivated medicinal shrub or small tree, Mussaenda raiatensis, the branch-bark and leaves used to make an infusion especially for children to drink. Syn. *bovo*. It is easily identified by its conspicuous very large white calyx tube that has the appearance of huge flower petals. Flowers, less conspicuous, are yellow.
voca v., adj. wrecked, as of a boat crashed on the reef. *kama voca* completely burnt.
voce, vocea v. to row or paddle (boat). *vocea* to row it. *vocera* to paddle (to a place). Fijians paddle facing the bow, traditionally using only one oar and no rowlock. It was actually paddling. They never rowed with two oars. They still do not favour the European custom of rowing facing the stern. *vakalutu ivoce* (Archaic) n. canoe song, usually sung by only two people, in rhythm with the movement of oars a specialty of the Yasawa archipelago.
ivocevoce n. paddle or oar for rowboat, blade of aeroplane propellor or electric fan.
voci, vocia v. to peel a skin-fruit (with the hands, as with banana, plantain, citrus), when the peel slips off easily. Idiom: *voci vakavudi* to relate everything fully and clearly. Let is all out, speaking freely. Lit. to peel off the skin as with plantain, easily and completely.
vocivoci n. puffer fish that contains deadly poison to be removed before eating, but best avoided by the novice.
ivoco n. anus. Syn. *icici*.
vodea adj. shallow, of a pool, lagoon. Also modernly, figuratively shallow, as of discourse, argument, the mind.
vodi v. to fail to penetrate, usually of a spear, knife, arrow, nail, but may be used figuratively: *tamata e vodi na vosa.* person(s) to whom words have no effect, fail to penetrate his/her/their mind(s). Syn. *sega ni coba*. Highlanders of VitiLevu were made by their priests to believe they were invulnerable to weapons. They used the word *vodivodi* for that invulnerability. It gave them courage and helped them be fearless in war.
vodo, vodoka v. to board (boat, bus, car), mount (horse).
ivodovodo n. fare to pay for passage on bus, boat, aeroplane.
vakavodo, vakavodoka v. to put on board (boat, bus, etc.).
vodre n. grasshopper. This is a sacred or symbolic animal of Batiki chiefs of Verata.
voivoi n. a cultivated shrub, Pandanus sp., leaves used for weaving mats. Propagation: grows best in coastal areas around damp soil. Roots are removed from the corm, which is planted shallow. Later surplus suckers should be removed if plant is to grow tall, with long leaves. Plants are often knocked

over when four or five feet tall to encourage more rooting, and longer leaves. Leaves are cut, boiled in water, then sun-dried. The thorny leaf-edges are stripped off (*toci*) with a shell (*kai*), or a knife. Smoothed, the leaves are often then coiled for storage, sale or transport. Unlike mats made of sedge (*kuta*), *voivoi* mats can be washed repeatedly in water. *voivoi ni valagi* introduced varieties, green leaves often striped or streaked with yellow or white, some with no leaf thorns. *Voivoi* may be listed as P. caricosus, P. thurstoni, P. joskei (all endemic to Fiji), or P. whitmeeanus, which is the most highly prized species for weaving mats. P. whitmeeanus probably originated in Vanuatu and was introduced aboriginally to Fiji. *Voivoi* was not formerly grown in the highlands of Viti Levu, where the only traditional mats were woven of sedge (*kuta*), that did not require cultivation. Syn. *kiekie*. (Lau, Kadavu) *kie*. (Nadro, Navosa) *yaba*. Ten *voivoi* leaves may be referred to a one *buki*. One hundred *voivoi* leaves are spoken of as being one *buto*. Approximatel one *buto* of *voivoi* is needed to make one sleeping mat (*idavodavo*).

voka n. low tide. *sa kui vakaukauwa na voka* the outgoing tide flows swiftly. *Sa gole na voka*. The tide has turned. *Sa tekivu di sobu na mati*. The tide has begun to fall. *na vokavoka* the tidal movement.

vokai n. Forest Gecko, Gecko vorax The babies hatch unattended. I found a baby one, five inches long, in the month of May on the lower branches of a tree. Their feet with adhesive discs help them climb. In captivity they can be encouraged to eat by hand feeding. They accept finely cut fruit, wet leaves and flowers of hibiscus (*se-ni-toa*), and wet leaves of the *bele* vegetable. With gentle handling, *vokai* become accustomed to humans but their bite is very painful and they have an edgy temperament. They may be found from three inches in length to 12 inches. They can move with startling speed to avoid danger, or to catch an insect. Viti Levu highlanders frequently ate them after grilling (*tavu*) over fire or hot coals, and some are eaten still. These geckos are not to be confused with iguanas, known as *saumure,* which are much larger. Some mainland Fijians have referred to iguanas as *vokai* but these days most Fijians have never seen a *vokai*. Similarly, the iguana is almost never seen due to predation by the mongoose and feral cats. A couple of the small gecko species are found in houses, and are usually known as *moko*.

vokete (Eng.) n. bucket. (Anglicism) *tekea na vokete* to kick the bucket, to die.

voki v. to shift direction suddenly, of the wind.

vola n. marking, sign, indicator. *iVolasiga* planet Venus, the morning "star".

ivola n. book, letter, marking. Indigenous Fijians never developed any system of writing or complex signing. *ivola* (of the body) birthmark. *ivola vakavula* monthly magazine. *ivola-ni-vuli* n. schoolbook. *ivolavosa* n. dictionary. *ivola-ni-baqe* bank book. *ivolatara* n. permit (as for driving). *na vale ni volavola* the office. *Vunivola Tudei* Permanent Secretary (of a Ministry, the top civil servant). *Na iVola ni Kawabula* The Register of Fijian Descendants, and official record maintained by the Native Lands Commission. It is said that a Fijian is "written down" *volai* as a member of one clan *mataqali,* usually the father's clan. The N.L.C once estimated that ten percent of Fijians are not registered.

vola, vola v. to write. *volai* written, "written down", as a Fijian may be written down as a member of a native clan in the official registry *Vola ni Kawa Bula*. European missionaries introduced the concept of writing. Previously this version of the word *vola* referred only to markings or an indicator or sign, as in *iVolasiga,* the planet Venus, morning star that indicates the coming of dawn. (Appearance of that planet can also indicate the recent setting of the sun.)

vola v. to surround, as in surrounding fish with a net. *vola na qele ni kanace.* encircle, surround the school of mullet.

dau vola-itukutuku (Anglicism) n. writer, reporter, journalist.

ivolavolai (Anglicism) n. writing.

veivolavolai (Anglicism) n. correspondence, letter-writing.

ivolasiga n. planet Venus ("morning star"). This has been the name of a Fijian-language weekly newspaper. No other planets are commonly known by name by Fijians today.

ivolavosa (Anglicism) n. writing, dictionary.

volau (Polyn.) n. boat-shed. *volau ni ta waqa* ship-building yard.
Idiom: *vakasa tale na waqa ti na kena volau* there is a recurrence, as of an old problem; also an analogy like the Prodigal Son, returning home.

ivolatara (Anglicism) n. permit, as for driving licence, ticket.

voleka near, nearby, almost. *vovoleka sara* very near(ly).
Idiom: *voleka na vanua e buli kina na matau.* something that is not accessible, as remote as the place where axes are made (unknown to early Fijians)

volekata near to (place, people, thing). *na baravi volekata na tauni.* the coast next to the town. *O Viwa e volekata na yanuyanu ko Bau.* Viwa is next to Bau Island. *volekati Suva.* next to Suva. *volekati ira* near or next to them (many).
veivolekati closeness (in a physical sense).
volekano (Eng.) n. volcano. (None is active in Fiji, and none within memory.) The word is rarely seen in print. This is one example of its spelling.
voli, volia v. to trade, buy, sell, exchange for things of equal value. *volitaka* to sell it. *volia mai* to buy. *na voli weleti* the buying of papaya. *volivoli* shopping. Such trading could be done only with people of unrelated social groups. With related social groups, village communities, mutual exchanges of goods involved festive ceremonies (*solevu*), still occasionally carried out. *dauvolivoli* shopper, buyer. *na volitaki weleti* the selling of papaya. *volivolitaki* n. marketing. *dauvolivolitaki* seller, salesperson, marketer. *veivoli* commerce, trade. *isoqosoqo cokovata ni veivoli* consumer cooperative. *volivinaka* to be a bargain. *volica* to be a bad buy. *voli-rawarawa* inexpensive. *voli-saulevu* expensive, pricey, "dear".
volia-volitaka v. to buy wholesale, then sell at retail (usually farm products). Most Fijians who sell in the market and by the side of the road have bought the produce that they are selling at retail.
volitaka v. to sell it. *dauvolivolitaki* n. salesman, sales woman, seller.
volivoli n. v., shopping. *dau volivolitaki* sellers, vendors. *dau volivoli* buyers, shoppers, consumers. *volivoli vakadinau* hire-purchase, installment purchase. *Volivoli* is an old place-name in a few different locations; it signifies the collection of Fijian goods submitted as tribute in olden days. Tributary paths from place to place were known as *sala volivoli*. Verata and Laucala were early centres that had a system of *sala volivoli*.
veivoli n. sales, marketing, as in *manidia ni veivoli* sales manager. *veivoli umauma* wholesale.
voli, volita v., n. to go around, to follow around *noqu voliti Viti* my going around Fiji. *E a soko wavoliti Viti Levu ena waqa o Seru.* Seru circumnavigated Fiji in the boat. See *wavoki*.
voli around, go about. *veilakoyaki voli* go around here and there. *qalo voli* swim about. In some cases the word is not directly translatable.
volivolita v. to surround. *era sa vakavolivoliti koya* they(many) surrounded him.
volipolo (Eng.) n. volleyball.
volo v. to dig for wild yams such as *tivoli, tikau, rauva* out in the bush.
Idiom: (Taveuni) *Lai volo!* Get out of the way, get out of here! Yelled at a child who is a nuisance.
vono n. v. (Tongan, Samoan *fono*) formal village meeting in Polynesian tradition.
vono n. shrub, Alyxia spp., Apocynacea, known for attractive flowers, usually white or cream-coloured. *vonokula* a pink var. that gives the name to Adi Pateresia Vonokula, Roko Tui Waimaro. Her names comes from Lau from an ancient marriage into the Waimaro super-tribe.
vono, vonotaka v. to inlay, to inlay with (perhaps shell, whaletooth into wood such as a warclub). Or to put pieces together, as in assembling something. *civavonovono* (Archaic) chiefly breast-plate of inlaid pearlshell with whaletooth, made by Tongans, some given by Bau to compliant lesser chiefs who cooperated with the extension of Bauan influence and power.
vonu n. giant sea-turtle, usually referring to the Green Turtle. Unlike the smaller Hawkbill turtle (*taku*), the Green is docile and usually does not defend itself by biting. It is vegetarian, favouring sea grass. Breeding takes place only at very specific sandy locations to which the turtle returns after a long absence. Sex ratio of newborn turtles depends on ambient temperature at incubation of eggs; higher temperatures around 30 degrees C. yield females while lower temperatures yield males. The name *vonu* also refers to the much rarer Leatherback, Dermochelys coriacea, *ika dina,* which is occasionally seen in Fiji waters, usually at sea rather than right by the shore, for apparently it does not breed here, and it has practically never been caught in the Fijian traditional turtle nets. In the Pacific, it has breeding grounds along the coast of Mexico. It is a much bigger turtle, up to perhaps 8 feet in length, the male weighing as much as two tonnes. The leatherback is the world's largest reptile. It is seen basking at midday, gathering body heat. At other times it dives very deep, to at least 3 thousand feet, feeding mainly on jellyfish and zooplankton, as they rise and fall in a daily cycle. Adults are more commonly seen in cold waters (40° F or less), except when they are breeding.

The Loggerhead turtle, one of the world's oldest species, is rarely seen in Fiji waters, mostly in the open ocean, lazing on the surface. Spending five years at sea as a diver and fisherman, I have seen one only once. Weighing 300 pounds or more, it has a huge, broad head with very powerful jaws that can bite through heavy clamshells that are almost two inches thick. It is carniverous but never wilfully attacks humans. This *tuvonu* never breeds in Fiji. Its main breeding grounds are very far away, mainly along beaches from Texas to North Caroline, and also at the coast of Oman. Eggs are laid in the sand, and covered, to hatch after about two months.

Turtle was a chiefly food, and social groups called Gonedau existed to catch turtle with nets (never spears), for their paramount chiefs at Verata, Bau, Cakaudrove. For the chiefs of Verata, the people of Qoma Island were traditional turtle fishermen. Turtle fishermen, and concept of paramount chiefs were of Tongan origin. Much ceremony attended the fishing for turtles. Turtle fishermen were sometimes also naval warriors, such as the Lasakau of Bau. Carving of the portions was a skilled occupation. At Bau, the turtle was killed by poking a *sasa* (coconut leaf midrib) up the turtle's nostril. The throat is then slit. Normally, the turtle heart beats long after the turtle is dead, a disturbing phenomenon for anyone to witness. Cutting up the turtle was a very specialised occupation, carefully done, with the various parts given out to various people. The blood solidifies by clotting. Put in a bowl, water accumulates above the clotted blood, and is discarded. The clotted blood is then cut, more or less in cubes, and is cooked with the meat and fat. It is is an extremely rich food.

Cakaudrove chiefs ate turtle eggs, often raw, sometimes cooked. Other than the eggs, the Tui Cakau was specially given the fatty part from inside the back of the turtle, a part called the *pito*, implying a navel in Tongan language. The shell and some leftover parts were reserved for the people of *Benau*, a seafaring people originally from Tonga, expert divers, fearless of sharks. As with whales, the meat is not marbled with fat, so a sauce or coconut cream are required, or the addition of fat. The fat congeals on cooking and turns a dark green colour, extremely rich in taste and can be eaten only in small quanitities.

Sanctity of the turtle, and the calling of turtles to the surface has been traditional at village Nacamaki, Koro Island, and at village Namuana, Vunisea harbour, Kadavu Island. Turtles are now an endangered species. Their main enemy is man, and also sharks. A large tiger shark can swallow a green turtle whole. *qoli vonu* fish for turtle (using nets). Syn. (Tonga) *fonu*.

voqa v., n. to rumble, echo, resound, deep reverberating sound. *na voqa ni ua*. The sound of the waves. *na voqa ni davui* the sound of the Trumpet shell horn. By ext. this can refer to the fuss made by "sounding off" in, for examples, letters to a newspaper editor.

voqataka v. to speak out insistently, persistently. *Eratou dau voqataka ena veiniusipepa*. They are always talking up in the newspapers.

vora, vorata v. to oppose, take a stand against, to resist.

veivorati n., adj. resistance, opposition, strongly opposed to each other.

voraki n., v. force or violence; forced against one's will.

vakavoraki-taka v. to force (someone, something).

voravora adj. very rough, of the sea, harsh of words, very severe of a person.

vore n. (Kadavu) pig. Syn. *vuaka*. (Rewa) *qo*.

vorivori adj. lecherous, lustful. Syn. *garogaro* (or) *garosa* (or) *yaga siri*.

voro, voroka v. to smash, break (skull, plates, glass, etc.). Modernism: *voroka na lawa* break the law.

voro adj. stuffed to the point of bursting, as in idiom *kana voro* stuff oneself with food. *voro leqa* terribly disturbed, bursting (*voro*) with worries (*leqa*).

vorowaqa sp. sailfish, Istiophorus sp. or swordfish Xiphia gladius. Most Fijians are familiar with neither. Sailfish is sometimes sold in the market but parasites have often made holes in the flesh. *waqa* boat.

vosa n. word(s), talk, language. *na vosa vakaViti* the Fijian language. *vosa ena vosa vaka neitou*. speak in our language (our dialect). *vosa-ni-vanua* n. dialect, communalect, local language. *daunivosa* (or) *gusu ni vosa* spokesperson (as a modern concept). *daunivosa* n. now adopted at Univ. of South Pacific for people who have studied linguistics. *matanaivosa* clever at talking, smart with words. *na ivolavosa* the dictionary. *yavu ni vosa* root-word, often modified, made transitive, by adding a suffix or prefix. *dewa ni vosa* alternative form of a verb, such as a transitive form, made by adding a prefix or suffix to the intransitive root-form. *yatuvosa* n. sentence (grammatical). *cai-vosa* (vulgar) v., adj. cheeky, too outspoken. *A vosa taumada* n. Foreword (as to a book). *vosa ena domo mamasu* speak in a pleading voice. *vosa veibasai* n. antonym, a word with opposite meaning. *malanivosa* n. part of speech. *matua-vosa* n. alphabet, script of a language. *wa ni vosavosa* n. telephone. *vosa ni susu* n. "first" language, one's primary language, spoken in childhood. Syn. (West) *tata*.

Idiom: *vosa vutubati* lit., speaks as if suffering from a toothache, i.e., reluctantly, unpleasantly, in a surly manner.

vosa v. to speak. *vosa vei koya* speak to him/her. *vosa taladrodro* speak fluently, flowingly. *vakalutu vosa* v., n. to wisecrack. *veisau vosa* v. to talk back. *na vosataki ni noda vosa* the speaking of our (many) language.

Idiom: *vosa tagau dua* speak briefly, lit. speak just the short length of one internode (as of bamboo, or *yaqona*); toward the end of a speech, the speaker may say "*Tagau dua . . .*" meaning "In brief" or "In summary" and summarise his main points.

veivosa n. expressions (in language, dialect).
vosa-vaka-ibalebale n. proverb.
vosavosa v. to talk excessively.
ivosavosa n. idioms, verbal expressions. *na ivosavosa vakaviti eso* some Fijian idioms. Syn. *veivosavosa*.
veivosavosa n. verbal expression, idioms, types of speech. Syn. *ivosavosa*.
vosaka v. to speak for the man, requesting a family for a certain woman in marriage. The request is accompanied by a whale-tooth. Acceptance of the whale tooth implies acceptance of the request. In cases of refusal, the offered tooth is taken but another tooth given to reciprocate,(*dirika* to respond negatively y reciprocating with a whaletooth.). *vosaki koya me watiqu* request her (through the family) to become my wife. Syn. *duguci*.
vosa-i-na-daku-taka v. to talk behind one's back.
veivosaki n. conversation. *ena nodaru veivosaki* in our (2) conversation.
veivosaki-taka v. to discuss it, talk it over. *veivosakitaki* discussed.
vosa mama v. to speak mutteringly, incoherently (as in one's sleep).
vosamana v. to foretell, prophesy (in the traditional Fijian way). This is usually done with ceremony, kava, frothing at the mouth or other shamanistic behaviour. The custom continues today.
Vosa Matua ni Pasifika e Cake n. branch of Austronesian language spoken by the migratory Lapita people from 1,000 B.C. that is the basis for the later development of Fijian and the Polynesian languages. A language first evolved from that in the central Pacific, later forming Fijian, Samoan and Tongan as separate languages. Cognates from that language persist today with many dozens of words mutually understandable. The word *Vosa Matua* was invented by Paul Geraghty. He has thought it necessary to create a very great number of modern Fijian words, particularly concerning Fijian grammar.
vosa-minimini v. to mutter hardly audibly, as when angry.
vosa muri, vosa muria v. to criticise, speak against, as of some decision or command, after it has been announced.
vosa-ni-vanua n. local or regional speech, dialect, communalect.
vosamuri-taka v. to have spoken, and then later speak against what was agreed to. To have "second thoughts" in an unpleasant way.
vosa-ni-susu (or) **vosanisucu** n. first language (that one spoke as a child).
vosataka v. to criticise, attack verbally, reprimand.
vosa-vakaca-taka v. to say bad things (about something or someone), to speak ill of . . .
Vosavakadua Chief Justice. This was also a name or quasi-title used by one of the prominent Fijian "prophets" (dissidents).
vosa-vinaka, vosavinaka-taka v. to express thanks graciously. This is a rather modern expression.
vosavosa 1. v., n. to grumble, grumbling, to complain.
vosavosa 2. v., n. speaking, talk. *vosavosa duadua* talking to oneself, as elderly people might do, or a delerious person.
ivosavosa 1. n. manner of speech, way of speaking or expressing oneself (dialect, slang or formal speech, personal manner).
ivosavosa 2. n. saying, expression, slogan, motto.
vosavosa i yalona v. to talk to oneself. Syn. *vosavoa duadua*.
vosavosa wale v. idle talk. *dau vosavosa wale* n. idle talker, gabbler.
vosayaco adj., influential (person), one whose words have effect to make things happen.
vosa-yalewa v. to propose marriage, usually in a formal sense, this done by elders for the prospective groom after they have been given to understand that the proposal will be accepted. Such formalities might only apply for high chiefs.
vosota n. patience, forgiveness. *dauvosota* patient, forgiving.
vosota v. to forgive, pardon, excuse, be patient with. *vosoti au* excuse me.
veivosoti n. reciprocal patience.
vosovosoti n. patience.
veivosovosoti n. profound, emphatic forgiveness with mutual understanding.
vota, vota v. to distribute, share out, often said of a *magiti* where the food and goods are shared out. (Careful judgement is required so that no people feel slighted; they certainly watch carefully.) *e vota*

mai na kabani distributed by the company. *votai* shared out, distributed (often in ceremony, according to custom). *na nomu ivotavota* (or) *ivota* your share.

Idiom: *votavota o Tuirara* criticism of a person's greed, implying that a village steward who distributes food at a formal distribution of food *magiti* could be favouring himself or his own people with a large share for himself.

votivoti adj. irritating, annoying (a problem, a person, physical abrasion).

voto-na n. thorn, spike. *votovotoa* or *veivotoki* thorny, prickly (lemon tree, sea urchin etc.) *na voto ni vai* the spike of the stingray.

votoka v. to prick, prickle, pierce, as a thorn or needle might do.

votu 1. v. to appear, become visible. *e votu mamaca* it appears clear(ly). *E laurai votu* It is clearly visible, apparent. Geraghty believes this is the origin of the place-name Votua, suggesting a location that has appeared after a lowering of the sea level or a rise in the level of the land.

votu 2. n. vowel. This word is a modern invention of teachers of Fijian language, unknown to the general public. Similarly, the new Fijian word *koso* has been invented to mean "consonant". And *tago-na* refers to "syllable".

vakavotukana v. to make apparent, cause to appear, reveal.

vou 1. adj. new (singular form). *vovou* (plural form). *ravouvou* n. "prince", young chief who is likely to inherit a traditional title other than in Fiji, though the word is used in children's stories. *vou vei au* (Anglicism) new to me.

Idiom: (Anglicism) *sucu vou* born again (among Evangelical Christians).

vou 2. adj. immature, green, of fruit.

Idiom: *bati vou* adj., n. one who likes to eat immature fruit (especially women and children). Jocularly, may be said of an older man who prefers younger girls.

vakavoutaka (Anglicism) v. to renew. *na vakavoutaki ni laiseni* the renewal of the licence.

ivovo n. leftovers, what is left over, as for food after a meal, or timber after construction.

vovou adj. new (plural form).

vu 1. v. to be the cause or origin, to be caused, to originate.

vu-na 2. n. origin, cause, reason. *yavu* house-foundation (a named house-site). *yavutu* place-name where a tribe (*yavusa*) was formed. *Na vu ni noqu biuti Suva* The reason for (or cause of) my leaving Suva. *vakavuna* v. to cause.

vu 3. n. ancestral spirit of one or more tribes (*yavusa*), originally a person who founded that social group, who may have become deified in a sense. In some cases the spirit could take the permanent or temporary form (*waqawaqa*) of an animal, or reside in a rock or tree. That representation (rock, tree, living creature) would be respected with avoidance or some respectful behaviour, perhaps even gifts, a small branch of leaves, or even a whaletooth in the case of Degei. But for the *vu* there is no supplication for special favour such as success in war. Among Fijians themselves, the term *kalou vu* is sometimes confused as a synonym for *vu*. And this is a topic one may not always discuss openly. Only some of the *vu* have names, or the names are forgotten probably because one is usually not encouraged to pronounce the name. By contrast, for *kalou vu*, temples were built and attended by just a few select people, services with offerings and solicitations, advanced through a priest *bete*, who would take care of food or any gifts presented for the *kalou vu*. The *kalou vu* did not necessarily ever have any previous human form. An authority as great as the late Solo Bulicokocoko referred to the spirit Tui Naikasi at village Nacamaki, Koro Island, as a *kalou vu*, yet in the formal chants calling the turtle, the people themselves refer to it as their *vu*. There has thus come to be some confusion among Fijians themselves as to usage of the terms *vu* and *kalou vu*.

When two kin-groups or tribes have the same ancestral spirit (*vu*), they are said to be *tauvu* to each other. For example, in Fijian, *Era veitauvutaki kina na vanua o Noco kei na vanua o Lau*. In English:- The Territory of Noco (in Rewa Province) is *tauvu* with the Territory of Lau. They have an historical intimacy, and may take liberties joking with each other. In some cases, this can be "hard" joking and they are said to be *tauvu dredre*. Formerly such relationships were often between two very specific places but in time this often becomes a relationship between both regions. In early times, for example, the relationship of Noco did not extend to all of Lau but only to Nayau if I remember correctly, and perhaps only to part of Nayau. Such relationships can become established after a very high level chiefly marriage between two places. Details are often forgotten.

The social relationship called *veitabani* refers to two specific places that have ancestral spirits (*vu*) that were cross-cousins (*tavale*) to each other. They may address each other as *Naita* and treat each other with very severe hard joking.

vu 4. (Anglicism) n. verb. *vuwale* intransitive verb. This Fijian word for "verb" has been invented and adopted by local teachers of language. The *vu* is considered the root-word, that in Fijian may be followed by one or more suffixes (called *dewa*, another invented word) that alter the meaning to make the verb transitive, and/or add various prepositions. For instance, *cici* is the root verb "run". *Ciciva* means to run for, or run to. And *civivaka* is to "run with" (say, carrying a knife), or ""run to get". *vu-vakavu* (Anglicism) n. transitive form of a verb, causing that verb to happen, e.g., *dara* is the verb to wear, put on (clothes, ring on finger). *vakadarama* is the *vuvakavu* to express the notion of causing the clothes, for example, to be worn. Such modern linguistic terms have been invented recently but are unknown to the general public.

vu 5. n.,v. to cough; or as a "cold" that implies coughing. *Sa manati au na vu.* I have a fit of coughing, have a cold that makes me cough. *vuvu* continued coughing.

vu ni kalou n. traditional midwife.

vu ni koli n. whooping cough. *koli* dog.

vuniduvu n. composer and choreographer of *meke* (traditional dance and songs). He is highly respected and rewarded for creating and "giving" the meke, which then belongs to the recipients who have asked for it. Syn. *dau ni vucu*.

vua = *vei koya* to him/her/it, for him/her/it. *Solia vua* . Give it to him/her/it. *na ka e sa yaco vua* what (that which) happened to him/her. *mai vua* from him/her, in relation to him/her. *cakacaka tiko vua na kaivalagi.* is working for the European.

vua v. to bear fruit. *Sa vua mai na moli.* The citrus is fruiting. *vua ni qele* n. harvest (in general), lit. fruits of the land. *Sa vuavuai vinaka na kumunilavo.* The money-collection was very successful (fruitful), an Anglicism.

vua-na n. fruit, harvest. *na vua ni painapiu.* the pineapple fruit. *na vua ni qele* the harvest, agric. produce.

vakavua v. to conquer (literally, with combat, said of a village or people).

vuabale v. to overflow (liquid, emotion). *Sa vuabale na noqu bilo.* My cup has overflowed, an Anglicism.

vuaira n. wind from northwest. Contrast with *vuaicake* (or) *tokalau* wind from the northeast, *tokalau cevaceva* wind from the southeast (the tradewind), *na ceva* the wind from the south. *vualiku* northwind, northeasterly, north, northeast (the proper, older meaning).

vuaka (Polyn.) n. pig, pork. *vuaka tagane* boar. *vuaka balavu* (Archaic) human cannibal meat, a term well recognized but now used very rarely, and only in joking. The pig was introduced by aboriginal Fijians. It was more efficient and less encumbering to hunt them when needed, rather than domesticate them. Only very small pigs were kept for a time as pets by Melanesian Fijians. On the larger islands, pigs are trapped, or with the aid of dogs, hunted with spears, only as needed for feasts, not as an everyday food. Several glands must be cut from the boar to avoid off-flavour. At large ceremonial food presentations, ten pigs are referred to as one *rara*. There might be two or more *rara* presented. Syn. (Kadavu, Nadro., Serua, Beqa) *vore*. (Rewa, Yasawa, Ba, Rakiraki) *qo*.

Idiom: *Matai via kana vuaka.* Refers to someone – a carpenter (*matai*) in this case -- who expects to share in compensation, as at a feast after completion of some work, when in fact he did little or nothing of the work itself.

Idiom: *vuaka balavu* n. cannibal meat, human body for eating. *balavu* tall (or) long.

vualiku n. north wind, north (as a direction) or northeast, northeasterly, the more "correct", older meaning. The prefix *vua* is an old term for wind. Syn: *tokalau*.

vuaviri n. overthrow (of a chief, or regime), military coup (May and September 1987, 2000, 2006). Before colonial times a very great number of chiefly lineages had been overthrown and replaced by outsiders.

vuaviri-taka v. to overthrow (it).

vuca adj. rotten.

vuce v., n. to swell, a swelling (of some part of the body).

vucesa adj. lazy.

vuci n. taro garden under natural irrigation, often swampy but where the water moves, even if slowly. The taste is considered better than that of dryland-cultivated taro. Anciently there were in a few places elaborate irrigated terraced taro gardens. Just a few were in use when Europeans first arrived.

vucu v. to chant. *dau ni vucu* (or) *vu ni duvu* composer and choreographer who creates traditional dances (*meke*), a position of great local respect.

vakavudua only once in a while, occasionally (not often), as in *sa rogo vakavudua voli ga na domona*. His/her voice is occasionally heard.

vude v. to bob up, as a head emerging from diving. Idiom: n., v. *vude* modern social dance that in Fiji involves a lot of bobbing up and down.

vudi n. plantain, and aboriginal introduction usually eaten as a cooked starch-food, often as sweetened pudding, with coconut cream (only in coastal areas). Sometimes listed as Musa balbisiana, though this genus is very labile and difficult to classify. The original varieties are now referred to as "true" plantain *vudi dina* to distinguish them from later introduced types. *vudi vula* is a tall plant with very plump fruit that often split as they ripen. This is not considered a defect by Fijians. Some also believe that the fruit of this variety (and also watermelon, by the way) will crack open if there is any thunder. Planting is by suckers and the mother plant naturally sprouts suckers. The leaves are useful as improvised mats or umbrellas, and stripped into sections, formerly used for "skirts" of both men and women.
    Idiom: *vocia vakavudi.* something done very easily, quickly with no effort, such as in removing the skin of plantain fruit, to gush forth with the whole story.

vudolo v., adj. snapped off, broken off, having a broken handle (usually spade, axe, garden tool), *vudolo rua* broken in two, as a boat crashed on a reef. Syn. *ramusu* or *kamusu*.

vueta, vuetaka v. to raise up, as with a fishing net; to rescue. *na tamata vuetaki ena wasawasa.* the people picked up at sea. *vueta na lawa* to raise the net. *Me vueti na lawa.* Raise the fishing net. Vueti was the name of a chief from Verata, who won a major victory for Degei in the Nakauvadra wars in the mid 1700s. Moving south to his father's home at Moturiki Island, he founded the tribe Vusaratu, and adopted the title Roko Tui Bau. With the Tui Kaba as his Vunivalu, he formed tribe Kubuna at Kubuna on the Tailevu coast and invaded a small island he named Bau. Significantly, Vueti is a Tongan name (Fueti), as is the name of his father, Vaula (Paulaho). There was very substantial early Tongan influence in Moturiki. The Tui Moturiki with an entourage had migrated to Tonga at least as early as the 1200s. Legend also tells of Tongan settlement on Moturiki.

veivueti n. AID, assistance (usually financial) in raising up, usually speaking of help to indigenous Fijians. *waqa ni veivueti* rescue boat. *Veivueti* name of a military operation that claimed to raise the status and economic well-being of the Fijians after the military coups of 1987.

vuga n. bush or tree, Metrosideros collina, Myrtaceae, with conspicuous red (sometimes pink or yellow) flowers all year. Prop roots at the base of the tree. Shaggy light grey bark. Slash is red, exposing yellow wood. Legend relates that *vuga* roots from Nakauvadra extend underground to Verata, or that the root was taken to Verata and planted, symbolizing the continuing blood relationship of the people. The Verata extension is known as the *Waka ni vugayali* ("Root of the *vugayali*"). Another legend relates that the root extends underground to the west, by Vuda and village Viseisei. The roots reportedly have blood-red sap, symbolic of the blood relationships descended from Lutunasobasoba, a late immigrant chief who promoted the new notion of paramount chiefs. Earlier Melanesian settlers from Vanuatu and the Solomons had never known the concept of paramount chiefs. *Vugayali* is legendary tree of Vugalei people, name of the last child of Degei, but from shame, Vugayali, with permission of Degei, changed his name to Kau. According to Basil Thomson, a bush called *vugayali* was cut down by Vueti in overwhelming village Narauyabe at the Nakauvadra mountain range in Ra. Narauyabe was the village of Tongan boat-builder Rokola, who was protecting the Ciri Twins who had killed Degei's pet fowl Turukawa. Trees known as *vugayali* still exist at Mt. Tomaniivei (= Mt. Victoria, highest mountain of Fiji, given its European name by Adolf Brewster.) The Fijian name means "From where does it flow", referring to this area as the source of the Ba River, Sigatoka River and the Rewa River.). The name is not Tomaniivi, "Adam and Eve", as is often thought. That tree is the totem of tribe Nacavodo at village Nasoqo, Nabobuco District, Naitasiri Province. These were a Waimaro people now living at the border of Provinces Naitasiri, Nadroga/Navosa, Ba, and Ra. One Vugalei author with some schooling, reports that the suffix *yali* comes only from the locals deeply regretting the loss of their tree that apparently had symbolic value to them. There is a slightly different species called *vugayalo* with flowers more starkly scarlet, and leaves that are more tender and shiny, and coloured a somewhat darker, duller green. Brewster consideres the name *vugayali* to be a mistake for *vugayalo*. In fact, they are two different plants as reported by the Forestry Department. Examples of each are grown for demonstration at Wainadoi Nature Gardens. Botanical identification is not yet determined.

vugo-na n. a set of specific mutual relationships within a family, also used as a form of address. For a younger person, *na vugoqu* usually refers to an aunt, or an in-law. It may also refer to the mother's brother, an uncle, but he is much more often referred to as *momo*. The elder person will also usually address the nephew or niece as *vugoqu*. The younger person will generally address *na vugona* as *mudrau* (probably an abbreviation of *kemudrau*, a respectful form of "you" because it is in plural form.) *Rau na veivugoni o Orisi kei Marica.* The two who are related as *vugona*, Orisi and Marica. Syn. *gaji*.

vuka, vukaca v. to fly. *vukaca* to fly some object, cargo or person(s). *manumanu vuka* n. bird. *waqavuka* n. aeroplane. *ika vuka* n. flying fish.

vuka-taka v. to fly (aeroplane, helicopter, passengers), also to send by air (as with air freight). *Sa vukataki na doka ni vale ena cagi laba.* The roof-top flew off in the hurricane.

vuka as in *yalo vuka* having an emotional reaction, as in being given a "start", sudden surpise or shock.

vuka n., adj. off-colour, as sullied, grey, pallid, mouldy, as human skin, mats or clothes might be. *vukoa* mould, mouldy.

vukavuka n. leprosy, preferably referred to as Hansen's disease, pre-existing in Fiji before arrival of Europeans. Infectious agent is Mycobacterium leprae, transmitted usually by droplets from nose or mouth in close contact over considerable length of time. Incubation takes five to 20 years. Some 95% of people are naturally immune though Dr. Corney, medical officer in Fiji, calculated in 1907 that leprosy was the cause of deaths of 0.8 percent of Fijians in his time. Symptoms appear on skin rashes, sores on feet, in deadening of nerves, stuffy or bleeding nose, eyes (glaucoma), disfigured limbs, erectile dysfunction, kidney damage. Treatment is by Multi-Drug Therapy over 12 months, though infectious dangers cease after first treatment. In 1890 a leper settlement was established on 138 acres purchased on Beqa for Fijian patients, with non-Fijians located at Walu Bay next to the then Colonial Hospital. In 1911, Makogai Island was established as a leper colony with 20 patients cared for by Roman Catholic sisters. It was closed in 1969 with the remaining 17 patients transferred to P.J. Twomey Hospital in Tamavua. Some 4500 lepers had been treated at Makogai and 1500 were buried there. To be remembered especially was Rev. Mother Mary Agnes who served on Makogai for 34 years, dying there at age 80 in 1955. She had been awarded the M.B.E. and the Legion of Honour. Syn. *sakuka, sakovi*.

vukavuka adj. as in *itukutuku vukavuka* (or) *itukutuku vuka* rumour. *rogoci vukavuka* heard as a rumour.

vuke, vukea v. to help. *vukei au* help me. *E keimami dau veivuketaka.* We (many) help with it.

ivukevuke n. assistant, deputy. *na ivukevuke ni jeamani* the deputy chairman.

veivukei n. help. *kerea na nona veivukei* ask for his help.

Vukelulu (or) **Siga Vukelulu** (Tonga, Pulelulu) n. Wednesday. Syn. (Lau) *Siga Vunau*. (Kadavu, Nadroga) *burelulu*.

vuki, vukica v. to turn, turn over. *tavuki* flipped over. (As a place-name Tavuki refers to a previous chiefly lineage overthrown.) *vuki vakanadaku* turn (one's) back on. *veivuki-yaki* adj., n. changeable, fickle, variable (as of the wind), unsettled. *vukivuki* of a baby, reached a stage of growth being able to turn over by itself.

Idiom: *vukica na uto* make a decisive, unexpected change. Being grilled on coals, breadfruit becomes charred, and is suddenly flipped over to avoid burning.

vuki n., v. (Colo East) method of cooking, food steamed in its own juices, contained in bamboo tubes, grilled over a fire. To avoid the bamboo being burned, it was frequently rotated, turned over, as implied in the name *vuki*. All cooking in the highlands was done by direct grilling over a fire (*tavu*) or *vuki*. There were no clay pots, and no use of the earth oven. The bamboo tubes were discarded after each use.

vuki prefix to words of people's behaviour or ability. *vuki totolo* swift, quick and responsive. *vuki bera* slow by nature. *vuki levu* awkward, clumsy, inept. *vuki matau* adept, clever. Vuki can be a feminine name.

vukitavali v. to unfasten, come unfastened.

vukitavu n. pudding specialty of village Nawaikama, Gau Island. Made of grated cassava and grated taro blended, boiled, and then grilled in bud-shaped packages of *ivi* leaf. Then *lolo buta* (caramelised coconut cream) is poured over it.

vukivuki restless, as in *moce vukivuki,* sleeping tossing and turning.

ivukivuki n. manners. (usually good), behaviour.

vei-vuki-yaki adj. as in *e dua na tamata veivukiyaki* an indecisive person, with a frequently changing mind.

vukoa n. mould, mildew.

vuku 1. n., adj. sensible, wisdom, wise, knowledgable, educated, intelligent.

Idiom: *yalewa vuku* midwife. *vukutaka* to be smart about (something).

Idiom: (Anglicism) *na yacana vakavuku* the scientific name.

vuku 2. in the expression *ena vuku ni* -- in the interests of. *ena vuku ni gonevuli* in the interests of schoolchildren.

vuku 3. in the expression *ena vuku ni --* concerning. *ena vuku ni tikina oqo* concerning this matter.

vuku 4. in the expression *ena vuku ni --* because of. *ena vuku ni kena levu.* because of its size.

vula 1. n. moon, month (Fijians used a lunar calendar). *na vula ko Noveba* the month of November. *vula vou* new moon, also an occasion for special Methodist services and competitive money collection. The household that gives the most money keeps on display for the next month a shield celebrating their generosity. *Sa taucoko na vula* (Anglicism) The moon is full, There is a full moon. *ena vula oqo* this month. *ena vula sa oti* last month. *ena vula mai oqo* next month. *mate ni vula* menstruation. Out in the villages, Fijians will recognise many of the signs of the changing months, the flowering or fruiting of certain plants, or the abundance of certain seafoods. At the end of this dictionary there is a list of the lunar months and the characteristic changing signs of nature.

vula n. species of bêche-de-mer (*dri*), Bohadschia spp, (several species, some with names slightly modified from *vula*), sold for the Chinese market, only rarely eaten by Fijians. It is whitish as indicated by the name, and otherwise appearance resembles *sucuwalu*, one of the main types without fleshy protrusions.

vakavulavula v. Idiom: do something by the light of the moon. *Au a vaka-vulavula mai ena bogi.* Last night I came by the light of the moon.

vulavula white. (Based on the word for moon (*vula*), which in fact has various shades of colour from white to yellow.)

vulaci v., n., adj. turned pale, pale(d), usually referring to a human face, as in *Sa vulaci na mataqu ena rere.* My face paled with fear. pallor, pallid. See *seavu, ceacea, ceavula*.

vulagi n. visitor, guest. *vulagi dokai* n. honoured guests, guest of honour. Modernly, in political parlance of Fijian extremists, *vulagi* also refers to people in Fiji who do not qualify legally as indigenous Fijians (*iTaukei*), though they may have been born in Fiji and lived all their lives there for several generations.

vulagi, vulagica v. to be unfamiliar (with something).

vulala v., adj. every dilute, usually of tea, *yaqona*. Syn. *waicala sara*.

vulawalu n. Crown of Thorns, a threat that damages the reefs, a name I learned from the late Rob Wright, noted authority on fishing in Fiji. There are efforts in some locations to eradicate it by collected them, or by injection of a chemical.

Vakavulewa (Anglicism) n. Constitution (of government).

vuli, vulica v. to study, learn (something). *koronivuli* n. school. *vuli tara* learn by experience, "hands-on" experience. *na ivakavuvuli* the teaching(s). *qase ni vuli* school-teacher. *gonevuli* schoolchild. *biu-vuli* school-leaver, one who has quit school. *vuli wale* free schooling (no school fees paid by parents), a concept that began to be discussed in Fiji as recently as 1995. *na vulici ni vosa vakaViti* studying, learning the Fijian language. *Na vuli nasi* the student nurse(s). Idiom: *vuli lokoloko* learn somethings such as a language by sleeping with one who knows it, a fast way to learn from the bed-partner. *lokoloko* soft pillow (artefact introduced from Polynesia).

vakavulica v. to teach (something or someone). *vakavuvuli* village pastor.

vakata-dredre (Archaic) for a chiefly girl, a ceremony performed until the fourth night after birth by old women with the implication that she should follow in their footsteps

vakatavulica v. to teach (something or someone). *na lesoni dau vakatavulici mai koronivuli* the lessons usually taught at school.

vakatavuvuli v. to practice, in order to master some skill.

vakavulici n. teaching(s) *na nodra vakavulici na luvedra* the teaching of their children.

veivakavulici n. teaching(s), education. adj. trained, taught.

vuli-vaka-vo n. school-leaver, quitting school before completion. Syn. *biu-vuli*.

vulo 1. n. ten whaleteeth, for ceremonial presentation. This counting system was used only at such very formal occasions.

vulo 2. n. strainer used for Fiji herbal medicine, usually cut from a sheet of natural, coarse fabric, the stipule, that grows at the base of the coconut palm fronds. Pieces of medicinal bark, root or leaf are tied in this as a little package through which water may be squished to obtain the essence. These day a piece of cloth may be used. *vulo-ni-ti* n. tea-strainer. *matavulo* n. mask. Little is known about the ancient use of masks. They were made only of plant fibres and human hair, never finely carved wood. No masks are used today (except balaclavas, worn by burglars. Wooden masks sold in tourist shops are not Fijian in design or function.

vulona (or) **tauvulona** v. to use a *vulo* strainer, usually in preparing Fiji medicine. *ivuloni* or *itauvulona* strainer.

vulua (or) **vuluwa** n. genital hair, pubic hair. See *modri*.

vulukano (Eng.) n. volcano. Fijians have no knowledge of volcanic activity. The last one occured in Vuna, Taveuni, in the mid-1300s, not remembered in Fijian oral history. (Volcano activity is well known in nearby Vanuatu.) This word is rarely seen in print. The spelling is not standard.

vuluvulu v. to wash (usually part of the body) with a rubbing motion, specifically wash the hands before or after a meal (since one eats with the hands). Basin and napkin are usually provided after meals. *ivuluvulu* n. the basin of water so used. No soap was known to indigenous Fijians.

vuna n. cause, reason (for something), source.

vakavuna v. to cause.

vunau, vunauca, vunautaka v. to preach. *vunauca na vavakoso* preach to the congregation. *vunautaka na tevoro*. preach about the devil(s). *Siga vunau* (Lau) Wedneday.

ivunau n. sermon. *na ivunau e tini* the ten commandments.

veivunauci n. advice.
Idiom: *veivunauci vaka i Ra kasala*. lit. give advice as a *kasala* fish does, that is, to be good at giving advice but failing to follow that advice oneself.

vunibati-na n. gums (of the human mouth). *bati-na* tooth. *gadro-na* palate.

vunidibi-na n. hip-joint of the human body.

vunikau n. plant, shrub, tree. *vu ni tiaina* banana plant; *vu ni painapiu* pineapple plant. Fijians have no separate words for herb, shrub, tree.

vunilagi n. horizon. *lagi* sky.

vuni adj. hidden, secret. *lako vuni* to go secretly.
Idom: *ka vuni* secret. Also, in context, private parts (of human body).

vuni, vunia v. to hide (oneself). *E dau vunia kina na matana*. He/she usually hides his/her face.

vuni, vunitaka v. to hide (something). *vunivuni* deceptively secretive.

vunivunitaki n. secrecy.

vuni- (followed by the name of a plant) n. plant names are usually given by adding this prefix to the name, as in *vuniweleti* papaya plant, *vuniwi* the *wi* tree (Spondias dulcis), *vunidalo* taro plant.

Vunilawa levu n. Attorney-general.

vunimarama n. distinguished woman, lady.

vunimemu 1. "it", in a game such as tag. 2. Idiom: "serves you right", or as Fijians often say, "good luck", intended as a sarcastic remark.

Vunisa n. title of the chief in certain places, such as Weilagi and Bouma, on Taveuni, and Vatulele, parts of Kadavu, and Noco in Rewa Province. The suffix *sa*, in this context, might refer to spears (as suggested to me by the recent chief at Weilagi, Ratu Jone Radrodro), or to an ancient particle meaning "tribe", as in the word *yavusa*. At Weilagi, the chief is also referred to as the Tui Taveuni but Vunisa is the traditional Fijian title. The title Tui was introduced from Tonga, via Verata, probably no earlier than the early 1700s.

vunitaba-na n. shoulder (of a person). *taba-na* arm.

vunisoco n. (Lau, Slang) person's rump, bum. Syn. *mu-na*. *vunisoco* lit. means citrus tree in Namosi, and is the name of a coastal village in that Province.

Vunivalu n. the most common traditional title (*itutu*) for a chief of a tribe (*yavusa*) in Fiji except in the west where the title Momo is common and even the concept of *yavusa* is foreign. *Vunivalu* is not a form of address and does not attach to the name of the chief or the the village or territory. In many places the chief goes through an installation ceremony to confirm the choice, especially if there might be any dispute, especially when lease-money is at stake. Under Tongan influence via Verata that title is often displaced in favour of Tui, followed by the location. Many of the older, local titles now play a secondary role to the title of Tui this or Tui that. Vunivalu is best capitalised when it refers to a specific chief.

vunivola (Anglicism) n. secretary. *Vunivola Tudei* Permanent Secretary (in government), head of a Department, serving a Minister.

vunivuni adj. deceptive, secretive, having a hidden purpose, of a person.

vuniwai (Medical) n. doctor.

vunoka (Medical) n. sprained ankle.

vunuki n. (Medical) eyesore where the eyelashes grow back inside the eyelid.

vuti-na n. fur, fuzz, down (light hairs as of a bird), of plants, human body or other animals. *vutivutia* hairy.

vuqa many. *vuqa tale* many other(s). *kei na vuqa tale* and many others, et cetera.

vakavuqa frequent, frequently.

vura 1. v. to arrive and be accepted formally by the hosts. A rather formal word.

Idiom: *A vura!* final words of a *isevusevu* ceremony as the guests are satisfied that they have been accepted formally.

vura 2. v. to appear quickly, to put in a sudden appearance.

vura 3. n. (Medical) benign tumour. Syn. *dabo*.

vuravura n. world. *Matabose kei Vuravura* United Nations. *e na vuravura taucoko* in the whole world.

vurai n. var. of very early yam, two types, *vurai balavu* and *vurai dra*.

vure v. spring up (water), come to mind (thought).

vure-na n. groin, pubic area of the human body.

vakavure, vakavureya v. to give rise to, bring up, to cause. *vakavureya na vakatataro* causes questions to be raised.

ivurevure (or) **vureniwai** n. spring (water). *ivurevure ni ilavo* source of money, income. *ivurevure ni vakasama* source of the thought.

vuru, vuruta (or) **vuruka** v. to crumble, pulverise (soil, biscuits, stale bread to make crumbs). *cavuru* crumbled, used for hair falling out, since some Fijian hair will not grow long; it breaks off, crumbling. *kavuru* is a stronger term. In traditional terms, *vuru, vuruta* could also refer to a light trimming of the hair to smooth the surface. This was done with a burning ember and the hair fell away as very small crumbs.

vuru n. stump of wood, partially burned (formerly used to singe in trimming the hair). *vuru (ni tavako)* "butt", cigarette butt. *ivuruvuru ni tavako* (or) *ka ni kavuru* ash tray. *vuru* may refer to a stump of burning ember but also an improvised torch in the country, as a burning coconut spathe (*bawara*), to walk outside at night.

vuru-memea v., adj. to fragment, crush into small pieces.

vuruvuru n. crumb, fragment.

vuruwaliso adj. glittering, sparkling, glistening, usually of light reflected.

vuseka adj., n. exhausted from physical labour.

vusi (Eng. pussy) cat, introduced by Europeans, often nowadays pronounced *vosi*. Only partially westernized Fijians keep cats domesticated in their own house, treating them as a close part of the family. There are substantial numbers of feral cats (and dogs) in the forests of the main islands. *daku ni vusi* hunchback.

Idiom: *suruta na vusi* lit. the cat sneezed on it, meaning that some plan or project has failed, there has been bad luck, someone's purpose has been foiled.

vuso n. froth, foam, spray (the sea, usually).

vuso v. to effervesce, to froth (the sea, beer). Can refer to a person or horse frothing at the mouth.

vusoya v. to squeeze, squish, as of laundry, to wash through the soap, and rinse out. Of Fiji medicinal plants, to squeeze out the liquid from leaves, roots, fruits. *Drauna tuki qai vusoi me wai ni lamea*. Leaves are beaten, then the liquid squeezed out as a medicine for thrush. (Typical procedure of native Fijian medicine.) See *vulo*.

vuso-na n. tip, upper tip or end, as of the growing tip of a plant or the top of a boat's mast, tip of a penis, source of a spring. *vuso ni iqaqalo* tip of the finger.

ivusoni n. sheath (of *voivoi* leaves for weaving mats), containing ten leaves. Ten *ivusoni* tied together can be called one *ivutu*. Ultimately the *voivoi* is often rolled into coils, tightened around two fingers, with the finer, top surface of the leaf on the outside of the coil.

vuso ni liga n. finger tip(s). *vuso-na* itself refers to the tip end of some long object.

vusoraka (or) **vusolaka** v. to launder (clothes) with heavy physical action of squishing water through the cloth. Suds or froth (*vuso*) are implicit.

vutevutea n., adj. very soft and smooth to the touch, usually of hair, human of animal.

vuti, vutia (Colo East) v. to pick (of certain fruits). Syn. Bauan *beti, betia*.

vuti-na n. body hair, fine fur or feathers, coat (horse).

vutia, vutia v. to pluck the feathers, as from a chicken, to be cooked. Might apply to other situations where the action is plucking, as modernly, with a woman's eyebrows.

vutivutika adj. hairy. *sere vutivutika* hairy chest. Syn. *vutivutia*.

vutia n. sea-grass, often the food of green sea turtles, growing in lagoons.

vuto, vutoca v. to ford (river crossing), to walk in shallow water, to wade. *ivutovuto* n. ford (of a stream or river), Irish crossing. *tui-vuto, tuivutona* to haul heavy things (such as firewood) in the water while wading, to ease the burden of carrying.

vutovuto n. sponge, coloured variously when fresh from the sea. Porifera sp. Used in coastal villages to clean pots and such things.

vutu adj. very painful. *vutu bati* (or) *vutu ni bati* have a painful toothache. *vutu na kete-na* constipation. *vuturi* tired with mental, physical fatigue.
Idiom: *vutu gu* to try with all one's strength, go to the limits of effort.
Idiom: *mata vutu* beautiful face.

vutu (or) **vutu kana** n. "edible" *vutu*. endemic nut-bearing coastal tree, Barringtonia edulis, Barringtoniaceae or Lecythidaceae. *Vutu kana* is semi-cultivated, edible, tasty and crisp when raw but sometimes boiled or roasted, as a starch-food on the main islands where it thrives in the wet climate, damp ground, and may be found at the Suva market (March) but fruits and flowers throughout the year. Inflorescence large, showy, pendant, with long white stamens tinged pink. Fruits oblong to 7 cm long, ripens to dark green or purple green, with persistent calyx, Syn. *vala* (old Oceanic name, Lau, Macuata, West., Kadavu), and in Melanesian English "cut nut". Care must be taken not to confuse it with a somewhat similiar looking poisonous species, *vutu ni wai* or *vutu gaga* B. racemosa. The fruit of a third species, B. asiatica, *vutu raka* or *vutu rakaraka* is also poisonous, formerly used as a fish-poison, and as floats for fishing nets; these nuts, the size of a fist, have four distinctive angles and a pointed tip, easily identified and very common around the shore. The beautiful flowers open only at night, falling to the ground by dawn. Grated seeds on the water serve as a fish poison but less effectively than Derris spp.
Idiom: *ta na vutu ni Kaba.* clever talker, fast, persuasive talker.

vutu, vutuka, vutulaka v. to pound, crush, mash. By ext. (extremely vulgar) fornicate, commit sodomy. Commonly refers to pounding of taro, breadfruit, or other starchy foods for making Fijian puddings *vakalolo*.
Idiom: *sinai vutuvutu* stuffed full.

vutu-gu v. to groan.

vutu-ni-yau very rich, as if stuffed full of wealth. Syn. *vakailavo*.

vaka-vutuvutu adj., as in *ibe vakavutuvutu*, mat with a border of finely shredded *voivoi* leaf.

vutulaki v. masturbate (male or female).

ivutu 1. n. pounder, pestle (of wood or stone) for pounding, as in making the starch-food mash for Fijian pudding *vakalolo*.

ivutu 2. n. ten taro corms, as presented at formal gatherings.

ivutu (senikau) 3. n. bunch (of flowers).

veivutu n., v. sodomy, buggery. Corpses of war victims were sometimes submitted to buggery by victorious warriors as a form of vengeance and degradation. Homosexuality as a recognized way of life was unknown to Fijians before the advent of Europeans (though trans-sexuals and trans-vestites were known and tolerated). *veivutu* may also refer to heterosexual intercourse with the vulgar implication of banging away. A very crude insult might accuse a woman: *Drau veivutu kei tamanu!* You fornicate with your own father!

vutu, vutuna v. to tie together in a bunch, flowers or leaves, usually for decorative purpose but also *makita* twigs for side-wall thatching of native houses. Also may apply to the bundling of taro. *Vutuna* can also refer to the French Polynesian islands Futuna, and Futuna people who ages ago settled in eastern Fiji under that tribal name Vutuna. *ivutu se ni kau* bunch of flowers.

vutu-coqa adj. packed in tightly, crushed together, as in a crowd. *e dua na basi ka sa sinai vutucoqa* a bus that is completely filled, packed tightly (with people). Syn. *osodrigi*.

vutugu v. to groan, as in deep pain. n. hopelessness, despair, emotional pain. *e na domo ni vutugu* with a voice of despair.

vutu-ni-kete n. severe stomach ache.

vuturi, vuturi-taka v. to be reluctant to do some work or fulfill some obligation, to avoid doing what is expected, due to fatigue, difficult conditions or discomfort.

veivutuni-taka v. to repent, regret (it).

vutuvutua adj. hairy, of the body. See *vutivutika*.

vu-vaka-vu n. new linguistic term referring to a causitive action, such as the word *vaka-rerea* to cause to be afraid, to cause fear. The relevant verb (in this case *rerea*) is preceded by *vaka*, or in some cases, the abbrev. form *va*.

vuvale n. household. *matavuvale* family (nuclear family of the household).

vuvu adj. n. jealous, jealousy, envious, envy. *E vuvutaka na noqu motoka vou.* He/she is envious of my new motor car.

vuvu n. stems of plantain cut to bind together, as for a floating raft for river travel and transport.

vuvu n. fish trap, usually made of bamboo, used in rivers and creeks.

vuvu adj. muddy, murky, of water. Syn. (Colo East) *bure*.

vuvu n. roof top, as in *delavuvu*, ridge of the house-roof.

vui, vuya v. to wash (the feet).

vuvula n. large fish, often in brackish water, rivers and mangrove, greyish above, shiny below, yellow dorsal fin, flesh soft and tasteless, Megalops cyprinoides. The fish schools seasonally at the shore of village Yadrana, Lakeba Island, and is considered their *"balolo"*, a celebrated annual harvest.

vuwawa n. (Medical) serious hernia of men that leaves testicles descended painfully, symptom also caused by elephantiasis.

W

The letter **w** is probably a little over-used in Fijian writing, where the letter **u** might suffice in some cases, or no letter at all. Regional variation of pronunciation complicates the matter. Readers tolerate various spellings that do not affect the understanding. The word for "flood" may appear as *waluvu* or as *ualuvu*.

wa n. string, cord, vine. The names of vines may be written as two words, or as one. *wa bosucu* may be written as *wabosucu*. Many types of vine are known to Fijians and some of them are useful. Regional names vary greatly. Common cordage has also been made from fibres of banana stems, and from inner bark of *vau* shrub stems and branches as well as sinnet (*magimagi*) from coconut husk fibre.

wa bosucu n. a fast-growing vine, Mikania micrantha, Asteraceae, climbs rapidly over other plants, even telephone poles, an extremely common introduced weed. Introduced from America circa 1900. Leaves useful to alleviate insect stings and to heal small cuts. Also may help protect *yaqona* bushes from sucking insects that transmit deadly virus. Many regional synonyms. (Rewa, Kadavu) *wabutako*. (West) *ovacia* or *ovaova*.

wa coro n. thin, strong vine, white sweet-smelling flowers, small black fruit. Useful for binding, Gynochthodes ovalifolia, Rubiaceae.

wa damu 1. n. Cuscuta campetris, Cuscutaceae, large round leaves boiled for hair dye. Syn. (Namosi, Nadrau, Wainibuka) *wa kurukuru*.

wa damu 2. n. Merremia peltata, Convolvulaceae, fast-growing, reddish thick-stemmed bush vine, common at all altitudes, large peltate leaves with white flowers, sprouting tips boiled as hair dye.

wa kalou n. Lygodium reticulatum, formerly used to secure thatch of chiefs' houses. A piece over the door helped keep out evil spirits. This fern grows by winding around other plants. Syn. (Kadavu) *komidri*.

wa ki n. used for tying thatch on roof. In Tailevu Province (Vugalei area) it is used for weaving *sova* baskets and modernly, laundry baskets, or small decorative baskets. One var. has thin stem, called *walaki* in the islands. (The name *walaki* is used for Flagellaria indica, very probably the same.) The main var. has thick stem. Called *wa ulo* in Colo East. Called *vakasara* in parts of Tailevu. Stem of the mature vine is very strong and woody, like rattan. For basket-weaving, very thin strips are cut in long lengths.

wa kurukuru: n. common running weed that covers vegetation, used for tying up bundles. White flowers Nov-Dec, signal that mussels (*kai*) are fully fleshed for eating. Flower petals drop away, leaving "wood roses" used modernly in floral decorations. Tiny seeds are airborne. Mashed-up leaves are applied externally to infections to draw out pus. Leaves and vines boiled with pandanus leaves for black colour. Botanical name is Morinda myrtifolis, Rubiaceae, in A. C. Smith, but *Na Ivolavosa VakaViti* lists it as Merremia peltata, Convulvaceae.

wa me n. vine, Freycinetia storckii, Panadanaceae, used in house-building, basket weaving, long leaves like pandanus, sweet-smelling white flowers attract bats. Fibre used in binding house rafters. Growth as a vine climbing trees with leaves only at the top of the plant, and aerial roots grow down to the ground. Syn. (Cakaudrove) *mere*.

walai n. Entada phaseoloides. Heavy forest rope. See *walai*, separately, below.

wa loa n. Rhizomorpha sp. black, shiny, formerly used for "kilts" or "skirts" for men and women. Syn. *sausauwai*. This and divided plantain leaves made the commonest forms of dress for early Fijians. The loincloth (*malo*), made from barkcloth (*masi*) was introduced from Tonga.

wa lutumailagi n. "vine fallen from the sky", Cassytha filiformis, a parasite common on the islands off Nadi and the nearby mainland. Ultimately it destroys the parent plant.

wa midri n. tree-climbing fern with edible fronds, Stenochlaena palustris, Blechnaceae. Sturdy vines used by highlanders in bindings, as for outrigger of *takia* paddling canoe. (Coastal Fijians used sinnet.)

warusi n. common climbing liana or shrub, Smilax vitiensis, Smilacaceae, by current fad (2006/2010) widely touted that an infusion of the woody roots, and also the leaves, serve an an aid for erectile dysfunction for men, *wai vakaukauwa*. As a placebo, it may still have some positive effect if people believe in it. No tests have been made of medical effectiveness. In the Suva market bottles sold for as much as F$5 in 2009. Some claim this is a general tonic and others say it cures headaches. More common, traditional use for the tough, thin stems has been for binding, for fish nets, and for weaving baskets. Stems usually smooth but some prickles, leaves with five veins, perianth, anthers, ovaries faded yellow, fruits purple or black. Flowers and fruits all year round. Syn. (Lau) *kadragi*.

wa sara n. a wild edible corm, considered a yam, often eaten raw, especially by highlanders of Colo East by my observation. This is probably the same as *wa yaka*. *Nai Vola ni Kau* gives *wa sara* as the Wainibuka name for *wayaka,* Pueraria lobata, Fabaceae. I believe the same name applies in Colo East. See *wa yaka* below.

wa ulo (Wainimala) n. Flagellaria gigantea, type of woody vine or rattan used in building. Strips of outer skin used in binding rafters in Colo East houses. Syn. *galo*.

wa vuka n. considered as a wild, edible raspberry shrub, with many recurved thorns, common in light forest, Rubus moluccanus, Rosaceae. Syn. *wa gadrogadro*.

wa yaka n. Peuraria lobata, Papilionaceae (or Fabaceae), edible long roots, flesh dirty white in colour, eaten mostly as famine food that can be eaten raw. Stems useful as cordage, formerly used for fishing nets. Cattle eat the leaves and the leaves are reasonably tasty to humans. New shoots in Sept., Oct. Hairy stem, three-leafed, flowers white tinged with purple. Grows wild. Syn. (Colo) *wa sara*.

wa ni culacula (Modernism) n. cotton or nylon thread (for sewing).

iwabale (Archaic) v., n. barkcloth cummerbund covering at least part of a man's chest and properly one shoulder, part of ancient formal chiefly costume, only in coastal areas and smaller islands, unknown in Viti Levu highlands where there was no mulberry barkcloth in earliest times. The higher the wrap, the more prestige implicitly asserted by the wearer. Wearing the *iwabale* could be dangerous presumption, virtually a challenge in ancient times. Modernly, *iwabale* may refer to anything worn over the shoulder, without chiefly implications. *wabale, wabaletaka* v. to put on or wear the *iwabale*.

wabibiri adj. refers to swollen, conspicuous muscles or veins. *Sa wabibiri na nomu ua.* Your muscles/veins really stand out.

wabobota adj. shiny smooth, usually said of a person's beautiful skin.

waboraki v. side-swipe, as with a "haymaker" punch.

wabunobuno v. to sweat heavily. *buno* to sweat.

wacava? How about it? What is up? How is it going? *Wacava na gaunisala i liu?* How is the road ahead?

wacece adj. dopey, with immaturity, irresponsibility implied, especially of girls.

wa-cegucegu v., adj. to pant, gasp, be out of breath. *cegu* to breathe.

waci (Vanua Levu) n. green vegetable, espec. *rourou,* the edible leaf of taro. (West) *bele,* edible green leaf vegetable.

waci poki (Taveuni) n. specialty food: leaves of taro rolled into small balls and cooked, usually fried with onions, in *lolo* (coconut cream). May contain meat or prawns.

wa-cimicimi v. to talk fast in a facile manner with glib deception. Syn. *wacemeceme, cimicimi*.

waciwaci n. tree, Sterculia vitiensis, Sterculiaceae, softwood rarely used for timber. The name applies to a village on Lakeba Island, famous for its early chief, the Tui Lakeba who married Sina-i-Takala, a female relative of the 30th Tui Tonga. Their son founded the Falefisi noble lineage in Tonga that connect to the nobility of Lakeba Island still today. Some people from village Waciwaci, Lakeba, moved over to Ono-i-Lau, and to Vatoa Island.

wadokau adj. hard, stiff, as of frozen food, or a stiff, unbending leg or arm, paralyzed or partly paralyzed. Syn. *dosa*.

wadra, wadrava v. to gaze vacantly, stare blankly in the air, or at something. See *ga balavu*.

wadredre adj. tight, taut (of a string, rope). Syn *tadre. dre, dreta* to pull.

wadrega 1. adj. chewy, dense, and thus of good texture, usually of taro, not soggy.
Idiom: *sa bau wadrega* that is difficult, hard to accomplish, impossible, literally hard to chew on. *drega* n. gum, glue.

wadrega 2. n. rubber band, or rubber that stretches on a spear-gun for spearing fish.

wadrovu adj. long or tall and erect or straight (person, post, tree).

wadru, wadruca v. to squeeze and pull between the thumb and the forefinger, as in removing the edible fern (*ota*) leaflets from the stem, or in stretching and smoothing cordage, or pandanus leaves (for weaving mats), or in "massaging" cured vanilla beans to condition and straighten them. This action has been the common way for clearing the nose of mucus. In Colo East the verb is *waru, waruca*. *wadruluka* to remove excess mucus from the nose by the same action of thumb and forefinger. This is still common practice among some people who have not yet adopted the use of handkerchiefs or toilet tissues. By extension, in slang, *wadruca* may refer to male masturbation from the motion of the hand.

wadua 1. n. (Music) bass string instrument improvised with a stick, a basin or tin or box for resounding, and a single string (literally *wa dua*) that is plucked.

wa dua n. 2. (Slang) homosexual man.

wadumu n. intestines. Syn: *wawa*.

wagugu v. to walk fast, purposefully. *gu* personal energy.

wahu (Hawaii), n. edible fish, Acanthocybium solanderi, very similar to the *walu*, but found in deeper water and thus previously not known to Fijians. For the differences, see *walu*.

wai 1. n. water. *e dua na bilo wai* a cup of water. *wai droka* (or) *waidranu* freshwater. *wai ni gunu* drinking water, *wai tui* saltwater. *waiwai* oil. Syn. (Tonga) *vai*.
Idiom: *wai ni vanua* ceremonial term for *yaqona*.
Idiom: *gunu wai ni bele* to be reprimanded.
Idiom: *wai ni diva, sega ni kabita.* the stuff of dreams, never achieved.

wai 2. n. medicine. *vale ni wai* n. medical clinic (usually without hospital facilities) where medicines are dispensed. Syn. (Tonga) *vai*.
Idiom: *E sega na kena wai.* There is no solution for that (problem), lit. no medicine for that condition. Sardonically, may refer to love having no cure.

wai 3. prefix, as in *wainimoli* citrus juice.

wai 4 n. river, stream, and as a name of river or stream, the prefix *Wai* is followed by the specific name, as in Wailevu ("Big River"), Waimanu, Wainadoi. *ulu-ni-wai* n. headwaters (of a river).

wai 5. (Archaic) n. ten blocks (*iqavi*) of Fiji sea-salt (*masima*) as a presentation, given at former traditional ceremonies. Village Lomawai at the Nadroga coast has been a centre of salt production. *Wai* may also refer to ten Fijian puddings (*vakalolo*) at formal occasions.

wai 6. n. women's genital fluids or the man's sperm. By ext., woman's vagina.

wai 7. (Slang) adj. drunk. *Sa wai tu o koya.* He/She is drunk.

wai 8. adj. as in *ulu wai* soft human hair, not crisp as in the "true" Fijian hair *ulu dina*. See *waiwaiya* of flowing hair.

waibuta n. fish broth, after boiling of the fish. This was the only soup drunk by Fijians and the only food actually boiled. Fijian clay-pot cooking effectively steamed the food, mostly in its own juices. Syn. *wai su*.

waicala adj. too dilute (of *yaqona*, tea, coffee), melting (ice, frozen things).

waicalataka v. to dilute, to cause something to melt, or de-congeal, such as coconut oil that may solidify in cold weather.

waidiva (or) **wai ni diva** n., v. futile dream or fantasy, usually for a person of the opposite sex. Syn. *dodomo lo*, lit. a secret lust.

wai dranu n. fresh water (in contrast to saltwater), not necessarily drinkable. Syn. *wai droka*. Drinking water is *wai ni gunu*. *wai drano* lake water.

wai droka n. fresh water (in contrast to salt water). Syn. *wai droka*.

waikama n. hot springs, as at Nasavusavu on Vanua Levu Island and several other places in Fiji.

wai lailai adj. of a beverage (*yaqona*, tea) too concentrated. Syn. *sosoko*.

wai laugunu n. potable water, drinkable water. *gunu* to drink.

wai levu adj. watery, dilute, as of *yaqona*, or soggy, as cooked taro may be.

Wailevu n. Rewa River, its traditional Fijian name.

wai loaloa (Modernism) n. laundry "blue" or washing soda as whitening. *vakawailoaloa-taka* to apply "blue" to one's laundry. *loaloa* dark, black.

wai-ni-mata-na n. tears. *qusia na wainimata-na* wipe away his/her tears. *mata-na* face.

wainimate n. medicine, chemical, drug. *wainimate ni co ca* weedicide.

waisou almost (happened) *Waisou sara!* That came really close to happening! *Waisou me kama na vale.* The house was almost burned down. Syn. *oisou*.

wai su 1. n. fish soup or broth from cooking fish. Fijians had no other type of soup or broth. Along the coast, where clay pots might be available, cooking pots that were round and short were used only to boil fish soup. Syn. *waibuta*.

wai su 2. n. (Kadavu) banana cooked in coconut cream (*lolo*), now used as a dessert. Desserts at meals are an adopted custom, not traditional.

vaka-wai-vinaka-taka v. to improve something by applying more water, usually to rinse off something such as dishes or a boat.

waite n. a snack food made by grating coconut and mixing that with bread or biscuits. This word can have various different spellings. Syn. *ouaite*.

waitui n. sea, salt water. *tuituina* salty, of food. Lauans used salt water from the lagoon as a condiment, kept in a whole coconut-shell at the house.

waiwai 1. n. vegetable oil, traditionally in coastal areas, that has meant coconut body oil, but also oils for muscle massage such as *dilo* oil. Coconut oil was extracted mainly three purposes, to keep the body warm in cold weather, as a base for body massage, and scented, to make the body look and smell attractive at special occasions. Extracted oil was never used for cooking or as any food ingredient. Highlanders of Viti Levu had no coconuts and never made any vegetable oils. *Waiwai* may refer modernly to cooking oil, corn oil, soya oil, as sold in supermarkets, though many Fijians still use lard because it is cheaper.

waiwai 2. n. fuel oil, diesel, petrol or lubricating oil. *vakawaiwai-taka na idini* oil the engine. *dramu waiwai* drum of oil.

waiwaiya (or) **waiwaia 1**. adj. fluid or flowing, as in *ulu waiwaiya* soft flowing hair of the head as of most Polynesians, Micronesians, Europeans and Orientals. Melanesian Fijians have tightly curled, compacted hair usually called "true hair", *ulu dina*. Among Viti Levu highlanders, it is tougher and even more tightly compacted (*maquru*). *Waiwiya* may also refer the fluid condition of liquids, such as coconut oil that congeals in cold weather.

waiwaiya 2. adj. senile.

waka-na n. root (of plant). Unless otherwise specified, *waka* means the root of *yaqona* (Piper methysticum), used in ceremonial presentations and to be consumed as a beverage. A huge root is sometimes referred to as *waka-tu*.

wakakau adj. very strong, firm and sturdy, as in *bulicaki wakakau* very strongly built, said of a man.

waka-tu n. tap-root. May refer to a large root of *yaqona*. See *waka-na*.

wakewake n. adj. bodily fatigue, physical weakness, from great effort. *na wakewake ni yagoda* our (many) bodily fatigue. Syn. *oca*.

waki, wakia v. to mix in, as ingredients. This is distinct from *uli, ulia* to stir, which applies to simple liquids such as tea. *wakia* can require more effort and materials that are not necessarily liquid.

wakiwakita adj. sticky, chewy, pasty, unsmooth, knotty (of wood), applies to viscous, sticky sap, such as breadfruit, chewing gum, paint that is too thick, needing a thinner, or to caramel candy, or doughy starchy mash (*mavu*) of Fijian pudding (*vakalolo*) in preparation.

walai n. useful and beautiful forest vine, Entada phaseoloides, Fabaceae, that can grow as thick as a man's arm. It contains pure drinkable water and serves to refresh the traveller in the bush. In the forest, children play by swinging on the vine, Tarzan-fashion. The seeds (known by a name derived from Tonga, *ilavo*) were formerly used as playing pieces in a game *veilavo*. The coin-shape of the seeds inspired Fijians to use their name for the English word money. The leaves of *walai* have been used medicinally by pregnant women. After cooking and washing, and draining, the seeds are eaten as food by kaiColo, who must first offer them in first fruits ceremony by late April (Waidina especially). There, they are combined with specially treated, grated wild yam to make a local food

wale 1. mere, merely. *Ia, e sega ni yaga na vakalelewa wale.* So, there is no use to be merely judgemental.

wale 2. of no particular importance, ordinary. *siga wale* any day except the sabbath. *tamata wale* ordinary person (not a chief or particularly important person). *E caka na lotu ena dua na vale wale.* Church takes place in an ordinary house. (That is the case for a couple of Christian denominations in Fiji.)

wale 3. without obligation, encumbrance or payment, or effect. *soli wale* "free" (in a commercial sense), given at no extra charge. *curu wale* free entrance. *vuli wale* free schooling, no tuition fees to be paid. *vodo wale* v. to get a free ride. *luvawale* naked. *E oga wale na boso.* The boss is busy to no effect, uselessly.

wale 4. as in *kana wale* to eat without any special garnish (*icoi*) such as meat or fish, just ordinary food like cassava or other starch-food.

walega only, perhaps more properly written as *wale ga*.

vakawale, vakawale-taka v. to neglect. *vakawaleni* n. neglected.

walesi (Eng.) wireless, radio. Walesi and Mere Walesi are also given names from Mary Wallis, author and wife of an American captain of the ship Zotoff in Cakobau's time. Her name was taken for a chiefly Bauan child, and has endured. *dauniwalesi* radioman, radio announcer. Syn. (Eng.) *retio*.

iwalewale 1. n. means, technique, way of doing things.

iwalewale 2. n. specific actions, behaviour (of a person), type of conduct, sometimes implied as bad or good. A more generalised word for type of behaviour or action is *ivukivuki*. Also the means (by which something may be done).

veiwali n., v. joke, to joke or laugh, a prevalent feature of Fijian culture.

wali, walia 1. v. to solve (problem). *walia na leqa* solve the problem. *na iwali ni leqa* the solution to the problem.

wali, walia 2. v. to oil or anoint (the body). *na waliwali* the oiling (of the body).

Idiom: *walia na vosa* speak words that smooth out a difficult situation, to "smooth-talk".

Idiom: *wali, walia* (a person) to cast a spell over a person of the opposite sex to gain their affection. This is usually said in teasing humour, though some believe it can be done by touching their body with a special oil. *E wali iko tiko?* Has a spell been cast over you? Are you in love?

waliso v. to glisten. Syn. *lisolisoa*.

waliso, walisoma v. to hasten, hurry up, do it with eagerness.

wa-lisoliso adj. active, agile, eager, in a hurry.

wa-litolito v. to look for something hastily this way and that.

walobi adj. hungry.

walokai adj. very hungry.

waloloi adj. very hungry.

waluvu n., v. flood, usually of a river. *Taukei ni Waluvu* Bauan name for the title of Waimaro chief at village Nairukuruku, Naitasiri Province, the *Taukei ni Bureburg,* purportedly able to control the floodwaters of the Wailevu (Rewa River). Syn. *ualuvu*.

walu 1. eight. *walu sagavulu* eighty. *tini ka walu* eighteen. *na ikawalu* the eighth. *walu na drau* eight hundred.

walu 2. n. kingfish, king mackerel, Spanish mackerel, Scomberomorus commersoni, a fine food-fish, named for its row of eight small fins along the back, behind the dorsal fin. It is caught by trolling close to the reef. The concept of trolling was introduced by Tongans and Samoans. The frozen *walu* steaks served by some restaurants are a poor version of a very tasty fish when it is fresh. *Walu* is often preferred for making marinated raw fish (*kododa*). It is very similar in appearance to the larger (to 120 cm) *wahu* or *wahoo*, Acanthocybium solanderi, usually a deeper-water fish previously unknown to Fijians (who did not fish beyond the reef) but now with the name *wahoo* borrowed from Hawaii. The *wahoo* is more elongate, cigar-shaped with a sharper snout while the *walu* is deeper and flatter with a blunter snout. Teeth of the *wahoo* lower jaw fit inside the teeth of the upper jaw while the teeth of *walu* are fairly matched. The *wahoo* generally dies with the eyes looking back that is not the case of the *walu*. Definitive indications of the *wahoo* is a small tag in the fork of the tail, and the number of dorsal spines twenty or more. The taste and texture and white colour are very similar. (Rob Wright's information from fisheries experts.)

walui, waluiya v. to scrape *voivoi* leaves or sedge leaves (usually with a sharp mussel shell), to soften and stretch the leaves prior to weaving mats. The spelling of this word varies.

wananavu adj. wonderful, wondrous, delightful. This word is often an exclamation. *Wananavu!* Great! splendid! perfect! Syn. *Daumaka!*

wa ni siwa n. fishing line, a concept from central Polynesia.

wa ni vicovico n. umbilical cord. *vicovico* n. navel.

wanono, wanonova 1. v. to stare, regard fixedly. It is normal for local children to stare relentlessly at strangers, and follow them around.

wanono, wanonova 2. v. keep a close eye on, examine closely, continue to scrutinize. *Wanonova matua sara na ka oqo.* Keep a very close eye on this thing. *Ena wanono tiko ko vuravura.* The world will be watching.

waqa, waqaca, waqara v. to light, lit (fire, lamp), burning. *Me waqa na cina.* Please light the lamp. *Sa waqa na buka.* The fire is lit. *waqawaqa ni buka* n. Piece of burning wood that can be used for lighting a fire. See *caudre*.

waqa 1. n. boat. *dau-ta-waqa* boat-builder. (Cakobau's boat-builder was an American black, probably earlier a ship's carpenter.) Syn. (Tonga) *vaka*.

Idiom: *waqa vata* (Anglicism) lit. "in the same boat", enduring the same conditions.

waqa 2. (Anglicism) n. envelope (as for letters). *waqa ni lokoloko* pillow-case. Such soft pillows were unknown to Fijians, but adopted from Tonga.

waqa 3. (Anglicism) n. book-cover. *waqa vavaku kaukauwa* hardcover. *waqa malumulumu* soft-cover.

waqabaca n., adj. sickly, often sick, weak.

waqaqa n. filiarasis infection that ultimately, after about ten years, may result in elephantiasis (*tauna*) with severe edema, thickened skin and swelling, especially of lower limbs and genitalia, or may cause blindness. Different species of the nematode affect different parts of the body. *ceke* elephantiasis specifically of scrotum and testicles. See also *tatuku, tauna*. Symptoms first come with fatigue, painful lymph glands, abdominal discomfort.

waqavuka (Anglicism) n. aeroplane. *rara ni waqavuka* or *iroro ni waqavuka* airfield, aeroport. *vuka* to fly.

waqawaqa 1. n. residence or visible form as taken by a spirit *kalou* or *kalou vu* that may exist in a rock, or sometimes in an animal such as a dog, shark.

waqawaqa 2. adj. wide eyed with fury, of facial appearance.

waqe (West) v., n. game. Syn. *qito*.

waqo adj. extremely skinny (person, animal), "skin and bones". This is thought to be an unhealthy condition. It may refer to a thin and weak plant. Of fruit, dried out, wasted.

waradi (Eng.) n. warrant, summons (court).

wara (Regional: Ra) no, not. Syn. *warai, sega*.
  Idiom: *'auria se wara!* take it or leave it!
  Idiom: *wara me soa* not a good match (do not belong together).

warai (Regional: Kadavu, Rewa, Namosi) no, not. Syn. *sega*.

waraka v. to wait for. *waraka na basi* wait for the bus; *waraki au* wait for me. *Wawa!* Wait! *waraka namaka* to wait with anticipation.
  Idiom: *Waraka qai Namuka!* Exclamation: It is futile to wait for it!

wararasa v., n. to sting painfully, as by a switch or perhaps a burn.

wa-ribariba v., adj. to be agile, quick in physical response; may apply to a hyper-active child. Syn. *waritorito*.

waro, waroca, warolaka v. to whack with a thin stick, usually hitting a child as punishment. *iwaro* n. thin stick so used, but may apply to a golf club. *qito wawaro* a rather affected, precious term for the game of golf.

warotu n. Fijian card-game with four players, or two, a version a "trump" *tarabu*. See *veimau*.

waru, waruta, waruka v. to stroke with the fingers, snot from the nose, leaflets from the edible *ota* fern, cured vanilla beans to straighten and smoothen them. Syn. *wadru, wadruca*.

warumisa v., n., adj. to sting, cause pain. By ext. may apply figuratively to stinging words, admonitions.

warumiso v., n., adj. extremely powerful (sporting team, strength of sun's rays, etc.), to do something powerfully.

waruta (Colo East) n. small wild terrestrial fern used as a condiment in place of salt which was usually unavailable in the highlands. Highlanders consider this condiment to be superior to salt. Not yet identified botanically. Curiously, this is also the name of a clan at Sabeto, western Viti Levu. (The local chief, Apisai Tora, notable retired politician, does not know any meaning for that clan name.)

wasa-liwa n. open ocean, deep ocean.

wasawasa n. sea, ocean.

wa-salulu v., n., adj. very wrinked, as of elderly person. *salulu* wrinkled, as of aged skin. See *sanuki* crinkled or wrinkled.

wase, wasea 1. v. to divide. In addition to the general meaning, this is commonly used for the dividing up of food at a food-presentation, before it is given out, a very common custom of ceremonies. It requires expert judgement to share out food or goods to the satisfaction of all recipients. *wase-i-rua, waseiruataka* v. to divide in two. *waseitolu* divided in three. *wasei vakatautauvata vei keda.* divided equally with us. *Erau sa veitawasei vakadua.* They (2) have divorced, separated permanently. See *vota* v. to share out.

wase, wasea 2. v. to sort out, classify, arrange in coherent types or amounts, put together those things that belong together.

wase, wasea 3 v. to discriminate, that can include ethnic or gender discrimination. Syn. *vakaduidui-taka*. This is rather a new notion to be talked about in Fiji, and a new use of the word *wasea*. *Kua ni wasea na mata tamata.* (Modernism) Don't discriminate people on the basis of race. See *veiwasei*, below.

veiwasei v. to discriminate. *Kua ni dau veiwasei ena soli veivuke.* Don't discriminate when distributing aid.

waselaka v. to share out or divide up carelessly, without careful judgement.

Vakatawase n. New Year's Day. This implies the division of the years, though years were never counted. Children may go about banging on tins; if they approach a house they may expect food, cake or candy, perhaps money.

iwase 1. n. portion from a division of things, such as food at a ceremonial food presentation (*magiti*).

iwase 2. n. food served and eaten, in conjunction with drinking of *yaqona*, usually eaten after the *yaqona* is drunk.

iwase 3. n. chapter (book), something divided off.

iwasewase n. share (as something is divided up), portion allotted.

iwase ni vuli n. (Anglicism) term of school.

iwase ni yaqona (vakaturaga) n. formal ceremony presenting uncooked food, usually part of series of ceremonies welcoming a chief. The original notion was that the food would counter-balance the drinking of *yaqona* though food is not eaten at the ceremony itself.

wa-sekaseka (or) **wa-seisei** (Archaic) n. chiefly necklace of finely split whaletooth, now seen only in museums. These were made by Tongans. Bauans gave them to highland chiefs who would cooperate with their purpose of Bauan domination with acceptance of Christianity.

"wash-down" (Eng, Slang) n., v. to drink alcohol, usually beer, after a session of drinking *yaqona*. *Yaqona* may potentiate the effects of alcohol.

waso adj. dried out, shrunken, shriveled, of a person, sick or old, or of an object, such *yaqona*, copra, or a dried fruit that has been exposed to the sun.

wasoma frequently, often, quite a bit.

wa-tabu n. plaited sinnet cord attached to head of *yaqona* serving bowl (*tanoa*) and stretched out in direction of important guest or chief. At the head of the *tanoa* there are attached two white cowry shells and one is attached to the distal end of the cord, closer to the guest(s). This is symbolic of a penis with two testicles. It it forbidden for anyone to walk in front of the *tanoa*. (At informal occasions, if necessary to cross in front, one would walk bowed down, and touch the bowl in passing.) All of this formality and ceremony, and the *tanoa* itself are Tongan introductions though the *watabu* itself is a Fijian innovation. Tongan bowls had the wooden nubbin but not the sinnet cordage.

wa-tatagi adj. very lovely, sweet, of singing voice(s). Syn. *memela sara*.

wate (Archaic) n. very emotional, erotic dance of women, welcoming successful warriors with their *bokola* (corpses for cannibal food). Syn. *dele*.

wati-na n. spouse. Also refers to a cross-cousin (*tavale*) of the opposite sex, a preferred marriage partner, but not yet married. Formerly, future marriage partners were sometimes selected for children. If a man and woman are seen together they will almost immediately be thought to be "married" informally. Brothers of a young woman may become violent if a Fijian man courts her without serious intentions. To be formally married (*vakamau*) in Church or civil registers is not always thought necessary except within traditional villages. As it now occurs in many other countries, Fijian couples may live together without any formal arrangements in urban areas. They may marry later or just remain as "partners".

veiwatini n. couple(s) of married people or co-habiting man and woman.

vakawati v., adj. to take a spouse, usually with no formal ceremony. All that is required is to live together (*tiko vata*), and after a time (in the case of young couples) for the man to present a whaletooth to the parents of the woman, a ceremony of bringing a whaletooth *ibulubulu*, asking forgiveness. In rural areas, if a man takes a young woman away from home for a night, he is considered as having married her. For modern ceremonies of formal marriage (with church, service and probably also, civil registry) the term used is *vakamau*, from a Tongan word "fakamau", adopted for Fijian Christianity. *vakawati vamatanitu* married by civil registry. *vakawati vaSamoa* (or) *vakawati vaSuva* just living together as a couple, in common-law marriage or as "partners".

iwau (Archaic) n. general word for wooden war-club. Specific types had specific names. *iula* throwing club. Other types: *bowai*, *gade* (pole clubs), *cali* (bladed club), *totokia* ("pineapple" club), *kiakavo* (spur club, often used in *meke*).

wa vau n. hibiscus fibre or cordage, from the inner bark of these small *vau* trees, used in tying parcels, tying up crabs or fish or fruit.

wa-velevele v., n., adj. restless, hyper-active, cannot sit still, of a child.

wavoki, wavokita v. to go around a place. *Au a wavokiti Lautoka* I went around Lautoka. *O laki ivei? Wavoki ga*. Where are you going? Just going around. *E rawa ni kau wavoki*. It can be carried around, is portable. *rai wavoki* look around. *E wavokita na vale e dua na bai*. A fence surrounds the house. *tamata wavoki* person with no fixed job or address, a drifter. Syn. *yavoki, yavokita*. See *wavoliti* and *voli, volita*.

iwavoki n. roundabout, place to turn around (as for a car). *sala wavoki* roundabout, indirect path (the more traditional meaning).

wavoki n. (Anglicism) round (as in boxing). *ena katolu ni wavoki* in the third round. Syn. (Eng.) *rauni*.

wavoliti around. *era vakaitikotiko wavoliti Korovou*. they (many) live around Korovou.

wavu 1. (Eng.) n. wharf, jetty.

wavu 2. (Eng.) n. bridge (usually a substantial one). *wavu lili* n. suspension bridge, hanging bridge such as the one that formerly crossed the Tovu River at village Nalele, Nadroga Province.

wavu 3. v. to stand upright, still (of a person, as in standing watchfully, or supporting a post, or a soldier at attention). See also *wavusasa*. *Sa wavu mai na drau ni uluna*. His/Her hair raised in fear.

wavukini (Eng.) n. pumpkin. Syn. *wavukeni, papukini*.

wavu sasa v. to be standing around with erect posture. If others are seated nearby, this could be considered disrespectful.

wawa n. intestines. Syn. *wewe*.
wawa, waraka v. to wait, waiting. *waraki koya*. wait for him/her .
iwawa n. feast to welcome someone who is awaited.
vakawawa adj. interim, temporary, tentative. *na matanitu tu vakawawa* the interim government. *na veivakadonui tu vakawawa* the temporary or tentative approval.
wawale adj. tired out (after some effort, work), worn out physically, of the whole body, or arms or legs, from exertion. Syn. *wawa*.
waya (Eng.) n., v. wire. *na waya ni talevoni*. the telephone wire. *waya votovotoa* n. barb-wire. *waya ni livaliva* n. electric wire.
  Idiom: *Sa bau waya* It's very difficult.
we-na n. trace, footprint, scar. *na we ni mavoa* the scar (of the injury). *na we ni yava* footprints (*yava* foot, leg). *we ni liga* n. fingerprint (*liga* hand).
wede, wedeva v. to flirt, act up, trying to be cute, showing off, usually to person(s) of opposite sex. *wedewede* n., adj. flirting. Lauan: *makamaka*.
wedru adj. soggy and soft, as of wet hair, food, or perhaps wet clothing or a wet mat. Syn. *sauwelu*.
weka-na n. family relative, colleague, associate. This includes people with any affiliation or association, indeed all people who are recognized as part of the extensive social network. *na wekana voleka* the close relatives (again a vastly wider network than that recognized by Europeans).
veiwekani v., n., adj. related by family or traditional relationship among different clans or tribes. *na veiwekani* n. the relatives (in Fiji that may include a very great number of people). In a sense, everybody is related to everybody else.
wele v., adj. idle, inactive; quiet, unconcerned, have the mind at ease (usually after tension), unmotivated or (small child) well behaved, tranquil, pacified.
vakawele gone v., n. to pacify a child, usually with a lullaby.
vakawelei v. to relax, take it easy. *na veika e rawa me vakawelei kina na yaloda*. things that can relax our (many) minds.
wele, weletaka v. to neglect. *Eda weletaka na noda itavi*. We (many) neglect our duty.
ivakawele n. toy, plaything, anything that helps one relax, such as hobby equipment.
welewelei adj. idle, relaxed, doing nothing.
vakawelewele v. to malinger, be neglectful, to neglect. *Me da kua ni vakawelewele*. Let us (many) not be neglectful. *na vakawelewele* the neglect, carelessness.
weleti n. papaya, Carica papaya, Caricaceae. Syn. (Rewa, Lau) *maoli*, (Lau) *leweti*. Introduced by Europeans. Green fruit eaten cooked by Lauans. Leaves and sap used as meat tenderiser though Fijians rarely bother. Mostly the fruit grows where seeds have been discarded, often near cement or concrete, because the plant does not thrive in acid soil. Trees are almost all male or female, some hermaphrodite. Only one male is needed for ten or more females. Fijians believe that cutting into a male tree may convert it to the more useful female. Tests made of this have not been successful. Fruits year-round. Skin of papaya fruit is used to treat boils known as *soso*, which is really a carbuncle. Syn. (Nadro, West, Macuata) *wi*.
weli n. saliva, spittle. *luka* nasal mucus.
weliwelia adj. slimy.
were, werea to garden, clean away weeds. *werekoro* v., n. to clean up the village as a community task, often for some special occasion, or as routine work.
  Idiom: *were ubiubi* deceptively to make like one is weeding, but in fact merely knocking the grass down, from laziness failing to cut the grass properly. Often used figuratively, for pretending to work at something.
were (or) **veiwere** n. yam garden.
were (West) n. house, formerly with thatching that makes the house appears rounded in shape despite its rectangular interior. Syn. *vale*.
weroka v. to repeat oneself, telling the same story over and over again, especially passing along rumours and gossip.
werowero (Lau) v., adj. n. keep repeating, tiresomely. "run off at the mouth".
weru-na n. guts of shellfish, the part that is not eaten.
wesi n. exhibition war dance (*meke wesi*) in which men dancers each brandishing a spear and a fan. The fan could be protective against hurled weapons but mostly signifies nonchalance in the face of the enemy. This dance features mainly in Vanua Levu, though in legend, it is a dance of the gremlins (*na iveli*) of Viti Levu.

iwewe ni gusu-na Idiom, as in: *Sa iwewe ni gusumu*. You are always talking, thinking only about it/him/her. Something has impressed or fascinated the person, focussing their attention.

wi n. a semi-cultivated tree-fruit, to altitude 500 meters, and thus unknown to highlanders in early times, Spondias dulcis, Anacardiaceae, relished by Fijians, fruiting around April, May, August to December. Fls small, white. Probably aboriginal introduction. Firm fleshed, it is too sour for most Europeans. The very firm, yellowish flesh is sweet only very close to the prickly kernel. Skin of the fruit remains green when ripe or turns yellowish, orange. Indians especially favour the fruit for pickles. *vili wi* to gather *wi* fruit. (*vili, vilika* to pick up, gather). Lves used to flavour meat; they have distinctive fruity smell when crushed. The bark is chalky, grey-brown, trunk is smooth and sometimes difficult to climb. Syn. *wikacu, wi'acu*.

Idiom: *vili wi* to lose out badly (sports, any competitive activity), with the implication of getting only the leftovers fallen on the ground. The "winner" climbs the tree and gets the best fruit. In fact, Fijians often reject fruit fallen on the ground, even if it is edible.

wili, wilika 1. (Anglicism) v. to read. Syn. *wilivola* (properly perhaps, *wili ivola*).

wili, wilika 2. v. to count. *wili leca* v. to mis-count.

wili-sese adj. infinite, uncountably large number.

wili-seva, wilisevataka v. to miscount. Syn. *wili leca*.

Idiom: *wiliseva na yalewa kalou* vast number, so big that literally, a woman-spirit could not count it.

wilibara (Eng.) n. wheelbarrow. *wili* n. wheel.

wili-gusu, wiligusutaka (Anglicism) v. to read out loud, to recite.

wilivanua (Anglicism) n. census. *Tabana ni Wilivanua* Census Department.

wilivola (Anglicism) n. v. to read. *vale ni wilivola (ivola)* n. library.

iwiliwili n. total count, total number added up. *Sa mai 84 toka na iwiliwili*. The count has reached 84. *vakaiwiliwili* adj. quantitative.

wini, winitaka (Eng.) v. to win, a word often used in sports. Idiomatically, this can mean for a man to succeed in having sex with a woman, or perhaps, the woman with a man.

wiri, wirica, wiricaka, wirilaka v. to spin, twist forcibly something that is held in the hand. Fast spinning action is also implied in the verb *cowiri-taka* to make something spin. *coco wiriwiri* to be spinning, rolling around. *vakaso wiriwiri* to be twirled, or spiralled as with the shape of a screw. *vakatawiriwiri* v. to be made to feel dizzy.

wirina v. to draw a circle, as in responding to a questionnaire, or in checking the proper answer to question on an exam paper. *wirina na isau ni taro* circle the answer to the question.

wiriwiri 1. n. Gyrocarpus americanus, Hernandiaceae, introduced Physic nut, shrub in wet zone, tree in dry zone where it thrives; soft and useless wood, poisonous fruit (dangerous to curious children). Leaves medicinal, used for diarrhoea. Cuttings used as living fence-posts, and for support and shade for cultivated vanilla vines.

wiriwiri 2. n. a soft-wood timber tree of coast and inland forest, Thespesia populnea, Malvaceae, also commonly called *mulomulo*. Easily cut and often used by Tuvalu people at Kioa Island for simple, small canoes (*bavelo*). Both Fijian names refer to a spinning action of the two-winged seeds that float down, rotating as they fall.

iwiriwiri 3. (Anglicism) n. dial, as on a radio, clock, electric or electronic device that is twisted to adjust it.

wiwi n., adj. sour, acidity.

Y

In Lau **y** precedes some names normally beginning with **a** as in the man's name Yaminiasi for Aminiasi, and the womens' chiefly title Yadi for the more commonly heard Adi in the rest of Fiji. In some cases the **y** is optional, and may be used or not used regionally, as in *iota* for yacht, *atu* or *yatu* for the fish tuna, or closely related species. In spelling the **y** is pronounced "*ya*".

ya-(number) each (used in Fijian as a prefix to the number); *yadua* each one; *yarua* every two, etc. *rakavi yavitu* rugby sevens (seven men on a side). *yatolu na tiaina* three bananas each. *E yatolu na dola na kena isau*. Three dollars each is the price.

yaba (Lau) n. mat. Syn. *ibe*.

yaba-taka v. to lie (falsehood), lie about.

yaba, yabaca v. to hold something next to a fire; warm something by holding it next to a fire, sometimes to smooth out wrinkles of cloth or matting.

yabaki n. year. Former meaning was annual harvest (mainly of yams, which figured in traditional Fijian lunar calendars, beginning late February or March), the "months" being separated approximately by natural phenomena relating to gardening work or marine harvests. See the end pages of this book for details of this indigenous lunar calendar. *ena veiyabakai* every year. *vakayabaki* annual(ly). *O sa yabaki vica?* How old are you? (to a child). *na cauravou yabaki 19* the 19-year old youth. *na tamata yabayabaki vata* the people of the same age. Early Fijians never counted months or years and the concept of "week" did not exist for them. They knew their age not in number of years but only as greater or less than others of the village, especially their siblings. Or they might say they were born before or after a certain well known public event. *kakana ni yabaki* n. seasonal food. *yabaki balavu* (Anglicism) n. leap year. *yabaki ni bula* n. age (of a person). Fijians normally report their age by the next year, not the last year, as in European custom.

yabe, yabeta v. to walk, stroll unencumbered. *o ira na yabe* those (many) who marched (as in a public demonstration). *tayabe* march, marchers, parade. *yabe vakawelewelei* to stroll casually, idly, with no purpose in mind. *ya* (or) *yaya* migration of land crabs toward the sea around November, December, for spawning in saltwater. *na iyabeyabe* n. the strolling, the stroll

yabia n. starch-flour (and by extension) the arrowroot plant, "true" *yabia*, Tacca leontopetalides, Taccaceae, and less commonly T. maculata, more often referred to as *yabia sa* in Fiji. The root can be poisonous but was eaten usually in the form of a well washed, flour-based pudding, especially in dry, sandy areas at low altitudes where it grows best. Hardly ever cultivated, *yabia* grows semi-wild in drier areas of Tailevu, other parts of Fiji but less common and even unknown in the interior, and where there is high rainfall. T. maculata is not found at sandy beach areas but rather in the dry hilly country below 350 meters. The true *yabia* grows widely throughout the Pacific from India across the eastern Polynesia. It may have reached Fiji naturally or, as John Parham suggested, have been introduced to Fiji by Polynesians who long ago favoured arrowroot as a more important food than it ever was to Melanesians.

yabia 2. (Regional) cassava, an introduced American plant that has assumed great importance in the Fijian diet. Name copied from the arrowroot name, possibly because both can be used to make starch. *yabia loa* refers to cassava starch, often used after laundry, to starch clothes in modern European context.

yabia ni vavalagi n. arrowroot, West Indian Arrowroot, Maranta arundinaceae, Marantaceae, origin in Brazil and Central America, an early introduction to Fiji, but not common and not grown or used by Fijians. This is the commercial species on the world market, used for arrowroot flour and arrowroot biscuits.

yabo, yabora (Ra) to kiss (traditional sniffing, nose to side of nose, or face). Syn. *regu, reguca*. Such Pacific Island sniffing may be done on greeting or farewelling friends, relatives, and formerly, to farewell a corpse in a ceremony called *ireguregu*. These days for babies and live adults, light cheek-kissing or forehead-kissing tends to replace sniffing.

yabo, yaboca v. to pass the hand over, touching lightly, as if checking something.

iyabo n. (Obsolete) man who has traditional role of handling the body of a dead chief, in only some areas of Fiji such as the Noemalu of Viti Levu. *bouta* or *bauta* serves in some places as a synonym; it is the function of one kin-group.

yaca-na n. name. *na yacamu* your name; *na yacaqu* my name. *vakayacana* v. to name. *vakatokayacataka* to decide on a name, formally give a name (usually to a person, boat, house-site), normally done with ceremony. *vakatokayacataki vei Seru* named after Seru (or for Seru). For many names one must ask permission to use it if some other people feel that they own the name *Na yacana vakavuku* n. The scientific name (this of course, a modernism). See *vakatoka*.

yaca n. namesake. *nomu yaca* your namesake (who may be addressed as *Yaca*). There were no surnames in Fiji until some Fijians began to follow that European custom. But in many cases both the Christian name and the family name might be given to someone quite outside the family. Formerly, a child was never given the name of its parent. Before Christian times a person might be given different names at different stages of life and even after death. If someone has been given the name of your father you may address that person as Father *Tamaqu*. Also, one's paternal uncles (father's brother) are considered as one's father.

yaca vata v. to bear a common name, as for example, in referring to all races of Fiji citizens as "Fijians" or all white people as Europeans.

yaca, yaca, yacaraka v. to grate (cassava, other root crops), scrub (laundry). *yacaraka* to scrub hard but by ext., may mean to beat up a person. Syn. *solo*.

yaco, yacova 1. v. to happen, occur, take place, become. *Ni yacovi iko na karamaca* . . . When you become extremely thirsty . . . . . *Ena yaco ni na dave na dra.* It will end up with bloodshed (lit., when blood will flow). See *vakayaco, vakayacora* v. to cause to happen.

yaco, yacova 2. until, reach (in time), as in *me yacova. me yacova nikua* up until today. *me yacova mai na vula oqo* up until this month. *me yavoca na macawa ka tu mai* until next week.

yaco, yacova 3. v. to arrive, extend to, reach (a place). *yacova na takete* reach the target, achieve the goal. *Au a yaco mai ena noa.* I arrived here yesterday. *yaco vata* arrive together. *Me vosa ga ena ka e yacova nona kila.* He should only speak about what he knows.

Idiom: *Eda na yaco vata ga ki Namuka.* lit. We (many) will arrive together at Namuka (at the same time, though by different boats), implying that haste or some improvement will not affect the outcome. You do it your way, I'll do it mine. It makes no difference.

vakayaco, vakayacora v. to bring about, to happen or cause to happen or occur, take place. *Sa vakayacori tiko na Adi Senitoa* Hisbiscus Festival (in Suva, in August, annually) is taking place, is underway. *na bose ka vakayacori tiko mai Tubou.* the meeting (or conference) that is taking place at Tubou. *na veika era rawa ni vakayacora na kai Idia ena noda vanua* the things the Indians can achieve (bring about) in our country.

iyacoyaco n. end, final outcome or result. *na iyacoyaco ni gaunisala* the end of the road. *Ia, sa kena iyacoyaco oqori.* Yes, that is what was going to happen in the end.

veiyacovi v., n. sexual intercourse (the appropriate, polite word), to have sexual intercourse. *mate dewa ni veiyacovi* sexually transmitted disease (STD).

yada n. widow.

yadi, yadia 1. (Ra, northern Tailevu) v. to raise up. **2.** v. to take *yadia na kuro* take the pot. *yadia mai na kuro* bring the pot here.

Yadi (Lau) n. chiefly title that precedes a woman's name, the same as Adi but in a form more common in Verata in earlier times, and also in Lau where names or words beginning with "a" are often preceded by a "y". Thus the man's name Aminiasi can become Yaminiasi in Lau.

yadra v. adj, awake, to wake up. *Sa yadra!* Good morning! *Sa yadra tu.* He/she is awake. *vakayadrati koya* wake him up. *yadra bogi* stay awake during most of the night, work at night. *yadra cecekala* wake with a start, suddenly.

yadra, yadrava v. to guard, watch for (something). *yadra* n. guard, watchman.

vakayadra, vakayadrava v. to to wake up (someone).

ivakayadra n. alarm clock. An old usage of this word was in describing the function of Turukawa, the pet fowl of legendary god Degei, that woke the chief each day at Nakauvadra. The Ciri Twins killed the fowl at a place called Conua, enraging Degei who expelled them. This is one of the best known of all Fijian legends.

yadra-vaka v. to be on the look-out for (something, someone).

yadre-na n. forehead. Syn. *edre-na.*

Idiom: *yadre toso* having a bulging, prominent, expressive forehead.

yadru n. mature bull, sometimes referred to as *bulumakau yadru*. Cattle are an introduced species. It is difficult to explain the origin of this word.

yadua each one, one each, every one. *na veitamata yadua* each and every person. *yadudua* absolutely each and every one (for more than one).

yadua-taka v. to do it one by one.

yadudua one at a time, each one. *lako yadudua* to go one at a time. *yadudua ni rua na itubutubu ni gone* each one of the two parents. *yarurua* two at a time, each couple.

yaga 1. n. adj. useful, necessary. *E sega na kena yaga.* It is of no use. *tawa yaga* useless.

yaga 2. n. spider shell, (French "lambis"), edible monovalve shellfish, usually found in dead coral areas, though hidden by camouflage colour of algae on upper side with bright orange underside, Lambis lambis, Strombidae. Two types, smaller one sold in the market, flesh removed with a fork. Larger one, Lambis lambis, is usually thrown in a fire, destroying the shell which is then cracked to remove the flesh. If boiled, the flesh becomes too touch and chewy. Perhaps because of the rubbery texture, some Fijians believe that eating *yaga* helps children who have speech problems (lisping, for example). Such a medicine called *wai ni vosa.* To preserve the shell for sale to tourists, the long protruding "neck" with two eyes at the end is tied with a string, and by this it is hung, till gravity causes the shell to drop. It is a spooky process to watch with the eyes looking at you. Feel guilty and cruel? Syn. (West, parts of Vanua Levu and Ra (*ega*).

-yaga 3. as a suffix, occasionally used at the end of a place-name, to indicate "place". On Kabara island, for example, there is a village Nakeleyaga, meaning "place useful for anchoring" boats.

vakayaga-taka v. to use. *na kena vakayagataki* its use, how it is used.

ivakayaga n. gratuity, usually money, given in appreciation of service rendered. Tipping, however, is not at all the custom in Fiji. This is an uncommon word of dubious origin.

yagai (or) **nagai** n. a tree, Canarium spp., Burseraceae, the Pili nut, an edible nut. Fiji has fewer species and varieties than western Melanesia, where it was a staple food in some areas before the advent of introduced root crops such as sweet potato and cassava. It has never been a significant item in the Fijian diet; any Fijian variety has a small nut with a very tough shell, not really a practical food. Generally now known in Vanuatu as Nangai, in Papua-New Guinea as Galip, and it is there sometimes gathered as a commercial nut-crop for eating and for oil production. In Indonesia the name is Kanari nut, and in parts of southeast Asia, the Pili nut. Other Fijian names are *kaucina, kaunicina, kaunigai,* the *gai* referring to the nut, as in *yagai*. The name *kaucina* "lamp-tree", indicates the usefulness of the nut-oil or resin as lamp-oil, though that type of artefact was unknown in the highlands of Viti Levu. Oil lamps, using coconut oil, were introduced on the coast by early Polynesians.

yagasiri n., v. fornication. Syn. *veidauci*, a more formal, proper word.

yago-na n. physical body of human or animal, hull of a boat. *o ira na yago vulavula* the (many) white people. *vakaukauwa yago* physical fitness.

yago-ni-mate n. corpse. *mate* dead.

yaka n. forest tree to 35 meters, Dacrydium nidulum, Podocarpaceae, a gymnosperm, branching only at the top to form a rounded crown, excellent furniture wood with conspicuous grain and colouring. Short, clustered needle-like leaves, adult lvs pointed, scale-like, 4 mm long, whorled. Small male cones, 9-12 mm, sometimes in groups. Female cones solitary at the tips of the needle-like leaves on separate trees from the males. Syn. *tagitagi*.

yakavi n. latter part of afternoon to dusk or early evening. *ena veiyakavi* every evening; *ivakayakavi* n. dinner. *vakayakavi* v. to have dinner. *yakavi siga* afternoon, in daytime. *tolu ena yakavi* three (o' clock) in the afternoon. A Fijian *yakavi* can extend much later than a European afternoon.

ivakayakavi n. evening meal. *vakayakavi* v. to have dinner. Formerly this meal was the second of the day, eaten just before sunset. There was no formal lunch, only occasional snacks in the middle of the day. Breakfast (*katalau*) was usually eaten at home only after several hours of early morning work in the food garden. It is now more common to have three meals a day, following the European custom.

yaki, yakia v. to beat up, give a hiding, a brutal beating and kicking. This may be done by several men on a single victim. Syn. *buturaka*.

yakiyaki n. a kind of Fijian sweet pudding (*vakalolo*) usually made of grilled breadfruit, sometimes with taro or cassava, with sweet, uncooked coconut cream (*lolodroka*), not caremelised coconut cream (*lolo buta*).

iyaku n. handful.

yaku, yakuta, yakulaka (or) **yakuraka** v. to pick out something with the fingers, usually food such as a piece of fish or pudding, something soft.

yaku-surasura v. to be sloppily done, as of some work, clothes worn, package wrapped, dance exhibition (*meke*).

yala, yalana v. to limit, to stop short, as of a road that ends abruptly, or of a meeting with limited time. *na iyalayalani* n. the limitation. *ka ni yalani* n. contraceptive. *Na itutu me yala ga vei au.* The (chiefly) title ends with me. (Such a statement was made by Ma'afu saying the the title of Tui Lau would be terminated after his death. Colonial authorities, however, revived the title for Ratu Sukuna and it was continued by Ratu Kamisese Mara.)

yala-na n. limit, extend to, end (of some physical thing). *tawa yalani* limitless; *iyalayala* boundary limit, border.

yala, yalaca 1. v. to extend to (some point of time or physically, to some place), to end in the sense of not extending further (than some boundary). *iyalayala* n. boundary.

yala, yalaca 2. v. to bring fire from one place to another with a burning brand, or to re-arrange burning logs in a fire to burn better, burn longer.

yala-taka v. to promise, to set a limit. *veiyalayalati* mutually promised, agreed, contracted. *Na Veiyalayalati* The Covenant (Bib.). *Na Veiyalayalati Vou* The New Testament. *veiyalayalati* n. committment, contract. *ivola ni veiyalayalati* n. written contract.

yalarua-taka v. to divide in two parts. *yala-limataka* divide in five parts.

yalava n. locally owned exclusive fishing grounds, many of them registered formally with the Native Land Trust Board. Syn. *qoliqoli*.

iyalayala n. boundary, limit, border. See *yala, yalaca*.

yalewa n. woman. *dabe vakayalewa* to sit like a woman, with both legs to one side. *gone yalewa* girl. *dau yalewa* womaniser, "girl chaser". *mata yalewa* man who always has eyes for the women. *Lewa!* common form of address used by men to a woman who is not higher in the social hierarchy than they are. *lasa vakayalewa* (of a woman) lesbian. *yalewa saumi* n. prostitute (very formal expression, little used.) *vakasalewalewa* n., adj. male homosexual, effeminate man.

yalewa ninini n. lit. "trembling woman", an attractive wild plant, Lycopodium cernuum, fairly common, used as body decoration at dances, or in flower arrangements.

yali adj. absent, away, missing, lost, and by extension, dead. *Sa yali ko koya* he/she is gone, absent; *Sa yali* It's not here, it's lost, gone. *Sa yali makawa.* It (or he/she) has been gone, missing, a long time. Syn. (West) *reva.* (Rewa) *leca.*

yali sa v. to walk here and there, wander about, pointlessly, doing nothing.

vakayalia v. to spend (or waste) money, time, or to lose (anything). *vakayalia na ilavo* spend money, lose money or fail to keep track of it. *vakayalia na nomu gauna* (Anglicism) to waste your time.

yalo n. spirit, mind, emotion or temperament, soul, ghost. *Yalo Tabu* Holy Ghost. *Yalo Bula* spirit of the dead. *na bula vakayalo* the spiritual life. *yalo vinaka* please, if you please (as an expression that stands alone, preceding a formal request). *kaci yalo* a mental illness when a person is not conscious of what he/she does or says.

vakayalo 1. adj. capable of reason, said of a child mature enough to be responsible. **2.** (Church) adj. spiritual.

yalo- a prefix in word combinations, describing a person's temperament (indicated by the second part of the word): *yalototolo* quick-tempered. *yalobalavu* slow but steady in attitude. *yalowai* immature, irresponsible. *yalomatua* reasonable, responsible. *yalodei* firmly consistent, stubborn.

yalo-na n. feelings, consciousness. *leca yalona* v. to be absent-minded..

veiyaloni of the same mind, in agreement.

Yalo Bula 1. n. "party person", always interested in music, parties, opposite sex. **2.** n. modern term for a "goon squad", a group of ruffians who try to intimidate an outspoken deviant.

yalo, yalova v. to beckon (to someone), to wave (the hand), This is normally a hand motion, or hand and arm motion, with the palm facing down, not up, as is European custom. It would be rude to beckon with the palm facing up. Hitch-hikers hold out a hand palm down, as if patting the air, clearly a request that the driver slow down and stop. *yaloyalo* v. to wave (greeting, farewell etc.)

yaloka n. egg. Formerly many Fijians did not eat birds' eggs, considering them disgusting, like saliva, they would say, though some would eat cooked turtle eggs. *yaloka ni gata* type of Solanum plant. ("snake's eggs"). *yaloka ni mata-na* eyeball(s). *yaloka ni vonu* lit. turtle eggs, fig. fried balls of leavened flour dough, often eaten sopped in tea as a breakfast. *vakalutu yaloka* to lay eggs.

yaloka ni mata-na n. eyeball. *dakudaku ni mata* eyelid.

yalolailai adj. timid, lacking courage.

yalomatua adj. reasonable, sensible, humble, respectful.

yaloqaqa adj. brave, courageous.

Yalo Tabu n. Holy Spirit, Holy Ghost.

yalototolo adj. quick to anger.

yalovinaka if you please, in good spirit. This is essentially a rather formal request to be of "good mind". As a single word it usually precedes a formal request.

yalowai adj. immature, lacking self-discipline and willpower, irresponsible.

iyaloyalo n. (Anglicism) cinema, movies. Properly, fully, the expression is *iyaloyalo yavala.* *retio yaloyalo* television. *sara iyaloyalo* to go to the movies.

yaloyaloturaga n. pupil (of the animal or human eye).

iyaloyalo yavala n. (Anglicism) moving pictures, movies.

yaloyalo v. to wave (the hand, in greeting, farewell, etc.). *yaloyalo vei koya.* wave to him/her.

yalu n. a common, wild, leafy-vine epiphyte that grows on trees, Dumb Cane, Toga plant, Epipremnum pinnatum, Araceae, used by Europeans as a decorative plant in Fiji and elsewhere. The sap is poisonous and even small quantities have a numbing effect on the skin. (More is seriously dangerous.) A pet parrot died from pecking at the leaves next to its cage. *Yalu dina* var. with very large leaves, the inside fibre of stem called *wa me*, twine for weaving baskets (*sova*). *Yalu tagane* var. with entire leaves, *yalu yalewa* var. with leaves having holes.

yalu (Archaic) n. ancient var. of *yaqona*, much prized for ceremonial presentations. The root is very large and grows horizontally in the ground, making it easy to harvest.

yalu, yaluma v. to reach out the arm to grab, grasp (something). *yaluyalu-lala* v. to reach out to take, but fail, empty-handed. *lala* empty.

yaluma 1. n., v. grief, to grieve, anguish, in agony, mental or physical.
yaluma 2. v. (Archaic) to retrieve, take, pass over to someone. Usually heard as *yaluma mai* get for me, retrieve for me.
yamaraka 1. v. to smash, knock down, as of a tree in a gale, a house in a hurricane.
yamaraka 2. v. to beat up, give a beating to someone. Syn. *buturaka*.
yamata n. military scout sent ahead to check the situation, spy (wartime). *yamata vuni* secret spy, an Anglicism sometimes seen in translated novels.
yame-na 1. n. tongue. *yameleka* n. tonsils. *dara yame* or *salayame* v. to stick out the tongue. *yame ni buka* n. flame, or "tongue" of fire.
Idiom: *yame-sa* "sweet-talk", liar.
yame-na 2. n. blade (knife, razor, axe).
yameyame 1. v., adj. talkative, voluble, glib, liar, smart and rapid talker.
yameyame 2. n. flames. *na yameyame ni buka* the flames from the fire.
yameca 1. v. to light up something, with light from a lamp, or flame from fire.
yameca 2. v. to deceive with clever, ingratiating words.
yamekemeke v. to be very unsettled in manner and feelings.
yamo 1. v. to go about at night, feeling one's way in the dark.
yamo 2. v. to fight at night in the dark. *yamoraka* beat up people under cover of darkness. Fijians would often attack from a concealed position, using the element of surprise.
yamo, yamoca, yamoraka v. to stroke with the hand, to massage with the hand, to grope for something with the hand. By extension, to "feel" a sexual partner.
yamosimosi v. to toss and turn, as in unsettled sleep.
vakayayamo v. to use one's hand(s) to find one's way around.
yamotu n. small patch of submerged reef separate from the main reef. *Motu* is an ancient Polynesian word for "island". Idiom: *Sa vakaua ga na yamotu.* said of a powerful person with great strength or great appetite. Lit. The reef-patch has waves.
yana, yanaka v. to wash off, clean off, especially shellfish, swilled about in water to separate them and remove sand or dirt.
yanaka v. to grope around with the hand, feeling for something, perhaps furtively. See *yamo, yamoca*.
yanaraka v. to scatter around as in flapping out a mat to remove crumbs, or dust. Also as in spreading out chunks of *yaqona* drying out in the sun. *yanaraka na lewe ni yaqona ena vata.* to spread out the pieces of kava on the drying-platform.
yani away (from the speaker, following a verb). *lako yani* go away (from where the speaker is located). The opposite of *mai* (in the direction of the speaker).
yanuca n. small island, now used only as a place-name for small islands, such as the tiny island where the Shangri-la Fijian Resort is located at the Nadroga coast of southwestern Viti Levu.
yanuyanu n. small island (not normally used for large islands like Viti Levu). *Yanu* is an ancient proto-Polynesian word for "small island". Occasionally *yanuyanu* might appear as the name of an island. There is one such just offshore of Lomaloma, Vanua Balavu Island.
yaqa, yaqava v. to sneak along crouching, usually to attack. Fijians are expert at such attacks, excellent as jungle fighters, exemplified when they were fighting Communists in Malaysia.
yaqona n. cultivated shrub, Piper methysticum, Piperaceae, aboriginal introduction from Vanuatu (the centre of its natural gene pool), used as a ceremonial and social beverage. The Polynesian name of *yaqona* is kava (or various versions of kava, such as ava, or awa.) and kava is the usual English word, more informally, grog. Speaking in high ceremony, Fijians may refer to it as *na wai ni vanua*.

The root (*waka*) and above-ground rhizome (*lewena*) are pounded or grated (formerly chewed into dry balls by men, usually) and infused in water, then strained and served. Saliva increased its potency and almost tripled the weight of the *yaqona*. In Lau, as in Tonga, the skin scrapings (*karikari*) or chips of skin (*civicivi*) of the rhizome are removed to make a whiter, less bitter beverage. Most coastal and small-island Fijians sun-dry the chopped-up plant-parts before use. Fiji highlanders, like the people of Vanuatu, traditionally use the fresh green plant, uncured, which is a much more potent intoxicant but a much smoother drink with fewer hangover effects when used as the highlanders use it. Fiji highlanders make a much less condensed mixture to drink as compared to the Vanuatu people where the beverage is prepared viscous and extremely concentrated.

Yaqona is a mild narcotic and diuretic that relaxes the muscles and the mind and allays thirst. (For this reason it was for Polynesians useful on long voyages when water was scarce.) Only excessive drinking inhibits or impairs movement such as walking, making it uncoordinated. Only extreme, continued consumption leads to addiction and results in dry, scaly discoloured skin and bleary eyes as well as disaffected behavious. Under normal consumption, the mind remains clear and a pleasant mood is engendered. Foreigners' initial impressions of the taste are usually negative. Serving conditions are not at all sanitary but fortunately, *yaqona* is an antiseptic, so the same cup may be used for serving many people. The physical and mental effects of *yaqona* are largely due to the concentration and relative amounts of some six major lactones. The kavalactone content depends on the variety of *yaqona*, the location of the plantation, and whether or not it is sun-dried (which reduces the concentration considerably). Normal concentration of kavalactone might vary between six percent and fourteen percent. A maximum in Fiji might reach fifteen to twenty percent, which is quite rare.

The plant is propagated only vegetatively by cuttings of the stem, and requires three years, preferably five years, before the whole plant is harvested. Main cultivars are either dark-skinned *yaqona* (*yaqona loa*), or lighter-coloured skin *yaqona* (*yaqona vula*). The lighter coloured type takes longer to mature (at least 5 years) but may be kept in a growing state as long as 20 years or more. It makes a smoother beverage, though the types and different cultivars are not distinguished in the market-place, or in traditional ceremony. Specific varieties include *kasa leka*, *dokobana* (and either may be *yaqona loa* or *yaqona vula*), *qila* (green skin, thick stem, short internodes), *yalu*, *honolulu* (bright green stems). No distinction as to variety is made in retail sales, and few if any differences are visible in the sun-dried product. In very formal presentations for a high chief the whole *yaqona* bush will be presented.

A cup of the beverage is in some areas traditionally drunk by a new chief to signal his formal installation in office. He/she is said to be *vagunuvi*. *Yaqona* is now a common social beverage but still, a minimum of ceremony attends its serving. Even the casual friendly visitor will say a few formal words as he sets down his gift. (*Sa dua na taga lala* . . This is but an empty bag . . .). Sailors and especially divers may offer a libation to the shark god Dakuwaqa, pouring a cup into the sea, before they themselves will drink. That will protect them from sharks, as long as they have avoided recent sexual intercourse. *Yaqona* is served at virtually all Fijian rites of passage, birth, marriage, death. It has been a part of almost all formal or official meetings and has been served in most offices, much as morning tea was part of the British ritual. Today, some of the Christian denominations forbid the use of *yaqona* and it has become forbidden in government offices. Nonetheless, a gift of *yaqona* is an essential ceremonial when presenting oneself (*isevusevu* ceremony), in being introduced to village elders.

Yaqona is not supposed to be drunk by a person alone, and once it is mixed (*lose*), that quantity should be consumed completely. Though now a popular drink, *yaqona* was formerly mainly the privilege of chiefs and priests and men as elders of the village. Its use in formal ceremony, reinforcing the social hierarchy by the order of drinking, is a custom introduced from Tonga, as is the use of the wooden *tanoa* serving bowl that was unknown before about 1800. Highlanders had no use for such protocol or severe social distinctions. They mixed their *yaqona* in a leaf-covered hole in the ground, knelt down, and sucked it up, lapped it up much as a dog drinks from a puddle, this being called *burau*. This may still be done in rural garden locations, especially by Viti Levu highlanders. Or more modernly, a cup may be fashioned from a leaf.

When sold in powdered form, *yaqona* root is normally adulterated with by at least a third of rhizome and scrapings of the skin. For this reason, many Fijians buy the unpounded kava and pound it themselves. Pounding is considered to make a better product than grinding, possibly due to the heat of the grinding process.

A person may engage a demon (*tevoro*) to gain power over another person, and is said to pour a *yaqona* to his devil. This is a Faustian concept. His disadvantage is that he must keep up serving *yaqona* to the demon and misfortune will befall him if he ever forgets. Such practices are believed to be quite current.

Some special words and phrases relate to *yaqona*:

na isevusevu root presented to host by a visitor to his host as a way of formal introduction.

na lose yaqona the mixing of the *yaqona* (or) one who mixes the yaqona.

na tu yaqona the formal serving of the *yaqona* (or) the one who serves the cup of *yaqona* to the chief or honoured guest.

rabe, rabeta to drink the next cup following the more important person, as a supportive gesture.

na ibili ni mua last round of serving, "one for the road".

na bulu yava round of *yaqona* served after departure of guest, when last comments and memories will be discussed. Memories may then be set aside.

ititoko, last cup before a person quits the session of *yaqona* drinking, lit. a walking stick.

yaqoyaqona n. a common weed, Macropiper aduncum (Piper timothianum and P. vitiense), Piperaceae, which resembles *yaqona* in appearance. Its main use perhaps is for making improvised *iqilai*, improvised pieces of shrub branch used as a hook for restraining clumps of grass with one hand while cutting with a knife in the other hand, or used as a hook to pull down fruit-tree branches, to pick the fruit. *Yaqoyaqona* is said to be the form of *yaqona* used as a beverage by the gremlins (*veli*) of the bush. Syn. *onolulu*. (West) *qonaqona*.

yara (or) **yaro** (Eng.) n. harrow, as used in farming, usually hauled by a steer, but some powered by diesel engine. *siviyara* v., n. to plough, an introduced concept.

yara-taka v. to haul, drag behind oneself. By extension, modernly, language teachers use the word *yara* to indicate a vowel or syllable that is drawn out in pronounciation, like the "o" in the word for cloud. *sa yara na "o"*. They sometimes indicate this by placing a macron above the vowel.
Idiom: *yara benu* ceremonial clapping when a chief has finished his meal. Lit., haul away the refuse. (*benu* garbage, refuse).

vakayarayara v. to keep on delaying, deferring, to prolong.

iyarabale n. dry dock, place where a boat can be hauled out (*yara*). Formerly referred to a low-lying stretch of land, place where a boat might be hauled across the land to reach the opposite sea. Both Vanua Levu and Kadavu have such places.

iyaragi n. weapon. *tagane vakaiyaragi* armed man. *na biu yaragi* the laying down of arms, the disarmament. Originally, this word referred only to indigenous weapons such as the club or spear.

yaraneke n., v. to cheat, as at playing cards, such as in the card game *tarabu* ("trump"). Such cheating is commonly done, considered playful and clever. Caught, the cheater will usually laugh. Syn. *eraneke*.

yarayara 1. here and there. *kacivaka yarayara yani vei ira* call out here and there to them. *Me tevu yarayara ena veico* spread it out on the grass. *E dau kele yarayara na motoka*. The cars park here and there (wherever they can). *moce yarayara* to sleep in various different places.

yarayara 2. to continue doing something. *tagi yarayara* to keep on crying. *vosa yarayara* to keep on talking. *talanoa yarayara* to yarn on and on.

iyarayara (Lau) n. small mat made specially for new born baby.

yaro n. sp. of endemic tree, mainly Premna protrusa (formerly P. taitensis), Verbenaceae, valued for durability of the timber, often used for house-posts, one of the best timbers for that purpose. Cream-coloured to yellow flowers, corollas to 9 mm in length, clusters of small (to 7 cm) 4-seeded globose black fruit, a drupe. *Yaro* is also P. serratifolia, a similar coastal species, very resticted in distribution, often near mangrove areas; its corollas are much smaller, only to 4 mm in length. Dried heartwood may scent body oil in the lowlands. (There was no body oil in the highlands of Viti Levu.) Syn. (Lau) *waro*.

yasa 1. v. to move about silently, usually secretly, with ulterior purpose (theft, violence, evesdropping).

yasa 2. n., adj. person who remains away from his village. After a long absence, returning even for a brief visit requires bringing of gift goods: kerosene, cloth, food. This costly custom keeps many Fijians from restoring close contact with their village when they have been long absent.

yasa ni at the side of. *E dua na vu ni niu e tiko ena yasa ni vale*. There is a coconut palm beside the house.

yasa-na n. side (physical location), part or section. *ena yasana kadua* on the other side. *e na veiyasa i Viti* in all parts of Fiji. *ena yasana vakara* on the western side (of Viti Levu Island). *tu e yasana* to stand aside, stand to one side.

Yasana n. province. Fiji has fourteen provinces, aside from Rotuma. *ena Yasana O Namosi*. in Namosi Province.

yasayasa n. region. *Yasayasa vakaRa* Western Region.

yaseyase n. lightning. *na lidi ni yaseyase* the lightning strike.

yasi n. sandalwood, Santalum yasi, Santalaceae, endemic in the central South Seas, Vanuatu, Fiji and Tonga. Greatly valued in the Orient, which led to an influx of U.S. trading ships for only ten years in the very early 1800s, till the plant became almost rare. This small, 2 to 12 meters, wild tree is becoming common again in Bua especially. Wilkes (1841) says its area was restricted to fifteen square miles, in barren and rocky land. Now it is also growing in Kadavu and a few trees are exhibited at the Nature Gardens at Wainadoi, some 22 km west of Suva. It is not easy to propagate because the young plant requires certain fungi and becomes a parasite on the roots of nearby trees. (Commercially, lemon trees are often used.) Fijians had never cultivated it and they never used it in body oil before contact with Tongans who used it traditionally, and Europeans who adapted it from Oriental custom. Inconspicuous florescence in the axils of leaves, tiny white florets turning pink, then rich red at maturity. Fruit round and small, 1.5 cm diam., green turning purple to black, with sweet pulp, seen mostly around August but exist throughout the year. Wood of the living tree has little of its fragrant scent that develops when it is dried. The tree grows to more than twenty feet, with a trunk up to six inches in diameter, the bark distinctively grey. Quite another, unrelated species of forest tree is also called *yasi*, from some similarities. To distinguish this other species, the term used is *yasi ni veikau* forest "sandalwood", or *yasiyasi*. See below. This counterfeit sandalwood sometimes raises false hopes for windfall money.

yasiyasi n. a forest tree, Syzygium spp., Myrtaceae, with extremely durable, springy, tough hardwood, formerly used for house-posts and for bows (for war) by highland Fijians. Bows were not used by Fijians for anything but war (not for sport, not for hunting or fishing). Lowlanders were more likely to use bows made from branches of mangrove *tiri*. By contrast, in Tonga bows were only ever used by chiefs, and only in sport such as shooting at rats.

yaso, yasova v. to howl, to yowl (dog, cat, person). *tagiyaso* v. to howl with grief, tears, crying, typically at funerals.

yatayata v., n. trembling, quiver usually of voice, incoherent mumbling as of a delirious speech.

yate-na n. liver. Idiom: *yate lailai* coward. *yate levu* courageous. The liver is considered to be the principal organ of the body and the focal point of one's courage. (The notion of the heart connected to romance or sentiment is a novel idea borrowed from Europeans.) *yate dei* firm, unyielding in spirit. Idiom: *Na yatemu e vaka na yate mai lagi!* lit. your liver is like liver from heaven. This is exaggerated flattery to impress a potential romantic partner.

Among the suits in a deck of cards, the hearts are known as livers *yate*. *kalavo* clubs, *siveti* spades, *daimani* diamonds.

yatevuso n. lung(s).

yati v. to move slowly, or clumsily, with effort, now a rarely heard word except in the idiom: *E na qai yati mai na Colo*: We will get there eventually, our persistence will be rewarded. Lit. implication is that the mountains will move slowly down to meet us if we struggle on. Originally this was supposed to be a saying of Vutia people who travelled up into the interior to trade their clay pots and mats for such items as *yaqona*. Carrying their heavy goods, this was an arduous climb.

yato, yatova v. take something by stealth, to snitch, grab. *na ka e yatovi rawa mai*. what can be grabbed.

yatu 1. n. row, and by ext. archipelago, as in *na yatu Lau* or *Na Tu-i-cake* the Lau archipelago. *yatu eliu* front row, in football the forwards. *yatu emuri* back row, in football, backfielders. Alternative is *iyatu*, though not for archipelago.

yatu 2. n. tuna, sometimes heard as *atu*. This may include the skipjack (*yatusewa*, with long stripes along belly), albacore (*yatu loa*, for its black back), yellow fin tuna (*yatu ni Toga*), and much more rarely the big-eye tuna (*yatu levu*, or dog-tooth tuna). Anciently, little distinction was made in Fijian languages because Fijians rarely caught any of these species; they did no trolling and hardly ever fished outside the reef. Today, these fish are caught commercially at sea, often 12 miles to 250 miles from shore, using long lines, 45-50 nautical miles long, with some 3,000 hooks, that may take 45 hours to lay out. Tuna migrate in a clockwise direction from south of Kadavu, around Fiji. They often follow lines of changed temperature (even a degree or two change), and lines of change in the current. December to January are often times of heavy catches but then a month may go by with very little catch at all. Depth of the lines is a vital matter. Yellow fin are found at 30 to 80 feet, with the big-eye somewhat lower. Largest catches are often at 100 to 200 feet. In waters less than 30 feet deep, one finds *walu*, crevally, and sharks, fish that are not valuable for export. Over-fishing and oriental competition, some of it illegal, has devastated the industry.

yatu, yatuna v. to line up in rows.

iyatuvosa n. (Anglicism) sentence (of speech, writing). This is of course a modern term, as are all words of grammar.

iyau 1. n. goods, wealth. *vutuniyau* rich, wealthy. All Fijian goods were perishable, usually food, mats, barkcloth or sinnet, salt, coconut oil. They represented power or prestige only as they were used, as in presentations (*magiti*, etc.) or ceromonial trading (*solevu*). Durable wealth such as whaleteeth were recent innovations, only in the 1700s, but only used in ceremonial presentations. Presentation wealth now also includes kerosene in 20 liter drums, bales of cloth. *vutu ni yau* rich, having many possessions.. *yaubula* n. wealth, precious goods. *vakayauyau* plentiful, abundant, in great number. *dauniyau* (Ang.) treasurer (as of an association, bank, organisation).

yau 2. n. dew. Syn. *tegu, bite*.

yau, yauta 3. v. to bear (carry), take, bring (of many things or people together), go together (of many people). *vakayayau* burdened, charged with burdens, carrying things around, plentiful, plentifully *Sa* *yau mai na tamata* A lot of people are coming here together in a bunch. *E yauti ira mai na lewe ni koro o Tukana.* Tukana is bringing the villagers here.

vaka-yauyau plentifully, in profusion, as in: *Sa drodro ga mai vakayauyau na wai-ni-mataqu* My tears just flowed down in profusion.

yauta adj. musty, soggy (clothes, sails), stale (biscuits).

yaubula n. wealth, riches.

yavala, yavalata v. to move, move it, to start (an engine). *Yavala!* Move! Get going! *yavavala* unsteady. *yavalavala* fidgety, in constant motion, unsettled.

yavala-taka v. to "work" or "run" (as of an engine)

yava-na 1. n. leg, foot. *yava veqa* (or) *yava teqa* (or) *yava vilovilo* bowlegged. *yava veitutu* knock-kneed. *yava saisaia* slender, weak legs. *gera* lame. *lokiloki* cripple. *qeteqete ni yava-na* n. bottom of the foot.

Idiom: *vale ni yava* house used casually by its owner, who stays there only occasionally. In Colo East the expression is *vale ni dua-na*. *yavayava ni toa* chicken legs (for eating).

Idiom: *Sa suasua na yavamu.* Lit. Your legs are still wet, implying you are new to this place, having just arrived ashore. You are a newcomer here and should not speak with assurance.

Idiom (Lau): *yava pepe:* has weak legs, usually from advanced age, infirmity but may be said of a baby or child.

yava-na 2. n. wheel. *yava ni lori* truck wheel. *yava ni motoka* motor-car wheel. Fijians had not invented wheels. They did use rollers under beached boats to get them into the water and human bodies were sometimes used to lubricate the movement.

veidre yava (Anglicism) **1.** v. to pull one's leg. **2.** v. to convince someone, to lure someone into doing something by using fair words.

yavato n. a very large white tree larval grub to 25 cm in length, eaten cooked or sometimes raw by some Fijians. They eat all but the very tip of the head and are delighted by the taste. It is the larval stage of Longhorn beetle, Cerambycidae; two Fijian species are Xixuthrus heyrovskyi and X. costatus. They live on rotting vegetation, especially on forest trees, often high on the tree. This is the animal totem throughout much of Namosi Province (specifically the super-tribe Nabukebuke), where the word should not be spoken. And nor should the word *kutekute* be spoken, which describes a later stage of the beetle's development. Similarly, the word *qou*, beetle, should never be pronounced. The Fijian name *vuka* applies to the Longhorn Beetle but that name is known to very few people.

"Operation Yavato" was an effort by the military revolutionary Sitiveni Rabuka claiming to uncover corruption in the previous government. Implied threats of exposure ensured compliance from other politicians. Results were never released to the public or used in court. Used figuratively, *yavato* implies secret plots and spying.

yavega-na (Colo East) n. armpit.

yavi, yavia v. to haul, as in hauling a boat ashore, or into the water, or to haul in an anchor. *yavia na wa ni siwa* haul in the fishing line. *me yavi na kelekele* haul up the anchor. See *yavi-rau*.

yavi, yavita v. to hit with a stick or club, to thrash.

Idiom: *yavita dole na mataisau* club the carpenter prematurely, i.e., judge a job prematurely before the work has been completed.

yavi rau traditional fishing along the coastal shore, many people manning a scare-line that encircles the fish and then is hauled in. The scare-line is a sort of rope, with leaves attached, that floats at the surface. The occasion is joyous, gathering fish for some upcoming feast, and sharing among the villagers. Similar traditional fishing took place on the Wainimala River in the highlands of Viti Levu, around village Nakorosule for example. Three villages might cooperate in a massive effort, particularly for migrating fish or seasonal fish caught in large numbers.

yavitu sevens, as in *rakavi le yavitu* rugby sevens, with seven men on a team.

iyavoi n. inter-planted crop, usually harvested before full maturity of the main crop. It makes more efficient use of land and helps avoid plant disease or pest problems common with monoculture. Examples are bananas or papaya interplanted among *yaqona*, or *dalo* among yams. Youngsters would not know this word.

yavu n. (Polyn. origin, "apu", heap) foundation, literally and physically, as in house foundation, or figuratively (modernly), refer to the basis of something. In each village, house-sites are named and dedicated to an extended family, though there may be no house built there. There may or may not be a stone foundation in place. Chiefly residences are referred to by the name of their house-site, and the name may refer to the chief himself and his immediate family. Traditionally, one should not pronounce a person's name. In principle, every house-site has a name and that name indirectly refers to the family that lives there. *tauyavutaka* to establish, to found. *E sega na yavu ni mataqali vosa vakaoqo.* There is no basis for this kind of talk.

Yavu ni Vakavulewa (Anglicism) n. Constitution (government).

yavuca n. improvised shelter to pass the night, bivouac, temporary camp.

yavula n. tarpon, Megalops cypriaoides.

yavusa n. tribe; largest kin-group resident often in one or a few villages or Territories (*Vanua*), usually composed of two or more clans (*mataqali*), each with one or more extended families (now often called by the standardized term *itokatoka*). This concept and three-fold social division did not exist in Fiji until the arrival of the major Nakauvadra immigration. It never became traditional in the western part of Viti Levu, which retained earlier Melanesian social structure. The conceptual structure of tribe, clan, extended family, has in most cases been super-imposed by the Fiji government. In fact, tribes are often political and economic agglomerations of peoples, clans and families that were originally unrelated. Often a village contains only one tribe but there are many exceptions. And in some areas, like Namosi, the tribe may extend over many villages. Tribes at different places may have the same name, and were once related, but are now separate and independent of each other (such as the Nabukebuke tribe in Namosi, in Rewa, and at Levuka, Ovalau). In personal life, many Fijians do not use the term *yavusa*, and really relate only the family, and to the clan, which usually functions as a unit in perceived rights and obligations.

yavutu (Polyn. origin) n. ancestral village of a tribe, where the tribe was formed, often as a political convenience after earlier wanderings or flights of escape, or separations of kin-groups from internal conflict or lack of land or water. All were high, fortified sites or ring-ditch fortifications hardly older than 300 years and virtually all have been abandoned as peace came under colonial governance. In many cases an ancestral spirit is associated with the *yavutu*. Younger Fijians today are not always familiar with the *yavutu* concept. A related concept is the *koro makawa* old village, where the people lived previously. Virtually all Fijian social groups have moved about considerably. They had no permanently settled homeland. The Native Lands Commission is based on Governor Gordon's misconceived assumption that all land "belonged" to some Fijian clan. In fact, most land was uninhabited, no-man's land, unused and too exposed to attack for anyone to live there. People lived very compactly in tiny enclaves.

iyaya n. gear, baggage, belongings, and by extension: *iyaya vakatagane* male genitals, private parts, the polite and usual term.

Idiom (Vulgar): *iyaya levu* large genitals, said usually in a mocking sense.

vakaiyaya-taka v. to furnish (house), supply with gear.

vakaiyau adj., adv. having a huge amount of gear, parcels, baggage, goods.

yayani adj. totally flat calm, of the sea. Syn. *vaka-lidi-maravu*.

yayani, yayani-taka (Eng. "iron") v. to iron (laundry). *vatu ni yayani* the iron (for laundry), *na iyaniyani* n. the ironing. Syn. *yani, yania*.

vakayauyau amply, in great quantity. *Sa drodro vakayauyau na wai ni mataqu.* My eyes were flooded with flowing tears.

yawa adj. far away, distant, and by idiomatic slang extension, "far out", unexpectedly extraordinary (of a person), astonishing, wierd.

Idiom: *yawa kalia* very remote, very far off the mark.

yawa n. distance. *E vica na kena yawa mai Beqa ki Suva?* How far is it from Beqa to Suva?

yawa (Tonga 'awa) n. breadfish, milkfish, bonefish, Chanos chanos, introduced from Tonga, where it was cultivated in ponds for chiefs at Ha'apai. It can tolerate brackish water. Tongans introduced *yawa* to freshwater Lake Masomo on Vanua Balavu Island. There is a joyous annual cerermony around October of swimming and catching these breadfish. Swimming stirs gases from vegetative matter in the water which incapacitate the fish that are then easily brought to shore. There is ritual associated with all this. A documentary of the occasion has been filmed by Sir Richard Attenborough. At sea, *yawa* are a fighting fish and may reach six feet in length. As a food, *yawa* has many bones. Syn. *awa*.

yawa kio n. freshwater bonefish, Albula sp. Has many bones, soft before they harden in cooking. Up to a meter in length. Silver skin, flesh very white.

yawaka v. to distance (usually oneself) from (some thing or place).

yayani, yayanitaka (Eng.) v. to iron (clothes, etc.). *vatu ni yayani* n. iron.

yedo! interjection of joy.

yota (Eng.) n. yacht. Syn. *iota*.

FIJI TRADITIONAL CALENDAR

Fijians lived by a lunar calendar with a climax of human activity around February, when they might begin to harvest the cultivated yam harvest. This is a "noble" crop, yams being prestigious at ceremonial food presentations. Cultivated yams were also the only basic food that could be stored in their natural state and kept for use much later in the year. All other vegetables and fruits were perishable. The word *yabaki* signified the annual yam harvest and that has been adopted as the word for "year". First fruits *isevu* of some crops were presented to chiefs or priests, and more modernly also the Christian church. Fijians never counted the years and had no concept of a weekly cycle. There were no dates on their calendar and no names of days, only lunar monthly cycles. They simply followed a seasonal calendar of events according to biological changes and climate changes of the year. The changes from month to month were signalled by the flowering or fruiting of certain plants, or by the sea, with the changes in the available seafood.

Highlanders of Viti Levu are of a different culture. They did not cultivate or honour yams to the degree of coastal Fijians. And they had no seafood, only aquatic life from the rivers. Much of this calendar does not apply to them. All too often when people speak of Fijians they are talking only of Fijians around the low-lying coastal areas and the smaller islands where there has been a heavy Tongan influence and different physical conditions with lagoons and reefs and groves of mangrove.

This traditional calendar of coastal Fijians has little or no relevance in the daily life of Fijians today, except for those who remain in the remote villages and live a subsistence life mainly from gathering and gardening, and fishing for their own food. For the rest of us, our interest in the calendar is mainly an interest in history and biology, and the practical matter of what fruits, vegetables or seafoods may be found at the market.

Of course with a lunar calendar there is no one-to-one correspondence with our months of the modern calendar. When we name the equivalents in European months it is only approximate. Also, in fact, the tropical climate has inherently variable seasons, not dependent only on the phase of the moon. We list here what is supposed to happen in each lunar month in following the seasons. Most of these observations have been cribbed from various previous writings; only a few are are original with this author.

Vula i Nuqa Levu.   January. Named for the great abundance of Rabbit Fish, Siganus vermiculatus, a small fish with fine texture delicious flavour. They are found close to shore in dense schools, passive and easy to catch in great numbers. Also the schooling surmullet or goatfish (*ki* or *deu*) caught in fish fences (*ba*). And young baby sharks (*bulubulu*) at the shore. Shellfish are plentiful, especially *kai koso, kuku, and kolakola* (Aetheria semilunata), the chiton (*tadruku*), the univalve *madrali* (Neretidae) and the sea-slug (*bosucu*) Onchidium that exudes a milky substance when squeezed. Land crabs (*lairo*) are spawning (*dere neke*) at the seashore, especially the red variety of *lairo*. And the small rock crab (*sara-valivali*) is full and rich (*momona*). The edible jellyfish (*drose*) are floating in abundance (and Fijians talk of "drinking" the jellyfish; they say it is *laugunu*, not eating it as a food which would be referred to as *laukana*. "Red tide" fish poisoning is a danger at this time.

The starch-food Polynesian chestnut (*ivi*) is gathered. Mango trees are fruiting, mainly important in the drier parts of the main island. (Mango hardly fruits on the wet southeaster side.) *Dawa* fruit is harvested and the *wi*. Breadfruit *uto* is fruiting abundantly. A sign of the time is the flowering of the timber tree *damanu*. Many flowers are blooming, used as *isaluwaki*, to make perfumed oil (only in coastal areas) or weave in garlands: *lagakali, bua ni Viti, caucau*. The *salato* shrub is developing thorns.

Vula i Sevu.   February. Turning point of the year. Beginning harvest of cultivated yam and setting up of yam storage shed *(lololo)* in the field. Presentation of first fruits to chief and Church. Plentiful harvest of breadfruit (*uto*), taro (*dalo*), cassava (*tavioka*), Polynesian chestnut (*ivi*), the fruit of the trees *wi* (Spondias dulcis), *dawa* (Pometia pinnata), and oranges. (Cassava and oranges are introduced plants). A sign of the time is the flowering of the timber tree *dakua salusalu*. In the fish fences one now finds the little fish *malevu, voro*, resembling and replacing the *ki* (goatfish).

Vula i Kelikeli.   March. Often rainy and a time from thunderbolts (*yaseyase*). Main harvest of cultivated yams, much to be stored. Long yams are harvested; some are buried. Certain varieties of breadfruit (*uto*) plentiful, *ivi* continues, and the *vutu kana* matures as an additional starch food. Avocados (introduced) are abundant. It is time to plant sweet potato (*kumala*).

The early, initial breadfruit cultivars fruited mainly in March and April but cultivars introduced later extended the season considerably.

Sea crabs (*qari*) are mature as are mud lobsters (*mana*) and the small crabs (*kuka*). Fishing is generally poor this month and next.

Signs of the time, this month or next, of the migratory shore-wading Golden Plover (*dilio*) that will depart Fiji for Alaska. Early flowering of reeds (*gasau*), *yalu* vine, and the *tokatolu* that will also come to fruit. In some places early harvest of *duruka* (Saccharum edule), the fruit of a vegetable grass so delicious grilled on a fire.

Vulu i Gasau. April. Often another rainy month. Conspicuous flowering of reeds *gasau*. Digging of long yams. Breadfruit fruiting in great abundance, citrus, including the shaddock (*moli kana*). Signs of the time include flowering of the trees *mako* and *damanu*. *Kavika* fruit is reaching the end of its season that began six months earlier, in October. *Dilo* nuts are rich in oil for massage. The *dilio* migratory birds are now departing Fiji.

Freshwater shellfish are out of season. But mud lobsters (*mana*), sea crabs (*qari*), and shellfish *kuka* are *daba*, full and rich for eating. The fish *tugadra* are plentiful in schools at the shore. This is a time for netting small fish, *daniva*, *salala*, *sara* by the shore. The catch will be poor for larger fish away from the shore.

Vula i Doi. May. The *doi* shrub (Alphitonia spp.) flowers (small and white) and fruits, as does the *vesi leka*. The short cultivated yam *uvi leka* reaches maturity for harvest, as does the *kawai* yam, especially in the drier areas of Macuata and Ra. Sweet potato (*kumala*) and arrowroot (*yabia*) are abundant in the places they grow best. *Tarawau* nuts come to harvest. The tree *yasiyasi*, false sandalwood, is fruiting. Along the coast there are many *salala* fish in schools. Month for late hurricanes, heavy storms and blustery winds called *cagi ni doi*. The end of this month is normally the end of the hurricane season. Sailing becomes much safer.

Vula i Werewere. June. Cool weather begins. The month to begin weeding (*werewere*), and planting the first yams. *Kawai* yams are plentiful, as are some of the wild yams such as *bulou*. Flowering occurs for *duruka* and *vico*. The coconut crab (*uga vule*) is *uro*, rich and plump on the few islands where it still thrives. There is a diminishing supply of oranges and *kavika*. Among fish, there are many *matu* Gerridae, and sardines (*daniva*). The trees *dilo* and *dakua salusalu* are fruiting. Humpback whales appear offshore, often with their young, having migrated past New Zealand to Fiji, on their way to Tonga before retreating again to the Antarctic. This will continue into July, or later. The giant sea turtles become scarce this month through August.

Vula i Cukicuki. July. Cold weather. Digging (*cukicuki*) and planting of yams by the end of the month. Harvesting sweet potato (*kumala*). Signs of the time include flowering of *moivi*, *drala*, *vasili*, and *vaivai ni vavalagi,* signals to begin planting yams. Flowering of *drala* attracts the Collared Lory, a lovely sight.

The relatively modern crop of maize (*sila*) matures in July and August. This is not sweet corn but tough field corn, elsewhere used only as animal feed, but in Fiji used as a human snack food, sold at the market. (Sweet corn would require purchased hybrid seed, not available to most farmers.) Deciduous trees such as *tavola*, *wi*, and *sinu*, will have lost their leaves in these cold months, July and August.

The fish *kesala* (*kerakera*) is spawning as is the *kawakawa*. And the octopus (*kuita*) are now becoming common. Fishing is good for *daniva*, *ose*, and *matua*.

Vula i Se-ni-drala (Vula-i-kawakawa). August. Cool, unsteady weather brings the end of the major *dalo* season that began around March. The tree *damanu* is flowering, as is the *drala* and the *kauceuti*. The mangrove (*tiri*) is fruiting, as is the *vaivai ni vavalagi*.

High season now for octopus. Schooling of the small sardine-like fish *vaya* and the *matu*. The fish *kesala* (*kerakera*) is still breeding, as is the *kawakawa*. The giant green turtle is now mating, drifting in couples at the surface of the sea (*veibalati na vonu*).

Vula i Vavakada. September. Month for staking out stick supports for yam vines (*na vavakada*). Also called *vula i kadrekadre* month for sprouting (of yams). Planting of *dalo* and *kawai*. Flowering of mango tree (introduced from India), *drala*, *buaniviti*, *mokosoi*, *wadamu*. Rock cod (*kawakawa*) is still spawning. Fruiting of *kaunigai* tree. Anciently the beginning of javelin-throwing sport *veitiqa*, after completion of planting. The Golden Plover *dilio* is now returning to Fiji from Alaska or Siberia on its annual migration. (No *dilio* eggs are ever found in Fiji.)

Vula i Balolo Lailai. October. Planting of *dalo*, *kawai*, and *via kana*. *Boro sousou* is in full growth, as in the medicinal *cagolaya* used for coughs and colds. First appearance of edible sea annelid *balolo* in some places. Maturity of breadfruit is beginning. *Kavika* fruit is in harvest this month and next. The introduced avocado (*pea*) is abundant on Taveuni especially from October through March. Beginning of the season for watermelon that will continue through February. Flowering of the *daiga*. Flowering of *mokosoi* tree, so much used for its scent and beauty in personal decoration behind the ear and floral garlands. The scented *misimisi* is fruiting. The deciduous Polynesian almond (*tavola*) is putting our fresh new leaves (*sovasova*). The noble timber tree *vesi,* Instia bijuga, is fruiting. The migratory bird *dilio* arrives in Fiji.

Vula i Balolo Levu. November. Second, larger appearance of *balolo* at some shores. Major pineapple and mango season (introduced plants) begins and *kavika* fruit is being harvested. *Dawa* and *vutu* are also fruiting. *Misimisi* is ripe.

The sea crabs (*qari*) are "full" of spawn (*momona*), and there is an abundance of the fish *walu*. Beginning of the hurricane season. Long distance sailing becomes risky due to storms.

Vula i Nuqa Lailai. December. Full hurricane season that might last through March or possibly April and a little later. Smaller concentration of schools of Rabbit fish (*nuqa*). The crevally (*saqa*) is spawning. Young sharks (*bulubulu*) now born, swimming close to shore, and sharks more inclined to bite. This is the rich *dere neke* time of the land crab (*lairo*) especially the *lairo vula*. In some areas the *balolo* may appear. The fish *walu* and the crevally (*saqa*) are breeding their young.

Can dig some early yams such as *vurai,* which also can be planted. Flowering of Flamboyant tree (*sekoula*), and the timber trees *buabua* and *kuasi,* both being species of Podocarpiaceae, also the *nuqanuqa*. Breadfruit mature, also mango, *kavika, dawa,* and pineapple with continued harvests.

www.ingramcontent.com/pod-product-compliance
Lightning Source LLC
Chambersburg PA
CBHW060507300426
44112CB00017B/2575